COMINTERN AESTHETICS

Comintern Aesthetics

EDITED BY AMELIA M. GLASER
AND STEVEN S. LEE

UNIVERSITY OF TORONTO PRESS
Toronto Buffalo London

ISBN 978-1-4875-0465-6 (cloth)   ISBN 978-1-4875-3064-8 (EPUB)
                                  ISBN 978-1-4875-3063-1 (PDF)

Library and Archives Canada Cataloguing in Publication

Title: Comintern aesthetics / edited by Amelia M. Glaser and Steven S. Lee.
Names: Glaser, Amelia, editor. | Lee, Steven S. (Steven Sunwoo), 1978– editor.
Description: Includes bibliographical references and index.
Identifiers: Canadiana (print) 20190200049 | Canadiana (ebook) 20190200081 |
    ISBN 9781487504656 (hardcover) | ISBN 9781487530648 (EPUB) | ISBN
    9781487530631 (PDF)
Subjects: LCSH: Literature – History and criticism. | LCSH: Communist
    International – Influence. | LCSH: Communism and literature – History – 20th
    century. | LCSH: Communism and culture – History – 20th century. | LCSH:
    Aesthetics – Political aspects – History – 20th century.
Classification: LCC PN51 .C66 2020 | DDC 306.345 – dc23 | 809/.04 – dc23

This book has been published with the assistance of the University of California,
Berkeley's Institute of Slavic, East European, and Eurasian Studies and Institute of East
Asian Studies; and the University of California, San Diego's Jewish Studies Program.

University of Toronto Press acknowledges the financial assistance to its publishing
program of the Canada Council for the Arts and the Ontario Arts Council, an agency
of the Government of Ontario.

Canada Council   Conseil des Arts
for the Arts   du Canada

ONTARIO ARTS COUNCIL
CONSEIL DES ARTS DE L'ONTARIO
an Ontario government agency
un organisme du gouvernement de l'Ontario

Funded by the   Financé par le
Government   gouvernement
of Canada   du Canada

Contents

Illustrations

Chronology: Comintern Aesthetics – Between Politics and Culture

DOMINICK LAWTON
UC Berkeley

The purpose of this chronology is to provide a basic guide and reference for the period that serves as the backbone of this volume. Many – indeed, most – of the nuances of its history are inaccessible through a timeline alone, and so have been left out; readers are encouraged to pursue this history in more detail by referring to the individual chapters of the volume. Visually, the timeline has been separated into two columns: one devoted to the political developments of the interwar years and the Third International's institutional history, from its birth as the self-designated vanguard of the world revolution to its collapse in the Second World War; the other to the radical and internationalist cultural ferment that surrounded, and was to a degree fostered by, the Comintern. However, this division is a contrivance of presentation. Far from assuming any clean separation of politics and culture (especially in this era), our goal is for readers to perceive their intertwining trajectories and to read the two strands of the timeline in conjunction with each other.

POLITICS	CULTURE
	Approx. 1912–14: Russian futurists energetically situate themselves within the international avant-garde, proclaiming their artistic independence and superiority with respect to Parisian modernism and Italian futurism.
1914: Second International of European socialists and social democrats breaks apart over member parties' support of their national governments in the First World War. Vladimir Lenin denounces this "social chauvinism" and calls for a more vigorously internationalist Third International.	

POLITICS

1916: Lenin writes *Imperialism, the Highest Stage of Capitalism*, which develops a Marxist theory of empire as a product of advanced capitalism. The text gives a foundation for linking anti-capitalist revolutionary socialism to anti-imperialism, arguing that revolution may spread from peripheral colonies to the core capitalist countries.

1917: February Revolution in Russia leads to overthrow of the monarchy and establishment of a bourgeois provisional government, uneasily sharing power with the Petrograd Soviet (Russian for "council") of workers' and soldiers' deputies. Months of political turmoil culminate in the October Revolution, resulting in Soviet power under Bolshevik leadership.

1918: Armistice between Allies and Central Powers formally ends the First World War. Civil war breaks out in Russia between the Bolshevik Red Army and anti-Bolshevik Whites. State-managed war communism instituted by Bolsheviks.

1919: Revolutionary failure in Europe with the bloody suppression of the revolutionary Spartacist Uprising in Germany and collapse of short-lived Soviet Republic in Hungary (in which Georg, or György, Lukács participates as a commissar). Third, or Communist, International (Comintern) officially convened at its First Congress in Moscow, chaired by Grigory Zinoviev.

CULTURE

1917: Foundation of Proletkult (Proletarian Culture), a mass organization with the project of creating a new, revolutionary, and genuinely socialist culture through literature, agitation, and the visual and performing arts. Key figures include Alexander Bogdanov, a former rival of Lenin's for Bolshevik leadership, and Anatoly Lunacharsky. Proletkult combines an ideology of autonomous proletarian culture with an ecumenical and experimental approach in practice, with the participation of a number of pre-war cultural luminaries; Lenin himself is sharply critical of the organization and the whole concept of "proletarian culture." On another end of the aesthetic spectrum are the futurists, who embrace the Revolution as an opportunity to realize their avant-garde aesthetic program.

1917–18: The Fine Arts Section of the Soviet People's Commissariat of Enlightenment (or Narkompros, headed by Lunacharsky) uses state funds to support independent avant-garde organizations in the visual arts ("Left Art" groups). Maxim Gorky founds the publishing house "World Literature" under the auspices of Narkompros, showcasing literature from around the globe translated into Russian.

1920: Second Comintern Congress held in July and August, with delegates from thirty-seven countries; Comintern's institutional structure established, including an Executive Committee (ECCI) in Moscow. At the congress, Indian communist (and Mexican Communist Party founder) M.N. Roy argues against Lenin's support for strategic alliances with bourgeois nationalists in the colonial world. First Congress of the Peoples of the East held by the Comintern in Baku in September. The Comintern modifies the First and Second International's slogan "Workers of the World, Unite!" to "Workers and Oppressed Peoples of the World, Unite!," emphasizing the International's anti-colonial agenda. Meanwhile, end of a decade of armed struggle in the Mexican Revolution.

1921: Red Army defeats White Armies, but its campaign to expand into Polish territory is repelled. Comintern begins to send emissaries to develop communist parties worldwide, including Europe and China. ECCI proclaims "United Front" policy of cooperation with reformists and social democrats, with the aim of winning over their rank and file to further revolutionary aims. New Economic Policy (NEP) instituted in the Soviet Union, a move away from war communism towards a provisional mixed public-private economy. Communist University of Toilers of the East (KUTV) opened in Moscow to train revolutionary cadre in the colonial world, attracting students from Ho Chi Minh, M.N. Roy, and Sen Katayama to African American communist Harry Haywood and Turkish poet Nâzım Hikmet.

1922: Benito Mussolini's Fascists take power in Italy. ECCI resolves that the Chinese Communist Party (CCP) enter a united front with the Guomindang, Sun Yat-Sen's bourgeois nationalist party, and offers the Comintern's resources and advisers to help build the Guomindang as well as the CCP. Official founding of Union of Soviet Socialist Republics (USSR).

1920: At Second Comintern Congress, establishment of short-lived Kultintern (Cultural International) under Lunacharsky, with mission to spread Proletkult internationally and eventually call a World Proletkult Congress. High points of Civil War culture with mass revolutionary spectacles in Petrograd and Vladimir Tatlin's planned Monument to the Third International (Tatlin's Tower). By year's end, Proletkult denounced by Bolshevik Central Committee and absorbed by Narkompros. All-Russian Association of Proletarian Writers (VAPP) founded in Moscow; it militates against aesthetic modernism, futurism, and the avant-garde and supports strictly proletarian writers, not bourgeois sympathizers.

1921: From Berlin, Willi Münzenberg founds Mezhrabpom, the Workers' Aid Organization (soon to sponsor close links between German and Soviet filmmakers via its Mezhrabpomfil'm studio). Ill and disaffected, Gorky leaves Russia for Italy. The critic Aleksandr Voronsky founds the journal *Red Virgin Soil*, which will combine a Marxist editorial line with a tolerant attitude towards bourgeois "fellow-travellers," including many of the most popular Soviet writers of the 1920s. State support withdrawn from Left Art groups.

1922: Jamaican-American poet Claude McKay travels to Moscow and helps redirect Comintern's attention towards the struggle of African Americans, speaking at its Fourth Congress. Association of Artists of Revolutionary Russia (AKhRR) formed, advocating for a strictly proletarian, technically realist art and against the avant-gardism of Left Art.

POLITICS

1923: After another failed uprising in Germany, crisis of the revolutionary movement and quashing of hopes for European revolution.

1924: Lenin dies, exacerbating power struggles for control over the Russian Communist Party (RCP) and Soviet state. Joseph Stalin begins to advocate for "socialism in one country" and an explicit shift of international communist priorities towards protecting and advocating for the USSR.

1925: Power struggles continue between Trotsky's "Left Opposition" and Stalin. Communist strength grows in China (with the May Thirtieth Movement) and India (with the Kanpur Congress of the Communist Party of India).

CULTURE

1923: Founding of first Society of Friends of the New Russia in Berlin to promote cultural exchange with the USSR. Founding of Soviet journals *On Guard*, by the group October (soon to control VAPP), expounding a militant proletarian position with an aesthetic opposed to formal experimentalism; and their opponents *LEF*, edited by the futurist poet Vladimir Mayakovsky, representing the avant-garde and their heirs (the "Left Front of the Arts" – including futurists, constructivists, formalists, and others). Leon Trotsky publishes *Literature and Revolution*, arguing that the path to a revolutionary socialist culture would require assimilating the traditions of the past, including a multiplicity of aesthetic forms; Trotsky objects to the idea of a single Party policy in art, and defends as necessary the transitional role of "fellow-travellers" (ideologically sympathetic non-proletarians) in the cultural process. In Moscow, the Russian poet Osip Mandelstam publishes an interview with Ho Chi Minh (under the name Nguyễn Ái Quốc).

1924: At the Fifth Comintern Congress, Lunacharsky again establishes a contact office to call for the creation of a new literary international.

1925: Central Committee of the RCP officially declares non-commitment to any one formal artistic tendency (although the necessity of eventual proletarian class hegemony in culture is upheld), effectively setting back VAPP's hopes for dominance and supporting a degree of tolerance for fellow-travellers. Mayakovsky tours North America, including Cuba, Mexico (where he is shown around by Diego Rivera), and the United States.

1926: Zinoviev and his ally Kamenev join Trotsky, forming the "United Opposition"; Zinoviev is removed from Comintern leadership and replaced by a collective dominated by Nikolai Bukharin, at this point Stalin's ally. Bukharin proposes the dawn of a new "third period" in postwar history, in which the revolutionary force of the European proletariat would grow and capitalist stability would unravel.

1927: Trotsky officially expelled from the Central Committee, RCP, and Comintern; other members associated with Trotsky's opposition purged. Disastrous failure of United Front policy in China when Guomindang massacres communists en masse in Shanghai, and civil war breaks out between communists and nationalists, lasting over two decades.

1928: Sixth Comintern Congress, where Stalin's doctrine of socialism in one country emerges dominant and the German Communist Party delegation defines social democracy as an ally of fascism (using the slogan "social fascism"). While Bukharin himself is marginalized by Stalin's mainstream, his "Third Period" concept is officially adopted: nationalist bourgeoisie of China and India are now declared counter-revolutionary.

1926: *On Guard* adapts to the previous year's Central Committee resolution by reconstituting itself as *On Literary Guard*, and debating how to improve the craftsmanship of "proletarian literature," but still maintaining a hard line against the futurists and their associates. Feuds among Soviet literary factions and institutions (including the On-Guardists and proletarian culture advocates, *LEF, Red Virgin Soil*, and others) continue.

1927: Lunacharsky's efforts bear fruit in the First International Conference of Proletarian and Revolutionary Writers in Moscow: writers from fourteen countries attend. International Bureau of Revolutionary Literature (IBRL) set up to coordinate "proletarian and revolutionary writers," including fellow-travellers, in capitalist countries. *LEF* reconstitutes itself as *New LEF*, opposed to belletristic forms and committing the avant-garde to a documentary "literature of fact."

1928: VAPP hosts first conference in Moscow and changes its name to Russian Association of Proletarian Writers (RAPP). "October" association founded in the visual arts (not to be confused with the earlier-mentioned literary group), uniting photographers, painters, muralists, and filmmakers from international communist circles (including Aleksandr Rodchenko and Diego Rivera). Inspired by previous year's International Conference in Moscow, Association of Proletarian Revolutionary Writers (BPRS) founded in Germany.

POLITICS

1929: Stalin's "revolution from above" is launched with accelerated collectivization of agriculture, the industrialization drive of the first five-year plan, and general purges of Party membership. Bukharin and sympathizers expelled from Comintern; intransigent theory of "social fascism" officially adopted by ECCI, with social democracy declared communism's greatest enemy. New York stock market crash initiates the Great Depression, an event perceived by Comintern as a vindication of the triumphalist "Third Period" theory.

1930: Purge Commission investigates Comintern members associated with "Left" (Trotskyite) and "Right" (Bukharinite) Oppositions. Continued Stalinization of Comintern (now officially directed by Stalin's protégé Viacheslav Molotov). ECCI adopts resolution defining African Americans as an oppressed nation (the "Black Belt," in Harry Haywood's formulation) within the US South.

1931: Comintern orders German communists to collaborate with Nazis in (failed) referendum to dissolve the Social-Democrat–controlled Prussian government. Following successful experiments in organizing the Chinese peasantry, Mao Zedong elected chairman of quasi-autonomous Jiangxi Soviet Republic.

CULTURE

1929: John Reed Clubs founded by Communist Party USA as American analogue to BPRS and RAPP. In USSR, RAPP and the movement for "proletarian literature" (with analogous proletarian movements in visual art – AkhRR – and music, all taking a far harder line against bourgeois fellow-travellers than did the "proletarian culture" efforts of Proletkult a decade earlier) expand steadily, fostered by militant new atmosphere of "cultural revolution" against bourgeois specialists in industry, "formalism" in art, and bourgeois influence in society; RAPP and its associates soon become dominant in Soviet culture.

1930: IBRL hosts Second Conference of Proletarian and Revolutionary Writers in Kharkov, with 100 delegates from twenty-three countries present. IBRL reformed as International Union of Revolutionary Writers (Russian acronym: MORP), explicitly conceived as Comintern's literary arm. *Roar China*, an anti-colonial play by the former *New LEF* editor Sergei Tret'iakov, tours Europe, with productions reaching New York and Guangzhou. Inspired by Soviet-Mexican revolutionary contacts and funded by Upton Sinclair, Sergei Eisenstein travels to Mexico to shoot a film about its history, *¡Que viva México!* Lukács summoned from Budapest to Moscow, where he largely remains until the mid-forties, a fixture of the Germanophone anti-fascist intellectual diaspora.

1931: *Literature of the World Revolution* founded as official journal of MORP, published in four (soon six) languages, with a multinational editorial board. In China, League of Left-Wing Writers and League of Left-Wing Dramatists issue programs to reach the masses.

1932: RAPP, by now hegemonic in Soviet culture but never officially part of the state, is formally disbanded when the Central Committee of the RCP issues a resolution "restructuring" Soviet culture by banning independent groups; Soviet literature reconstituted under a centralized Writers' Union, with Gorky invited back from Italy to serve as its head. Mezhrabpomfil'm invites a delegation of African Americans, including Langston Hughes, to the USSR to shoot an anti-racist film; Hughes tours Soviet Central Asia. Eisenstein's *¡Que viva México!* project implodes due to political and financial controversies. *Literature of the World Revolution* renamed *International Literature*.

1933: Adolf Hitler appointed chancellor of Germany, quickly consolidates dictatorial control, and begins liquidation of Social Democratic and Communist Party opposition. Nonetheless, Comintern's commitment to "social fascist" line at first barely wavers.

1933: Debates in Soviet journals over the nature of "socialist realism," which has been proclaimed as the generic and programmatic essence of Soviet art. Now unable to stay in Berlin, Lukács becomes an editor of the heterodox Germano-Soviet journal *Literary Critic* (*Literaturnyi kritik*) and a Soviet literary theorist, justifying socialist realism with respect to nineteenth-century novelistic realism and the heritage of German philosophical aesthetics.

1934: Socialist and communist workers in France band together in anti-fascist strikes and actions. Georgi Dimitrov, a Bulgarian communist framed by the Nazis for setting fire to the Reichstag, is released from jail and appointed general secretary of Comintern by Stalin; Dimitrov pushes for more cooperation with social democrats to fight fascism, softening the Comintern's "social fascism" position.

1934: First Congress of the Soviet Writers' Union in Moscow, where Gorky, Andrei Zhdanov, and other literary luminaries and Party figures expound on socialist realism, firmly institutionalizing it without clearly defining it, to an audience including numerous well-known international fellow-travellers. The British section of the International Union of Revolutionary Writers founds the journal *Left Review*, which will last until 1938, publishing a range of prominent left-wing and anti-colonial writers.

POLITICS

1935: Seventh (and final) Comintern Congress held in Moscow, reversing positions to officially declare a newly broad "Popular Front" against fascism in collaboration with peasants, the petty bourgeoisie, and social democrats (no longer maligned as fascists). This directive also buoys Mao to engineer a Second United Front with the Guomindang to resist Japanese aggression.

1936: Popular Front governments elected in France and Spain; the latter faces a right-wing coup attempt led by Francisco Franco, triggering the Spanish Civil War between Republicans and Nationalists. Comintern mobilizes International Brigades of volunteers to aid the Republican side.

1937: In the USSR, with the Great Terror in full swing, the Comintern is decimated by Soviet security forces; many nations' communist parties, in exile in Moscow, are practically eradicated. Stalin uses the Spanish Civil War as an opportunity to strike at left-wing ideological foes abroad, with internecine attacks by Spanish communists and Soviet agents on Trotskyist and anarchist forces.

1938: Trotsky attempts to organize an anti-Stalinist Fourth International; its founding conference is held outside Paris with thirty delegates attending.

1939: The Nationalists emerge victorious in the Spanish Civil War, brutally suppressing their opponents. The Popular Front comes to a halt when Stalin signs the Molotov-Ribbentrop Pact of non-aggression with the Nazis; with the outbreak of another world war, the Comintern resurrects Lenin's analysis of twenty-five years before to declare the conflict an inter-imperialist war, like the First World War, and urges workers to stay uninvolved.

CULTURE

1935: First Congress for the Defence of Culture held in Paris, bankrolled by the Comintern to redefine its internationalist cultural activity as humanist and anti-fascist; attendance is very high, particularly among American, European, and Soviet writers. MORP replaced by the International Writers' Association for the Defence of Culture. Founding conference of the CPUSA-backed League of American Writers in New York City.

1936: All-India Progressive Writers' Association, soon to become South Asia's most powerful literary force, hosts its inaugural conference in Lucknow. Spanish intellectuals form the Alliance of Anti-fascist Intellectuals for the Defence of Culture.

1937: Second Writers' Congress in Defence of Culture takes place in Madrid, Valencia, Barcelona, and Paris, while numerous writers worldwide with anti-fascist sympathies head to Spain to join the Republican forces. Meanwhile, the Terror begins to claim numerous victims from the Soviet literary and artistic world.

1938: Debate between Lukács and Ernst Bloch over the legacies of modernism (specifically German expressionism) and realism in *Das Wort*, Comintern-affiliated journal of the exiled German intellectual diaspora.

1939: In response to Stalin's actions in Spain and the Molotov-Ribbentrop Pact, numerous anti-fascist intellectuals drawn into the Comintern's orbit throughout the 1930s grow disaffected and cut ties with communism.

1941: In China, the anti-Japanese Second United Front ends in January when Guomindang troops attack Communist Party forces. In June, Germany invades the USSR, and the Comintern immediately changes its line to propagandize for the Soviet war effort; due to the Comintern's (by now) threadbare infrastructure and membership, its contribution is minimal.

1942: In China, the CCP holds a Forum on Literature and Art at Yan'an: Mao's speech propounds the need for a revolutionary mass culture that addresses workers and peasants, proclaiming literature and art as subordinate to socialist politics.

1943: The moribund Third International is officially dissolved. Its final resolution argues that different nations' working classes face divisions that are practically irreconcilable.

1947: Founding of Cominform, or the Information Bureau of Communist and Workers' Parties, to coordinate communist parties in the Eastern bloc under Soviet dominance. Dissolved in 1956 after rapprochement between Nikita Khrushchev's USSR and Josip Broz Tito's Federal People's Republic of Yugoslavia.

Editors' Note

The breadth of languages, regions, and alphabets covered in this volume has necessitated some variance in spelling and transliteration. We have chosen to Romanize all non-Roman alphabets in order to make the formal poetic innovation more accessible to a broad English-language readership. In citations from the original Russian, we have followed the United States Library of Congress transliteration system. We have followed the Hanyu Pinyin Romanization system for transliteration from Chinese. Yiddish has been transliterated following the YIVO system of orthography.

In the case of well-known figures and place names, we have opted to use the most common spelling in English for broader recognition: thus, Mayakovsky (rather than Maiakovskij or Maiakovskii); Peretz (as opposed to Perets). Unless otherwise noted, all translations are by the author of the relevant chapter.

COMINTERN AESTHETICS

Introduction: Comintern Aesthetics – Space, Form, History

STEVEN S. LEE
UC Berkeley

The aim of this volume is to remap world literature and culture from the perspective of world communism – that is, from the perspective of a leftist, anti-capitalist modernity that ascended in the years after the 1917 Bolshevik Revolution. In the 1920s and 30s, this alternative modernity witnessed, for instance, Vladimir Mayakovsky writing "Afro-Cuban" poetry that was later translated by Langston Hughes in Moscow; Sergei Eisenstein shooting a film in Mexico based partly on the murals of Diego Rivera, another traveller to Moscow; and the Beijing opera star Mei Lanfang's own 1935 visit to Moscow, where his lectures and gender-bending performances inspired, among others, Eisenstein and Bertolt Brecht.[1] After persisting through much of the twentieth century, this largely forgotten modernity decisively imploded (along with the Soviet Union itself) by century's end, but, as the volume shows, we can still use it to articulate internationalist alternatives to the flattened, commodified cultures of neoliberal globalization.

Communism provided a different world system – most obviously conveyed in a geopolitical sense through the notion of a "Second World" that, during the Cold War, coloured maps of Eastern Europe, vast swaths of Asia, as well as parts of Africa and Latin America in red.[2] However, the focus of this volume will be an earlier moment when communism's allure was more dispersed and open-ended – again, the 1920s and 30s, the time of the Third Communist International, or Comintern. Founded by Vladimir Lenin in 1919 to foment world revolution, the Comintern advanced not just proletarian struggle but a wide variety of radical causes – struggles against imperialism and racism in settings as varied as Ireland, India, the United States, and China. Notoriously and from the organization's outset, these causes grew ever more subservient to Soviet state interest and Stalinist centralization, but this volume shows how the cultural and political networks emerging from the Comintern have long outlived its 1943 demise. The chapters that comprise this volume track these networks through a multiplicity of artistic forms geared towards advancing a common, liberated humanity. As a whole, the volume captures the failure of a Soviet-centred world revolution, but also shows its enduring allure into the present.

Though *Comintern Aesthetics* covers a wide range of forms alongside contexts, the one that recurs most frequently here is literature. This focus is largely because existing models of cultural circulation have themselves tended to foreground literature and have emerged from ongoing debates about the meaning of world literature. The volume intervenes in these debates by eschewing models of world literature that, by typically foregrounding the West, tend to mirror the flows of capital and empire. For instance, Franco Moretti – drawing from Immanuel Wallerstein's world-systems theory, which charts the global economy's ever-shifting centre, semi-periphery, and periphery – has suggested that the centre of the modern novel can be understood as France and England; the semi-periphery, the United States and Southern and Eastern Europe; and the periphery, countries in Africa, Asia, and Latin America. Likewise, Pascale Casanova has posited Paris as the centre for her "world republic of letters," in which writers from around the world compete for the cultural capital bestowed by French scholars and literary critics. One benefit of such models is that they help to free literary studies from national constraints and from an exclusively Western orientation; indeed, Casanova suggests that writers in the postcolonial periphery are often more innovative precisely because of their distance from the cosmopolitan (Parisian) centre.[3] At the same time, however, Casanova foregrounds literary modernism in a way that approximates the Cold War divide between the communist East and capitalist West – the Cold War recast as a clash between Western modernism and Eastern realism or socialist realism.[4] Accordingly, lost in both Casanova's and Moretti's models is the literature of the world revolution – literature produced beyond or explicitly against the limits of Western capitalism and empire.[5] A desire to counter these models explains the relative (but by no means absolute) absence of the West in the present volume, which covers China, Southeast Asia, India, the Near East, the Soviet Union, Eastern Europe, Germany, Spain, and the Americas – all sites where the Comintern or its affiliates had an active presence – and certainly the list could go on. Our aim is not to seal off a supposedly singular communist or Soviet bloc, but to blur the boundaries between East and West, North and South, national and international. We also aim to provide a foundation for further research extending the networks covered here.

Accordingly, since the Cold War's end there has been a growing body of scholarship aimed at reconstructing leftist political and cultural genealogies across national lines. For instance, as has now been well established, Maxim Gorky's state-supported World Literature Publishing House (1919–25) addressed such issues as racism and cultural hierarchy, and prominently featured non-Western titles; the Soviet Union of the 1920s and 30s inspired such luminaries as Lu Xun, André Malraux, and Pablo Neruda; and Moscow's apparent elimination of racial discrimination, coupled with the Comintern's policies against Jim Crow, resonated with many prominent African Americans.[6] One key inspiration for this volume has been Michael Denning's notion of a "novelists' international," which at the turn of the twentieth century first emerged through alliances between writers and socialist movements; was deeply influenced by competing Soviet notions of proletarian culture in the 1920s and 30s; but then reappeared in the form of postcolonial and magical realist texts in the postwar years. (Denning calls magical realism the now-canonical "aesthetic of globalization" – that is, world literature's current dominant form – and then traces its roots back to proletarian literary movements.)[7] Despite its emphasis on the novel, one of the appeals of Denning's international is that it allows for a variety of narratives (for example, factory and tenement novels using techniques like documentary and reportage) that unfold differently in different settings. *Comintern Aesthetics* deepens his manifesto-like piece by gathering the work of many different regional experts and also broadens it by encompassing architecture, painting, poetry, theatre, music, and film in addition to novels – in other words, not just world literature but world culture. By providing the most comprehensive-to-date glimpse of the twentieth century's revolutionary cultures, the volume seeks to recapture a long-lost moment in which the aesthetic could not only transform perception but also highlight alternatives to capitalism – namely, an anti-colonial world imaginary foregrounding national, racial, class, and gender equality.

This project is easier said than done in light of the Comintern's troubled history and the often vexed relationship between radical politics and culture. The Comintern's subservience to Soviet state interests and Stalinist realpolitik is undeniable; indeed, Stalin, who was always suspicious of the organization's cosmopolitanism, ultimately dissolved it to appease his Second World War allies.[8] Meanwhile, it is tempting to think of "Comintern aesthetics" as synonymous with the coercion of artists and writers by state and party or, more specifically, with Soviet socialist realism. In response, the volume highlights the gap between the entropic actuality of the Comintern (more on which later) and its unrealized and perhaps unrealizable dream: to balance centripetal control with local struggle, internationalism, and nationalism. As the chapters here demonstrate, this dream of world revolution persists through the aesthetic – through specific cultural forms that continue to survive the Comintern's and Soviet Union's downfalls. These forms are by no means limited to socialist realism, which was enshrined only in 1934, that is, fifteen years after the Comintern's founding, but include a wide range of experimental realisms and modernisms. Taken together, the studies gathered here transgress standard realism-versus-modernism divides in search of a broader understanding of the relationship between artist and masses, representer and represented, individual and collective. What kinds of cultural production best bridge these divides? Which were (or are) able, on a global scale, to stir opposition to social and political oppression? Mining the often oppressive, utopian history of twentieth-century communism, the pieces here try to work through, if not resolve, these ever-urgent questions. The volume uses specific aesthetic forms to track the Comintern's utopian promise and

0.1   Ai Weiwei, *Working Progress (Fountain of Light)*, 2007. Courtesy of Ai Weiwei Studio.

dispersed networks, and then follows these forms to understand how this promise and these networks have been carried forward into the present.

Working Progress

To illustrate the continuing relevance of Comintern forms, let us begin not in Leningrad but Liverpool, not in the interwar years but in 2007 – with Tate Liverpool's exhibit "The Real Thing: Contemporary Art from China" and, in particular, Ai Weiwei's chandelier installation piece *Working Progress (Fountain of Light)*. There are many ways of reading this work – a seven-metre-tall, three-ton tower covered with lights and glass crystal (figure 0.1). "Working Progress" is a play, of course, on "Work in Progress," which perhaps references the fact that the work on which it is based, Vladimir Tatlin's 1920 *Monument to the Third International* (figure 0.2), was never completed. "Working Progress" can also be read as a reference to the enormous growth of China over the past three decades – a progress that works. But, of course, "Working Progress"

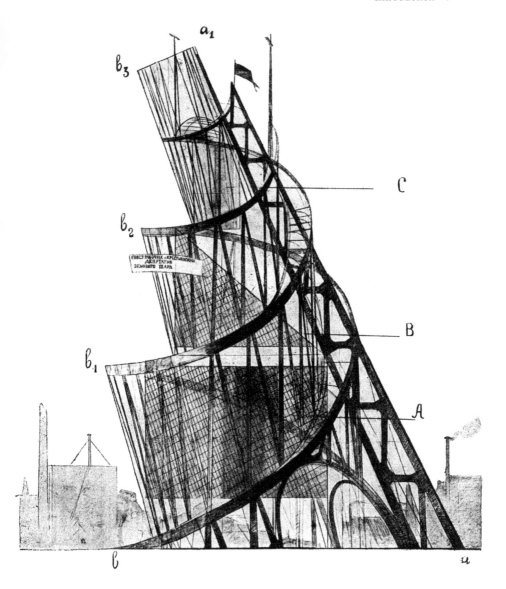

0.2 Vladimir Tatlin, Monument to the Third International, 1920.

also conveys a more cynical meaning: working as cheating, as in "working the system." From this perspective, the title links progress to duplicity, progress to fraud. The revolutionary fervour of the Comintern and the Soviet avant-garde repeats itself in the capitalist fervour of contemporary China.

How are we to connect Tatlin's 1920 Comintern monument and Ai's 2007 reworking of it? Simple continuity does not seem to apply: in his comments on the piece, Ai discerns a critique of progress or the illusion of progress built into the original structure, stating: "The spiral is a dynamic upward motion that ultimately goes nowhere."[9] To reinforce this sense of illusion, he placed the work on a barge floating beside Tate Liverpool so that it could be reflected in water (figure 0.3). In his conceptual notes he writes: "The reflection of the chandelier in water is the positive. It is related to both the earth and sky, screwing out of one and into the other, as spirals are able to extend outwards and downwards" (39). The spiral and its reflections thus point in opposite directions – again, a dynamic motion that goes nowhere. Ai adds that the spiral form of Tatlin's Tower "defeats the very intellectual ideal it was meant to symbolize: ironically, it becomes a metaphor for the way in which power ultimately collapses in upon itself, for the romantic sentiments with which the rational mind is eternally in conflict always prove to be its undoing" (40). In short, Ai's invocation of Tatlin's tenuous structure emphasizes the failure of communist internationalism and the sentiments undergirding it – revolutionary romanticism in tension with rational thought. Observing Tatlin's use of glass, Ai notes: "Glass served to emphasize the degree of clear, enlightened thinking behind Lenin's theories of an ideal social system ... Whenever Man experiences a bout of revolutionary thinking, he always ends up boxing – caging, in this case – himself in" (38).

Following Ai's lead, we can use Tatlin's Tower to reflect on both the promise and disappointment of the Comintern's history, including the organization's enlistment of radical art. But, while Ai reads the tower's two intertwined spirals as a metaphor for romanticism struggling against reason, they can also be read as the convergence of experimental art and radical politics, constructivist form and revolutionary function. Intended not just as the Comintern's monument but also its headquarters, the iron spirals were to have supported (as Ai notes) three glass structures, each spinning at different speeds. A large cube at the base was to have rotated once a year and hosted the organization's polyglot congresses, which worked to apply Marxist-Leninist theories to both industrial and pre-industrial societies, to both Western powers and their colonized subjects. For instance, the year of the tower's unveiling, the Comintern's Second Congress (with delegates from thirty-seven countries) famously supported "oppressed nations" in their fight against "oppressor nations," effectively making anti-imperialism a key part of the world revolution.[10] Above the congress cube, Tatlin planned a pyramid rotating once a month, which was to have housed the Comintern's executive committee. In the 1920s this committee

0.3 Ai Weiwei, *Working Progress (Fountain of Light)*, 2007, floating beside Tate Liverpool. Courtesy of Ai Weiwei Studio and Tate Images.

included the Indian communist and Mexican Party co-founder M.N. Roy, who over the course of several congresses stressed Asia's importance for the revolution; as well as Sen Katayama, a founder of communist parties in Japan and the United States, who was instrumental in directing the Comintern's attention to the plight of African Americans.[11] Finally, a cylinder at the tower's top was to have rotated once a day and housed information and propaganda offices. This was to be the centre of the Comintern's wide-ranging cultural initiatives, for instance, its sponsorship of bodies like the International Union of Revolutionary Writers (publisher of the journal *Literature of the World Revolution*, renamed *International Literature* in 1932, with editions in six languages); and Mezhrabpom (International Workers Aid), a famine relief organization which, under the wily Berlin-based communist Willi Münzenberg, distributed Sergei Eisenstein's *Battleship Potemkin* in Germany and, through its Mezhrabpomfil'm studio in Moscow, produced groundbreaking works like Vsevolod Pudovkin's *Storm Over Asia* (1928). Reinforcing the tower's utopian reach, radio broadcasts were to emanate from its peak and agitational slogans projected onto surrounding clouds.[12] In short, Tatlin captured the hopes of a fantastically dispersed albeit top-down world revolution – what Brigitte Studer has recently described as "a hierarchical but polycentric internationalism," which, however, "gave way in time to a concentration on Moscow."[13]

For Ai, Tatlin's use of spirals presaged this concentration, that is, the inward collapse of these utopian designs – a collapse reinforced by the tower's incompletion due to a lack of materials, but also, one could argue, due to the Comintern's increasing restrictiveness. Following Ai's and Tatlin's leads, we can track this collapse by following two intertwined tracks, the political and the cultural. First the political: From its inception (that is, not just under Stalin, but also under Lenin), the Comintern demanded discipline, as indicated by the twenty-one conditions that local parties had to fulfil to be considered for membership – for instance, the requirement "to give unconditional support to any Soviet republic in its struggle against counter-revolutionary forces."[14] This demand for discipline became ever more pronounced and beholden to Soviet foreign diplomacy throughout the organization's erratic history. For much of the 1920s, a "united front" policy sought to broaden communism's appeal to workers, but the Comintern went back and forth on whether to ally with the leaders of mainstream unions and reformist parties.[15] From the middle of the decade, Stalin's theory of "socialism in one country" asserted that Soviet socialism was no longer dependent on a larger, world revolution, which instead was dependent on the Soviet state's survival.[16] "Socialism in one country" affirmed the Comintern's turn to Stalinist centralization; indeed, the organization soon became a theatre for Stalin's elimination of his Bolshevik rivals. His consolidation of power along with united front failures (most notably in China), as well as the perception that global capitalism was entering a crisis phase, provided the backdrop for the Comintern's ultra-sectarian Third Period (1928–33), during which social democrats were vilified as "social fascists" whose "conciliators" had to be purged from communist ranks worldwide.[17] Hitler's 1933 election – at the very least facilitated by the Third Period view that German social democracy posed a greater threat than Nazism[18] – then prompted the Comintern's about-face call for a Popular Front against fascism. However, this tactical shift, which allowed for alliances with social democrats and fellow travellers, remained secondary to Stalinist centralization and paranoia – as evidenced by the purge of anarchist and Trotskyite anti-Franco forces during the Spanish Civil War (1936–39).[19] The Popular Front was suspended after the 1939 Molotov-Ribbentrop Non-Aggression Pact, but abruptly resumed after the German invasion of the Soviet Union in 1941.

Much recent scholarship has worked to nuance these stages – in particular, to emphasize local agency against notions of the Comintern as monolith – and ultimately this volume will follow suit. However, it is undeniable that local agency existed alongside an overall trend towards centralization[20] – a trend that we see again when turning from the political to the cultural track: During the Civil War and New Economic Policy (NEP) years, the Soviet state adopted an ecumenical approach to revolutionary culture, but in 1928 a state-sanctioned cultural revolution elevated doctrinaire "proletarian" writer and artist groups over "bourgeois specialists," that is, pre-revolution intellectuals. This cultural revolution was related to the Comintern's Third Period: both were part of Stalin's move against the so-called "right opposition" led by Nikolai Bukharin.[21] And, just as the Third Period gave way to the more inclusive Popular Front, the cultural revolution gave way to the 1934 founding of the Union of Soviet Writers, which included "bourgeois specialist" members but also marked the official enshrinement of socialist realism.[22] In short, the cultural experimentation of the 1920s gave way to artists and writers as Party functionaries – "engineers of human souls" charged with depicting "reality in its revolutionary development."[23]

Given these long-established political and cultural tracks, *Working Progress*'s cautious take on revolution – the inward collapse of intertwined spirals, the tower and its reflection working against one another – seems all the more apt. And yet, as *Comintern Aesthetics* shows repeatedly, creative expression need not be beholden to historical failure. As has been widely noted, Ai does not simply provide a monument to disillusion, but instead reconfigures Tatlin's Tower into a critique of contemporary China's hyper-development, here captured by the chandelier pieces that gaudily drape the tower – markers of capitalist excess appended to the scaffolding of revolution.[24] Behind Ai's criticism of Lenin lies an implicit criticism of the current Chinese Communist Party and its corruption-plagued embrace of free markets. Not simply stripped of its radical underpinnings, Tatlin's Tower here re-emerges as contemporary protest art – to be sure, a far cry from revolution, but affirmation nonetheless of the ongoing allure of Tatlin's utopian design. In other words, the radical aesthetic vision outlasts the political one; the aesthetic experiments surrounding the Comintern persist long after communism's official collapse. From this perspective, we can see Ai's work not simply as a critique of revolution but also of the very notion of historical progress: the opposite screws connote historical cessation, enabling us to rethink (but not neglect) well-trodden narratives about the 1920s and 30s, for example, the turn from world revolution to Stalinist centralization, from avant-gardism to socialist realism.[25]

The many different cultural works examined in this volume do something similar to *Working Progress*: taken together, they point to the elusive, irruptive persistence of what we are calling "Comintern aesthetics," which, as we will now see, cross historical boundaries like interwar versus postwar; spatial boundaries like East versus West; and formal boundaries like modernism versus realism. Understanding this concept requires unpacking each of these two terms, "Comintern" and "aesthetics" – tracking the Comintern's applicability across multiple contexts and cultures, and regearing the aesthetic so that it is able to encompass multiple forms, media, and political applications.

Interwar/Postwar, East/West, Modernism/Realism

But first we must recognize the virtue of failure. Paradoxically, the fact that the utopian ambitions behind the Comintern and its monument remained unrealized is precisely what allows these ambitions to remain intact. Had Tatlin's Tower been constructed, its allure would have quickly tarnished as the home of a top-heavy bureaucracy subservient to Stalinist centralization and terror. Indeed, architect Takehiko Nagakura has depicted a completed tower in contemporary St. Petersburg as just another ruin bearing testimony to the failed Soviet utopia (figure 0.4).[26] But the fact of the tower's incompletion holds the benefit of reinforcing the dispersed quality of Comintern aesthetics – the circulation of these leftist networks around a centre which was never realized, or which collapsed in on itself like a black hole, or which proved to be the "no-place" of utopia.[27] In other words, if the history of the Comintern is a troubled history, its (unintended) lack of a centre makes it possible to salvage (if not quite redeem) the organization as a catalyst not just for artistic innovation but also for ongoing, global struggles for equality. Moscow was an aspiring but failed centre, a fact that enables us to emphasize some of the more non-centripetal aspects of the Comintern's revolution and, more to the point, prevents Comintern aesthetics from becoming just one more centre-periphery model of world culture.[28] Thus, for instance, in his discussion in this volume of the Comintern's 1920 Congress of the Peoples of the East, Harsha Ram suggests that the "Bolsheviks' undeniable cultural Eurocentrism ... was to some extent counterbalanced by their striking reconfiguration of Marxist doctrine in accordance with the 'zig-zag' rather

0.4 Still from *Tatlin's Tower – Monument to the Third International*, 1999. Producer/ Director: Takehiko Nagakura; Computer Graphics: Andrzej Zarzycki, Takehiko Nagakura, Dan Brick, and Mark Sich.

than stadial path of non-European history" – a "zig-zag" affirmed by Velimir Khlebnikov's eccentric "abstraction of time" and "decolonization of space" in his "supersaga" *Zangezi* (1920–22). Likewise, Katerina Clark's discussion of Soviet, German, and Chinese cultural responses to the failed united front in China (that is, the 1927 Shanghai massacre) reinforces the notion of what has been called a "socialist global ecumene" – one that breaks from vertical, centre-periphery models of internationalism and allows instead for multiple, overlapping networks.[29] Snehal Shingavi's contribution tracks some of these networks by showing how the All-India Progressive Writers' Association navigated both British and Soviet influences, as well as the local exigencies of 1930s Indian anti-imperialism. Sarah Ann Wells extends the ecumene further by showing how, that same decade, modernist Brazilian artists and writers turned to the Soviet Union to articulate a "global simultaneity," which served to counter (arguably still extant) notions of South American "belatedness." Meanwhile, within Soviet borders, an official nationalities policy promoted a diverse range of cultures, which were to be "national in form, socialist in content."[30] Though this policy has frequently been seen as a mummifying prescription, always beholden to

Soviet state interests, Nariman Skakov shows how, particularly in spaces far removed from Moscow (for example, the Central Asia of Andrei Platonov in the 1930s), vibrant expressions of national form were indeed possible.[31]

From this decentred perspective, the Comintern provided a platform for situating ethnic and national struggles within a larger, international movement and, in doing so, helped set into motion the postcolonial wave that crested after the Second World War, that is, after the Comintern's demise.[32] Tony Day makes this point clear by tracking the emergence of a world literary space corresponding to the non-aligned "Third World" of the 1955 Afro-Asian Conference in Bandung, Indonesia – a space marked by a dynamic socialist realism that refused both colonial masters and top-down decrees, and emphasized local understandings of fate and natural law. Similarly, Kate Baldwin connects the prominent role of African Americans in the interwar international left (the focus of Jonathan Flatley's and Christina Kiaer's chapters) to the more flexible leftism of the postwar years – namely, a black feminist transnationalism that articulates coalitions through "quotidian, mundane, heartfelt connections." And Katie Trumpener shows how, in East Germany after the Second World War, interwar leftist networks were recoded into a unique decolonization model that cast Nazi aggression as an outgrowth of Western imperialism and racism. She also tracks echoes of these networks in postwar media circulation, particularly the radio airwaves that fostered the East German dissident and tamizdat movements of the 1960s and 70s. Through Baldwin's, Day's, and Trumpener's contributions, the left of the Comintern becomes more familiar and, perhaps, palatable. They help us to forge bridges between interwar revolution and more contemporary forms of activism – feminist, anti-racist, postcolonial, anti-authoritarian.

In short, *Comintern Aesthetics* unearths a lost genealogy for present-day activism, demonstrating ways of connecting the local and the global, the personal-as-political and world revolution. Such connections can be understood not only in historical (interwar/postwar) terms but also in spatial ones – namely, East and West. Specifically, the volume seeks to unseat the Cold War partition of the international left into Eastern and Western camps by revealing continuities that have long been obscured. For instance, the key Western Marxist thinker Antonio Gramsci famously argued that, to forge radical hegemony, attention must be paid to civil society and, in Stuart Hall's words, to "the ethical, the cultural, the moral."[33] For Gramsci, revolution depended on a "'cultural-social' unity through which a multiplicity of dispersed wills with heterogeneous aims are welded together with a single aim, on the basis of an equal and common conception of the world."[34] Gramsci thus eschewed top-down directives from a Leninist vanguard in favour of a more inclusive, holistic view of revolution – one lending itself to a variety of struggles in which all aspects of life were part of an ongoing war of position to alter "common sense." However, as Ernesto Laclau and Chantal Mouffe have shown, such efforts to nuance Marxist theory and practice were in fact extensions of Comintern strategies: Gramsci himself was a Comintern veteran, spending 1922–24 with the organization in Moscow and subsequently butting heads with it in his capacity as Italian Communist Party head.[35] The larger point here is that much of what is considered canonical leftist thought in the West emerges from concrete experiences with and participation in the leftist circuits tracked in this volume. To be sure, these experiences often ended negatively – again, Moscow was ultimately a failed revolutionary centre. And yet, their formative role helps to explain why the culmination of this failure – namely, the Soviet collapse – proved so debilitating for the global left; why the decline of "Eastern" Marxism coincided with the suddenly common-sense view, all around the world, that there was no alternative to global capitalism.[36]

But perhaps more relevant here is how the blurring of East-West, centre-periphery allows us to reconsider not just political genealogies but the very notion of aesthetic form. Our starting point is the earlier-noted casting of the Cold War as a clash between modernism and realism. Since we tend to think of realism and, in particular, socialist realism as the mandatory aesthetic of the Soviet Union, and since socialist realism was originally enshrined during the interwar years and was subsequently promoted around the world through Comintern channels, it is tempting to think of Comintern aesthetics as synonymous with socialist realism. In contrast, modernism breaks free from the limits of top-down aesthetic prescriptions by leaving room for experimentation, iconoclasm, and ironic playfulness. However, as Clark emphasizes in her magisterial *Moscow, the Fourth Rome*, within Soviet and Soviet-influenced literary circles through the early 1930s, there was no absolute divide between modernism on one hand and realism and socialist realism on the other. For instance, the earlier-mentioned journal *International Literature* published episodes one through ten of Joyce's *Ulysses* in 1935 – that is, one year after the official launch of socialist realism. Accordingly, Christina Kiaer shows in her chapter how modernist experimentation persisted in the Soviet Union even after all of the country's artists were consolidated into single, state-controlled unions in April 1932. Also troubling the modernism-realism binary, Enrique Fibla-Gutiérrez and Masha Salazkina present an ideologically diverse group of Spanish film viewers who sought models for a new national realism from such canonically "modernist" figures as Sergei Eisenstein and Vsevolod Pudovkin. In turn, examining 1930s Yiddish poems written in the style of Spanish Republican placards, Amelia Glaser not only links Jewish tradition, the Spanish Civil War, and communism, but also crosses the seeming divide between artistic experimentation and political propaganda. And Evgeny Dobrenko's chapter shows how, across Eastern Europe after the Second World War, socialist realism gave way to a vibrant, ecumenical "socialist literature."[37]

Without discounting the state's control over the arts, its enshrinement of socialist realism, and the subsequent reverberations in leftist circles around the world, this volume seeks a dynamic understanding of the aesthetic – one that encompasses multiple forms and contexts, and exceeds both the realism-versus-modernism debate and the East-West binary grafted onto it during the Cold War. This understanding is what we already begin to find by unpacking one of the origin moments for this debate: the Bloch-Lukács-Brecht exchanges about expressionism that played out over the 1930s in the pages of *International Literature* and another Comintern-affiliated, Moscow-based journal, *Das Wort*. To varying degrees, these thinkers were all committed to a Soviet-led world revolution; yet, while Bloch and Brecht embraced the fragments and alienation effects that we would now label modernist, Lukács (writing from Moscow) famously clung to the nineteenth-century realist novel as the literary form best suited to unveiling the capitalist world.[38]

However, on closer examination, these exchanges trouble the modernism-realism divide via an expansive notion of realism that is central to Comintern aesthetics.[39] In a 1938 reply to Bloch published in *Das Wort*, Lukács defines the major realist writer as one who "fashions the material given in his own experience, and in so doing makes use of techniques of abstraction, among others. But his goal is to penetrate the laws governing objective reality and to uncover the deeper, hidden, mediated, not immediately perceptible network of relationships that go to make up society."[40] Thus, for Lukács, realism can encompass modernist abstraction as long as abstraction ultimately gives way to a "new immediacy" that departs from what he views as the superficial, politically misguided abstraction and immediacy of expressionism. This new immediacy – "life as it actually appears" – allows us to observe

> the whole surface of life in all its essential determinants, and not just a subjectively perceived moment isolated from the totality in an abstract and over-intense manner. This, then, is the artistic dialectic of appearance and essence. The richer, the more diverse, complex and 'cunning' (Lenin) this dialectic is, the more firmly it grasps hold of the living contradictions of life and society, then the greater and the more profound the realism will be. (39)

Despite Lukács' fixation on the realist novel, it is in this effort to capture a contradictory totality that we find common ground among him, Bloch, and Brecht. They are united in their efforts to interrupt, in the words of Jed Esty and Colleen Lye, our "quasi-natural perception of reality as a mere given," even if they disagree about the nature of reality.[41]

Comintern aesthetics brings to the fore this intricate, capacious understanding of the real, as well as of a realism that allows for the formal innovations that we would typically associate with modernism. It allows, too, for the vernacular cultures that many of the volume's contributors engage, despite Lukács' own wariness about folk art.[42] The key here is an expansive understanding of realism that sidesteps any binary opposition to modernism. This is the realism articulated by Brecht in an article that was submitted to but rejected by *Das Wort* in Moscow:

> Realistic means: discovering the causal complexes of society / unmasking the prevailing view of things as the view of those who are in power / writing from the standpoint of the class which offers the broadest solutions for the pressing difficulties in which human society is caught up / emphasizing the element of development / making possible the concrete, and making possible abstraction from it.[43]

In short, in determining whether a work adheres to realism, the focus should not be on the technical, on form, but rather on whether the work provides an "accurate image of the real social forces at work under an immediately visible surface" (84). From this perspective, realism becomes, in Fredric Jameson's words, "not a purely artistic and formal category" but rather an idea that "governs the relationship of the work of art to reality itself, characterizing a particular stance towards it." Jameson adds: "The spirit of realism designates an active, curious, experimental, subversive ... attitude towards social institutions and the material world."[44] Thus, Brecht (along with Jameson) defines realism not by any single form but by what it is able to accomplish in the world.

Building from this understanding of realism, Esty and Lye's "peripheral realisms" project seeks to grasp the post–Cold War world system by situating critical realism "within a genealogy of ethnic and postcolonial studies and within an expanded field of literary practice not solely organized by the historical referent of the nineteenth-century European nation-state."[45] Comintern aesthetics does just this by turning from Western Europe to the Third International, but, as we have seen, though the Comintern's history can be woven into postcolonial genealogies, it also adds to the mix the spectres of revolutionary failure and Stalinist terror. Indeed, within this context, realism itself becomes fraught, given its association with state-mandated socialist realism, which Lukács himself helped to articulate. This history also touched Brecht in troubling ways: Adorno describes his plays as combining innovation and didacticism, but then critiques him for failing to grapple with or counter real social problems – and, in particular, for providing (in the 1930 play *The Measures Taken*, discussed in Clark's contribution) a possible apologia for the Moscow trials.[46]

In the face of such quandaries, it is not enough to think about Comintern aesthetics solely as a new spin on realism or socialist realism. Instead, as a whole, the volume seeks to reorient the aesthetic itself away from art and literature per se (for example, the formal distinctions between realism and modernism) and towards a "sensual, cognitive experience that is capable of resisting abusive power's self-justification."[47] These are the words of Susan Buck-Morss, who has been instrumental in turning attention away from Kantian aesthetics (centring on a transcendental, masculinist subject who "purges himself of the senses") to an "aesthetic system of sense-consciousness, decentred from the classical subject, wherein external sense-perceptions come together with the internal images of memory and anticipation."[48] That is, the aesthetic here refers to inner and outer sensations mediated by the body's surface, and Buck-Morss shows how, in the 1930s, when confronted with this "aesthetics of the surface," Walter Benjamin was able to discern its competing political applications: while the "aestheticized politics" of fascism worked as an anaesthetic to "numb the organism, to deaden the senses, to repress memory" (18), in contrast, the "politicized art" of communism was to lay bare fascism's manipulation of the senses and turn attention to actual material relations. Following Benjamin's lead, Buck-Morss forwards a radical aesthetic that foregrounds the sensory rather than any particular form – an aesthetic bound not to art or realism but to "corporeal, material nature." Like Lukács and Brecht, she seeks a critical grasp of capitalist totality, but, unlike Lukács and (to a lesser extent) Brecht, she doesn't specify what successful, progressive politicized art should look like, only what it is supposed to accomplish – namely, a sensory experience that allows for "critical cognition, and therefore a potential source of resistance against oppressive cultural practices."[49]

This understanding of the aesthetic is appealing not only because it allows for a variety of expressive forms (in a way wholly compatible with Jameson's "spirit of realism") but also because it allows us to register both the promise and the failure of Comintern aesthetics. Buck-Morss's expanded aesthetic makes it possible to grasp not just the multiple artistic styles and methods competing for primacy within the interwar left but also the contradictory experiences and sensations that the history of the Comintern necessarily elicits – not just "realism" and "modernism" but also what Richard Wright described as the "horror" and "glory" of twentieth-century communism.[50] Such broadly felt experiences of illusion and disillusion came to fill in the failed, then absent centre of the Third International, and Buck-Morss's sensory aesthetic enables us to register this – to register, without necessarily discarding, the unfulfilled hopes of twentieth-century communism.

Ultimately, then, the volume identifies not only a variety of forms but also feelings. The key here is a socialist way of feeling that continues to reverberate across spatial and historical contexts – Comintern aesthetics as a means of forging collective, mobilizing emotions.[51] For instance, Kiaer describes how a 1932 Soviet animated film about the oppression of Afro-Cubans used an "emotional key" to generate empathy across national and racial lines, in the process showing "how feeling and emotion are just as integral to communist consciousness as analyses of social processes."[52] Jonathan Flatley complicates such feelings by stirring in the negative: in his discussion of Langston Hughes's frequently dismissed revolutionary poems, he uses the blues to identify a feeling of being both beaten and unbeatable, which then proves central to Hughes's effort to bridge his poetic "I" to the "we" of which he is part. Likewise, Bo Zheng notes the mobilizing role of anger in workers' theatre from 1920s China, while Xiaobing

Tang's discussion of 1930s Chinese street theatre foregrounds "a communal experience affecting and bringing together both performer and spectator." Taken together, these pieces show that, even after the avant-garde's demise and the enshrinement of a doctrinaire, non-"lyrical" socialist realism, and even after the 1943 collapse of the Comintern and the 1991 "end of history," Comintern aesthetics still persists as a certain feeling that encompasses realism/modernism and horror/glory. It is a feeling connecting the many places and moments in which this often tragic history unfolded, filtering down to the present through a variety of unexpected channels – from postwar "international" architecture, as Vladimir Paperny and Marina Khrustaleva show, to Eastern European samizdat/tamizdat, to contemporary Chinese art and performance.

This journey brings us back to Ai Weiwei's *Working Progress*. From the perspective of Comintern aesthetics, it becomes possible to see it anew as more than a disavowal of the revolutionary past that it references or as just another example of contemporary protest art, but rather as a present-day regearing of the liberatory potential of Comintern aesthetics. In addition to Ai's earlier-quoted lines about the futility of "romantic sentiments" and "revolutionary thinking," the catalogue accompanying *Working Progress* notes that "for the artist it is best described as a model of the human mind, trapped in the confines of a dogmatic political and ideological framework, and that, if set free, would be capable of achieving so much, ironically in the very name of the self-same constraining cultural framework."[53] From this perspective, *Working Progress* expresses a fascinating tension between anti-communist dissidence and a desire to break free from dogma so as to realize the thwarted dreams of Tatlin's Monument to the Third International. Rather than the naïve "romantic sentiments" and bloodless "revolutionary thinking" chided by Ai, what is needed to process this tension is a layered feeling that allows us to grasp simultaneously world revolution, its failure, and its still-unfolding afterlives.

Organization of the Volume

The volume is comprised of three overlapping, interconnected parts. The first ("Space") tracks the wide geographical dispersion of leftist cultural and literary networks during the interwar years, mirrored somewhat by the range of artistic modes addressed in the section: novels, poetry, theatre, painting, and film. Sometimes manifested through physical travel, but more often through the circulation of texts and ideas, these networks were bound together by the political and cultural allure of the Soviet Union. Both beyond and within that country, the Comintern inspired new ways of imagining a liberated yet interconnected world, including, for instance, sober critical and socialist realisms as well as the iconoclastic "geopoetics" of the avant-garde.[54] However, these wide-ranging visions always had to be attendant to local conditions; in the section, translation (and, often, gaps in translation) emerges as the fabric articulating together Comintern aesthetics. Indeed, the image of a variegated fabric or netting helps to eschew the centre-periphery model too often applied to world literary cultures.

The second part ("Form") focuses on disrupting the boundaries ostensibly separating modernism and realism, art and propaganda. Though the pieces here may seem more national (or ethno-national) than international in focus, together they point to a shared, multi-sited effort to broaden our understanding of the aesthetic – often for the sake of showing how visions of world revolution could adapt to and benefit from local cultures and contexts. The chapters in this section do this either by finding a middle ground (or middle period) between modernism and realism or by pointing to an expansive, haptic understanding of the aesthetic that sidesteps altogether such binaries as art versus propaganda and artist versus audience.

Finally, the third part ("History") unsettles received historical narratives about the Comintern's rise and fall by advancing from the 1920s and 30s to the Cold War and into the present. Though several of the pieces here document the often fatal missteps of the interwar years – in effect, providing eulogies for Comintern aesthetics – they also highlight afterlives in postwar art and activism. The volume ends by urging contemporary artists, activists, and scholars to draw not just historical lessons but tools from Comintern aesthetics – the most important of which is an attunement to today's ever-worsening global class divides from the perspective of a defeated but latent alternative world system.

NOTES

1   On Hughes and Mayakovsky, see Ryan James Kernan, "The *Coup* of Langston Hughes's Picasso Period: Excavating Mayakovsky in Langston Hughes's Verse," *Comparative Literature* 66, no. 2 (Spring 2014): 227–46; and Steven S. Lee, *The Ethnic Avant-Garde: Minority Cultures and World Revolution* (New York: Columbia University Press, 2015), 47–82. On Eisenstein in Mexico, see Anne Nesbet, *Savage Junctures: Sergei Eisenstein and the Shape of Thinking* (London: Tauris, 2003), 116–56; and Masha Salazkina, *In Excess: Sergei Eisenstein's Mexico* (Chicago: University of Chicago Press, 2009). On Mei Lanfang in Moscow, see Katerina Clark, *Moscow, the Fourth Rome: Stalinism, Cosmopolitanism, and the Evolution of Soviet Culture, 1931–1941* (Cambridge, MA: Harvard University Press, 2011), 192–208.

2   Of course, the notion of an undifferentiated Second World (versus an industrialized capitalist First World and a non-aligned anti-colonial Third World) obscured infighting among communist states, most notably between the Soviet Union and China. Mao Zedong famously offered his own three-world theory that foregrounded imperialism rather than capitalism-versus-socialism: the United States

and the Soviet Union comprised the imperialist First World; developing countries in Asia, Africa, and Latin America comprised the Third World; and developed countries in between comprised the Second World. Alexander C. Cook, "Third World Maoism," in *A Critical Introduction to Mao*, ed. Timothy Cheek (New York: Cambridge University Press, 2010), 296–7.

3 Franco Moretti, "Conjectures on World Literature," *New Left Review* 1 (2000): 54–68; Pascale Casanova, *The World Republic of Letters*, trans. Malcolm DeBevoise (Cambridge, MA: Harvard University Press, 2005).

4 Michael Denning, *Culture in the Age of Three Worlds* (New York: Verso, 2004), 53–4; Joe Cleary, "Realism After Modernism and the Literary World-System," *MLQ* 73, no. 3 (2012).

5 For a critique of Casanova and Moretti on precisely these grounds and an assertion of world literature's (specifically, the postcolonial novel's) advancement of world-historical becoming and transcendence of capitalism, see Pheng Cheah, *What Is a World? On Postcolonial Literature as World Literature* (Durham, NC: Duke University Press, 2016). Interestingly though, revolution does figure into Casanova's world republic: according to her, Paris achieved its literary pre-eminence partly due to its own revolutionary pedigree, namely, "the overthrow of the monarchy, the invention of the rights of man – an image that was to earn France its great reputation for tolerance toward foreigners and as a land of asylum for political refugees" (*World Republic*, 24). For Moscow as a centre of 1930s world letters, see Clark, *Moscow*; and Rossen Djagalov, "The People's Republic of Letters" (PhD diss., Yale University, 2011), 13–49.

6 On the World Literature Publishing House, see Maria Khotimsky, "World Literature, Soviet Style: A Forgotten Episode in the History of the Idea," *Ab Imperio* 3 (2013): 119–54. On the many authors from around the world drawn to the Soviet cause, see Jürgen Rühle, *Literature and Revolution: A Critical Study of the Writer and Communism in the Twentieth Century*, trans. Jean Steinberg (New York: Praeger, 1969); and Clark, *Moscow*. On African Americans and Soviet communism, see William Maxwell, *New Negro, Old Left: African-American Writing and Communism Between the Wars* (New York: Columbia University Press, 1999); Kate Baldwin, *Beyond the Color Line and the Iron Curtain: Reading Encounters Between Black and Red, 1922–1963* (Durham, NC: Duke University Press, 2002); and Glenda Elizabeth Gilmore, *Defying Dixie: The Radical Roots of Civil Rights, 1919–1950* (New York: W.W. Norton & Co., 2008).

7 Denning, *Culture in the Age of Three Worlds*, 51, 55–61, 64–7, 69. For a recent elaboration of the novelists' international, including its key institutions and recurring themes, see Rossen Djagalov, "The Red Apostles: Imagining Revolutions in the Global Proletarian Novel," *SEEJ* 61, no. 3 (Fall 2017): 396–422.

8 On Stalin's low regard for the Comintern, see, for instance, Sheila Fitzpatrick, *On Stalin's Team: The Years of Living Dangerously* (Princeton, NJ: Princeton University Press, 2015), 103.

9 Ai Weiwei quoted in Karen Smith, "Ai Weiwei," in *The Real Thing: Contemporary Art from China* (London: Tate, 2007), 38. Further page references are inserted parenthetically in the text.

10 Lenin called for communists to support "revolutionary movements among the dependent and underprivileged nations (for example, Ireland, the American Negroes, etc.) and in the colonies." See V.I. Lenin, "Draft Theses on National and Colonial Questions for the Second Congress of the Communist International," https://www.marxists.org/archive/lenin/works/1920/jun/05 .htm; and Robert J.C. Young, *Postcolonialism: An Historical Introduction* (Oxford: Blackwell, 2001), 129–34. On one hand, this gesture to anti-imperial, anti-racist struggle can be seen as a precursor to "the pluralist approach of the post-war national liberation movements, starting with that of Mao in China" (Young, *Postcolonialism*, 134). On the other hand, Lenin's outreach to (typically bourgeois-led) national liberation movements was contested by the Indian communist M.N. Roy, who argued that Asia was already ripe for full-fledged proletarian revolution. Lenin's position arguably reflected a Eurocentric position that consigned Asia to "backwardness" for strategic purposes. See Hélène Carrère d'Encausse and Stuart R. Schram, *Marxism and Asia* (London: Penguin, 1969), 27–31.

11 To be sure, Roy's arguments were frequently sidelined (see Carrère d'Encausse and Schram, *Marxism and Asia*, 41–5), and in 1929 he was expelled from the Comintern due to his "inability to form the mass party of the proletariat that he had advocated" for India (Young, *Postcolonialism*, 148). Roy also bungled an assignment to China, where, amid Chiang Kai-Shek's 1927 massacre of communists, he revealed to a Guomindang official Stalin's secret plan to reorganize the Guomindang. See Young, *Postcolonialism*, 148; and Michael Weiner, "Comintern in East Asia, 1919–39," in *The Comintern: A History of International Communism from Lenin to Stalin* by Kevin McDermott and Jeremy Agnew (New York: St. Martin's, 1997), 177–8. On Katayama's more auspicious career as a Comintern luminary, see Hyman Kublin, *Asian Revolutionary: The Life of Sen Katayama* (Princeton, NJ: Princeton University Press, 1964). For his promotion of African American causes in Moscow, see Claude McKay, "Soviet Russia and the Negro," *Crisis* 27 (December 1923): 63.

12 On cultural bodies under the Comintern's aegis, see Clark, *Moscow*, 38, 160. On Münzenberg's career as a communist film mogul, see Sean McMeekin, *The Red Millionaire: A Political Biography of Willi Münzenberg, Moscow's Secret Propaganda Tsar in the West* (New Haven, CT: Yale University Press, 2003), 174–92. For a more nuanced view of Münzenberg, see Sarah Wilson, "Comintern Spin Doctor," *English Historical Review* 127, no. 526 (June 2012): 662–8. On the specific features of Tatlin's Tower, see Nikolai Punin, *Pamiatnik III Internatsionala* (Petrograd: Otdel izobrazitel'nykh iskusstv NKP, 1920), 1; Nikolai Punin, "O pamiatnikakh," in *O Tatline*, ed. I.N. Punina and V.I. Rakitin (Moscow: RA, 1994), 16–17; and Svetlana

Boym, *Architecture of the Off-Modern* (New York: Princeton Architectural Press, 2008), 8–10.

13 Brigitte Studer, *The Transnational World of the Cominternians* (London: Palgrave Macmillan, 2015), 24. Accordingly, in designing the Monument (which he originally planned to commemorate the October Revolution), Tatlin found it necessary to adapt to state demands and preferences. See Pamela Kachurin, "Working (for) the State: Vladimir Tatlin's Career in Early Soviet Russia and the Origins of *The Monument to the Third International,*" *Modernism/modernity* 19, no. 1 (January 2012): 24–31.

14 Jane Degras, ed., *The Communist International: 1919–1943 Documents*, vol. I, *1919–1922* (London: Oxford University Press, 1956), 171, https://www.marxists .org/history/international/comintern/documents/volume1-1919-1922.pdf.

15 McDermott and Agnew note: "By never clearly delineating the limits of contact with socialist organizations the authors of the united front tactics prepared the ground for 'deviations' in the communist movement, since the Bolsheviks were the ultimate arbiters of what was the 'correct' path at any given time" (*Comintern*, 33). Thus, a Comintern functionary could alternately be condemned for overreliance on reformist parties ("rightist deviation") or for premature faith in bottom-up, worker-led revolution ("leftist deviation"). For instance, after a failed German revolution in 1923, Comintern official Karl Radek (associated with Trotsky) was criticized for his overly optimistic support of revolutionary workers there (McDermott and Agnew, *Comintern*, 38, 44–5). In contrast, the Comintern repeatedly demanded that Chinese communists ally themselves with the bourgeois nationalist Guomindang, and then blamed the latter's 1927 betrayal of this alliance on the Chinese communists' both overreliance on and underestimation of the bourgeoisie (Carrère d'Encausse and Schram, *Marxism and Asia*, 57).

16 McDermott and Agnew, *Comintern*, 50–1.

17 Ibid., 68–75, 82–90.

18 For an in-depth account of the Comintern's and German Communist Party's ineffectual, factionalist responses to Nazism, see E.H. Carr, *The Twilight of the Comintern, 1930–1935* (London: Macmillan, 1982), 45–82.

19 For a definitive first-person account of this purge, see George Orwell, *Homage to Catalonia* (San Diego, CA: Harcourt, 1980), which remarkably also preserves the fleeting, utopian "foretaste of Socialism" that Orwell encounters in Republican Spain (104).

20 For a recent historical study that allows for both top-down and bottom-up understandings of the Comintern, see Jacob A. Zumoff, *The Communist International and U.S. Communism, 1919–1929* (Chicago: Haymarket, 2015).

21 According to Sheila Fitzpatrick, proletarian writing – which in theory meant writing by and for workers but in fact was led by young communist intellectuals interested more in "literary politics rather than the actual production of literature" – simply provided Stalin with a "predefined opposition platform and support"

against Bukharin. That is, the brief ascendance of proletarian art and writing during the cultural revolution was not related to Stalin's own aesthetic preferences. See
Sheila Fitzpatrick, *The Cultural Front: Power and Culture in Revolutionary Russia*
(Ithaca, NY: Cornell University Press, 1992), 104, 113–14. Similarly, McDermott
and Agnew show how Stalin embraced the Third Period in part to outmanoeuvre
Bukharin – even though Bukharin was the first to theorize the Third Period based
on his view of shifting international circumstances (*Comintern*, 68–77).

22 Fitzpatrick, *The Cultural Front*, 144.

23 Andrei Zhdanov, "Soviet Literature: The Richest in Ideas, the Most Advanced
Literature," *Soviet Writers' Congress 1934*, https://www.marxists.org/subject/art/
lit_crit/sovietwritercongress/zdhanov.htm. For in-depth accounts of this transition from avant-gardism to socialist realism, see Vladimir Paperny, *Architecture
in the Age of Stalin: Culture Two* (Cambridge: Cambridge University Press, 2002);
Boris Groys, *The Total Art of Stalinism: Avant-Garde, Aesthetic Dictatorship, and
Beyond* (Princeton, NJ: Princeton University Press, 1992); and Susan Buck-Morss,
Dreamworld and Catastrophe (Cambridge, MA: MIT Press, 2000). For an engagement of Paperny, see Nariman Skakov's contribution to this volume (chapter
seven); for an engagement of Groys and Buck-Morss, see Harsha Ram's contribution (chapter one).

24 Bernard Fibicher, "Descending Light," in *Ai Weiwei* (London: Phaidon, 2009),
115–16; Philip Tinari, "Chairs and Visitors," in *Ai Weiwei: Works 2004–2007*
(Zurich: JRP|Ringier, 2007), 11; Andrew Cohen, "Ai Weiwei," *ArtAsiaPacific* 74
(2011): 80. On the figure of the spiral as a long-view critique of capitalism, drawing
from Giovanni Arrighi's study of "recurrent macroeconomic patterns," see Lauren
Goodlad, "Introduction: Worlding Realisms Now," *Novel* 49, no. 2 (2016): 193,
196–7.

25 Accordingly, as many have argued, Tatlin's Tower points not just to a liberated
future but also to "celestial rhythms" (day, month, and year), as well as to the
mythic and pre-modern (for example, its uncanny resemblance to the Tower of
Babel). In a recent book, I connect this Janus-faced orientation to the messianic
cessation of Walter Benjamin's Angel of History, as well as to Leon Trotsky's
theory of combined and uneven development. See Steven S. Lee, *Ethnic Avant-
Garde*, 5–12; Svetlana Boym, *Another Freedom: The Alternative History of an
Idea* (Chicago: University of Chicago Press, 2010), 211; John Milner, *Vladimir
Tatlin and the Russian Avant-Garde* (New Haven, CT: Yale University Press,
1983).

26 Boym, *Architecture of the Off-Modern*, 80. See pages 28–37 for other renderings of
Tatlin's Tower in late and post-socialist Russia. Interestingly, Aleksei German, Jr.'s
recent film *Under Electric Clouds* (2015) centres on an unfinished spiraling tower –
commenced by an oligarch, halted after his death, and then recommenced by his
daughter – in a near-future, apocalyptic Russia. Perhaps to confirm the Tatlin
reference, messages are projected onto the clouds nearby (if not from) the tower,

though these are advertisements for glossy lifestyle magazines, not revolutionary slogans.

27 This sense of incompletion reflects Mikhail Bakhtin's juxtaposition of the world of the absolute epic and the fundamentally continuing and incompletable world of the present captured by the novel. From this perspective, the world envisioned by *Comintern Aesthetics* has always been a work in progress. See Bakhtin, "Epic and the Novel," in *The Dialogic Imagination: Four Essays*, ed. Michael Holquist (Austin: University of Texas Press, 1981), 16.

28 As Nirvana Tanoukhi notes in response to Moretti and Casanova, the problem with such efforts to map literary space is their tendency to elide spatial differentiation – the deep-seated but productive contradictions lurking in a given place. Nirvana Tanoukhi, "The Scale of World Literature," *New Literary History* 39 (2008): 599–617.

29 Kris Manjapra, "Communist Internationalism and Transcolonial Recognition," in *Cosmopolitan Thought Zones: South Asia and the Global Circulation of Ideas*, ed. Sugata Bose and Kris Manjapra (New York: Palgrave Macmillan, 2010), 159–77.

30 For overviews of Soviet nationalities policy, which also emphasized territorial "self-determination" and promoted local elites and cultures, see Yuri Slezkine, "The USSR as a Communal Apartment, or How a Socialist State Promoted Ethnic Particularism," *Slavic Review* 53, no. 2 (Summer 1994); Ronald Grigor Suny, *The Revenge of the Past: Nationalism, Revolution, and the Collapse of the Soviet Union* (Stanford, CA: Stanford University Press, 1993); Terry Martin, *The Affirmative Action Empire: Nations and Nationalism in the Soviet Union, 1923–1939* (Ithaca, NY: Cornell University Press, 2001); and Francine Hirsch, *Empire of Nations: Ethnographic Knowledge and the Making of the Soviet Union* (Ithaca, NY: Cornell University Press, 2005).

31 Providing a precedent for the Soviet periphery's relative flexibility, Eric Blanc shows how, prior to 1917, social democrats in the Russian Empire's Central and Eastern European borderlands pushed Bolshevism towards its eventual promotion of national particularism. Eric Blanc, "Anti-Imperial Marxism," *International Socialist Review* 100 (Spring 2016), http://isreview.org/issue/100/anti-imperial-marxism.

32 Indeed, as Robert Young points out, the interwar years can be seen as an earlier, overshadowed postcolonial moment, one that witnessed the collapse of the Austro-Hungarian, Ottoman, and Russian empires after the First World War. Young, *Postcolonialism*, 117–20. For postwar Soviet efforts to foster anti-colonial Third Worldism, see Djagalov, "Peoples Republic of Letters," 96–156.

33 Stuart Hall, "Gramsci's Relevance for the Study of Race and Ethnicity," *Journal of Communication Inquiry* 10, no. 2 (1986), 18–19.

34 Antonio Gramsci, *Selections from the Prison Notebooks*, quoted in Ernesto Laclau and Chantal Mouffe, *Hegemony and Socialist Strategy* (London: Verso, 2001), 67–8. See also Hall, "Gramsci's Relevance," 22.

35 Laclau and Mouffe, *Hegemony*, 61–5. See also Michael Denning, *The Cultural Front: The Laboring of American Cultures in the Twentieth Century* (New York: Verso, 1997), 99–100; McDermott and Agnew, *Comintern*, 60.

36 Beyond Margaret Thatcher's "there is no alternative" slogan, for more on the Soviet collapse's deleterious impact on the Western left, see François Furet, *The Passing of an Illusion: The Idea of Communism in the Twentieth Century*, trans. Deborah Furet (Chicago: University of Chicago Press, 1999).

37 Clark, *Moscow*, 160–2, 179. See also Christina Kiaer, "Lyrical Socialist Realism," *October* 147 (Winter 2014): 56–77. For an overview of postwar debates on the "openness" or "closure" of socialist realism from the 1950s to the 1990s, see Thomas Lahusen, "Socialist Realism in Search of Its Shores," in *Socialist Realism without Shores*, ed. Thomas Lahusen and Evgeny Dobrenko (Durham, NC: Duke University Press, 1997), 5–26.

38 Georg Lukács, *The Historical Novel* (London: Merlin, 1962).

39 By contrast, as Joe Cleary points out, Western scholars seeking to overcome the realism-modernism binary have typically relied upon the expansiveness of modernism. A key precedent here is Eric Auerbach's *Mimesis*, which, for instance, praises quintessentially "modernist" works like Virginia Woolf's *To the Lighthouse* for its "realistic depth." Joe Cleary, "Realism After Modernism," 256. Benita Parry has built upon modernism's expansiveness through her notion of "peripheral modernisms," which joins formerly colonized sites through a focus on uneven economic development rather than centre-periphery relations. Stylistically, peripheral modernist literature is marked by alienation devices and "narrative modes that undermine realism" – for instance, the incorporation of multiple temporalities and self-consciousness about a text's own viability. Benita Parry, "Aspects of Peripheral Modernisms," *Ariel* 40 (2009): 38. For a related study of "irrealism" in the semi-periphery of the modern capitalist world system, see the Warwick Research Collective, *Combined and Uneven Development: Towards a New Theory of World-Literature* (Liverpool: Liverpool University Press, 2015).

40 Georg Lukács, "Realism in the Balance," in *Aesthetics and Politics* by Theodor Adorno et al. (London: Verso, 1977), 38. Much of this debate was compiled in this particular book, further page references to which are inserted parenthetically in the text.

41 Jed Esty and Colleen Lye, "Peripheral Realisms Now," *MLQ* 73 (2012): 277. Interestingly, Thomas Lahusen tracks how, in the Soviet Union and Eastern Europe, postwar efforts to demarcate the boundaries of socialist realism seemed to favour Brecht over Lukács – the latter critiqued by Soviet critics both for too hastily abandoning "left expressionism" and for blurring the distinction between critical realism and socialist realism. Lahusen, "Socialist Realism," 10–11.

42 Lukács critiques expressionist painting's incorporation of folk art (which for Bloch indicated a connection to "ordinary people") by tying it to an elitist, retrograde

primitivism. Folk art and other markers of cultural heritage are useful to him only when "characterized by a dynamic, progressive movement in which the active creative forces of popular tradition, of the sufferings and joys of the people, of revolutionary legacies, are buoyed up, preserved, transcended and further developed" ("Realism in the Balance," 54). Despite this loophole, Lukács seems generally wary of folk cultures and vernacular traditions. By contrast, several of this volume's contributors – for instance, Tony Day, Jonathan Flatley, Harsha Ram, Snehal Shingavi, and Xiaobing Tang – highlight the progressive potential of seemingly past-bound cultures.

43   Bertolt Brecht, "Against Georg Lukács," in Adorno et al., *Aesthetics and Politics*, 82. Further page references are parenthetically inserted in the text.

44   Fredric Jameson, "Reflections in Conclusion," in Adorno et al., *Aesthetics and Politics*, 205. Jameson develops these ideas in *The Antinomies of Realism* (New York: Verso, 2013), which connects realism to the mid-nineteenth-century bourgeois body and the affects it registers in an eternal present. For overviews of Jameson's shifting views on realism – for instance, from the 1977 essay I have quoted to his 1998 book on Brecht – see Carolyn Lesjak, "History, Narrative and Realism: Jameson's Search for a Method" in *On Jameson: From Postmodernism to Globalization*, ed. Caren Irr and Ian Buchanan (Albany, NY: SUNY Press, 2006), 27–50; and Colleen Lye, "Afterword: Realism's Futures," *Novel* 49, no. 2 (2016): 347, 353–4.

45   Esty and Lye, "Peripheral Realisms Now," 279–80. For similar efforts to expand realism, often via postcolonial settings, see the 2016 *Novel* special issue on "Worlding Realisms" (*Novel* 49, no. 2); Ulka Anjaria, *Realism in the Twentieth-Century Indian Novel: Colonial Difference and Literary Form* (Cambridge: Cambridge University Press, 2012); and Paul Nadal, "Remittance Fiction: Human Labor Export, Realism, and the Filipino Novel in English" (PhD diss., UC Berkeley, 2017).

46   Theodor Adorno, "Commitment," in Adorno et al., *Aesthetics and Politics*, 186–7.

47   Buck-Morss, *Dreamworld and Catastrophe*, 101.

48   Susan Buck-Morss, "Aesthetics and Anaesthetics: Walter Benjamin's Artwork Essay Reconsidered," *October* 62 (1992): 13. Further page references are inserted parenthetically in the text.

49   Buck-Morss, *Dreamworld and Catastrophe*, 101, 336n89. Tellingly, Buck-Morss sidesteps the realism versus modernism debate. Though she notes the ability of expressionist artists to register "the material impress" of modernity's "technological shattering" of the body, she notes too how photomontage registers the fragmented body but then, in accord with fascist aesthetics, pieces "the fragments together again in images that appear impervious to pain" ("Aesthetics and Anaesthetics," 34). In short, there is nothing intrinsically progressive about modernist formal experimentation.

50   Richard Wright, "I Tried to Be a Communist," *Atlantic Monthly* 174, no. 3 (September 1944): 54; quoted in Denning, *Culture in the Age of Three Worlds*, 52.

51 I am drawing here from Jonathan Flatley's generative work on socialist feeling, specifically his readings of Andrei Platonov's "socialistic communities organized not around use value or mutual exploitation, but the meeting of two *toskas* – two longing, melancholic affects meeting halfway, but never quite joining." Jonathan Flatley, *Affective Mapping* (Cambridge, MA: Harvard University Press, 2008), 188–9.

52 This emphasis on feeling resonates with Kiaer's emphasis elsewhere on the haptic and emotional in early socialist realism. According to her, socialist realist painting of the early 1930s worked "at the boundary between private emotion and publicly oriented feeling," and in doing so provided a glimpse of "socialism as an alternative affective economy." Kiaer, "Lyrical Socialist Realism," 60, 77.

53 Smith, "Ai Weiwei," 40.

54 In addition to Ram's piece in this volume on Khlebnikov's "geopoetics" (chapter one), see Anindita Banerjee and Jenifer Presto, "Introduction: Toward a Russian Geopoetics, or Some Ways of Relating Russia to the World," *Slavic Review* 75, no. 2 (Summer 2016): 247–55.

PART ONE

Space: Geopoetics, Networks, Translation

World Literature as World Revolution: Velimir Khlebnikov's *Zangezi* and the Utopian Geopoetics of the Russian Avant-Garde

HARSHA RAM
UC Berkeley

Segodnia snova ia poidu
Tuda, na zhizn', na torg, na rynok,
I voisko pesen povedu
S priboem rynka v poedinok!

Today once more I shall march forth
To life's bazaar, the marketplace:
My ragtag regiment of songs
Will mute the market's breaking wave!

– Velimir Khlebnikov, 1914[1]

The convergence of revolutionary politics and artistic-literary vanguardism has long been regarded as a striking feature of early Soviet culture.[2] Yet, the significance of this convergence for the history and theory of world literature has yet to be clearly posed. This evaluation requires that we go back to the years prior to the bureaucratic constitution of Soviet literature, with its familiar themes of socialist construction and the brotherhood of peoples, to a time when utopian visions of world revolution fostered by the Comintern coexisted with the extreme privations of war communism (1918–21). It was during these years of revolutionary hope, material destitution, and uncertain state patronage that Russia's avant-garde poets and artists further radicalized their ongoing turn to formal abstraction. By analytically decomposing the linguistic and artistic raw materials of the creative process and reconstituting them as a new means to signify the coordinates of space and time, the Russian avant-garde strove to generate a planetary internationalism of aesthetic form commensurate with world revolution. This vision was grounded in the specificities of Eurasian history and geography, of which Russia was territorially the largest, albeit historically the most recent component. At the same time, the regional "geopoetics" of the

Russian avant-garde point beyond the Eurasian landmass to the structuring principles of the modern artistic and social utopia. Unrealized and essentially unrealizable, Russian avant-garde utopianism produced a "cultural surplus" or "supplement" that resonates to this day as an implicit corrective to policies pursued by the Bolsheviks during the heady initial years of the Comintern. This cultural surplus, most abundantly found in the writings of the futurist poet Velimir Khlebnikov (1885–1922), also highlights the limits of the modern social imaginary upon which recent theories of world literature have been founded.

This chapter focuses on the dual legacy of Russian avant-garde utopianism, at once an immediate echo of the Russian Revolution as well as of Marxist debates on socialist internationalism and uneven development, and a deeper quest to determine the coordinates of space-time as the basis of a new planetary system of linguistic communication and social organization. It begins by recapitulating pertinent aspects of existing theories on world literature before turning to the Russian Revolution as an alternative configuration of aesthetics and politics. From these broader contexts, related to Lenin's theory of imperialism and Comintern debates on anti-colonial revolution, the chapter then examines the twin legacies, theoretical and literary, of Velimir Khlebnikov. Khlebnikov's poetic practice, above all his "supersaga" *Zangezi* (*Зангези*, 1922), presents itself as an encyclopedic updating of human knowledge that yokes the archaic authority of the poet-prophet to an urgently topical yet strikingly heteroglot vision of planetary life – past, present, and future. At once a metatheoretical reflection on space-time and a series of "world-texts"[3] that enact or embody an unevenly unified globe, Khlebnikov's work, alongside that of the constructivist artist Vladimir Tatlin, represents a significant chapter in revolutionary modernism whose pertinence to the theory and practice of world literature awaits further exploration.

World Literature: Beyond the Nation and the Market

The configuration of world literature today substantially remains a publishing and teaching reflex of Western liberal multiculturalism, a reflex strengthened in recent decades by the accelerating flow of goods and people across national boundaries that we commonly associate with globalization. Indeed, genealogies of world literature that harken back to Goethe, Marx, and Auerbach perhaps do no more than invoke the "prehistory" of globalization, earlier restructurings of the globe taking place in the wake of the Napoleonic wars and again in the aftermath of the Second World War. Then as now, the recovery of the non-Western cultural archive for the enrichment of the Western liberal imagination was the byproduct of an expanding world market inscribed within a geopolitical order marked by intense interstate rivalries.

Goethe's celebrated advocacy of world literature reflected the need, widely felt in the wake of a quarter-century of "horrifying wars" brought to a conclusion by the Congress of Vienna, to forge a qualitatively new relationship between nations in which "confusion and mutual conflict" would give way to "more or less free intellectual commerce [*mehr oder weniger freien geistigen Handelsverkehr*]."[4] Goethe's vision was of an expanding traffic in texts in which the dynamics of translation and cross-cultural appraisal would play an essential role in mitigating international antagonisms without, however, eliminating the nation itself: "The peculiarities of a nation," Goethe explained to Thomas Carlyle, "are like its language and its currency [*Münzsorten*]: they facilitate commerce [*Verkehr*], indeed they alone make it fully possible."[5] In this sense, the "connections between original and translation most clearly express the relationship of nation to nation."[6] Goethe advocated a circulatory model of global literary exchange facilitated by the "ever increasing rapidity of interaction [*vermehrenden Schnelligkeit des Verkehrs*]" and ever more cosmopolitan habits of reading and taste.[7] Goethe's ideal of "free intellectual commerce" betokened the unfettered material circulation and reception of texts that traversed national boundaries without undermining national particularities. Yet, it was ultimately not the competitive book trade as such that for Goethe established literary value, but the semiotic capacity of language itself to represent and communicate national difference. Goethe's repeated references to *Verkehr*, then, were at once an acknowledgement of the rising significance of global trade and a metaphorical analogy serving to designate the interaction between national languages through the medium of translation. Eliding the material world into language, Goethe's marketplace of texts offered an idealized space of mediation and exchange within which to mitigate the risks of international conflict. It is no coincidence, then, that the fleeting lines dedicated to world literature in Marx and Engels's *Manifesto of the Communist Party* (1848) take up and reformulate Goethe's articulation of the relationship between nation-states and the global market:

> All old-established national industries have been destroyed or are daily being destroyed ... In place of the old local and national seclusion and self-sufficiency, we have intercourse in every direction [*ein allseitiger Verkehr*], universal inter-dependence of nations. And as in material, so also in intellectual production. The intellectual creations of individual nations become common property. National one-sidedness and narrow-mindedness become more and more impossible, and from the numerous national and local literatures, there arises a world literature.[8]

The *Manifesto* replaces Goethe's idealized vision of the literary market with a striking account of the creative destruction whose accomplishment was to be the historical task of the bourgeoisie. For Marx and Engels, world literature could never be the mere accumulation of national literatures rendered in translation: it was the dialectical outcome of the deterritorialization and recon-stitution of the globe wrought by the very market mechanisms in which Goethe had sought an alternative to war.[9]

Contemporary theories of world literature continue to read as powerful cultural analogues to geopolitics. For Pascale Casanova, Paris represents the capital of a "world republic of letters" marked by cosmopolitan centres and restlessly assertive national peripheries,[10] while Franco Moretti's formulation of the global diffusion of the modern novel as a "compromise between European patterns and local reality"[11] strikingly echoes Benedict Anderson's account of the spread of print nationalism from Europe to all corners of the contempo-rary world system.[12] Moretti's hypothesis of two competing models of cultural change, the "tree" and the "wave," are by his own admission nothing more than naturalized metaphors for the nation and the market: "Trees and branches are what nation-states cling to; waves are what markets do ... Cultural history is made of trees *and* waves."[13] The recuperative nature of the world literary en-terprise might thus justifiably be seen as the global projection of a typically Western configuration involving two distinct but intersecting logics of power, the first economic and the second territorial, in which the restless cosmopoli-tanism of the market is shaped and channelled by a network of allied or com-peting spatially bounded nation-states.[14]

By that very logic, alternative models of world literature might well be ex-pected to arise when the socio-economic underpinnings of the world market, and the Westphalian system of nation-states into which it is inscribed, have entered a profound crisis. One such crisis was the Russian Revolution, which sought to liberate physical need and cultural creativity from the sway of the market and challenge the division of the globe imposed by the Western powers. Among the most significant long-term cultural consequences of the October Revolution was the establishment of Soviet literature as the first state-sponsored multilingual and multi-ethnic literature of the twentieth century, anticipating by half a century the re-emergence of world literature in the West as an expres-sion first of postwar liberal multiculturalism and then of neoliberal globaliza-tion. Soviet literature at once reified the nation and relativized its importance by inserting it into a federal structure that reconfigured relations between local, regional, and central actors. Ethnicities were reconstituted as national repub-lics, while the state would displace the market – with decidedly mixed results – as the principal guarantor of cultural production, publication, and distribution.

The Utopian Geopoetics of the Russian Avant-Garde

Prior to the consolidation of Soviet literature, whose undeniable achievements and catastrophic failures cannot be elaborated here, it was principally the task of the Russian avant-garde, alongside Russia's other modern and modernist artistic currents, to ponder the cultural significance of the revolution for the modern social imaginary.[15] The convergence of revolutionary politics and artistic-literary vanguardism, I would contend, points beyond ideological sympathy or aesthetic analogy to a deeper quest on the part of the Russian avant-garde: an ongoing desire to contemplate the historic ruptures of 1914–17 according to a regional (Eurasian) and ultimately global "internationalism of aesthetic form."[16] This internationalism of form, at once an investigation and an abstraction of time-space, is perhaps the most extravagantly ambitious moment in Russian literature's rich tradition of geopoetic reflection: as such it might also offer an alternative genealogy for contemporary conceptualizations of world literature. As the "operative category … for the modes of inscription of the Earth into a literary text," geopoetics, I would suggest, is irreducible to geopolitics without constituting a purely autonomous realm.[17] It embraces the mimetic-representational elements by which space is conventionally designated and demarcated but subjects these elements to an imaginative-projective reinscription. The distinction between mimetic representation and imaginative reinscription will become abundantly evident in the pages to come.

The geopoetics of the Russian avant-garde, although facilitated by a singular convergence of revolutionary change and artistic experimentation, should not be viewed as irreducibly Russian. Indeed, its deeper logic mirrors what Louis Marin has identified as the characteristic structural tension of "the modern literary-political utopia": "on the one hand, the free play of the imagination in its indefinite expansion measured only by the desire, itself infinite, for happiness in a space where the moving frontiers of its philosophical and political fictions would be traced; on the other hand, the exactly closed totality rigorously coded by all the constraints and obligations of the law binding and closing a place with insuperable frontiers that would guarantee its harmonious functioning."[18] Marin's observation is perhaps nothing more than a spatial rendering of the constitutive contradiction between utopia as a state of "being" – the perfected place that is at the same time a no-place, whose first modern articulation was Thomas More's *Utopia* (1571) – and utopia as an experience of "becoming," an anticipatory impulse or desire which, far from merely offering the "premature and illusory solution of social contradictions," represents what Ernst Bloch once called "cultural surplus," the concentrated dream-image of unfulfilled human potential whose realization is projected onto an alternative future.[19] The underlying contradiction, proper to utopian thought, between "totality and infinity, … closure and liberty"[20] is readily reflected in the powerful tension between the emancipatory potential of the Russian Revolution, whose aesthetic analogue would be the cubo-futurist and Russian formalist liberation of the signifier – locally dubbed the "self-sufficient word [*samovitoe slovo*]" – from the constraints of conventional meaning and everyday use,[21] and its totalizing or authoritarian impulse, which the poet-artist would claim by reviving the Prometheanism of the nineteenth-century romantics who, in the words of Shelley, had elevated the poet-artist to the rank of an unacknowledged legislator of mankind. The emancipatory and totalizing components of the revolutionary impulse would thus seem to find a clear literary analogy, first in Russian futurism's insistence on the associative polysemy and autonomy of poetic language and then in the subordination of that polysemy to a set of abstract universal principles invoked and buttressed by the poet-artist's prophetic authority.

Between Totalization and Rupture: The Mediating Function of Geopoetics

In suggesting that Stalinism inherited from the Russian avant-garde its understanding of art as a means for the radical transformation – rather than mimetic representation – of everyday life, Boris Groys controversially isolated the second element of this opposition, that of aesthetic totalization, as the defining cultural reflex of the artistic avant-garde no less than of the revolutionary vanguard party: "It is in avant-garde art," writes Groys, "that we find a direct connection between the will to power and the artistic will to master the material and organize it according to laws dictated by the artists themselves ... Under Stalin, the dream of the avant-garde was in fact fulfilled, and the life of society was organized in monolithic artistic forms, though of course not those that the avant-garde itself had favored."[22] Groys implicates Stalin and the Russian avant-garde in a shared impulse towards aesthetic mastery, even as he acknowledges the radical divergences in their actual artistic or political practice.

By way of contrast, Susan Buck-Morss has insisted upon a constitutive "temporal" distinction between Russian artistic practice and Bolshevik policy: "the 'time' of the cultural avant-garde," she argues, "is not the same as that of the vanguard party." If avant-garde artistic practice "interrupted the continuity of perceptions and estranged the familiar," thereby seeking to *"rupture* the continuity of time," the Bolshevik party promoted a "chronological perception of revolution," the "cosmological *continuum* of historical progress" that was in sharp contrast to the *"lived* temporality of interruption, estrangement, arrest ... the phenomenological experience of avant-garde practice."[23] If Groys's formulation lopsidedly focuses on the Russian avant-garde's "totalizing" impulse in order to create a conceptual continuum implicating Russian revolutionary modernism in the rise of Stalinist aesthetics, then Buck-Morss highlights a poetics of "rupture" broadly characteristic of radical modernism worldwide, without defining its Russian specificity. Moreover, it is surely mistaken to equate the Bolsheviks' historical vision with "chronological perception." For Lenin, revolutionary progress was anything but linear, being shaped by conditions of profoundly uneven development. While the arguments of Groys and Buck-Morss find some justification in the context of Stalin's embrace of "socialism in one country" beginning in late 1924, they fall significantly short of grasping the Eurasian and

properly global dimensions of Bolshevik policy and avant-garde artistic practice in the years immediately following the Russian Revolution.

To grasp fully the impact of the October Revolution on the Russian avant-
garde, it is necessary to explore how the antinomy of formal emancipation and
conceptual totalization was geographically and historically mediated by Russia's
avant-garde poets and artists. This aspect is significantly ignored by Groys, who
identifies the fundamental gesture of the Russian avant-garde with Kazimir
Malevich's quest for "something irreducible, extraspatial, extratemporal, and
extrahistorical to hold on to, [at the far end of] the process of destruction and
reduction." In Groys's reading, the radical objectlessness of Malevich's *Black
Square* (1915) becomes the Russian avant-garde's defining expression, a visual
analogue to the futurist poet Velimir Khlebnikov's search for a "purely phonetic
'transrational' language" that could "organize the entire world on a new audial
basis."[24] Lost in Groys's account is the process by which Velimir Khlebnikov – the
central figure of this chapter – reached his poetic universalism: a febrile process
of reduction and abstraction, to be sure, but one that had first to calibrate and
reconfigure the basic coordinates of time and space. Khlebnikov's "transration-
alism" (*zaum'*), far from being a "purely phonetic" game with the building blocks
of sound, was, we shall see, first and foremost a *geo*-poetics, one evolving in close
tandem with the politics and cultural polemics of the day.

Like its counterparts elsewhere in the world, the Russian avant-garde strove
to overcome the "backwardness" of local culture by adapting and radicaliz-
ing the artistic innovations then emanating from Europe. At the same time, it
shared with other avant-garde movements a competitive and agonistic understanding of global literary-artistic space that permitted – indeed necessitated –
bold assertions of regionalism and nativist cultural pride. The constitutive
tension between indigeneity and internationalism was particularly apparent in
the Russian avant-garde, whose regionalism was realized through an ongoing
search for cultural continuities common to the Eurasian landmass as a whole,
and whose internationalism was manifested through the establishment of epistemological or aesthetic principles deemed universal and yet irreducible to
Western bourgeois culture. Closer in spirit and intent to the "peripheral" modernisms of Latin America and India than to the fauvist or cubist experiments in
Europe of which they were acutely aware, Russia's avant-garde painters sought
to rehabilitate the marginalized folk traditions of the Slavic peasantry and the
decorative arts of the Eurasian landmass.[25] This tendency, dubbed neoprimitivism in 1913, was arguably the most explicit act of *self*-orientalization that
Russian culture had yet witnessed, one that at once encompassed as well as
transcended Russia's boundaries. The painter Natal'ia Goncharova explained
the goals of neoprimitivism with startling clarity: "At the beginning of my development I learned most of all from my French contemporaries ... Now I shake
the dust off my feet and leave the West ... My path is toward the source of all

arts, the East ... I aspire toward nationality and the East, not to narrow the problems of art but, on the contrary, to make it all-embracing and universal."[26] In Goncharova's declaration, the East is at once a geographical marker, a set of cultural particularities, and the source of an alternative universality.

The eastward turn of Russian painting found an unexpected verbal correlative in the Russian futurist proclamation of the radical autonomy of the verbal sign. Inspired by Slavic philology and folklore studies but ultimately transcending the very regionalism that was its originating impulse, the futurist principle of the "self-sufficient word," alongside the rise of abstraction in the Russian visual arts, might be read as a means of seizing the monopoly over the aesthetic realm, over "literariness itself," a monopoly that had been associated for over a century with Paris.[27] Viewed as a manifestation of regionalism, the Russian avant-garde can be seen to point to a new set of spatio-temporal coordinates, tied initially to Russian-Eurasian history and geography and thence to the coordinates of world revolution. Never fully realized and self-consciously utopian, the legacy of the Russian avant-garde reveals an alternative geopoetics of world literature that would no longer be defined exclusively by the cultural assumptions and political ascendancy of the West.

This geopoetic mediation, in which the Eurasian region came to be seen as the catalyst for a new global imaginary, was most ambitiously and vividly achieved by the futurist poet Velimir Khlebnikov. Khlebnikov's earliest reflections on the patterns of Eurasian history were rooted in Slavic philology and motivated by the neoprimitivism of the pre-revolutionary avant-garde, just as his long-standing quest to ascertain the "laws of time" (to be elaborated later in this chapter) arose well before the watershed of October 1917, which the poet even claimed to have foreseen. At the same time, Khlebnikov's post-revolutionary writings show a marked tendency to approximate the lively debates on national and social liberation then being conducted by Bolshevik leaders and their interlocutors in the Comintern, debates whose import the poet sought to absorb and translate into his own evolving epistemology of space-time.

The convergence of Khlebnikov's poetic utopianism with the Comintern's celebrated "eastward turn" in 1920, then, is the historical context and literary-theoretical object of the pages to come. It was precisely this convergence – of geopolitics and geopoetics – that produced the poet's culminating work, the supersaga *Zangezi*, in which an alternative vision of world history and world geography is adumbrated. Like much of Khlebnikov's poetry, the work of a poet's poet, *Zangezi* failed to elicit widespread comprehension among the wider public; yet, its impact on select figures of the Soviet avant-garde and left intelligentsia was profound.[28] Staged three times in 1923 by the celebrated Soviet constructivist Vladimir Tatlin (figure 1.1) in the Petrograd Museum of Artistic Culture – itself a Tatlin-led institution and arguably the world's first museum dedicated exclusively to contemporary art – *Zangezi* stands alongside

1.1 Poster advertising the Tatlin production of *Zangezi* in Petrograd, 1923. Courtesy of the Russian Museum, St. Petersburg.

Tatlin's own unrealized Monument to the Third International (1919–20) as an immensely ambitious attempt to generate an artistic form and a set of constructive principles equal to the global resonance of the Russian Revolution.

The pages to come move systematically from context to text. I account first for the wider stakes of the revolutionary era, animated by ongoing debates on imperialism, uneven development, and world revolution. I then explore how these debates came to be refracted within a specific locale: Baku, capital of the recently Sovietized republic of Azerbaijan, site of the 1920 Congress of the Peoples of the East, and briefly home to the vagabond futurist poet Velimir Khlebnikov. I move then to the poet's own theories of time-space, whose discovery the poet ascribed to his sojourn in Baku. I then turn to *Zangezi* itself, elaborating its earliest production history, its salient themes and structure, and arguing ultimately for its status as a "world-text," one that evokes a unified planetary scale of spatial representation even as it consciously juxtaposes symbolic forms and discourses arising from distinct times and places.

1920: Uneven Development and the Eastward Turn of the Comintern

In class warfare, space is merely tactical, not the political goal,
whereas for the nation-state, time is tactical, and space is everything.

– Susan Buck-Morss, *Dreamworld and Catastrophe*[29]

The Second International of Europe's socialist parties had collapsed in the carnage of the First World War as a result of conflicting loyalties to class and nation as the drumbeat of bellicose patriotism eclipsed international workers' solidarity.[30] The Third Communist International arose under entirely different conditions: launched in Moscow in 1919 under Bolshevik leadership, its goals were intimately tied to the success and survival of the October Revolution, while its larger vision derived from the stringent critique of the emergent world order found in Lenin's *Imperialism, The Highest Stage of Capitalism* (*Imperializm, kak vysshaia stadiia kapitalizma*, 1916). Lenin's pamphlet was nothing less than an attempt to analyse the early twentieth century as a new and historically distinct stage in the history of global capitalism in which free competition had been displaced by the ascendancy of monopolistic finance capital and the colonial partition of the world had definitively been achieved by the hegemonic capitalist states. Now truly planetary, the emergent twentieth-century world order was nonetheless neither homogeneous nor stable, marked as it was temporally by the "*uneven and saltatory nature* of its development [*neravnomernost' i skachkoobraznost' v razvitii*]," and spatially by the "lack of correspondence [*nesootvetsviia*] between the development of productive forces and the accumulation of capital on the one hand, and the division of colonies and 'spheres of influence' for finance capital on the other."[31] Crises of overaccumulation in advanced capitalist nations were resolved through the export of capital to overseas colonies, yet the frenzied pursuit of land and raw materials exacerbated inter-imperial rivalries, whose inexorable outcome was war. It had also produced a "universal system of colonial oppression and financial suffocation by a handful of 'advanced' countries of the vast majority of the world's population."[32] As Giovanni Arrighi has astutely observed,[33] the novelty of Lenin's theory lay not so much in its interpretation of modern empires as a function of capital, but rather in Lenin's increasing sense of the planetary condition of uneven development, the result of great-power rivalry; of the "vast diversity of economic and political conditions" resulting in "discrepant rates of growth" between nations;[34] as well as of the disjuncture between competing metropoles and peripheries, whereby a small group of core nations was able to subject the greater part of the world to varying kinds of dependency or domination. Unevenness was not merely the defining characteristic of the contemporary world, but equally its potential breaking point. Classical Marxism had identified the bearer of that rupture as the European working class; Lenin's compass pointed eastward, to Russia itself, and to the national liberation movements of Asia working in tandem with progressive forces worldwide.[35] The Russian Revolution of 1905 had set off profound reverberations in Iran, Turkey, and China: what would be the consequences, in Eurasia, of 1917?

With the failure of the 1919 Hungarian and German revolutions, the Bolsheviks concluded that the European proletariat could no longer be counted upon to chart the direction of world revolution or to offer immediate aid to the beleaguered Soviet state. "The European revolution has seemingly receded," stated Trotsky, such that the "way to Paris and London lies through the cities of Afghanistan, Punjab and Bengal."[36] Convoked in Moscow in June 1920, the Second Congress of the Comintern thus signalled a significant turn to the East: although more than 90 per cent of the over two hundred delegates were Russian or European, the congress called for "the closest possible alliance of all national and colonial liberation movements with Soviet Russia."[37] This call became the impetus for the Congress of the Peoples of the East, held later that year (1–8 September) under Comintern auspices in recently Sovietized Baku, during which it was proclaimed that "all Communists – Russian, French, British, Italian and so on – have now become Asians, and are resolved to help every revolutionary movement in the East and in Africa."[38]

The Baku Congress of the Peoples of the East, counting over two thousand delegates,[39] was not merely the first gathering of revolutionaries in history to foreground the participation of non-Europeans, principally from the Muslim world: it was also a chaotic attempt at theorizing the concrete conditions of anti-colonial revolution and of relating local contingencies specific to the non-West to global communist strategy. Generating more enthusiasm than clarity, the Baku Congress affirmed the Leninist position that the backward conditions in which Asia languished might permit the circumvention of capitalism altogether, a leapfrogging of history that Lenin had also embraced as Russia's own path.[40] No less important were the role of the peasantry in regions where the proletariat was at best minimally present and the difficult correlation, under colonial conditions, between national and social revolution. The national aspirations of oppressed peoples were to be welcomed, if supplemented and ultimately supplanted by social revolution.

How might we rethink the significance of the Baku Congress beyond the immediate context of Bolshevik tactics and revolutionary strategy? Nergis Ertürk has recently made the bold and suggestive claim: "*Comparative Literature might reclaim the history of this congress as an alternative genealogy for the discipline*, an experiment in displacing the discipline's other founding stories: Goethe's invention of *Weltliteratur* in conversation with Eckermann, Leo Spitzer and Erich Auerbach's missed encounter with an Orientalized Istanbul."[41] Ertürk notes the cacophony of languages spoken at the Baku Congress, which resonated in sharp contrast to the woefully inadequate translation facilities provided by the Bolshevik authorities, leading to a "leveling of linguistic multiplicity" that had equally blemished previous congresses of the Comintern. As such, the congress – or better still the gap between the heteroglot reality of the congress (including dissenting and untranslated voices) and the homogenized Russian stenographic record of its proceedings (figure 1.2) published shortly thereafter in Petrograd – might be read as a latter-day communist reworking of the biblical

1.2 Cover of the Russian stenographic edition of the proceedings of the Baku Congress, 1920.

story of Babel, whose "unfulfilled promise," Ertürk suggests, was an "immanent, heterogeneous common in alterity" that would take the place of a "transcendent God." Such a promise, it should be noted, was decidedly *not* articulated in the actual speeches of Bolshevik leaders, who viewed differences of national culture, religion, and language as temporary impediments to revolution to be tactically conceded where necessary. Michael Kemper has rightly observed of the Baku Congress that "a discussion of [the] specificities of Muslim societies or of Islam was conspicuously absent," a lacuna filled by generic references to "Oriental backwardness" unabashedly drawn from "a European Orientalist perspective."[42] One might argue that the Bolsheviks' undeniable cultural Eurocentrism, "anti-Orientalist in form but Orientalist in content,"[43] was to some extent counterbalanced by their striking reconfiguration of Marxist doctrine in accordance with the "zig-zag" rather than stadial path of non-European history.[44] Whether this reconfiguration would occur in response to actual conditions on the ground, or according to the political, economic, and diplomatic exigencies of the newly emergent Soviet state, still remained to be seen. In short, the Second Congress of the Comintern, along with the Baku Congress of the Peoples of the East, marked a significant shift of focus within the world communist movement towards Asia and what we today call the global South, a shift that would ultimately – though not immediately – mirror the actual pattern of world revolution in the twentieth century. At the same time, both gatherings betrayed the Bolsheviks' characteristic tendency to derive theoretical principles from the concrete historical moment, which also meant the shifting realm of diplomacy and military manoeuvre, thereby anticipating the role of the Comintern in instrumentalizing world revolution in the service of Soviet foreign policy.[45] Whatever the limitations of the Baku Congress, its "unfulfilled promise," that of a renewed Eurasian and world literary common, was arguably realized by one of its most unlikely eyewitnesses, the Russian futurist poet Velimir Khlebnikov.[46]

Khlebnikov in Baku, or the Utopian Geopoetics of Eurasia

Esli ia obrashchu chelovechestvo v chasy
I pokazhu, kak strelka stoletii dvizhetsia,
Neuzheli iz vashei vremen polosy
Ne vyletit voina, kak nenuzhnaia izhitsa?

If I turned humankind into a timepiece
And showed you how the hand of the centuries moved,
Wouldn't war itself, like an obsolete letter,
Fall away from the newsprint of time?

                                                            – Velimir Khlebnikov, 1922[47]

Khlebnikov was born in a remote and rudimentary encampment in the Kalmyk steppe, north of Astrakhan, near the Caspian Sea. Far from Russia's metropolitan centres, this southern Volga region was, both biographically and mythopoetically, the poet's point of origin, one that offered him an alternative optic through which to view the Russian tradition. Rooted in Russia's borderlands, which the poet regarded as a crossroads rather than a periphery, Khlebnikov's literary geography would acquire an increasingly expansive vision, one the poet himself characterized in 1913 as "continent-wide [*materikovym*]" rather than narrowly "Great-Russian [*velikorusskim*]."[48] Khlebnikov's poetic and scientific quest mirrored the centrifugal impulse of his geographical trajectory to a remarkable degree, and never more than during his final years, which coincided with the immediate reverberations of the Russian Revolution and the Comintern's "turn to the East."[49]

    Beginning in 1919, the poet travelled widely through Ukraine and southern Russia, both then lacerated by civil war, crossing the Caucasus Mountains via Daghestan to reach Baku in the autumn of 1920.[50] In October, soon after the Baku Congress, the poet was appointed as educational collaborator to the local branch of the Soviet news agency BakKavRosta, where he was tasked with composing versified slogans for agitational posters, before receiving the nominal post of lecturer to the Political Education Department of the Volga-Caspian Fleet. These were months of material destitution and febrile concentration, during which the poet arrived at the definitive version of his mathematically derived theory of history. As the poet would subsequently declare: "I found the pure laws of time in 1920 while living in Baku,"[51] a startling claim echoed in a letter of February 1921 to none other than the celebrated theatre director Vsevolod Meyerhold: "As for me, I have achieved the promised revolution [*переворота*] in the understanding of time, a revolution that embraces several scientific fields."[52] Living in Baku until mid-April 1921, Khlebnikov then sailed across the Caspian to Iran as part of the Red Army's interventionist campaign in support of a revolutionary uprising in the Iranian province of Gilan: barefoot and dressed in tattered robes, he would be hailed by local villagers as a "Russian dervish." Returning to Russia with the evacuation of the Red Army from Iran, Khlebnikov would spend the last months of his life working on the final redaction of his culminating work, the supersaga *Zangezi*, before dying of a debilitating illness that took his life in June 1922.

How might we relate Khlebnikov's physical peregrinations and poetic-scientific experimentation to the intellectual ferment and geopolitical pressures of the time? Khlebnikov's movements during Russia's Civil War mirror to a striking degree the successes and failures of the Red Army in Ukraine, southern Russia, the Caucasus, and Iran. Yet, beyond the broadly emancipatory goals of revolution, Khlebnikov's writings ignore Hegelian-Marxist categories in favour of the poet's own idiosyncratic reworking of time, space, and language. Reporting to his sister on an evidently disastrous lecture given that winter at Baku's Naval University before an audience of no doubt bemused sailors and workers, Khlebnikov wrote: "I informed the Marxists present that I was Marx squared [*Marks v kvadrate*], and to those who preferred [the prophet] Muhammad I said that I was the continuation of the preachings of Muhammad, who had fallen mute and substituted numbers for words. I titled the lecture 'The Quran of Numbers.'"[53] These brief lines point whimsically to the poet's astonishing intellectual hubris: Khlebnikov saw his legacy as ultimately surpassing all prior forms of cognitive enquiry, a synthetic vision that would reconcile but also supersede art, science, and the Near Eastern lineages of prophetic revelation. It is not within the socialist traditions of Marx or Lenin, then, that we must situate Khlebnikov's planetary vision. Coinciding geopoetically but not conceptually with the Bolshevik and Comintern goal of world revolution, the writings of Khlebnikov's last years offer a kind of supplementary internationalism of poetic-scientific cognition in which the civilizational and spiritual energies of West and South Asia, which historical materialism had ostensibly rendered obsolete, would be mobilized alongside Khlebnikovian science in the service of a new global imaginary. This global imaginary finds its fullest expression in *Zangezi*, a text that incorporates and enacts Khlebnikov's theory of time, space, and much more. A cursory outline of the essential aspects of Khlebnikovian theory, as evidenced by his manifestos, his correspondence, as well as his speculative opus *The Tables of Fate* (*Doski sud'by*), is thus an essential prerequisite to any reading of *Zangezi* itself. These texts also constitute one of the most ambitious attempts at a utopian reconstitution of language and epistemology ever attempted by a modern poet.

Throughout his life, Khlebnikov sought to uncover the underlying laws governing history: to recognize its patterns, he believed, was to anticipate and ultimately neutralize the cycles of violence that periodically engulfed humanity. Khlebnikov measured historical time by calculating the days between watershed events. Nations, he argued, did not rise and fall at random: on the contrary, all human vicissitudes, including war and peace, were punctuated by consistent lapses of time whose regularity was in turn governed by precise mathematical relations. A letter by Khlebnikov to the painter Pëtr Miturich written just months before Khlebnikov's death makes this point succinctly: "Here is my fundamental law of time: in time a negative shift takes place in 3^n days, while a positive one takes place in 2^n days." Thus "between [Russia's] conquest of Siberia in 1581 and Russia's rebuff [by Japan] on 15 February 1905 at the Battle of Mukden, $3^{10} + 3^{10}$ days were to pass."[54] How should we interpret this extraordinary claim? Let us first note that Khlebnikov's understanding of time was founded on an entirely conventional belief that human history was first and foremost a set of events, empirically datable just as a datum of science is verifiable. Yet, in combining these data into new syntagmatic sequences – be they mathematical equations or lines of verse – Khlebnikov broke entirely with the conventional notion of time as a flow of contiguous, successive moments: "The new relationship to time brings to the fore the operation of division and asserts that distant points may be more identical than two neighbouring ones," he declared in 1919.[55] Causality was no longer a matter either of immediate context or of a linear historical process, but of establishing the relatedness of events possibly centuries apart. Moreover, an attentive reading of the letter to Miturich points to a spatial logic no less than a temporal one. Even as a "mathematical" abstraction of time – based on exponential expressions of twos and threes – is seen to govern the logic of victory and defeat in battle, it is accompanied by a "geographical" abstraction of space – an East/West axis which, alongside the laws of time, governs the waxing and waning of Eurasian nations and empires. Khlebnikov saw "temporal" repetition as necessarily complemented by "spatial" reversal, such that Japan's crushing victory over Russia in 1905 was also the geographically predetermined overcoming of Russia's own centuries-long eastward expansion into Siberia. By correlating time *and* space, Khlebnikov was able, at least in part, to overcome the difficulty of reconciling historical concretion with an abstract principle of temporal repetition.

Khlebnikov scholarship has responded in predictably polarized ways to the poet's epistemology of time-space. Lada Panova has sought to debunk the "cult" of Khlebnikov as poet-prophet by questioning the originality of Khlebnikov's mathematization of history, pointing to the poet's debt to the occult numerological explorations of his predecessors, the Russian symbolists.[56] Yet, Panova's suggestive exercise in intertextual parallelism ignores Khlebnikov's own repeated insistence that his theories had definitively superseded religion by reducing the conundrum of fate to a tangible set of mathematical formulae predicated on the "immanent" unfolding of history: indeed, Khlebnikov's utopianism is, if anything, a radical "secularization" of religious eschatology.[57] Henryk Baran similarly – and with some justification – situates Khlebnikov's poetics in "mythical thought" predicated on a "transcendent pattern" according to which "different levels of reality" – macrocosm and microcosm – may be "homologized."[58] Yet, it remains to be seen whether Khlebnikov's laws of time can be assimilated without residue to the cyclical nature of myth, and whether they are not rather a distinctly modern and modernist response to the crisis of nineteenth-century linear historicism. Ronald Vroon, by contrast, insists that "Khlebnikov's vision was conditioned by a deeply rational, essentially empirical attitude to spatio-temporal reality" based on experimental verification: "Firstly the poet gathered and juxtaposed historical data; he then analysed the frequency of events of a specific type and drew corresponding mathematical equations with which this frequency could be described ... Finally the mathematical formulae would be tested, firstly by drawing on additional information about the past that would either confirm their efficacy or require their modification, secondly by generating prophecies about the near or distant future."[59] Vroon correctly distinguishes Khlebnikov's inductive method – obsessive though hardly rigorous – from the essentially intuitive-mystical premise of his symbolist precursors, but falls well short of clarifying the epistemological rupture it represents as a singular expression of avant-garde utopianism.

The striking convergence, manifested in Khlebnikov's work, of poetry and science is best understood as part of the broader historical arc of the Russian avant-garde. The Italian historian of architecture Manfredo Tafuri long ago traced the "contradictory" evolution of the Russian avant-garde from the Russian formalists' initial reduction of art to its constitutive material components to the subsequent reinsertion of art and literature, with Soviet constructivism, into a productivist ideology devoted to the planned construction of a socialist society. The avant-garde, for Tafuri, was not a hermetic celebration of the irrational forces of the imagination: rather, its anti-traditionalism served to destroy antiquated notions of art and society whose negation paved the way for new rationalizations of time and space, labour and capital.[60] Tafuri's stark thesis is usefully nuanced by Julia Vaingurt's distinction between the "instrumental" rationality of the Soviet state, rooted in notions of productivity, functionality, and efficiency, and the "non-utilitarian" rationality of the Russian avant-garde, which was "ultimately hypothetical and exploratory."[61] Khlebnikov's hyper-rationalization of the constitutive elements of time, space, and language (to be explored further in the coming pages) might thus be seen as the literary correlative to the Russian constructivists' declared aim of replacing art with a universal set of technical principles, methodically derived and perceived to be functioning within an immanent system. These technical principles would eventually be subordinated to the decidedly external goals of socialist modernization, the vision of a planned society governed by scientifically derived laws. At the same time, as Hubertus Gassner has argued, constructivist production art contains "a utopian surplus value that transforms even the individual utilitarian object into a *pars pro toto* of a cosmos harmonically structured by rhythmic movements. This utopian surplus lends their objects their aesthetic and ethical value and even bathes them in an aura of artistic autonomy – precisely the quality the Constructivists struggled to nullify on their flight into bare functionalism."[62] Gassner's essentially Blochian argument is as pertinent to the poetry of Velimir Khlebnikov as it is to the constructed objects of Vladimir Tatlin and Aleksandr Rodchenko. The poet's legacy rests on a distinctly archaic – or at the very least neo-romantic – model of poetic-intellectual labour that had yet to be subordinated to the technocratic demands of the socialist state, even as it willingly embraced the goal of a rationally organized society. Khlebnikovian science blended positivist content – the empirical quantification of historical intervals in calendar time – with the form of prophetic utterance, with its utopian promise to fulfil and renew human destiny. As such, it merits our interest, not for its accuracy but as an avant-garde geopoetic meditation on a region convulsed by revolution and war.

Khlebnikov's poetic-scientific legacy has been frequently hailed as marking a "temporal turn" equivalent to contemporaneous ruptures in science and advances in technology. Barely months after Khlebnikov's death, Russian art historian Nikolai Punin, a gifted champion of the avant-garde who would perish in Stalin's labour camps, wrote that "a new feeling for time" was the "general and singular trait of the twentieth century." If, in the past, "time was assumed to be successive, a flat, continuous sequence," then "our era," he claimed, had been inaugurated by the revelations of Einstein and Khlebnikov.[63] There is indeed much in the rhetoric of Khlebnikov's manifestos to corroborate Punin's thesis, although they echo Einstein less than they parody Khlebnikov's great international rival, the Italian futurist Filippo Marinetti. In Khlebnikov's manifesto "The Trumpet of the Martians" (*Truba marsian*, 1916), the futurist movement's youthful rebellion against the cultural establishment is figured as an act of political secession that unilaterally establishes the "independent state of *time* (devoid of space) [*nezavisimoe gosudarstvo* vremeni (*lishennoe prostranstva*)]."[64] The conflict between innovation and tradition is here staged as a struggle between nations – nations, moreover, that diverge precisely as time differs from space: "We have founded the state of time ... leaving to the states of space the chance to reconcile themselves to its existence by leaving it alone, or by engaging it in a frenzied struggle."[65] These curious lines require careful unpacking. Marinetti and the Italian futurists had married a grandiloquent embrace of accelerating time to a bellicose commitment to the militarized Italian state, acting within a world marked by intense interstate rivalries.[66] Khlebnikov's response was to mimic Marinetti's agonistic register while inverting its intent. By abstracting the spatial logic of interstate rivalry at the heart of the Great War and then applying it to time itself, Khlebnikov sought to carve out a revolutionary poetic-scientific realm, governed by the revealed laws of time and its youthful exponents, as a utopian alternative to the political state. The utopian revolutionary potential of this statement should not be underestimated: it anticipates the youth focus of the New Left by several generations. Yet, this leap into the fourth dimension of time also points to an aporia at the heart of Khlebnikov's literary-scientific endeavour. Khlebnikov's declared hypostasis of time had initially to deflate the importance of space, including one of the most potent forms of spatialization available – the nation-state. As Khlebnikov's great contemporary, the poet Osip Mandel'shtam, put it: "Khlebnikov contemplated language as a state [*myslil iazyk kak gosudarstvo*], but one by no means situated geographically in space, but rather in time."[67] Yet, Mandel'shtam's astute formulation ignores an essential slippage in Khlebnikov's rhetoric: in attacking space, Khlebnikov fell back on the very idiom of territorial integrity that is the military precondition of national sovereignty. The unit of Khlebnikovian time thus paradoxically remained geographical, more specifically, territorial, even as his "state of time" acquired an increasingly emancipatory transnational form.

In the poet's final years, the temporal utopia that Khlebnikov sought to liberate became increasingly identified with the Eurasian landmass itself, as it was awakening, through war and revolution, to its historical destiny. In 1918, some six months prior to the founding of the Comintern and some two years before its articulated turn to the East, Khlebnikov authored several manifestos that amounted to a sweeping act of global decolonization. In "An Indo-Russian Union" (*Indo-russkii soiuz*), never published in Khlebnikov's lifetime and surviving in draft form, the poet in part proclaims:

1. The organization aims to defend the shores of Asia from sea pirates and to create a single maritime border.
2. As we know, the bell that sounds for Russia's freedom will have no effect on European ears.
3. As with social classes, political states can be divided into oppressor states and oppressed states.
...

5. The great nations of the Continent of ASSU (China, India, Persia, Russia, Siam, Afghanistan) belong to the list of oppressed states.

6. The islands are oppressors, the continents are oppressed ...

7. Maximize maritime frontiers, while abolishing land frontiers entirely.

8. A united Asia has arisen from the ashes of the Great War ...

9. Donning the heavy armour of the positive sciences, we hasten to the aid of our common mother.

10. The will of Fate has ordained that this union be conceived in Astrakhan, a place that unites three worlds – the Aryan world, the Indian world, the world of the Caspian: the triangle of Christ, the Buddha, and Muhammad.

...

12. We speak as the first Asians to take cognizance of their insular unity.

13. May the citizens of our island pass from the Yellow Sea to the Baltic, and from the White Sea to the Indian Ocean, without ever encountering a frontier.

14. May the tattooed patterns of nation-states be wiped from Asia's body by the will of Asiatics.

15. May the separate regions [udely] of Asia be united into an island.

16. We, the citizens of the new world, freed and united because of Asia, parade in triumph before you.

...

19. Our path leads from the unity of Asia to the unity of the stars, and from freedom for the continent to freedom for all of Planet Earth.

...

24. To begin our new life, we snatch India from the clutches of Great Britain. India: you are free. The first three to call themselves Asians are setting you free.[68]

This remarkable manifesto combines the performative speech-acts proper to an emancipation proclamation with the generic logic of utopian thought.[69] As such, it fuses two distinct rhetorical operations: a metaphorical projection onto a radically utopian "non-place" and a metonymic displacement of contemporary geopolitics, palpable here as a series of recognizable toponyms, and in the topical allusions to contemporary debates within the world communist movement on national and social liberation. These topical references are invoked only to be subject to a utopian reinscription, culminating in the neologistic acronym ASSU, which two scholars have recently glossed as the "Asian Union of Free Regions [Aziiskii soiuz svobodnykh udelov]."[70] Attentive readers will have noticed a curious equivocation in the text: Is Asia an island (Points 12, 13, and 15) or a continent (Point 5)? Given the antagonism of islands and continents (Point 6) – a topographical rendering of the struggle between empires and colonized nations – how could Asia be both? Leading Khlebnikov scholar A.E. Parnis reads this equivocation philologically as a "slip of the tongue" on the poet's part.[71] I would suggest that we are in fact dealing here with a deeper structural inconsistency, proper to utopian writing, between openness and boundedness.[72] The manifesto, like many of Khlebnikov's works, vacillates between two equally utopian impulses: the first being one of outward expansion, from the erasure of national boundaries to the final goal of planetary liberation; the second being one of closure, with ASSU declared an impregnable island ruled by a "laboratory for the study of time," which would serve as the "Supreme Administrative Soviet of Asia."[73]

It becomes clear, then, that Khlebnikov's utopia was at once – like Sir Thomas More's island-commonwealth – a unified and bounded state governed by the poet-scholar, and – like world revolution – an ever-expanding, self-emancipating realm outside of space as such, a "state of time." In the poet's final years, the Eurasian landmass itself – a region embracing Russia as well as regions more conventionally regarded as Asiatic – emerged as Khlebnikov's organizing geopoetic figure, bringing together a specific if mobile geographical matrix and a scientific enquiry into the abstract patterns underlying history. A mathematical abstraction of time was thus complemented by the decolonization of space, a utopian operation of metaphorical projection and metonymic reinscription that Khlebnikov would repeatedly identify as "Asia."[74]

One final aspect of Khlebnikovian theory remains to be sketched before we turn to his culminating work. In several manifestos closely related to *Zangezi*, the poet strove to supplement his long-standing mathematization of time with an additional geometricization of space. Just as numbers (above all, exponentials of two and three) were declared the base unit of time, so too letters (understood initially in phonic terms, but increasingly as graphemes) were found to be the base unit of space. Khlebnikov's central claim was that the initial consonantal sound of any word served to define its deeper semantic import, determined by the abstract spatial pattern that the sound was said inherently to possess.[75] Khlebnikov determined the geometrical value of each consonant by accumulating lists of – generally Slavic – words beginning with the same letter, whose deeper connectedness it was the poet's task to ascertain. In the manifesto "Our Fundamentals" (*Nasha osnova*, 1919), a list of *l* words, such as "*lodka* [boat], *lyzhi* [skis] ... *ladon'* [palm of the hand], *lapa* [paw]," and so forth, points to the following conclusion: "The meaning of *l* is the conversion of a body stretched along the axis of movement into a body stretched in two directions perpendicular to the axis of motion ... Let us consider a sailor in a boat: his weight is distributed over the broad surface of the bottom of the boat. The point where force is applied is spread out over a wide area, and the wider the area the less the weight. The sailor loses weight. For this reason we may define *l* as the decrease of a force at any given point brought about by an increase of the field of contact. A falling body comes to rest when it comes into contact with a large enough surface." At this very point, Khlebnikov shifts his attention from the abstract spatial value of *l* to its concrete application within contemporary history: "An example of such a shift in the social order is the shift from tsarist to Soviet Russia, since in the new order the weight of power was transferred onto an incomparably wider area of those bearing power: a sailor – the state – is supported by the boat [*lodka*] of broad popular sovereignty."[76]

How are we to understand this startling correlation of articulated sound and political history? Khlebnikov broke his universal writing system down into a list of graphic signs or – better still – phonemes capable at some future point of generating universally accepted graphemes. Like the letter *l*, each phoneme was said to correspond to a precise if abstract geometrical expression. This series was in turn subdivided into opposing pairs, termed "negative twins."[77] Thus Khlebnikov would substantiate his claim, made in *Zangezi*, that the letters *r*, *k*, *l*, and *g* were the "real protagonists" of the Russian Revolution by recoding recent Russian history as a war between opposing letters: *l* versus *g*, *r* versus *k*.[78] These letters, the sonic-spatial forces behind the Russian Revolution, are glossed in *Zangezi* as follows:

> L (Л): the cessation of a fall, or of motion in general, halted by a plane that is transverse to the falling point.
> G (Г): the movement of a point at right angles to the principal motion, away from it. Hence height.
> R (P): a point that penetrates a transverse area.
> K (K): the encounter and hence the halt of multiple moving points in one motionless point. Hence the ultimate meaning of *k* is calmness; immobilization.[79]

From this admittedly truncated list, it becomes clear that Khlebnikov sought to translate sounds into distinct spatial trajectories, produced by the interaction of points, lines, and planes, in an ongoing dialectic of movement and stasis. Just as numbers dictated the outcome of history, sounds served to determine the mobile logic of human geography. The alliterative patterns of words thus became a key to understanding the migrations of peoples, the impact of invasions, the pulse of revolution and reaction. The letter *l*, in impelling the collapse of vertical hierarchy (the letter *g*) onto the transverse principle of democratic horizontality, emerged as nothing less than the final resting point of the Russian Revolution, its utopian state of blissful stasis.

However implausible, Khlebnikov's theory of letters merits some basic conceptual parsing. In linguistic terms, Khlebnikov interpreted phonemes as if they were morphemes, attributing the generation of meaning to the basic differential units of sound. Poetic alliteration was thereby transformed into a generalizable semantic law: initial consonantal letters were seen to embody a kind of spatial inner form, whose geometrical-pictorial contours coexisted with a given word's everyday meaning, determining the semantic "halo" it shared with all other words beginning with the same letter. These inner forms, deemed universal, held the potential to generate ideograms that would supersede existing languages as well as the purely conventional nature of alphabetic writing. The extraordinary leap from linguistic structure to political history, made repeatedly by Khlebnikov both in his theoretical writings and in his poetic practice, rested on the intuition that spatial manipulation was the basis both of world history and the linguistic sign: "The simple bodies of language – the sounds of the alphabet – are the names of various kinds of space, the list of the occasions of its life. An alphabet shared by many nations is a short dictionary of the spatial world."[80] And elsewhere: "Power, the laws of nation-states, is a closed body in space [*Vlast', zakony gosudarstv, zamknutoe telo v prostranstve*]. A spatial *yes* ... we can seize them like lumps, like mountains of space-beasts, with a whole positive number."[81] According to Khlebnikovian epistemology, then, the dynamics of force were registered spatially in letters, while its vicissitudes in time could be calculated by numbers.

If Khlebnikov's semanticization of the basic units of language was an attempt, rationalist in essence, to overcome the arbitrariness of the linguistic sign, then its wider social purpose was, once again, universalist and utopian, namely to "find the general unity of world languages on the basis of the units of the alphabet."[82] This goal is most clearly articulated in the remarkable manifesto "Artists of the World!" (*Khudozhniki mira!*), published posthumously in 1928 but authored in 1919 for *Art International* (*Internatsional iskusstva*), an abortive journalistic initiative of the Visual Arts Department (IZO) of the People's Commissariat for Enlightenment, which, if realized, could well have furnished the basis of a Comintern aesthetic.[83] "Artists of the World!" is the clearest codification of Khlebnikov's "spatial dictionary" and the most lucid articulation of its global purpose. Here, Khlebnikov presents language transactionally, as a means of exchange and a mode of equivalence. If, in times past, language "had undermined enmity" by allowing a "union of people to exchange the values of reason for one and the same equivalent sounds," then today's world, typified by a post-Babelic cacophony of tongues, was no less than an anarchic form of linguistic capitalism. The planet had been reduced to "a series of verbal markets [*riad slovesnykh rynkov*]" in which "each order of sound-money [*kazhdyi stroi zvuchnykh deneg*] claims supremacy; in this way languages as such serve to divide humanity and wage phantom wars." If Goethe had regarded literary exchange through translation as an alternative to war, then Khlebnikov viewed heteroglossia itself as the linguistic equivalent to financial speculation: both exacerbated the volatility and arbitrariness of exchange-value, while a "single written language," like the ideographic characters of the "Chinese and Japanese peoples," could bring humanity together. "Silent graphic signs," the poet concluded, "will reconcile the diversity of tongues" by serving as "mute money" in the "conversational markets."[84]

Khlebnikov's "Artists of the World!" invites a brief comparison with Ernest Fenollosa's *The Chinese Written Character as a Medium for Poetry*, a foundational theoretical text of Anglo-American poetic modernism. Published posthumously by Ezra Pound in 1920, Fenollosa's slim treatise made its public appearance just a year after Khlebnikov's manifesto was completed. Near-contemporaneous documents with analogous "Sinophilic" claims, both essays allow for a useful juxtaposition of the American and Russian avant-gardes, in their imagist and futurist manifestations, within the context of global modernism. Both Fenollosa and Khlebnikov discerned in the Chinese writing system an archaic articulation of the relationship between visual sensation and conceptual abstraction. For Fenollosa, the earliest Chinese characters were "shorthand pictures of actions or processes" that "served to throw light upon our forgotten mental processes." This process was none other than metaphor itself, "the use of material images to suggest immaterial relations."[85] In unifying the immediate visual impact of imagery with the cognitive dynamism implied by metaphorical condensation, Fenollosa's formulation provided the impetus for a significant revolution in modern American verse. Christopher Bush has recently argued that Western poetic modernism's fascination for the Chinese writing system was at once a speculative ethnographic projection – the potent fantasy of an archaic mode of imagistic cognition lost to the West but vestigially present in the East – and an implicit dialogue with new technological media such as photography and the cinema, whose visual immediacy and logic of montage posed a direct challenge to the inherited conventions of poetic syntax and metaphorical association.[86] Khlebnikov's intervention, I would argue, was no less motivated by ethnographic impulses and technological concerns; yet, both these factors resonated differently on Eurasian soil. Fenollosa's intuitions had served to recuperate difference, while Khlebnikov's proposal was an act of cultural solidarity, all the more astonishing in the wake of the Russo-Japanese war of 1905. In his 1916 "Letter to Two Japanese" (*Pis'mo dvum iapontsam*), for example, Khlebnikov asserted that "Asia is not just some northern land peopled by a multinomial [*mnogochlenom*] of nations, but is also *a cluster of written characters out of which the word 'I' must emerge* ... Asia has a will of her own."[87] If Fenollosa, in the telling words of Pound's preface, "looked to an *American* renaissance," such that "the exotic was always a means of fructification,"[88] then Khlebnikov's theory was based on a shared act of cultural self-emancipation binding Russia and Asia together as one.[89]

I have thus far sketched the barest outlines of Khlebnikov's theory of numbers and letters as markers of time-space. Some scholars have argued that Khlebnikov never achieved the unification of his mathematical theory of time and his linguistic theory of space, which remain juxtaposed rather than integrated in his work.[90] Carla Solivetti, by contrast, sees Khlebnikov's theory of space no less than of time as subject to the shared principle of "alternating opposites": just as time is governed by a tug of war between the odd and even numbers 2 and 3, so too space is controlled by contrasting pairs of letters capable of inducing inverse effects in the real world.[91] The convergence of numbers and letters is indeed central to the prophetic revelation articulated in *Zangezi*. However incomplete, Khlebnikov's search for the universal patterns of time-space might also be regarded as Khlebnikov's utopian resolution to the question of world literature. To a remarkable degree, the poet's scientific theories and poetic practice revolved around the challenges posed by the nation-state and the market, the two intersecting forms of the modern world system that have structured the project of world literature since Goethe. Not only did Khlebnikov's mathematization of time and geometricization of space expose the underlying patterns of interstate conflict and market competition, they also pointed to a rationally organized global utopia in which war would be eradicated and speculative gain rendered obsolete: "As the rays of fate become exposed," he wrote, "the concept of nations and states vanishes; all that remains is a single humanity, whose every point is linked by regular laws."[92] The price of Khlebnikov's utopianism was considerable: the attribution of idiosyncratic semantic values to the linguistic signifier, the elimination of all randomness in human evolution in favour of historical regularity, leading ultimately to an extreme rationalization of time-space itself as the basis of world harmony. It would be difficult to find a better illustration of the emancipatory and expansive elements of utopian thought, alongside the impulse towards totalization and closure. Let us now see how this abstractly utopian vision came to be embodied in Tatlin's theatrical representation as well as in Khlebnikov's literary practice.

Khlebnikov's *Zangezi* and the Legacy of Tatlin

Zangezi (1922) is arguably the supreme creative expression of Khlebnikov's search to renew poetic form in the wake of his claim to have discovered the underlying regularities of time-space.[93] An amalgam of prophetic utterance, densely alliterative verse, exuberantly neologistic wordplay, and quasi-scientific data purporting to elucidate the phonic-spatial and rhythmic-temporal laws of Eurasian and world history, *Zangezi* is, in essence, an avant-garde *Gesamtkunstwerk*, one that seeks to reconcile the architectonics of cubism and constructivism, the dynamism of theatrical performance, and the disintegration of epic narrative into lyric fragments, the latter being the consistent response of Russia's poets since Pushkin to the receding viability of epic form (figure 1.3).

The opening lines of *Zangezi* herald the text as a radical generic innovation. *Zangezi*, we are told, is a "supersaga [*sverkhnovest'*]," "put together from independent fragments [*samostoiatel'nykh otryvkov*], each with its own special god, special faith and statute ... Each has been granted the freedom to profess

1.3 Cover of the first edition of *Zangezi*, 1922, designed by Pëtr Miturich.

its own faith. The constructive unit or building block of the supersaga is the first-order narrative [*povest' pervogo poriadka*]. It resembles a statue made of different blocks [*glyb*] of stone of varying colour, its body consisting of white stone, its cloak and attire of blue, its eyes of black. It is carved out of the multicoloured blocks of the word, each with its own structure [*stroeniia*]. Thus do we find a new kind of operation in the realm of verbal affairs. A story [*rasskaz*] is architecture with words. Architecture with 'stories' is a supersaga [*Zodchestvo iz 'rasskazov' est' sverkhpovest'*]. The artist's building block is no longer the word, but the first-order narrative."[94]

Khlebnikov's account of the compositional principles of *Zangezi* closely parallels debates in the visual arts during the dramatic transition from prewar cubo-futurism to Soviet constructivism. The division of the text into twenty-one distinct verbal "planes [*ploskosti*]," composed separately between 1920 and 1922, recalls cubism's fracturing of linear perspective into elementary geometrical forms and simultaneous angles of vision, a method *Zangezi* explicitly acknowledges as the basis of language as well: "Words do not exist, there are only movements in space and its parts ... Planes, the lines defining an area, the impact of points, the divine circle, the angle of incidence, the fascicule of rays proceeding from a point or penetrating it – these are secret building blocks of language."[95] The emphasis here on movement, on space as a kinetic field of forces, recalls the Italian futurists' critique of cubism's inability to move beyond static three-dimensionality, while Vladimir Tatlin explicitly pointed to Khlebnikov's feeling for the sculptural plasticity of sound as analogous to constructivist design, with its commitment to the "tectonics" and "texture" of constructed objects.[96] Tatlin's declaration that his staging of *Zangezi* constituted a multi-media "performance [*predstavlenie*] + lecture + exhibition of material constructions" mirrors Khlebnikov's own desire to erase the distinction between poetry, art, and the metalanguage of science.[97] Tatlin's *Zangezi* was a precocious instance of what we now understand as performance art, as well as an attempt at bringing both poetry and performance into contact with material culture. The constructivists' insistence on technical rigour, on the transparent and rational organization of artistic space and the surface tactility of materials deployed, also finds ample resonance in *Zangezi*. The geometricization of space evident in Tatlin's stage design (figure 1.4) was at once a search for theatrical equivalents to Khlebnikov's theory of language and an extension of Tatlin's own guiding principles, above all the organizing role of an upwardly thrusting line, often diagonal or sloping, which marks many of Tatlin's counter-reliefs as well as his celebrated Monument to the Third International.[98]

The formal homologies between Tatlin's monument and his staging of *Zangezi* merit closer attention, both intrinsically and for the ways they point to an incipient Comintern aesthetic. In both play and monument, a vertical axis perpendicular to the earth serves to structure political organization and

1.4 A sample sketch, in charcoal on paper, of the set design for the Tatlin production of *Zangezi*: clearly visible here is the dominant diagonal line organizing the vertical axis linking the hero, Zangezi, to the masses below. Courtesy of the A. A. Bakhrushin State Central Museum of the Theatre, Moscow.

discursive power: just as the monument's glass cube, pyramid, and cylinder, each independently rotating at different velocities representing the span of a year, a month, and a day, respectively, arrange the deliberative, executive, and propagandistic-informational arms of the Comintern in an upward movement of ascending authority and planetary reach, so too the play arranges its various discursive "planes" in a hierarchical order that culminates in the figure of Zangezi himself (figure 1.5). To be sure, Tatlin's Monument to the Third International dissolves the neo-romantic aura of the Khlebnikovian poet-prophet into a rigorously functional "information office," situated at the tower's apex and dedicated, in the words of art historian Nikolai Punin, to the "publication of proclamations, brochures and manifestos – in a word, all the various means of broadly informing the international proletariat, and in particular a telegraph ... and a radio station, the masts of which rise above the monument" (figure 1.6)[99] In other words, the functionalism of the monument, while

1.5 Image from Tatlin's 1923 production of *Zangezi*: beyond directing the play and designing the sets, props, and costumes, Tatlin can be seen here playing the hero, Zangezi. Courtesy of the Russian State Archive for Literature and Art.

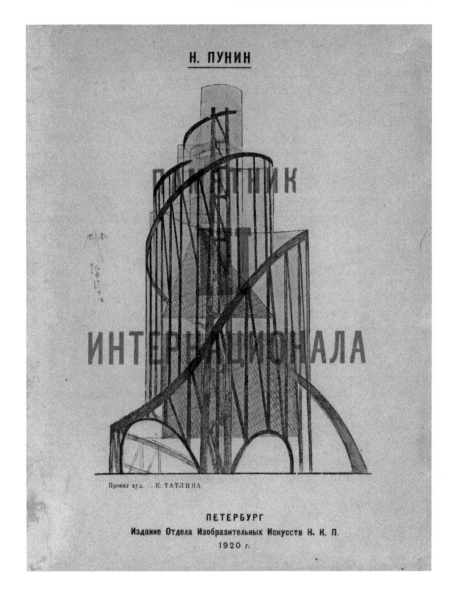

1.6 Front cover of Nikolai Punin's brochure *Monument to the Third International* (Petrograd, 1920): here, at least three of the four geometrically shaped interiors – glass cube, pyramid, and cylinder – are clearly visible.

necessarily abolishing the figure of the poet-prophet, displaces his symbolic role onto modern technology and the artist-technician who has mastered it.

Curiously, Punin did not notice the role of Tatlin's diagonal in reconciling and supporting the monument's other upward lines, specifically the vertical axis constituted by the four rotating glass stories of the monument (the cube, pyramid, cylinder, and hemisphere) and the iron spirals that gird it from without.[100] In Tatlin's monument, a diagonally tilted line mediates between the politically functional vertical principle and the largely symbolic double-helix, itself leaning at the earth's axial tilt, which Punin viewed as the "ideal expression of emancipation" from "all animal, earthbound, and reptilian [*presmykai-ushchikhsia*] interests," the material expression of a materialist transcendence of matter.[101] Tatlin's *Zangezi*, while lacking a corresponding spiral framework, once again inserts a diagonal axis, which appears to offer a dialectical mediation between the authoritarian principle of vertical hierarchy culminating in Zangezi's eyrie and the horizontal space of the vox populi. This diagonal axis, I hypothesize, may well have theatrically arranged the supersaga's heterogeneous linguistic planes, broadly corresponding to Khlebnikov's Eurasian geopoetics.

The structural homologies between Tatlin's monument and his production of *Zangezi* point suggestively to a nascent Comintern aesthetic, one that married avant-garde utopianism to the goals of the Comintern at a time when Russian revolutionary modernism was evolving beyond pure abstraction towards an architectonics of space-time. The avant-garde's engagement in revolutionary politics imposed a set of shifting realignments between utilitarian function and aesthetic form. Overall, Khlebnikov's literary works were in profound and often precise consonance with the techniques of modernist art – above all that of montage – without seeking to dissolve art and the artist into industrial production, the path soon to be taken by many of Khlebnikov's counterparts in the left avant-garde. Tatlin's own resistance to this imperative is in consonance with his life-long devotion to the poetry and vision of Khlebnikov.[102]

Zangezi: A World-Text

Let us now turn from Tatlin's production to the text itself. Both conceptually and theatrically, *Zangezi* is structured as a spatial dynamic enacted between multiple discourses or sign-systems. The most potent aspect of this spatial dynamic is an overarching yet tilted vertical axis, apparent from the stage directions that precede the play proper:

> The mountains. Above a clearing there rises a steep and shaggy crag that resembles an iron needle seen through a magnifying glass. Like a pilgrim's staff leaning against a wall, it stands beside the steep slopes of layers of rock overgrown by a forest of pines. A bridge-like platform connects it to the bedrock, the result of an

avalanche that fell on the clifftop like a straw hat. This platform is Zangezi's favourite place. He comes here every morning and recites his songs.[103]

At the apex of this leaning vertical axis, constituted physically by the "bridge-like platform" linking the mountaintop to the steep crag, we find Zangezi himself, while the base of the axis is peopled by the common folk situated below. Inscribed physically into the play's landscape, the vertical axis was more generally identified by Khlebnikov as the privileged space of prophetic insight as well as its transmission: "*What is vision?* Vision is a kind of specially calculated time ... When the priest [*zhrets*] descends the steps of this staircase from the lofty tower where he resides, a human can see [*chelovek vidit*]."[104]

The play's rudimentary plot is largely sustained by the verbal encounter between prophet and the masses, an encounter closely modelled on Friedrich Nietzsche's *Thus Spoke Zarathustra*, *Zangezi*'s most significant intertext, as well as on the long succession of prophets from the biblical Moses to the nineteenth-century Iranian religious reformer Mirza Ali Mohammad Shirazi, known as the Bab.[105] While no less oracular than *Zarathustra*, *Zangezi* is nonetheless significantly more dialogic, containing a range of "first-order narratives" attributed to agents other than the prophet-hero himself. Among these we find birdsong, registered in the form of onomatopoeia (Plane 1), the glossolalia of the gods (Planes 2 and 11), the everyday language of the common folk, some true believers, others sceptics, but all witnesses to the written or spoken words of Zangezi himself, which they are free to embrace or reject (Planes 3, 4, 5, 6, 7, 13, 14, 17).

These diverse voices and discourses stand at varying degrees of dialogical proximity or distance to the discourses of Zangezi. They range from the non-human (the animal and the divine) to the banally human, each internally differentiated according to avian species, world religions, and the gamut of human responsiveness, from adoration to mockery. Yet, Khlebnikov's proclamation of "complete confessional freedom" is ultimately belied by the text's operative hierarchy, which subordinates the diversity of human and non-human discourses to Zangezi himself as the new source of authority. Thus the enchanting morning chorus of birds (Plane 1) is interrupted by the menacing figure of a boy-hunter bearing a cage, and the distinctly pagan and polytheistic "assembly of the gods of all nations" (Plane 2) ends with their flight (Plane 11), precipitated by the substitution of the initial consonant b (*б*) in *бог* (god) by m (*м*), producing *мог[у]*, "I can." The chorus of the birds and the gods, like the everyday prattle of human speech, resonate as verbal relics, preserved for posterity like geological sediments but ultimately superseded by Zangezi's own prodigious verbal inventiveness.

Zangezi dominates the play by superseding, but not eliminating, his interlocutors. His dominance is based on the novelty and urgency of his message, the related revelations of a universal language and a universal theory of space-time. These include the "astral language [*zvezdnyi iazyk*]" of semanti-cized consonants (Planes 7, 8, 12); neologistic word-creation [*slovotvorchestvo*], based on the manipulation and substitution of existing as well as imaginary morphological units – Russian roots, prefixes, suffixes, and finally consonants – (Planes 9, 10, 13, 14); chromatic "sound-writing [*zvukopis'*]," which identifies sounds with colours (Plane 15); and Khlebnikov's mathematical theory of time, here serving to illuminate the patterns of Russian revolutionary history from the Decembrist uprising of 1825 to the assassination of Count Mirbach, the German ambassador to Moscow, in 1918 (Plane 18, anticipated by Plane 4). These revelatory discourses are in turn bookended by two exquisitely lyrical monologues (Planes 6 and 19), moments of intense self-reflexivity that allow for a more conventionally imagistic elaboration of Zangezi as hero. The text culminates in a play-within-the-play, a kind of comedic folk mysterium involv-ing the allegorical figures of Grief and Laughter (Plane 20), which embody the alternative dénouements – whether of tragedy (suicide) or comedy (resurrec-tion) – available to the hero, and arguably to human history itself.

However singular in its structural innovations and verbal exuberance, *Zangezi* might be regarded as one of a series of works of world literature since Goethe's *Faust* to merit Franco Moretti's epithet of "modern epic" or "world-text [*opera-mondo*]." These works, states Moretti, retain "many struc-tural similarities to a distant past," while pointing to a "*supranational dimen-sion of represented space* ... a broader entity – a continent, or the world-system as a whole." Moreover, it is Moretti's claim that world-texts characteristically arise in the semi-periphery of the modern world system or, more precisely, in "sites of combined development: *where historically non-homogeneous social and symbolic forms, often originating in quite disparate places, coexist in a confined space*," such that "the Before-and-After is transformed into an Alongside."[106]

Zangezi's status as a world-text is based on several distinct dimensions of its complexly unfolding drama. The lyrical monologues of Planes 6 and 19 provide a rich series of global or cosmic world-images, always mediated by or even identified with Zangezi himself. From his initial and profoundly alienated self-image as a "butterfly who has flown/ into the hall of human life/ To trace my dusty script/ ... On fate's unyielding windowpane,"[107] Zangezi grows into the Anthropos or Cosmic Man, a distinctly archaic symbol of collective humanity, at once a cosmogonic myth and an image of human evolutionary and revolu-tionary potential.[108] As such, he is co-terminous with the earth's topography, binding microcosm and macrocosm, with "rivers for hair:" the name Zangezi is itself likely an amalgam of the Rivers Zambezi and Ganges, symbolizing the un-ion of Asia and Africa, an idiosyncratically Hindu figuration of the Comintern rallying cry of anti-imperialist solidarity.[109] Zangezi then presents himself as "master-carpenter of humanity's timepiece," a striking shift from an archaic organicist model of the cosmos to a distinctly mechanistic understanding of nature, here coupled with a Nietzschean summons to acknowledge the death of God and transcend the existing limits of humankind:

Planets of Earth! Forward, march!
Just suppose somebody throws
A net of numbers over the world,
Did he really elevate our minds?
No, our mind is a lot more alone!
Once [we were] snails and slugs
Now it's the life of eagles!
In colours ever more of the rainbow!
Hooray!
The world will be covered
By a network of overhead roads
Hooray!
If someone says you are God
Respond with rage: "What slander!"
God comes up to my legs!
Are heels and shoulders the same?
Hooray!
People are melted ice.
Higher and higher we fly.
In a great race
Of frenzied horses
The Planet Earth a tiny ball
Held in the palms of our hand.[110]

As butterfly, Zangezi can be seen to symbolize the realm of spirit chafing at the burden of material embodiment and mundane life; as Anthropos or Cosmic Man, Zangezi represents the ideal equivalence of the human body and the physical and subtle universe; and as master-carpenter, Zangezi represents modern scientific reason, which permits human mastery over the universe, but at the cost of exacerbating the alienation of mind from matter until the definitive self-transcendence of humankind is achieved. Martin Heidegger once argued that "what distinguishes the essence of the modern age" is that "the world *becomes a picture at all*," objectified by scientific investigation, shrunk – as in the passage quoted earlier – into a "tiny ball" to be studied and transformed at will.[111] Yet, while Khlebnikov generally presents the modern era, and his contribution to it, as the evolutionary culmination of human cognitive endeavour, he also anachronistically situates the modern "world-picture" alongside markedly older cosmologies, and he does so within an overarching structure that is essentially synchronic (architectural and montage-based) rather than diachronic.

This structure is hierarchical, in prioritizing Zangezi's own utterances, yet also open-ended, in that its theatrical unfolding is dialogic and incomplete.

What is true of the world-picture, which is at once a representation of the world and the self-imaging of Zangezi as world-subject, is also true of the competing realms of discourse in Khlebnikov's supersaga. Here, too, a multiplicity of semiotic systems prevail.[112] At one extreme, we have the onomatopoeic twitter of the birds and the glossolalia of the gods: their utterances are not so much *trans*-rational as *pre*-rational, pure signifiers that preclude translation in the absence of any decoding mechanism. In their realm, vocalization is accompanied by a heightened sense of localized space and physical embodiment: the yellow bunting is associated with reeds and the branches of the walnut tree, while the Zulu creator-god Unkulunkulu "listens attentively to the sound of a beetle tunnelling its way through the beam of his wooden body."[113] For birds and gods, then, there is no path from embodied particularity to universalizing abstraction: hence their utterances are limited to their realm and kind. Human speech, by contrast, while all too comprehensible, is limited to the banalities of common sense. It reflects either general doxa or knee-jerk responses to Zangezi's speeches. It cannot initiate or innovate; it is merely the passive recipient of revelation, which it frequently confuses with entertainment. It is the *profanum vulgus* of the Roman poet Horace, in opposition to the *sacerdos musarum*, updated to reflect the avant-garde's quest for the radical renewal of society through cognitive-artistic transformation.

Zangezi's discourse, while unified and integrated by the presence of the hero, can in turn be differentiated into three principal modes: the scientific-interpretive, the prophetic-revelatory, and the poetic-imaginative. Together they give rise to a hybrid or mixed regime of signs in which various linguistic functions vie for temporary dominance. The scientific-interpretive modality is primarily metalingual in its function; it is oriented chiefly towards the code at hand and its successful decipherment. It is not so much *trans*-rational as *hyper*-rational: it seeks to master and coordinate the potentially infinite relay of signs by inaugurating a system of precise equivalences between signifier and signified. It is impersonal and taxonomic, its quintessential expression being the glossary, such as those found in Planes 4, 8, 9, and 15. Zangezi's "prophecies" are frequently no more than the discursive elaboration of the principles found in these glossaries, their crucial task being to exemplify in narrative form the newly reconstituted relationship between code (numbers and letters) and context (history and geography). When thus instantiated, each code is seen to point beyond itself to the referential world, claiming to regulate the temporal rhythm of event and counter-event as well as the spatial dynamic of territorial loss and gain. The prophetic-revelatory modality thus combines a heightened referentiality of context – world history and geography – with a recoded message whose sheer newness places it at loggerheads with the doxa of received opinion and the traditional idiom of faith. The efficacy of the prophetic-revelatory mode does not, however, consist solely in the novelty of its recoding. It also evinces a pro-foundly pragmatic interest in the charismatic authority of the prophet and the receptivity of his audience. In *Zangezi*, the prophet's authority is consistently asserted but often resisted: the repeated derision of Zangezi by the populace and the willful destruction of his manuscripts reported in the play's epilogue point to the inverse image of the prophet, that of the scapegoat or martyr. In this sense, the prophetic-revelatory mode is caught between a radically innova-tive relationship between code and context and a profoundly conventional re-lationship between addresser and addressee. The latter, an "I/you" relationship rooted in religious and literary traditions dating back millennia, offers a finite range of subject-positions and affective responses from which to choose: from prophet-martyr to cosmic man to trickster-god in the case of Zangezi; from credulous enthusiasm to derisive mockery in the case of his audience.

Finally, the poetic-imaginative mode focuses on the poetic resources of lan-guage itself. It serves as a powerful counterbalance to the extreme rationalization of time-space realized by the scientific-interpretive mode. The poetic mode is clearly evident in the exquisite if conventionally lyrical dramatic monologues found in Planes 6, 19, and 20. It is also palpable in those passages that give full force to the principles of neologistic word-creation, arguably the one element of Khlebnikov's poetics to resist easy decoding. Thus Khlebnikov describes the flight of the "gods of speech," outmoded by the onslaught of Zangezi's "astral alphabet," in this way: "*Letury letiat v sobesa/ Tolpoiu nochei ischezaev./ Potokom krylatoi etoty,/ Potopom nebesnoi netoty.*"[114] These lines – essentially untranslatable like all of Plane 13 from which they are taken – have been rendered by Paul Schmidt as follows: "Ledglings in flight, seeking their selfland,/ Flocking through darkness to vanishment./ A swelling of heavenly neverings,/ A swirling of wing-welling overings."[115] These verses reconcile a broad adherence to the grammatical and syntactical norms of the Russian language with a level of morphological experimentation that func-tions in excess of any taxonomy or glossary offered by Khlebnikov himself. The sheer exuberance of Plane 13 eclipses its referential function as an account of the gods' flight, or as a coherent illustration of the metalinguistic principles under-lying Zangezi's "astral language." As such, it is perhaps the most vivid example in *Zangezi* of the *trans*-rational (*заумь*), in contradistinction to the *pre*-rational and the *hyper*-rational. In this context, it is worth recalling Osip Mandel'shtam's powerful admonition not to misread Khlebnikovian trans-sense as a kind of sha-manistic abracadabra. Mandel'shtam viewed Khlebnikov's morphologically mo-tivated wordplay as nothing less than the "historically unrealized path of Russian linguistic destiny [*istoricheski nebyvshii put' rossiiskoi rechevoi sud'by*]," a kind of counterfactual history in which what could have been – and what still could be – supplemented the actual path of linguistic evolution.[116]

Zangezi, then, is a radically diverse text, heterogeneous by virtue of its very structure. To be sure, the supersaga strives consistently to subordinate

the burgeoning diversity of its discursive registers to the extraordinary pronouncements of the main hero. As a diachronic elaboration of the hero's encounter with the people, *Zangezi* grounds its authority upon the figure of the
poet-prophet, making him the emissary of a revolutionary utopia, at once historical and linguistic, which renders all other discourses obsolete. In this sense,
the text invites us to identify its universality as one with the figure of Zangezi
himself, the harbinger of a new secular world order in which time and space
have been definitively codified and linguistic diversity reduced to one rational
means of planetary communication. By abolishing all particularisms of faith
and nationality, *Zangezi* may count as the Russian avant-garde's most ambitious
attempt at fulfilling the totalizing impulse of all literary-social utopias.

At the same time as being a "supersaga" composed of "independent fragments," *Zangezi* preserves the very differences it seeks to supersede. From birdsong to the guttural ululations of pagan deities, the text explores the full gamut
of semiotic and sonic possibility. *Zangezi* straddles the archaic charisma of the
prophet and the authority of modern scientific method, moving between the
animal and the mundanely human, the divine and the superhuman. It also repeatedly shifts generic registers, from lyric monologue to prose dialogue and
from quasi-scientific exposition to tragicomic mystery play. These shifts alone
frustrate any sense of incremental or teleological movement. The play ends in a
comedic spirit, whose deepest promise is renewal or resurrection, but at the cost
of diminishing the aura of Zangezi as prophet. The text's dénouement is open-
ended, the inverse of utopian closure. The homogenizing intent of Zangezi's
prophetic revelations is held in check by the text's formal heterogeneity.

How then might we read *Zangezi* as a text of world literature? Its immediate
context was the first post-revolutionary years, during which the carnage and
privations of war communism coexisted with hopes of world revolution. While
having little or nothing doctrinally in common with Marxist thought, *Zangezi*
articulates an internationalism of poetic and cognitive innovation designed to
unify the human race in tandem with the goal of world revolution. In *Zangezi*,
the utopian promise of planetary unity coexists with the reality of a radically
uneven world in which the archaic and the primitive, past, present, and future are seen to be coeval with the modern. It is precisely this unevenness to
which Lenin pointed as a singular feature of the contemporary world system,
and which Trotsky would later generalize as the "law of combined and uneven
development."[117] Khlebnikov's speculations on space-time, like his linguistic
experimentation, read overtly as a search for patterns underlying and correlating all phenomena. Yet, even as they sought to resolve the unevenness of
space-time into deeper regularities, Khlebnikov's theories led in practice to a
montage-based poetics of radical juxtaposition. Events remote in time could
be yoked together, generating a Eurasian and ultimately global alternative history in which the ancient, the contemporary, and the merely possible were

in intimate dialogue. In a manner characteristic of the Russian avant-garde, Khlebnikov straddled the emancipatory and the totalizing impulses of the October Revolution. He echoed the Comintern's call for world revolution, and mirrored its centripetal tendencies, with the poet-prophet displacing the vanguard party centred in Moscow. To a greater extent than any other Russian artist of the time, however, Khlebnikov offered the antinomies of utopian thought a geopoetic mediation rooted in the cultural history and political geography of Eurasia. This geopoetic vision, regionally grounded yet abstracted to a universal vision of space-time, is one further example of what has been called the "utopian supplement" or "cultural surplus" of the Russian avant-garde, a dimension that to date has been largely identified with Soviet constructivism in the visual arts. In Khlebnikov's case, this supplement was nothing less than a mythopoetic solution to the global condition of uneven development, one that reconciled the archaic force of Near Eastern prophecy with the scientism of Western modernity. That the Bolsheviks had little use for Khlebnikov's vision is perhaps the best evidence one could adduce of the gap that divided them. But there is more at stake here than the familiar story of the collisions and collusions between Russia's artists and the state, which has fuelled so many histories of Russian culture. As a regional but resolutely internationalist response to the worldwide predicament of uneven modernity, the Russian avant-garde, like the revolution which shaped its trajectory, points to alternative narratives and paradigms for world literature as a whole, beyond the prevailing models that assume the universality of the market and the nation-state. Khlebnikov's lasting legacy to world literature, then, is surely neither his pseudo-scientific theorization of time-space nor his ideographic Esperanto, symptomatic as they are of avant-garde utopianism, but the countervailing montage-based form that informs *Zangezi* as well as much of his poetry. Khlebnikov's poetics embraces the juxtaposition of historically and generically distinct registers and sign-systems, while still insisting on the contiguously based agglomeration of regional geographies, irradiating outward from the crossroads of Eurasia to the world at large. And for Khlebnikov, Eurasia was at once the arena for East/West conflict and heir to a utopian legacy of overlapping cross-cultural exchanges upon which to build a different template of world literature.

NOTES

1 Velimir Khlebnikov, "Segodnia snova ia poidu," *Tvoreniia* (Moscow: Sovetskii pisatel', 1986), 93. All translations from the Russian are mine unless otherwise indicated.
2 On the relationship between the Russian avant-garde and post-revolutionary politics, see Paul Wood, "The Politics of the Avant-garde," in *The Great Utopia: The*

Russian and Soviet Avant-Garde (New York: The Guggenheim Museum, 1992), 1–24; and T.J. Clark, "God Is Not Cast Down," in *Farewell to an Idea: Episodes from a History of Modernism* (New Haven, CT: Yale University Press, 2001), 225–97. It should be noted that the term "avant-garde" was not widely used in Russia, either before or after the revolution, to designate the phenomenon of radical or revolutionary modernism: the canonization of the term is essentially retrospective, accomplished by Camilla Gray, *The Great Experiment: Russian Art 1863–1922* (New York: Harry N. Abrams, 1962). See John E. Bowlt and Olga Matich, "Introduction," *Laboratory of Dreams: The Russian Avant-Garde and Cultural Experiment*, ed. John E. Bowlt and Olga Matich (Stanford, CA: Stanford University Press, 1999), 3–5. By contrast, the term "vanguard party" to describe the leading role of the Social Democratic Party in fomenting revolution was coined by Lenin in 1902 in his pamphlet "Chto delat'?" [What Is to Be Done?], in *Polnoe sobranie sochinenii V.I. Lenina* [*The Complete Works of V.I. Lenin*], 5th ed. (Moscow: Izdatel'stvo politicheskoi literatury, 1969), 6:83–90.

3 See Franco Moretti, *Modern Epic: The World System from Goethe to Garcia Marquez* (London: Verso, 1996): I return to Moretti's argument at the end of this chapter.

4 Johann Wolfgang Goethe, "Vorwort zu Carlyles *Leben Schillers*" (1830), in *Sämtliche Werke, Briefe, Tagebücher und Gespräche*, ed. Friedmar Apel et al. (Frankfurt: Deutscher Klassiker Verlag, 1999), 1/22:870. See also Fritz Sprich, *Goethe and World Literature* (New York: Hafner Publishing, 1949); John Pitzer, "Goethe's 'World Literature' Paradigm and Contemporary Cultural Globalization," *Comparative Literature* 52, no. 3 (Summer 2000): 213–27; Stefan Hoesel-Uhlig, "Changing Fields: The Directions of Goethe's *Weltliteratur*," in *Debating World Literature*, ed. Christopher Prendergast (London: Verso, 2004), 26–53; and Hendrik Birus, "The Goethean Concept of World Literature and Comparative Literature," in *Comparative Literature and Comparative Cultural Studies*, ed. Steven Tötösy de Zepetnek (West Lafayette, IN: Purdue University Press 2003), 11–22.

5 Goethe, Letter to Thomas Carlyle, 20 July 1827, in *Sämtliche Werke, Briefe*, 2/10:497.

6 Johann Wolfgang Goethe, Letter to Thomas Carlyle, 1 January 1828, in *Werke herausgegeben im Auftrage der Grossherzogin Sophie von Sachsen*, ed. Gustav von Loeper et al. (Weimar: Böhlau, 1908), 4/43:222.

7 Goethe, "Vorwort zu Carlyles *Leben Schillers*," in *Sämtliche Werke, Briefe*, 1/22:826.

8 Karl Marx and Friedrich Engels, *Manifest der Kommunistischen Partei* (Offenbach: Verlag Olga Bonario und Herbert Baum, 1997), 37–8; *The Communist Manifesto*, ed. Frederic Bender (New York: W.W. Norton and Company, 1988), 58–9. See also S.S. Prawer, *Karl Marx and World Literature* (Oxford: Oxford University Press, 1978), 138–65.

9 I am indebted here to the insights of Pheng Cheah and Aamir Mufti. See Pheng Cheah, "What Is a World? On World Literature as a World-Making Activity," *Daedalus* 137, no. 3 (Summer 2008): 26–38, esp. 32: "Marx's immanent critique of world literature inverts Goethe's trade metaphor. Whereas Goethe mistook the real referent for a metaphor for world literary relations, Marx sees the material world, a world created in the image of the bourgeoisie, whose economic activity breaks down parochial barriers and national exclusiveness, as the concrete basis of world literary relations, which are merely the autonomized products of alienation." See also Aamir R. Mufti, "Erich Auerbach, and the Death and Life of World Literature," in *The Routledge Companion to World Literature*, ed. Theo D'haen, David Damrosch, and Djelal Kadir (London: Routledge, 2011), 75: "For as a concept of bourgeois society, *Weltliteratur* is fundamentally a concept of exchange, that is, a concept that recodes an opaque and unequal process of appropriation as a transparent one of supposedly free and equal interchange and communication."

10 Pascale Casanova, *La République mondiale des lettres* (Paris: Seuil, 2008), 62–3: "The accumulation of literary resources is thus necessarily rooted in the political history of states. More precisely, one might suppose that the two phenomena – the formation of the state and the emergence of literature in the modern languages – arise from the same principle of 'differentiation.'"

11 Franco Moretti, "Conjectures on World Literature," *New Left Review* 1 (January/ February 2000): 64; see also Moretti, "World-Systems Analysis, Evolutionary Theory, *Weltliteratur*," in *Immanuel Wallerstein and the Problem of the World: System, Scale, Culture*, ed. David Palumbo, Bruce Robbins, and Nirvana Tanoukhi (Durham, NC: Duke University Press, 2011), 67–77.

12 See Benedict Anderson, *Imagined Communities: Reflections on the Origin and Spread of Nationalism*, 6th ed. (London: Verso, 1990).

13 Moretti, "Conjectures on World Literature," 67.

14 See John Agnew, *Geopolitics: Re-visioning World Politics* (London: Routledge, 1998).

15 The modern social imaginary, in Charles Taylor's words, is "not a set of ideas; rather, it is what enables, through making sense of, the practices of a society." In the West it is closely associated with "certain social forms," namely "the market economy, the public sphere, and the self-governing people, among others." See Charles Taylor, *Modern Social Imaginaries* (Durham, NC: Duke University Press, 2004), 2. The Russian revolution clearly posed a challenge to the Western social imaginary, as an alternative path to modernity.

16 See Neil Larsen, *Determinations: Essays on Theory, Narrative and Nation in the Americas* (London: Verso, 2001), 12, on the response of the historical avant-garde to the crisis of the First World War: "For what is generated in the wake of imperialism's first and subsequent global crises is not an international aesthetic culture *per se* ... Rather it is an experience of *aesthetic form itself* as 'international'... A 'revolutionary' world aesthetic, rather than a tradition, canon or culture, stands forth

as the poetics of the new (anti-)imperialist internationalism, both proletarian and all-purpose liberal-humanist ... All conceive of and even (re)produce themselves as instances of a *Weltliteratur* different from the one envisioned by Goethe, and even, perhaps, by Marx and Engels."

17 The term "geopoetics" appears to have been coined by the French-Scottish poet and intellectual Kenneth White in 1979. I take up the term as defined by the Italian poet-scholar Federico Italiano in "Geo-Introduzione," in *Geopoetiche. Studi di geografia e letteratura*, ed. Federico Italiano and Marco Mastronunzio (Milan: Edizioni Unicopli, 2011). Italiano sees geopoetics as the "hybrid fruit of an epistemic translation" between the disciplines of geography and literary criticism and theory (11–12), an "operative category for the understanding of geographical knowledge and for the modes of inscription of the Earth into a literary text" (18). Geopoetics is thus principally interested in how spatial-geographical, territorial, and ecological-environmental markers are aesthetically encoded in a text, revealing a specific inscription of the earth or some part of it in a literary artifact.

18 Louis Marin, "Frontiers of Utopia: Past and Present," *Critical Inquiry* 19, no. 3 (Spring 1993): 403–4. On utopia, see also Robert C. Elliot, *The Shape of Utopia: Studies in a Literary Genre* (Chicago: University of Chicago Press, 1970); Louis Marin, *Utopiques: Jeux d'espaces* (Paris: Les Editions de Minuit, 1973), 249; Ruth Levitas, *The Concept of Utopia* (Syracuse, NY: Syracuse University Press, 1991); and Fredric Jameson, *Archaeologies of the Future: The Desire Called Utopia and Other Science Fictions* (New York: Verso, 2005). See also notes 21, 55, 56, and 57.

19 Ernst Bloch, "Art and Society," in *The Utopian Function of Art and Literature: Selected Essays*, trans. Jack Zipes and Frank Mecklenburg (Cambridge, MA: The MIT Press, 1988), 40.

20 Marin, "Frontiers of Utopia," 406.

21 The precise formulation was "the self-sufficient word beyond everyday life and customary usage": see Velimir Khlebnikov, "Svoiasi" (1919), in *Sobranie proizvedenii*, ed. N. Stepanov (Leningrad: Izdatel'stvo pisatelei v Leningrade, 1933), 2:9. N. Stepanov, in *Velimir Khlebnikov* (Moscow: Sovetskii pisatel', 1975), 31–3, notes that new notions of aesthetic autonomy were introduced into Russian poetry from the realm of abstract art. On the utopianism of the Russian avant-garde, and of Velimir Khlebnikov in particular, see Stepanov, *Velimir Khlebnikov*, 248–55; and Dubravka Oraic-Tolic, *Khlebnikov i avangard* (Moscow: West-Consulting: 2013).

22 See Boris Groys, *The Total Art of Stalinism: Avant-garde, Aesthetic Dictatorship, and Beyond*, trans. Charles Rougle (Princeton, NJ: Princeton University Press, 1992), 7, 9.

23 Susan Buck-Morss, *Dreamworld and Catastrophe: The Passing of Mass Utopia in East and West* (Cambridge, MA: The MIT Press, 2000), 49, 55, 62, emphasis partly added.

24 Groys, *The Total Art of Stalinism*, 15, 18.

25 On the regionalism of the Russian avant-garde, see Jane Sharp, *Russian Modernism between East and West: Natal'ia Goncharova and the Moscow Avant-garde* (Cambridge: Cambridge University Press, 2006), 22–62, 174–220. On neoprimitivism in Indian modernism, see Partha Mitter, *The Triumph of Modernism: India's Artists and the Avant-Garde* (London: Reaktion Books, 2007), 29–122. The most striking example of Latin American neoprimitivism is the Brazilian Oswald de Andrade's "Cannibalist Manifesto," in *100 Artists' Manifestos: From the Futurists to the Stuckists*, ed. Alex Danchev (London: Penguin, 2011), 262–6.

26 Natal'ia Goncharova, "Preface to Catalogue of One-Man Exhibition, 1913," in *Russian Art of the Avant-Garde: Theory and Criticism 1902–1934*, ed. and trans. John E. Bowlt (New York: Viking Press, 1976), 55, 60. The term "neoprimitivism" was coined during the same year by the Russian avant-garde painter Aleksandr Shevchenko in his brochure *Neoprimitivizm: Ego teorii, ego vozmozhnosti, ego dostizheniia* (Moscow: Tip. 1-oi Moskovskoi Trudovoi arteli, 1913). On the relationship between painterly and poetic neoprimitivism in Russia, see D.V. Sarab'ianov, "Neoprimitivizm v russkoi zhivopisi i futuristicheskaia poèziia 1910-kh godov," in *Russkaia zhivopis'. Probuzhdenie pamiati* (Moscow: Iskusstvoznanie, 1988), 324–41.

27 I have elaborated this argument at greater length in my article "Futurist Geographies: Centre, Periphery, and the Struggle for Aesthetic Autonomy: Paris, Italy, Russia, 1909–1914," in *The Oxford Handbook of Global Modernisms*, ed. Mark Wollaeger (New York: Oxford University Press, 2012), 313–40.

28 See the powerful review of Tatlin's staging of *Zangezi* by Nikolai Punin, "Zangezi," *Zhizn' iskusstva* (22 May 1923): 10–12, republished in N. Punin, *O Tatline* (Moscow: Literaturno-Khudozhestvennoe Agenstvo "RA," 1994), 62–4. Punin's account may be compared to more critical reviews of the same production by Sergei Iutkevich, "Sukharnaia stolitsa," *Lef* 3 (1923): 181–2; and A.B. Tufanov, "K postanovke poèmy 'Zangezi' Velemira Khlebnikova," *Krasnyi Student* 7–8 (1923): 29–30. For Tatlin's critics, the primary weakness of his production lay in its rejection of conventional theatricality, exemplified by the use of non-professional actors and the absence of a clear boundary between theatrical and non-theatrical space. For more scholarship regarding the Tatlin production, see note 102 of this chapter.

29 Buck-Morss, *Dreamworld and Catastrophe*, 25.

30 An excellent recent account of the Communist International and the Baku Congress can be found in Robert J.C. Young, *Postcolonialism: An Historical Introduction* (Oxford: Blackwell Press, 2001), 113–39. See also Julius Braunthal, *History of the International, 1864–1914* (New York: Praeger, 1967); Cosroe Chaqueri, *Documents inédits du Comintern: L'Orient et la IIe Internationale* (Tehran: Antidote Publications, 1984).

31 Vladimir Lenin, *Imperializm, kak vysshaia stadiia kapitalizma, Polnoe sobranie sochinenii V.I. Lenina*, 5th ed. (Moscow: Izdatel'stvo politicheskoi literatury, 1969), 27:359, 396, emphasis added.

32 Ibid., 305.

33 Giovanni Arrighi, *La geometria dell'imperialismo* (Milan: Feltrinelli, 1978), 22; compare Alex Callinicos, *Imperialism and Global Political Economy* (Cambridge: Polity Press, 2009), 64, 88.

34 Lenin, *Imperializm, kak vysshaia stadiia kapitalizma*, 394.

35 See Lenin, "O lozunge Soedinennye shtaty Evropy," in *Polnoe sobranie sochinenii V.I. Lenina*, 26:354, emphasis added: "*Uneven economic and political development is the indisputable law of capitalism.* From this it follows that the victory of social-ism is possible initially in a few countries, or even in one taken individually." See also Lenin, "Doklad na II vserossiiskom s'ezde kommunisticheskikh organizatsii narodov vostoka 22 noiabria 1919," in *Polnoe sobranie sochinenii V.I. Lenina*, 39:327: "Hence, the socialist revolution will not be solely, or chiefly, a struggle of the revolutionary proletarians in each country against their bourgeoisie – no, it will be a struggle of all colonies and countries oppressed by imperialism, of all dependent countries, against international imperialism."

36 Leon Trotsky, "Pis'mo L. Trotskogo v TsK RKP(b) o podgotovke elementov 'aziatskoi' orientatsii," 5 August 1919, in *Komintern i ideia mirovoi revoliutsii. Dokumenty* (Moscow: Nauka, 1998), 147–8.

37 "National and Colonial Questions" (Session 5, 28 July 1920), in *Workers of the World and Oppressed Peoples, Unite! Proceedings and Documents of the Second Congress, 1920*, ed. John Riddell (New York: Pathfinder Press, 1991), 285. See also James W. Hulse, *The Forming of the Communist International* (Stanford, CA: Stanford University Press, 1964), 193–4.

38 Mikhail Pavlovich, "Piatoe zasedanie," in *Pervzyi s'ezd narodov Vostoka. Baku 1–8 sent. 1920g. Stenograficheskie otchety* (Petrograd: Izdatel'stvo Kommunisticheskogo Internatsionala, 1920), 139; for the English text, see Mikhail Pavlovich, *To See the Dawn. Baku 1920. First Congress of the Peoples of the East* (New York: Pathfinder Press, 1993), 145.

39 G.Z Sorkin, *Pervyi s'ezd narodov Vostoka* (Moscow: Izdatel'stvo vostochnoi literatury, 1961), 21. See also Solmaz Rüstamova-Tohidi, "Sobytie, predan-noe zabveniiu," accessed 7 December 2015, http://azcongress.ru/2010/09/19/sobyitie_predannoe_zabveniyu/.

40 Grigorii Zinov'ev, "Pervoe zasedanie," in *Pervzyi s'ezd narodov Vostoka*, 71; Pavlovich, *To See the Dawn*, 71.

41 Nergis Ertürk, "Baku, Literary Common," 14 September 2014, accessed 25 January 2015, https://stateofthediscipline.acla.org/entry/baku-literary-common, emphasis added.

42 Michael Kemper, "Red Orientalism: Mikhail Pavlovich and Marxist Oriental Studies in Early Soviet Russia," *Die Welt des Islams* 50 (2010): 448–9.

43 Ibid., 469.

44 Compare Zinov'ev, "Pervoe zasedanie," 41, emphasis added (Pavlovich, *To See the Dawn*, 72), who contrasts the "fast, impetuous and powerful stream" of the

European proletariat with "another stream, which is as yet not strong enough, *which in some places takes a zigzag course* – this is the movement of the oppressed nationalities which have not yet chosen the road they will follow." The contrast between linear and zig-zig-like (*zigzagoobraznyi*) paths of historical development belongs to Lenin: see "Protiv boikota" (1907), in *Polnoe sobranie sochinenii V.I. Lenina*, 16:8–9.

45 One might argue that Bolshevik sincerity was put to the test as early as 1921, when the Soviet government concluded treaties with Turkey and Iran and a trade agreement with Britain, at which point Bolshevik policies towards the East became considerably more muted: see Stephen White, "Communism and the East: The Baku Congress, 1920," *Slavic Review* 33, no. 3 (September 1974): 492–514; and Kemper, "Red Orientalism," 454. For an alternative account of the Comintern in Asia that is more sensitive to Marxist theory, see Hélène Carrère d'Encausse and Stuart R. Schram, *Marxism and Asia* (London: Allen Lane/The Penguin Press, 1969).

46 It must be said that there is as yet no definitive scholarly consensus concerning the poet's presence at the Baku Congress. Ultimately, however, Khlebnikov's physical presence at the congress is not essential to my argument, which is amply corroborated by Khlebnikov's wider geographical and creative trajectory during the last years of his life. Khlebnikov's presence at the congress has been confirmed by Sofiia Starkina in her recent biography *Velimir Khlebnikov* (Moscow: Molodaia Gvardiia, 2007), 238–9. Andrea Hacker, "To Pushkin, Freedom, and Revolution in Asia: Velimir Khlebnikov in Baku," *Russian Review* 65, no. 3 (July 2006): 439–69, also assumes his presence there, offering a useful historical account of Baku in 1920 in addition to precious commentary on Khlebnikov's poetry. Ronald Vroon, "A Russian Futurist in Asia: Velimir Khlebnikov's Travelogue in Verse," in *Writing Travel in Central Asian History*, ed. Nile Green (Bloomington: Indiana University Press, 2013), 181, cautions that the "concrete dates of [Khlebnikov's] journey from Kharkov to Baku [in 1920] are not known," but accepts Starkina's findings. However, leading Khlebnikov scholars Henryk Baran and A.E. Parnis insist that "in early September 1920, while the Congress was taking place, Khlebnikov was in Rostov and not Baku." See Henryk Baran and A.E. Parnis, "'Anabazis' Velimira Khlebnikova: Zametki k teme," in *Evraziiskoe prostranstvo. Zvuk, slovo, obraz*, ed. Viacheslav Vs. Ivanov (Moscow: Iazyki slavianskoi kul'tury, 2003), 277. Even if Khlebnikov missed the congress, he was clearly in Baku by October, several weeks later.

47 Velimir Khlebnikov, *Doski sud'by* (Moscow: Rubezh stoletii, 2000), 6.

48 Velimir Khlebnikov, "O rasshirenii predelov russkoi slovesnosti," in *Neizdannye proizvedeniia*, ed. N. Khardzhiev and T. Grits (Moscow: Khudozhestvennaia literatura, 1940), 341–2.

49 There is now a significant body of scholarship on Khlebnikov's "Eurasianism": see M. Loshchits and V.N. Turbin, "Tema vostoka v tvorchestve V. Khlebnikova,"

Narody Afriki i Azii 4 (1966):147–60; V. Ivanov, "Struktura stikhotvoreniia Khlebnikova 'Menia pronosiat na slonovykh,'" *Trudy po znakovym sistemam 3,* no. 198 (1967): 156–71; Salomon Mirsky, *Der Orient im Werk Velimir Chlebnikovs* (Munich: Otto Sagner Verlag, 1975); P.I. Tartakovskii, *Poèziia Khlebnikova i vostok 1917–1922* (Tashkent: Izdatel'stvo "FAN" Akademii nauk, 1992); and Aleksandr Parnis, "'Tuda, tuda, gde Izanagi....' Nekotorye zametki k teme 'Khlebnikov i Iaponiia,'" in *Iskusstva avangarda: Iazyk mirovogo obshcheniia. Materialy mezhdunarodnoi konferentsii 10–11 dekabria 1992g* (Ufa: Muzei sovremennogo iskusstva "Vostok," 1993), 90–102; Harsha Ram, "The Poetics of Eurasia: Velimir Khlebnikov between Empire and Revolution," in *Social Identities in Revolutionary Russia,* ed. Madhavan K. Palat, (Basingstoke: Palgrave Publishers, 2001), 209–31; Ronald Vroon, "Quarrat Al-'Ayn and the Image of Asia in Velimir Khlebnikov's Post-Revolutionary *Oeuvre,*" *Russian Literature* 50 (2001): 335–62; A.E. Parnis, "Evraziiskie konteksty Khlebnikova: ot 'kalmytskogo mifa' k mifu o 'edinoi Azii,'" in *Evraziiskoe prostranstvo,* 299–344; Susanna Soojung Lim, "'L'esprit du continent,' ou le Japon, l'Eurasie et l'Empire dans l'oeuvre de Velimir Khlebnikov," *Slavica Occitania* 33 (2011):177–212; Harsha Ram, "Spatializing the Sign: The Futurist Eurasianism of Roman Jakobson and Velimir Khlebnikov," in *Between Europe and Asia: The Origins, Theories and Legacies of Russian Eurasianism,* ed. Mark Bassin, Sergey Glebov, and Marlène Laruelle (Pittsburgh, PA: University of Pittsburgh Press, 2015), 137–49.

50 Concerning Khlebnikov's travels of 1920–21 through the Caucasus, Azerbaijan, and Iran, see Tat'iana Vechorka, "Vospominaniia o Khlebnikove," in *Zapisnaia knizhka Velimira Khlebnikova,* ed. A. Kruchenykh (Moscow: Izdanie Vserossiiskogo Soiuza Poetov, 1925), 21–30; D. Kozlov, "Novoe o Velimire Khlebnikove," *Krasnaia nov'* 8 (1928): 177–88; A. Kosterin, "Russkie dervishi," *Moskva* 9 (1966): 216–21; A.E. Parnis, "V. Khlebnikov v revoliutsionnom Giliane (novye materialy)," *Narody Azii i Afriki* 5 (1967): 156–64; O. Samorodova, "Poet na Kavkaze: Vospominaniia," *Zvezda* 6 (1972): 188–9; and Aleksandr Parnis, "V. Khlebnikov v Bakrosta," *Literaturnyi Azerbaidzhan* 7 (July 1976): 117–19.

51 Khlebnikov, "Otryvok iz dosok sud'by" [An extract from the Tables of Fate], *Sobranie proizvedenii,* 5:471.

52 Khlebnikov, Letter to V.E. Meyerhold, 18 February 1921, *Sobranie proizvedenii,* 5: 318.

53 Khlebnikov, Letter to V.V. Khlebnikova, 2 January 1920, *Sobranie proizvedenii,* 5: 316.

54 Khlebnikov, Letter to P.V. Miturich, 14 March 1922, *Sobranie proizvedenii,* 5:324.

55 Khlebnikov, "Nasha osnova" [Our Fundamentals], *Sobranie proizvedenii,* 5:241–2.

56 Lada Panova, "Numerologicheskii proekt Khlebnikova kak fenomen Serebrianogo veka," in *Velimir Khlebnikov i Doski sud'by: tekst i konteksty. Stat' i materialy* (Moscow: Tri kvadrata, 2008), 393–455.

57 Compare Khlebnikov, "Otryvok iz Dosok sud'by," [An extract from the Tables of Fate], *Sobranie proizvedenii*, 5:472. "The face of time had been written in words on old canvases such as the Quran, the Vedas, the Gospels and other doctrines. Now, with [the discovery of] the pure laws of time, the very same great face is being painted by the brush of number; a new approach has thus been applied to the cause of my predecessors." N. Stepanov, *Velimir Khlebnikov*, 253, has argued that "for all its utopianism, [Khlebnikov's] new cosmogony was founded on a materialist understanding of physical regularities related in large part to his understanding of language."

58 Henryk Baran, "Temporal Myths in Xlebnikov: From 'Deti Vydry' to 'Zangezi,'" in *Myth in Literature*, ed. Andrej Kodjak, Krystyna Pomorska, and Stephen Rudy (Columbus, OH: Slavica Publishers, 1985), 63–88.

59 Ronald Vroon, "Matematicheskaia mistika: k voprosu o nauchnosti istoriosofskikh vzgliadov Velimira Khlebnikova," in *Nauchnye kontseptsii XX veka i russkoe avangardnoe iskusstvo* (Belgrade: Izdatel'stvo filologicheskogo fakul'teta Belgradskogo universiteta, 2011), 51, 60. See also Andrea Hacker, "Mathematical Poetics in Velimir Khlebnikov's Doski sud'by," *Vestnik obshchestva Velimira Khlebnikova* 3 (2002): 127–32; and Raymond Cooke's excellent synthesizing statement in *Velimir Khlebnikov: A Critical Study* (Cambridge: Cambridge University Press, 1987), 152: "The mathematical predictions of the scientist and the prophetic visions of the artist merge to form a single framework for both the literary and the non-literary."

60 Manfredo Tafuri, *Progetto e utopia. Architettura e sviluppo capitalistico* (Bari: Laterza, 1973), 55. See also Tafuri, "Il socialismo realizzato e la crisi delle avanguardie," *Socialismo, città, architettura. URSS 1917–1937*, 2nd ed. (Rome: Officina Edizioni, 1971), 41–88; as well as Frederic Jameson, "Architecture and the Critique of Ideology," in *The Ideologies of Theory: Essays 1971–1986*, vol. 2, *Syntax of History* (Minneapolis: University of Minnesota Press, 1988), 35–60.

61 Julia Vaingurt, *Wonderlands of the Avant-Garde: Technology and the Arts in Russia of the 1920's* (Evanston, IL: Northwestern University Press, 2013), 126: "Khlebnikov's insistence on the existence of the fourth dimension, the imaginary space that must exist parallel to three-dimensional reality, without ever merging with it, lays bare the basic device of the [Stalinist] state: simulation of reality."

62 Hubertus Gassner, "The Constructivists: Modernism on the Way to Modernization," in *The Great Utopia*, 299. See also Benjamin H.D. Buchloh, "From Faktura to Factography," *October* 30 (Autumn 1984): 82–119; Maria Gough, "*Faktura*: The Making of the Russian Avant-garde," *Res* 36 (Autumn 1999): 32–59; and Maria Gough, *The Artist as Producer: Russian Constructivism in Revolution* (Berkeley: University of California Press, 2005), esp. 10–11, 14, 59, 63–6, 191–4.

63 N.N. Punin, "Khlebnikov i gosudarstvo vremeni," in *Mir Velimira Khlebnikova. Stat'i, issledovaniia 1911–1998* (Moscow: Iazyki russkoi kul'tury, 2000), 1160–1.

64   Khlebnikov, "Truba marsian" [The Trumpet of the Martians], in *Sobranie proizvedenii*, 5:152.

65   Khlebnikov, "Lialia na tigre" [Lalia Rides a Tiger], in *Sobranie proizvedenii* 5:213.

66   F.T. Marinetti, "Fondation et Manifeste du futurism," in *Enquête internationale sur le Vers libre et Manifeste du futurisme* (Milan: Éditions de "Poesia," 1909).

67   Osip Mandel'shtam, "Buria i natisk" (1923), in *Polnoe sobranie sochinenii i pisem* (Moscow: Progress-Pleiada, 2010), 2:137.

68   Velimir Khlebnikov, "Indo-russkii soiuz," ed. A.E. Parnis, published as an appendix to "Evraziiskie konteksty Khlebnikova: ot 'kalmytskogo mifa' k mifu o 'edinoi Azii,'" in *Evraziiskoe prostranstvo*, 336–9. For a more detailed discussion of this manifesto, see my article, "The Poetics of Eurasia: Velimir Khlebnikov between Empire and Revolution," in *The Transformation of Russian Social Identities*, ed. Madhavan K.Palat (Basingstoke: Palgrave Publishers, 2001), 209–31.

69   See Louis Marin, "Thèses sur l'idéologie et l'utopie," in *Utopiques: Jeux d'espaces*, 249.

70   See Jean-Claude Lanne, "'Astsu': Tentative de topographie futurienne," *Modernités russes* (2001): 125–37; and A.E. Parnis, "K deshifrovke odnoi mifologemy Khlebnikova: ot 'Ostrova vysokogo zvezdnogo dukha' k sviashchennomu ostrovu," *Russian Literature* 55 (2004): 353–70.

71   Parnis, "Evraziiskie konteksty Khlebnikova," 336n81. Parnis argues that Khlebnikov's utopian goal was the establishment of a "mega-island" named ASSU and that he merely misspoke when referring to Asia as a continent. Yet, this argument ignores Khlebnikov's repeated references to the "continent of time" or the following statement of 1912: "I know about the mind of continents, which is quite unlike the mind of islanders. *The son of proud Asia cannot be reconciled with the peninsular reason of Europeans*" (Khlebnikov, "Teacher and Pupil: On Words, Cities and Peoples" [Uchitel' i uchenik. O slovakh, gorodakh i narodakh], *Sobranie proizvedenii*, 5:178–9, emphasis added). My point is that these topographical designations are not to be taken literally, but as metaphors for openness versus closure.

72   See Louis Marin, "Frontiers of Utopia"; and Fredric Jameson, "Of Islands and Trenches: Neutralization and the Production of Utopian Discourse," in *The Ideologies of Theory. Essays 1971–1986*, 2:75–101, esp. 95.

73   Khlebnikov, "Azosoiuz" [a parallel manifesto written in 1918], published in Parnis, "Evraziiskie konteksty Khlebnikova," 340.

74   See Christopher Kendrick, "More's Utopia and Uneven Development," *boundary 2* 13, nos. 2/3 (Winter–Spring 1985): 236–66, esp. 238: "Utopian work does not dispose of, or overturn, ideological problems (whose privileged form is the antinomy) ... but rather neutralizes them, i.e. re-poses them on another (imaginary) plane." The "imaginary plane" in Khlebnikov is "Asia" as an emancipated "state of time."

75 Khlebnikov, "Nasha osnova," *Sobranie proizvedenii*, 5:235–6. On Khlebnikov's theory of language, see Iurii Tynianov, "O Khlebnikove," in Khlebnikov, *Sobranie proizvedenii*, 1:25–6; Carla Solivetti, "'Azbuka uma' Velimira Khlebnikova," *Russian Literature* XXIII-II (February 1988): 169–84; M.S. Kiktev, "Khlebnikovskaia 'azbuka' v kontekste revoliutsii i grazhdanskoi voiny," in *Khlebnikovskie chteniia. Materialy konferentsii 27–29 noiabria 1990g* (1991), 15–39; Carla Solivetti, "Lingvisticheskie prozreniia Velimira Khlebnikova," *Russian Literature* LV-I/II/III (January–April 2004): 405–29; Dubravka Oraic-Tolic, *Khlebnikov i avangard*, 52–9.
76 Khlebnikov, "Nasha osnova," *Sobranie proizvedenii*, 5:237.
77 Khlebnikov, *Zangezi, Sobranie proizvedenii*, 5:340.
78 Ibid., 330.
79 Ibid., 332–3.
80 Khlebnikov, "Khudozhniki mira!" in *Sobranie proizvedenii*, 5:219–20.
81 Khlebnikov, "Iz zapisnykh knizhek," in *Sobranie proizvedenii*, 5:268.
82 Khlebnikov, "Svoiasi" (1919), in *Sobranie proizvedenii*, 2:9.
83 The creation of IZO marks the greatest proximity to have arisen between the Russian radical avant-garde and the new Soviet state. The journal was to have reflected the internationalist goals of the post-revolutionary era: see Aleksandr Parnis, "Khlebnikov i neosushchestvlennyi zhurnal 'Internatsional iskusstva.' Novye materialy," in *Na rubezhe dvukh stoletii. Sbornik v chest' 60-letiia Aleksandra Vasil'evicha Lavrova* (Moscow: Novoe literaturnoe obozrenie, 2009), 530–56.
84 Khlebnikov, "Khudozhniki mira!" *Sobranie proizvedenii*, 5:216, 220.
85 Ernest Fenollosa, *The Chinese Written Character as a Medium for Poetry*, ed. Ezra Pound (San Francisco: City Lights Books, 1964), 9, 21, 22.
86 Christopher Bush, *Ideographic Modernism: China, Writing, Media* (Oxford: Oxford University Press, 2010), 19–29.
87 Khlebnikov, "Pis'mo dvum iaponstam," in *Sobranie proizvedenii*, 5:155, emphasis added.
88 Ezra Pound in Fenollosa, *The Chinese Written Character*, 3, emphasis added.
89 For an excellent survey of Khlebnikov's linguistic postulates in the context of Russian intellectual and cultural history, see Solivetti, "Lingvisticheskie prozreniia Velimira Khlebnikova."
90 See N.N. Pertsova, "O 'zvezdnom iazyke' Velimira Khlebnikova," in *Mir Velimira Khlebnikova*, 359–71, esp. 370–1.
91 Solivetti, "'Azbuka uma' Velimira Khlebnikova," 174–5.
92 Khlebnikov, "Nasha osnova," *Sobranie proizvedenii*, 242.
93 On the structuring principles of the "supersaga," and of *Zangezi* specifically, see N. Khardzhiev, "Ot redaktsii," in *Neizdannye proizvedeniia* (Moscow: Khudozhestvennaia literatura, 1940), 11–12; Vladimir Markov, *The Longer Poems*

of Velimir Khlebnikov (Berkeley: University of California Press, 1962), 25–9; Iu
Tynianov, "O Khlebnikove," in *Mir Velimira Khlebnikova*, 217; Dubravka Oraic,
"Sverkhpovest," *Russian Literature* XIX (1986): 43–56; Henryk Baran, "Temporal
Myths in Xlebnikov: From 'Deti Vydry' to 'Zangezi,'" *Myth in Literature*, 63–88;
R.V. Duganov, "Ia umer i zasmeialsia, ili teatr nevozmozhnogo," in *Zangezi.
Sverkhpovest'* (Moscow: Diagilev tsentr, 1992), 4–10; Ronald Vroon, "Genezis
zamysla 'sverkhpovesti' 'Zangezi' (k voprosu ob evoliutsii liricheskogo 'ia' u
Khlebnikova)," *Vestnik Obshchestva Velimira Khlebnikova* 1 (1996): 140–59.
Khlebnikov's earliest explication of the compositional principles of a complex hy-
brid genre similar to the supersaga, which he calls "differential dramatic creation,"
can be found in his letter to Vasilii Kamenskii, 8 August 1909, in *Neizdannye
proizvedeniia*, 358.

94 Khlebnikov, *Zangezi, Sobranie proizvedenii*, 5:317.
95 Ibid., 333.
96 V. Tatlin, "O Zangezi," *Zhizn' iskusstva* 18 (1923): 15, republished in English,
"On Zangezi," in *Tatlin*, ed. Larissa Zhadova (New York: Rizzoli International
Publications, 1988), 148–9.
97 Tatlin, "O Zangezi," 15.
98 On Vladimir Tatlin's Monument to the Third International, see Christina Lodder,
Russian Constructivism (New Haven, CT: Yale University Press, 1983), 55–67;
as a case study by which to understand the relationship between radical artists
and the nascent Soviet state, see Pamela Kachurin's "Working (for) the State:
Vladimir Tatlin's Career in Early Soviet Russia and the Origins of *The Monument
to the Third International*," *Modernism/modernity* 19, no. 1 (January 2012): 19–41.
Kachurin argues against both an abstractly formal and a purely instrumental-ca-
reerist reading of the monument, suggesting that "multivalent aesthetic, symbolic,
political and economic imperatives" coalesced in Tatlin's project. On Tatlin's
monument, see also Steven S. Lee, *The Ethnic Avant-Garde* (New York: Columbia
University Press, 2015), 6ff.
99 N. Punin, *Pamiatnik III Internatsionala* (Petrograd: Izdanie Otdela
Izobrazitel'nykh iskusstv N.K. P., 1920), 1.
100 By contrast, formalist critic Viktor Shklovskii, in "Pamiatnik Tret'emu
Internationalu," *Zhizn' iskusstva* (January 1921): 5, noticed that the "spiral is falling sideways supported by a sturdy leaning structure."
101 Punin, *Pamiatnik III Internatsionala*, 3.
102 Concerning Tatlin, Khlebnikov, and *Zangezi*, see Lodder, *Russian Constructivism*,
esp. 31–2, 205–12; John Milner, *Vladimir Tatlin and the Russian Avant-Garde*
(New Haven, CT: Yale University Press, 1983), 196–202; F.I. Syrkina, "Tatlin's
Theatre," in *Tatlin*, 155–79; as well as the informative notes by A.E. Parnis,
in *Tatlin*, 396–400; Anatolii Strigalev, "Retrospektivnaia vystavka Vladimira
Tatlina," in *Vladimir Tatlin. Retrospektiva* (Cologne: DuMont Buchverlag, 1993),
41–5, 266; Tat'iana Liuboslavskaia and Irina Arskaia, "Postanovka Tatlinym

sverkhpovesti Velimira Khlebnikova 'Zangezi,'" and "Tatlin i Khlebnikov: K nekotorym aspektam stsenicheskoi interpretatsii 'Zangesi," in *Vladimir Tatlin. Leben, Werk, Wirkung. Ein Internationales Symposium veranstaltet von der Städtischen Kunsthalle Düsseldorf und dem Kunstwissenschaftlichen Institut des Kulturministeriums der UdSSR, Moskau*, ed. Jürgen Harten (Cologne: DuMont Buchverlag, 1993), 348–52, 389–93, respectively; Linda Schädler, "Synthesis of the Arts: Tatlin's Staging of *Zangezi* – A Total Work of Art?" in *Tatlin. New Art for a New World. International Symposium* (Basel: Museum Tinguely, 2012), 271–4.

103 Khlebnikov, *Zangezi, Sobranie proizvedenii*, 5:317.

104 Khlebnikov, "Otryvok iz dosok sud'by" [An extract from the Tables of Fate], *Sobranie proizvedenii*, 5:518.

105 On Khlebnikov and Nietzsche, see Betsy F. Moeller-Sally, "Masks of the Prophet in the Works of Velimir Khlebnikov: Pushkin and Nietzsche," *Russian Review* 55, no. 2 (April 1996): 201–25; and Henryk Baran, "Khlebnikov and Nietzsche: Pieces of an Incomplete Mosaic," in *Nietzsche and Soviet Culture: Ally and Adversary*, ed. Bernice Glatzer Rosenthal (New York: Cambridge University Press, 2010), 58–83. Regarding Khlebnikov's close interest in nineteenth-century Iranian religious reformers, see Baran and Parnis, "'Anabazis' Velimira Khlebnikova."

106 Moretti, *Modern Epic*, 2, 5, 50, 52, emphasis added.

107 Khlebnikov, *Zangezi, Sobranie proizvedenii*, 5:324. My rendering of Khlebnikov has relied in part on Paul Schmidt's translation of *Zangezi* in *Collected Works of Velimir Khlebnikov*, vol. 2, *Prose, Plays and Superplays*, ed. Ronald Vroon (Cambridge, MA: Harvard University Press, 1989), 337.

108 Concerning the archetype of the Cosmic Man, see Marie Louise von Franz, "The Cosmic Man as Image of the Goal of the Individuation Process and Human Development," in *Archteypal Dimensions of the Psyche* (Boston: Shambhala Publications, 2004), 133–57.

109 See V.P. Grigor'ev, *Slovotvorchestvo i smezhnye problemy iazyka poèta* (Moscow: Nauka, 1986), 222–34, esp. 224. I would argue that Khlebnikov's particular imaging of the Cosmic Man has Indic (Hindu) sources, both Puranic and Vedic, combining the iconographic attributes of the mountain-dwelling hermit god Shiva (from whose locks the river Ganges flows) and the Vedic figure of Adipurusha (*Rg Veda*, 10:90).

110 Khlebnikov, *Zangezi, Sobranie proizvedenii*, 5:357. I have relied heavily on Paul Schmidt's translation of this passage in *Collected Works of Velimir Khlebnikov*, 2:365–6.

111 Martin Heidegger, "The Age of the World Picture," in *The Question Concerning Technology and Other Essays*, trans. William Lovitt (London: Garland Publishing, 1977), 130.

112 My account of *Zangezi*'s multiple sign-systems has been influenced by Roman Jakobson, "The Speech Event and the Functions of Language," in *On Language*, ed. Linda R. Wugh and Monique Monville-Burston (Cambridge, MA: Harvard

University Press, 1990), 69–79; as well as by Gilles Deleuze and Félix Guattari, "587 av. J.-C: Sur quelques régimes de signes," in *Mille Plateaux. Capitalisme et schizophrénie* (Paris: Les Editions de Minuit, 1980), 140–84.

113 Khlebnikov, *Zangezi, Sobranie proizvedenii*, 5:319.
114 Ibid., 340–1.
115 *Collected Works of Velimir Khlebnikov*, 2:351.
116 Osip Mandel'shtam, "Vulgata: (Zametki o poèzii)," in *Polnoe sobranie sochinenii i pisem* (Moscow: Progress-Pleiada, 2010), 2:143.
117 See Lev Trotskii [Leon Trotsky], "Osobennosti razvitiia Rossii" [The Peculiarities of Russia's Development], in *Istoriia russkoi revoliutsii* [A History of the Russian Revolution], vol. 1, *Fevral'skaia revoliutsiia* [The February Revolution] (Berlin: Granit, 1931), 20–1: "A backward country assimilates the material and intellectual achievements of the advanced countries. But this does not mean that it follows them slavishly, reproducing all the stages of their past ... Compelled to strain after the advanced countries, a backward country does not observe the established sequence: the privilege of historical belatedness – and such a privilege exists – allows, or rather compels, the adoption of what is ready in advance of any established deadlines, leaping over a series of intermediary stages." For applications of Trotsky's theory within the realm of literary analysis, see Ruth Jennisen, "Combining Uneven Developments: Louis Zukofsky and the Political Economy of Revolutionary Modernism," *Cultural Critique* 77 (Winter 2011): 146–79; and Warwick Research Collective, *Combined and Uneven Development: Towards a New Theory of World-Literature* (Liverpool, UK: Liverpool University Press, 2015).

Chapter Two

Berlin–Moscow–Shanghai: Translating Revolution across Cultures in the Aftermath of the 1927 Shanghai Debacle

KATERINA CLARK
Yale University

This chapter[1] is related to a larger study in which I look at the dynamic of what Kris Manjapra has recently called "the socialist global ecumene" or, more specifically, part of the "transcolonial ecumene" formed within it.[2] By this term, Manjapra means an "ecumene" in the modern sense of a far-flung or worldwide community of people committed to a single cause and engaged in discussions, lobbying, and writing aimed at working towards a common, Marxist-based program, at generating a common discourse. In Manjapra's somewhat idealized account, this ecumene involves not relations between powerful centres and their dependencies, but rather lateral connections of the worldwide like-minded. In generating this discourse, communist and Comintern bodies and personnel played a major role.[3]

In reality, of course, though a lot of lateral intercourse took place among committed leftists during the late 1920s and early 1930s, the period that I am discussing, the metropole – Moscow – also played an important role in fostering and mustering what can only be called a putative ecumene. But one should not just dismiss the ecumene as yet another example of an insidious Soviet cultural imperialism with the foreign participants as unwitting pawns. Many of the writers involved, whether they were affiliated with the Party or the Comintern or not (and many important ones were not, such as Mulk Raj Anand, discussed in another piece by me),[4] were relatively independent members of the ecumene and, though committed anti-colonialists, drew in their writings on a variety of influences, generally including some modernist works. Moreover, it should not be assumed that the Comintern was a monolithic body and that all its leaders were of one mind on all issues or used the same vocabulary. Its official platform, including in literature, changed at least twice during the seven years, 1927–33, covered in this chapter.

The writers I will be discussing, as de facto members of the (putative) ecumene, had to negotiate for themselves the competing draws of the national, the transnational, and the international. An underlying problematic for them in their commitment to a particular version of internationalism was the way in which, as Glyn Salton-Cox put it, "the clichés of national tradition simultaneously constitute and undermine an ethic of internationalist solidarity."[5] Resolving the two also had more strictly literary dimensions after the Soviet promulgation of socialist realism as *the* national (Soviet) literary method, which was also to serve, potentially, as a hegemonic, transnational literary tradition. It should be noted, however, that the term "socialist realism" was coined only in 1932, and the First Congress of the Soviet Writers' Union, which gave it an official definition, met only in 1934, so the texts I will be discussing are essentially pre–socialist realist. Nevertheless, the writers had to negotiate between their vernacular literary traditions and values and the emerging common rhetoric of the ecumene.

My chapter will confine itself to looking at texts generated in Berlin, Moscow, and Shanghai between 1927 and 1933 that directly or indirectly respond to the 1927 debacle and its aftermath. That is to say, they engage in some way the April 1927 rout of communists in Shanghai by Chiang Kai-shek's Nationalists, who dominated the Guomindang, and the subsequent repression of communists throughout the country – especially of Soviet advisors – causing most advisors and many Chinese communist activists to retreat to the Soviet Union. Alternatively, these texts treat some aspect of the series of communist-led attempts at uprisings in China made over the ensuing years that likewise ended in failure.

This chapter will analyse common themes and strategies used by writers, dramatists, and filmmakers to represent this defeat, which was devastating for the international communist movement. The commonality between texts from the three cities was fostered both vertically – works on revolutionary China incorporated material disseminated by authoritative communist or Comintern bodies or officials – and horizontally (or laterally) – works incorporated material derived from interactions with others in the various far-flung networks of the ecumene or from non-communist printed material coming from other countries.

Literary exchanges between the three cities on the subject of the debacle occurred despite the huge distances and political and organizational obstacles. These exchanges took place not only because leftists in all three cities heeded the Soviet platform. Not a single template was adopted in all the texts I am discussing, although most of those who produced them shared a similar set of assumptions. The commonalities were fostered in part by networks established by the Comintern, which facilitated communication: educational institutions in Moscow, such as the international section of the Communist University of Toilers of the East (KUTV; *Kommunisticheskii universitet trudiashchikhsia vostoka*) and the Sun Yat-sen University, where friendships and other links were formed with fellow students from other countries; a cluster of literary journals, starting in 1927, published in Moscow under the auspices of the Comintern comprising semi-parallel editions in French, Russian, German, and Spanish (also briefly in Chinese), which were linked in turn with journals in other countries such as the *New Masses* in America; and a series of literary conferences (Moscow 1927, Kharkov 1930, Paris 1935, London 1936, Spain 1937) attended by delegates from many countries. In these various ways writers, ideas, and texts circulated and interacted throughout the world.

Actually, however, the two kinds of interaction I have identified – the lateral, or horizontal, and the vertical – cannot be readily disaggregated. A clear example of this difficulty can be seen in the impact of Ėmi Xiao (Xiao San) on Russian and German texts about China. Ėmi Xiao, a communist and graduate of KUTV (where he became friends with, inter alia, the leading Turkish writer Nâzim Hikmet[6]), moved on to become a Comintern-assigned political leader in China and in 1927 led insurgents in the Shanghai workers' suburb of Chapei.[7] Like several other Chinese communist leaders, he turned from politics to literature after the debacle; from 1930 he operated in Moscow as a writer, as the chief liaison between Moscow and the newly formed League of Leftist Writers in Shanghai, and as the broker for publishing Chinese works in the Comintern-sponsored journal *Internatsional'naia literatura*, where he was on the editorial board.[8] He also served as an intermediary from revolutionary China to Berlin writers in that, at the Kharkov literary congress of 1930, he talked to both Anna Seghers and Egon Erwin Kisch about the Shanghai uprising and was one of the sources they drew on in their writings about China.[9]

Most of the German and Soviet works on China I will be discussing were published first in Moscow and then in Berlin in German translation, or vice versa, so writers and filmmakers in both cities who engaged the topic of China were drawing on common texts, but texts promoted officially – a further, institutional example of links that are effectively both vertical and lateral. Berlin was, during the years I am covering, a centre for the German left and the headquarters of the Comintern in Europe. The German capital functioned as the gateway to Europe for Soviet culture and culture producers, seen in Karl Schlögel's title for his book on the subject, *Berlin Ostbahnhof Europas* (Berlin: Europe's Eastern Railway Station).[10] In the late 1920s and early 1930s, Berlin and Moscow leftist culture were drawing closer thanks to a growing exchange of writers, filmmakers, films, and printed material, not to mention joint film productions by Mezhrabpomfil'm (covered in Katie Trumpener's piece in chapter fifteen of this volume).

Clearly, translation was endemic to the project of international revolution, both metaphorically, given the aim of implementing in individual countries a scenario that was putatively transnational, but also literally. Edwin Gentzler and Maria Tymoczko remark in their introduction to *Translation and Power*: "Colonialism and imperialism were and are made possible not just by military might or economic advantage but by knowledge as well ... Translation has been a key tool in the production of such knowledge and representations."[11] Analogously, the Comintern-sponsored literary journals that emanated from Moscow and other leftist publishing enterprises in the three cities played an important role in making foreign literary texts accessible to those who could not read them in the original, but these enterprises were also aimed at the dissemination of a particular "knowledge" and particular "representations."

The dynamic I have identified, then, is in some ways comparable to the one that Antoinette Burton and Isabel Hofmeyr discuss in their introduction to the edited collection *Ten Books That Shaped the British Empire: Creating an Imperial Commons*, but, though there were distinctly neo-imperial elements to the fostering of the ecumene by the Comintern, we are looking at a relatively early stage in the evolution of a hegemonic discourse within literature. Moreover, as Burton and Hofmeyr point out (and was certainly true of the putative ecumene), the "imperial commons" was far from uniform but rather was "both integrated intellectually *and* perpetually disintegrated by the myriad subjects and agents who constructed, lived inside, and sought to exceed its territorial and epistemological frames."[12] Though Èmi Xiao in his many official speeches to international writers' gatherings consistently called for Chinese writers to follow Soviet literary models and directives from Moscow, and though his own literary efforts were crudely propagandistic, the others I am discussing were less rigidly wedded to authoritative models.[13] For example, German accounts of contemporary China tended to focus on revolutionary uprisings in Shanghai factories and were thus out of synch with the new, post-1927 Bolshevik and Comintern line on China, which emphasized peasant revolt and the formation of provincial communes.

Though one cannot readily disaggregate vertically derived material and laterally or horizontally derived material in the literary texts and films about revolutionary China from these years, I am somewhat artificially distinguishing between the two in accounting for the provenance of material used in the texts I am describing and the correspondingly different uses to which the material was put. In the works I will be discussing, the accounts presented of factory and living conditions in Shanghai and of the organization of strikes and other revolutionary events, accounts that inform the bulk of a given text and provide a rationale for radical action, largely draw on horizontally derived sources. This approach is especially evident in the case of texts about China generated in the late 1920s and early 1930s by some of the leading leftist writers in Germany (Bertolt Brecht, Friedrich Wolf, Anna Seghers, Egon Erwin Kisch, Karl Wittfogel). Their accounts of Shanghai factories and the Chinese revolution were indebted to such sources as a series of reports from Shanghai published in *Frankfurter Zeitung* between November 1929 and November 1930, written by Agnes Smedley (an American journalist and leftist activist who, though never a member of the Communist Party of the United States of America, was possibly, as Ruth Price claims, a Comintern agent in China).[14] They were also derived from these German writers' discussions with individuals from the sizeable body of Chinese – mostly students – living in Germany at the time, many of them part of the "Circle for the Chinese Language," which was effectively a Chinese Communist Party section within the Communist Party of Germany, with which the Chinese Party in Germany had been melded after 1927.[15] As mentioned, in the cases of Seghers and Kisch, another important source was the conversations they had with Xiao at Kharkov, during which they were able to learn about the 1927 debacle first hand; for Kisch, an additional source was a clandestine trip he made to China resulting in the 1933 book *China geheim* (Secret China), published in Russian as *Razoblachënnyi Kitai* in 1934.[16] A further common source, known to have been used by Wolf and Seghers, was the 1926 *New China: Report of an Investigation* by Colonel Cecil L'Estrange Malone (Malone was not a communist), which appeared in German translation in 1928 as *Das neue China*.[17]

Here, however, I will focus not on such relatively horizontally derived aspects of the texts on revolutionary China from these years, but rather on those that have been derived more vertically from injunctions, Party rhetoric, and authoritative texts. I intend to show that, in the works on China that appeared in these cities, the overall trajectory of the plot, many of the political discussions set up between characters, and, particularly, a work's ending seem to represent expansions or other appropriations of tropic elements from authoritative communist texts, some of them in turn derived from earlier, pre-communist intellectual traditions. These tropic elements – motifs, symbols, metaphors, expressions from Party discourse, plot functions adapted from official versions of events – were commonly deployed in texts about China, but cannot be said to form a coherent master narrative; at best they could be considered elements of an embryonic master narrative, which could not be claimed to have been derived from Soviet literary texts about the debacle itself. In fact, unexpectedly perhaps, Soviet authors produced very little coverage of the years of revolutionary devolution, 1927–30, in contrast to the extensive coverage of the years 1923–27. The debacle and its aftermath attracted greater attention among German leftist writers (also to be noted is André Malraux's *Man's Fate* [*Condition humaine*] of 1933, which I am not treating here). However, this finding does not mean that, during these years, Soviet texts on China did not appear in the Soviet Union or in other countries. But, rather than represent the recent debacle, most of the Soviet texts that appeared or were promoted after the crisis were recycled versions of pre-1927 texts or in some other way anachronistic.[18]

A good example of the anachronistic text would be V.I. Pudovkin's silent film *Storm over Asia* (originally titled *The Heir to Genghis Khan* [*Potomok Chingis-khana*], 1928). That there was particular political direction in making this film seems highly likely; when Pudovkin filmed much of it in Buryat, Mongolia, over twelve weeks starting in April 1928, he was assisted by A.I. Oshirov (1901–31), a Buryat Mongol and Comintern agent who worked among the Buryats in Mongolia.[19] The film essentially provides a compensatory narrative of successful revolution in Asia. It is ostensibly set in Mongolia and based on an earlier novella, *The Heir to Genghis Khan* by Ivan Novokshonov (who also collaborated with Osip Brik on the screenplay). The novella remained unpublished in the 1920s, was revised in the 1930s, and was first published in 1966, well after Novokshonov had been repressed in 1937, so one cannot ascertain for sure what was in the first 1920s variant, completed shortly before the film script assignment; the version of the novella that appeared in the sixties differs from the screenplay in several significant respects, which suggests that, in writing the screenplay based on the original novella, the plot was revised to fit in with the post-debacle moment. Among the differences, the novella (unlike the film) devotes considerable space to describing the experiences of the central character, Bair, as a novice in a Buddhist lamasery and to the Bolshevik struggle and victory over the forces of Baron von Ungern, an eccentric and sadistic asian-ophile whose personal army captured Mongolia in 1921 before being defeated (and he executed) by the Bolsheviks.[20] In the film, the antagonists are instead the British military forces, who appear to have occupied the area, and European fur traders who look American. In actuality, the English and Americans did not have any significant presence in Mongolia at this time, let alone a military one. Also, the film ends with a resounding triumph of the forces of the Mongolians against the British, while the novella ends with Bair seeking out his childhood love in the Mongolian capital, Urga, only to find her destroyed by prostitution and disease. The changes to the plot and the consequent historical inaccuracies were, I would suggest, designed to render the setting more of a generic Asia or, more specifically, a version of China, which had a large European military presence and where, in the analysis of Lenin and others, the British represented imperialism incarnate.

The film premiered in Moscow on 10 November 1928, but was swiftly exported for screening overseas. Already in December it opened in Berlin and was renamed *Storm over Asia* (*Stürm nach Asien*) – in keeping with the intention to make it a generic tale of Asian revolution. This premiere was followed by one in Budapest (April 1929), and then in Holland and England in February 1930.[21] It was also screened among many other films in New York. This film, however, was not promoted as widely as another Soviet text on China, Sergei Tret'iakov's play *Roar, China!* (1925), which had opened on 23 January 1926 at Meyerhold's theatre in Moscow. The text was a pre-1927 product, but it was widely promoted after 1927, especially in Germany. The first foreign production of *Roar, China!* was in Frankfurt on 9 November 1929, followed by performances in Leipzig, Münster, Remscheid, Hamburg, Halle, Karlsruhe, and

Dortmund. In Cologne it was performed on 1 May 1930 in a stadium with seating for 6,000. In the spring of 1930, Meyerhold brought his Moscow production to Germany, where it was staged in Berlin, Breslau, and Cologne. The play was also performed on a range of international stages, including in Japan, England, Vienna, Australia, New York (October 1930), and even China (Canton 1930, Shanghai 1933), and the script appeared in translation in many languages; it was so popular that these translations often went through multiple editions.[22] To some extent, the play's popularity and multiple productions were because it struck a chord, but the productions were largely fostered "vertically," actively promoted by Soviet authorities. The All-Union Society for Cultural Links with Foreign Countries (VOKS), affiliated with the Soviet Commissariat for Foreign Affairs, sent copies of the text to assorted foreign theatres, including a fruitless dispatch to Turkey of a version in Russian and a translation into German (but not into the necessary Turkish).[23]

In a sense, *Roar, China!* was potentially a unifying text to rally the ecumene in this difficult, post-debacle moment. It functioned as something of an establishing text, a synecdoche for the struggle against imperialism and class oppression in Asia. In the play there are no Guomindang nationalists aligned with the communists. Its characters are just coolies, oppressor foreigners, compradors, and a Chinese union organizer. Consequently, it could be appropriated for the post-1927 moment.

With the determined export of *Roar, China!* all over the world, the Soviet Union was purveying an account of China that was anachronistic, because it suggested that the dynamic of that country's glorious revolutionary years (1925–27) still obtained. The plot of the play, when presented after 1927 as it was, implicitly defied the actuality of the downward curve, of the revolution's devolution. Subsequent texts about China, in particular those published in Germany where the play was widely staged in 1929–30, though in subject matter addressing the debacle and its inglorious aftermath, picked up the general trajectory of *Roar, China!*. Also, in the play the oppressed Chinese are represented by coolies, not by factory workers. In this first five-year plan moment, most of the major texts about the debacle (German and Chinese) took industrial Shanghai and its workers as their subject matter.[24]

Roar, China! is based on an actual event or, more specifically, on newspaper reports of an actual event. As recounted in the Tret'iakov script, after the inadvertent drowning of an American businessman in a Chinese provincial town on the Yangtze River during a confrontation with boatmen, officials from a foreign naval vessel, "The Cockchafer," stationed there demand that those responsible for the drowning be handed over for summary execution or, failing that, two members of the Boatmen's Union be surrendered to die in their place; if not, the gunboat will fire on the populace. The terrified mayor feels compelled to order executions. Here we will look only at the play's ending. In it one character, Stoker, tells an assembled crowd that the foreigners are leaving because "in Shanghai there is a revolution." He challenges the forces of capitalism and imperialism with the words: "Count your hours. Your end is near. China is roaring ... Shoot! I may fall, but ten will rise in my place." A student picks up his cry, shouting: "Roar over the whole earth! Roar, China in the ears of all the world! Roar, China the story of this crime."[25]

Following this play, most representations of revolution in texts about China from 1927–33 culminate in the masses "roaring," or, at any rate, some form of future revolutionary triumph is implied as some assemblage of the masses lets forth a resounding cry. In the case of *Storm over Asia*, this "roar" was less feasible, given that it is a silent film and hence has no sound track. The finale doesn't have a sonic "roar," but there are shots of Asiatic horsemen galloping furiously over the plains. The horsemen prevail over the forces of English imperialism, who are driven back by a mighty wind, which could be seen as a visual correlative of the unstoppable revolutionary "roar."

Most of the literary works about recent revolutionary events in China that were published between 1928 and 1933 in Berlin, Moscow, and Shanghai end not with a revolutionary triumph per se, but with some deafening roar that implies massive revolutionary resistance. The outcome, what happens after the "roar," is not represented, as the text breaks off at that point. What constitutes the "roar" varies. Anna Seghers's "1 Mai Yanschupou," published in the German communist newspaper *Rote Fahne* on May Day, 1932, is a story about Shanghai textile workers organizing a strike; in the story's climactic final moment, as a crowd of rebellious workers assembled on a square confront the troops who have come to put them down, the workers close ranks and let out a defiant response in sound.[26] There is, however, a difference from the ending of *Roar, China!* Seghers describes her workers as forming "a single rumbling, jeering mass," using the verb "*brummen*," which can be translated into English as "rumble" and is, therefore, a somewhat lesser sound than the "roar" of *Roar, China!*; the title of Tret'iakov's play is rendered in German as *Brülle, China!*

The German communist writer Friedrich Wolf's play *Tai Yang erwacht* (Tai Yang Awakens, 1930) provides another version of the revolutionary "roar." The play is set after the Shanghai debacle of 1927, as is evident in several references to the "treachery" of Chiang Kai-shek. It was also the first Western literary work to mention Mao Zedong (the play alludes to his rallying the Southern peasants).[27] As its title proclaims, the play chronicles the political awakening of Tai, a young textile worker in Shanghai, who is employed with her younger sister, Ma, in a silk factory owned by a Chinese, Tschu Fus, who is a patriot. In principle, Tschu Fus is against the foreign capitalists but (a common plot function in leftist texts of this period) resigns himself to accepting the support of the foreign powers when his workers become restive. At first Tai is reluctant to be politically involved and refuses to join any form of protest because she believes protesting only results in the strikers being mown down on the streets by the capitalists. But, in the end, she comes to recognize that a sudden death in a street protest is preferable to the slow death that she and her fellow workers are undergoing at the factory bench (one of them already has contracted tuberculosis from the steam and the long hours). Tai's conversion is partly motivated by the love plot. She is at first attracted by the good life and material plenty she enjoys when she becomes the factory owner's mistress; but, in that position she comes to see more directly the true dynamic of ruthless exploitation and how ready the owners are to use extreme means to quieten the factory workers. However, her ultimate conversion occurs when she is attracted to a factory agitator, Wan. Feelings are mutual, but both lay them aside to work for the cause. In the final scene, Tai has returned to the factory with leaflets urging the workers to demonstrate the next day in support of revolutionaries who are converging on Shanghai from other towns – suggesting, in other words, a reversal of the debacle. Her comrades, including her younger sister, opt to resist whatever the cost.

As with Brecht's plays, songs play a major role in this text. There are about five songs, but the most important is "The Mango Tree." Allegedly an ancient folk song (as far as I have been able to ascertain a fabricated one), the leftist workers have appropriated it for the cause and added verses (implying that traditional Chinese culture can blend with the Marxist-Leninist). In the adapted version, branches of the ancient mango tree fall down and some turn into lances, while others form a torch or the shaft of a weapon until there are "hundreds of weapons, thousands of weapons, ten thousand."[28] It is also clear from essays Wolf wrote at about this time, such as "Art as a Weapon" (*Kunst als Waffe*) of 1928, and also from the critical importance in the play's plot of an underground printing press and the distribution of revolutionary pamphlets, that the "weapons" spawned by the tree are not just arms, but also agitational texts.[29] This song becomes a weapon in the play's finale: as Tai and Ma and their comrades set off to join the uprising, they break into song, but the mango tree song is also picked up by workers on every floor of the factory and reverberates in a deafening din, a "roar." Wolf was using here a strategy employed, as mentioned, by virtually all of the writers I am discussing – to break off the story at the moment when the rebellious workers are about to confront the forces of state power, at which point, historically, they were crushed; but in fiction, films, and plays, that point of debacle is not reached. Rather the "roar" of the oppressed in its various forms reaches a crescendo as the curtain falls, or the novel or film ends.

Though these writers may well have taken the trope of the "roar" from Tret'iakov's play, it is not actually Tret'iakov's own but is effectively derived from the manifesto of the 1920 Congress of the Peoples of the East in Baku, a congress that was organized by the Comintern and attended by delegates from all over what later came to be called the Third World. This manifesto identifies

Britain as imperialism incarnate and China as her principal victim. After listing British imperial iniquities in a series of countries, the manifesto pronounces:

> This shall not be! ... The peoples of the East have long stagnated in the darkness of ignorance under the despotic yoke of their own tyrant rulers, and under that of the capitalist conquerors. But the roar of the world-wide conflict, and the thunder of the Russian workers' revolution, which has released the Eastern peoples of Russia from their century-old chains of capitalist slaves, has awakened them, and now aroused from their sleep of centuries, they are rising to their feet ... hearing the call to a holy war.[30]

We will note that the phrases the "peoples of the East have long stagnated in the darkness of ignorance" but have now been "awakened ... from their sleep of centuries" could easily have been lifted from an imperialist tract, though this standard imperialist rationale for colonization is, in the manifesto, given a revolutionary, anti-imperialist twist – they are "rising to their feet."

Another of the songs in *Tai Yang erwacht* is "The Internationale," the hymn of the international communist movement. This text is closely associated with Tai's progressive coming to consciousness over the course of the play. Early on, her resistance to the strike movement comes out when some of her fellow workers sing a snatch of the song, "Wake up [*Wache auf*], the damned of the earth," and Tai responds, "Quiet. I won't hear this song, this song that leads us all into unrest, struggle and death ... I will not 'wake up' when waking up for us means strike, death and firing in the streets."[31]

It might appear that this opening line of "The Internationale" gives the play its title, but the German version of "The Internationale" does not use the verb "*erwachen*" for "to wake up," as does Wolf's title, but a related verb "*aufwachen*." Moreover, in this crucial line of "The Internationale," which inflects so much literature about China of this time, there are variations from language to language. Several versions enjoin the oppressed to "stand up": "*debout*" in the original French of 1871, "stand up" in some of the English versions, "*vstavai*" in Russian. But a second injunction is found in some English versions of the song – "Arise ye workers from your slumber" – and "*Wacht auf*" in German. This sense of emerging from sleep is also conveyed in the Russian translation of Wolf's title, *Tai-ian probuzhdaetsia*.

By using "*erwachen*," Wolf is not following "The Internationale" but rather the title of the Frankfurt school theorist Karl Wittfogel's highly influential 1926 work on China, *Das erwachende China*, in which he outlines his theory of the Asiatic method of production, a text that was almost immediately published in Russian as *Probuzhdaiushchiisia Kitai*.[32] An extract on the Asiatic method taken from this book appeared in *Rote Fahne* right after the Shanghai debacle, as if authoritative and relevant to the current situation of China.[33] But the theory was, in fact, controversial and became especially so in the context of the highly acrimonious debates between Trotsky and Stalin over the causes of the debacle and the way forward, which played a critical role in the ultimate ouster of Trotsky in late 1927. Trotsky had attacked Stalin for allying himself with the Guomindang nationalists and maintaining that a broad-based (in class terms) alliance of those opposed to the imperialists could be the only way forward for China, which had not as yet entirely thrown off its feudalism and was, consequently, not ready for a fully proletarian revolution. The theory of the "Asiatic mode of production," however, contended that, because arid Asiatic societies were so dependent on the regulation of water to ensure a livelihood for their agrarian masses, they were controlled by a despotic ruling clique; in the wake of the debacle, the suggestion that the socio-economic organization of pre-capitalist Asia was distinct from that of feudal Europe and possibly even post-feudalist was anathema, because it contradicted the Stalinist thesis that China was still largely feudal. Consequently, though this theory was espoused by Marx in the early 1850s, after the debacle it was denounced in officially sponsored Soviet scholarly discussions of it.[34] In other words, Wolf's opting to foreground "*erwachen*" rather than "*aufwachen*" in his play, a trifling-seeming difference, is potentially an example of the general dynamic that Burton and Hofmeyr suggest in their introduction to *Ten Books That Shaped the British Empire* (cited earlier), pointing out that the "imperial commons" was far from uniform but "both integrated intellectually *and* perpetually disintegrated by the myriad subjects and agents who constructed, lived inside, and sought to exceed its territorial and epistemological frames."[35] In a sense, Wolf opted for a version of the concept that came from vernacular intellectual enquiry, if a communist one.

The notion of China "waking up" has a long prehistory in German intellectual life. Notably, Herder proclaimed China a highly patriarchal and "despotic realm" cut off from the rest of the world – "a nation thrust into a corner" – which consequently "has remained for thousands of years at the same point." It "has stood still in its education" and made no advances in the sciences. In sum, and these words are Herder's famous verdict that was often repeated: "The empire is an embalmed mummy, wrapped in silk, and painted with hieroglyphics: its circulation is that of a dormouse in its winter's sleep."[36] Hegel was blunter: he presented a similar analysis but gave greater emphasis to the "despotism of the Sovereign" that stultified "Spirit," and declared that China has no history – in other words, it has had no linear progression.[37] We will note, in both accounts, a European condescension of the sort that typifies the colonialist mentality; colonialists also see Asians as "sleepy" or "barbaric," or both.

One might have assumed that the Marxist leaders would use different vocabulary, but, in fact, the notion of China (or of Asia generally) as being in the sleep of centuries typifies their remarks. Marx, in an article of 7 July 1862, remarked that "Oriental empires continually exhibit an immutability" and pronounced China to be a "living fossil."[38] "The English cannon," he also contended, "forc[ed] upon China that soporific drug called opium." He concluded wryly: "It would seem as though history had first to make this whole people drunk before it could rouse them out of their hereditary stupidity."[39] But Marx also maintained that Asians, and the Chinese in particular, were already emerging from their torpor.

Lenin, in his pronouncements, was even more positive about the revolutionary promise of moribund China. In his speeches, he did not use the terminology of the "mummy" or the "fossil" but rather, and repeatedly, versions of "awakening" as in "The Internationale." In one article, "China Renewed," he declared that "four hundred million backward Asians [that is, the Chinese] have awakened [*prosnulis*] to political life. A fourth of the population of the globe has gone, so to speak, from sleeping to the light, to movement, to struggle."[40] In an article titled "The Awakening of Asia," where he used for "awakening" the word "*probuzhdenie*," a version of the standard Russian title for Wolf's play and the title for the Russian edition of Wittfogel's *Das erwachende China*, he declared that "world capitalism and the Russian movement of 1905 have awakened Asia [*razbudili*]." He continued on to say: "Hundreds of millions of people, who are downtrodden and have gone to seed in a medieval stagnation, have woken up [*prosnulos*] to a new life and to a struggle for the fundamental rights of man, for democracy ... The awakening of Asia and the struggle for power by the most advanced proletarians of Europe is a sign that at the beginning of the twentieth century a new phase [*polosa*] in world history has opened."[41] Later, in a speech to the Second All-Russian Congress of Communist Organizations of the Peoples of the East in 1919, he declared: "Now it remains for our Soviet republic to gather around herself the peoples of Asia who are awakening in order to conduct the struggle against international imperialism together with them."[42]

One sees a different version of the "awakening" in a Soviet post-debacle text, which was important at the time and widely promoted but is largely forgotten today: Oskar Ėrdberg's collection of short stories on China, *Kitaiskie novelly*. Russian editions of this book appeared in 1929, 1930, and 1932; an English translation, *Tales of Modern China*, in 1932; and a German translation, *Die drei Grundsätze des Mister Kung, u.a. chinesische Novellen*, likewise in 1932.[43] Oskar Ėrdberg was, in fact, one of several pseudonyms assumed by Sergei Razumov, who as Oskar Tarkhanov worked in China with the Soviet representative Mikhail Borodin from 1925 to 1926 as a political advisor to the Southern government of Sun Yat-sen in Canton (Guangzhou), specializing in agrarian issues. In 1926–27, he served as an advisor to the agrarian commission of the Guomindang, where he met the then relatively unknown Mao Zedong, at the time head of the peasant section of the Central Committee of the Communist Party of China. After the 1927 debacle, Ėrdberg/Tarkhanov fled with Borodin by car through the Gobi Desert, where he was wounded in the shoulder blade by a stray bullet. He took the Trotskyite position in the 1927–28 debates about China, and was excluded from the Party and exiled to Arkhangelsk, but he quickly recanted in 1928, was reinstated, and produced this book.

Tales of Modern China is ostensibly based on Ėrdberg's own experiences. Most chapters indicate the time as 1926–27, when the narrator, implied to be Ėrdberg, experienced the events described. But, of course, Ėrdberg was translating back from post-1927 in his recounting of his experiences. Fairly consistently, the "tales" attack the Guomindang, who are represented as corrupt, brutal, licentious, and ever-ready to form alliances with foreign capitalists, despite their claims to be anti-foreign and dedicated to the cause of national liberation. The tales also suggest that, at this pre-debacle time, lower-class Chinese recognized the falsehood of the Guomindang and preferred the communists and their independent organizations.

The book is highly constructed. Each of the tales has its narrative arc leading to a politically motivated conclusion, and the collection as a whole also has its own similar narrative arc. Somewhat as in *Tai Yang Awakens*, but here not in the story of one individual but in a generalized form, the book traces a progression to ever greater consciousness on the part of the lower-class Chinese. But the primary trope is not an awakening but rather a revolutionary spirit arising phoenix-like from the ashes of 1927.

To illustrate this trajectory, I will confine myself to discussing two stories from the collection; one is from early in the book, while the other is its last story (in the first edition).[44] The first of these two stories, "Around a Bowl of Rice" (*U vedra s risom*), allegedly records an incident of 9 July 1926. This story is set in a minor provincial town, where one evening the narrator finds workers gathered around a cauldron of rice. His interpreter translates for them a speech the narrator delivers, which was intended to instil in them a sense of international worker solidarity. But the listeners are sullen and resistant, preferring to cling to their misplaced faith in religious superstitions and a local capitalist entrepreneur. While the translator is speaking, the narrator has a vision of "millions of builders of the New China thronging together from their medieval towns that are encircled by silent [*glukhimi*] walls – our flags before them." "I saw columns of people," he reports, "rising up out of the mud, from disunity [*razobshchennosti*], from slavery, from the stench of the past."[45] One can note here elements to be found in standard Marxist-Leninist texts on Asiatics: medieval, slavery, rising up. But two particular and interrelated words in this passage – "wall" and "silent" – function as motifs with metaphorical resonance. They recur in most of these tales and are, in effect, Ėrdberg's own figurative renderings of concepts common to Marxist-Leninist discourse. The "wall" that encircles Chinese towns, at the time a realistic detail, figuratively condemns the Chinese to a medieval stage of development and also walls them off from what would lead to their own liberation. "Silent" is actually (my) inaccurate translation for the Russian word used, "*glukhoi*," which means deaf, impervious to sound: not only do the Chinese workers in "Around a Bowl of Rice" not "roar," they do not hear the sound of revolution, are sullen even. But "*glukhoi*" also has another meaning – remote, god-forsaken – comparable to Herder's "a nation thrust into a corner." And, of course, in this context it also means far from Moscow. The "*glukhoi*" wall of resistance that the narrator bemoans in "Around a Bowl of Rice" could be seen as a figure for what in fact happened in China in 1927; all the communist agitation of 1923–27 was to no avail.

The implication of the doomed fate of the revolution is countered as the collection progresses. This story establishes, if you will, the first stage on the Chinese masses' road to consciousness to be de facto charted over the course of the collection: with each new story, the Chinese emerge as successively more conscious. This approach is a reverse trajectory to the actual historical trajectory, which was to debacle. The crushing defeat of 1927 is not explicitly present but implicitly evoked when, in one entry, suddenly and without explanation, the narrator is no longer in coastal China but in Xi'an, and then, in the next, he is further away in the Gobi Desert; in other words, the last stories imply the rout of the Soviet advisors and their flight westward, as Èrdberg's Soviet readers, and quite likely his German readers as well, would have surmised.

The culminating story in Èrdberg's collection, "The Red Scarf" (*Krasnyi sharf*), datelined 2 December 1927 in Sharan-Sumè, that is, in the Gobi Desert, ostensibly recounts events from the narrator's flight back to the Soviet Union over the Gobi Desert, though once again he does not make the circumstances explicit. The group fleeing the debacle passes the Great Wall of China, which the ravages of time and weather have reduced to "piles of stones."[46] After that, the terrain becomes more and more barren until it is just sand, a metaphor for the 1927 debacle. "We were in the most god-forsaken [*glukhoi*] corner of the Gobi," the narrator reports.[47] The epithet "*glukhoi*," which has functioned throughout this book as a sign of the ignorance and backwardness of the Chinese often leading to their unresponsiveness, could be seen here as a metaphor for the revolutionary nadir. In this locale, the narrator recalls, there had been "mighty towns before which the world trembled." He elaborates: "Eight centuries ago under the Great Khan, Italian masters built fountains that disgorged wine, kumis, and sincera into silver pools – the height of luxury – but now the Mongol horsemen who inspired fear in the local farmers no longer terrorize [*trevozhat*] and the Great Wall is reduced to pitiful remnants."[48] All is buried under the sand.

The invocation of the great imperial conquerors provides an epic setting for the otherwise barren landscape and elevates the struggle of the Soviet envoys in China. The vast empty expanse of the desert also becomes a site where internationalism can be enacted without the hindrance of messy actuality.

The narrator catches a mirage-like glimpse on the horizon of a small group approaching from the opposite direction. When they arrive, it emerges that this group comprises Chinese students from KUTV and Sun Yat-sen University, who are returning to China to continue the revolutionary effort. The two groups exchange news from Moscow and China, mixing up as they do Chinese, English, and Russian words but "understand[ing] each other so well as if [they] had spent [their] lives together" – as if they had come from an ecumene.[49] For revolutionary internationalists, language is no barrier.

A red scarf from one of the Chinese flutters in the wind and seems to the narrator to be laughing "at the sands [of the Gobi Desert], under which are buried the great empires of the past, but which are powerless to hinder ... these youths from KUTV and [Sun Yat-sen University] from going to China and arousing millions of her sons." The two groups shake hands and proceed on, in opposite directions, one back to Soviet Russia, the other to China, and the narrator closes the text with a sublime vision of the sun setting over the "boundless ocean of sand ..." Ėrdberg's pregnant suspension points (a common technique in all these tales) leave open the possibility of a "boundless ocean" of revolutionary masses from all countries. In an earlier story, "Three principles of Mr. Kung," a title adopted to name the German translation of the tales, the narrator invokes a revolt to which there would be no end;[50] here the boundless spatial expanse matches the boundless temporal expanses of international revolution. The use of suspension points to imply a counterfactual triumph of the Chinese revolutionary movement was a common feature of the works discussed here, particularly of *Tai Yang erwacht*.

Here, also, we palpably sense the neo-imperialist element in these anti-imperialist tracts about China. Ėrdberg was, of course, a Soviet writer intent on establishing his fealty after a Trotskyite lapse, but one of the variables in representations of the Chinese revolution among the works I am treating is the extent to which the impetus for revolution is seen as coming from "Moscow." This viewpoint is true of Tret'iakov's *Roar, China!*, where an activist tells a disheartened Chinese that "there is such a country" where they make short work of imperialist oppressors.[51] In the finale of *Storm over Asia* as laid out in Osip Brik's original script, the galloping horsemen are headed for an idealized version of Moscow beckoning from afar.[52] Moreover, in an earlier scene of the finished film, the final words of a martyred partisan leader to his comrades gathered at his bier are "Listen to Moscow." However, the non-Soviet writers (other than Ėmi Xiao) tended to omit mention of "Moscow" or its emissaries; if there is a non-Chinese advisor among the characters, he is not Russian but more likely a generic Western European leftist – in *Tai Yang erwacht*, Peer is such a figure. Generally, where the characters have come from, why they are there, and what their leadership role is portrayed to be is somewhat murky, but the inclusion of such figures in the plots of works on the Chinese revolution could be seen as partial gestures in the direction of the mentor figure, who will assume a crucial function in full-blown socialist realist literature.

The technique of implying revolutionary triumph, but breaking the narrative off just before an encounter between revolutionary forces and agents of capitalist power reaches its crescendo, was also used in the most famous Chinese literary account of post-debacle China, Mao Dun's[53] highly popular novel *Midnight* (1933), which appeared in Russian as *Pered rassvetom* (Before the Dawn) with a title change meant to express the hope that in China a new day would dawn.[54] The novel ends at "midnight," the last moment before the world of Shanghai's capitalist class and that of the feudal landlords with it will, the text implies, come crashing down. The novel presents a panoramic account of China during the turbulent time around 1930 and has a very complicated plot involving large numbers of characters, most of whom are linked either by family connections or by a common workplace, commercial connections, or erotic liaisons (mistresses, concubines). As is perhaps already apparent, in writing this novel Mao Dun was inspired in part by Émile Zola's "encyclopedic treatment of social forces" in his series of twenty novels set in France's Second Empire, collectively known as *Les Rougon-Macquart*, which follows two branches of a family over five generations.[55] Zola had been important to many Chinese leftist writers of the interwar years; in fact, Èmi Xiao had taken on Èmi as his name from Zola's first name, Émile. Mao Dun's *Midnight* also provides an example of how members of the putative ecumene drew in their writings on a variety of influences, not just those emanating from Moscow; the prominence given to steamy sex in Dun's plot, for example, is closer to Zola's naturalism than to communist novelistic conventions.

Midnight treats not five, but three generations of one (Chinese) family. It focuses on the unravelling of the world of a leading Shanghai "captain of industry," Wu Sun-fu. Wu's family came from the provinces and some of them still live there, a plot device that enables Mao Dun to cover both the Chinese countryside and the city, to be as encyclopedic in one book as Zola was in twenty. Wu Sun-fu's father, old Mr. Wu, stands for the old China, which has been swept away in the turmoil. He had been full of reformist zeal in his youth, but now clings to a primer that served as a sort of bible for him, the *Supreme Book of Rewards and Punishments*. Fan Po-wen, Wu Sun-fu's cousin and a poet, says: "When he lived in the country, he existed like a mummy [shades of Herder]. The country was his grave in which he could decompose easily."[56] In this modern city of Shanghai, old Mr. Wu feels alienated and soon succumbs to a heart attack. Exit the old China.

Indigenous Chinese capitalism founders, too, ceded to the imperialists. The novel presents a number of patriotic Chinese industrialists who resist foreign capital and fight for an independent Chinese industry, but are ultimately forced by the impact of the Depression, the Chinese civil war, and strikes to ally with foreign capitalists, a common theme of European communist writing on China after 1927 (seen also in *Tai Yang erwacht* and in several of Ėrdberg's tales). In *Midnight*, this common theme is amplified with a wealth of detail, focused on the machinations of the stock exchange during these turbulent years, where Mao Dun's capitalist Chinese are embroiled in risky ventures involving selling short and selling long on the stock market. Mao Dun depicts a dog-eat-dog world, where individual investors are seeking to outsmart and destroy each other.

In the novel, the initial response of the local capitalists to their desperate situation is, predictably, to try to recoup their losses by squeezing their exploited workers ever harder: reducing wages, dismissing employees, and adding extra hours for no more pay. The result is widespread strikes and even a call for a general strike, which would deliver a coup de grâce to the Chinese owners' teetering factories. Their managers try to defuse the situation and circumvent the strike movement through cunning, using spies to identify communists and arrest them, and also through persuasion. Important, too, in the depiction of the factory milieu is the widespread dissatisfaction among the workers with the yellow trade unions, that is, nationalist-oriented trade unions founded by the Guomindang in 1927, which Mao Dun represents as allies of the capitalists. The workers in the novel want to form their own trade union, in other words, the "red," that is, communist, trade union, established by the Chinese Communist Party (CCP) in 1929, which in fact had trouble recruiting large numbers of members in those years.[57]

Though the capitalists are divided in the novel, the communists do not present an image of unity and solidarity either. As in Friedrich Wolf's *Tai Yang erwacht* and Anna Seghers's "1 Mai Yanschupou" (1932), the focus is on organizing strikes among female factory workers in silk factories. But Mao Dun, himself (like Ėmi Xiao) a political leader in the 1920s – an insider – presents a much more complex and less heroic account of that subject, including representations of internal conflicts in the communist movement.

In sections treating the strike movement, Mao Dun effectively airs the controversies over tactics debated within the CCP, the Bolshevik Party, and the Comintern that came to a head in 1930–31. In his treatment of this topic, Mao Dun essentially conflates the conflicts within the CCP (and vis-à-vis the Bolsheviks and the Comintern) about the correct action to take in the attempted "fourth uprising" of 1930 with the fateful Stalin/Trotsky polemic of 1927 concerning the reasons for the debacle of that year and the way forward for China. In late 1920s China, many communists subscribed to the view that appropriate moments for revolutionary action came in "waves." Thus the defeats of late 1927 were explained as being due to a "trough" between two revolutionary waves.[58] Stalin and the Comintern had originally supported the idea that a new revolutionary tide was coming in China and that the communists could initiate a "fourth uprising," but, after some initial successes, including the capture and brief occupation of Changsha, a move encouraged by the Comintern, they began to contemplate the consequences of failure and advised delay. Nevertheless, the impulsive head of the CCP, Li Li-san, became impatient and sent the Chinese Red Army into action. When the new military efforts resulted in another debacle, the Executive Committee of the Comintern sent a letter to the CCP; at an urgent meeting of its Central Committee held on 23–26 November 1930, Li Li-san was dismissed from his posts and summoned to Moscow to answer for his errors.

This disagreement has some similarities with the acrimonious exchange between Stalin and Trotsky of 1927. Stalin's "Questions of the Chinese Revolution," in response to the 1927 debacle and to Trotsky's attacks on his position, argued that "[the Trotskyite opposition] does not realize that the revolution in China cannot develop at a fast pace ... The opposition demands the immediate formation of Soviets of workers', peasants' and soldiers' deputies in China ... [but] they cannot be formed at any moment – they are formed only when the tide of revolution is running high [*period osobogo pod"ema revoliutstionnykh voln*]."[59]

These two controversies, which were played out at the highest levels of the two communist parties and the Comintern, are, in effect, echoed in *Midnight* in the much smaller arena of a disagreement about organizing a general strike among factory workers in Shanghai (such a strike would constitute, in its own way, the officially sought "fourth uprising"). A version of the "fourth uprising" was, essentially, also the subject of Wolf's *Tai Yang erwacht* and Seghers's "1 Mai Yanschupou," but the divisions within the movement in these texts are muted. Mao Dun's account of the strike meetings focuses on these divisions but conflates the Li Li-san position with that of Trotsky. In a climactic strike meeting, a young female Party organizer who has come to oversee the meeting, Tsai Chen, is said to be from a wealthy background and "dressed like one of the girls from the silk factory, but her sophisticated expression and manner proclaim her to be an intellectual" and therefore, by the codes of the day, a Trotskyite; true to that role, she turns off some of her colleagues with her "formulas" and "jargon." Tsai is impatient for a general strike to break out immediately. She mouths the Li Li-san line about the "tide" of revolution being high, thus demanding revolutionary action, and reprimands those who advocate more caution and more preparation, saying: "You're wrong! ... You're disregarding the fighting spirit of the masses at a time when the tide of the revolution is in full flood ... You're taking a rightist view of things!" A humbler participant in the discussion, Ma Chin, disagrees with Tsai. She feels there are flaws in Tsai Chen's "formula," but "with her scanty knowledge and experience she is unable to explain just where [and it is] not in her nature to make hasty statements." "You're forgetting our general line," she responds. Another colleague in the Party objects that a general strike could never be organized in one night, given that their organization among workers has been "completely wrecked." She asks for a day's delay to organize the strikers properly, but Tsai rejects the request, branding that position with Lenin's negative term "tailism" (*khvostizm*) – lagging behind – which Trotsky invoked in 1927 to denigrate Stalin's China policies.[60] Then Tsai and other Party officials hurry off to further meetings, as if indifferent to the fact that they are probably condemning the silk-worker lambs to needless slaughter.

Mao Dun has, then, conflated two moments (and two arguments) in the history of communist revolution in China and controversies over it in the CCP, the Comintern, and the Bolshevik Party. He has translated major historical events into fictional form, recast the actors in them from the major realm to the minor and local, and distilled all the specific details of the historical events into a mini-plot.

During the debate over when the silk workers should strike, Su Lun, one of the participants, is sympathetic to the more cautious Ma. She points out: "While Tsai Chen deals in theories ... Ma Chin bases herself on facts. And facts are the one thing we shouldn't ignore." This exchange has relevance not only to the clashes over China policy between Stalin and Trotsky or the CCP and the Comintern, but also to the whole issue of a Comintern aesthetic. A central issue of debates within the leftist literary world at this time was over whether literary works should privilege "facts." In early 1930s Germany, a heated argument was taking place among leftists, centred on two articles published in *Die Link-skurve* in 1931 and 1933 by Georg Lukács. The argument pertained to central concerns of leftist writers in those years and attracted the attention of the editors of the Moscow Comintern-affiliated journal *Internatsional'naia literatura*, which printed the Lukács articles and some responses. Though Lukács did not attack Brecht directly, the articles were effectively aimed at him and his associates in the German leftist avant-garde who advocated alternative approaches to conventional "realism."[61] In a series of 1930s essays, Lukács argued against giving priority to facts, or "details," in literary works, essentially because they threatened to undermine any overarching, ideologically inflected and teleological structure – any master narrative. Mao Dun took a similar position. Though he tried to remain both faithful to the integrity of realistic details and "strictly empirical" in his depictions, he was also committed to being "ideological and analytical." As Marston Anderson stated in his book *Limits of Realism*, "Mao Dun labored, through both the scale and the artifice of his fiction, to reconcile the detail to the structure and the individual to history."[62]

Given the centrality of this literary debate among leftists of the ecumene in the years I am discussing, is it possible to talk about a Comintern aesthetic, per se? As has already been established, most of the German, Soviet, and Chinese writers treated here drew on sources that provided a wealth of empirical detail about the dreadful conditions in Shanghai's factories and the resultant uprisings.

But elements of some sort of embryonic master narrative were deployed by all the writers I mentioned, if in different ways.

Though Brecht was an unacknowledged target of the Lukács attack on the avant-garde fetish for facts, actually, in his main Chinese text of these years, his play (or more precisely oratorio) *The Measures Taken* (*Die Massnahme*, 1930), it could be said that he essentially veered over into allegory. Yet, Brecht also incorporated documentary material when the oratorio was performed. More specifically, and somewhat dialectically, he screened footage from a recent film about the Shanghai uprising, in all probability the Soviet director Iakov Bliokh's *Shanghai Document* (*Shankhaiskii document*, 1927), as a backdrop to what was taking place on stage, making the performance yet another example of Soviet/German cross fertilization (though a short-lived one, for the censors soon intervened).[63]

The Measures Taken was allegedly written partly under the influence of Lenin's essay "The Infantile Disease of Leftism" (1920), published in volume 25 of a German edition of Lenin's works, which came out in April 1930. Some of Lenin's phrases appear in the text without acknowledgement, though, since Brecht began work on his play in January 1930, this essay cannot have provided the initial impetus. "The Infantile Disease" sent a volley in Lenin's ongoing campaign against assorted communists and factions in Russia and Germany whose positions at various points he found heretical. However, in delivering the volley, Lenin made a strong statement about the need for Party hegemony, for "discipline," and for "*besposhchadnost*," a term that roughly means ruthlessness and mercilessness and, as such, is counterposed to human pity or empathy, two qualities decried in this work.

Unlike the other texts discussed here, *The Measures Taken* is not about Chinese revolutionaries, but about Europeans in China. In the opening scene, four "agitators" present themselves to a "Control Chorus" of the Party to account for their recent visit to Manchuria and report that they had been obliged to execute a "young comrade" whom they had recruited near the frontier to help them with their agitational work there. These decisions were the "measures taken"; for the rest of the play, the agitators proceed to justify the execution to the Control Chorus by recounting the events leading up to the killing in a narrative re-enactment, each agitator assuming in turn the role of the young comrade.

In the play, the agitators tell how, when they are about to cross into China, they each don a mask to disguise themselves as Chinese. Then, once their narrative brings them to Mukden (Shenyang, in Manchuria), they describe for the Control Chorus three incidents in which the young comrade is set a task by the agitators. In their eyes, he fails each time because he has not acted as an agent of the Party's will and in accordance with the guidelines set out in the "classics" (of Marxism-Leninism), but rather is moved by pity to intervene on behalf of the oppressed. The third of these incidents leads to a critical confrontation between the young comrade and the agitators. The young comrade argues that a general strike should be called, insisting: "The unemployed can wait no longer. Nor can I ... There are too many paupers." The agitators retort that "there are not enough fighters," and the workers, though growing in political consciousness, are ignorant of how many regiments the government has. On orders from the Party, the agitators have decided to postpone armed action until the delegates of the farmers' organizations have arrived in the city. The young comrade ignores their injunctions to "silence," takes off his mask, and shouts to all who can hear: "We have come to help you! We come from Moscow!" Without his mask, the young agitator is exposed. Someone shouts: "Foreigners! Throw the troublemakers out!" Locals begin to assemble for a strike but are unprotected. The agitators, sensing disaster, knock down the young comrade to silence him and then lift him up and leave the city in haste. They are pursued and have to take quick stock of the situation, concluding that they have no recourse but to kill the young comrade, "even if he does not agree," and destroy his body though "IT IS A FEARSOME THING TO KILL [emphasis Brecht's]." The young comrade does agree, responding with a curt, "Yes" and adding that they should put him "in the lime pit." After the agitators have shot him and thrown him into the pit, they return to their work, which is "successful" in spreading "the teachings of the classics." Or so the Control Chorus reports as they conclude the play with the words: "In yet another country the revolution advances. In another land the ranks of the fighters are joined. We agree with what you have done."[64] Again, the revolution is represented as triumphant here, as in most other texts of the time generated by leftists. In fact, this exchange bears comparison with the earlier described scene where advocates of immediate, "spontaneous struggle" argue with those who contend that the strikers must wait until the provisions to ensure a victorious outcome are in place.

I will not engage here the rightfulness of the extreme "measures taken," an issue that troubled many communists at the time and even the German Communist Party.[65] Later, Adorno weighed in as well, remarking that "what [Brecht] justified was not simply, as he long sincerely believed, an incomplete socialism, but a coercive domination in which blindly irrational social forces returned to work once again ... The wild roar of *The Measures Taken* drowns out the noise of the disaster that has overtaken the cause, which Brecht convulsively tries to claim as salvation" – the "disaster" obscured by the "roar" being, in this case, not the debacle of Shanghai in 1927 but what has happened to Marxism at the hands of the Soviet leadership.[66] More germane here, however, is an idiosyncratic feature of the play, the characters' donning of masks. The group put on masks when they cross the border. At that point they are instructed: "You are not Karl Schmitt from Berlin, you are not Anna Kjersk from Kazan, and you are not Peter Sawitch from Moscow. One and all of you are nameless and motherless, blank pages on which the revolution writes its instructions."[67] In a sense, then, there is no death, only an imperfect text which has to be "edited."

The mask's ostensible purpose is functional. The masks are to obliterate ethnic particularity enabling the wearers to blend in with the Chinese. As the head of the Party headquarters at the border says: "From this hour on ... You are unknown workers, fighters, Chinese, born of Chinese mothers, with yellow skins and speaking Chinese in fever and in sleep."[68] Seemingly, the dichotomy of self and mask has been resolved in that, even in states when one might most forget oneself and reveal one's identity (in sleep or in a fever), the mask stays firmly on.

With their masks on, the small group expand the range of their already mixed national identity (German and Russian), suggesting the possibility of a transnational Party and, hence, also a transnational, or even universal, cultural system, something that many in the Russian and German leftist avant-gardes had long sought. The agitators acquire a transnational identity as they cross a border, but, arguably, that border is both actual and metaphoric. Here we see an instance of the phenomenon where the national and the international are not distinct but imbricated with each other. Masking entails assuming a transnational identity, but also means absolute allegiance to a particular country. At the point when the agitators put on their masks, they do not so much become Chinese as opt for *total* commitment to the Soviet model.

By masking, as the agitators transcend their individual selves, they also accept a simplification of the world. In that sense, the play could be read as a parable about subsuming the self to the master narrative. While Brecht's work ostensibly poses the question as to whether the Party should use extreme measures against the well-intentioned and loyal Party member, it is also, on a more metalevel, about using "extreme measures" in representation. The mask in the play is both a thematic and an aesthetic strategy. The two (form and content, or aesthetics and politics) are for Brecht not distinct, as Benjamin argued in "The Author as Producer."[69] Politics and aesthetics are intertwined, not just at the crude level of "repression" (of art by the state). The mask is an artifice that facilitates a non-realistic narrative. Realistically, the agitators would not have been taken for Chinese merely because they were wearing Chinese masks. Thus, at the point when they cross the border and put on their masks, the drama leaves realism behind (the agitators are suddenly able to speak Chinese, a version of speaking in tongues) and crosses into a highly stylized theatrical tradition (Brecht drew from the Japanese tradition of Noh drama).

In donning their masks, the characters also lose their national identities. But, in actuality, Brecht himself did not lose sight of his own in writing this play. It was ostensibly about China, and no doubt that was the case to some degree; part of the background to the play's composition was the stint in China that Gerhart Eisler, brother of the composer for *The Measures Taken*, Hanns Eisler, had undertaken in November 1929 when he was sent under cover from Moscow to Mukden and Shanghai to work on the reorganization of the CCP (Germans had easier access to China at this time than Soviet citizens).[70] But, at the same time, Brecht was using "China" here as a place to go to comment on the organization of an attempted revolutionary uprising in Saxony.[71] Friedrich Wolf, similarly, has explained that, in *Tai Yang erwacht*, he had written a play about revolution in China rather than Germany partly because, at that time, it had become impossible to represent German revolution directly, but he wanted the play's heroine to be taken as an example by oppressed Germans.[72] The national and local converges with the international. Another symptom of this convergence can be seen with the first German production in Frankfurt of *Roar, China!*, which premiered on 9 November 1929, the tenth anniversary of the ill-fated German revolution of 1919. Are distinctions lost in such convergence? When, in Ėrdberg's "Around a Bowl of Rice," the Korean Pando translates the narrator's speech about the brotherhood of revolutionary internationalism to a group of workers who are impervious to its message – "sullen" – readers must ask themselves whether a foreigner speaking a bookish Chinese (Mandarin) could, in any case, reach uneducated, provincial Chinese who in all probability speak a dialect. The limits of translation, unacknowledged here, plagued the would-be ecumene, as did the mandate to translate.

The masking of the characters in *The Measures Taken* could be read as being about adopting a unitary belief system and common "language" in a polyglot society. This interpretation seems surprising given that, while Brecht was a Marxist materialist, he was opposed to anything that whiffed of reified dogma. The mask of Marxism-Leninism, itself a simplification of the original Marxism, would obscure life's complexity, its eddies and flows. But there are several ways in which this oratorio should be seen as open-ended rather than monologic. Though the summary execution of the young comrade in *The Measures Taken* is endorsed by the higher Party authority represented by the Control Chorus, the countervailing position remains on the table because of the presence of dialogue as a central animating principle for the play. Brecht regarded the text as unfinished and looked to his worker participants to critique it at each rehearsal, so it was always in the process of being written. Even after the oratorio premiered, he refused to regard the text as final. Symptomatically, the play's songs are peppered with question marks, and "discussion" is the title of several of the play's scenes.

Were all to have donned the mask, were all differences of "language" to have been obliterated, and so on, a cultural-cum-political ecumene of sorts would have been achieved, but not a very ecumenical one. In practice, as this chapter has shown, rather than follow a single "master narrative" throughout their works on China, the cultural producers discussed here deployed intermittently versions of a common set of tropes and plot functions derived from Marxist-Leninist, Stalinist, or Comintern discourse. But the translation was not literal.

NOTES

1 All the translations into English throughout the chapter are my own unless an English edition is cited.

2 Kris Manjapra, "Communist Internationalism and Transcolonial Recognition," in *Cosmopolitan Thought Zones: South Asia and the Global Circulation of Ideas*, ed. Sugata Bose and Kris Manjapra (London: Palgrave Macmillan, 2010), 172, 159.

3 Manjapra, "Communist Internationalism and Transcolonial Recognition."

4 Katerina Clark, "Indian Leftist Writers of the 1930s Maneuver between India, London and Moscow: The Case of Mulk Raj Anand and His Patron Ralph Fox," *Kritika* 18, no. 1 (Winter 2017): 63–87.

5 Glyn Salton-Cox, "Cobbett and the Comintern: Transnational Provincialism and Revolutionary Desire from the Popular Front to the New Left" (PhD diss., Yale University, 2013), 3.

6 Saime Göksu and Edward Timms, *Romantic Communist: The Life and Work of Nazım Hikmet* (London: Hurst & Co., 1999).

7 Wang Zhengming, *Xiao San Zhuan* (Chengdu: Sichuan wen yi chu ban she, 1985), 222, cited in Weijia Li, *China und China-Erfahrung in Leben und Werk von Anna Seghers* (Bern: Peter Lang, 2010), 70–1.

8 Most of my biographical information on Xiao comes from the Russian State Archive of Socio-Political History (RGASPI) F 495 op 225 d 96, ll, 58–65, 90, 111–23.

9 Zhengming, *Xiao San Zhuan*, 244, cited in Weijia, *China und China-Erfahrung*, 170.

10 Karl Schlögel, *Berlin Ostbahnhof Europas. Russen und Deutsche in ihrem Jahrhundert* (Berlin: Siedler, 1998).

11 Edwin Gentzler and Maria Tymoczko, eds., *Translation and Power* (Amherst: University of Massachusetts Press, 2002), xxi.

12 Antoinette Burton and Isabel Hofmeyr, "Introduction: The Spine of Empire? Books and the Making of an Imperial Commons," in *Ten Books That Shaped the British Empire: Creating an Imperial Commons*, ed. Antoinette Burton and Isabel Hofmeyr (Durham, NC: Duke University Press, 2014), 23.

13 For example, Èmi Xiao, "Zadachi kitaiskoi revoliutsionnoi literatury. K plenumu Mezhdunarodnogo biuro revoliutsionoi literatury," *Literaturnaia gazeta*, no. 48 (19 October 1930): 1 (Xiao's address to the Plenum of the International Bureau of Revolutionary Literature [IBRL or MBRL] in October 1930, a warm-up to the Kharkov conference).

14 Ruth Price, *Lives of Agnes Smedley* (New York: Oxford University Press, 2005).

15 Weijia, *China und China-Erfahrung*, 69–70, 81.

16 Egon Erwin Kisch, *Egon Kisch berichtet: China geheim* (Berlin: E. Reiss, 1933); published later as *China geheim* (Berlin: Aufbau-Verlag, 1950); in Russian as *Razoblachënnyi Kitai*, trans. Vera Gurvich (Moscow: Gos. izd. khud. Lit., 1934); in English as *Secret China* (London: John Lane, 1935).

17 Cecil L'Estrange Malone, *Das neue China und seine sozialen Kämpfe* (Berlin: Allg. Dt. Gewerkschaftsbund, 1928).

18 An important partial exception would be the collection of short works on China: Oskar Ėrdberg, *Kitaiskie novelly* (Moscow: Molodaia gvardiia, 1929); see discussion on this work later in the text.

19 Some have said that Oshirov spent some time in the diplomatic mission in China, but I have been unable to find corroboration on that.

20 Willard Sunderland, *The Baron's Cloak: A History of the Russian Empire in War and Revolution* (Ithaca, NY: Cornell University Press, 2014).

21 *Storm over Asia* received a prize at the First International Film Festival in Moscow in 1935 and was screened at the Paris World's Fair in 1937. Actually, however, the actor who played the central character, Bair, defected with his family to Paris in 1930, and his name was struck from the credits. They were reinstated only in 1985 when the film was re-edited and given sound.

22 A.F., "Sovetskaia p'esa za rubezhom. 'Rychi Kitai!' v Evrope, Amerike i Azii," *Literatura mirovoi revoliutsii*, no. 4 (1932): 125–7 (A.F. is probably Aleksandr Fevral'skii, a great enthusiast for the Meyerhold theater and, consequently, the success he reported for the play may be exaggerated); Benno Reisenberg, "'Brülle China,'" *Frankfurter Zeitung*, 11 November 1929, evening edition; Walter J. Meserve and Ruth I. Meserve, "The Stage History of *Roar China!*: Documentary Drama as Propaganda," *Theatre Survey* 21 (1980): 1–13; Ėmi Xiao, "Literatura kitaiskoi revoliutsii," *Internatsional'naia literatura*, nos. 3–4 (1934): 334.

23 State Archive of the Russian Federation (GARF) F 5283 op 4 (Turtsiia), e/kh 55, l.57, l.58.

24 Iakov Bliokh's film *Shanghai Document* (*Shanghaiskii document*), filmed in 1927 and released in 1928, opens with scenes of coolies but, in the second half, which covers the debacle, foregrounds industrial workers. Space constraints do not permit me to cover this text.

25 Sergei Tret'iakov, *Roar China, an Episode in Nine Scenes*, trans. F. Polianovska and Barbara Nixon (New York: International Publishers, 1931), 86–9.

26 Anna Seghers, "1 Mai Yanschupou," *Rote Fahne* 14, no. 94 (1 May 1932).

27 Friedrich Wolf, "Tai Yang erwacht. Ein Schauspiel," in *Gesammelte Werke in sechzehn Bänden*, vol. 3, *Dramen* (Berlin: Aufbau Verlag, 1960), 163.

28 Wolf, "Tai Yang erwacht," 113.

29 Fridrikh Vol'f, "Slovo pered zanavesom," *Literatura mirovoi revoliutsii*, no. 5–6 (1931): 161–2.

30 Manifesto of the Congress of the Peoples of the East in Baku (1920), https://www.marxists.org/history/international/comintern/baku/manifesto.htm; originally published in *Kommunist international*, no. 15 (December 1920).

31 Wolf, "Tai Yang erwacht," 112.

32 Karl August Wittfogel, *Das erwachende China. Ein Abriss der Geschichte und der gegenwärtigen Probleme Chinas* (Vienna: Agis-Verlag, 1926). Also K.A. Wittfogel,

Shanghai-Kanton (Berlin: Vereinigung Internationale Verlags-Anstalten, 1927); K.A. Vittfogel, *Probuzhdaiushchiisia Kitai*, trans. D. Strashunskii (Leningrad: Priboi, 1926).

33 K. Wittfogel, "Chinas Bewässerungssystem," *Rote Fahne*, 7 May 1927.

34 For example, *Diskussiia ob aziatskom sposobe proizvodstva po dokladu M. Godesa*, Obshchestvo marksistov-vostokovedov pri leningradskom otdelenii kommunisticheskoi akademii i Leningradskom vostochnom institute im. A. Enukidze (Moscow: Gos. sotsial'no-ėkonomicheskoe izdatel'stvo, 1931).

35 Burton and Hofmeyr, "Introduction: The Spine of Empire? Books and the Making of an Imperial Commons," 23.

36 Johann Gottfried von Herder, *Outlines of a Philosophy of History of Man*, trans. T. Churchill (New York: Bergman Publishers; first published London, 1800), 296, 298; Johann Gottfried Herder, *Ideen zur Philosophie der Geschichte der Menschheit*, Band 2 (Berlin and Weimar: Aufbau Verlag, 1965), 17, 20.

37 Georg Wilhelm Friedrich Hegel, *The Philosophy of History*, Part I, *The Oriental World*, trans. J. Sibree (New York, Dover Publications, 1956), 116, 124, 131–2, 138.

38 Karl Marx, "Chinese Affairs, *Die Presse*, 7 July 1862.

39 Karl Marx, "Revolution in China and in Europe," *New York Daily Tribune*, 14 June 1853.

40 V.I. Lenin, "Obnovlënnyi Kitai," in *Polnoe sobranie sochinenii*, vol. 22 (Moscow: Institut marksizma-leninizma pri TsK KPSS, 1958), 189.

41 V.I. Lenin, "Probuzhdenie Azii," *Pravda*, 7 May 1913.

42 V.I. Lenin, "Doklad na 2-om vserossiiskkom s"ezde kommunisticheskikh organizatsii narodov Vostoka," 20 December 1919, reprinted in V.I. Lenin, *Polnoe sobranie sochinenii*, tom 39, iun'-dek 1919 g (Moscow: Politizdat, 1970), 330.

43 Ėrdberg, *Kitaiskie novelly*; Oskar Sergeevič Ėrdberg, *Die drei Grundsätze des Mister Kung, u.a. chinesische Novellen* (Vienna, Berlin: Verlag f. Literatur u. Politik, 1932).

44 Later Russian and English editions of 1932 end with "The Precious Stone," which has the dateline Kazan, 1928; this story stresses the multicultural aspect of the Soviet Union, claiming even that the Volga is not a Russian river: "[the area] where the Volga flows is inhabited by Tatars, Mari, Mordvinians, and Chuvashians." Oskar Ėrdberg, *Tales of Modern China* (Moscow: Co-operative Publishing Society of Foreign Workers, 1932), 179–90, quotation at 189.

45 Ėrdberg, *Kitaiskie novelly*, 28.

46 Ibid., 154.

47 Ibid., 155.

48 Ibid.

49 Ibid., 159.

50 Ibid., 110.

51 S. Tret'iakov, *Rychi, Kitai sobytie v 9-i zven'iakh* (Moscow-Leningrad: Gos. Izd., 1930), 40.

52 A. Karaganov, *Vsevolod Pudovkin* (Moscow: Iskusstvo, 1973), 95.

53 Mao Dun (or Mao Tun) was the pseudonym of Shen Dehong. His publications in Russian include the following: Mao Dun, "Kitaiskoi steny net mezhdu nami" (pered s"ezdom pisatelei), *Pravda*, 25 July 1934; *Kolebaniia roman*, trans. S. Sin, ed. Vasiliev and V.G. Rudman (Leningrad: Goslitizdat, 1935).

54 V.I. Rudman and Kho Fu, "Tvorcheskii put' Mao Dunia" in *Pered rassvetom* by Mao Dun, roman, perevod s kitaiskogo Kho Fu i V.I. Rudman (Leningrad: GIKhL, 1937), 61; see also Mao Dun, "Miatezh (glava iz romana Rassvet)," trans. Pukhov, *Internatsional'naia Literatura*, no 5 (1935).

55 Marián Gálik, *Mao Tun and Modern Chinese Literary Criticism* (Wiesbaden: Franz Steiner Verlag GMBH, 1969), 37; Marston Anderson, *The Limits of Realism: Chinese Fiction in the Revolutionary Period* (Berkeley: University of California Press, 1990), 42, 127.

56 Mao Tun, *Midnight*, trans. Hsu Meng-hsiung and corrected A.C. Barnes (Peking: Foreign Language Press, 1957), 31.

57 Weijia Li, *China und China-Erfahrung*, 87.

58 See also I. Stalin, "Voprosy kitaiskoi revoliutsii (tezisy t. Stalina dlia propagandistov, odobrënnye TsK VKP(b)," *Pravda*, 21 April 1927; Leon Trotsky, *Problems of the Chinese Revolution*, with a new foreword by Max Shachtman (Ann Arbor: University of Michigan Press, 1967), 29 .

59 Stalin, "Voprosy kitaiskoi revoliutsii" *Pravda*, 21 April 1927, 3.

60 Leon Trotsky, "The Chinese Revolution and the Theses of Comrade Stalin," 17 May 1927, reprinted in *Problems of the Chinese Revolution*, 17; "tailism" (*khvostizm*) is a term coined by Lenin. He first used it to describe the "Economists," those who argued that the Communist Party should not take the lead in a revolutionary situation, but should allow economic events – crises, strikes, unrest – to unfold on their own. The Party would then pick up on the tail of these events. Lenin insisted that, since the Party was the vanguard, it should lead.

61 Georg Lukács, "Willi Bredels Romane," *Die Linkskurve*, no. 11 (November 1931): 23–7; "Germanskaia proletarskaia kritika o romanakh Villi Bredelia," *Literatura mirovoi revoliutsii*, no. 2 (1932): 107–10; Georg Lukach, "Reportazh ili obrazotvorchestvo? Kriticheskie zamechaniia po povodu romana Otval'ta" and Ernst Otval't, "Roman fakta (otvet Georgu Lukachu)," *Internatsional'naia literatura*, no. 2 (1933): 91–104, 105–9, respectively.

62 Anderson, *Limits of Realism*, 128, 150.

63 "Die Zensurmaschine arbeitet. Filmzenen in 'Tai Yang' verboten," *Berlin am Morgen*, 20 January 1931.

64 Bertolt Brecht, *Die Massnahme: Zwei Fassungen, Anmerkungen* (Frankfurt am Main: Suhrkamp, 1998), parallel 1930 and 1931 versions, 65–85; Bertolt Brecht, "The Measures Taken" in *The Jewish Wife and Other Short Plays by Bertolt Brecht*, trans. Eric Bentley (New York: Grove Weidenfeld, 1992), 99–102, 106–8.

65 For example, Alfred Kurella, "'Vysshie mery' Bert Brekhta, *Literatura mirovoi revoliutsii*, no. 1 (1932): 70.

66 Theodor Adorno, "Commitment," in *Theodor Adorno, Walter Benjamin, Ernst Bloch, Bertolt Brecht, Georg Lukács, Aesthetics and Politics* (London: Verso, 1977), 187.

67 Brecht, *Massnahme*, 18–21; "The Measures Taken," 81–2.

68 Brecht, *Massnahme*, 20–1; "The Measures Taken," 82.

69 Walter Benjamin, "The Author as Producer," in *Selected Writings*, vol. 2, *1927–1934*, trans. Rodney Livingston et al. (Cambridge, MA: Belknap Press of Harvard University Press, 1999), 769–70.

70 Jost Hermand, "Unvorhersehbare Folgen: Die drei Eislers und Brechts 'Massnahme,'" *Brecht Jahrbuch*, no. 30 (Madison: University of Wisconsin, 2005), 365.

71 Alfred Kurella, "'Vysshie mery' Bert Brekhta," *Literatura mirovoi revoliutsii*, no. 1 (1932): 70.

72 Friedrich Wolf, "Weshalb schrieb ich 'Tai Yang erwacht'?" in *Aufsätze über Theater* (Berlin: Aufbau Verlag, 1957), 370.

Chapter Three

India–England–Russia: The Comintern Translated

SNEHAL SHINGAVI
UT Austin

The issue of Comintern aesthetics grows more vexed the farther one moves away from those countries in or which became the Second World.[1] This situation is not because the influence of the Comintern over activists, artists, and parties was any less profound, but rather because the lack of state patronage for an official style meant that artists were able to shift much more rapidly between stylistic and aesthetic choices (sometimes in search of other sources of patronage). Artists working within the parameters of an official state style were innovative and important, but artists in other parts of the world, especially the colonial countries, were at the intersection of various kinds of intellectual, political, and aesthetic commitments. Moreover, new research about the Comintern has demonstrated convincingly that "notwithstanding the overarching Soviet domination [of the Comintern], the national sections did enjoy a certain degree of relative autonomy."[2] In India, for instance, there were clearly artists who were connected to the Communist Party and worked very closely with the literary movement, which was most closely associated with (though not run by) the Party, but, even then, those writers were influenced by more than just that movement.[3] More confoundingly, since the Comintern had no official aesthetic policy, disaggregating one literary form from others becomes a more difficult proposition.

Even though by the 1920s the Comintern had directed "European Communists to work among colonial emigres and migrants in the metropole," and individual émigrés like Shapurji Saklatvala and R. Palme Dutt, who joined the Communist Party, inspired other Indians to do the same, the work was necessarily uneven,[4] and aesthetics were not always a priority. The resulting picture is not one in which the Comintern was irrelevant or Soviet policy towards the arts was not meaningful, but one in which the aesthetic and political notions put forward through various organs of the Communist Party were translated, reinterpreted, reimagined, and refigured.[5] The translational problem is all the more important given that the idea of the Comintern was not monolithic. To put this matter as sharply as possible, the Comintern had two poles – solidarity and obedience (masked by the two slogans "communist internationalism" and "socialism in one country") – which were uneasily in tension by the time of the Fifth Congress of the Comintern; the aesthetic movements inspired by international communism varied sharply as a result. Added to this problem is the fact that parties affiliated to and individuals influential within the Comintern were subject to change from congress to congress, as purges and dismissals based on the needs of the Soviet Union's shifting foreign policy became routine. Relying on formal affiliation to the Comintern, then, produces an incomplete and inadequate picture of the range of literary movements and artists who were drawn into the orbit of communist internationalism (rather than the more narrowly defined Comintern) and who travelled throughout the world in order to discuss, debate, and disseminate their own ideas and work. Writers and artists from countries that were still undergoing anti-colonial processes of their own were exemplary of this problem of multiplied affiliation, since the Comintern changed its approaches to the colonial question repeatedly in the interwar and Cold War periods.[6] The resulting picture is not one of a hub-and-spokes model, where the ideas of the Comintern or of Soviet literary critics were simply regurgitated as they radiated outwards from the Muscovite centre, but one of collaboration, critique, compromise, and, most importantly, co-constitution.[7] The Indian case, perhaps, allows us to consider the possibility of not merely critiquing the notion of an official Comintern style but also the idea of any modernist aesthetic at all. Unless we understand aesthetics to mean patterns of patronage, there is no singular modernist style, even if there is a singular modernity.[8]

At the same time, there is no doubt that the period from 1917 until the Second World War inspired Indians (both in London and in British India) to take communism more seriously.[9] The success of the Russian Revolution had certainly made the issue of international socialism feel like an imminent possibility. At the same time, the growth of labour militancy in the metropolis as well as in British India added to the feeling that the prospects for revolution were not fanciful. Between 1923 and 1926 (following the General Strike), the membership of the Communist Party of Great Britain (CPGB) nearly tripled.[10] In India, general strikes in Bombay led by the textile workers shut down the city in both 1919 and 1920. Between 1921 and 1926, there were 1,282 strikes in British India, with more than two million workers participating.[11] At the same time, the Communist Party of India (CPI) was not a dominant force in these actions or through much of the independence struggle.[12] The CPI was initially formed in Tashkent in 1920 by M.N. Roy along with several Indian émigrés in the Soviet Union.[13] It was not until 1925 that the CPI established itself in India proper. Shapurji Saklatvala, British MP and member of the CPGB, made his first trip to India to visit Indian communists only in 1927.[14] As a result, the Comintern had few direct connections with communist organizations in British India. Rather, the Comintern had to rely on the deeper connections between the CPGB, Indian leftists in England, and the fledgling communist movement in India in order to advance its policies on the colonial question and to direct the labour movement in India.[15] As Sobhanlal Datta Gupta has noted, "the CPGB [was] the most important mediating factor between the CPI and the Comintern from the mid-1920s to the 40s," acting "as the CPI's guardian, if not, at times, its surrogate, in the Comintern."[16]

In 1935, Mulk Raj Anand, Muhammad Din Taseer, and the communists Jyoti Ghosh, Pramod Sen Gupta, and Sajjad Zaheer met in London to draft what would later become the Manifesto of the All-India Progressive Writers' Association (AIPWA). In part, this meeting was a direct result of the participation of Indian writers in the 1935 Paris Congress for the Defence of Culture, an anti-fascist meeting in which several of the key tenets of socialist realism would be defended, but where close contacts would be made between Indian writers and committed (communist) writers from the European continent. The London meeting was the culmination of decades of collaboration and translation between Indian and Russian writers, beginning with Tolstoy (who corresponded with a number of Indian writers about Indian politics) and Maxim Gorky (whose novel *Mother* was smuggled into British India).[17] By this point, too, the Russian Communist Party had already begun an extensive translation project (under the direction of Anatoly Lunacharsky and Maxim Gorky) to translate "Oriental literature" into Russian, though this program had dwindled by 1925 due to a lack of translators.[18] The meeting was also the result of deep collaboration between several members of the group and the CPGB and a few of its reading groups, in which Indian students in London would have had access to Russian literature in English translation.

Zaheer, in particular, went back to India and used his contacts to help knit a network of writers together around the manifesto, but also in response to the British censorship of a controversial Urdu short-story collection, *Angaaray* (1935).[19] In April 1936, while India was still under British rule, the AIPWA held its inaugural conference in Lucknow.[20] The meeting was designed to bring together writers to defend artistic freedoms against the twinned challenges of colonial censorship and religious orthodoxy. As Katerina Clark has observed: "The association was the Indian iteration of a series of Moscow-oriented writers' organizations that sprang up in different countries during these years, partly in response to the 1935 Paris Congress, which had founded the Association internationale des écrivains pour la défense de la culture, with which IPWA [AIPWA] voted to become affiliated."[21] But the goals of the AIPWA went beyond free speech issues to embrace a wide range of social and political concerns.[22] The Manifesto of the All-India Progressive Writers' Association read, in part:

1. It is the duty of Indian writers to give expression to the changes in Indian life and to assist the spirit of progress in the country by introducing scientific rationalism in literature. They should undertake to develop an attitude of literary criticism which will discourage the general reactionary and revivalist tendencies on questions like family, religion, sex, war and society, and to combat literary trends reflecting communalism, racial antagonism, sexual libertinism, and exploitation of man by man.

2. It is the object of our association to rescue literature from the conservative classes – to bring the arts into the closest touch with the people ...

3. We believe that the new literature of India must deal with the basic problems of our existence today – the problems of hunger and poverty, social backwardness and political subjection.

4. All that arouses in us the critical spirit, which examines customs and institutions in the light of reason, which helps us to act, to organize ourselves, to transform, we accept as progressive.[23]

The manifesto was not only responding to the heady spirit of the agitations for India's independence, but also attempting to redirect India's future towards a wide range of concerns: social redistribution, gender equality, scientific rationality, and political reform.[24] While initially dominated by Urdu writers, the linguistic orbit of the association was vast: "almost no contemporaneous Indian writer in any language, including English, would remain unaffected by its reach;"[25] though, it bears underlining, few anglophone Indian writers were members of the AIPWA for very long. The Progressive Writers' Movement grew over the next decades to become the most important and largest literary movement in South Asia's history. Even at this early stage, the movement's emphasis (as the AIPWA Manifesto put it) on "bring[ing] arts into the closest touch with the people and [making] them the vital organs which will register the actualities of life," and focusing on a population largely illiterate in the vernacular languages and nearly entirely incapable of reading in English, seemed to come very close to ideas held by Soviet artists.[26]

One of the reasons it is important to situate anglophone writing within the orbit of the communist-influenced All-India Progressive Writers' Association – even though it was not entirely determined by its gravitational pull – is because anglophone writers have been used as evidence in the partisan debates about AIPWA to demonstrate that the progressive movement deteriorated into a Party-controlled socialist realism; that the AIPWA's intolerance towards "art for art's sake" drove serious artists from its ranks.[27] Contrary to the critical consensus, Indian anglophone writing had its origins between the movements for a communist international and nationalist anti-colonialism. Anand's *Apology for Humanism* is usually read as an attempt to chart out a political course that is separate from progressivism and has given succor to critics who want to distinguish Anand from the formal left.[28] Ahmed Ali, who had an explicit falling-out with the leadership of AIPWA, especially Sajjad Zaheer (later head of the Communist Party of Pakistan), was explicit that the reason he left the movement was because the AIPWA was too tightly controlled by the agenda of the Communist Party of India: "The fanfare that accompanied the first All-India Progressive Writers' Association meeting in 1936 was largely political and stamped with a certain ideology ... When an open attempt was made in 1938–39 to give the movement a direct communist turn, the creative section moved away from it. Even Premchand would have done so had he been alive, for he was never a communist anyway, though he was progressive in the sense most of us understood the word."[29] In this view, communist involvement repelled rather than shaped Indian aesthetic developments.

Nevertheless, even before he broke from the AIPWA, Ahmed Ali made claims that were indistinguishable from the very ideologies he was criticizing: "The artist lives in society, and as its product he cannot escape tendencies which work in that society in that particular period. Feudalism has produced an aristocratic art, democracy a more popular one; capitalism now has produced an exclusive art expressing all despair and contradictions inherent in it; and side by side the proletariat has created and is creating an art of its own, which is more human and free from obscurity and contradiction."[30] As such, the impact of AIPWA on the thought and craft of the anglophone novelists of the period (as well as their centrality to the development of the AIPWA) is unmistakable, as is the political critique these novelists made against both British imperialism and comprador religious forces. Ahmed Ali and Mulk Raj Anand are considered two of the "founding fathers" of anglophone writing in India and were both involved in the earliest stages of organizing the AIPWA. Anand helped to pen the first draft of the manifesto, while Ahmed Ali helped to organize meetings in Lucknow. Anand's novels, *Untouchable* (1935) and *Coolie* (1936), both draw attention to the plight of young labourers and their exploitation by Hindu orthodoxy and colonial capitalism – although sometimes when writing about them Anand could be cagy about their politics.[31] Ahmed Ali's novel *Twilight in Delhi* (1940) documents the slow devastation suffered by Delhi's cultural establishment as British colonialism reorganized the city for its own imperial purposes. The poet Sarojini Naidu, who was also Gandhi's lieutenant during the Salt Satyagraha (1930), addressed several of the meetings of the AIPWA. And even though Bhabani Bhattacharya, Raja Rao, K.S. Venkataramani, and others never joined the AIPWA, it would not be difficult to demonstrate that their work, too, dealt with the same issues that the manifesto laid out.[32]

In these early years (roughly 1935–40), the definition of what it meant to be "progressive" was still in flux, and even though most took it as a "kind of euphemism for socialist realism," there were still many in the group who were committed to a politics of social justice but less convinced of the need to defer formal innovation.[33] However, as the movement developed, and it became more important for the Communist Party of India to exert influence in the AIPWA and use the association as its cultural arm, the AIPWA began to alienate writers who saw its doctrinaire approach to literary form unacceptable.[34] At the same time, writers who remained within the orbit of the AIPWA objected both to the accusation that theirs was not an innovative realist art and that their emphasis on social problems reduced their art to mere propaganda.[35] Part of the reason the scholarship on the All-India Progressive Writers' Association is so partisan has to do with the fact that the movement would undergo a number of splits, all of which produced different accounts of the association's history and its aesthetic contributions.[36] Moreover, as Meenakshi Mukherjee reports, the debates that started in the 1930s in the ranks of the AIPWA continued to inflect literary debates after independence as well:

> But opposition between those who used literature to highlight injustice and oppression, and the writers who focused on the predicament of the individual in a fragmented society, persisted for many decades to come. In fact the rift might have even grown wider over the years. Harish Trivedi has pointed out how in 1943 when *Tar Saptak* was published, Agyeya [Sacchidanand Hiranand Vatsyayan] and [Gajanan] Muktibodh could co-exist in the same volume; but in subsequent decades their admirers are in such sharply opposed camps that the importance of one can be claimed only by denying literary merit to the other.[37]

Anglophone writers, too, became partisans in these post-independence literary debates.

Mulk Raj Anand and Ahmed Ali are counted among the ranks of both the supporters and detractors of the AIPWA because of the changing nature of the category "progressive," which at this early stage was capacious enough to absorb both socialist realism and experimental modernism. Mulk Raj Anand's essay "On the Progressive Writers' Movement" and Ahmed Ali's "Progressive View of Art" are both included in Sudhi Pradhan's collection, *Marxist Cultural Movement in India*, but without any sense that this editorial decision was a controversial move. In his essay, Anand argues in defence of perhaps the most left-wing account of literary criticism (though it contains the germ of the terms that separated him from the later AIPWA):

> Lenin's occasional essays and notes on literature are examples of this method and the viewpoint behind them differs from the approach of the mere sociologist and of the dilettante critic, because, whereas the latter seems to conceive Marxist criticism as the answer to the question to what class a writer belongs, the former judges the artistic quality of a writer's work by relating it to the history of the time in which the writer lived, the conditions under which he worked, the social problems

that were pressing for solution during his life, the relationships of the classes of the time, and withal the depths of understanding of the writer and the intensity of his realization of the social reality of the time.[38]

Ali, too, begins his essay by talking about the beginnings of "proletarian" art in India, but then lays out the debate over what counted as "progressive":

At the very out-set I must point out that "progressive" should not be taken to be synonymous with revolutionary. It does, however, mean trying for the betterment of our social life. It implies the banishment of mysticism ... and all that which stands in our way of attaining freedom. It also means the acceptance of realism as a primary factor in the arts and literature ...

The word progressive, then, implies the consciousness of what we are, what we were, what we should or can be. It is dynamic in essence and stands for action. In order to appreciate it we must be conscious of our condition today: We are in the mire – we were not in the mire – how can we get out of the mire?[39]

Both of these essays contain terms that either the communist-affiliated wing of the AIPWA or those who left the AIPWA could find to support their positions. Anand's defence of Lenin's historical materialist reading practice is coupled with his belief that good writing and class allegiances may not work in the same direction. Ali's sense that "progressive" and "revolutionary" art were separate entities did not prevent him from endorsing socialist realism as the form that literature would need to take in the modern period. Also, at least one critic has suggested that, despite his later criticisms of the AIPWA as being too closely dominated by the Communist Party, Ali's early definitions of "progressive" were even more restrictive than the communists.[40] At a minimum, though, all critics are forced to acknowledge that Anand, Ali, and many of the anglophone writers of the period would have been considered progressives.[41]

At the same time, the intimate connection between progressive literature and socialist realism meant that the literature of the period continued to be treated as if it were aligned with Comintern aesthetic ideology. People closely affiliated with the Communist Party of India saw utopia as the unique monopoly of the socialist realist imagination. This position was more or less accepted by the AIPWA; literature should be directed towards the people, should lift their political spirits, and should show them the direction towards revolution and utopia. Those who had political disagreements either with the CPI or with this particular literary program were quickly called bourgeois renegades, a term that they then began to claim. The disagreements that Trotsky, Brecht, and Breton had with this particular vision for art while still being communists should reflect how politicized the aesthetics of utopia actually were[42] That not everyone holding this view of socialist realism was a card-carrying member of the

Communist Party should also reveal how socialist realism was not only politics but also a genre that provided a pathway to patronage. It should also be clear, then, that Indian modernists, at least at the early stages of both the *Nayi Kahani* (New Story) and the *Nayi Kavita* (New Poetry) movements in Hindi, were also committed socialists, just not always members of the Communist Party. Anglophone literature was remarkably free of these Party literature debates because of the idea that only vernacular literatures could reach the masses – so there was no one form or style that dominated anglophone literature from South Asia nor a theory that connected it to politics as such. Despite its liminal status, however, anglophone fiction and anglophone criticism were still important to the ways that debates about vernacular writing were conducted; even here, aesthetic and political ideas were constantly being shuttled back and forth in English.[43]

Additionally, there has been an implicit attempt to draw a line between form and content without recourse to history, meaning that, in most discussions of socialist and communist art, there is an assumption of politics inherent in the form. How did it come to be that South Asian realism was identified with communism and the left, and South Asian modernism was identified with anti-communism and the state? In Pakistan, in Urdu, this identification happened as a result of the close connection between the *Halqa-e-Arbab-e-Zauq* (the circle of the men of taste) and the state, which gave it patronage and resources; in India, in Hindi, it happened as a result of the heatedness of the debate between certain sections of the *Akhil Bharatiya Pragatisheel Lekhak Sangh* (AIPWA) and those who rejected their commitment to a certain pattern of socialist realism; and in English, in both nations, the dominant belief that the "people" spoke in the vernaculars meant that anglophone literature was freed from the responsibilities of programmatic partisanship or any consistent movement, especially since the dominant source of publishing was in the West. Important questions are therefore raised concerning what is meant by progressive literature and about the artists who may have been striving to produce it. In addition, what might happen to our picture of Indian and Pakistani literary history, as well as the history of modernism more generally, if we began to read texts differently? The partisan debates that were conducted in the mostly post-partition (1947) era presumed that form followed politics: the *ghazal* was necessarily decadent and feudal, experimentalism and modernism were uniquely bourgeois, and realism and plain-spokenness were requisite for a commitment to the people (defined usually as the peasantry, but written more for urban, educated middle-class readers). This categorization is not the result of a theoretical error but of the way that all critical debates between movements were carried out. In India, the debate between the AIPWA and the Hindi modernists used formal differences as stand-ins for political difference, which is to say that socialist realism was seen to be politics masquerading as literature, while modernism was seen as form without content. If, following Jameson, we periodize literature not according to the development of movements but according to the changes in the relations of production, it becomes much more obvious how debates between movements mask other more important ideological debates.

Bhisham Sahni, the important Hindi playwright and later head of the AIPWA, most forcefully makes this claim, namely that there was no way to distinguish between various kinds of generic differences at a certain level – which meant that politics and literary form could not be bound together or diagnostic of one another. Sahni describes how, in the post-independence milieu in Hindi literature, it became impossible to pin style down:

> The cultural circles began to change thus after independence. People began to leave Allahabad, which had been the center of Hindi literature ... This trend had an effect on the form and nature of literary activities. Various schools also fought with each other. The tendency to claim territory and plant a flag also increased. Previously, there was more naturalness to literary production. Afterwards, stories took ideologies on and began to propagate "movements" – "New Story," "Sensitive Story," "Anti-Story," "Contemporary Story," etc.[44]

Sahni was, importantly, noticing how the pre-independence nationalist coalition, which held together a number of competing ideas and politics, had fractured as soon as independence had been achieved. Now, artists and intellectuals were stressing their differences with one another rather than what held them together:

> The development of multiple schools was also damaging – literary works were all labelled. Works and writers, too. Camps developed. It was difficult to label a work. If you removed the writer's name from a work it was hard to say to which category it belonged. It was very easy to affix a label to a writer. And that's precisely what happened.[45]

Sahni describes how forms of patronage and circles of affiliation developed that obscured style almost completely by the 1950s and 1960s with the proliferation of a whole series of journals, each with its own stylistic brand (*Nayi Kahaniyan, Sarika, Sanchetna,* and so on). However, Sahni is also describing the pattern of affiliation in Hindi that took longer to develop because of the closer association of writers with one another. The case of Indian anglophone literature, where writers were much more geographically separated from one another, shows how this development had also been taking place earlier.

In 1935, near the time that he and a few others were composing what would become the Manifesto of the All-India Progressive Writers' Association, Mulk Raj Anand published his slim novel *Untouchable.* The novel described a day in the life of a young sweeper, Bakha, and the kinds of humiliations and trials he had to endure under the twin problems of Hindu caste-based chauvinism and British colonialism. At the end of his day, Bakha finds himself serendipitously at a rally being held sometime during Gandhi's tour in 1932–33 to explain why he had conducted his "epic fast" against Ramsay MacDonald's decision to grant special reserved seats in government to the "untouchable" (now Dalit) constituency, something known as the Communal Award.[46] Bakha is at first immediately drawn to Gandhi's humanity and kindness:

> The Mahatma raised his right arm from the folds of his shawl and blessed the crowd with a gentle benediction. The babble of voices died out, as if he had sent an electric shock through the mass of humanity gathered at his feet. This strange man seemed to have the genius that could, by a single dramatic act, rally multi-coloured, multi-tongued India to himself. Someone stood up to chant a hymn. The Mahatma had closed his eyes and was praying. In the stillness of the moment, Bakha forgot all the details of his experience during the day, the touched man, the priest, the woman in the alley, his father, Chota, Ram Charan, the walk in the hills, the missionary and his wife. Except for the turbaned, capped and aproned heads of the men and women sitting on the grass before him, his eyes seemed intent on one thing and one thing alone, Gandhi, and he heard each syllable of the Hindu hymn.[47]

The passage is remarkable as a piece of free indirect discourse, as Bakha's consciousness merges with the omniscient narrator's to turn a day in which Bakha has only experienced the terror of caste chauvinism into one where caste, language, and colour dissolve into an appreciation of Gandhi's "genius." What has been built up over the course of a harrowing series of daily humiliation is allowed to flow into the narrator's mind, proof of the pliability and decency of nationalist understanding. Yet, this unity-through-Gandhi is clearly at odds with the itemized depiction of the range and number of people (also "multi-coloured, multi-tongued") who have embarrassed and hurt Bakha throughout the day. So great is Bakha's admiration for Gandhi that he is even persuaded momentarily not to object to the Hinduism that endorses his oppression. What exactly does Bakha understand to be happening here?

The passage is important in the novel for at least two reasons. First, and most significantly, is how much it relies on a political ideology being transformed into a feeling, of a capacious humanism that exceeds class and caste divisions in India. The Hindu hymn in question is "*uth jaag musaafir,*" a song reported in Gandhi's book *The Epic Fast* (1932) to have been sung at one of Gandhi's meetings. That Anand read this account of the meeting is proven by the fact that he lifts Padraaja Naidu's translation of it verbatim into his novel. But it is significant that, in Anand's gloss of the song, it becomes a "Hindu hymn" despite the repeated use of the Persian word "*rab*" in the original, a term used by people of all faiths in India to refer to divinity. Naidu's translation of the hymn is, additionally, both idiosyncratically Victorian and Christian.[48] Moreover, neither of these options – Christian or Hindu – would have appealed to most politically conscious low-caste Indians at the time of the speech or to the supposedly multi-faithful audiences that Gandhi was supposed to have drawn out. Perhaps that is the reason the hymn is followed by a dramatic intervention: "Then his [Bakha's] attention began to flag." But even Bakha's momentary boredom, attributable possibly to Anand's chauvinism about low-caste attention spans, folds back out into hopefulness about national unity: "The brown and black faces below him were full of a stilled rapture. He sought to feel like them, attentively absorbed."[49] As such, the form of the passage is forced to oscillate between the optimism of a national utopia and the pessimism of the low-caste critique of it.

Second, the passage reflects the novel's contradictory posture towards aesthetics and form. Anand was fascinated by Joyce's novel *Ulysses*, which inspired the day-in-the-life structure of the book and its repeated shifts between styles as well as its peripatetic main character.[50] Joyce's stream of consciousness and stylistic virtuosity were, in fact, a much more conspicuous part of earlier versions of Anand's novel until the novel was edited – by many including Gandhi – into having a more realist feel. Elements of Joycean modernism are still present in the novel, including the multiple shifts of perspective and focalization even in the passage just quoted, but these shifts have become much more subdued in the final draft. Nevertheless, both modernism – with its unwillingness to prefer dramatic closure to aesthetic closure – and realism – with its injunction on dramatic resolution – are both present in the novel. This dualism is a result, perhaps, of both historical and stylistic demands: historical, because the outcome of anti-colonial nationalism was both open and closed in the years before independence; stylistic, because important aesthetic debates were being conducted internationally over the meanings of modernism and realism. It may also have had dramatic purposes: whether or not Bakha, as a representative of the "depressed classes," could actually be convinced to trust the nation and its citizens is a genuine question in the development of his consciousness and character. In overdetermined ways, the stylistic, dramatic, and historical ambivalence of the passage all clash together.

But the politics of this passage also matter. In 1932, when he would have been holding meetings like the one described, Gandhi was locked into a bitter debate with Bhimrao Ambedkar, then the most important leader of India's Dalit community. Ambedkar had campaigned vigorously for the Communal Award – which would have guaranteed representation on the basis of "depressed caste" status rather than counting the Dalits as Hindus – but had been manipulated into giving it up once Gandhi began one of his famous fasts from

Yeravda Prison.[51] Gandhi had worried that granting special reservations to the "depressed castes" would result in both dividing the nationalist movement and creating another competitor in his negotiations with the British for independence. He had already felt that Muhammad Ali Jinnah's argument that Muslims represented a separate nation had caused too much division and made it easier for the British to claim there was no India deserving of independence. Ambedkar, on the other hand, felt that Gandhi's Congress Party was moving too slowly if at all on the question of caste. The result was a period of much confusion and debate, both about the possibilities that nationalists would only betray the low caste and about whether Gandhi could be relied upon to have unilateral control over the decisions made in the nationalist movement.

At the same time, 1932 is important for another reason: it was the end of the Comintern's "Third Period."[52] It is exactly in the middle of the expulsion of M.N. Roy from the Comintern and his replacement by Gangadhar Adhikari as head of the Communist Party of India. Roy, who had been the leading Indian communist in the Comintern and famous for his debates with Lenin over the national question, lost favour with the leadership of the Comintern in 1928 over the shift in policy at the Sixth Congress of the Comintern. Roy had previously argued in 1922 that national liberation would require a revolution led by the peasantry and the proletariat, and that the national bourgeoisie would never openly lead a struggle for independence. Roy now argued that the Indian situation had changed: the British now needed the Indian bourgeoisie to develop the Indian economy in order to resolve the economic crisis that imperialism had created for them. The result was his "decolonization" thesis, arguing that, because of this shift, the British would need to decolonize India through a compromise with the Indian bourgeoisie in which independence would be granted gradually and incompletely through "Dominion status." Indian communists, therefore, should now work within the Indian National Congress Party. The Sixth Congress of the Comintern had taken the opposite position on the possibility of collaboration with the Indian National Congress.[53] Roy was summarily expelled, a common practice in the post-1924 era of "Bolshevization."[54] The Communist Party of India would then continue its anti–Congress Party position until 1935, when the famous Dutt-Bradley thesis argued that it was now possible to bring the Indian National Congress into a fight against imperialism and fascism.[55] This shift in policy towards the British dovetailed with the Comintern's popular front, anti-fascist policies.[56] One other consequence of the debates in the Comintern was that the "Indian Communist Party was put under the supervision of the Communist Party of Great Britain."[57] In addition, while several of the writers who became important leaders already had connections to the CPGB, this new relationship between the CPI and the CPGB would have a direct bearing on the political direction of Indian communism.[58] This change would ultimately shift the focus of the Indian communists towards London and away from Moscow.

Another important thinker who was an admirer of the Comintern was Jayaprakash Narayan, the leader of the Socialist Party. In the 1930s, though, before he had become disillusioned with both Nehru and Soviet communism, Narayan was crucially involved in the mass contact campaigns that the Congress Party was undertaking at that time. The aim of his newly minted Congress Socialist Party, as he described in "Why Socialism?" was "to elucidate certain problems arising out of the present stage of the national movement and the problem of its future direction."[59] Narayan had hoped that the pamphlet would open up a discussion with Congress Party workers to answer some of the more basic objections to socialism and also convince the Congress Party to adopt a more radical program that would make it possible to transform the Congress Party from a limited to a mass organization.[60]

Narayan knew this program would immediately put him into conflict with the leadership of the Congress Party, much of which was closely allied to the large landlords in India and some of which relied on capitalist patronage in order to fund their operations. However, Narayan had been relying on a perspective anticipating that Nehru's presidency in the Congress Party would open up space for more radical debates within the Indian National Congress, so that any movement in the direction of a more radical program would immediately shift the Congress Party towards a mass-based party. In this project, Narayan relied on a theoretical understanding of the relationship between the Congress Socialist Party and the Indian National Congress in which entering the latter allowed the socialists to get closer to the real anti-imperialist forces in the country. Narayan put it this way: "The argument advanced is that by remaining within the Congress, [the Congress Socialist Party] is strengthening the bourgeois hold over the anti-imperialist elements within the Congress. Nothing can be further removed from reality, however. The very purpose of the Party remaining in the Congress is to weaken by inside propaganda and opposition, that hold; and ripen the anti-imperialist elements for a final break with it."[61] Narayan imagined that, by pushing the Congress Party towards developing a mass, populist base, he would be forcing a rupture within it: the bigger the movement grew, the harder it would be for Gandhian ideas to hold on to the reins of the movement. Narayan's vision of socialism without working class self-emancipation put him squarely in the camp of the Second International.

Anand was clearly within the orbit of both sections of this left. Several critics have noticed his relationship with M.N. Roy.[62] But ideas closer to those of Jayaprakash Narayan were articulated in his autobiographical essay, *Apology for Heroism*:

> But I did not let my imagination blind me to the fact that my hatred of Imperialism was bound up also with my disgust for the cruelty and hypocrisy of Indian feudal life, with its castes, creeds, dead habits and customs, and its restrictive religious

rites and practices. I was one of many groping young men of my generation who had begun to question everything in our background, to look away from the big houses and to feel the misery of the inert, disease-ridden, underfed, illiterate people about us. The more authority humiliated us and insulted our intelligence by suppressing books and ideas, the more hungrily we devoured knowledge of the outside world, the more avidly we sought to contact others in Europe and Asia who we knew were thinking like us. And whether our dearest friends and nearest relations liked it or not, whether the Sarkar tortured us or talked to us persuasively, we had set our hearts on our liberation and those of other oppressed peoples, whoever they were, wherever they were and of whatever shape, size, and colour.[63]

This political move – an appreciation of the problems of the underclass and low caste as part of the project of anti-colonialism – is at the heart of the formal choices in the novel. Anand and the other "groping young men of his generation" comprised a section of the radical middle class that saw in the discrimination faced by other oppressed groups a reflection of the chauvinism and censorship that they encountered. Imperialism and Hindu orthodoxy, having run their course together, have driven the middle class to seek out collaborators in "other oppressed peoples." This politics of internationalism and inter-caste solidarity would push the limits of the official politics of Indian nationalism. But Anand was seemingly untroubled by the need to choose between various versions of socialism and communism.

This politics, too, is a part of the architecture of the original passage's ambivalence, its multiple and contradictory (because emergent, in Raymond Williams's sense) structures of feeling that are trying very hard to come to some resolution about what it means for humanity to be united.[64] What might it mean to say that Indian nationalism now produced a situation in which the communist might find important collaborators within the nationalist mainstream, or to argue that now was a period in which nothing was possible in the fight against imperialism except for political retrenchment? The other crowd, importantly, that Bakha encounters earlier in the day, after he accidentally touches an upper-caste man, offers a different way of thinking about a united humanity or an inevitable nation:

But the crowd which pressed round him, staring, pulling grimaces, jeering and leering, was without a shadow of pity for his remorse. It stood unmoved, without heeding his apologies, and taking a sort of sadistic delight in watching him cower under the abuses and curses of its spokesman. Those who were silent seemed to sense in the indignation of the more vociferous members of the crowd an expression of their own awakening lust for power.[65]

These are almost certainly the same people he encounters later in the day, but here, the crowd is menacing and cruel, unable to see him as a part of their collectivity. The drama, however, is identical to the later moment in the novel – a large mass of people, convened because they have been called by a singular figure, and Bakha's contradictory alienation from and desire to merge with them. Here, the terms are closer to what we might describe as naturalism – with its attendant pessimism about crowds, belief in the animal qualities of human nature, and its penchant for set piece scenes in which individual difference is bullied. Anand, too, would have been responding to the kinds of communal violence that had occurred throughout India, most recently in 1922–23, which allowed the British to conclude that Indians were not fit to govern themselves.

As a result, Anand interestingly vacillates between seeing Bakha as an animal and seeing him as the perfect industrial worker:

> Little pieces of straw flew into the air as he shoveled the refuse into the chimney, the little pieces settling on his clothes, the slightly bigger ones settling on the ground where he had to collect them again with his broom. But he worked unconsciously. This forgetfulness or emptiness persisted in him over long periods. It was a sort of insensitivity created in him by the kind of work he had to do, a tough skin which must be a shield against the most awful sensations. Stooping down over the baskets full of straw, he gathered shovelfuls and cast them into the grate till it seemed congested and he could take no more. Then he picked up a long poker and prodded the fire. Quickly it flared up, suddenly illuminating the furnace with its leaping red, gold and black flames, an angry consuming power, something apart, something detached from the heaps of straw it fed on.
>
> The blood in Bakha's veins tingled with the heat as he stood before it. His dark face, round and solid and exquisitely well defined, lit up with a queer sort of beauty. The toil of the body had built up for him a very fine physique. It seemed to suit him, to give him a homogeneity, a wonderful wholeness to his body, so that you could turn round and say: "Here is a man." And it seemed to give him a nobility, strangely in contrast with his filthy profession and with the sub-human status to which he was condemned from birth.[66]

Here, Anand has to torque very hard against the real productive processes of scavenging and sweeping labour, which all relied on very primitive techniques and technologies, in order to transform Bakha into an industrial labourer. The "furnace" is surely a makeshift oven, unlikely to have a "chimney" as much as a crude opening, and low-caste labourers almost definitely could not afford anything that resembled a "shovel." Sweepers would never have the accumulated capital to afford anything other than makeshift instruments and improvised disposal processes. Instead, we are offered socialist realism – with pokers, flames, repetitive Fordist movement, a gritty kind of work that nevertheless produces the hyperbolic "nobility." Here, even non-capitalist relations of production produce visions of capitalist modernity and redeem Bakha from his handling of night soil by focusing on the much more euphemistic "straw." This style is one way that the novel sutures the beginning to the ending of Bakha's day, when he overhears his favourite solution to the problem of caste: "When the sweepers change their profession, they will no longer remain Untouchables. And they can do that soon, for the first thing we will do when we accept the machine, will be to introduce the machine which clears dung without anyone having to handle it – the flush system."[67] The futurist, utopic nature of this vision is belied by the fact that, in contemporary India, half the population lacks access to indoor toilets, let alone the flush system.

Anand cannot decide at various points in the novel whether he should be looking at Bakha and seeing a man of the future, an animal, an alienated proto-intellectual, a newly sexualized young man, or a good worker. For Anand, these were all important guises for Bakha to take on because they represented, in various ways, figures for what different intellectuals recognized as the chief problems standing in the way of national independence: lack of modernity; lack of education; the separation between the intellectual and the masses; the restrictions on sexuality posed by religion; and the lack of economic development (respectively). But this indecision is not because of a failure on the part of Anand as a novelist; rather, it seems more likely that Anand is responding in different ways and with different aesthetic ambitions to the same kind of political and aesthetic questions that were posed by communists of all stripes about how to resolve the social contradictions that imperialism and capitalism generated in India. While the Communist Party of India may have had certain political lines, because those lines were subject to change, and because there were other competing left-wing organizations that also drew their inspiration from the Comintern, meant that it was possible to have contradictory views on resolving the problems India faced.

For instance, Agyeya, the pen name of S.H. Vatsyayan, was a member of the Hindustan Socialist Republican Army. If we look at Agyeya's *Shekhar: Ek Jivani* (1942–43), which lays out many of the early formal innovations of Hindi's modernist aesthetic, we have to be struck by its insistence on rebellion, its foregrounding of national and international politics, its deep desire for a revolutionary overhaul of every aspect of life: the family, sexuality, religion, caste, even nationalist organizations. So, at the beginning of *Shekhar* we are given this explanation for what constitutes a rebel:

> It's not my argument that Karl Marx was simply born or that Shelley didn't learn anything from the world, or that Trotsky wasn't as affected by his world as much as he affected the world. What's unique about a revolutionary's spirit is that it remains revolutionary even when it embraces the modern ideas that are flying around as part of its development, since it is more advanced than the most advanced sections of its times. That's why Einstein is a revolutionary despite being born in reactionary Germany, and despite being cradled in the womb of the world's greatest, the

most fiery, intense, world-historical event of the Russian Revolution, Stalin never became a revolutionary. He simply remained to pick up the scraps ...

If this is the case, is it pointless to propagandize about revolutionary ideas? No, but if the ideas are being disseminated in the hopes that they will produce new revolutionaries, or that they will give rise to revolutionary possibilities, then they will prove fruitless. But if the objective is to recruit existing revolutionary forces, collect the existing will to revolution, to give it a line of march, then this objective will come to fruition.[68]

In *Shekhar*, Agyeya not only hints at his early disagreements with the ways that the AIPWA was organized around a narrow set of politics, but he also traces a different left-wing tradition, an anti-Stalinist socialism that traces its lineage through Marx, Percy Bysshe Shelley, Trotsky, and Einstein. Here, too, is the early critique of progressive writing as futile propaganda, but instead of noting its artlessness, Agyeya points to a different theory of literary and political propaganda that attempts to draw around itself a variant of the vanguard. Even more acerbically and perhaps more subtly, Agyeya offers up a glimpse of a theory of why socialist realism can never be revolutionary while avant-garde art uniquely can. The function of art in revolutionary contexts is not, Agyeya argues, to convince the unconvinced through pedantry, but rather to lead the existing forces by embracing the spirit of rebellion as modernity. Mixed with this criticism is the art-for-art's-sake formulation, too. A few paragraphs later, he writes:

The most important thing for an artist, after mastering a working knowledge of art's internal force, is to have a pure reverence for art itself; and similarly the most important thing for a revolutionary is to have a devotional attachment to revolution. That's the only way that he acquires the ability to lose himself in his work, to devote his entire subjectivity to it, and still have the power to judge it objectively; it's the only means by which his drifting is intentional drifting, when he dies it's because he wants to sacrifice his soul, if he loses himself in the world, it's because he understands his personality.[69]

This statement is the refrain that has become familiar in a sort of depoliticized modernism, whose primary antagonist has to be committed to literature of a certain kind, but here, the critique of ideological conformity is married to a left-wing theory of social reorganization. Here the relationship to the utopian project of the European avant-garde is complete: the hope that aesthetic force produces political transformation and social revolution.

If Anand is sometimes accused of producing boilerplate socialist realism (despite his distance from the AIPWA), the charge is never leveled at his contemporary Raja Rao, whose novel *Kanthapura* (1938) describes the period of nationalist agitation in a small village in Uttar Kanara immediately following Gandhi's Salt Satyagraha (1930). *Kanthapura* was perhaps a one-of-a-kind experiment in anglophone writing in India, as Rao attempted to marry the novelistic form to the *sthalapurana*, an oral epic tradition narrating the history of a pilgrimage site. Its breathless polysyndetons not only exploded the realist sentence of tight adjectival phrases but also allowed for a different pattern of political explanation to enter into the novel. The novel's narrator is a grandmother named Achakka who, early on in the novel, describes how politics entered into the claustrophobic world of women's homes:

> Our Rangamma is no village kid. It is not for nothing she got papers from the city ... But there was one thing she spoke of again and again – and, to tell you the truth, it was after the day the sandal merchant of the North came to sell us his wares and had slept on her veranda and had told her of the great country across the mountains, the country beyond Kabul and Bukhara and Lahore, the country of the hammer and sickle and electricity – it was onwards that she began to speak of this country, far, far away; a great country, ten times as big as, say, Mysore, and there in that country there were women who worked like men, night and day; men and women who worked night and day, and when they felt tired, they went and spent their holiday in a palace – no money for the railway, no money for the palace – and when the women were going to have a child, they had two months' and three months' holiday, and when the children were still young they were given milk by the Government, and when they grew older still they went to the universities free, too, and when they were still more grown-up, they got a job and they got a home to live in and they took a wife to live with and they had many children and they lived on happily ever after. And she told us many marvelous things about that country.[70]

In the place of the usual set piece of union militant who excoriates about the evils of capitalism, Rao's novel offers the almost fairy-tale version of socialist utopia in the Soviet Union, complete with its emphasis on the centrality of women's rights in the workplace. Unlike the socialist realism of the period, which produced the political speeches at the end of the novel as a kind of pseudo-epiphany, Rao's novel puts its political themes at the beginning and then watches them unfold. And contrary to the claims of some critics who have called the novel "distinctly non-Marxist" and "Gandhian," it is clear that the novel holds out the possibility of far more radical solutions than those on offer from Indian nationalism.[71]

Indian authors working in the 1930s and 1940s were not involved exclusively in communist circles. They travelled variously (England, France, Germany, Italy, Mexico, China, Japan, Indonesia, Turkey, Egypt, the United States, and the Soviet Union); they participated in Party-led and non–Party-led international organizations, especially the International Conference Against

Fascism (1935); they were involved in Communist Party organizations as well as organizations both formally expelled from the Comintern and those that were never a part of the Comintern; their intellectual interests were necessarily varied as they tried to adapt European theories of history to their own colonial contexts. Their models of internationalism were both communist and non-communist, including pan-Islamism and pan-Asianism.[72] Their models of communism and socialism were also varied, coming from admixtures of second (especially because of the British Labour Party), third, and fourth international strands. And, most importantly, they were also deeply swayed by the political importance of the national liberation struggle, which meant that they also held very strong nationalist allegiances. They defined themselves at various times as socialist, communist, humanist, secularist, progressive, internationalist, and Gandhian.[73] Their ranks included both those who were more closely identified with socialist realism, those who were classicists, and those who identified self-consciously with modernism and the avant-garde. The term "Comintern aesthetics" holds a different meaning for this group of writers (whom Kris Manjapra calls "anti-colonial cosmopolitans") as they tried to stitch together, from various strands, a politics that made sense from various sources that did not hold an exclusive monopoly on anti-colonial answers.[74] The ban on the Communist Party in India by the British government until the Second World War also meant that the influence of the Comintern was necessarily uneven, selective, and not always aesthetic. From both perspectives – that of the Comintern and that of the colonial artists – the relationship between the Comintern and the colonial writers (at least partly) influenced by it was neither unidirectional nor (merely) hierarchical, but rather one node in a larger network of filiation, fellowship, and friction. Even in those places where a "Soviet style" emerged and was self-consciously defended, the layers of influence embedded in the translation of that style into an Indian context betray the orthodoxy of its claimants.

Translation, then, becomes an important heuristic for explaining how influence works in unexpected ways and with novel consequences, where the original is less important than the consequences for the transmission of novelty into new contexts. Translation worked in three distinct spheres: first, in the process of transferring Comintern policies into colonial contexts, including those instances where Comintern policy was being debated frontally (including the Soviet-sponsored Indian Military School in Tashkent); second, in trying to imagine how a given prescribed relationship between art and politics was to be imagined in relationship to other aesthetic traditions (the translation of several Russian authors into Indian languages that was being conducted in Moscow) as well as in the various Indian languages, including English; and third, in the relationship between Indian writers and British communists. In the first case, the expulsion of M.N. Roy from the Comintern in 1929 and the shift in official support behind G.M. Adhikari, beginning in 1933, already set the stage for splits and factional strife within the Communist Party of India.[75]

Simultaneous to this project of disaggregating multiple political strands within a (translated) Comintern politics is a recuperative aesthetic project. Aesthetically, it is worth underlining that the Cold War, an ambient anti-communist rhetoric, and the robust needs of a new nationalism all played immense roles in the shaping of Indian literary history. Various aesthetic movements had communist affiliations but they later came to be dissociated from their political roots and commitments and became more easily and commonly read as anti-communist instead. For instance, the most important literary and cultural organizations of the 1930s and 1940s – the AIPWA and the Indian People's Theatre Association (IPTA) – had both communists and Nehruvian nationalists as members, and both initially endorsed both socialist realist and experimentalist projects. Modernist projects had both Trotskyist and capitalist supporters. These movements then began to split and fracture on both aesthetic and political lines the farther one moved from the moment of nationalist independence, and different sources of patronage, publication houses, and political alliances all began to differentiate themselves (in part a feature, too, of state-led capitalist development in India). The only way to understand the Comintern as an important part of the development of Indian literature is to understand it under the sign of translation, to see not only the political influences of Indian literature but the dynamic interplay between anglophone writing and the various vernacular traditions as well.

NOTES

1   D. Hallas, *The Comintern: A History of the Third International* (London: Bookmarks, 1985), 106–25.
2   S.D. Gupta, *Comintern and the Destiny of Communism in India: 1919–1943, Dialectics of a Real and a Possible History* (Kolkata: Seribaan, 2006), 15.
3   S. Zaheer, *The Light: A History of the Movement for Progressive Literature in the Indo-Pak Subcontinent*, trans. A. Azfar (Karachi: Oxford University Press, 2006).
4   J. Zumoff, "'Is America Afraid of the Truth?' The Aborted North America Trip of Shapurji Saklatvala, MP," *The Indian Economic and Social History Review* 53, no. 3 (2006): 407.
5   Katerina Clark, "Indian Leftist Writers of the 1930s Maneuver among India, London, Moscow: The Case of Mulk Raj Anand and His Patron Ralph Fox," *Kritika: Explorations in Russian and Eurasian History* 18, no. 1 (2017): 63–87. Katerina Clark's excellent essay on the relationship between Ralph Fox and Mulk Raj Anand demonstrates just how deep the connection between the Communist Party of Great Britain and Indian writers actually was and just how much it was not monolithic.

6 For instance, the Third Congress of the Comintern oversaw the marginalization of the Berlin group of Indian revolutionaries (Virendranath Chattopadhyaya, Pandurang Khankhoje, G.A.K. Luhani, Bhupendra Nath Datta, and others) in favour of M.N. Roy, since he had already acquired a reputation at the Second Congress of the Comintern over his debates with Lenin (Gupta, *Comintern and the Destiny*, 76). The debate had centred on the question of whether or not the nationalist bourgeoisie of the colonial countries was a revolutionary force, a debate that remained unsettled until the directive from the Sixth Congress of the Comintern (1928) on the colonial question, following the betrayal of the Chinese communists by the Guomindang, that national bourgeoisies (and some national liberation struggles) were wholly reactionary.

7 Kris Manjapra has made this point in a different context: "What if the decentralized and contingently arising epicenters of Indian anti-colonialism were located abroad, sending catalytic effects in multiple directions including towards the site of territorial contestation? This represents a fundamental rethinking of notions of 'territorial' and 'diasporic' politics." Kris Manjapra, "Communist Internationalism and Transcolonial Recognition," in *Cosmopolitan Thought Zones: South Asia and the Global Circulation of Ideas*, ed. Sugata Bose and Kris Manjapra (New York: Palgrave Macmillan, 2010), 160).

8 Frederick Jameson, *A Singular Modernity: Essay on the Ontology of the Present* (London: Verso, 2002).

9 I will use "British India" to differentiate the geographic entity that existed before partition (1947), and "India" and "Pakistan" to represent the post-independence, post-partition dispensation.

10 Zumoff, "Aborted North America Trip," 411.

11 Ibid., 413.

12 B. Ranadive, *The Independence Struggle and After* (New Delhi: National Book Centre, 1988), 60.

13 Kris Manjapra, *M.N. Roy: Marxism and Colonial Cosmopolitanism* (New Delhi: Routledge India, 2010).

14 Zumoff, "Aborted North America Trip," 432.

15 J. Callaghan, "Racism, the CPGB and Comintern in the Inter-War Years," *Science & Society* 61, no. 4 (1997/1998): 515. Callaghan does argue, however, that because Party membership plummeted in 1931 to 2,555 members, and because the Party never had "more than 18,000 members in the inter-war years," it was difficult for the CPGB to sustain protracted, engaged, serious anti-colonial work in all of the colonies, including India.

16 Gupta, *Comintern and the Destiny*, xviii, 302.

17 A. Maurya, "Indian and Russian Literary Mutuality," *International Conference on Arts, Design and Contemporary Education* (June 2015): 39, https://doi.org/10.2991/icadce-15.2015.5.

18 M. Friedberg, *Literary Translation in Russia: A Cultural History* (University Park: Pennsylvania State University Press, 1997), 4.

19 S. Zaheer, A. Ali, M. uz-Zafar, and R. Jahan, *Angaaray: The Firebrands*, trans.
    S. Shingavi (New Delhi: Penguin, 2014).
20 P. Gopal, *The Indian English Novel: Nation, History, and Narration* (New York:
    Oxford University Press, 2009), 17.
21 Clark, "Indian Leftist Writers," 72.
22 T. Ahmed, *Literature and Politics in the Age of Nationalism: The Progressive Episode
    in South Asia, 1932–56* (London: Routledge, 2009), 3.
23 H. Malik, "The Marxist Literary Movement in India and Pakistan," *The Journal of
    Asian Studies* 26, no. 4 (August 1967): 651.
24 Ahmed, *Literature and Politics*, 11–37.
25 Gopal, *Indian English Novel*, 2.
26 M.R. Anand, "On the Progressive Writers' Movement," in *Marxist Cultural Move-
    ment in India*, ed. S. Pradhan (Calcutta: National Book Agency, 1979), 21.
27 A. Mufti, "Towards a Lyric History of India," *boundary 2* 31, no. 2 (2004): 252.
28 M. Fisher, "Interview with Mulk Raj Anand," *WLWE* 22 (1973): 81. Fisher notes:
    "Even in the early days of his career, in the 1930s, for example, when Anand was
    closely connected with the Progressive Writers' Association (PWA) and personally
    accepted the idealistic goals of Marxism, he never viewed the writer as one whose
    purpose was chiefly propagandistic or political."
29 A. Ali, "The Progressive Writers Movement and Creative Writers in Urdu," in
    Marxist Influences & South Asian Literature, ed. C. Coppola (East Lansing: Asian
    Studies Center, Michigan State University, 1974), 43–5.
30 A. Ali, "Progressive View of Art," in *Marxist Cultural Movement in India*, ed. S.
    Pradhan (Calcutta: National Book Agency, 1979), 67.
31 M.R. Anand, "The Making of an Indian-English Novel," in *Untouchable* (London:
    Penguin, 1940).
32 C. Coppola, ed., *Marxist Influences and South Asian Literature* (Delhi: Chanakya
    Publications, 1988), 11. For instance, the manifesto reads: "the new literature of
    India must deal with the basic problems of our existence today – the problems of
    hunger and poverty, social backwardness and political subjugation, so that it may
    help us to understand these problems and through such understandings help us
    act."
33 Priya Joshi, *In Another Country: Colonialism, Culture and the English Novel in India*
    (New York: Columbia University Press, 2002), 208.
34 K.A. Ali, *Communism in Pakistan, Politics and Class Activism 1947–72* (New York:
    I.B. Tauris, 2015), 7. Bhisham Sahni insisted that the Communist Party never ex-
    erted any programmatic control over the AIPWA, though by the time he assumed
    its presidency, the AIPWA had more or less become uniformly pro-communist;
    see Bhisham Sahni, *Today's Pasts*, trans. S. Shingavi (New Delhi: Penguin Books,
    2015), 364–6. Interestingly, Sahni was much more sensitive to the Communist Par-
    ty's control over the Indian People's Theatre Association; see Sahni, *Today's Pasts*,
    215–6.

35 C. Coppola, "Ahmed Ali (1910–1994): Bridges & Links East & West," *Journal of South Asian Literature* 33/34, nos. 1/2 (1998/1999): 114.

36 K.A. Ali, *Communism in Pakistan*, 7.

37 M. Mukherjee, "Mapping an Elusive Terrain: Literature," *India International Centre Quarterly* 33, no. 1 (Summer 2006): 82.

38 Anand, "On the Progressive Writers' Movement," 9.

39 A. Ali, "Progressive View of Art," 78–9.

40 Ahmed, *Literature and Politics*, 45. As Talat Ahmed observed, "it was his [Ali's] contribution that struck a sectarian, dismissive note."

41 M. Prabha, *The Waffle of the Toffs: A Sociocultural Critique of Indian Writing in English* (New Delhi: Oxford & IBH Publishing, 2000), 20–36.

42 Leon Trotsky, *Literature and Revolution*, ed. William Keach, trans. Rose Strunsky (Chicago: Haymarket Books, 2005).

43 Almost every major writer in Hindi during this period also read in English.

44 Sahni, *Today's Pasts*, 241.

45 Ibid., 244.

46 S. Chahal, *Dalits Patronised: The Indian National Congress and Untouchables of India, 1921–47* (Delhi: Shubhi Publications, 2002).

47 Anand, *Untouchable*, 144.

48 Pyarelal, *The Epic Fast* (Ahmedabad: Navajivan Publishing House, 1932), 122, http://www.mkgandhi.org/ebks/epic_fast.pdf.

49 Anand, *Untouchable*, 145.

50 M.R. Anand, "On the Genesis of *Untouchable*: A Note," in *The Novels of Mulk Raj Anand*, ed. R. Dhawan (New Delhi: Prestige Books, 1992).

51 C. Jaffrelot, *Dr. Ambedkar and Untouchability* (New York: Columbia University Press, 2005), 68.

52 M. Worley, "The Communist International, the Communist Party of Great Britain, and the 'Third Period,' 1928–1932," *European History Quarterly* 30, no. 2 (2000): 185–208.

53 R. Chandavarkar, "From Communism to 'Social Democracy': The Rise and Resilience of Communist Parties in India, 1920–1995," *Science & Society* 61, no. 1 (Spring 1997): 101.

54 Gupta, *Comintern and the Destiny*, 9.

55 N. Redfern, "British Communists, the British Empire and the Second World War," *International Labor and Working-Class History* 65 (Spring 2004): 133.

56 Chandavarkar, "From Communism to 'Social Democracy,'" 103.

57 Clark, "Indian Leftist Writers," 66.

58 Redfern, "British Communists," 117.

59 J. Narayan, "Why Socialism?" in *Jayaprakash Narayan: Selected Works*, ed. B. Prasad (Delhi: Manohar, 2001), 1.

60 Ibid., 86.

61 Ibid., 87.

62 Kris Manjapra notes: "Through his critique of fascism, M.N. Roy was a figure of admiration for many leaders of the All-India Progressive Writers' Association … along with the Indian People's Theatre Association … Among those Indian members of this international writer's movement who admiringly spoke of M.N. Roy were Abu Syed Ayub, Humayun Kabir and Sudhindranath Datta in Calcutta, Khwaja Ahmad Abbas in Bombay, Mulk Raj Anand in London, Abburi Ramakrishna Rao in Hyderabad and Gopal Mittal in Lahore. Mulk Raj Anand even incorporated M.N. Roy as a character in one of his novels [The Sword and the Sickle]" (Manjapra, *M.N. Roy*, 131–2).

63 M.R. Anand, *Apology for Heroism* (New Delhi: Arnold-Heineman Publishers, 1946), 53–4.

64 R. Williams, *Marxism and Literature* (New York: Oxford University Press, 2009).

65 Anand, *Untouchable*, 49.

66 Ibid., 20.

67 Ibid., 155.

68 Agyeya, *Shekhar: A Life*, trans. S. Shingavi and V. Dalmia (New Delhi: Penguin, 2017) 15–16.

69 Ibid., 18.

70 R. Rao, *Kanthapura* (New York: New Directions, 1963), 29.

71 H. Trivedi, "Gandhian Nationalism: *Kanthapura*," in *Literature and Nation: Britain and India, 1800–1900*, ed. R. Allen and H. Trivedi (Abingdon: Routledge, 2000), 114.

72 P. Mishra, *From the Ruins of Empire: The Intellectuals Who Remade Asia* (New York: Farrar, Strauss, and Giroux, 2012).

73 S. Shigavi, *The Mahatma Misunderstood: The Politics and Forms of Literary Nationalism in India* (London: Anthem Books, 2013).

74 Manjapra, *M.N. Roy*, xix.

75 S.N. Talwar, *Under the Banyan Tree: The Communist Movement in India, 1920–1964* (New Delhi: Allied Publishers, 1985), 176.

Chapter Four

Seeing the World Anew: Soviet Cinema and the Reorganization of 1930s Spanish Film Culture

ENRIQUE FIBLA-GUTIÉRREZ
Elías Querejeta Zine Eskola

MASHA SALAZKINA
Concordia University

The hour is coming when Spanish cinema will trespass its borders in order that a new cinema, one for which our fallen comrade has fought so much, becomes a reality. Much of the credit will be due to Juan Piqueras. The logical triumph of a revolutionary Spanish art will herald the future of a new Spain, forged in the anti-fascist trenches of the country.

> – *Frente Rojo* and *Adelante* newspapers on the death of film
> critic Juan Piqueras[1]

On 6 February 1937, eight months after the execution of film critic and Spanish Communist Party member Juan Piqueras by fascist forces, the first articles about his death began to appear in both national and international newspapers. Georges Sadoul would write in the newspaper *Commune* to condemn his assassination, lamenting that Piqueras "could have been, in the midst of the Civil War, the organizer of an important and truly Spanish cinema."[2] Piqueras had been forced to stop near the Venta de Baños (Palencia) train station in July 1936 to take care of a stomach ulcer. There, he was unfortunate enough to encounter the advance guard of Franco's forces, in revolt against Republican Spain. A label from a Moscow hotel, to where Piqueras had presumably recently travelled, was deemed enough cause for his arrest. When he was searched, they found among his possessions the manuscript of an anti-fascist article about the creation of a Spanish Federation of Proletarian Film Clubs, which he had published in the Marxist film journal *Nuestro Cinema* in October 1933, and an authorization from the French communist cooperative Ciné-Liberté to manage the exchange of newsreels for the Popular Front.[3] Filmmaker Luis Buñuel and fellow film critic Antonio Del Amo, who also belonged to the Spanish Communist Party, attempted to rescue him in those first chaotic days of the Civil War, but the roads were closed and Piqueras was executed around the end of July.

These three figures – Piqueras, Buñuel, and Del Amo – are key protagonists in the largely forgotten story of Spanish radical film culture of the late 1920s and early 1930s. That short-lived culture, brought to an end by the outcome of the Civil War, began with the circulation and appreciation of Soviet cinema in Spain and ultimately took aim at transforming Spanish cinema into an instrument for promoting the social revolution to come. Its main outlet was the journal *Nuestro Cinema*, described by Georges Sadoul as the "best film journal in Capitalist Europe."[4] The journal released thirteen issues from 1932 to 1933, and four more in 1935, creating a shared proletarian cinematographic imaginary through its editorials and articles written by Piqueras, Del Amo, and Spanish critics, writers, and artists such as Rafael Sender, César M. Arconada, Buñuel, and Josep Renau; translations of articles from Béla Balázs, Sergei Eisenstein, Ilya Trauberg, Vsevolod Pudovkin, Joris Ivens, Léon Moussinac, Georges Méliès, and René Clair; and its film stills, illustrations, and advertisements. The journal had a marked internationalist spirit and included an "International News" section that covered Europe, the Soviet Union, North America, Latin America, and Asia. This dimension was highlighted in the journal's self-promotion, which declared it was "the only truly international Spanish journal, written by international collaborators and inspired by an international direction."[5]

Beyond *Nuestro Cinema*, Piqueras, Buñuel, and Del Amo were also involved in Comintern-aligned cultural organizations such as the French section of the International Union of Revolutionary Writers (AEAR, Association des écrivains et artistes révolutionnaires)[6] and its local Spanish branches, largely organized around the journal *Octubre*, which, in its first (June 1933) and second (July 1933) issues, already promoted a joint anti-fascist and anti-imperialist front under the slogan "United against the imperialist war!"[7] Their activities were also made visible through the proletarian newspapers *Pueblo* and *Mundo Obrero*, which were managed by the famous Comintern propagandist Willi Münzenberg.[8] Through their ties to the Communist Party, they were in dialogue with many of the leftist artists and intellectuals who were participants in the thriving experimental cinematic culture in Europe and the Soviet Union.

These histories of the Spanish intellectuals' and artists' collaborations provide us with an opportunity to explore the transnational dimension within interwar European leftist culture. All too often this history has been narrated through an exclusion of Spanish cinema from this key moment in the institutional development of cinema across Europe. As we will see in the following pages, the personal trajectories of our three leading figures – who made the transition from the cultural avant-garde to the forefront of political struggle in a few years – display an exemplary sensitivity to the context in which the Comintern intervened.[9] The goals of this chapter, therefore, are twofold. First, it focuses on the cultural activities of the Comintern beyond Soviet Russia and Germany, considering instead the Comintern-aligned cinematic front elsewhere in Europe.

Until recently, the discussions of the relationship of the Comintern to cinema have largely circled around Willi Münzenberg and Francesco Misiano, and examined the role of the Mezhrabpom Studio, which produced and exported many of the most important films of the period made in Soviet Russia, resulting in their wide circulation across Europe.[10] This chapter follows instead the cultural networks supported by the Comintern and the role they played in the creation of a lively international cinematic culture in Spain.

While it is indisputable that the Spanish Civil War was one of the great epicentres of the internationalist communist experience of the period, an importance amplified by foreign film productions focusing on Spain during that time (most notably, perhaps, through Joris Ivens's and Roman Karmen's famous films),[11] surprisingly little scholarly attention has been paid to the Spanish context preceding these developments, often assuming its intrinsic poverty. Therefore, the second goal of this chapter is to demonstrate the vibrancy of film culture in Spain of the 1920s and 30s and the degree to which its key figures were active participants on the international leftist scene.[12] Most accounts of Spanish cinema of that period generally omit the important relationship between leftist politics and aesthetics and the role Comintern-aligned activities played in the various attempts to transform the country's film culture. This transformation was a process that could not be reduced to a mere reflex of Soviet cinema, but instead allowed for the ideologically and artistically complex negotiations between the local and transnational motivations and effects of that relationship. As such, the first part of this chapter focuses more explicitly on the situation facing the Comintern in Spain, while the remainder is concerned with the dynamics of the reception accorded Soviet cinema, taking a particularly close look at the position and role of *Nuestro Cinema* in this process.

The paradox at the heart of this story taps into the very problem that plagued the Comintern leaders throughout the 1920s and 30s: how to create an "authentic" proletarian culture within the confines of the bourgeois sphere, taking advantage of the politicization that had generated a splinter progressive bourgeois sector as a reaction to the rise of fascism. In Spain, the Spanish bourgeoisie's desire for modernization and dissolution of an old order opened a window of opportunity for leftist politics to spread via cultural production and appreciation of revolutionary aesthetics. Antonio Marichalar's review in the journal *Revista de Occidente* – founded in 1923 by philosopher José Ortega y Gasset as an elitist cultural referent for a new enlightened Spain – of the first screening of Sergei Eisenstein's *Battleship Potemkin* (*Bronenosets Potemkin*, 1925) gives a perfect example of how Soviet cinema was seen as a model for translating revolution to the Spanish cultural elite. According to Marichalar, Eisenstein's film "is not a communist but a revolutionary film. Its effect is not to persuade, convince, praise, or propagate something. Its objective is to disturb one's spirit ... A film like this can ignite anyone with a minimum instinct of rebellion and critical spirit. It can turn him against constituted power, regardless of his convictions and the regime he supports."[13] The challenge facing pro-communist cultural activists was to find a way to transfer these revolutionary energies aroused by Soviet aesthetics from minority intellectual circles to the proletarian masses. Piqueras, Buñuel, and Del Amo sought to use the Comintern's support to provide a solution to this problem.

The PCE and the Comintern in Context

To understand the dissemination of a leftist political aesthetic in Spain, it is necessary to look at the political and cultural aspects of the Spanish Communist Party's relationship to the Comintern during this period. The Spanish Communist Party (PCE, Partido Comunista de España) was formed as a split from the Spanish Socialist Workers' Party (PSOE, Partido Socialista Obrero Español) in 1920, and was officially recognized as the Third International representative in Spain in November 1921.[14] Spain in the 1920s underwent the Primo de Rivera dictatorship (1923–30), which gave way to an authoritarian regime lead by General Berenguer (1930–31), finally ending in the proclamation of the Second Republic (14 April 1931). In response to this authoritarian political culture and its legacy, Comintern policy towards Spain during the Second Republic was split between those who thought the country was in the ideal state for a proletarian revolution and those who believed that the defence of the democratic Republic was more important to assure a future workers' rule. The end of the Primo de Rivera dictatorship and the overthrow of King Alfonso XII interested the Soviet Union, which until then had paid very little attention to Spain, despite the marked cultural and political changes the country was experiencing.[15]

The PCE only had around 1,000 members at the beginning of 1931, and it initially failed to gain significant presence in the first months of the Spanish Second Republic due to its ambivalent attitude towards the Republican government. For Party militants, the Republic was seen as a hopelessly bourgeois enterprise. Among other factors, the competition with the anarchists for loyalty among the Spanish workers, and the repression of strikes by the government, made it difficult for the PCE to be anything but oppositional. Nevertheless, the PCE's membership grew steadily as the cultural and political relationships between Spain and the Soviet Union intensified and the volatile political situation called for unexpected – in relation to Comintern directives – changes in political strategy.[16] Indeed, the relationship between the Spanish leaders of the PCE and foreign Comintern representatives was often strained in the years leading up to 1936, in part due to the initial ignorance in Moscow of the Spanish social and political reality.[17] In October 1932, the entire executive of the PCE was summoned to Moscow and replaced due to their support for the democratic Republic; José Bullejos, Party leader, had advanced the slogan "For the defence of the Republic" after a failed coup by General Sanjurjo in Seville.[18] This position clashed with the Comintern's program to attack socialists and anarchists. In 1933, Heinz Neumann, who had been in the German Communist Party (KPD) with Willi Münzenberg, was sent to Spain on behalf of the Comintern to reorganize the PCE.[19]

These manoeuvres should be put within the context of the rise of the fascist threat in Germany with Hitler's seizure of power in 1933, which increasingly concentrated Stalin's attention on a rising military threat. In response, Communist Party policy gradually changed from one of supporting international revolution to one that called for the defence of the true socialist state (the Union of Soviet Socialist Republics, USSR), even if this orientation meant the subordination of revolutionary activity elsewhere. By 1935, the Popular Front strategy against fascism was adopted at the Comintern's Seventh World Congress, a policy enthusiastically greeted by the PCE.[20] The Soviet Union's warming to progressive political factions of the Republic nullified the policy of attacks on other progressive forces (socialists and anarchists). Third Period policies were abandoned with relief, since in Spain this strategy could only prove negative for the workers.[21] Shortly after, when the Civil War broke out, the desperate need for Soviet aid consolidated relations between the PCE and the Republican government, united this time under the Popular Front against fascism.

A Transversal Fascination: The Comintern and Intellectual Circles

Although the PCE was in constant political turmoil, it did develop a cultural policy that it hoped to make attractive to the new cultural elite represented by the "Generation of '27" (Generación del 27).[22] As already mentioned, the PCE was not a strong political force in 1931; although in the following years the Party membership grew steadily, it was still far less popular than the PSOE, the leading left-wing political force, and was even smaller than the different anarchist movements of the time. This weakness was mirrored in its problems creating a popular cultural policy, since most intellectuals were suspicious of the all-encompassing state associated with Soviet communism, preferring either the bourgeois liberalism of the republicans or the more libertarian strains of leftism, such as anarchism, which abhorred centralized governments and defended personal freedom.[23] To try to turn this situation around, the PCE received help from the Comintern representatives, who most likely recommended the recruitment of intellectuals to the cause as per the Comintern policy in France and Germany.[24] Indeed, the Communist International had already started a large-scale operation to promote both the USSR's image abroad and to attract intellectuals from all over the world to communist-related organizations.

Led by Willi Münzenberg, former Young Communist International head and KPD member, the operation involved the management of several newspapers

and magazines across Europe, as well as sponsoring talks to international
worker organizations, including one in New York. It was under these auspices
that Mezhrabpom Film Studio, a production and distribution company (under
the name Prometheus Film) with headquarters in Berlin but physically located
in Moscow, was created.[25] Among the films it produced were *Storm over Asia*
(*Potomok Chingis-Khana*, Vsevolod Pudovkin, 1928), *The End of St. Petersburg*
(*Konets Sankt-Peterburga*, Vsevolod Pudovkin and Mikhail Doller, 1927), and
The Road to Life (*Putyovka v zhizn*, Nikolai Ekk, 1931), which were some of the
first Soviet films screened in Spain.

While Willi Münzenberg's activities have received significant attention, his
relationships with key Spanish cultural figures related to film have been largely
unexplored. From 1933, after fleeing Berlin, he oversaw anti-fascist propaganda
in Paris,[26] which put him in contact with many Spanish intellectuals such as
Julio Álvarez Del Vayo, who had helped introduce Soviet cinema into Spain in
the late 1920s.[27] When the 1934 Asturias October revolution failed, Münzenberg became actively engaged in helping many of the political refugees who fled
to France. This activity threw him into the same spheres as Piqueras, who was
hosting some of those same refugees in his Paris house.[28] Likewise, Piqueras's
job in Paris selecting films for the distribution and production company Filmófono had to put him in contact with Münzenberg through Prometheus, the
distribution branch of Mezhrabpom that managed the international circulation
of Soviet films.[29]

The German propagandist became an important connector in the international solidarity campaign with the Spanish Republic during the Civil War. He
was in contact with Buñuel,[30] who was in Paris working for the Spanish embassy to coordinate the production, exhibition, and circulation of documentaries and newsreels in solidarity with the Republic.[31] Del Amo worked as the
assistant director and cameramen for these films, presumably with a camera
that Buñuel had given him.[32] The particular trajectory of Del Amo, from a
twenty-year-old film critic for *Popular Film* magazine, to Piqueras's disciple and
director of *Nuestro Cinema* in Spain, to PCE member, to battlefront newsreel
filmmaker in only four years, is exemplary of the vertiginous rhythm of cultural
and political transformations in the Spain of those years. It also testifies to the
success of the Comintern's recruitment of intellectuals as the political situation
in Spain radicalized. As we will examine in the next paragraphs, the propagation of Soviet culture happened transversally across Spanish society, catching
the attention of a broad spectrum of intellectuals from leftist poets to bourgeois
amateur filmmakers.

From afar, the USSR appeared as the materialization of the kind of society
that was being demanded by scientists, writers, artists, teachers, and filmmakers. It seemed to have successfully merged progressive culture and politics with
economic planning in a decade during which the economic slump was taken

to signal the death knell of capitalism. These cultural figures created the first "friends of the Soviet Union" associations and even become active members of the PCE. As described by Julián Marías, Spanish intellectuals had become politicized in the wake of the loss of the colonies in 1898, known as "El Desastre del 98" (the '98 Disaster); their anxieties about Spain's supposed backwardness fed their own self-image as the vanguard that would push their country into modernity.[33] For them, it was of primary importance to break down the wall isolating Spanish intellectuals from international, or at least European, contexts, rallying to Miguel de Unamuno's famous phrase, "Spain remains to be discovered, and it will only be discovered by Europeanized Spaniards."[34] However, this sense of a national project did not necessarily produce any single political identity, but was, instead, directed towards the urge for economic, cultural, and political modernization of Spain under a variety of ideological guises.

With the radicalization of the political context after the Primo de Rivera dictatorship (1923–30), critics, writers, poets, filmmakers, artists, scientists, and journalists, who could see Spain's backwardness compared to other European countries, started to become politically involved at different levels of militancy. Some took an institutional approach, attaining appointments to positions of power – the symbolic figure here being the first president of the Second Spanish Republic, Manuel Azaña, lawyer and writer. Others – such as poet Rafael Alberti and writer María Teresa León – made use of the Republic's policy of cultural exchange and travelled to countries like Germany, from where they could visit the Soviet Union.[35] Given the reality of a semi-industrialized economy, widespread rural poverty, harsh working conditions, and the growing power of worker organizations, it is not surprising that Soviet culture and society, which was also rapidly modernizing a country known for its uneven development, would seem to be a model for the Spanish intellectual elite.

But the fascination with Soviet society and culture was not only an affair of the left, since bourgeois creative sectors also turned their attention to the USSR. Even the amateur film section of the Catalan Excursionist Centre (CEC, Centre Excursionista de Catalunya), a stronghold of the powerful and conservative Catalan industrial elites, admired Soviet filmmaking. In issue ten of its journal, *Cinema Amateur*, for instance, the CEC published a translated article from the American Society of Filmmakers by Karl Freund that included praises for Eisenstein's montage.[36] For the CEC, the expressive qualities of Soviet montage were a much better example of what could be done with film than the elaborate production numbers in Hollywood, given the material limitations of working without sound and with limited quantity of film stock available. Likewise, the CEC's strong anti-commercial film bias made the Soviet film industry a logical place to look for suggestions, in spite of the organization's lack of sympathy for communism. Issue eleven also devoted the "foreign collaboration" section to Soviet cinema, in this case with an article by V. Solev on Soviet sound experimentation, focusing on the "drawn sound" films by E. Sholpo in his Petrograd laboratory.[37]

Antonio Bonet is another good example of this class-crossing bourgeois admiration for Soviet cinema, which the Comintern capitalized on. Bonet was a prominent architect and member of the Group of Spanish Artists and Technicians for Contemporary Architecture (GATEPAC, Grupo de Artistas y Técnicos Españoles Para la Arquitectura Contemporánea), which put out a journal called *AC Documents of Contemporary Activity* (*AC Documentos de Actividad Contemporánea*). It is surprising to find numerous mentions of Soviet cinema in its issues among pleas and plans for an elitist, rationalist architecture and design. For example, the fourth issue of 1931 contains an article devoted to Nikolai Ekk's *The Road to Life* as "the first Soviet sound feature."[38] What is even more surprising is that the anonymous article, quite possibly written by Bonet himself, praises the communal aspect of Soviet society. Considering the difficulties facing the circulation of Soviet films in Spain at the time, it is noteworthy that the article is contemporaneous to the release of the film (1 June 1931) in the USSR, showing how connected certain intellectuals were to the cultural life of the Soviet Union.

The bourgeois intellectual imagination was also captivated by both the will for experimentation and the utopian transformative projects taking place in the USSR, so much so that the radical politics of a worker revolution were left to one side. Coming out of a dictatorship and decades of relative cultural isolation, the newness of the Soviet project – which was arriving late to Spain, compared to other European countries – appealed greatly to these self-fashioned Spanish intellectuals precisely as a stimulating horizon onto which to project their hopes and aspirations for a different Spanish society in cultural terms. This attraction to "all things Soviet" by cultural tastemakers coexisted with the rejection of an old and seemingly discredited Catholic bourgeois code. Similarly, a host of younger intellectuals such as Del Amo, Buñuel, Alberti, León, Arconada, and Piqueras staked their work on the Soviet experiment, which meant sometimes violently disassociating from the countless political, cultural, and social projects of the previous decades that had all failed to lift either the standard of living or the tone of the country. Film, the new medium that had so rapidly put itself at the centre of mass culture, seemed to provide a unique instrument for shaking off the pessimism of a culture nostalgic for a failed empire and producing the mindset, at least, of a modern European state, just as it had done, or so it was sometimes claimed, in the USSR.

In a way, this strong attraction to the USSR reflected the extreme crisis of the Spanish mindset, which was desperately striving to break with the conditions that made the past rather than the future the privileged image of utopia but without a clear image of what the socio-political future was supposed to look like or what role was to be allotted to the "masses" or the "people" in this transformation. The Soviet Union seemed a viable model to follow for some intellectuals, but for many others it was "more than a revolution, a social dissolution."[39] These ideological disparities reflect the complexity of what Gerald Brenan called "the Spanish labyrinth": the complex political and social paths, often blocked, folding one on the other, into which intellectuals led themselves, identifying their pursuit of power with their pursuit of a better future.[40] In the following sections, we go into this labyrinth through cinema, exploring the relationship between politics and aesthetics that made the USSR an appealing project in the eyes of the Spanish leftist citizen and the bourgeois amateur alike.

Learning Revolutionary Aesthetics; the Appeal of Soviet Cinema in Spain

Nuestro Cinema can't but accept, on good terms, a cinema capable of freeing us from today's ideological poverty. That is, a cinema with depth, with an open mind, with social content ... A cinema that was born with Eisenstein, with Pudovkin.

– Juan Piqueras, 1932[41]

In most historical accounts of the cultural relationships between Spain and the USSR, the Civil War overshadows the key prior period (1929–36), when a number of intellectuals, directly or indirectly within the Comintern orbit, actively encouraged Soviet film appreciation with an eye to creating a revolutionary Spanish cinema. In the following sections, we provide an overview of the critical reception accorded Soviet cinema and the discourses associated with it in Spain during the late 1920s to early 1930s, placed within the broader context of the Spanish film culture of the time.

The absence of a strong Spanish film industry during the Primo de Rivera dictatorship had permitted French and American domination of the Spanish market, with local competition confined to the "españolada" – cheap productions based on popular melodramatic romances and old values, one-act farces, and basic comic sketches. Spain exported, and imported, an image of a stratified and ignorant society that had very little to do with the everyday reality of the country, but that was nonetheless hugely popular. Moreover, the centrality of Spanish cultural production in previous centuries to the construction of both European and Latin American culture was completely eclipsed by this new "backward" image, relegating Spain to the periphery of cultural production and academic attention – where it has more or less remained ever since. Spain's rich cultural history would be re-appropriated by both conservative and liberal nationalists from time to time,[42] but, beyond its borders, Spain was fixed in the public imaginary as an exotic failed empire, always in the shadow of what happened in Paris.[43]

The advent of the Second Republic in 1931 promised to drastically change the cultural landscape of the country. Education and the creation of a new national cultural policy became a priority for the liberal authorities, who attempted to unite Spaniards through their rich artistic heritage.[44] At the same time, a local film industry began to develop in Madrid and Barcelona, although most films reproduced the "españolada" model. Critics were divided between those who accepted this type of cinema as a necessary first step in the consolidation of a Spanish film industry and those who opposed it tout court. For the latter group, the models to follow were the films of Eisenstein, Pudovkin, and (perhaps more surprising to us today) Olga Preobrazhenskaia, which retold the narrative of the "Russian people," creating a new history of proud citizens (referred to at the time as "the masses"), busy in the collective construction of a promised future. As one review of Preobrazhenskaia's *Baby ryazanskie* (*El Pueblo del Pecado* [*Women of Ryazan*], 1927) – the first commercially exhibited Soviet film in Spain – remarks:

> *El Pueblo del Pecado* resembles no other film. It's unique. It has nothing of the other movies. It doesn't even have a protagonist. In *El Pueblo del Pecado* the protagonist, allow me the expression, is everyone: the people, the masses. The Russian people with their habits, with their tremendous passions, with their eagerness for social sense.[45]

It is important to highlight that, as elsewhere in Europe, the exhibition of Soviet films was mainly confined to film clubs and special screenings, as we will see in detail later. This marginalization – for obvious political reasons – coincided with the expansion of the theatrical exhibition system in Spain, which by 1935 had 3,450 screens – although only 1,550 of them were equipped with sound systems[46] – ranking among the highest in Europe.[47] It is also important to locate the development of such networks within the complex Spanish historical context as a still semi-industrialized economy, without official diplomatic ties to the USSR, and having inherited seven years of relative isolation from the avant-garde culture that had spread throughout Europe in the years of the Primo de Rivera dictatorship.[48]

The story of Spanish cinema in this period, when told at all, is largely seen as completely dependent and dominated by the French intellectual circles of the time. Although the influence and importance of the French avant-garde on Spanish intellectuals is without question,[49] this line of scholarship has overlooked the significance of a circle of intellectuals moving in an informal network dedicated to creating a "new Spanish cinema" that would not be a copy of Hollywood and would be politically charged. It is true that the avant-garde in Spain was more concerned about the circulation of new works conforming to their vision of cinema (the creation of an avant-garde culture itself) than making films, but one must consider the difficult political and economic context of the country in terms of production and financing. The first important production companies – with more than one film produced in a year – did not appear until 1932 (Orphea in Barcelona and CIFESA in València), and it was not until 1935–36 that other such companies were founded (for example, Filmófono, Exclusivas, and Alianza Cinematográfica Española). Either way, Spain produced a peak 37 feature films in 1935, compared to 45 in the USSR, but still far from the 525 produced in the United States, 200 in Britain, and 115 in France.[50] Given these factors, the film cultural explosion of the late 1920s and early 30s experienced by Spain is even more remarkable,[51] offering a unique example of a national cinema in the making, heavily influenced by the Soviet Union's successful film policy of promoting didactic, avant-garde, and political works over commercial films.

The traditional narrative of film history placed France at the centre of inter-war avant-garde cinema. Recent scholarship has revisited this thesis[52] and, in the process, further emphasized the impact of early Soviet cinema on cinema worldwide, which began to be explored in scholarship and criticism in the late 1960s to early 70s.[53] In the interwar period, with most European countries in political turmoil and facing radical social and cultural transformations, Soviet cinema provided an apparently perfect synthesis of avant-garde aspirations. Its formal innovation both reflected and set in motion the disruption of an es-tablished social and political regime in the name of a utopian future. It was a cinema that could both reflect and advance the new world order formally, thematically, and in its very organization.[54] Piqueras described this Soviet cinema as the synthesis of "emotion" and "education" when describing the film *Turksib* (Viktor Turin, 1929), a documentary on the construction of the Siberia-Turkestan railroad.[55] In his essay "Educational and Cultural Meaning of Soviet Cinema," the critic finds it important to quote the film director's as-sertion: "The central theme of Soviet art is the building of a socialist society, the new life that emerges in the Soviet Socialist Republics. Our reality provides the artist's creative genius an infinite variety of themes. And these new themes demand to be treated in new ways."[56]

Statements like the one just quoted provided a new generation of Spanish film critics with a language of revolutionary aesthetics that offered the capacity to dissolve the old conservative order. While the role of early Soviet cinema as a historical point of reference for building a national film industry and a culture of film education has been generally acknowledged, the appeal of the Soviet model to "peripheral" countries in Europe like Spain and Italy is only begin-ning to be explored.[57] Its appeal in more distant contexts, such as Latin Amer-ica, has also been recently explored by Sarah Ann Wells, establishing suggestive parallelisms with the Spanish context.[58] To ascribe this attraction solely to fas-cist nationalists' search for possible models of a propagandistic visual regime overlooks the existence of competing modes of nationalist discourses within the Spain's cultural and political spheres of the time, such as the ones promoted by Spanish or Catalan leftist intellectuals throughout the 1920s and 30s. For them, cinema provided a unique opportunity to change the country's backward and stereotyped narrative, creating a new image and institutional model that could encourage the much-desired leap into general modernization.[59] Soviet cinema provided considerable inspiration for this transformation. And, although many of the Soviet films that inspired the Spaniards belong to what we generally consider the "avant-garde," it was their "realist" capacity – understood as a privileged relationship between the art form and the social material and cultural reality it represents – that held most sway in the discourse of the time.

Take, for instance, the words of anarchist critic and director Mateo Santos, responding to a question in a survey published by the journal *Cine Art*: "What orientation (aesthetic, ideological, educational, etc.) should the national production follow?" Santos replied: "The only one possible: that which displays in the celluloid an image and a landscape that can be identified as genuinely Spanish."[60] Santos had regularly defended the need for a Spanish proletarian film culture in journals such as the Marxist *Nuestro Cinema* and *Popular Film*, a politically and content-wise diverse publication – albeit more eschewed towards a libertarian approach – where he was the editor. It's notable that he does not refer to Soviet aesthetics here, expressing instead the generalized sentiment among Spanish leftist critics that a future national cinema should develop its own form of realism.

In this sense, Soviet aesthetics was the model of what *could* be done but, as critic and writer César M. Arconada remarked, not what *should* be done, point by point. Instead of copying the Soviets, the Spanish left proposed using the Soviet film industry as an inspiration to develop a form of realism that corresponded to Spanish reality.[61] When, in 1935, *Nuestro Cinema* asked five well-known intellectuals – Benjamin Jarnés, Francisco Ayala, Antonio Espina, Federico García Lorca, and Ramón J. Sender – about Soviet cinema, they all highlighted the undeniable importance of Soviet filmmaking as an educational and cultural model for Spain, praising both technique and content, although Sender specified that content should also be "local," mentioning the importance of linking revolutionary thought with the "national means of expression."[62] Spain hadn't experienced a proletarian revolution, so the transformation of capitalist culture would have to begin from within the system, anticipating the uprising that would "build a new era of justice, where proletarian cinema and art will develop in complete unity with life."[63] In contrast to the sleek studio productions of Hollywood and their European imitators, Soviet aesthetics made it imaginable to create works that would point to a revolutionary culture to come, propagandizing among the masses in order to effect a grass roots ideological change. More optimistically, it would be a change in which the masses would recognize cinema as their instrument, rather than that of the entertainment industry. As Piqueras's earlier quote remarks, the aim was to free the worker from the ideological poverty of mainstream films and the false image of Spanish society that they reflected.

Soviet film's emphasis on the collective over the individual provided the perfect framework for a new narrative foray with which to experiment, taking as its subject the fragmented nature of Spanish society itself, but resolving that discord, à la the Soviet example, with the aid of a state willing to strongly unite the people for the construction of a common good – a new and just society. This idea greatly appealed to those tired of the endlessly unresolved struggle for cultural and political hegemony in Spain. It provided a serious alternative to cinema as mindless entertainment and distraction, offering instead a space for collective cohesion that mixed the old and the new with a glorious future in mind. Most importantly, if Spanish art was to aid in the proletarian revolution, it had to get rid of the individualism that characterized the despised bourgeois intellectual. Arconada claimed:

> It is convenient to say that art is naturally a vehicle towards a proletarian world. But when arriving at the end of the journey, one must descend from it. It's not acceptable to travel alone, in a carriage of aesthetics, like an ordinary Oscar Wilde, with impertinence and individual artistic pride.[64]

Arconada, like Piqueras and Santos, defended the idea of the collective subject that would be at the centre of a national film project for Spain. The collective principle would work from the top to the bottom: the filmmaker wouldn't "travel alone," but alongside fellow technicians and workers. And the "carriage" would not be made solely of aesthetics, but of social content and pedagogical intentions. While this vision was most powerful and clearly articulated among the radical leftist circles in the 1930s – which will be our focus later in the essay – the appeal of Soviet cinema needs to be further explored within a broader cultural context, beyond the creation of a specifically proletarian film culture, through the variety of circulatory networks that shaped its reception in Spain.

Film Clubs and the Bourgeois Introduction of Soviet Films in Spain

Although the focus of this chapter centres on how the Comintern capitalized on Spanish intellectual circles of the time to advance a particular proletarian film culture, it is important to stress that the cultural relationship between the USSR and Spain happened both on an official and an unofficial level.[65] The varied channels through which the Comintern managed to consolidate a proletarian film culture – despite the ban on commercial circulation of Soviet films, which only ended during the Spanish Civil War – were quite distanced from the commercial film industry.[66] Specifically, film clubs emerged as a key space for the propagation of revolutionary ideology throughout the country, to the delight of Comintern-aligned organizations. Such clubs were, at first, an instrument of the cultural bourgeoisie. Buñuel introduced avant-garde films in Spain in sporadic sessions organized in the Residencia de Estudiantes (Madrid) during the mid-1920s. In 1928, Ernesto Giménez Caballero – director of the journal *La Gaceta Literaria*, the most importance tribune for the cultural expression of the so-called Generación del 27 – founded the Cineclub Español, where Buñuel and Piqueras soon became involved in the programming. Although bourgeois in nature and not meant for workers at all, the Cineclub Español became the centre of avant-garde film culture in Spain throughout its three seasons (1928–31), providing an outlet for Soviet cinema to be shown for the first time in Spain and inaugurating a film club culture, which would rapidly spread throughout the country after the end of the Primo de Rivera dictatorship.

Informal relations between Spanish and Soviet film culture had started in the late 1920s. In 1927, Julio Álvarez Del Vayo – the future minister of foreign affairs during the Civil War – travelled to the Soviet Union and, like many sympathetic intellectuals, was put in contact with VOKS (All-Union Society for Cultural Relations with Foreign Countries) and Sovkino (the centralized state-owned cinema organization) representatives.[67] Del Vayo was an admirer of Soviet film and would later help Eisenstein in Mexico, where Del Vayo worked in the Spanish embassy, when the Soviet director encountered problems with the Mexican authorities upon arrival in that country.[68] In his 1927 visit, Del Vayo attempted to buy Soviet films in order to circulate them in the Spanish market. By early May 1929, he had received copies of Pudovkin's *Storm over Asia* (1928), Ivan Pravov and Olga Preobrazhenskaia's *Women of Ryazan* (1927), and Iakov Protazanov's *The Lash of the Tzar* (*Belyy oryol*, 1928), although details about these transactions are not known.[69] Shortly afterward, on 20 January 1930, the first showcase of Soviet films was organized by the Cineclub Español in its ninth session, with a special presentation by Del Vayo on Soviet cinema, where he spoke about his experience visiting Russian directors and studios during his trips to the USSR.[70] Curiously enough, only one of the films that he had supposedly purchased just a few months earlier was screened.[71] The program mentions the screening of Preobrazhenskaia's *Women of Ryazan* and an earlier version of *Ivan the Terrible* directed by Turi Taritsch.[72]

As is the case with most such events across Europe (except perhaps for Léon Moussinac's cultural work in France),[73] the context of this first Soviet film showcase was far removed from the original proletarian audiences intended for these films. The Cineclub Español membership was largely bourgeois, and the screening took place in the lavish Ritz Hotel in Madrid. This class inversion is partially explained by the fact that the state still prohibited the mass-market exhibition of Soviet films, presumably because of their inflammatory nature.[74] However, these reasons did not apply to an audience of inoffensive bourgeois intellectuals – that is, in the eyes of the authorities – unconnected to any labour movement. What the authorities didn't fully understand was the role of the Cineclub as a pedagogical institution. In its own programming notes, the Cineclub mentioned that "the Cineclub Español has been the first Spanish film school," going on to enumerate the number of directors, producers, and distributors involved in the association.[75] It successfully created the first relevant network of alternative cinemas in Spain. Although it was bourgeois in nature, the Cineclub Español was of interest to the Comintern, which was already actively attempting to recruit intellectuals in Spain by the early 1930s.[76] Indeed, the fact that Piqueras and Buñuel were involved in different capacities in the Cineclub Español and the Cineclub Proa Filmófono, while remaining in the orbit of the PCE and Communist Party of France (PCF), raises the question of whether the Comintern wasn't at least surreptitiously involved in the enterprise, especially in regards to how exactly the copies of Soviet films were obtained.

The selection of Soviet films for the Cineclub Español was made by Piqueras, whose admiration of Soviet cinema had grown together with his political alignment with the PCE. Piqueras himself wrote the review of the screening devoted to Soviet cinema for the newspaper *El Sol*, admitting that "cinematographically speaking we had some references of Russia. But we didn't know anything about the USSR."[77] With these words, Piqueras was, on the one hand, acknowledging the sparse information about the Soviet Union available to Spanish citizens of the time (1929–30) and, on the other, conveying the strong fascination and interest for the USSR that those films aroused in film club audiences. The film showings happened, opportunely, on the eve of the proclamation of the Second Republic, after which Eisenstein's *The General Line* (*Staroye i novoye*, 1929) was shown in Barcelona and Madrid. In August, a local delegation of "Friends of Russia" (Amigos de Rusia)[78] in Alicante had also screened the film. By October of that same year, Catalan architect and urban planner Antonio Bonet was organizing a one-day Soviet film festival with the help of VOKS, screening Eisenstein's *Battleship Potemkin*, Trauberg's *Blue Express* (*Goluboy ekspress*, 1929), and a documentary.[79]

Beyond the realm of bourgeois intellectual cinephiles, Soviet aesthetics also circulated in the more politicized settings of film clubs open to the working class. With different levels of autonomy and political agendas, these film clubs shared the objective of inciting a political "awakening" through proletarian aesthetics, transforming the bourgeois intellectual type into what they envisioned to be proletarian intellectuals, directly or indirectly at the service of the communist cause. Examples of these film clubs include the Cineclub Frente Revolucionario, Sindicato Banca y Bolsa, Cineclub FUE, Socorro Rojo Internacional, and Juventud Roja.[80] These alternative networks of exhibition and distribution created the conditions for the emergence of the radical film culture that reached its highest point during the Civil War, providing the aesthetic models to produce propaganda films and graphic art. These earlier cinematic experiences that the film clubs provided found their way into films like *Aurora de Esperanza* (Antonio Sau Elite, 1937), produced during the war to promote solidarity among the fighting workers, and the posters of José Renau (figure 4.1) for that film and others like *Chapaev* (Georgi Vasilyev and Sergey Vasilyev, 1934) and *We Are from Kronstadt!* (*My iz Kronshtadta*, Efim Dzigan, 1936).

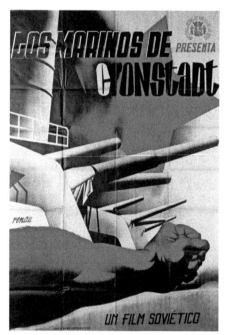

4.1 Josep Renau's posters for *Chapaev* (top) and *We Are from Kronstadt* (bottom). Courtesy of the CRAI Biblioteca Pavelló de la República (Universitat de Barcelona). Copyright Fundació Josep Renau, València.

But, beyond specific aesthetic models that came to be mobilized during the Civil War, starting from the early 1930s Soviet cinema provided a vision of aesthetic and political education that would resonate powerfully among the intellectuals who were embarking on the creation of a new social and political culture. We will now turn to the evolution of this particular understanding of cinema, which shaped the reception of Soviet cinema as a model for the Spanish left.

Soviet Cinema and the Synthesis of Education and Emotion

In 1930, critic Guillem Díaz-Plaja, who went on to teach the first Spanish university course devoted to cinema, wrote *A Culture of Cinema* (*Una Cultura del Cinema*), the first book about cinema published in Catalan and certainly one of the first to be published in Spain. He emphasized cinema's ability to capture the fast-paced changes of modern life (cars, factories, typewriters, telephones, and so on), its valorization of a sensory culture as opposed to an intellectual one, and its potential as an educational instrument, which could contribute to Spain's much-needed social and cultural modernization. In the last sentence of the book, Díaz-Plaja mentioned that "Russia is the key to the cinema of the future,"[81] and included a multilingual bibliography with the most relevant books published to date on Russian cinema, bringing forward the theme advanced in his quotation from Sergei Eisenstein that "cinema has to be a bridge between reason and sentiment."[82] Díaz-Plaja had borrowed from Eisenstein the idea of "cinema dialectic" and proposed it as a didactic model for Spanish cinema.

This model was broadly based on the different approaches of Russian film-makers discussed in the book, such as Sergei Eisenstein, Dziga Vertov, and Vsevolod Pudovkin. These filmmakers promoted cinema as a form of intellectual education, in particular through specific uses of montage techniques. They saw film as a formidable instrument for epistemological and cognitive – as well as political – transformation, which allowed spectators to understand the inner workings of society. Eisenstein, in particular, promoted this idea, giving conferences throughout Europe in the late 1920s. He stated the goals of the Soviet film industry as follows: "The aim of our cinema is not to create entertainment or an enjoyable distraction. For us cinema is always a very serious issue, which has an instructional and cultural nature."[83] His method for such "instruction" was based on the dialectical juxtaposition of images, from which a new meaning would emerge. Eisenstein summarized this process in his lecture "The Principles of New Russian Cinema" (translated and published in *Nuestro Cinema*): "From the image to the emotion, from the emotion to the thesis."[84] This formula allowed for enormous pedagogical implications, and, in Díaz-Plaja's interpretation, this cinema would be "a link between the language of logic and the language of images, to create a cine-dialectic representative of humanity's aspirations."[85] This concept, of course, had a formidable propagandistic potential for the different nationalisms that coexisted in Spain, which needed to mobilize the masses around their respective visions of the country. In particular, Catalan nationalist intellectuals from widely different ideological positions were attracted to the USSR because of its explicit defence of self-determination, included in the Soviet Union's 1918 constitution.

Not surprisingly, when the recently elected autonomous Catalan government created a Catalan Cinema Committee in 1933,[86] it drafted an official policy towards cinema as an instrument of culture, including key references to cinema in the Soviet Union, especially regarding the institutionalization of film education.[87] The famous Moscow Film Institute, (VGIK) was, of course, not an unusual point of reference for the institutionalization of film education in Europe and elsewhere. While this process in Europe and North America took place gradually over the course of the 1930s through to the 1960s, in the Soviet Union, by the late 1920s to early 1930s, the professional and academic institutionalization of film education was nearly complete and subsequently served as a model internationally for film training. It combined practice with theory and embraced artistic experimentation as a standard curricular requirement for students, all within a centralized educational structure.[88]

This approach to film education attracted critics like Díaz-Plaja who, in an article in *Cinema Amateur* titled "The Role of the Amateur in Educational Cinema," mentioned the need to go beyond "theoretical divagations" and create an official film school that would create "the vision of Catalonia for the eyes of the young."[89] Although ideologically distant from its Catalan enthusiasts, the Soviet VGIK was the most successful example they could turn to for their institutional plans in Catalonia. According to Josep Carner i Ribalta, one of the main figures in the Catalan Cinema Committee, the film school had been almost ready to open in the summer of 1936 alongside a 16 mm production studio, but the Civil War disrupted such plans.[90] Either way, the documentary film production of the Generalitat de Catalunya Propaganda Commissariat and its production company Laia Films during the war – including instructional documentaries from Ramón Biadiu and the weekly propaganda newsreel *España al Día* – can be linked to the long-standing admiration for Soviet cinema and, especially, to Ribalta's trip to Moscow in 1936, during which he visited the Soyuzkino studios and came back to Catalonia with a handful of educational documentaries that surely influenced Laia titles such as *Catalonia Martyr* (*Catalunya Màrtir*, 1938), *Conquest of Teruel* (*Conquista de Teruel*, codir. Manuel Berenguer, 1938), and *Transformation of the Industry at the Service of War* (*Transformació de la indústria al servei de la guerra*, 1938).[91] These works, alongside foreign revolutionary films, were projected to soldiers in the Aragon front by the mobile exhibition services of the Propaganda Commissariat.[92]

The detail that Díaz-Plaja provides regarding Soviet film culture shows that the scholarly consensus according to which Spain was an isolated and completely peripheral cultural context needs to be revised. Many Spanish intellectuals and educators were aware of the situation of film in the USSR. Their information derived both from articles in the journals already cited and from books on Soviet cinema published in other languages, such as Léon Moussinac's 1928 *Soviet Cinema* (*Le cinema Soviétique*), which was translated into Spanish in 1931, and René Marchand and Pierre Weinstein's *Art in the New Russia: Cinema* (*L'Art dans la Russie Nouvelle: Le Cinema*, 1927) – from which Díaz-Plaja copied the "Tekhnkium" (as VGIK was referred to at the time) class list. By this time too, there were first person accounts from Spanish intellectuals who had travelled to the Soviet Union: for instance, Julio Álvarez Del Vayo, who in 1925 had published *The New Russia* (*La Nueva Rusia*); Rafael Alberti, whose articles appeared in the newspaper *Luz*, titled *News from a Poet in the USSR* (*Noticieros de un poeta en la USSR*, July–August 1933); and Josep Pla, whose account of his 1925 trip to Russia was printed in the newspaper *La Publicitat* and later published as a book titled *Trip to Russia* (*Viatge a Rússia*).[93] Finally, some books on Soviet cinema were published in Catalan, like Josep Palau's *Soviet Cinema: Cinema and Revolution* (*El cinema soviètic: cinema i revolució*, 1932).[94] But the most important outlet for Soviet film culture–related news was certainly Piqueras's *Nuestro Cinema*, which included articles from foreign and Spanish correspondents in the USSR, filmmakers like Sergei Eisenstein and Joris Ivens, institutional figures from the Soviet film industry, and well-known international critics such as Léon Moussinac or Béla Balázs. We now turn to this mostly overlooked journal, which became a central node for the organization of a new Spanish radical film culture. As in most leftist circles, the journal's approach to cinema was greatly influenced by the heated debates and irreversible split between socialist realism and avant-garde positions.

Nuestro Cinema and the Organization of a New Spanish Film Culture

Piqueras had been the Spanish delegate at the Second Congress of Independent Filmmaking in Brussels (1930), and later allegedly travelled to the Soviet Union to visit its film industry (circa 1934–35). In Paris, where he worked for Filmófono selecting films to be distributed in Spain, he had ample opportunities to meet the international avant-garde. From the last months of 1929, when he helped select the Soviet films screened in the ninth Cineclub Español session, until his murder in 1936, he wrote dozens of articles devoted to this cinematography. For Piqueras, the discovery of Soviet cinema marked a progressive break with the canonical avant-garde of René Clair, Germaine Dulac, and Salvador Dalí – so much so that he abandoned his role as assistant director in Clair's *Freedom for Us* (*À nous la liberté*, 1931), accusing his friend of indulging in a bourgeois humanist exercise instead of adopting a true social perspective, as in the Soviet films he now admired.[95]

At this point, it is worth noting that the very period when Soviet cinematic culture (to large extent due to Piqueras's efforts) found its way to Spain was the period of transition from the 1920s avant-garde to the 1930s realism; perhaps nowhere was this divide as dramatic as in the Soviet Union, where the diversity of post-revolutionary modernist and avant-garde movements came to be gradually replaced by a state-imposed unitary doctrine of socialist realism. This transition in the Soviet context took place over a decade and was accompanied by intense polemics – political and aesthetic – as well as institutional and ideological power struggles, which Piqueras tapped into and helped translate into the Spanish context.[96]

What did Piqueras find in Soviet cinema of the late 1920s to early 30s that attracted him so much as to break with the avant-garde circles in favour of what he called a "united front facing the screen, in which our worker and peasant base is included alongside the intellectual and revolutionary base that has created vital organizations for the new political and cultural movement in Spain"?[97] The answer is not straightforward, but if we analyse his writings and the editorial direction of *Nuestro Cinema*, we can see that Piqueras's fascination with Soviet cinema was rooted in its organizational force and ability to reflect the "reality" of a working class completely absent from mainstream Spanish cinema. This quest for material organizational structures that could impact social reality led him to align himself with materialist approaches to cinema, such as those advocated by French critic Léon Moussinac, who followed a similar intellectual and aesthetic trajectory.[98] The quest for socialist realism was intended as a response to the urgent needs to introduce the lives of the workers in the public sphere, rather than as a reaction against avant-gardist experimentation.[99] Such a turn towards notions of realism among the radical left in Spain was (as was also the case in Italy for critics such as Umberto Barbaro and later Guido Aristarco, or even Cesare Zavattini) not so much a matter of aesthetic principle. Instead, it served as a possibility for a productive relation between film and its material and social context.[100] The idea that "Soviet cinema has assigned itself the role of showing, as is, the life of the working class to capitalist country audiences"[101] certainly appealed to those deeply discontent with the escapist nature of Spanish cinema. The visibility and exploration of the life of the working classes in Soviet films was constantly highlighted in the numerous articles on Soviet cinema published in the journal – many of them translated contributions from foreign collaborators, due to the censorship of Soviet cinema in Spain.

The way critics discussed realism in *Nuestro Cinema* was varied and at times contradictory,[102] but in many ways it most closely resembled the position occupied by the journal's contemporary Soviet literary and artistic faction known as Factography – in particular in what Joshua Malitsky describes as Factography's characteristic "recognition of the interrelation of form and content, a turn toward genres that emphasize the immediacy of everyday experience, and a new dialectical relationship between media language and industry."[103] Coincidentally, the name Piqueras chose for the journal, *Nuestro Cinema*, echoed a key 1928 article by Sergei Tret'iakov, "Our Cinema." Although Tret'iakov is never mentioned explicitly in Piqueras's writings, "Our Cinema" can be read as a programmatic roadmap for *Nuestro Cinema*'s quest against capitalist cinema's "ideological poverty" and "taming of the masses."[104] Factography's own highly problematic relationship to the advent of socialist realism, and its ultimate complicity with it,[105] was mirrored in its Spanish appropriation. The fact that *Nuestro Cinema* focused on contemporary Soviet films and criticism (from 1930 onwards), therefore underrepresenting the more experimental Soviet cinema and writings of the 1920s, is quite revealing of the aesthetic politics favoured by Piqueras (figure 4.2).[106] With this particular understanding of cinematic realism, *Nuestro Cinema* followed Tret'iakov's dual conception of cinema's role as both "intellectualizer" and "emotionalizer" in the construction of a "new reality."[107]

For instance, César M. Arconada praised Buñuel's *Land without Bread* (*Las Hurdes*, 1933), arguing that beyond films "which show us what we want to see," there were others that "show us what we wouldn't normally see because of multiple reasons: because it is ugly, sad, vulgar, or bitterly poor."[108] Arconada celebrated Buñuel's turn to "realism" and his departure from a "complicated intellectualism," without devaluating his previous films *Un Chien Andalou* (1929) and *L'Age d'Or* (1930), which Arconada also described as "magnificent."[109] Such a conception of the new realism as a logical consequence and the maturation of avant-garde experimentation is best illustrated in Arconada's description of *Las Hurdes* in relation to Buñuel's career: "the world, in its classic form, in its vertical and concrete lines, has been reintegrated to his deepened and misplaced surrealist eyes."[110] This position was shared by other materialist critics, exemplified in Moussinac's description of documentary filmmaking as a "rude but fine path to activism."[111]

The aesthetically conservative positioning of many of the foreign (that is, non-Spanish) contributions to the journal can be seen in the choice of authors, who were often not critics or filmmakers but institutional and political figures. For example, the first issue of the journal includes the international communist leader Karl Radek's famous attack on Dziga Vertov's film *Enthusiasm* (1931) as a confusing "cacophony."[112] In that same issue, Anatoli Lunacharsky – former People's Commissar for Education, representative of the USSR to the League of Nations, and appointed ambassador to Spain in 1933[113] – was chosen to describe "the state of Soviet cinema," offering a vaguely reconciliatory position aesthetically and emphasizing cinema's progressive development.[114]

The most prominent foreign contribution on Soviet cinema in the journal was Ivan Anisimov – literature professor and future director of the Gorky Institute of World Literature – whose lengthy essay on Sergei Eisenstein was

4.2 Overview of Soviet cinema's trajectory in *Nuestro Cinema*, issue 8–9, January–February, 1933. The more "avant-garde" works of the 1920s, except for *Battleship Potemkin*, are conspicuously absent. Courtesy of Filmoteca Catalunya.

translated from the journal *Literature of the World Revolution* and published throughout issues 3, 4, and 5 of *Nuestro Cinema*. Anisimov's otherwise seemingly celebratory piece nonetheless critiques Eisenstein for "his inability to fully articulate a dialectic alternative to bourgeois individualism" in his films, thus displaying a narrow-minded "petit bourgeois" ideology.[115] The attack escalates to the point of accusing Eisenstein of adopting a "technological fetishism that is the ideology of technique-driven intellectuals ... From a gigantic social process, he only sees a technical shell."[116] This harsh "anti-formalist" position was never explicitly supported by *Nuestro Cinema*'s own Spanish critics, who preferred, as mentioned earlier, to focus on the material implications of developing and organizing a social cinema in Spain.

In this sense, the article (signed by Soyuzkino's deputy director G. Liss) on the Soviet film industry's organizational efforts towards "the cause of culture and instruction, in helping the propaganda and stirring of the Party, the government, and the proletarians; in one word, in building the new socialist society" seems to resonate more with the writings of Piqueras than concrete criticisms of specific films or filmmakers, or debates concerning "formalism" versus "realism."[117] It is in this spirit that the critic gathered news on the creation of a Soviet film archive, school, and other related institutions (as detailed by Eisenstein himself) that had helped develop filmmaking in small national contexts with a weak film industry, something of great interest to those looking to create a new film culture in Spain.[118] And, most importantly in terms of *Nuestro Cinema*'s main objective of educating readers, the journal underscored advances in critical film spectatorship in the USSR, from where writer Ramón J. Sender reported, describing audiences as "more sharp every day, educated by the professional press," ultimately reflecting how Soviet cinema "reproduced every modality of Soviet social organization."[119]

From the very beginning of his engagement with Soviet cinema, Piqueras, in an article written in 1931, celebrates the specifically educational role of Pudovkin's, Dovzhenko's, and Vertov's new films as Soviet cinema's greatest achievements.[120] The ability of Soviet film culture to go well beyond artistic production, becoming an all-encompassing educational and social process, seized his imagination. This didactic dimension of the cinematic apparatus was also the driving principle in Piqueras's later projects for a Spanish Federation of Proletarian Film Clubs and an amateur proletarian cinema. This last project was aimed at overcoming the difficulties of production in Spain, envisioning a grassroots cinema that "depicts the life and essential struggles of the proletariat in the world, that shows its ideas and initiatives, its labors and problems."[121] Although these projects either failed or had short lifespans due to lack of funding and institutional support, all together they represented the most comprehensive Spanish attempt to emulate the USSR's cinematic model. The fact that some of Piqueras's ideas would be re-appropriated by anti-Franco militant film movements in the 1970s testifies to their long-lasting impact on the oppositional imaginaries in Spain. For example, in their 1976 analysis of Spanish cinema, Marxist collective Marta Hernández explicitly highlighted Piqueras's proposal for a Federation of Proletarian Film Clubs as a point of reference "concerning its direct relationship with a plausible production of proletarian films."[122] It is another long-term ramification in the worldwide genealogies created by the early Soviet cinema throughout the twentieth century.[123]

Conclusion

As we have seen, Soviet cinematic culture resonated strongly among a wide array of Spanish and Catalan intellectuals, critics, politicians, and educators in the late 1920s and early 30s. Although formal innovation and disruption of established artistic canons were important factors for them, we argue that the most appealing element of Soviet film culture was its pedagogical role in the construction of a new national(ist) narrative. Different Comintern-aligned initiatives, from the PCE to the PCF, and other internationalist organizations such as the AEAR, used this appeal – and the organizational force of Soviet cinema described by *Nuestro Cinema* – to tap into the cultural and cinematographic circles of the time. This new model of cinema promised to accomplish what countless well-intentioned Spanish projects had failed at in previous years: a definitive break with the past through a radical transformation of the national means of expression.

The political context accelerated exponentially what Piqueras, Del Amo, Buñuel, and many others had started as a fad among Spanish cinephiles for Soviet films. Their initial artistic admiration rapidly evolved into a larger aesthetic and political commitment in tandem with the rise of political forces on the left after the end of the Primo de Rivera dictatorship and the beginning of the worldwide economic slump. As Moussinac described in one of the last issues of *Nuestro Cinema*, Soviet film had convinced the "intellectual elite" that the coupling of formal experimentation and social orientation was only truly possible when following the USSR's model, regardless of the medium of expression (literature, art, science, and so forth).[124] For Moussinac, this interconnection was the reason why, despite all the difficulties (in reference to censorship), Soviet cinema had successfully attracted "not only the sympathies of increasingly larger social layers, but also a part of the bourgeois intellectual elite." Moussinac ended the article remembering that "such a task demands a specific will, theoretical and practical preparation, and technical organization" – a set of attributes that can be extended to the tireless efforts of Piqueras and other leftist intellectuals to create a proletarian film culture in Spain.

When the Fascist rebellion against the Second Republic in 1936 plunged the country into Civil War, this revolutionary film culture, at least partially under the influence of the Comintern's turn to the Popular Front strategy, created more space for the kind of engaged cinema that intellectuals had long been calling for. The conflict boosted the production of newsreels in defence of the Republic, and the screening of Soviet films increased with the end of censorship, especially at the front. In October 1936, Communist Party leader José Díaz gave a speech after a projection of Efim Dzigan's *We Are from Kronstadt* in the Cine Monumental of Madrid, where he praised the struggle of the "red sailors," reminding the audience that this fight was the fight they were going to experience in the following months.[125] By the time Díaz gave that speech, the foundational work had been done on the cinema front. According to a newspaper report, a few weeks later Antoni Coll, a Republican soldier, emulated a famous scene from the film – in which a Bolshevik soldier destroys an enemy tank with a hand grenade – by taking down several nationalist tanks.[126]

The Comintern had successfully introduced Soviet films in Spain through its network of intellectuals and was now ready to harvest the fruits of a well-planned cultural policy alongside other leftist forces. The film industry was collectivized by the anarchist CNT-FAI (Comisión Nacional del Trabajo, Federación Anarquista Ibérica) and the socialist UGT (Unión General de Trabajadores) in Barcelona and Madrid in the first weeks of the war, although the Communist Party also participated through its own distribution and production company, Film Popular (1937–39), and through the production efforts of the Republican government's Ministry of Education and Public Instruction, headed by PCE member Jesús Hernández Tomás.[127] The Spanish Federation of Public Spectacle Industries (FEIEP, Federación Española de la Industria de Espectaculos Publicos), with which all film workers were affiliated, sent a warm greeting to the Comintern during its 1937 foundational congress, describing Soviet leaders as "the most faithful interpreters and conductors of the working class."[128] As *Nuestro Cinema* had predicted in 1933, the widespread circulation of proletarian films pointed to "the inevitable surrender of studios, laboratories, factories, and cinematographers to the workers who labour in them."[129] Only six years after the ninth Cineclub Español session in the Ritz, which screened the Soviet films selected by Piqueras, a proletarian militant film culture had been created in Spain with the cooperation of a radicalized bourgeois intelligentsia – a culture that would thrive throughout the Civil War years, disappear during the first decades of Franco's regime, and re-emerge in the venues of an underground anti-dictatorship Marxist-driven movement of the late 1960s and early 70s.

Indeed, the scope and appeal of Soviet cinema has proven transhistorical as well as transnational throughout the twentieth century. In Spain, forty years after the last issue of *Nuestro Cinema* was published, critics Carlos and David Pérez Merinero devoted a book (*Del cinema como arma clase*, 1975) to Piqueras and the history of his journal. As elsewhere during this period of "the long sixties," they turned to the 1920s–30s Marxist film criticism as a viable point of reference for militant thought and practice in the 1970s:

> Cinema has to be, if it wants to achieve its historical mission, an instrument of culture and education against the chloroform of consciences. This pedagogical role has to focus especially on offering the proletariat lessons that can be used in their current struggle for liberation.[130]

The pedagogical and transformative capacities of Soviet cinema identified by Piqueras, in particular the films of Eisenstein and Pudovkin – "a cinema capable of freeing us from today's ideological poverty" (1932) – thus made their way into the long sixties. This programmatic position re-emerged in the form of writings, alternative exhibition spaces, production cooperatives, and films, attempting to finally realize what had begun and was lost in the Venta de Baños train station where Piqueras stopped to rest in July 1936.

NOTES

1   Juan Manuel Llopis, *Juan Piqueras, El "Delluc" Español*, Textos / Ediciones Filmo-
    teca 1A-B (Valencia: Filmoteca, Generalitat Valenciana: Generalitat Valenciana,
    Conselleria de Cultura, Educació i Ciencia, Institut Valencià d'Arts Escèniques,
    Cinematografia i Música, 1988), 112–13. Translation by Enrique Fibla (applicable
    to all translated texts in the article, unless otherwise indicated).
2   Llopis, *Juan Piqueras*, 114–15.
3   Román Gubern, *Luis Buñuel: The Red Years, 1929–1939*, English ed., Wisconsin
    Film Studies (Madison: The University of Wisconsin Press, 2012), 252.
4   Georges Sadoul, "Les Rebelles Ont Fusillé Le Louis Delluc Espagnol Juan
    Piqueras," *Regards*, 28 January 1937, 159.
5   *Nuestro Cinema* 14 (January 1935). Issues 14–17 of the journal had no page num-
    bers; applicable to all other such references.
6   As we will see later, Buñuel worked for the AEAR during the Civil War coordi-
    nating the production and distribution of newsreels in defence of the Republic.
    A less-known fact, which I recently discovered while consulting Piqueras's file in
    the dictatorship's archives, is that Piqueras was working in 1936 for the Alliance
    du Cinéma Indépendant (which directly depended on the AEAR). See "Juan
    Piqueras to Cine Teatro Club," 20 May 1936, Fichero General Político-Social
    (ES.37274.CDMH/9.8.10), Expediente N° 00056261, Centro Documen-
    tal de la Memoria Histórica, Salamanca. For more information, see Enrique
    Fibla-Gutiérrez, "Traduire l'avant-garde: Léon Moussinac, Juan Piqueras et la
    pédagogie critique de cinéma," *1895: Mille huit cent quatre-vingt-quinze, Revue
    d'histoire du cinéma*, no. 84 (Spring 2018): 41–67.

7 M. De los Angeles Egido León, *La Concepción de La Política Exterior Española Durante La II República: (1931–1936)*, Aula Abierta (Madrid: Universidad Nacional de Educación a Distancia, 1987), 589.

8 Willi Münzenberg was a key figure for the USSR's internationalization policy, both as a propagandist and a recruiter of intellectuals for the communist cause. For more information on his trajectory, see note 10.

9 Recently, there have been a few English-language works on such networks. See Enrique Fibla-Gutiérrez, "Film Called into Action: Juan Piqueras, Léon Moussinac, Harry Alan Potamkin and the *Internationale* of Film Pedagogy," *Screen* 58, no. 4 (1 December 2017): 412–36, https://doi.org/10.1093/screen/hjx041; Fernando Ramos Arenas, "Film Criticism as a Political Weapon: Theory, Ideology and Film Activism in *Nuestro Cinema* (1932–1935)," *Historical Journal of Film, Radio and Television* 36, no. 2 (2 April 2016): 214–31, https://doi.org/10.1080/01439685.2016.1167466; Eva Touboul, "Entre Divertissement et Arme: Le Cinéma Selon *Nuestro Cinema* (1932–1935)," in *COLLECTION Les Travaux Du Crec En Ligne*, no. 2, ed. F. Etienvre et S. Salaün, (2004), 184–208, http://crec-paris3.fr/wp-content/uploads/2011/07/10mfranco.pdf; Gubern, *Luis Buñuel*.

10 See, for example, Kasper Braskén, *The International Workers' Relief, Communism, and Transnational Solidarity* (London: Palgrave Macmillan, 2015), https://doi.org/10.1057/9781137546869; S. McMeekin, *The Red Millionaire: A Political Biography of Willi Münzenberg, Moscow's Secret Propaganda Tsar in the West, 1917–1940* (New Haven, CT: Yale University Press, 2003); Sarah Wilson, "Comintern Spin Doctor: Willi Münzenberg, Artiste En Révolution, 1889–1940," *English Historical Review* 127, no. 526 (2012): 662–8.

11 For example, *Ispaniya* (Esfir Schub, 1939), where Karmen is listed as camera operator, or the famous *The Spanish Earth* (Joris Ivens, 1937), in which Ernest Hemingway and John Dos Passos collaborated. See Sonia García López, *Spain Is Us: La Guerra Civil Española En El Cine Del Popular Front, 1936–1939*, Història (València: Universitat de València, 2013).

12 See also Fibla-Gutiérrez, "Film Called into Action"; Enrique Fibla-Gutiérrez and Pablo La Parra-Pérez, "Turning the Camera into a Weapon: Juan Piqueras's Radical Noncommercial Film Projects and Their Afterlives (1930s–1970s)," *Journal of Spanish Cultural Studies* 18, no. 4 (2017): 341–62, https://doi.org/10.1080/14636204.2017.1380148.

13 Antonio Marichalar, "Visto y Oído," *Revista de Occidente*, no. 95 (May 1931): 195–7.

14 María Teresa Gómez, "The Long Journey: The Cultural Politics of the Communist Party of Spain, 1920–1939" (PhD diss., McGill University, 1999), 83.

15 Already, the last decades of the nineteenth century witnessed a generational intellectual change. The Free Institution of Education (ILE, Institución Libre de Enseñanza), founded in 1876, became a pivotal institution in the modernization of the country's old-fashioned knowledge production system. It established the

Students' Residence (RE, Residencia de Estudiantes) in 1910 to place promising students from all over Spain into an environment in which were fostered creative interests in different cultural realms such as poetry, writing, theater, painting, or film. Among its pupils we find key leftist intellectuals such as Antonio Machado, Rafael Alberti, Federico García Lorca, Luis Buñuel, as well as those with more ambiguous political sympathies like Salvador Dalí. Its mission was not only to embrace avant-garde thought, but also to popularize a version of modernism contoured to the needs of Spanish society. To meet these ends, it created the Committee for Extended Studies (JAE, Junta de Ampliación de Estudios), which established the first grant system for Spanish intellectuals to travel abroad.

16 By 1934 the PCE had 25,000 members, and by 1936 it had grown to 100,000, with an increasing political weight in the Republican governments during the Civil War, when Jesús Hernández Tomás was appointed head of the Ministry of Education and Fine Arts (Ministerio de Instrucción Pública y Bellas Artes).

17 Edward Hallett Carr and Fernando Santos Fontenla, *El ocaso de la Comintern, 1930–1935* (Madrid: Alianza Editorial, 1988), 317.

18 Gómez, "The Long Journey," 231.

19 Babette Gross, *Willi Münzenberg: A Political Biography* (East Lansing: Michigan State University Press, 1974), 242.

20 Edward Hallett Carr, *The Comintern and the Spanish Civil War*, 1st American ed. (New York: Pantheon Books, 1984), 1; Carr and Santos Fontenla, *El ocaso de la Comintern*, 311–40.

21 The constant conflicts between anarchists and communists during the Civil War later proved the negative consequences of this strategy. In May 1937, an open armed conflict between them exploded in Barcelona, causing more than 1,000 dead and seriously debilitating the Republic's opposition to the advancing Francoist troops. See Manuel Aguilera, *Compañeros y Camaradas: Las Luchas Entre Antifascistas En La Guerra Civil Española* (San Sebastián de los Reyes [Madrid]: Actas Editorial, 2012).

22 Historians use this phrase to refer to the artists, writers, and poets that came to the fore of Spanish cultural production in the 1920s and 30s, heavily influenced by avant-gardist culture and modernity. Many of them gathered in Seville in 1927 to commemorate the 300th anniversary of the death of Baroque poet Luis de Góngora (hence the name).

23 This divergence in political affiliation of leftist intellectuals can be exemplified in the crossed accusations between the journals *Popular Film* (directed by anarchist Mateo Santos) and *Nuestro Cinema* (directed by communist Juan Piqueras). The latter accused the former of using its lack of political consistency to advance the interests of capitalist film companies and even defend Nazi film policy. See Juan Piqueras, "En Torno a Una Polémica de Popular Film," *Nuestro Cinema*, no. 13 (October 1933): 213. *Popular Film* replied by accusing Piqueras of "wanting everyone to think ... as ordered by the USSR, who pays for it." See Mateo Santos,

"Posiciones: La de Juan Piqueras y La Mía," *Popular Film*, no. 384 (21 December 1933); Jean Bécarud and Evelyne López Campillo, *Los Intelectuales Españoles Durante La II República*, 1. ed, Estudios de Historia Contemporánea Siglo XXI (Madrid: Siglo Veintiuno Editores, 1978); Coloquio sobre Historia Contemporánea de España, *Los Orígenes Culturales de La II República*, 1. ed., Historia (Madrid: Siglo Veintiuno Editores, 1993).

24 León, *La Concepción de La Política Exterior Española*, 541. The Comintern maintained its control over the PCE throughout the 1930s via its liaisons Victorio Codovilla (until 1937) and Palmiro Togliatti (until 1939). N. LaPorte, K. Morgan, and M. Worley, *Bolshevism, Stalinism and the Comintern: Perspectives on Stalinization, 1917–53* (London: Palgrave Macmillan UK, 2008), 171–2; A. Elorza and M. Bizcarrondo, *Queridos Camaradas: La Internacional Comunista y España, 1919–1939*, La España Plural (Madrid: Planeta, 1999).

25 Gross, *Willi Münzenberg*, 148.

26 Ibid., 270.

27 Ibid., 271. Alvarez del Vayo was a Soviet film enthusiast and would be appointed Minister of Foreign Affairs in 1936. According to Babette Gross, Del Vayo and Münzenberg had met in Berlin years before, where the former worked in a Latin American newspaper and the latter was beginning his career as a propaganda impresario for the USSR.

28 Llopis, *Juan Piqueras*, 138.

29 Founded by businessmen Ricardo Urgoiti in 1929, the company would be of vital importance for both Buñuel and Piqueras, providing financial support as their main employer in the early 1930s. The former would be hired as director of the film production department in 1934, and the latter was responsible of selecting films for Spanish distribution from France. Although Urgoiti was not a communist, he was indeed aligned with a left-wing ideology, actively supporting the Republic after the fascist rebellion. He can be considered as a key "financial benefactor" of the film culture analysed in this chapter, both as employer of its most relevant figures and as financial supporter of Piqueras's *Nuestro Cinema*.

30 In an interview with fellow Spanish exiled writer Max Aub, Buñuel acknowledged that in August 1936 he carried money from the Spanish Republic war ministry in Madrid to Münzenberg in Paris, although the details of the operation, especially what the money was for, are unknown. See Max Aub, *Buñuel, novela* (Granada: Cuadernos del Vigia, 2013), 156.

31 Gubern, *Luis Buñuel*, 262.

32 Ibid., 245.

33 Julián Marías Aguilera, "España Ante La Historia y Ante Sí Misma 1898–1936," in *Historia de España*, vol. XXIX, no. 1 (Madrid: Espasa-Calpe, 1993), 59–60.

34 "España está por descubrir, y sólo la descubrirán españoles europeizados" (Translation EF). Marías Aguilera, "España Ante La Historia," 68.

35 They were given a scholarship from the Committee for Extended Studies (Junta de Ampliación de Estudios) to research new forms of theatre in France and Germany. For a complete account of their journeys, see Allison Taillot, "El modelo soviético en los años 1930: los viajes de María Teresa León y Rafael Alberti a Moscú." *Cahiers de civilisation espagnole contemporaine*, no. 9 (11 December 2012), https://doi.org/10.4000/ccec.4259.

36 Freund Karl, "I Qué Es Muntatge?," *Cinema Amateur* 1, no. 10 (January 1936): 62–3.

37 V. Solev, "Música Absoluta Amb Só Dibuixat," *Cinema Amateur* 2, no. 11 (Spring 1936): 88–9.

38 "El Primer Film Sonoro de La URSS," *AC Documentos de Actividad Contemporánea*, no. 4 (1931): 29.

39 Luis Araquistaín, "Comentarios: La Nueva Dialéctica Histórica," *El Sol*, 18 May 1925.

40 See Gerald Brenan, *The Spanish Labyrinth: An Account of the Social and Political Background of the Civil War*, Canto ed. (Cambridge: Cambridge University Press, 1990).

41 "*Nuestro Cinema* no puede admitir – amistosamente – más que un cinema capaz de librarle definitivamente de la pobreza ideológica del de hoy. Es decir, un cinema con fondo, con ideas amplias, con contenido social ... Un cinema que nació con Eisenstein, con Pudovkin." Juan Piqueras, "Itinerario de Nuestro Cinema," *Nuestro Cinema*, no. 1 (1932): 1.

42 For a comprehensive account of the relationship between culture and nationalism in Spain, see Sandie Eleanor Holguin, *Creating Spaniards: Culture and National Identity in Republican Spain* (Madison: University of Wisconsin Press, 2002); Jordana Mendelson, *Documenting Spain: Artists, Exhibition Culture, and the Modern Nation, 1929–1939*, Refiguring Modernism 2 (University Park: Pennsylvania State University Press, 2005).

43 See, for example, Eric Hobsbawn's description of the country: "Spain was a peripheral part of Europe, and its history had been persistently out of phase with the rest of the continent from which it was divided by the wall of the Pyrenees." Eric J. Hobsbawm, *The Age of Extremes: A History of the World, 1914 – 1991* (New York: Vintage Books, 1996), 156.

44 This policy earned the opposition of most political factions. The Catholic conservatives criticized its lack of religious content, radical leftists saw it as bourgeois intellectualism and asked for an end to the censorship of Soviet film, and regional nationalists in Catalonia and Basque Country were insulted by the absolute centrality of Spanish language and culture in these initiatives.

45 "El Pueblo Del Pecado," *ABC*, 30 March 1930.

46 Compared to countries like France, Germany, or Italy, Spain was very slow to equip its theatres with sound technology – mainly due to economic reasons – although Western Electric had already fitted out 500 sound cinemas in Spain by

June 1932. See Bernard P.E. Bentley, *A Companion to Spanish Cinema*, Colección Támesis, Serie A, Monografías 266 (Rochester, NY: Tamesis, 2008), 54.

47   Emilio C. García Fernández, *El cine español entre 1896 y 1939: Historia, industria, filmografía y documentos* (Barcelona: Ariel, 2002), 247.

48   The Residencia de Estudiantes in Madrid was an exception to this isolation, but it was just a small oasis in a cultural desert regarding avant-garde and revolutionary artistic expressions.

49   Here are just a few examples: Poet and writer Louis Aragon, who had broken with the surrealists after his support of Stalinism, exercised some influence on Luis Buñuel. See Román Gubern, *Los Años Rojos de Luis Buñuel*, 1a ed. (Madrid: Cátedra, 2009), 316. Juan Piqueras was himself influenced by fellow Marxist film critic Léon Moussinac, a member of the PCF, who introduced him, together with Louis Delluc, into the film circles of Paris, where he met Georges Sadoul, Jean Cocteau, and Germaine Dulac, among other important cultural figures of the time. See Llopis, *Juan Piqueras*, 136. Many of these intellectuals collaborated at some point in Piqueras's journal *Nuestro Cinema*, which he directed from Paris, where Buñuel also lived intermittently.

50   Román Gubern, *El Cine Sonoro En La II República (1929–1936)*, 1. ed., Historia Del Cine Español 2 (Barcelona: Editorial Lumen, 1977), 71, 82; Steven P. Hill, "A Quantitative View of Soviet Cinema," *Cinema Journal* 11, no. 2 (1972): 21, https://doi.org/10.2307/1225047. Both references exclude documentary and educational films.

51   In his study of the film magazines from 1930 to 1939 in Spain, scholar Aitor Hernández Eguílez identifies at least fifty-eight film-specific magazines published throughout those vibrant years. See Aitor Hernández Eguíluz, *Testimonios en Huecograbado: El cine en la 2ª República y su prensa especializada 1930–1939* (Valencia: Instituto Valenciano del Audiovisual y Cinematografía, 2010), 28.

52   Ian Christie, "Eastern Avatars: Russian Influence on European Avant-Gardes," in *The Emergence of Film Culture: Knowledge Production, Institution Building and the Fate of the Avant-Garde in Europe, 1919–1945*, ed. Malte Hagener (New York: Berghahn, 2014), 143–61; Malte Hagener, *Moving Forward, Looking Back: The European Avant-Garde and the Invention of Film Culture, 1919–1939*, Film Culture in Transition (Amsterdam: Amsterdam University Press, 2007); Masha Salazkina, "Moscow-Rome-Havana: A Film-Theory Road Map," *October* 139 (1 January 2012): 97–116, https://doi.org/10.1162/OCTO_a_00082.

53   See, among others, Annette Michelson, "Film and the Radical Aspiration," in *Film Culture Reader*, ed. P. Adams Sitney (New York: Cooper Square Press, 2000), 404–22; Peter Wollen, "The Two Avant-Gardes," *Studio International* 190, no. 978 (December 1975): 171–5.

54   As the scholars previously mentioned have shown, tensions between different avant-garde factions soon emerged, especially after the Stalin-imposed turn to socialist realism. Art and politics were either *too close* or *too apart* for them.

Although still formally innovative, the tie of Soviet aesthetics to Stalin's national project was not accepted by many members of the avant-garde, a conflict epitomized by Lois Aragon and André Breton's fallout in 1933 (known as the "Aragon affair").

55 Juan Piqueras, "Sentido Educativo y Cultural Del Cine Soviético," *El Sol*, 1 January 1931, 8.

56 Ibid.

57 Masha Salazkina, "Soviet–Italian Cinematic Exchanges: Transnational Film Education in the 1930s," in *Emergence of Film Culture*, 180–98; Enrique Fibla-Gutiérrez, "Revolutionizing the 'National Means of Expression': The Influence of Soviet Film Culture in Pre-Civil War Spain," *Catalan Journal of Communication & Cultural Studies* 8, no. 1 (1 April 2016): 95–111, https://doi.org/10.1386/cjcs.8.1.95_1.

58 Sarah Ann Welles, "Parallel Modernities? The First Reception of Soviet Cinema in Latin America," in *Cosmopolitan Film Culture in Latin America*, ed. Rielle Edmonds Navitski and Nicolas Poppe (Bloomington: Indiana University Press, 2017), 151–75.

59 Ilya Ehrenburg famously notes in his 1932 account of the first months of the Second Republic, *España, República de Trabajadores*, that the anachronisms of Spanish society were unparalleled. He vividly describes the differences between urban and rural: millionaires in luxury cars and illiterate peasants travelling by donkey; lavish meals in the Ritz in Madrid and malnourished children in remote villages. Il'ia Grigorevich Ehrenburg, *España, república de trabajadores*, trans. N. Lebedef (Barcelona: Melusina, 2008), 9.

60 "Una Encuesta Sobre Cine Español," *Cine Art* 1, no. 12 (1934): 26.

61 Arconada had by now written two novels inspired by Soviet realism (*Turbina* in 1930 and *Los pobres contra los ricos* in 1933).

62 "Segunda Encuesta de Nuestro Cinema: Convocatoria y Cuestionario," *Nuestro Cinema* 2, no. 17 (1935): 66–7.

63 César M. Arconada, "Hacia Un Cinema Proletario," *Nuestro Cinema*, no. 8–9 (January–February 1933): 94.

64 Ibid., 102.

65 Although in this chapter we focus more on unofficial (non-government) initiatives, we should mention briefly the importance of the All-Union Society for Cultural Relations with Foreign Countries (VOKS, Vsesoiuznoe Obshchestvo Kul'turnoi Sviazi s zagranitsei) and the Friends of the Soviet Union (AUS, Amigos de la Unión Soviética), the two most important official venues aimed at disseminating a positive image of Soviet culture and society among Spanish citizens. The former was in the USSR and was administratively subordinate to the Comintern and its Foreign Relations Secretary, while the latter was controlled by the International Committee of Soviet Union Friends (which itself was subordinated to VOKS) and had different branches across Spain, with a central office in Madrid. In the absence of an official Soviet diplomatic mission, these organizations filled

that space and helped disseminate a positive image of Soviet culture while at the same time gathering useful information about the Spanish society and its key intellectual figures for the Comintern's use. M. Garrido Caballero, "Las Relaciones Entre España y La Unión Soviética a Través de Las Asociaciones de Amistad En El Siglo XX" (Tesis doctoral, Universidad de Murcia, 2006).

66 As an example, in December 1935 critic Antonio Del Amo gave notice in the PCE journal *Pueblo* that the Cineclub GECI (Group of Independent Film Writers / Grupo de Escritores Cinematográficos Independientes) and the AUS were sponsoring a screening of the Soviet adaptation of Ostrovsky's classic play *The Storm*, followed by a presentation by several AUS members who had recently travelled to the USSR and wanted to share their impressions of the journey. Antonio Del Amo Algara, "Cineclub GECI: Groza, Film Soviético de V. Petrov," *Pueblo*, 28 December 1935, 97.

67 Daniel Kowalsky, *Stalin and the Spanish Civil War* (New York: Columbia University Press, 2004), 333.

68 Gubern, *Los Años Rojos*, 284.

69 Kowalsky, *Stalin and the Spanish Civil War*, 334. Since Soviet films were banned in Spain and diplomatic relationships with the USSR non-existent at that time, one wonders how these prints actually got to Del Vayo or, rather, if they actually ever did.

70 "La Novena Session Del Cineclub," *El Sol*, 21 January 1930.

71 However, *Storm over Asia* was shown in the eleventh session in April 1930. See Llopis, *Juan Piqueras*, 306.

72 We have been unable to identify what film this is. It may be a lost film, although it is quite possible that the title and/or director name were incorrectly transcribed in the Spanish press.

73 See Timothy Barnard, "From Impressionism to Communism: Léon Moussinac's Technics of the Cinema, 1921–1933," *Framework* 42 (2000), https://www.frameworknow.com/vol-42; Bert Hogenkamp, "Léon Moussinac and The Spectators' Criticism in France (1931–34)," *Film International* 1, no. 2 (February 2003): 4–13, https://doi.org/10.1386/fiin.1.2.4; Léon Moussinac, Valérie Vignaux, and François Albéra, *Léon Moussinac: Un intellectuel communiste, critique et théoricien des arts* (Paris: Association française de recherche sur l'histoire du cinéma, 2014).

74 María Antonia Paz Rebollo and Julio Montero Díaz, "Las Películas Censuradas Durante La Segunda República. Valores y Temores de La Sociedad Republicana Española (1931–1936)," *Estudios Sobre El Mensaje Periodístico*, no. 16 (2010): 369–93.

75 *Cineclub Español*, May 1931, Program handout, Filmoteca Española, Madrid, ARA/15/01. This handout included a brief history of the organization, a summary of the films projected, and a reflection on the cultural and educational importance of the organization (it would be the last session of the Cineclub).

76 The specificities of the Spanish context demanded a less hard-line Third Period approach, since the first objective of the PCE was to increase its membership and political influence.

77 Llopis, *Juan Piqueras*, 300.
78 This organization was a precursor of the AUS, and continued to exist in parallel during the following years.
79 Daniel Kowalsky mentions the celebration of this one-day festival in his account of Soviet-Spanish cultural relations before 1936, quoting a letter from Antonio Bonet to VOKS from 26 August 1931 (GARF, f. 5283). Kowalsky, *Stalin and the Spanish Civil War*, 335.
80 Asier Aranzubia Cob, "Julián Antonio Ramírez: Inventario de Actividades Fílmicas," *Ikusgaiak* 6 (2003): 148.
81 Guillem Díaz-Plaja, *Una Cultura Del Cinema: Introducció a Una Estètica Del Film* (Barcelona: Publicacions de La Revista, 1930), 114.
82 Ibid., 107.
83 Sergei Eisenstein, "Los Principios Del Nuevo Cine Ruso," *Nuestro Cinema*, nos. 8–9 (January–February 1933): 105. Conference presentation in Paris transcribed to Spanish by Juan Piqueras.
84 Ibid., 108.
85 Ibid., 107.
86 The committee was officially constituted in 1933 and later renamed Generalitat de Catalunya Propaganda Commissariat during the Civil War.
87 The document was drafted using several memorandums written by candidates to occupy the committee's direction, among them Domènec Giménez i Botey – one of the main figures of the Catalan Excursionist Amateur Cinema Section. Domènec Giménez i Botey, "Quina Hauria d'ésser La Funció Dels Organismes Oficials per Utilitzar l'acció Del Cinema Com a Instrument de Cultura," 6 May 1933. For a translation of segments of the document, see Masha Salazkina and Enrique Fibla-Gutiérrez, "What Should the Role of Official Institutions Be in Relation to the Use of Cinema as an Instrument of Culture?" *Film History* 30, no. 1 (2018): 168, https://doi.org/10.2979/filmhistory.30.1.08.
88 See Masha Salazkina and Nathalie Ryabchikova, "Sergei Eisenstein and the Soviet Institutional Models for the Study of Cinema, 1920s–1940s," in *Sergei M. Eisenstein: Notes for a General History of Cinema*, ed. Naum Kleiman and Antonio Somaini (Amsterdam: Amsterdam University Press, 2016), 405–14; Masha Salazkina, "(V)GIK and the History of Film Education in the Soviet Union, 1920s–1930s," in *A Companion to Russian Cinema*, ed. Birgit Beumers (Hoboken, NJ: John Wiley & Sons, 2016), 45–65, https://doi.org/10.1002/9781118424773.ch2.
89 Guillem Díaz-Plaja, "Funció de l'amateur En El Cinema Educatiu," *Cinema Amateur* 1, no. 2 (Winter 1933): 36.
90 Josep Carner-Ribalta, *De Balaguer a Nova-York Passant per Moscou i Prats de Mollo. Memories* (Paris: Edicions Catalanes de Paris, 1972), 148–50.
91 Ibid., 167–8. For more information on the work of Ramón Biadiu and the Generalitat de Catalunya Propaganda Commissariat's relationship with the USSR, see José María Caparrós Lera, Ramon Biadiu Cuadrench, and Miquel Porter i

Moix, *Petita història del cinema de la Generalitat: 1932–1939* (Mataró: Robrenyo, 1978); Mercè Biadiu Ester, *Ramon Biadiu (1906–1984): Cineasta d'avantguarda* (Súria; Manresa: Ajuntament de Súria; Centre d'Estudis del Bages, 2007); Josep Puigsech Farràs, *La Revolució Russa i Catalunya* (Vic: Eumo, 2017); Ramón Breu, *La Catalunya Soviètica: El Somni Que Venia de Moscou*, primera edició, Sèrie H (Badalona: Ara Llibres, 2011); Enric Ucelay da Cal and Joan Esculies, *Macià Al País Dels Soviets*, primera edició, De Bat a Bat 35 (Barcelona: Edicions de 1984, 2015).

  92 R.S. Noguer, *El Cine En La España Republicana Durante La Guerra Civil (1936–1939)*, Colección Cinereseña (Bilbao: Mensajero, 1993), 217.

  93 Josep Pla, *Viatge a Rússia: Notícies de l'URSS: Una Enquesta Periodística*, 2. ed., L'Ancora 27 (Barcelona: Destino, 1990).

  94 Josep Palau was a critic for *Mirador* journal, a key outlet for bourgeois modernist ideas in Catalonia during the 1920s and 30s. Like Domènec Giménez i Botey and Guillem Diaz-Plaja, Palau was involved with the Catalan amateurs and published in their journal, *Cinema Amateur*.

  95 Juan Piqueras, "En Torno a René Clair," *Cinegramas*, no. 78 (8 March 1936).

  96 For a detailed analysis of this shift, see Ramos Arenas, "Film Criticism as a Political Weapon."

  97 Juan Piqueras, "Hacia Una Federación Española de Cineclubs Proletarios," *Nuestro Cinema* 2, no. 13 (1933): 216.

  98 For a detailed analysis of this trajectory, see Barnard, "Moussinac's Technics of the Cinema"; Moussinac, Vignaux, and Albéra, *Léon Moussinac*.

  99 The defence of a social cinema rooted in realism was also shared by anarchist critics such as José Peirats, who in 1935 published a book titled *What a Social Cinema Could Be* (*Lo que podría ser un cinema social*), in which realism – and the documentary genre in particular – was underscored as the most important feature of the medium. Similar positions were defended in realms such as literature and graphic arts. See, for example, José Renau's defence of a "new realism" for graphic arts in his book *The Social Function of Advertisement Posters*. José Renau, *Función Social Del Cartel Publicitario* (Valencia: Tipografía Moderna, 1937), 28.

100 Salazkina, "Moscow-Rome-Havana: A Film-Theory Road Map," 106–7.

101 Kurt Kersten, "Los Problemas Del Cine Soviético," *Nuestro Cinema*, no. 4 (September 1932): 117.

102 Also highlighted by Ramos Arenas, who comments that Piqueras chose to "overlook this contradiction," putting "film theory in the service of ideology. Ramos Arenas, "Film Criticism as a Political Weapon," 222–3.

103 Joshua Malitsky, "Ideologies in Fact: Still and Moving-Image Documentary in the Soviet Union, 1927–1932," *Journal of Linguistic Anthropology* 20, no. 2 (December 2010): 357, https://doi.org/10.1111/j.1548-1395.2010.01074.x.

104 Sergei Tret'iakov, "Our Cinema," reprinted in *October* 118 (October 2006): 27–44, https://doi.org/10.1162/octo.2006.118.1.27.

105 E.A. Papazian, *Manufacturing Truth: The Documentary Moment in Early Soviet Culture* (DeKalb: Northern Illinois University Press, 2009).

106 When the journal published a special issue on film history in 1933, it included a full-page illustration devoted to the "Soviet Trajectory," including stills from mostly recent films, except for *Battleship Potemkin* (Sergei Eisenstein, 1925). The other films included were *Storm over Asia* (Vsevolod Pudovkin, 1930), *The General Line* (Sergei Eisenstein, 1929), *Road to Life* (Nikolai Ekk, 1932), *Ivan* (Alexander Dovzhenko, 1932), *Golden Mountains* (Sergei Yutkevich, 1931), *Les Tartares* (Piotr Tchardynine, 1926), and another a full-page photomontage of *The Blue Express* (Ilya Trauberg, 1930) as well as a film identified as *Arsenal Humano* (?) by director Alexander Room, which probably corresponds to *Arsenal* (Alexander Dovzhenko, 1929).

107 Tret'iakov, "Our Cinema," 36. See, for example, Pedro Vigues's description of Soviet cinema as the "antithesis of bourgeois cinema ... It's not only in the technical aspect that Soviet cinema creates its means of expression; its avant-garde visual angles ... but the differentiating element is manifested ... in its social stance." See Pedro Vigues, "Individualismo y Colectivismo En El Cinema," *Nuestro Cinema*, no. 14 (January 1935).

108 César M. Arconada, "Luis Buñuel y Las Hurdes; El Film," *Nuestro Cinema*, no. 15 (February 1935): 9.

109 Ibid.

110 Ibid.

111 Barnard, "Léon Moussinac's Technics of the Cinema," 8.

112 Karl Radek, "'La Sinfonfa de La Cuenca Del Don' de Dziga-Vertoff y 'Sola', de Llya Trauberg," *Nuestro Cinema*, no. 1 (June 1932): 18–21.

113 Lunacharsky died on 26 December 1933 in France on his way to take office as ambassador in Madrid.

114 A.W. Lunacharsky, "El Cinema Soviético: El Cinema Revolucionario Soviético," *Nuestro Cinema*, no. 1 (June 1932): 14.

115 Ivan Anissimov, "El Cinema Soviético: Los Films de Eisenstein," *Nuestro Cinema*, no. 5 (August 1932): 74, 76. Anisimov's last name is incorrectly spelled with two s's.

116 Ibid., 73.

117 G. Liss, "El Cinema Soviético y el Segundo Plan Quinquenal," *Nuestro Cinema*, no. 6 (November 1932): 171–4. Translated from Russian by M. Villegas López.

118 Eisenstein, "Los Principios Del Nuevo Cine Ruso."

119 Ramon J. Sender, "Notas Sobre El Cinema Soviético," *Nuestro Cinema*, no. 13 (October 1933): 220.

120 Juan Piqueras, "'Tres Evoluciones Ideológicas En El Cine Soviético," *La Gaceta Literaria*, no. 105 (May 1931).

121 Juan Piqueras and Lisa Jarvinen, "Our Amateur Cinema in 'Nuestro Cinema,'" *Cinema Journal* 51, no. 4 (2012): 142–3.

122 Marta Hernández, *El Aparato Cinematográfico Español*, Akal 74; 51 (Madrid: Akal, 1976), 172.

123 Salazkina, "Moscow-Rome-Havana: A Film-Theory Road Map," 97–116; Fibla-Gutiérrez and La Parra-Pérez, "Turning the Camera into a Weapon, 341–62; Fibla-Gutiérrez, "Traduire l'avant-garde," 41–67; Welles, "Parallel Modernities?" 151–75.

124 Léon Moussinac, "El Cinema Soviético Tiene Quince Años," *Nuestro Cinema*, no. 15 (February 1935): 2.

125 José Díaz, *Tres Años de Lucha* (Paris: Editions de la Librairie du Globe, 1970), 112.

126 The story was probably a propaganda manoeuvre from the Republican government to lift the moral of the soldiers defending Madrid, although it was recounted in at least six different sources (*El Sol, ABC, El Mono Azul, Heraldo de Madrid, Ahora, Solidarida Obrera*). See José Cabeza San Deogracias, "Buscando Héroes La Historia de Antonio Col Como Ejemplo Del Uso de La Narrativa Como Propaganda Durante La Guerra Civil Española," *Historia y Comunicación Social*, no. 10 (2005): 37–50.

127 Gubern, *Luis Buñuel*, 268.

128 José Cabeza San Deogracias, *El Descanso Del Guerrero: Cine En Madrid Durante La Guerra Civil Española (1936–1939)* (Madrid: Ediciones Rialp, 2005), 170.

129 Juan Piqueras, "Historiografia Del Cinema," *Nuestro Cinema*, nos. 8–9 (January–February 1933): 44.

130 Carlos Pérez Merinero and David Pérez Merinero, eds., *Del Cinema Como Arma de Clase: Antología de Nuestro Cinema 1932–1935* (Valencia: F. Torres, 1975), 19.

Chapter Five

The Panorama and the Pilgrimage: Brazilian Modernism, the Masses, and the Soviet Union in the 1930s

SARAH ANN WELLS
University of Wisconsin, Madison

In 1933, a Brazilian journal surveyed various writers and public figures with the question, "Where is Brazil heading?" This question captures the oscillating apocalyptic and optimistic tones of the decade's cultural production, one of many attempts to both diagnose impending political and economic crises and reroute them towards alternate economic, political, and artistic paths. In his answer to the question posed by the journal, the influential Brazilian avant-gardist Oswald de Andrade offered one such path: "Where is Brazil heading ... To Russia!"[1] With his response, Oswald joins a growing group of Brazilian intellectuals and artists who sought out overlooked points of contact with the Soviet Union as a means of participating in and fashioning a global imagined community. Brazilian artists and intellectuals had only recently begun to find in the partial, uneven, and juxtaposed modernities of the Soviet Union a connection to their understanding of Brazil's position in the world, one that attempted to short circuit both the prerogative of Paris and the burgeoning superpower of the United States. They began to consider, as scholars would decades later, that the most daring of experimental practices of historical modernism might not be found in Paris, London, or New York, but rather in Leningrad and Moscow – or in Recife, Rio de Janeiro, and São Paulo.

This chapter focuses on the impact of the Soviet Union on the trajectories of two key Brazilian modernists: the writer, editor, and communist Patrícia Galvão and the modernist painter Tarsila do Amaral. Aided by their growing interest in Soviet art and politics, Galvão and Tarsila (as she is known in Portuguese) helped to inaugurate the two genres that will come to characterize 1930s late modernist production in Brazil: the proletarian novel and its painterly equivalent, known in Brazilian cultural history as "social painting."[2] I explore the strategic, if ultimately truncated, possibilities the Soviet Union afforded artists and intellectuals by analysing how these artists employed two figures: the panorama and the pilgrimage, both of which sought to envision a world whose increasing connectedness possessed utopian dimensions for artists on the peripheries of global capitalism.

Such world-making impulses can be seen as a response to the "imperial dreams" and, more broadly, new forms of perception in the nineteenth century that sought to apprehend increasingly larger stretches of the globe. These phenomena are epitomized in the apparatus of the panorama.[3] Immersing viewers in global scenes, the historic panorama concealed its operations in order to produce an ideally seamless sense of worldliness; the term is a neologism borrowing from Greek, meaning "all-seeing."[4] Yet, as Toscano and Kinkle suggest in their *Cartographies of the Absolute*, the panorama need not only represent an ideological blind spot, a shorthand of the "dangers" of totalization. Instead, this mode of envisioning also contains glimpses of the "gaps and dislocations" apparent in any attempt to view the world as a whole[5] – attempts that should not be discarded but explored from their varying sites of envisioning. The panoramic experiences I analyse in this chapter exceed the more precise and narrow apparatus of the historical-technological panorama and include the virtual and metaphoric: they include various iterations of modernist experiments with the global, from inventive maps to graphic design, correspondence, little magazines, the novel, travel itineraries, and oil painting, all of which sought to produce a sense of global simultaneity from a particular vantage point.[6] What I am interested in is how artists and intellectuals borrowed from the effects of these kinds of immersive global experiences of visuality to recast the panorama's imperial dreams from outside Euro-American centres, enabled in no small part by their literal and figurative journeys to the Soviet Union. If one of the constitutive elements of the panorama is the "blindness" of the interior, the location from which the spectator watches, it does not follow that all locations themselves are neutral in their seeming opacity. In this way, I argue, the invocation of the Soviet Union helped artists and intellectuals to produce Brazil's contemporaneity during the period, implicitly questioning the characterization of belatedness that plagued (and, arguably, continues to plague) approaches to modernism on the continent.[7]

Many of Latin America's most important modernists of the late 1920s through the 1940s were fascinated by the Soviet Union. In the South American context, Argentina proved the most robust environment for Soviet-inflected modernism in the form of dozens of little magazines and influential artists, particularly writers, as well as serving as the heart of the Comintern's South American sphere.[8] Peru was the birthplace of the influential postcolonial Marxist intellectual José Carlos Mariátegui, who died in 1930, leaving behind an unparalleled experimental, anti-colonial, pro-indigenous leftist journal (*Amauta*, 1926–30); as well as Latin America's most formidable avant-garde poet, César Vallejo, who, beginning in the 1930s, produced hundreds of pages on the problems of art and politics as inflected by his newly acquired communist identity and travels to the Soviet Union. To these cases we can add the most famous Latin American poet of the twentieth century, the Chilean Noble Prize–winner

Pablo Neruda, who joined several of his contemporaries in crafting odes to Stalingrad in the early 1940s. In addition, prominent writers such as Jorge Luis Borges (Argentina) and Alejo Carpentier (Cuba) engaged in debates about the impact of Soviet art, especially cinema, during the modernist period. Their views differed vastly and their interests in turning to the Soviet case were idiosyncratic, but all registered, even if begrudgingly (as in the case of Borges), its importance for any discussion of modernism. Beginning in the 1930s in particular, the late modernist turn towards the Soviet Union expanded the project of the earlier continental avant-gardes to inscribe themselves onto a global map that often seemed intent on disavowing their protagonism.

In this context, Brazil possessed no precise equivalent to a formidable figure like Mariátegui or Vallejo. Yet, Brazilian intellectuals and activists would develop an organized and active Communist Party (PCB, Partido Comunista Brasileiro), which would incorporate key modernists in the 1930s. Often irrespective of their individual political affiliations, Brazilian intellectuals throughout the twentieth century would also find a shared sense of identity with what they often labelled the "colossus" that was the Soviet Union: a country that, like Brazil, was enormous, diverse, and semi-agrarian, on the hither side of Europe, and on the cusp of industrialization and rapid progress.[9] The Soviet Union's seemingly miraculous surmounting of what was depicted as centuries of lethargy and the promise of its Great Leap presented tremendous potential for Brazil; a country that the press repeatedly depicted as barbaric and lawless had very quickly become a world protagonist. Because Brazilian intellectuals had long seen their own country, "the sleeping giant," in similar terms, a doubled discourse of identification and promise, of diagnosis and change, characterized their discussions of the Soviet Union, with its "audacity" and independence with respect to world politics and culture.

While the Brazilian Communist Party was founded in 1922 – inspired by earlier anarchist and socialist movements and the Russian Revolution itself – it was not until the 1930s that we find modernist artists taking up the Soviet promise with gusto. This particular historical juncture, which saw both a turning away from the euphoria of the earlier Brazilian avant-gardes and the politicization of the aesthetic sphere, is central to the reception of Soviet culture in Latin America. This reception includes the country and continent's first exposure to Soviet avant-garde cinema during the late 1920s and early 1930s, and, in a more widespread fashion, the boom of affordable translations of Russian literature (mainly from the nineteenth century, but also including writers such as Gorky) that flooded South America vis-à-vis new technologies and publishing houses designed to address an expanding mass readership. In addition, the period also saw the publication of Brazil's first leftist periodicals run by intellectuals and artists seeking a broader base (as opposed to the ephemeral, if compelling, anarchist press and communist dailies of the 'teens and 1920s).

Finally, and also beginning in the 1930s, the masses became a site of political and aesthetic potential throughout the continent. The figure of the masses was far from transparent: it appeared to forever betray its cohesiveness because of the very heterogeneity it claimed to embody.[10] Moreover, it was both adopted and produced by a variety of different aesthetic and political orientations, including nationalist and proto-fascist movements. As a figure, it was both index and icon for major debates of the 1930s, drawing together these previously separate realms, politicizing the aesthetic and aestheticizing the political. Everyone, it seemed, spoke its language. In this context, Soviet cultural production provided a set of verbal and visual tropes that promised participation in an increasingly broader panorama, beyond the Latin American–North Atlantic axis; invoking the idea of a potentially global mass offered a means of participating in the construction of a contemporaneity that seemed, for artists in and beyond Brazil, on the cusp of becoming truly expansive.

Patrícia Galvão: Print Culture, the Proletarian Novel, and a Global Mass Aesthetic

The work of writer and activist Patrícia Galvão (1910–62) constitutes the most ambitious effort to join together the political and aesthetic avant-gardes during the 1930s in Brazil. Indelibly marked by the seminal Brazilian modernist movements in literature and painting of the late 'teens through the 1920s, both her work and her life provide a key point of inflection of the influence of Soviet art and political discourse in the transition between her predecessors, with their emphasis on ludic experimentation, and the late modernists of the 1930s and 1940s, with their emphasis on the urgency of the socio-economic and political. This transition was by no means seamless, and Galvão's work demonstrates a conflicted struggle between the imperatives of political and aesthetic experimentation that often appeared, to many of her contemporaries, to be mutually exclusive.

In the periodical she co-founded and co-edited, *The Man of the People* (*O homem do povo*, 1931–32), and in *Industrial Park* (*Parque industrial*, 1933), Galvão negotiated a series of questions that would retrospectively define the artistic movements of the 1930s, a moment in which, in the words of an article in *The Man of the People*, "the most absurd tendencies clash in their effort to conquer the working masses"[11]: How can the mass be at once the vanguard? How can the representative speak for the whole? How can the global speak to the local? Galvão frequently borrowed from the visual in her search for forms that would speak at once to both the interconnected yet uneven status of the globe, its simultaneous discontinuity, and Brazil's role within it, as well as to the increasingly prominent figure of the masses. This dual interest was shaped by her recent conversion to communism, a position she would abandon in the

second half of the decade after suffering both disillusionment at the Party's proletarianization phase and violent political repression and imprisonment at the
hands of the anti-communist regime of Getúlio Vargas (1930–45).[12]

Galvão's modernist debut did not hint at either the radical leftist commitments or bold experiments that would characterize her 1930s work. In her
first public appearances, the more prestigious modernists present constructed
her as an enigmatic figure of desire, the modernist muse. A portrait printed
in the popular magazine *Para Todos* and dated 27 July 1929 shows "Pagu"
(her nickname) smoking in flapper-style clothes; naming the famous artists
whom she accompanies, it praises her for "abolishing the grammar of life"
and describes her as a "lioness": "the ultimate product of São Paulo."[13] Ostensibly seductive, feral, wild, Pagu was an example of what Liz Conor has called
"the spectacular modern woman," or *melindrosa*, as she was known in Brazil:
a form of self-fashioning afforded to women in the early twentieth century
through their manipulation of visual "techniques of appearing."[14] The velocity
at which Galvão's techniques of appearing would change in the following years
allows us to trace, as in no other artist, the rapid but far-from-seamless transition between the modernism of the 1920s to its late modernist formulation
as global leftist critique.

Yet, Galvão's trajectory does not merely reflect this transition but was also
instrumental in shaping it. In 1930, just a year after she appeared as the feral
muse in *Para Todos*, Galvão travelled to Buenos Aires, where she met both Brazilian and Argentine communists. Upon returning to Brazil in 1931, she and
her partner, Brazilian modernism's enfant terrible Oswald de Andrade, joined
the PCB. The years that follow reveal an astounding body of work, in the largest
possible sense. Oswald will attribute his own "conversion" to Galvão's political,
aesthetic, and affective influence; in an inversion of the earlier modernist-muse
relationship, he will go on to emulate her use of pro-Soviet language in his own
fiction, beginning with the preface to his experimental novel *Seraphim Ponte
Grande* (1933). Inaugurating the Brazilian iteration of the proletarian novel,
Galvão also ushered in the conversion of key modernists to the communist
cause, embodying the modernist artist-activist.[15]

Galvão's first iteration of Soviet influence appears in the little magazine *The
Man of the People*.[16] *The Man of the People* bridges the earlier experimental
period with Galvão's newly politicized orientation through strategies that seek
to produce the global mass in ways her predecessors had not. Throughout, the
earnestness of its new-found leftism intermingles with a lacerating irony that
showcases the at times uncomfortable marriage between avant-garde irreverence and the burgeoning communist allegiance of its editors. Its founding,
prompted by the editors' new leftism, was inflected by the recent global economic crash that, they hoped, would draw the world together in a shared experience, apocalyptic (revelatory) with respect to the contradictions of capitalism.

They write in their programmatic statement in the first issue: "In the world there is super-production of everything and never was there so much misery."[17] Crisis, they believed, would allow for the "synthetic rupture" that Lukács argued would render visible capitalism's workings.[18] Throughout its eight issues, the journal claims no party affiliation but grants its strongest support for a "revolutionary left" that supports national interests, while frequently expressing admiration for the Soviet Union.

Each issue of *The Man of the People* contains six pages in an unusually large, tabloid form. It employed modernist typography – experiments with capitalization, fonts, and the size of letters – inspired by Brazil's first avant-garde periodical, *Klaxon* (1922–23), whose aesthetics drew from Dada, among other sources. The playfulness of *The Man of the People*'s avant-garde predecessors can be found as well in the pseudonyms of the contributors, varying nom de guerre/plume that reflect the high-low and internationalist orientation of the periodical, as well as its typographical experiments: "Âlcool Motor," GÂS ASFIXIANTE," "Reporter Z," "ZUMBI," "COBRA," "Spartacus," and "Mademoiselle Chiquinha Della-Oso," a fashion consultant (likely Galvão). Coupled with the journal's sardonic, polemical tone, these attributions signal *The Man of the People*'s avant-garde pedigree, as the rebellious offspring of the *Revista de Antropofagia* (*Cannibal Journal*, 1928–29), with its unprecedented combination of the ludic, postcolonial, and psychoanalytic.

The Man of the People marks its difference with these avant-garde predecessors, however, in its title, which seeks out a very different audience. In their effort to produce a popular idiom while working on a budget, the editors interwove the typographical experiments with film stills in unexpected or contrapuntal juxtapositions of content and images. The journal also featured a regular cartoon by Galvão, which recounts the adventures of a young revolutionary with humour and defiantly rudimentary sketches accompanied by brief, slangy captions. Galvão's cartoon invites identification with the heroine, depicted in simple, modernist (short skirt, beret) clothes as she engages in direct action: metafictionally founding a journal, resisting sexist overtures, protesting, getting arrested. Drawing on the concision, brevity, and rapid-fire cuts of the newly popular form of the cartoon, Galvão also recasts the modernist muse as political activist.

In the column "Woman of the People" (A mulher do povo), Galvão also attempts to address the specificity of women's experience. In strident language, she puts forth a prescient critique of the facile importation of what she sees as bourgeois and Eurocentric – what would later be dubbed First-World feminism – to the Global South, evading larger structural (economic) concerns.[19] At the same time, her column is not immune to tensions that run throughout *The Man of the People* in its casting of the mass as the vanguard. In an article in the last issue entitled "Normalinhas" (the word for those "little girls" who attended public school), Galvão's voice drips with anger as she accuses the group of misdirected energies, easy dupes for capitalist mass culture. The voice here oscillates, at once positioning itself as part of this group (Galvão had, in fact, been one of such students and will soon write detailed accounts of its forms of sociability in her novel *Industrial Park*) but also above it, a member of a new communist vanguard. Describing these young women in the third person as "ignorant of life and of our moment!," she subsequently shifts to the second person to berate them.[20] Her tone oscillates to simultaneously critique and exhort, swinging between the author's own identification with the mass that she also wants to guide. On the visual plane, this column reinforces the sense of uplift that the journal itself wrestles with: it is juxtaposed with a photograph of two girls, one swarthy and one blondish, holding hands, with the caption "two girls of the People [*do povo*] ready to fight for the proletarian cause." The photograph is also framed with a heading, "Revolutionary Happiness." Since the girls are not identified with any proper names, we are left to wonder if they are Brazilian potentialities, Soviet actualities, or in fact representatives from some other part of this worldwide revolution. As throughout the periodical, here the disparate is yoked together under the same space on the printed page, the public school girls intoxicated by cheap romances and the young girls ready to fight for the revolution.

Galvão's drawings and columns point us back to a constitutive tension of the journal: its desire to be at once "of the mass" and "of the vanguard." For example, rather than listing the founders, the periodical's masthead attributes its directorship to the eponymous "man of the people." This ventriloquism, wherein the artist/intellectual throws his or her voice into mass body, will become a feature of cultural production in the 1930s: "So we will debate all social, economic, and financial problems in an accessible way [*em forma popular*], in order to be understood by the less educated mass of the population, so that they might learn to voice their own opinions."[21] As this quote reveals, the ventriloquism is contradictory: the man of the people is simultaneous the director/producer and consumer of the journal; while supplanting the role of vanguard, he nevertheless still needs to be guided by the editors.

The same tension is apparent in the little magazine's fascinating heterogeneity, its admixture of materials, and the variety of its regular columns. It moves among politics ("Pamphlet and Doctrine"), economics ("Economic Barometer"), the arts ("Stage, Screen, and Circus"), and even sports (one column espouses the organic links between soccer and communism.)[22] While this eclectic mix is constitutive of the periodical as a medium, *The Man of the People* is quite unparalleled among its contemporaries in its desire to see every facet of daily life as part of a larger struggle in which the man of the people's devotion to sports and cinema would be equivalent to his investment in the number of tons of steel produced that quarter in the Union of Soviet Socialist Republics (USSR).

As these strategies indicate, *The Man of the People* borrows from earlier modernist strategies of parataxis to a different effect. While their predecessors had employed the paratactic in what amounted to an implicit celebration of Brazil's "uneven" modernity as a source of avant-garde potential, in *The Man of the People* this juxtaposition is drawn onto the same temporal plane and expanded out spatially, seeking to produce the simultaneity of the global present.[23] The column "World Summary" in particular encapsulates the journal's program to invest in new, popular forms as a means of bringing the world to the viewer/reader in a synthetic, entertaining, and unapologetically leftist stance. The article "Juicy Carrion" promises to bring to the eponymous man of the people, "who leaves home early for the factory, office, or warehouse and so has only a few minutes during his streetcar ride," the opportunity to consume "rapid, concise, and concrete news" of the world in "just four lines." Unlike "carbon paper, slavishly summarizing the news from the telegraph," however, the editors insist that their world coverage will be at once "dense" and "distilled." They promise to "juice the telegrams" to offer the very best to their busy man of the people, as in the following:

Nine million workers unemployed in the U.S. (Hip, hip Hoover!). Thälmann Communists thrashing Hitler's Nazis. Strikes in Spain. Yet another state of emergency in Cuba ... 300,000 red soldiers in Soviet China (30,000,000 inhabitants), beating back, in hand-to-hand combat, the imperialist bandits. The five-year plan realized in four. Trotsky's house in flames ... Etc. Etc. Etc. The world convulsing. Combusting. Volcano. Revolution.

On one hand, the editors appropriate the paratactic strategies of the earlier avant-gardes to underscore the clash between disparate global forces – "Hitler's Nazis" with "strikes in Spain." At the same time, they reorient the cannibal trope from the import-export model, with its implicit acceptance of the one-way street of colonial expropriation, towards an imagined plane of global simultaneity. The world's central struggles thus "juiced" to their essence, the digestive process takes place: "the teeth of the man of the people will break down this news, which, for its part, stimulates the appetite of solid, healthy stomachs."[24] Along with the paratactical, telegraphic writing that had characterized the early Oswald, this article also rewrites his privileged trope of cannibalism as a trope of postcolonial appropriation of Western knowledge. Redeploying the cannibal trope from its origins in the avant-garde stance, the article projects it into the stomachs of the masses, in a kind of planetary digestion. In the fifth issue, for example, world news will also be presented as "the tastiest of telegrams," including a general strike in Oslo, the lockout of unemployed workers in Copenhagen, and a group of young women strikers in Johannesburg who prevented strike-breakers from entering a factory. In both cases, current world events, rather than a mythic past as wellspring or origin story, provides the journal with its motivation: inspiring and frustrating moments unfold before the viewer/reader.

This present is also fashioned in terms of telescoped scales, in which the Soviet Union serves as a connecting vector. The column "The City, the Country, the World" showcases this ambition: the local (São Paulo), national (Brazil), and global are seen as interlocking, rather than discrete realms. In this sense, *The Man of the People* not only describes but also produces a global struggle that interpellates Brazilians as part of a broader struggle: "The world is spectator to a gargantuan struggle between life and death, enacted between the communist sector, represented by the Soviet Union, and the capitalist sector, represented by five-sixths of the globe."[25] From its opening manifesto, ironically titled "Order and Progress" (the Positivist slogan that adorns the Brazilian flag since its formation as a republic in 1889), the magazine declares this purpose. Signed by the pseudonym "Black Helium," "Order and Progress" is a declaration of this new global order that does not eschew but rather repositions the national as part of a potential vanguard: "We want the national revolution as a stage of planetary harmony that the age of the machine promises us." This founding editorial proceeds to pendulum between the Soviet Union and Brazil, between the potential being realized in the foreign country and the truncated potential of their own, as the speaker surveys this new global order he is also attempting to shape: "We admire contemporary Russia, despite its disorder," it states. Later, after praising Russia's advances in metalwork, the editors turn back towards Brazil: "From a country possessing the greatest reserve of iron and the highest level of hydraulic power, they've made a country of dessert. Coffee, sugar, smokes, bananas." And yet, "we eat apples from California, cod and sardines from abroad, in spite of our own abundant fields of fruit, our rivers, and sea."[26]

In this sense, the magazine's panoramic impulse, which maps out the world as clashing forces, indexes the desire to participate in an alternative cosmopolitanism. It sketches a world divided in which Brazilians might have the choice of allegiance, the opportunity to cast off their colonial subjugation and align themselves with struggles occurring abroad.

This impulse is especially evident in the frequent discussions about India, markedly unusual for a Brazilian periodical of this time (albeit present in the PCB daily *Classe Operária* [*Working Class*], which its founders undoubtedly read.) *The Man of the People* underscores the similarities between the two as large, diverse nations suffering under imperialism. In all capital letters and bold print, the editors proclaim in one unsigned piece: "BUT WHAT HAVE WE GOT TO DO WITH ALL THIS? PLENTY! INDIA IS OUT OF WHACK FROM IMPERIALIST EXPLOITATION: SHE HAS SHOUTED, SHE HAS PROTESTED AGAINST THE DOMINATION OF THE PARASITIC VINES THAT OPPRESS AND SUCK THE LIFE OF THE WORLD." The typography clearly strains here in an attempt to issue forth a public scream, positing a virtual collectivity that includes ethnic, national, and linguistic difference. While India's imperial subjugation is blatant, Brazil's is less explicit, "stealthier": "They say that Brazil is for the Brazilians. But its railways and ports are British and French. Its mines are British. Its dams are American. Its industry is Italian."[27] Drawing on the paratactic forms of modern print journalism, the Indian and Brazilian contexts are linked here in a map of exploitation and burgeoning resistance, triangulated through the USSR. In comparing them, Brazilian leftists sought to produce their own anti-imperialist panoramas.

Galvão's experience with the little magazine undoubtedly shaped *Industrial Park*, which sought to build on *The Man of the People*'s anti-imperialist panorama through the genre of the novel.[28] While it had scant impact upon its publication in 1933 (when Galvão was only twenty-two), this novel will retrospectively be seen as among the first in a boom of Brazilian and Latin American proletarian novels of the 1930s. Yet, her approach is quite different from the socialist realism that will become prominent throughout the decade; like *The Man of the People*, *Industrial Park* is poised between the avant-garde experimental novel of the 1920s and the new genre of the proletarian novel, which will become associated above all with the more celebrated communist writer Jorge Amado.

Like *The Man of the People*, *Industrial Park* features a slangy orality and draws from popular visualities to interrogate what Galvão saw as the genre's trenchant focus on a bourgeois, individual history. The novel's chapters are divided into brief sections, separated by a modernist graphic icon, suggesting a kind of cinematic cut. In its emphasis on clashing forces, it is also indebted to Soviet montage, to which Galvão was exposed very briefly, seeking to adopt forms from the cinema to the page. Just as Eisenstein had proclaimed the cinema would override the individual, she hoped to undermine the novel's traditional emphasis on individual perspectives in favour of a new, collective subject.[29] In this respect, Galvão's strategies also dovetail with Walter Benjamin's Soviet-inflected vision of the writer in "The Author as Producer," originally delivered as a talk at the Institute for the Study of Fascism. Contemporary with *Industrial Park* and part of the broader proletarianization of the early to mid-1930s, "The Author as Producer" rethinks the materialities of writing as a means of reconceiving literary form and genre: "There were not always novels in the past, and there will not always have to be," Benjamin states.[30] Drawing on Sergei Tret'iakov's distinction between the "operating" and the "informing" writer, Benjamin depicts an author "intervening" and "struggling" through the very materials of his or her prose. Like Galvão, for Benjamin the new writing that would emerge from the Soviet imperative would upset both the role of the expert and of the genre itself, inaugurating a radical shift in our understanding of both artwork and authorship.[31]

While *The Man of the People* approached this dual problem through the piecemeal, ephemeral, and contingent modes proper to modern journalism (a key site for Benjamin of "The Author as Producer" as well), *Industrial Park* attempts to import these same strategies into a thick description of a city and people immersed in a crisis. Beginning with its epigraph, the novel locates us squarely in an "economic depression that afflicts the whole world and whose repercussion we began to feel in the month of October 1929." As in *The Man of the People*, the global crisis is also an opportunity for experiments with simultaneity that signal the interconnectedness of the globe. Here, Galvão takes on the additional challenge of inflecting this "global" – as much fashioned as described – through the particular textures of a city that, in turn, functions as a microcosm of these same struggles. In what is arguably Brazilian literature's most heterogeneous depiction of mass experience, *Industrial Park* depicts faces, voices, and bodies struggling with interlocking problems of class, race, gender, nationality, and sexuality. These disparate perspectives encounter one another – and often clash – around a centripetal event, the fomentation and suppression of a strike. Three characters in particular are instrumental in the strike narrative and demonstrate Galvão's attempt to metonymically stage the mass as a disparate but linked collectivity. While not protagonists, they are accorded a certain gravitas in the novel. Didactic arrows, they point towards the masses they are supposed to metonymically represent: Otávia is a school-girl-turned-activist factory worker whom critics tend to read as autobiographical; Rosinha, a Lithuanian immigrant, nods to Rosa Luxemburg and encapsulates the immigrant experience. Most powerfully, Alexandre, an Afro-Brazilian dockworker and leftist leader who dies a martyr, shot down by the police during a protest, is modelled after an activist who played a key role in Galvão's radicalization, Herculano de Santos. De Santos was assassinated by the police in 1931 at a rally protesting the Sacco and Vanzetti case, organized by the PCB, before being able to realize his dream of travelling to the Soviet Union. His death inspired mass protests and a collective ceremonial burial when the police denied his family the right to his body.[32]

Yet, Galvão does not manage the strike plot as a realist novel would, through pacing and accumulative detail in which each character's "coming to consciousness" would be reflected in a broader narrative arc. Instead, she presents us with a kaleidoscopic panorama, a constantly mutating collection of voices and bodies drawn from strikingly disparate scenes from the rapidly industrializing, ethnically diverse, and class-stratified city of São Paulo: brothels, boarding houses, factories, street protests, salons of the wealthy, schools, streetcars, and Carnival all make an appearance. Chapter titles connect different social spaces, pointing simultaneously to an episode taking place within the chapter and a broader global phenomenon: "Racial Opiate," "Where Surplus Value Is Expended," "A Bourgeois Vacillates," "Where They Talk about Rosa Luxemburg," and, unsurprisingly, "Proletarianization." In this way, the chapters and their titles suggest the telescoping of scales in the column "The City, the Country, the World" of *The Man of the People*, where vectors with clear communist resonance traverse increasingly broader contexts, at once irreducibly local and global.

The year following the publication of *Industrial Park* was a culminating one in Galvão's turn towards the Soviet Union.[33] In 1934, the PCB urged her to travel to the country she had long imagined and evoked in the novel and little magazine: "I was going to see Russia. I was going to encounter a different world of struggle, and I expected so much from that world."[34] Departing Brazil, Galvão would now corporeally enact the global panorama she had fashioned in *The Man of the People* and *Industrial Park* in an unprecedented itinerary for a Brazilian of the time: from New Orleans and Hollywood to China, Japan, and the Soviet Union, before concluding in Paris prior to her return to Brazil.[35] It was only in 2005 that her experiences there would become public through the publication of her memoir, in the form of a long letter written to her second husband, under the title *Paixão Pagu* (*Pagu-Passion*). This strange text is marked by her profound disillusionment with communism, forming part of the more widespread "repentance" genre of the political and aesthetic vanguards of the historical modernist period.[36] Part confessional, part testimony, part renunciation, the memoir was drafted in 1940 as Galvão waited out the end of her prison sentence for her communist sympathies. Her next work of fiction would be a novel, co-authored with her now-husband Geraldo Ferraz, *A Famosa Revista* (1945), a scathing critique and repudiation of the PCB.

Her memoir interests me precisely for its anguished, retrospective exploration of the 1930s enthusiasm for the political-aesthetic promises housed in the Soviet Union. Galvão writes the account as a way of wrestling with the tremendous sacrifices she has made in the name of communism; it is also an essay of a self divided or doubled in its aesthetic and political commitments. It is constructed as a series of trials that the first-person narrator faces: imprisonment for her leftist sympathies by local and national authorities, followed by tests to prove her loyalty to the PCB, culminating in a final test, her pilgrimage to the USSR. Prior to this culmination, she is sent from one city in Brazil to another and, as the proletarianization imperative becomes official during the Third Period, is made to seek work in a variety of places: as a tailor's assistant, line worker at a bottling factory, maid, metalworker, usher at the cinema. Her self-fashioning as a proletariat is superimposed upon her newly repentant self, the ex-Party member, in a fraught act of self-translation or masking (as in a personae) that resonates, albeit with a very different relationship to the state, with Katerina Clarke's analysis of the Stalinist intellectual within the Soviet Union during the same period.[37]

Towards the end of the account of her Soviet journey, Galvão utilizes the train ride to and from Moscow as a metaphor for the way in which expectations and realities surrounding the Soviet Union become confused and superimposed in her mind as she (materially) experiences the encounters she had (virtually) fantasized in Brazil:

> All of my readings of texts rained down like an avalanche, linking themselves to my desires, my life, my past observations, my fantasizing. I postponed as long as I could the paradisiacal visions, uniting, through the jolts and bumps of the train, Shakespeare and a mythological Ancient Greece, riven through with tractors and airplanes that rained down wheat instead of bombs and, above all, marching youth: all with dazzled [*deslumbrado*] eyes.[38]

The description invokes the panorama of *The Man of the People* and *Industrial Park*, but now criticized as a fantastical superimposition of unrelated icons for eyes that are at once "dazzled" and "blind." The last lines of her memoir are characterized by an ironic hindsight. As she leaves Moscow, "the sky was a sky of planes and over there, in the tribune, at the heart of the young people in a line, the supreme leader of the Revolution. Stalin, our guide. Our chief."[39] A few years prior, she or one of her co-editors of *The Man of the People* had constructed its participation in the global vanguard by invoking Stalin, signing with the pseudonym "Estalinho" ("little Stalin") an article discussing the ways in which journalists – "proletarians of the pen" – were obligated to produce anti-communist propaganda in Vargas-era Brazil.[40] The affectionate use of the diminutive, and the freedom to take on the personae of Stalin as a sign of the irreverence of the periphery, is precisely what will be undercut repeatedly in the years following the little magazine's publication. By the late 1930s, Galvão will abandon the PCB, along with her fascination with the global mass as a paradoxical vanguard.

Tarsila do Amaral: Painting and Pilgrimage

Shortly before Galvão travelled to the Soviet Union, Tarsila do Amaral, arguably the most influential Brazilian visual artist of the early twentieth century, made her own pilgrimage there. This shared experience of two very different modernists indicates the importance of the Soviet Union for experimental artists of the period, even as the proletarianization of the 1930s seemed to foreclose the very possibilities opened up under its banner. While the two women frequented the same circles in the 1920s, and overlapped briefly as romantic partners of Oswald de Andrade (indicating the close-knit nature of Brazil's historical avant-gardes), their artistic biographies and role in the intellectual and aesthetic sphere of modernist Brazil were quite different. Where Galvão was from a self-described "petit-bourgeoisie" family, living in the worker's neighbourhood of Bras until the age of sixteen "in a proletarian atmosphere,"[41]

Tarsila belonged to the elite São Paulo society from which many of the modernists of the 1920s also emerged. Tarsila was also older, travelled, and accomplished; during the 1920s, Galvão as the young muse frequently depicted her admiration for Tarsila's artistic prowess.

Moreover, while they made similar pilgrimages during the same period – the long journey to Moscow followed by a trip to Paris before returning to Brazil – both their experiences and the art works they produced under the influence of the Soviet Union differed in significant respects. Galvão's trip to the French capital (her first) included links to provocateurs Louis Aragon and André Breton, as well as to the group "À la Lumière du Marxisme," which edited international socialist editions; Tarsila's, by contrast, was a kind of homecoming for an artist who had received Cubist training there during the 'teens, and whose political activism was limited to a brief stint painting worker housing in the Parisian suburbs.[42]

Why would Tarsila, an artist who expressed few explicit political convictions either before or after her pilgrimage, a member of Brazil's elite, and an ardent admirer of the Parisian artistic milieu, make the risky journey to Moscow? Her Soviet pilgrimage points to the critical juncture of the mid-1930s, in which "Soviet cultural leadership was a distinct possibility throughout the transatlantic intellectual world, even for Paris-based intellectuals, a reality often ignored in cultural histories."[43] For Tarsila, to be an artist in the world meant participating in this alternate itinerary, a participation that would be significantly less fraught than Galvão's. While drawing on the rhetorical and visual strategies of Soviet art, ultimately she found it less a nodal point for an urgent global present than a repository for buried treasures: icons ignored by modernity, ethnic and national particularities that paralleled her unique vision for her own homeland and for Brazilian modernism. Her approach less reverent, more modestly iconoclast, she remained less scathed by the Soviet adventure than her literary contemporary.

There are many fruitful points of comparison between Tarsila's early work, prior to her discovery of Russia, and a nativist variant of the Soviet avant-gardes with whom she would only become familiar and influenced by in the 1930s. The primitivism and influence of naïve art that characterized her early work resonates, albeit without the Marxist inflection, of the neo-primitivism of key Soviet artists such as Natalia Goncharova. Indeed, the Latin American avant-gardes more broadly – from Oswald to Mariátegui to the Mexican artists and intellectuals Eisenstein encountered in the early 1930s – often looked to models of national or regional autochthony, not only to reinvent art and make it new but often as a creative if problematic solution to the problem of underdevelopment.[44] In contrast to Galvão, Tarsila's incipient interest in the Soviet context is inflected by the romantic strain of Brazil's historical avant-gardes: the construction of new beginnings through a search for national essences, in

particular the non-Western treasures ostensibly lying in wait for artistic exploitation, an interest that links Brazilian and Russian artists, here shorn of the
dimension of class struggle. No image is more iconic of this quest than Tarsila's
startling *Abaporu* (1928), considered the visual equivalent of Oswald de Andrade's
1920s manifestos and poetry. Along with her earlier representations of Brazil's
abundant flora and fauna, this singular figure captured a gesture of the first
avant-gardes: the euphoric sense of discovering Brazil through experimentation with proportions, colours, and the human body itself, while drawing on
the (creatively interpreted) tradition of the indigenous Tupi, the large ethnolin-
guistic group that Brazilian intellectuals crafted as an origin. *Abaporu* became
the icon of Oswald de Andrade and Oswald Costa's avant-garde cannibalism,
and was published along with the seminal "Cannibal Manifesto."

In 1930, Tarsila sold paintings from her personal collection – like Oswald
de Andrade, her family had lost a chunk of their coffee plantation fortune in
the 1929 crash – to pay for a trip to the Soviet Union, inaugurating a two-year
period of her first and last experience with Comintern aesthetics. Her own
month-long imprisonment in São Paulo upon returning to Brazil (due to her
Soviet trip and presumed left-wing sympathies) would put a definitive end to
this short-lived but intense enthusiasm. "Now I am seeing what Russia is," she
will also write home to her family.[45] "So much fantasy surrounds her!" The
phrase is ambiguous: Is the fantasy her own, prior to her arrival, or those of
others? Does seeing, rendering visible, dispel the seduction that motivated her
journey? As Tarsila's account suggests – and as Galvão also discovered in her
much more fraught pilgrimage – it is impossible, and ultimately unproductive,
to separate the two. These virtual and material trips to the Soviet Union meant
taking myth and fantasy seriously, as Tarsila had long done.

Revolutionary fervour notwithstanding, Tarsila appears fundamentally
interested not in the Soviet Union's promise of futurity but in folk religious
culture, an interest that echoes her fascination with the Brazilian baroque
and indigenous cosmologies. Before leaving for the Soviet Union, Tarsila reflected on the promise of the foreign land in this same spirit of avant-garde
ethno-national "discovery": "The legends that surround the snowy land of
Lenin exercise an inexplicable seduction on my spirit. This is why I want to
visit Moscow: to appreciate her new constructions, as well as her animated
people [*povo*], with their utterly unique and healthy mentality, their natural
laws and lungs able to breathe the air of the healthiest of freedoms."[46] In this
description, the "new constructions" take a backseat to the mythic "snowy
lands" with their "inexplicable seduction." In a letter to Mário de Andrade,
her close friend and the so-called "pope" of Brazilian modernism, she mar-
vels at collections of icons that would inspire his own folkloric investigations
into "deep Brazil."[47] In the letter to her family, she notes, without dwelling
on, the destruction of churches or their conversion into secular museums,

mentioning that religion is still preserved in some small towns. In her obligatory trip to Lenin's tomb, what most impresses her is its sense of worship,
"religious pilgrimage," and "sect." "I'm imbued with the spirit of the People
[povo]," she writes. And, while she notes the era's commonplace of the Great
Leap – "admirable what such a barbaric people has achieved in such a short
amount of time!"[48] – she is drawn to what seems to be old in this land of energetic progress. In a 1944 article, she would continue to write of her fascination
with Leningrad, now completely stripped of its politics, in terms of these striking architectural features: "the Asiatic city of strange architecture, where the
church cupolas recall gigantic onions draped in gold and shrieking colours."[49]
Her sketches from Moscow are focused in particular on statues and cupolas, vertical structures that draw our eyes upwards, away from the work begin
done on the ground.[50] Painterly from beginning to end, Tarsila's pilgrimage
exhibits none of the urgent angst of Galvão's.

Still, Tarsila's Moscow period affords us a glimpse of a cultural exchange
between the Russian and Brazilian contexts, motivated by a leftist orientation
if not circumscribed by it. This brief look again contrasts with Galvão's production and subsequent narrative, where the Soviet Union appears only as a
beacon and ultimately frustrated object of desire, or heartbreak: a promise for
global participation held out and then deferred. The highlight of Tarsila's visit to
Moscow would be an exhibition of her 1920s paintings there.[51] While she writes
home to both friends and family that it was a success, it does not appear to have
turned out quite as expected. Her work was introduced at the museum with a
preface on "decadent Western art"; this was the year of the Kharkov conference
that set the terms for socialist realism, bad timing for the reception of Tarsila's
defamiliarizing, euphoric shapes and colours. Aracy Amaral reproduces some
of the negative comments included in the visitor's book the museum provided:
Tarsila is accused of not understanding the proletarian cause; her striking colour palate is seen to be alienating; and so forth. Still, the Soviet government
ends up purchasing one of her works, the painting *The Fisherman* (*O pescador*,
1925) for its Central Museum of Western Art (part of the Hermitage), a purchase that allowed her the funding to continue her travels around the country.[52]
The Fisherman (figure 5.1) is an earlier work that typifies Tarsila's interest in
saturated colours and naïve art; in the foreground, a lone Afro-Brazilian fisherman, in profile and with his features undetailed in a kind of lush abstraction, exercises his trade, dwarfed by an exuberant nature and the whitewashed
houses that surround him. In addition to her exhibit, Tarsila also gave a talk on
Brazilian art while in Moscow.

Tarsila's partner, the writer, psychiatrist, and future art critic Osorio César,
functioned as Galvão had for Oswald de Andrade: he guided her burgeoning
passion for the Soviet Union, inflecting her pilgrimage. César would write his
own travelogue from the period, *Where the Proletariat Leads ... (Panoramic*

5.1 Tarsila do Amaral, *The Fisherman* (*O pescador*), 1925. Copyright Bridgeman Images.

Vision of the USSR) (Onde o proletariado dirige ...[Visão Panorâmica da URSS], São Paulo, 1932): "The Soviet Union is now at the forefront. We all want to know what is happening in that Socialist republic whose expanse encompasses one-sixth of the world."[53] As do articles in *The Man of the People*, César empha- sizes the Soviet Union's large size as a sign of its world prowess and the need for Brazilians, themselves part of a huge, peripheral nation on the rise, to reorient their gaze to what they have overlooked. César's use of the term "panorama" in the title invites comparisons with the visual strategies that structure Galvão's contemporaneous print production, in which the invocation of the Soviet Union serves as a springboard to envision the world's global connectedness. Here, the panorama invokes the Brazilian traveller's own participation in a cos- mopolitan identity: not just to "know what is happening" in the great "colos- sus" but to *see* it, to render it visible, albeit in a less jarring, clashing sense than the juxtapositions which defined Galvão's approach to the global present. This cosmopolitan desire is reinforced by the book's preface by Henri Barbusse, the

5.2 Tarsila do Amaral, cover design for *Where the Proletarian Leads* ... (Osorio César), 1932.

French novelist, communist, and Esperantist (and later the author of a hagiographic biography of Stalin.)

César's book also features a cover design by Tarsila herself (figure 5.2), as well as sketches from her Soviet journey. These images indicate a first step towards the later social paintings that mark her interest in the Soviet Union and represent her second significant collaboration with a writer-partner after *Abaporu*.[54] On the cover of *Where the Proletariat Leads*, dark outlines of buildings, smokestacks, and bridges usher in Tarsila's first approaches to industrial space. More abstract and less detailed than her later short-lived "social period," these figures occupy the majority of the cover and lift our eyes vertically: a signature of her Soviet sketches. While most of the cover is in black and white, a red square in the corner frames the author's name, yoking him through into a broader communist community. The title is written by hand, scrawled diagonally across the bottom of the cover in lower-case letters in an almost naïve scrawl that suggests a desire to mimetically encapsulate the earnest hand of the proletariat of the title.

This book indicates the steps taken by Tarsila to reroute her artistic orientation away from the exuberance of *Abaporu* and its promise of renewal through autochthony, while not abandoning it entirely. In addition to Tarsila's own sketches, César's work contains archival images that offer us a clue to the influences that mark her brief Soviet period. These include a portrait of Lenin speaking by A.J. Alexandrovitch, the leader perched at a podium in the foreground; in the backdrop, the ubiquitous smokestacks that are reflected in the cover. On the following page, a photograph, dated 1931, of a large mass of people celebrating the October Revolution; the crowd spills out as far as the eye can see in a diagonal sweep that directs our gaze towards the edges of the frame. When she returned to Brazil, Tarsila drew on such images to create the two paintings that will define what is known as her brief but potent "social" period: *Second Class* (*Segunda Classe*, 1933) and *Labourers* (*Operários*, 1933).[55] This same year, she also gave a talk at the São Paulo Modern Artists Club (CAM, Clube de Artistas Modernas) on Soviet poster art, based on examples she brought back from her travels. She would subsequently donate these to the Museu de Arte de São Paulo (MASP), inaugurating an archive for future artists and providing a certain symmetry to the purchase of her own painting by the Soviet state.[56]

If *Industrial Park* is considered the first proletarian novel in Brazil, *Labourers* (figure 5.3) has been deemed its painterly equivalent. A line of smokestacks recalls images from *Where the Proletarian Leads*, including the cover and the image of Lenin, drawing our eye upwards. At the same time, the decentred pyramid of faces pushes at the painting's frame, suggesting a seemingly infinite continuity. Aracy Amaral suggests that the painting might have also drawn inspiration from the more avant-garde, photo-montage posters of Soviet artists like Valentina Kulagina, noting her 1930 poster for International Women's Day – with a sea of textile workers positioned similarly to the right of the setting of their trade, arranged in a pyramid shape – as a possible source (as well as a possible object in the exhibit Tarsila organized upon her return).[57]

In both *Labourers* and *Second Class*, Tarsila shifts towards the physiognomies of the proletariat and the precariat, respectively. (*Second Class* seems to depict itinerant families without work, while *Labourers* depicts factory workers.) Tarsila's only approach to the masses in her oeuvre, *Labourers* replaces *Abaporu*'s sense of wonder with rows of proletarian faces. The painting is clearly located in an industrialized São Paulo, the subject of *Industrial Park* and a very new location for her paintings, which had tended towards mythical spaces

5.3   Tarsila do Amaral, *Labourers* (*Operários*), 1933. Copyright Romulo Fialdini/
Tempo Composto.

or small, often tender or toy-like villages from the Brazilian interior. In both
paintings, the artist underscores both the plurality and specificity of the mixed-
race faces increasingly identified in the 30s with Brazil's national identity. In
Labourers in particular, these faces retain the integrity of specific features (some
modelled after Tarsila's friends and acquaintances), in contrast to earlier paintings like *The Fisherman*, while also complementing one another as a mass. In
contrast to the exuberant, pulsating colours of her earlier modernist paintings,
the palate here is more sober in its diversity: peaches, tans, and deep browns
playing off one another across a variety of phenotypes through shadows, lip
tones, hair colour, and hijabs, giving us a figure of unity in diversity, the multi-
ethnic, multiracial and multinational (immigrant) scene of São Paulo also
depicted in *Industrial Park*.

In addition, those pulsing smoke stacks, drawn in much less detail than the
faces, adapt Tarsila's earlier interest in the power of naïve painting to the new
imperative to position the human figures against a backdrop that determines

them. Essentially, the painting inverts her earlier work; where, in paintings like *The Fisherman* and *Abaporu*, the background and foreground seemed to envelop the figures with a sense of non-deterministic, celebratory harmony, these workers stare back at the viewer, and possibly at the artist herself. For its part, *Second Class* also seeks to register the increasingly prominent and unstable figure of the masses, a problem virtually absent from the earlier work of Tarsila and her cohort. Here, the faces are those of migrant workers from the Brazilian interior, as intricately detailed as in *Labourers*, who also stare back at the viewer as if interrogating her.

In contrast to the Soviet paintings that inspired these works, however, Tarsila's subjects are more melancholic and implicitly ruminating, a gaze that resists a clear-cut political ascription. In this sense, they recall an earlier variant of Brazilian modernism: the struggle of elite artists and writers to comprehend the "enigma" of Brazilian national identity.[58] Ultimately, Tarsila's collective are more *povo* (folk) than *mass*. Thus, despite the shared inspiration from the Soviet context, including the desire to meet the gaze of the masses, Tarsila's adaptation of Soviet poster art and discursive celebration of the proletariat to her own "elevated" interpretation of socialist realism through oil painting in the end contrasts with Galvão's contemporaneous work. Rather than an effort to agitate the Brazilian cultural sphere through an injection of urgency that draws on mass culture forms, Tarsila shapes icons of Soviet visuality (the smokestack, the sea of workers' faces) to her particular vision. Rather than invest in the strategies of juxtaposition that telescoped city, nation, and world, Tarsila continues her quest for something like a national essence, mythic, if irreducibly specific.

As Aracy Amaral points out, Tarsila's social paintings lack the sense of agitation, futurity, or movement of the works of Soviet poster art or photographs of crowd scenes that were their possible inspiration and that appear in *Where the Proletariat*. Tarsila's gaze seeks to produce an intimacy that, at its root, maintains a kind of romantic stasis, even in her most leftist period, a moment that she too would subsequently disavow. As they fashioned their global visions through their Soviet pilgrimages, these two artists ultimately embodied quite different approaches towards the fraught present.

Conclusion: Cinema and the Afterlives of the Soviet Avant-Gardes

It is a historical irony that the discovery of the Soviet Union by Brazilian artists and intellectuals occurred during the Third Period.[59] This moment in the Comintern's history exhibits parallels with Brazil's own "October Revolution," which in 1930 brought Getúlio Vargas to power, reorienting Brazil's exuberant first-wave modernism towards state-sponsored, culturally nationalist forms. The artistic flourishing of the 1920s would not expire but would be forced to mutate, either confronting political repression from the left or subsumed into

Vargas's conservative revolutionary program in which poets, novelists, painters, and filmmakers were incorporated into state policy. Vargas's administration thus overlapped in certain respects with Stalin's program to subsume avant-garde energies into the state.[60] The audacious experiments of the first wave of the avant-gardes would become, through a targeted program of appropriation and censorship – of Gramscian coercion and consent – either bureaucratized or censored. What Brazilian artists and intellectuals sought out in the Soviet Union as a radical alternative, in other words, would not be very different from what was taking shape back at home. Thus, it is no surprise that the 1940s accounts of the Soviet Union by key modernists would be disillusionment: not only given the repercussions of Stalinism but also in its uncanny photographic negative back home in the virulently anti-communist milieu of contemporaneous Brazil.

Yet, this period did not mark an end to the reception of the Soviet Union by Brazilian artists and intellectuals. In fact, the marriage of formal experimentation and the pressing force of the masses, itself a means of positioning Brazil (and Latin America) globally, will only continue throughout the twentieth century. In the continent's flourishing experimental leftist art movements of the 1960s and 1970s, Soviet art will become once again a way of thinking the union of national-popular anti-imperial politics and aesthetic avant-gardes. During this period, a different medium becomes the site of this transculturation of Soviet aesthetics: cinema emerged to replace print and painting as the site where Brazilians engage with the Soviet Union.[61]

As the cosmopolitan travelling medium par excellence, cinema afforded a different iteration of the pilgrimage to the Soviet Union of the 1930s. With film form, this travel is not only spatial but also temporal: cinema is a particularly potent form of time and space travel, from its production to its circulation, distribution, and reception. The cinema is the panorama's most influential heir, and it would render that particular form of spatial-temporal travel obsolete, offering more powerful ways of positioning the viewer and the immersive, vicarious experience of (planetary) travel it seeks to produce. In the wake of the optimism surrounding the Cuban Revolution (1959), filmmakers from Brazil and throughout Latin America returned to early Soviet avant-garde cinema, often positing it as an alternative to both the national military dictatorships and the ever-increasing influence of globalizing US mass culture. The influential notion of "Third Cinema" – Latin America's contribution to postcolonial film theory – posits an alternative to Hollywood as well as to the New Wave, and thus it is no coincidence that the Soviet Union once again pops up as an alternative to the models of the United States and France with which the historical avant-gardes of the 1920s and 1930s had also struggled. The most important experimental leftist filmmakers of the 1960s, including Glauber Rocha, Nelson Pereira dos Santos, and Leon Hirszman, cut their teeth on screenings of Soviet films, where the half-lives of Eisenstein and Pudovkin found a new venue in young artists searching for an alternative to Hollywood and its South American imitators: glossy, high-production and formulaic productions that seemed to eschew the raw reality of the national-popular.[62] Their formative years were marked by the optimism of the presidency of Juscelino Kubitshek (1956–61), whose campaign slogan "fifty years in five" has its own debt to earlier Soviet political discourse.

As Brazil's democratically elected left gave way to a right-wing military regime (1964–81), in a pattern that would be repeated throughout South America, the employment of earlier Soviet film aesthetics began to take on an untimely edge. Brazilian experimental filmmakers would appropriate what they read as the frustrated utopias of 1920s Soviet avant-garde aesthetics. In this context, they began to opt for modes of pointedly belated appropriation over the presentist urgency of the 1930s writers and artists, for whom citation of the Soviet Union constituted, as we have seen, a calling card for participating in global contemporaneity. Instead, these filmmakers invoked and extended the truncated promises of early Soviet avant-garde film form – which had little or no direct influence on filmmakers of the early to mid-twentieth century – into the optimism and subsequent despair of the second half of the century. In contrast to their predecessors in the historical avant-gardes, Brazilian and Latin American filmmakers of the 1960s and 1970s achieved renown for their particular strategies that de-emphasized technological virtuosity and underscored the power of cutting, non-actors, and didactic anti-imperialist critique. Telescoping contemporary struggles with experimental strategies of earlier Soviet cinema, Brazilian filmmakers were thus allowed into a global conversation hereto denied to their predecessors, while paying homage to the late modernists who had first experimented with alternative panoramas and pilgrimages, the Soviet Union their lodestar for strategic envisionings of the globe.

NOTES

1   Originally published in *Diário de Notícias* (Rio de Janeiro, 28 May 1933); reprinted in Agosto de Campos, ed., *Pagu, Patrícia Galvão: Vida-obra* (São Paulo: Brasiliense, 1982), 326. Unless otherwise noted, all translations from Portuguese are mine.

2   I describe this period as "late modernism" to distinguish it from the earlier experimental period of the 1920s, and further develop this periodization in *Media Laboratories: Late Modernist Authorship in South America* (Evanston, IL: Northwestern University Press, 2017). In texts from the 1930s in Brazil, the period is at times referred to as *pós-modernismo* to indicate a similar distance with respect to their experimental precursors.

3   See Angela Miller, "The Panorama, the Cinema, and the Emergence of the Spectacular," *Wide Angle* 18, no. 2 (1996): 34–69, esp. 34. See also Markus Krajewski,

World Projects: Global Information before World War I (Minneapolis: University of Minnesota, 2014).

4 Miller, "Panorama," 34, 43.

5 Alberto Toscano and Jeff Kinkle, *Cartographies of the Absolute* (London: Zero Books, 2015), 55. Toscano and Kinkle are resolutely Euro-American in their focus.

6 In his inversion of North/South relations, *América Invertida* (1943), for example, the Uruguayan artist Joaquín Torres-Garcia clearly echoed the Belgian variant of surrealist remapping of the world to locate Russia at the centre of a new globe (1929).

7 A common error is to equate the Boom of the 1960s and 1970s with Latin America's entry into modernism, overlooking the vast production of the continent's historical avant-gardes of the 'teens through the 1930s. Fernando Rosenberg's reading of geopolitics from the specific location of Latin American modernism offers a compelling counterpoint, and has informed my reading of the period here and elsewhere. See Fernando Rosenberg, *The Avant-Gardes and Geopolitics in Latin America* (Pittsburgh, PA: University of Pittsburgh, 2006). See also Michael Denning, "The Novelists International," in *Culture in the Age of Three Worlds* (London: Verso, 2004), 51–72. Denning's argument reads the Latin American Boom as a response to the proletarian novel – not equivalent to official socialist realism – of the first decades of the twentieth century. His attention to this genre allows him to move beyond entrenched, Cold War–driven opposition between Soviet realism and US modernism.

8 The Brazilian Communist Party (PCB, Partido Comunista Brasileiro) grew in part through its close ties with the more developed Argentine Communist Party in the 1930s. See Marco Santana, "Moscow in the Tropics: The Third Period, Brazilian Style," in *In Search of Revolution: International Communist Parties in the Third Period*, ed. Matthew Worley (London: I.B. Tauris, 2004), 360–72. On the Argentine context during the 1930s and 1940s, see John E. Eipper, "On Utopia, Infiltrators and Five-Year Plans: Argentine Populist Writings and Early Soviet Russia," *Journal of Latin American Cultural Studies* 7, no. 1, (1998): 95–110.

9 With the notable exception of Eisenstein's justifiably famous sojourn in Mexico and, in particular, Masha Salazkina's compelling model of comparative modernisms and modernities on the periphery, *In Excess: Sergei Eisenstein's Mexico* (Chicago: University of Chicago Press, 2009), and her more recent overview, "Eisenstein in Latin America," in *The Flying Carpet: Studies on Eisenstein in Honor of Naum Kleiman*, ed. Joan Neuberger and Antonio Somani (Paris: Éditions Mimésis/Images, Médiums, 2017), 343–66, the Soviet reception of the first half of the twentieth century in Latin America is understudied. I explore the early reception of Soviet film in "Parallel Modernities? The First Reception of Soviet Cinema in Latin America," in *Cosmopolitan Visions: Latin American Film Culture, 1896–1945*, ed. Rielle Navitski and Nic Poppe (Bloomington: University of Indiana, 2017), 151–75.

10 The literature on the masses in Latin America during this period is voluminous. For one example, see José Luis Romero, *Latinoamérica: Las ciudades y las ideas*

(Mexico: Siglo Veintiuno, 1986), 159–60, 409–16. Romero defines the masses in growing urban centres, from Mexico City to Buenos Aires, as neither right- nor left-wing; they are what exceed political classification, its surplus.

11 ZUMBI, "Contras os carangueijos do movimento syndical," *O homem do povo*, no. 4 (1931): 2; in the facsimile edition (São Paulo: Impr. Oficial do Estado, Divisão de Arquivo do Estado de São Paulo, 1985), 36. Galvão co-founded and produced *The Man of the People* with Oswald de Andrade and Oswaldo Costa, another *antropofagista* writer.

12 Galvão was the first woman incarcerated in Brazil for political reasons. Vargas began a severe repression of leftists in the wake of a failed communist rebellion in 1935, imprisoning thousands of artists, activists, and intellectuals, including many non-communists, Tarsila do Amaral among them.

13 Reprinted in de Campos, *Pagu, Patrícia Galvão*, 304. The fascination with Galvão's modernist gesture, dress, and body is repeated in accounts of her in the 1930s, including observations of her behaviour at her various trials for political subversion in the latter part of the decade: "Ultra-modern in ideas and dress, 'Pagu' calmly awaited her hearing while she smoked many cigarettes from a long holder." Dan Shupe, "News in English: Local," *Diário de Notícias* (Rio de Janeiro, 23 February 1946): 2. At her trial by the National Security Tribunal, she was described as "extremely dangerous, very intelligent, speaking diverse languages, an intellectual orator of the red ideology who makes use of printed materials." (As cited in K. David Jackson and Elizabeth Jackson, "Afterword," in *Industrial Park*, trans. Elizabeth and K. David Jackson (Lincoln: University of Nebraska, 1993), 120–1.

14 Liz Conor, *The Spectacular Modern Woman: Feminine Visibility in the 1920s* (Bloomington: Indiana, 2004). See also Vicky Unruh, "Las ágiles musas de la modernidad: Patrícia Galvão y Norah Lange," *Revista Iberoamericana* 64, nos. 182–3 (Enero-Junio 1998): 271–86. Evidently, given the long equation of women with the body, there are risks in overemphasizing the "body work" of women artists and activists, but it is important to recover this ephemeral archive.

15 Oswald depicts himself in the character Jorge D'Alvellos in *The Staircase* (*A Escada*, 1934), the last volume of his *Exile Trilogy*, "narrating his conversion to Marxism, instigated by Mongol," a character clearly modelled after Galvão, also known as "Pagu" (Risério in de Campos, *Pagu, Patrícia Galvão*, 19). For her part, in *Industrial Park*, Galvão had fashioned the character Alfredo de Rocha – a wealthy man who becomes a leftist sympathizer, only to be expelled from the Party rather quickly for his inability to take the revolution seriously – after Oswald.

16 The journal would be destroyed by a group of law students who resented the anti-nationalist, anti-military, and anti-Catholic stance it repeatedly and provocatively took.

17 Oswald de Andrade, "Ordem e progresso," *O Homem do Povo*, no. 1 (São Paulo, 27 March 1931): 1; facsimile, 17.

18 See Toscano and Kinkle, *Cartographies of the Absolute*, 79.

19   *O Homem do Povo*, no. 1 (27 March 1931): 2; see also Risério in de Campos, *Pagu*, *Patrícia Galvão*, 19. In this context, Vargas's 1932 electoral code, which granted women the right to vote – first exercised in the presidential elections of 1934 – is relevant. *The Man of the People* and *Industrial Park* were thus published during the time in which Brazilian women's first official civic-political participation became possible.

20   *O homem do povo*, no. 8 (13 April 1932): 2; facsimile, 60. This passage gives a sense of her anger and also the way in which her prose incorporates orality in a kind of urgent, "undisciplined" speech: "If you all, instead of those twisted books you read, and the syphilitic kisses you offer, turned your eyes a bit towards the revolutionary avalanche that is gathering across the world; if you studied, *really* studied, in order to understand what's happening right now, you would be able to – with the conviction of real proletariats ... – come out in front, with a contemporary mentality, as authentic pioneer women of a new age."

21   Oswald de Andrade, "Ordem e progresso."

22   *O Homem do Povo*, no. 4 (1931): 4; facsimile, 38.

23   On this aspect of the earlier Oswald, see Roberto Schwarz, "The Cart, the Tram, and the Modernist Poet," in *Misplaced Ideas: Essays on Brazilian Culture*, trans. John Gledson (London: Verso, 1992), 108–25.

24   Aurelinio Corovo, "Sumario do mundo: A carniça está gostosa," *O homem do povo*, no. 1 (27 March 1931): 5; facsimile, 2.

25   Raul Maia, "The City, the Country, the World," *O homem do povo*, no. 3 (1931): 3; facsimile, 31. For an acute article that pits the Soviet Union's progress against Brazil's parasitic capitalism, see Spartacus, "Os amigos da Light," *O homem do povo*, no. 4 (1931): 3; facsimile, 37.

26   Oswald de Andrade, "Ordem e progresso." A particular feature of Latin American communism, Brazil included, is its national-popular orientation and its anti-imperialism directed in particular against the United States. See Ronald Chilcote, *The Brazilian Communist Party: Conflict and Integration, 1922–1972* (Oxford: Oxford University Press, 1974), 8.

27   "Hontem, hoje, amanha: O Brasil é dos brasileiros?" *O homem do povo*, no. 5 (1932): 6; facsimile, 46. Similarly, *The Man of the People* also ferociously and satirically covered in several issues the Prince of Wales's visit to Brazil, fawned over by the mainstream press, as an example of the coloniality of power.

28   For a synthetic introduction to the novel and to Galvão in English, see Elizabeth and K. David Jackson, "Translators' Preface," *Industrial Park*, 1993. *Industrial Park* is one of Denning's examples in "The Novelists International" of the "short, sometimes crude, but electrifying works often written by figures who did not go on to careers as novelists" (54), a kind of "subaltern modernism," the "first self-conscious attempt to create a world literature" (53).

29   See, for example, Eisenstein's "Montage of Attractions," originally published in *Lef* in 1923, with its emphasis on liberation from the hero-driven plot. See Sergei

Eisenstein, *Film Form and Film Sense*, trans. and ed. Jay Leyda (New York: Meridian Books, 1960), 230–3. I analyse *Industrial Park*'s dialogue with cinema and other techniques of mechanical reproduction more extensively in "Mass Culture in and the Laboratory of Late Modernism in Patrícia Galvão's *Industrial Park*," *Luso-Brazilian Review* 53, no. 1 (1 June 2016): 55–76.

30 Walter Benjamin, "The Author as Producer," in *The Work of Art in the Age of Its Technological Reproducibility, and Other Writings on Media* (Cambridge, MA: Harvard University Press, 2008), 82.

31 While ultimately unsuccessful in her goal, Galvão wanted the novel to be printed with large letters and ample spaces between sentences, approaching the more accessible forms of the cinema and advertising. See Thelma Guedes, *Pagu: Literatura e revolução. Um estudo sobre o romance* Parque industrial (Cotia, São Paulo: Ateliê Editorial; São Paulo: Nankin Editorial, 2003).

32 In her memoir, Galvão will credit Herculano and another fellow activist, Maria, for "guiding me on the streets of revolt, for having showed me all the faces of oppression, for putting me in contact with true misery." Patrícia Galvão, *Paixão Pagu: a autobiografia precoce de Patrícia Galvão* (Rio de Janeiro: Agir, 2005), 87–8.

33 There are precedents to these Soviet pilgrimages: the first Brazilian delegate in the Comintern period, Antônio Bernardo Canellas, took a PCB-delegated trip in 1922. His anarchist sympathies led to the Comintern denying the PCB membership. After Canellas's spectacularly undisciplined performance at the First Congress, Trotsky famously labelled him the "South American phenom." In 1930, the prominent communist (and interlocutor of Galvão) Astrojildo Pereira travelled to Moscow and returned with plans to foment a revolution in Brazil. Shortly thereafter, he would be expelled by the PCB, during the proletarianization phase.

34 Galvão, *Paixão Pagu*, 137.

35 While in France, she joined the Communist Party there under the false name "Leonnie," narrowly escaping deportation to Germany or Italy by the intervention of a Brazilian diplomat. See de Campos, *Pagu, Patrícia Galvão*, 22, 262.

36 Galvão will also repudiate communism repeatedly and publicly in publications throughout the 1940s to the 1960s.

37 See Katerina Clark, *Moscow, the Fourth Rome: Stalinism, Cosmopolitanism, and the Evolution of Soviet Culture, 1931–1941* (Cambridge, MA: Harvard University Press, 2011), 41. Many leftist artists were expelled from or left the PCB for not adhering to the new proletarianization line under Stalinism, most notably the socialist realist writer Rachel de Queiroz, the most lauded woman novelist of 1930s Brazil.

38 Galvão, *Paixão Pagu*, 149. *Deslumbrado* can also mean "dazed" or "blind."

39 Ibid., 150.

40 Estalinho, "Ideologia criminosa," *O homem do povo*, no. 6 (1932): 7; facsimile, 58.

41 Galvão, *Paixão Pagu*, 56.

42 Compare Aracy Amaral, *Tarsila: sua obra e seu tempo* (São Paulo: Ed. 34: Edusp, 2003), 349.

43 Clark, *Moscow, the Fourth Rome*, 27.

44 Compare Schwarz, "The Cart, the Tram, and the Modernist Poet"; Unruh, "Las ágiles musas." For an intriguing parallel, see Harsha Ram, "Futurist Geographies: Uneven Modernities and the Struggle for Aesthetic Autonomy: Paris, Italy, Russia, 1909–1914," in *The Oxford Handbook of Global Modernisms*, ed. Mark Wollaeger (Oxford: Oxford University Press, 2012), 313–46.

45 Aracy Amaral, *Tarsila*, 413. In this same lengthy letter home, she is particularly interested in women's issues: daycare centres, reproductive rights, divorce, equal pay for equal work, campaigns to eradicate prostitution.

46 Tarsila do Amaral, *Tarsila por Tarsila* (São Paulo: Celebris, 2004), 155; originally published in the *Diário da Noite*, São Paulo, 26 March 1931.

47 Mário de Andrade and Tarsila do Amaral, *Correspondência Mário de Andrade e Tarsila do Amaral*, org. Aracy Amaral (São Paulo: EdUSP, 1999), 112, my translation. In a letter dated 31 July 1929 from Odessa, she writes: "We've got ahold of folklore music that you're going to love" (113).

48 Aracy Amaral, *Tarsila*, 414–5, 415–6.

49 Tarsila do Amaral, *Tarsila por Tarsila*, 155.

50 See, for example, the sketches in Aracy Amaral, *Tarsila*, 343, 348.

51 Compare de Andrade and Amaral, *Correspondência*, 112. In a letter to Mário de Andrade from Leningrad, dated 9 July 1931, she asks him to send his works and those of others to David Vigodsky, "charged by the Soviet government to write a history of contemporary Latin American literature for a major Soviet encyclopaedia he is preparing"; while well-acquainted with Argentine authors, she writes, he knows little of Brazilian literature and art.

52 This painting was later moved in 1935 to the State Hermitage Museum (Ibid., 113).

53 Osório César, *Onde o proletariado dirige ... (Visão Panorâmica da URSS)* (São Paulo: Edição Brasileira, 1932). I would like to thank Michael Hironymous at The University of Texas at Austin for his help tracking down archival material, and especially Tarsilinha for granting the rights to reproduce Tarsila's art here.

54 Compare de Andrade and Amaral, *Correspondência*, 121; *Tarsila do Amaral* (Madrid: Fundación Juan March, 2009), 238.

55 During the mid to late 1930s, Tarsila would also begin two other paintings that can be considered part of the same period, *Seamstresses (Costureiras*, 1939–68) and *Orphanage (Orfanato*, 1935–49), both of which will only be completed much later. With their interest in working-class women's labour, in the double sense of the term, both paintings resonate with *Industrial Park*.

56 Compare Aracy Amaral, *Tarsila*, 370, 372. In this context, it is worth noting another key figure in the broader map of Comintern aesthetics: the communist muralist David Alfaro Siqueiros, whose exile and travels would influence artists throughout the continent, inspiring pictorial accounts of mass struggle that would reverberate from Buenos Aires to Los Angeles. Among them were Tarsila and Candido Portinari, the major Brazilian muralist of the 1930s. In 1933, CAM hosted

a conference by Siqueiros, who was in Brazil on his way for a stint in Argentina (Ibid., 365), where he would also have an enormous impact on painters.

57 "A gênese de *Operários*, de Tarsila." In *Textos de Trópico de Capricórnio: artigos e ensaios (1980–2005)*, vol. 1, by Aracy A. Amaral (São Paulo: Editora 34, 2006): 57–62, esp. 60–1; see also Aracy Amaral, *Tarsila*, 377.

58 A. Amaral notes the more pronounced melancholy in Tarsila's paintings, in contrast with their Soviet inspiration. The canonical text of Brazilian modernist melancholy is by Paulo Prado, who moved in similar circles to Tarsila, *Retrato do Brasil: ensaio sobre a tristeza brasileira* (*Portrait of Brazil: Essay on Brazilian Sadness*).

59 By the time the Comintern's popular front policy would trickle down to the PCB, both Galvão and Tarsila had already been imprisoned and disillusioned. The popular front policies would have afforded both artists more room to explore their different approaches to modernist humanism.

60 See Clark, *Moscow, the Fourth Rome*; Boris Groys, *The Total Art of Stalinism: Avant-Garde, Aesthetic Dictatorship, and Beyond* (London: Verso, 2011). The Soviet Union's emphasis on culture, Clark shows in her study of 1930s and 1940s Moscow, could also serve a compensatory function for the military and technological lag the Soviet Union was perpetually hoping to overcome (Clark, *Moscow, the Fourth Rome*, 11) – comparable to the South American context.

61 A key example is Glauber Rocha's "An Esthetic of Hunger" (1965), written while he was reading and viewing Eisenstein, whose influence is visible in Rocha's early film *Barravento* (1962). "An Esthetic of Hunger" influenced film discourse in Brazil, France, and Italy, as well as throughout Latin America. See Glauber Rocha, "An Esthetic of Hunger," in *Brazilian Cinema*, by Randal Johnson and Robert Stam (New York: Columbia University Press, 1995): 68–71. Another example would be Leon Hirszman's failed project, inspired by Eisenstein's also incomplete *Que viva México*, to create a twelve-film series entitled *Que viva América*. Hirszman and Rocha are the Brazilian filmmakers most inspired by Eisenstein.

62 In addition to numerous films that explicitly cited Eisenstein in their form, 1969 saw the publication of the first Brazilian edition of Eisenstein's *Reflexões de um cineaste* in São Paulo (an edition had been published in Lisbon in 1961); Dwight Macdonald's *El cine soviético: una historia y una elegía* was published by Sur in Buenos Aires in 1956.

Chapter Six

Polycentric Cosmopolitans: Writing World Literature in Indonesia and Vietnam, 1920s to 1950s and Beyond

TONY DAY
Independent Scholar

Even though little translated into other languages and scarcely marketed or noticed in Europe, the Americas, Africa, or China, the modern literatures of Southeast Asia express "world" culture, the product of global, cross-cultural interactions extending over continents and seas for centuries. But how should we describe the discursive world(s), the global cultural spaces, which have shaped, and been shaped by, the arts of Southeast Asia in specific, world-historical terms? In my essay, I focus on several writers from before and after the Second World War whose literary work expresses some kind of "socialist realism." My aim is to give this term, when applied to Southeast Asian writing, a global meaning, whether or not the socialist realism in question is homegrown or borrowed from elsewhere. I also want to show that, whatever its temporal or cultural point of origin, socialist realism in Southeast Asia has never ceased to develop in diverse ways that expand and deepen our understanding of the genre.

World Republic of Letters or Writers' International?

There are a number of approaches to the question of how to describe a literary and aesthetic form in global terms.[1] Drawing on Immanuel Wallerstein's "world-systems" model of the modern capitalist global economy, consisting of an unequal relationship between a dominant "core" and subservient "peripheries," comparative literature scholar Pascale Casanova defines what she calls the "world literary space" of the mid-nineteenth to late twentieth centuries:

> [This space is] organized in terms of the opposition between, on the one hand, an autonomous pole composed of those spaces that are most endowed in literary resources, which serves as a model and a recourse for writers claiming a position of independence in newly formed spaces (with the result that Paris emerged as a 'denationalized' universal capital and a specific measure of literary time was

established); and, on the other, a heteronymous pole composed of relatively deprived literary spaces at early stages of development that are dependent on political – typically national – authorities.[2]

This bipolar global world of literary activity is reproduced within each "national space," where "national" and "international writers" compete with one another. Such literary antagonisms are homologous to the tug and pull between "the autonomous and unifying pole of world literary space," centred in a cosmopolitan centre like Paris, and "the inertial forces that work to divide and particularize by essentializing differences, reproducing outmoded models, and nationalizing and commercializing literary life" at home in a writer's "national space."[3] Mediating in a crucial way between the cosmopolitan literary centre and the "relatively deprived literary spaces" of the peripheries is translation.

Casanova lays primary emphasis on modernism and its influence, via the translations of the work of such leading innovators of literary form as James Joyce and William Faulkner, on the development of literature in "peripheral" regions around the world. If "modernism" is a keyword for conceptualizing world literature in one way, some kind of "realism," whether "socialist" or "magical," is another.[4] Michael Denning argues that "the international of writers" who shared the African American writer Richard Wright's (1908–60) perception of "the similarity of the experience of workers in other lands ... [and of the possibility] of uniting scattered but kindred peoples into a whole"[5] began to take shape even before the October Revolution of 1917, as exemplified by the writings of the Russian Maxim Gorky (1868–1936), whose 1907 novel *Mother* and early short stories were quickly translated into European languages.[6] According to Denning, "proletarian literary movements," which dealt variously with workers' movements, subaltern living conditions, or the migration of workers from the countryside to the city, developed in four different situations: countries with communist movements and regimes; nations with repressive authoritarian governments; the creole countries of the Americas; and "the colonized regions of Asia and Africa."[7]

It makes sense to draw on and combine critical ideas and approaches from both Casanova and Denning as we look for expressions of socialist realism in Southeast Asia during the era of the Comintern (1919–43) and the early years of the Cold War. In the discussion that follows, Denning's idea of an "international" of realist writers helps us understand why Southeast Asian writers adopted certain styles and read certain authors and not others in the quest for modernity in the context of a struggle for postcolonial national independence and identity. Casanova's model of the "world republic of letters," notwithstanding her great interest in Third World authors who achieved international recognition through translation, is so explicit in its reliance on Wallerstein's Eurocentric model of the world system that it, in fact, brings the variety of global orientations to be found among Southeast Asian intellectuals and artists into sharp relief. While Casanova is too critical of nationalism to be helpful with developing an approach to Southeast Asian writers who were cosmopolitan in outlook yet also intensely committed to participating in the development of their national communities, her insights into the key role played by translation in creating world literature are important for encouraging an examination of the way translation shaped literary imaginations in Southeast Asia during the period that interests me here.

Polycentric Cosmopolitans

Both before and after the Second World War, ideas, literary aesthetics, and modular literary forms flowed from New York, London, Amsterdam, and Paris, as well as from Moscow, Cairo, Shanghai, and Beijing, to Southeast Asia, even though these centres were visited by only a few literary sojourners from the region, most of whom continued to write in their own native and/or national languages rather than in those of their former colonial overlords. But this flow of literary models to Southeast Asia from centres elsewhere was always circuitous and mingled with local currents. Both before and after the war, the cosmopolitanism of Southeast Asian writers never developed in or was oriented towards a single Western or Asian literary-imperial centre. Southeast Asian literature-worlds became visible instead on polycentric maps that included the major cities of Southeast Asia, former capitals of defunct pre-colonial kingdoms, villages, and regions where authors were born and raised speaking regional languages or dialects, as well as distant places of origin for imported literary models from Europe, America, the Soviet Union, the Middle East, and China.

Two examples must suffice here to give a sense of what I am calling the "polycentric cosmopolitanism" of Southeast Asian writers in the interwar period before I turn my attention to writing during the early years of the Cold War. Semaoen (1899–1971) was a labour activist in the Dutch Netherlands Indies; member of the first mass nationalist party, the Sarekat Islam (Association of Islam), at the age of fifteen; the first chairman of the Indonesian Communist Party, which was formed on 23 May 1920; and a contributor to as well as editor of the communist newspaper *Sinar Hindia* (*Light of the Indies*). In 1919 he was tried and convicted of "inciting and spreading hatred in speech and writing" and sentenced to four months in jail.[8] While there he wrote a novel, the *Hikajat Kadiroen* (*The Story of Kadiroen*), which was published first in 1920 in serial form in *Sinar Hindia*, then as a book by the Communist Party of Indonesia in 1922. Semaoen's novel provides a good Indonesian example of the process by which literary models from elsewhere were "shaped by native habits of mind."[9] The hero of Semaoen's work, Kadiroen, progresses from good son, to upright official in the colonial civil service, to communist convert, to leftist journalist dedicated to the people's welfare and is a pious Javanese Muslim as well as a "positive hero" in the pre–socialist realist sense described by Katerina Clark in her study of the Soviet novel.[10] Here is how Kadiroen is described when first introduced to the reader:

> Kadiroen was of medium build, but he had great strength within. He was good looking, with fine dark skin. His large, clear eyes shone steadfastly when they looked at anyone – a sign that he had a noble character, disliked wrongdoing, and was brave, loyal and trustworthy. He treated his peers with respect and would not insult or hurt others. Everyone liked him.[11]

As the novel progresses, the assimilation of Marxist ideas to Javanese and Islamic ones continues. Semaoen borrowed from various Western literary genres,[12] but the dominant model for the novel is a kind of socialist realism. The most interesting way in which socialist realist ideas merged with Javanese-Islamic ones lies in Semaoen's use of the Malay-Arabic word "*kodrat*" (power, omnipotence, especially with reference to Allah) to mean "natural law" or "destiny." Semaoen gives *kodrat* a meaning that resembles the idea of "necessity" in the writing of the Marxist historian Lukács, in both a historical and stylistic-aesthetic sense.[13] Not only are superfluous, "contingent" stylistic details entirely absent from the lean narrative style of *The Story of Kadiroen*, but, thematically, everything from romantic relationships to human destiny is governed by *kodrat*. This theme is clearly present in the words of the communist cadre, whose speech Kadiroen is sent by his Dutch superiors to monitor, which converts him to communism:

> Comrades! I have explained to you the path of destiny [*djalanja kodrat*], in the past, present, and future ... When we have understood the progress of an age, then we have a duty to follow the trend and demands of that age, so that we, and our children and grandchildren will be prosperous and honourable, especially at the end of this age. Because we are at present in a time of hardship, we must therefore move forward to herald the coming of the age of happiness, that is the ultimate age of communism ... That is our obligation, because we are destined [*kodrat*] to follow Allah's laws in the course of each age [*Allah poenja wet-perdjalanan-djaman*].[14]

The *Hikajat Kadiroen* is Semaoen's only literary work. He wrote the novel two years before visiting the Soviet Union in 1921 at the age of twenty-two to attend the First Congress of the Toilers of the Far East, where he met Lenin and gave a report on the history of the Indonesian Communist Party as a "block within." The report was a revelation that influenced the Comintern's decision to recommend the same "block within" approach to fostering communism in China.[15] Only 1,500 copies of the *Hikajat* were printed in book form in 1922. We do not know what Semaoen had been reading when he composed it. When Pramoedya

Ananta Toer (who will be discussed later) wrote about Semaoen and his novel in 1962, he could only find a synopsis of the text.[16] Not until the year 2000, after the fall of the dictator Suharto, did *Hikajat Kadiroen* reappear in print.

At first glance, the prolific literary output and political views of the anti-capitalist but anti-communist Vietnamese writer Vũ Trọng Phụng (1912–39) stand in marked contrast to Semaoen's own. By the mid-1930s, Vũ Trọng Phụng was famous for his realist works of reportage about gambling, house servants, relations between Vietnamese women and French legionnaires, and venereal disease and prostitution, reports that indicted colonial capitalism and its social effects. These works formed but a small part of his oeuvre. In Peter Zinoman's words, "in a career spanning less than ten years, [Vũ Trọng Phụng] published eight novels, four books of narrative nonfiction, and hundreds of stories, plays, essays, editorials, and articles."[17] In his writings, Vũ Trọng Phụng, who received six years of education in a French school, directly cited "more than sixty" foreign writers and referred to others, including ancient Greek playwrights and Shakespeare; Corneille, Racine, and Molière; and "a wide array of romantics and neo-romantics, mid-nineteenth century realists and early twentieth-century social realists, symbolists, naturalists, modernists, and Catholic neo-traditionalists." In short, Vũ Trọng Phụng was "never a disciple of any particular foreign writer or international literary movement."[18]

And yet, in 1936 he published a novel, *The Storm (Giông tố)*, which was the first Vietnamese novel to portray a communist secret agent.[19] As a protagonist, the Comintern agent Hải Vân is both different and similar to Kadiroen. Hải Vân comes from a scholarly rather than a simple peasant background. Unlike Kadiroen, who pursues a highly successful career in the Dutch colonial bureaucracy before leaving it after joining the Communist Party, Hải Vân cannot follow the family tradition of service in the imperial bureaucracy because of the French conquest of Vietnam. Like the communist and writer Semaoen, the character Hải Vân is radicalized and educated through imprisonment. Somewhat different from Kadiroen, whose family values never come into conflict with his dedication to the needs of the people, but in parallel to leading figures in the early Communist Party in Indonesia and Vietnam, Hải Vân dedicates himself to "a new life of wandering and adventure," in which he pledges his devotion, not to family, but to "all of society ... all of humanity." But here the similarity of Hải Vân to both the highly rational Kadiroen or the "sanitized accounts of the history of the inter-war communist leadership put forward by the [Vietnamese Communist] Party after it assumed state-power in 1954" ends.[20] Far in excess of Kadiroen's outstanding but mundane abilities as a socialist realist "positive hero" but similar to the reputed prowess of the Indonesian Comintern agent Tan Malaka, who was fictionalized in the *Patjar Merah Indonesia (Scarlet Pimpernel of Indonesia)* novels of the 1930s as a messianic hero with magical abilities, Hải Vân possesses superhuman powers.[21]

While in jail he learns how to tell fortunes; he is also a master of geomancy. "He is fluent in Chinese and a master of disguise ... He possesses some knowledge of Western medicine and is a skilled hypnotist. He is an able marksman and a formidable martial artist. He even knows how to prepare a decent opium pipe. Hải Vân owes his easy facility in these areas and many others to the curriculum taught at the Stalin School."[22] As Hải Vân explains to his son, "Students there are trained in swordsmanship, shooting, diving, swimming, driving cars, flying planes, Western and Japanese martial arts and political subversion ... They also learn rhetorical techniques to win over the masses, how to master the arts of disguise and intimidation, and how to run a security organization and an intelligence service."[23]

Hải Vân shares one skill with Kadiroen, however, that provides an important clue for understanding the localization of the Marxist concept of history throughout Southeast Asia: his "profound knowledge of the workings of *số mệnh* – a key concept in Sino-Vietnamese popular religion that may be translated crudely as 'fate.'"[24] "Hải Vân's speech is infused with the notion that *số mệnh* represents a powerful, determinative force in human affairs that overwhelms individual agency," Peter Zinoman observes.[25] Stalinist communist literary critics who attacked Vũ Trọng Phụng's work after 1954 strongly disapproved of Hải Vân's "superstitions," particularly in light of the author's open expression of contempt for the communist movement under Stalin in essays published in 1937.[26] A leftist critic in 1937 faulted Vũ Trọng Phụng for emphasizing nationalism over internationalism in his novel, to which he responded, as Zinoman notes, "by pointing out that Vietnamese internationalists frequently employed nationalist language and symbolism in their political appeals ... [and arguing] that he had no choice but to depict this contradiction." In Vũ Trọng Phụng's own words: "My realistic pen is absolute ... I only describe people as they actually are, not ... as they ought to be."[27]

In 1960 Vũ Trọng Phụng's works were banned, not to reappear on bookshelves in Vietnam until the late 1980s. Semaoens's nearly total literary obscurity in postwar Indonesia, where leftist writing was totally suppressed between 1965 and 1998, and the long hiatus in the availability of Vũ Trọng Phụng's realist and anti-capitalist but mostly anti-communist masterpieces in the Democratic Republic of Vietnam indicate the difficulty of tracing a continuous history of the development of a socialist realist literary aesthetic in Southeast Asia. But such a history continued to unfold after the end of the Second World War, as can be seen by examining literary developments in Indonesia and Vietnam in the early years after independence. My case studies from the early years of the Cold War suggest that "world literary spaces" in Southeast Asia were not confined to the national, political, or ideological boundaries within which writers lived. Rather, they extended across the globe according to various coordinates that corresponded more closely to the non-aligned cultural locations of the

Africans and Asians who met in Bandung in 1955 to discuss the formation of a "Third World" than to the Cold War boundaries decreed by American or Soviet ideologues.[28]

These coordinates came into view for writers from Indonesia at the first international conference on Indonesian literature held in Amsterdam on 26 June 1953.[29] Sticusa, the Foundation for Cultural Cooperation that had been established as a result of the Cultural Accord between the Netherlands and Indonesia in 1949, sponsored the meeting. The agreement guaranteed a Dutch cultural presence in post-independence Indonesia; continuing Dutch economic dominance was already a source of friction and national debate. In a congress (*kongres*) on the "national culture" held in Jakarta in August 1950 to discuss the implications of the Cultural Accord, the pre-war debate about how to create a "modern" Indonesian culture resurfaced. On the one hand, the Indonesian minister for education, training, and culture, Ki Hadjar Dewantara (1889–1959), who had founded a school system before the war that drew on traditional Javanese as well as avant-garde Western concepts, rejected a Dutch- and Western-centric notion of modernity and declared that the Cultural Accord was a diplomatic defeat for Indonesia. He urged that Indonesia independently seek closer cultural ties with Asia.[30] As he had during the 1930s, on the other hand, the Sumatran writer and editor Sutan Takdir Alisjahbana (1908–94) argued that Indonesians should embrace Western culture and continue to seek access to it by cementing close, postcolonial cultural relations with the Netherlands. Most of the other speakers and discussants at the conference attacked the neocolonial nature of the Cultural Accord and criticized Western European and American cultural influences on the developing national culture of Indonesia.[31] Notwithstanding what appears to have been a consensus among participants on the negative features of the 1949 cultural agreement with the Dutch, the conference resolved to support it in principle.

Three concerns that emerged from the August 1950 conference came to form the principal leitmotif of literary debates in Indonesia in later years: what to do about regional and Asian cultures in the pursuit of modernity; what to do about postcolonial cultural influences from Europe and the United States in independent Indonesia; and, finally, notwithstanding both these concerns, how to satisfy the participants' strong desire for cultural dialogue with the rest of the world. These issues were immediately addressed in two important cultural manifestos that were published that same year: one issued by the liberal Gelanggang (Arena) group founded by a number of writers and painters in 1946 and associated with the weekly journal *Siasat* (*Strategy*);[32] the other from the Marxist cultural organization Lekra (Institute of People's Culture), which was founded on 17 August 1950 in response to the failure of the congress on national culture a week earlier to repudiate the Cultural Accord.[33] Despite their divergent politics, both manifestos used similar language to claim the whole world, and not just the positive aspects of past or future cultural relations with the Netherlands, as a source for the development of modern Indonesian culture.

It may be an expression of Casanova's centre-periphery world literary struc-ture that the first international conference on Indonesian literature was held in Amsterdam on 16 June 1953. Although he was already widely recognized as Indonesian's greatest writer, the young Pramoedya Ananta Toer (1925–2006) was not one of the featured speakers (by his own choice perhaps[34]), but he was in the audience, since he and his family were spending several months in the Netherlands under the auspices of Sticusa. The morning proceedings of the conference were opened by the young Dutch professor of linguistics and authority on Old Javanese and Indonesian literatures, A. Teeuw, and it was not until the afternoon that the two important Indonesian participants and invited speakers at the conference, Takdir Alisjahbana and Asrul Sani (1926–2004), had a chance to speak. Takdir, the more senior, was a strong supporter of the Cultural Accord with the Netherlands, as we know. In his remarks Takdir traced his familiar themes: the coming of Western modernity to Indonesia via Dutch colonialism and the social disruptions caused by the process of modernization and the resultant rise of individualism.

Asrul Sani spoke next. Dutch-educated, a poet, short story writer, essay-ist, editor of several important literary journals, Asrul had already been living in Amsterdam for several years with his wife, Siti Nuraini, a noted poet and translator of Dutch, German, and French literature.[35] Pramoedya Ananta Toer heard Asrul's speech and reacted critically to it in an article he published in July 1953, accusing Asrul of being a "salon intellectual" and a spokesperson for, in the words of Keith Foulcher's summary of Pramoedya's argument, an "uprooted intelligentsia who have little to contribute to the condition they are identifying."[36] Asrul would have agreed that the uprootedness of Indonesia's writers was their key problem. In Pramoedya's view, however, there was no conflict between East and West, as Asrul and Takdir both asserted. Pessimism and other expressions of post-revolutionary letdown in Indonesian culture and literature at the moment were not cultural diseases or Western imports, but simply byproducts of an ongoing creative process, which it would be point-less to criticize.

In a strongly worded essay published before his departure for the Netherlands, Pramoedya had also criticized the concept of artistic purity and detachment. In these and other essays, as well as in his short stories, particularly the *Tjerita dari Djakarta* (*Tales from Djakarta*) published in the 1950s, Pramoedya began making the case for a more socially engaged kind of Indonesian literature than could be found in the writings of the Generation 45.[37] His intellectual development during this period was shaped by his reading and involvement in literary polemics, but also by his travel abroad and the work he did as a translator.[38]

The Question of Translation

During the 1950s, Indonesian journals and newspapers were full of translations of short stories and poetry by foreign authors; novels and plays by an eclectic range of writers, modern and ancient, famous and less well known, also appeared in book form.[39] Translations of Western critical theory also made their way into print, especially in leftist newspapers and journals where socialist realism was much discussed.[40] In 1950 Pramoedya published translations of Steinbeck and Tolstoy. He later commented that translating *Of Mice and Men* taught him about "not interfering in his protagonists' affairs, and depicting the stirrings of their hearts only by the evidence of the senses: sight and sound."[41] The style Pramoedya is alluding to here is documentary reportage, of which both Steinbeck and Vũ Trọng Phụng were masters, which Pramoedya discovered when he carried out research in the 1960s into the serialized short stories by Eurasian and Malay writers at the turn of the twentieth century. During the years 1955–56, Pramoedya again published a number of translations, the most important of which was *Ibunda*, a translation of Gorky's *Mother* (1907), a work that Katerina Clark, drawing on Pushkin's definition of translators as "post-horses of civilization," describes as "that post, or station, where Bolsheviks coming out of the old intelligentsia tradition were able to stop and take on fresh horses to bear them on into Socialist Realism itself."[42] Three short translations of non-fictional works by Pramoedya suggest how translation served to connect him to the leftist "international" of world literature during the Cold War.[43]

In late 1955 and the first half of 1956, Pramoedya published three translations in the journal *Indonesia*, a major forum for critical thinking about Indonesian society and the arts that was edited at this time by Armijn Pané (a famous pre-war intellectual and writer), the legal authority Mr. St. Mohamad Sjah, and Boejoeng Saleh, a poet, prolific writer on cultural and sociological topics, and leftist polemicist. In the first of these translations, "Kesusasteraan dan Publik,"[44] Pramoedya presents his readers with a discussion of the development of what he interpreted as "realism" in late nineteenth-century Germany from a sociological study of literary taste written by a German professor of English literature, L.L. Schücking. A passage from the opening paragraphs of Schücking's chapter strongly suggests that there is a close historical parallel between the cultural world Schücking describes and the situation in mid–twentieth-century Indonesia, with its literary world dominated by middle-class urban intellectuals in an atmosphere of deepening political and economic crisis, a situation ripe for even a belated advent of revolutionary realism:

> In Germany naturalism (or realism) came remarkably late. In France its most eminent representative, Emile Zola, had written his famous novels in the seventies ... In Germany at that time the main buttress of art was a cultured middle class

[*parapendukung seni adalah kelas pertengahan jang berbudaja*], largely made up of higher officials, which mainly in consequence of the political stagnation that followed the victorious wars, restricted itself in every field to the careful guarding of traditions ... The sense of hollowness of the religious conceptions that continued to dominate the school and the life of the State ... the increasing hardness of the conditions of existence, due to growth of competition, as reflected in the growing importance of the women's question; the increase in the elements of conflict in social and political life ... the trivializing influence of the great cities [*pengaruh sehari-hari daripada kota-kota besar*] – all these things combined to lead certain social groups into a passionate struggle [*perdjuangan jang bersemangat*] in various fields of everyday life against what they felt to be empty phrases ... The path of art is no Sunday stroll [*pelantjongan dihari minggu*] through pretty country with a young flock, but an everyday pilgrimage [*perdjalanan djemaah jang dilakukan tiap hari*] that does not shirk the investigation of any site [*penjelidikan atas tiap daerah*].[45]

The suggestion in the last line of the passage just quoted, that "naturalist" (which for Pramoedya meant "realist") writers need to investigate "any" and every "site" of the everyday world, is one that Pramoedya returned to in the first of two translations that appeared in the March 1956 issue of *Indonesia*. On 25 September 1953, the Chinese author and feminist Ding Ling gave a speech to the Second Congress of Representatives of China's Literature Workers titled "Settling Down among the Masses," which was later translated into English and published in 1954 as "Life and Creative Writing" in *Chinese Literature*, a journal edited by the eminent novelist and People's Republic of China (PRC) minister of culture from 1949 to 1965, Mao Dun, featuring essays and literary works from contemporary China published by the Foreign Languages Press in Beijing.[46] It is here that Pramoedya evidently found an essay by a leftist writer from the global "international" that helped articulate his own concerns about the need for Indonesian writers to engage with the everyday life of ordinary people.

Along with many other Indonesian cultural commentators, Pramoedya had already written about the need for urban artists to reorient themselves to the countryside, where the mass of the Indonesian people lived. In January 1956, Pramoedya published an essay praising the "popular tendency" in a new gen-eration of writers, even though they were still just cultural "tourists having an adventure in a new place [*merupakan turis yang mengembarai daerah baru*]" rather than serious investigators of real life.[47] Pramoedya's principal targets in this piece were the middle-class, Europeanized literary idealists like Asrul Sani, who had called for a "return to the village" in his 1953 Amsterdam address without ever enacting such a return himself.

Ding Ling opens her lecture by criticizing the very same sort of writers, who "sit back in their arm chairs and indulge in idle talk, in the attempt to fill the emptiness of their life [*duduk kembali dikursinja dan membiarkan diri dalam pergumulan soal-soal jang sia-sia, dalam usahnja untuk mengisi kekosongan hidupnja itu*].[48] What writers need to do, says Ding Ling, is "experience life," which Pramoedya translates as *merasumi hidup*, "penetrate" or "soak in" life, using a word for "experience" that connotes spirit possession or memorable food. "If we really wish to create new characters and produce good books, we must settle down among the masses [*mulai turun tangan ditengah-tengah rakjat*] and establish close and friendly relations with the people around us."[49] In China at least, "the writer is provided with excellent conditions and a broad path to literary creation. Wherever he goes, he is welcome ... The masses around him, anxiously hoping that he will write a good book about them and for them, expect him to stay long with them and tell him everything he wants to know."[50]

Ding Ling's essay forcefully asserts the same kind of artistic commitment to understand and serve the needs of ordinary people that Pramoedya could have found expressed by many other contributors to *Chinese Literature*. His essay "Literature as a Tool," published in March 1953 in one of the several journals edited by H.B. Jassin,[51] has the stylistic clarity and polemical punch of the essay he translated by Ding Ling. Pramoedya engages with Soviet and Chinese ideas about the social function of literature in this essay, but in a critical fashion, arguing for a distinction between literature as a "tool [*alat*]" in the hands of the autonomous writer and literature as a "means to an end [*diperalat*]" at the service of someone else's cause. In the latter sense, the instrumentalization of literature, when taken out of the hands of the author, poses a danger to "the truth of creativity as a personal and intellectual necessity [*membahayakan hakikat penciptaan sebagai keharusan pribadi dan keharusan budi*]."[52] Pramoedya's position on creativity and the inviolability of the writer's inner freedom represents a significant deviation from official models of socialist realism in the Soviet Union and China, and is strikingly similar to Ding Ling's allegiance to her own "subjectivity," which was the cause of her downfall in 1958.

Near the end of her essay, Ding Ling touches on a subject that Pramoedya addressed in his December 1954 lecture, to which he returned several times in articles written after his visit to China in October 1956: the economic well-being of the writer as a fundamental right and precondition for his or her ability to perform the job of being a creative artist.[53] It is not surprising, therefore, that Pramoedya selected "The life and Organization of Soviet Writers," chapter two of George Reavey's *Soviet Literature To-Day*, for translation, the second piece translated by Pramoedya to appear in the March 1956 issue of *Indonesia*.[54] Gorky's *Mother* must have been on his mind at this time; his translation of the novel was probably intended for publication on a date as close as possible to planned celebrations for the twentieth anniversary of Gorky's death (18 June 1936).[55] In the chapter Pramoedya translated, Reavey wastes no time in pointing out that Soviet writers had access to state-subsidized housing, including country *dachas* where "writers may retire and isolate themselves either for work or when recovering from illness [*dimana parapengarang boleh beristirahat atau memisahkan diri sendiri baik untuk bekerdja ataupun beristirahat sewaktu baru baik dari sakit*]."[56] Soviet writers were prospering largely due to the huge expansion in the number of readers after the war, so that an "edition of 100,000 to 500,000 is more like the norm for more popular books," compared to the 3,000 to 4,000 copies usually printed for literary works in Indonesia.[57] The standard serialization of novels in literary magazines and the Stalin Prize were also sources of income for the best authors.

But Soviet writers were not just exemplary because of their economic well-being. Reavey quotes from the wartime diary of the woman poet, journalist, and translator Vera Inber, as she explains the difference between being an independent writer and one who belongs to the Communist Party:

Formerly, it was like this: I would write, let us say, a successful thing [*karja-karja jang menghasilkan sukses*], and I was glad [*dan aku merasa gembira*]. Failure was bitter. But it was my personal sorrow and joy only [*Tetapi hal itu adalah kesedihan dan kegembiraanku seorang diri sadja*]. But now I think: *in what measure is that which I write useful for Soviet literature*, which, in its turn, appears only as a part of the great thing – the flourishing of my country [*kesedjahteraan tanahairku*], the first Socialist country in the world? *Each literary work, if logically continued, must be transformed into action* [*Tiap karja sastera, bila diikuti setjara mantik, haruslah didjelmakan kedalam tindakan*].[58]

Reavey discusses other matters in his chapter, such as Soviet writers' unions and organization, that were of interest to Pramoedya, but the passage I have just quoted would have been the most resonant for him. The declarations of Ding Ling, the Chinese writer, and Vera Inber, the Soviet poet, both women, expressed the same socialist ideals that gradually form in the mind of the illiterate mother and hero of Gorky's novel, a character who would reappear in several guises in Pramoedya's later writing.

The three translations by Pramoedya that appeared in *Indonesia* in 1955–56 served as windows onto non-Indonesian worlds, both past and contemporary, in a way that brought them closer to home. Schücking's history of the formation of literary taste in late nineteenth-century Germany offered Pramoedya a case study that he could develop into a historical parallel; in later years, he uncovered an entire history of realist literature in Indonesia stretching back to the later years of the nineteenth century, to which he would add his greatest work. Ding Ling's essay was a model of clear reasoning and an articulation of international socialist realist literary principles, but it also gave voice to a liberated female subjectivity, the ultimate symbol for Pramoedya of Indonesia's emerging national identity in the postcolonial world. Finally, Reavey's discourse on

Russian writers and their dedication to and support from the Soviet state established a benchmark for how to improve the working conditions of Indonesian writers so that they could escape their current poverty of body and mind, better to serve the building of the Indonesian nation. As Pramoedya argued in an essay he wrote in 1954 in response to those who questioned the international status and value of Indonesian literature: "Internationalism [*Keinternasionalan*] doesn't exist if it doesn't start from the national itself. The international can only be attained if an author is capable of recognizing his own and his country's problems [*masalah-masalah diri/bangsanya*] in a fundamental way, and by himself draws parallels with problems faced by those who live in the world at large, so that his own problems become ones that belong to the world itself."[59]

The three short translations we have been considering show us Pramoedya engaging with an "international" of socialist realist ideas from around the world, discovering parallels as well as differences concerning the situation of writers in Indonesia. The fact that these translations served to connect Indonesia to Europe, China, the Soviet Union, and world history itself says something obvious but important about the global reach and coherence of the socialist realist "international." Greatly facilitating the creation of socialist internationalism was the availability of both contemporary and classical writings from China and the Soviet Union in well-distributed, state-sponsored translations into English and many other languages.[60] Nothing like this kind of organized literary outreach was carried out by the non-communist bloc during the Cold War. By comparison, the propagation and local reception of liberal "modernism" in Southeast Asia was more uneven and problematic. Modernist literary texts were scattered across many different languages and across different media, if you include Western film as a major vehicle for modernism that was avidly viewed and discussed in Southeast Asia during the Cold War. Almost none of the books Casanova considers central to the modernist canon, such as the novels of James Joyce or William Faulkner or the plays of Henrik Ibsen, were translated into Indonesian or Vietnamese during this period. In the case of leftist "international" texts, however, not only were many of the most important works available in languages Southeast Asian writers could read, but the themes that most concerned these writers – anti-imperialism, populism, nationalism, the difficulty of being oneself as part of the collective effort to build a communist state – were all present in such works, facilitating the translation of socialist realist ideas and aesthetic forms into Southeast Asian literary practices.

Mayakovsky in Hanoi, Gorky in Jakarta

As in Indonesia, experimentation with literary forms that could express modern kinds of individuality and new kinds of national community, as well as vigorous debates that pitted advocates of "art for art's sake [*nghệ thuật vị nghệ thuật*]" against proponents of "art for life's sake [*nghệ thuật vị nhân sinh*]," were well underway in Vietnam by the mid-1930s.[61] Hue Tam Ho Tai, who has studied these debates, stresses the lack of congruence at that time between aesthetic allegiances and political ones, with the "leading defender of pure art, Hoài Thanh ... already leaning towards communism at the time of the debate." Hue Tam Ho Tai also establishes the international, world literary orientation and content of the debates. Vietnamese intellectuals, who gained full access to newspapers in French when censorship was lifted in 1935 soon after the formation of the Popular Front in 1934, invoked "foreign critics and writers to support their particular views on the relationship between art and politics."[62]

As the struggle to build not just a new nation but a strong state, founded on a class-based social order, and artistic forms that the masses could understand intensified in North Vietnam during the early 1950s, many writers found that, in the words of the painter Tô Ngọc Vân, they had two selves, one that "serves the nation and the masses" and one "that serves art."[63] The two selves collided in widespread conflict in intellectual circles in the North during the crisis years of land reform. The nature of the conflict is illustrated best in the controversy that erupted in literary journals and newspapers over the writing and opinions of a young army writer and painter named Trần Dần (1926–97).[64]

Trần Dần began his literary career in 1946 as a poet interested in folk traditions. Joining the Communist Party in 1948, he was one of the first cadres to be trained in Chinese rectification (that is, forced public recantation) techniques, which were introduced in Vietnam in 1951 to bring intellectuals into line with official programs and views.[65] His experiences in the decisive Vietnamese victory over the French at Điện Biên Phủ led to the writing of a novel, one of the earliest fictional accounts of that famous battle and a huge success with the public. What distinguished Trần Dần's novel from the many other accounts of the war was his attempt to represent soldiers and their subjective experiences in all their complexity, rather than resort to the prescribed formulas of what Trần Dần, according to one of his friends and later defenders, called "smoke-and-fire literature," war novels full of guns, loud noise, exemplary heroes, but no people.[66] Trần Dần was sent to China between 10 October and 12 November 1954 to work on the narrative script for a film about the battle of Điện Biên Phủ, just at the time that a well-known Chinese literary critic and Chinese Communist Party member, Hu Feng, openly challenged the authority of the Party to dictate how literature should be written. On his return to Vietnam, Trần Dần became the spokesman for a group of army writers who demanded creative freedom and an outspoken critic of writers who conformed to Party dictates.[67] Disciplined by the army and confined to quarters for three months after he asked to resign from both the army and the Party in May 1955, Trần Dần responded by writing a poem, "Nhất định thắng" (We Must Win).[68]

Trần Dần's poem, with its " insistent, haunting rhythm [that] pulls the reader into the poet's heart"[69] and its equally insistent negation of the chief symbol of the Vietnamese Workers' Party,[70] ends on a triumphal and loyal note, as the poet walks on, "seeing the streets and the houses/ Not the falling rain/ Only the sun rising/ upon the red flag."[71] "We Must Win" was published in February 1956 in the first issue of a literary magazine started by a group of young writers who expressed more zealous commitment to than rebellious deviance from the ideals of the revolution. But the authorities read "We Must Win" as an expression of Hu Feng–like "subjectivism," which threatened the authority of the state-sponsored Association of Art and Literature and the official aesthetic standards it sought to promote. Trần Dần was denounced as a reactionary and arrested. It took his attempted suicide, the news of the cultural effects of de-Stalinization in the Soviet Union, and the temporary relaxation of controls on intellectuals during the Hundred Flowers Movement in China (January 1956–June 1957) to rehabilitate Trần Dần and force a (short-lived) re-examination by the Party of its policies towards intellectuals and artists.[72]

Trần Dần's "We Must Win" explored the subjectivity and indeterminacy of living in newly independent, post-revolutionary North Vietnam, issues that Pramoedya Ananta Toer would have found entirely familiar. In its free verse form, typographic layout, fervent nationalism, and unabashed celebration of the defiantly lyrical "I," "We Must Win" is also powerfully reminiscent of the poetry of Vladimir Mayakovsky (1893–1930), the famous poet of the Russian Revolution whose work was available in Vietnamese translation by 1953, if not before, and well known to Trần Dần.[73] Mayakovsky's verse offered Trần Dần and his friends a stirring example of cosmopolitan modernist poetry that was at once lyrical and realist, but also critical of the shortcomings of the communist revolution. Challenged by his friend Hoàng Cầm to explain why his poetry sounded so much like Mayakovsky's, Trần Dần reportedly replied: "A profound influence is only possible when there is a similarity of thought! It is true that I am influenced by Mayakovsky, but the most important influence is the impact that the Vietnamese revolution and its realities have had on me. It is thus that bit by bit I will become myself."[74] Indeed, Trần Dần's poetry expresses a nationalist sensibility and a commitment to the autonomy of the self that seems entirely congruent with Pramoedya's thinking about Indonesian literature in the 1950s. Of the creative process, Pramoedya wrote in 1950:

The creative process is utterly individual in character, and can occur only after formation of the mysticum as a conditio sine qua non. This mysticum, a condensed personal freedom, which liberates the I from the world outside it, and which places the I beyond reach of the power of Time – a condition in which there is only the I in its servant relationship to the Lord, with all the evidences of His lordship – it is here that the [artistic] creator manifests himself with the Creator by means of his [artistic] statements. And, if you'll forgive me for saying so, precisely because this experience is so individual in character, it needs no validation by anyone else.[75]

Such thoughts could not be further from the canonic Soviet socialist realism of the 1930s!

Pramoedya translated Gorky's *Mother* in 1956, using both English and Dutch-language versions of the novel, but it wasn't until he composed his four novels on the Indonesian nationalist movement during his imprisonment on the island of Buru in the 1970s that we can trace the full impact of *Mother* on his thinking and literary practice. In 1962 Pramoedya wrote a series of lectures on "*realisme sosialis*" where, on the first page of the introduction, he hails Gorky as the most famous practitioner of the kind of socialist realist writing, exemplified best by *Mother*, that he wants to discuss. Later on, Pramoedya refers to Gorky's *My Childhood* and the autobiographical method Gorky uses to portray "the blows and oppression that he suffered from the capitalist-bourgeois class," noting further that it "isn't surprising that he allied himself with his grandmother, a beggar woman, and took her side in opposing his grandfather."[76] Once Pramoedya begins examining the socialist realist literary tradition in Indonesia in his lectures, it is clear that Gorky's writing and ideas were of greatest use, not as models to imitate but as examples that helped him identify the characteristics of an autonomous Indonesian tradition of socialist realist writing, one that has its origins in stories published in the Malay-language press by Eurasian and Malay writers at the turn of the twentieth century. These stories were written in unadorned, everyday Malay in a reportage style and were based on real events, usually murders, thefts, and interracial conflict. The "Story of Nyai Dasima" by G. Francis in 1896, for example, relates the downfall of a concubine who leaves the European master who has educated her and given her a child in order to regain her native identity in the village, only to be murdered for her money by Samioen, an evil Muslim.[77] Pramoedya's heroine Nyai Ontosoroh in the Buru tetralogy is based on the mother character from Gorky's novel but also on *nyai* (concubine) characters like Dasima from the turn-of-the-century reportage literature in Java. Pramoedya's discovery of realist reportage writing about colonial oppression at the turn of the century, combined with the biography of his grandmother and the memory of his own beloved mother,[78] enabled him to localize, to Indonesianize, the "plot formula Gorky worked out for *Mother* (i.e., the disciple acquires the likeness of the mentor and hence acquires 'consciousness')" in a novel way.[79] In Pramoedya's reworking of the formula, not only are the mentor/disciple roles reversed, with the "mother" Nyai Ontosoroh teaching the young Dutch-educated aristocrat Minke, who comes to live in her house as a quasi-adoptive son, how to become an Indonesian nationalist. But it is Nyai Ontosoroh and other female characters in the novels, rather than the male nationalist hero, who are shown to travel the "road to consciousness" and who become the real force for revolutionary change in the tetralogy.[80]

"A literary work can only be conceived in the mind," Trần Dần wrote in an essay for the literary journal *Nhân Văn* (*Humanism*) published on 30 September 1956, "and it can only be born from an emotion in the spirit of the writer. It only obeys the demands of the inner heart, and only becomes concrete when a fire breaks out in this inner heart."[81] The subjective realm of an "inner quest," where the first kind of liberation from colonial oppression had to take place before any other kind of revolution could be fought, is where Trần Dần, Pramoedya, and many other socialist realist writers in Southeast Asia translated and communed with the cosmopolitan "literature-worlds" that came to inform their writing.

NOTES

An earlier version of this chapter appeared as "Still Stuck in the Mud: Imagining World Literature during the Cold War in Indonesia and Vietnam," in *Cultures at War: The Cold War and Cultural Expression in Southeast Asia*, ed. Tony Day and Maya H.T. Liem (Ithaca, NY: SEAP Press, Cornell University, 2010), 131–69. I am grateful to the editor of SEAP Press for permission to reprint portions of my earlier essay here.

1 See also Tony Day, "Locating Indonesian Literature in the World," *Modern Language Quarterly* 68, no. 2 (June 2007): 173–93.
2 Pascale Casanova, *The World Republic of Letters* (Cambridge, MA: Harvard University Press, 2004), 108.
3 Ibid., 109.
4 Michael Denning, "The Novelists' International," in *The Novel, Volume 1: History, Geography, and Culture*, ed. Franco Moretti (Princeton, NJ: Princeton University Press, 2006), 703–25. For a related essay, see Timothy Brennan, "Postcolonial Studies between the European Wars: An Intellectual History," in *Marxism, Modernity, and Postcolonial Studies*, ed. Crystal Bartolovich and Neil Lazarus (Cambridge: Cambridge University Press, 2002), 185–203. Brennan argues that "postcolonial studies" has its origins in interwar Marxism rather than in intellectual movements associated with decolonization after the Second World War.
5 Denning, "The Novelists' International," 703–4. Denning is quoting from Wright's memoir *Black Boy*.
6 Ibid., 706–7. Denning mentions several other European, North American, and South Asian writers born in the mid to late nineteenth century as well as the Chinese short story writer and essayist Lu Xun (1881–1936) as major, pre-1917 socialist realist authors. I follow Denning (and Pramoedya Ananta Toer) in decoupling the timing and nature of the appearance of "socialist realism" in Southeast Asia from the chronology and morphology of its development in the Soviet Union.
7 Ibid., 711–12.

8   H.M.J. Maier, "Written in the Prison's Light: The Hikajat Kadiroen by Semaoen," *RIMA* 30 (Winter/Summer 1996): 1–18, quote at 5. This essay serves as an introduction to an English translation of Semaoen's novel, "The Story of Kadiroen," published in the same issue of *RIMA*. For the history of the founding of the Communist Party in Indonesia and Semaoen's role in it, see Ruth T. McVey, *The Rise of Indonesian Communism* (Ithaca, NY: Cornell University Press, 1965).

9   Katerina Clark, *The Soviet Novel: History as Ritual*, 3rd ed. (Bloomington: Indiana University Press, 2000), 63.

10 Ibid., 46–67.

11 Semaoen, "The Story of Kadiroen," trans. Jan Lingard, *RIMA* 30 (Winter/Summer 1996): 19–139, quote at 26.

12 Paul Tickell, "Novels, Politics and Values: Political Discourse and Modern Identities in Semaoen's Hikajat Kadiroen," *RIMA* 30 (Winter/Summer 1996): 142, 150. In his afterword to the translation of *Hikajat Kadiroen*, Paul Tickell points out that another source of themes in the novel is the Western detective novel, with its emphasis on the rationality of the individual, an attribute also highly valued in Islam. The adventures of the American writer John Russell Coryell's hero Nick Carter appeared in 1914, for example, in serial form in a popular Malay-language newspaper published in Java that would have been available to Semaoen.

13 Tickell, "Novels," 147; Katerina Clark, *Moscow, the Fourth Rome: Stalinism, Cosmopolitanism, and the Evolution of Soviet Culture, 1931–1941* (Cambridge, MA: Harvard University Press, 2011), 134.

14 Semaoen, "The Story of Kadiroen," 87; Semaoen, *Hikajat Kadiroen* (Semarang: Kantoor P.K.I., n.d.), 113–14. *Kodrat* is translated as "destiny" in the passage. The phrase "Allah's laws in the course of each age" is a translation for *Allah poenja wet-perdjalanan-djaman*, which means literally "Allah's law (from Dutch *wet*) for the course of the age." Here and elsewhere in the novel it is clear that Semaoen understands the Marxist concept of history in terms of *kodrat* and the omnipotence of Allah, which incorporate and transcend all other forms of causation, including Dutch colonial law.

15 Ruth McVey, trans. with comments, "An Early Account of the Independence Movement, by Semaun," *Indonesia*, no. 1 (April 1966): 46–7.

16 Pramoedya Ananta Toer, *Realisme-Sosialis dan Sastra Indonesia [Socialist-Realism and Indonesia Literature]* (Jakarta: Lentera Dipantara, 2003), 64.

17 Peter Zinoman, *Vietnamese Colonial Republican: The Political Vision of Vũ Trọng Phụng* (Berkeley: University of California Press, 2014), 1.

18 Peter Zinoman, "Provincial Cosmopolitanism: Vũ Trọng Phụng's Foreign Literary Engagements," in *Traveling Nation-Makers: Transnational Flows and Movements in the Making of Modern Southeast Asia*, ed. Caroline S. Hau and Kasian Tjapira, Kyoto CSEAS Series on Asian Studies 3 (Singapore: NUS Press, in association with Kyoto University Press, 2011), 129.

19 Zinoman, *Vietnamese Colonial Republican*, 94–104; and Peter Zinoman, "Hải Vân, *The Storm*, and Vietnamese Communism in the Inter-War Imagination,"

in *Southeast Asia over Three Generations: Essays Presented to Benedict R. O'G. Anderson*, ed. James T. Siegel and Audrey R. Kahin (Ithaca, NY: Southeast Asia Program Publications, 2003), 125–43. Vũ Trọng Phụng was well informed about Comintern and Indochinese Communist Party policy. The serialization of the novel, Zinoman also points out, coincided "precisely with the rise of the Popular Front and the surge of local political journalism that arose in its wake." See *Vietnamese Colonial Republican*, 94.

20 Zinoman, "Hải Vân," 132.

21 For more on the Comintern agent Tan Malaka (1897–1949), who recorded his wandering and adventures in Europe, the Soviet Union, Indonesia, China, and Southeast Asia in his autobiography and was mythologized as the character Patjar Merah (Scarlet Pimpernel) in a series of popular novels published in Sumatra between 1938 and 1940, see Noriaki Oshikawa, "*Patjar Merah Indonesia* and Tan Malaka: A Popular Novel and a Revolutionary Legend," in *Reading Southeast Asia*, ed. Audrey Kahin, Roberta Ludgate, and Dolina Millar (Ithaca, NY: Southeast Asia Program, 1990), 9–39.

22 Zinoman, "Hải Vân," 133. The "Stalin School" in the novel is based on the real University of the Toilers of the East in Moscow, which was founded in 1921. Vietnamese communists began training there in 1925. See Sophie Quinn-Judge, *Ho Chi Minh: The Missing Years* (Berkeley: University of California Press, 2002), 54.

23 Quoted in Zinoman, "Hải Vân," 133.

24 Zinoman, "Hải Vân," 134.

25 Ibid.

26 Zinoman, *Vietnamese Colonial Republican*, 117–28.

27 Ibid., 101.

28 For more case studies that support this claim, see my "Still Stuck in the Mud."

29 See Keith Foulcher, "On a Roll: Pramoedya and the Postcolonial Transition," Indonesian Studies Working Papers No. 4 (Sydney, AU: The University of Sydney, January 2008): 3, 7–9, https://pdfs.semanticscholar.org/22a9/ff189454d65aaa84dec9fd798976e0151a99.pdf.

30 Keith Foulcher, *Social Commitment in Literature and the Arts: The Indonesian "Institute of People's Culture" 1950–1965* (Clayton, AU: Monash University Centre of Southeast Asian Studies, 1986), 16.

31 See *Cultureel Nieuws Indonesië 1950* 1 (October 1950): 1–31.

32 On Gelanggang and the writers associated with it, see A. Teeuw, *Modern Indonesian Literature*, vol. 1 (Leiden: KITLV Press, 1994), 115, 126–34; Martina Heinschke, "Between Gelanggang and Lekra: Pramoedya's Developing Literary Concepts," *Indonesia* 61 (1996): 145–69.

33 The best history and analysis of Lekra, including translations of writings by the major Lekra writers, is still Foulcher, *Social Commitment*.

34 Foulcher, "On a Roll," 8n12 cites Pramoedya's recollection in his memoirs that he remained silent throughout the seminar.

35 For more on Asrul and his writing, see my "Still Stuck in the Mud," 142–4.

36 Foulcher, "On a Roll," 8.

37 See Pramoedya Ananta Toer, *Tales from Djakarta: Caricatures of Circumstances and Their Human Beings* (Ithaca, NY: Southeast Asia Program Publications, 1999).

38 In addition to attending the Amsterdam conference in 1953, Pramoedya went to China in October 1956 as an official guest of the conference commemorating the twentieth anniversary of the death of the writer Lu Xun. He returned to China in October 1958 after heading the Indonesian delegation to the Asian and African Writers' Conference in Tashkent. See Hong Liu, *China and the Shaping of Indonesia, 1949–1965* (Singapore and Japan: NUS Press and Kyoto University Press, 2011), 244–53.

39 For an informative overview of the translation of foreign literature into Indonesian during this period, with a focus on the work of Trisno Sumardjo, who translated many of Shakespeare's plays, and Koesalah Soebagyo Toer, Pramoedya's younger brother, who specialized in works by Russian, Romanian, and Czech writers, see Maya H.T. Liem, "Bridge to the Outside World: Literary Translation in Indonesia, 1950–65," in *Heirs to World Culture: Being Indonesian 1950–1965*, ed. Jennifer Lindsay and Maya H.T. Liem (Leiden: KITLV Press, 2012), 163–90.

40 Foulcher, *Social Commitment*, 37–9. In May 1954, Pramoedya published a translation of an article on the importance of the Soviet example for the development of socialist realism in China by a leading and rigidly doctrinaire Party literary theorist, Zhou Yang. See Tjau Jang [Zhou Yang], "Realisme Sosialis – Jalan Kemajuan bagi Kesusastraan Tioghua," *Harian Rakjat*, 8 May 1954, cited in Foulcher, *Social Commitment*, 38n4. An English version of this essay, which Pramoedya may have used for his translation, can be found in Chou Yang [Zhou Yang], *China's New Literature and Art: Essays and Addresses* (Peking: Foreign Language Press, 1954), 87–102. Later that same year, Zhou, described by C.T. Hsia as "a ruthlessly ambitious man, constantly exhorting writers to follow the Mao Tse-tung line in literature and periodically initiating attacks on unorthodox writings and writers," led the assault on the "subjective idealist" critic Hu Feng, about whom more later. See C.T. Hsia, *A History of Modern Chinese Fiction*, 3rd ed. (Bloomington: Indiana University Press, 1999), 331 and passim.

41 Pramoedya Ananta Toer, "*Perburuan* 1950 and *Keluarga Gerilya* 1950," trans. Benedict Anderson, *Indonesia* 36 (October 1983): 37.

42 Clark, *The Soviet Novel*, 52.

43 There is no space here to examine the full significance of even these translations for understanding Pramoedya's thinking during a major period of change in his career as a writer and critical thinker. The best studies of Pramoedya's intellectual development during the mid-1950s are Heinschke, "Between Gelanggang and Lekra"; Foulcher, "On a Roll"; and Hong Liu, "Pramoedya Ananta Toer and China: The Transformation of a Cultural Intellectual," *Indonesia* 61 (April 996): 119–43.

44 L.L. Schücking, "Kesusasteraan dan Publik," trans. Pramoedya Ananta Toer, *Indonesia* 6, nos. 10–12 (Oktober–November–Desember 1955): 384–92.

The English translation is "Literature and Public," chapter four of Schücking's *Die Soziologie der literarischen Geschmacksbildung*, first published in 1923, from E.W. Dickes's English translation, published in 1944 as *The Sociology of Literary Taste* (London: Kegan Paul, Trench, Trubner and Co.) in the International Library of Sociology and Social Reconstruction series edited by Karl Mannheim.

45 The English translation is from Schücking, *Sociology of Literary Taste*, 26–7; the Indonesian versions of selected passages are taken from Pramoedya's translation of L.L. Schücking, "Kesusasteraan," 384–85. A few lines below the passage I have just quoted, Schücking identifies those who led the early Naturalist movement in Germany as "only small groups of journalists in the great cities that took up the cudgels for the new trend in art" (27), a striking anticipation of, if not direct stimulus to Pramoedya's own investigations, lectures, and publications in 1962–63 on the history of an indigenous "socialist realism" that developed in early twentieth-century Netherlands Indies Malay literature.

46 Hong Liu, "Pramoedya," 125n24 identifies the text and provenance of the original speech but not the title and location of the English translation used by Pramoedya. See Ting Ling [Ding Ling], "Life and Creative Writing," *Chinese Literature* 3 (1954): 152–8. Pramoedya's translation appeared as Ting Ling, "Hidup dan Penulisan Kreatif," *Indonesia* 7, no. 3 (Maret 1956): 102–10.

47 Pramoedya Ananta Toer, "Tendensi kerakyatan dalam kesusastraan Indonesia terbaru" [The Popular Tendency in the Latest Indonesian Literature], *Star Weekly*, no. 525, 21 January 1956, reprinted in Pramoedya Ananta Toer, *Menggelinding I [On the Move I]* (Jakarta: Lentera Dipantara, 2004), 456.

48 Ting Ling [Ding Ling], "Life and Creative Writing," 153; Ting Ling, "Hidup," 103. Pramoedya's translation of "indulge in idle talk" adds a vulgar connotation that gives the phrase extra sting.

49 Ting Ling [Ding Ling], "Life and Creative Writing," 155; Ting Ling, "Hidup," 106.

50 Ting Ling [Ding Ling], "Life and Creative Writing," 157.

51 "Kesusasteraan Sebagai Alat," *Mimbar Indonesia*, 17 March 1953, reprinted in Pramoedya, *Menggelinding*, 222–31. For more on Jassin, see my "Still Stuck in the Mud," 138–41.

52 "Kesusasteraan Sebagai Alat," 230.

53 See Hong Liu, "Pramoedya," 130, on Pramoedya's observations about the economic security of contemporary Chinese writers.

54 George Reavey, *Soviet Literature To-Day* (New Haven, CT: Yale University Press, 1947), 30–44. Pramoedya's translation appears as George Reavey, "Hidup dan organisasi pengarang Soviet," *Indonesia* 7, no. 3 (Maret 1956): 194–205. George Reavey (1907–76) was an Irish surrealist poet born in Russia, Samuel Beckett's first literary agent, and a prolific translator of twentieth-century Russian poetry, including that of Mayakovsky, into English. I do not know whether or not Pramoedya read any of Reavey's literary translations.

55 In his memoirs, Pramoedya recounts that he was desperate for money after his
    second marriage. "Fortunately, around this time, a poet and friend of mine, A.S.
    Dharta, stopped by the house with an English-language copy of Gorki's novel
    Mother to see if I would be interested in translating it into Indonesian. The 6,000
    rupiah that he proceeded to count out convinced me I was up to the job." See
    Pramoedya Ananta Toer, *The Mute's Soliloquy: A Memoir*, trans. Willem Samuels
    (New York: Hyperion East, 1999), 227. There was considerable interest in Gorky
    in Indonesia at this time and a strong appreciation for the international stature of
    Russian writers generally.

56 Reavey, *Soviet Literature*, 31; Reavey, "Hidup," 195.

57 Reavey, *Soviet Literature*, 32. Pramoedya gives the Indonesian figures in a long arti-
    cle he published in February 1957, "Keadaan Social Parapengarang Indonesia" [The
    Social Situation of Indonesian Writers], *Star Weekly*, 12 January 1957, reprinted
    in Pramoedya, *Menggelinding*, 524. In another article published in *Siasat* a month
    later, Pramoedya cites the same figures from Reavey and adds further comparative
    material from France, Britain, Czechoslovakia, China, and Burma; see "Keadaan
    social para pengarang: Perbandingan antarnegara" [The Social Situation of Writers:
    An International Comparison], *Siasat* 502 (20 February 1957): 25–6.

58 Reavey, *Soviet Literature*, 34; Reavey, "Hidup," 197. Italics in English are in the
    original.

59 "Perjuangan Kesusastraan Indonesia Yang Lalu Dan Yang Akan Datang" [The
    Struggle of Indonesian Literature Past and Future], in Pramoedya, *Menggelinding*,
    325. Foulcher discusses this and related essays from the late 1950s in "On a Roll,"
    17–19, and shows that Pramoedya thought cosmopolitanism, national identity,
    social commitment, and the expression of the writer's individuality were necessar-
    ily interconnected in the writing of "Indonesian" literature.

60 For an excellent study of the process through which, by means of translations and
    other forms of cultural exchange, China became part of the international socialist
    world after 1949, see Nicolai Volland, "Translating the Socialist State: Cultural
    Exchange, National Identity, and the Socialist World in the Early PRC," *Twentieth-
    Century China* 33, no. 2 (April 2008): 51–72. "The translation of a new breed of
    socialist literature," Volland writes, "became an especially important factor in this
    process: the simultaneous consumption in a dozen countries of Soviet popular
    novels, and of representative literary works produced everywhere in the socialist
    world, could make a direct impact on local audiences, reaching more people than
    all other forms of cultural exchange" (70).

61 See Neil Jamieson, *Understanding Vietnam* (Berkeley: University of California
    Press, 1993), 100–75; Hue Tam Ho Tai, "Literature for the People: From Soviet
    Policies to Vietnamese Polemics," in *Borrowings and Adaptations in Vietnamese
    Culture*, ed. Truong Buu Lam (Honolulu: Center for Asian and Pacific Studies,
    University of Hawaii at Manoa, 1987), 63–83; and Tuan Ngoc Nguyen, "Socialist

Realism in Vietnamese Literature: An Analysis of the Relationship between Literature and Politics" (PhD diss., Victoria University (AU), 2004), http://eprints. vu.edu.au/279/. Vietnamese writers were introduced to Soviet socialist realism through French translations in the 1930s. The first Soviet literary work translated into Vietnamese was part of Gorky's *My Childhood*, which appeared in 1936; the first of four different translations of Gorky's *Mother* was published in 1939; see Nguyen, "Socialist Realism," 72–84.

62 Tai, "Literature for the People," 64. Tai points out that Vietnamese writers relied mainly on French sources and accounts of the Soviet literary debates of the 1930s, even though some of them had attended the Workers' University of the East in Moscow: "The French critics who wrote for *l'Humanité* or *Monde* were ... more than transmitters, albeit selective, of a received line; they adapted it and even advanced their own interpretation of what was politically committed and proletarian literature" (65). For more discussion of literary debates in Vietnam during the 1940s and early 1950s, see my "Still Stuck in the Mud," 155–8.

63 Nguyen, "Socialist Realism," 82.

64 Ibid., 121–63; Georges Boudarel, *Cent Fleurs Écloses dans les Nuit du Vietnam: Communisme et Dissidence 1954–1956* [*A Hundred Blooming Flowers in the Night of Vietnam: Communism and Dissidence 1954–1956*] (Paris: Jacques Bertoin, 1991).

65 Rectification was not the only revolutionary Chinese concept that gained currency in Vietnam starting in 1950. Mao's "Talks at the Yan'an Conference on Literature and Art" was translated into Vietnamese in 1949; the essay collection by Zhou Yang, from which Pramoedya made a translation in 1954, appeared in Vietnamese as *Văn Nghệ Nhân Dân Mới* (*The People's New Literature and Art*), also in 1954. For more on revolutionary Chinese literary and ideological influence on Vietnam in the 1950s, see Nguyen, "Socialist Realism," 173–83.

66 Quoted in Kim N.B. Ninh, *A World Transformed: The Politics of Culture in Revolutionary Vietnam, 1945–1965* (Ann Arbor: The University of Michigan Press, 2002), 128, from Hoàng Cầm's biographical account of Trần Dần published in the 20 September 1956 issue of *Nhân Văn* (*Humanism*), one of two literary journals started by dissidents in 1955. For a partial English translation of Hoàng Cầm's biography, see Hoa Mai, ed., *The "Nhan-Van" Affair* (N.p.: The Vietnam Chapter of the Asian Peoples' Anti-Communist League, n.d.), 43–51. The complete biography in French translation appears in Boudarel, *Cent Fleurs*, 26–46.

67 Hirohide Kurihara, "Changes in the Literary Policy of the Vietnamese Workers' Party, 1956–1958," in *Indochina in the 1940s and 1950s*, ed. Takashi Shiraishi and Motoo Furuta (Ithaca, NY: Southeast Asia Program, Cornell University, 1992), 165–96.

68 For a text, translation, and discussion of this poem, see my "Still Stuck in the Mud," 159–62.

69 Ninh, *A World Transformed*, 139–40. According to Ninh, the "honest and raw" quality of the poem was partly because Trần Dần never planned to publish it. While Trần Dần was away in a village as part of a land reform team, the poet Hoàng Cầm, who wanted to include something from his friend in the first issue of the new literary journal *Giai Phẩm Mùa Xuân* (*Fine Works of Spring*), went ahead without the author's permission and published it.

70 Nora A. Taylor, "Raindrops on Red Flags: Tran Trong Vu and the Roots of Vietnamese Painting Abroad," in *Of Vietnam: Identities in Dialogue*, ed. June Bradley Winston and Leakthina Chau-Pech Ollier (New York: Palgrave, 2001), 120. Trần Trọng Vũ is Trần Dần's son and a highly successful painter based in Paris. In an installation exhibited in 1999, Vũ commented on and celebrated his father's famous poem.

71 Quoted and translated in Ninh, *A World Transformed*, 139.

72 Ibid., 140–1.

73 A collection of six poems by Mayakovsky, translated by the poet Hoàng Trung Thông (1925–93), was published in 1953 and again in 1954. In 1957, a volume titled *Thơ Mai-a-cốp-xki* (*Poems by Mayakovsky*) appeared, translated by Hoàng Trung Thông and Trần Dần, with an introduction by the poet Lê Đạt, who was himself the author of verse that recalled the spirit and typography of Mayakovsky in which he extolled the "New! New!/ Always new!/ Fly high/ Fly far/ Above the signs of the old/ Above the deteriorating sidewalks/ Surpassing today/ Surpassing tomorrow, the day after,/ Always surpassing." See Lữ Huy Nguyên and Đào Ngọc Du, eds., *35 năm văn học, 1948–1983* [*Thirty-five years of literature, 1948–1983*] (Hà Nội: Nhà xuất bản Văn học, 1983), 208–9, 214; and Ninh, *A World Transformed*, 137–8. For more on the reception of Mayakovsky in Vietnam during this period, see my "Still Stuck in the Mud," 163–4.

74 Boudarel, *Cent Fleurs*, 30.

75 Pramoedya, "Perburuan 1950," 28.

76 Pramoedya, *Realisme-Sosialis*, 27. Pramoedya based the first of what was going to be a series of novels about the Indonesian nationalist movement, *Gadis Pantai* (*The Girl from the Coast*), on the life of his maternal grandmother, who had been sold by her father as a concubine to a local aristocrat around the turn of the twentieth century. *Gadis Pantai* was published in serial form at the end of 1962. The manuscripts of the remaining novels in the series, together with all of Pramoedya's research materials on early twentieth-century socialist realist fiction from Indonesia, were destroyed when he was arrested on 13 October 1965. See Pramoedya Ananta Toer, *The Girl from the Coast*, trans. Willem Samuels (New York: Hyperion East, 2002).

77 See my "'Self' and 'Subject' in Southeast Asian Literature in the Global Age," in Kathryn Robinson, *Asian and Pacific Cosmopolitanisms: Self and Subject in Motion* (Basingstoke, UK: Palgrave Macmillan: 2007), 26–7. In contrast to Semaoen, who stressed the positive side of Islam in *Hikajat Kadiroen* in line with the "block

within" policy of the Indonesian Communist Party in the 1920s, Pramoedya consistently portrays Islam in a negative light in his writing.

78 Pramoedya, *The Mute's Soliloquy*, 126. "When I was growing up, I didn't know my mother's name ... But each time I think of her, especially when I'm trying to write, my mother is always vaguely present, hovering in my father's shadow."

79 Clark, *The Soviet Novel*, 65.

80 For a discussion of the transposition of another *nyai* character from a story published in 1900 to the pages of the second novel in the Buru tetralogy, *Anak Semua Bangsa* (*Child of All Nations*), in which Pramoedya endows the oppressed woman from the colonial story with subjectivity and a nationalist consciousness, see my "'Self' and 'Subject,'" 28–9.

81 "Let Us Struggle for the One Hundred Flowers Blooming Policy," in Mai, *The "Nhan-Van" Affair*, 59–64.

PART TWO

Form: Beyond Realism-versus-Modernism
and Art-versus-Propaganda

Chapter Seven

Culture One and a Half

NARIMAN SKAKOV
Stanford University

In 1924, Mikhail Bakhtin worked on the lengthy article titled "Towards Questions of Methodology of Aesthetics of Verbal Art" – one of his major theoretical works of the early period. The notion of boundary and its place in the discourse of culture preoccupied the thinker, who, at the time of writing, found himself on the margins of the intellectual life of the young Soviet state. But the experience of liminality was not perceived as something negative. On the contrary, the fringe retained an enormous cultural potential. Bakhtin put it in these words:

> One must not, however, imagine the realm of culture as some sort of spatial whole, having boundaries but also having internal territory. The realm of culture has no internal territory: it is entirely distributed along the boundaries, boundaries pass everywhere, through its every aspect ... Every cultural act lives essentially on the boundaries: in this is its seriousness and significance; abstracted from boundaries it loses its soil, it becomes empty, arrogant, it degenerates and dies.[1]

This rather dense passage intricately reflects the period's general fascination with the possibility of infinite expansion and the obsession with things marginal, peripheral, and liminal. The wholeness of culture is achieved through its dispersed constituents.[2] In the same year, 1924, Iurii Tynianov wrote a seminal essay, "Literary Fact," in which the formalist critic argued that the literary, and by extension cultural, process can be understood as a relationship between centre and periphery that constantly swap places:

> It is not only the *borders* of literature – its "periphery," its liminal regions – that are fluid, but also its very "centre." It is not a matter of some primeval, successive stream moving and evolving in the centre of literature while new phenomena flow in only at the edges – no, these new phenomena themselves take place in the very centre, and the centre itself moves away to the periphery.[3]

Tynianov makes a claim – radical for the time and strongly resonating with Bakhtin's – that there is no such concept as an immobile permanent centre. Grand narratives of culture rise and fall. The only thing that always remains in place is a process of interchange, and it is remarkable that the critic conceptualizes this idea in (proto)postcolonial terms. The notion of periphery is central.

The present chapter is a story of how the notion of boundary and its cultural significance changed throughout the late 1920s and the 1930s. The transformation of the Third Communist International's political stance, the modification and manipulation of Soviet nationalities policy, and the evolution of the aesthetics of modernism were inherently interlinked, and the concept of boundary served as a constant refrain throughout the tumultuous period of Soviet history. In the 1930s, after the Soviet Union's major socio-political upheaval and the turn towards building socialism in one country, the geographical impetus of modernism found its home on the fringe of the country: the republics of Central Asia. The space provided an intensely alienating, defamiliarizing, and disorienting experience – just the type that lies at the core of modernist aesthetics. It was also an essentially heterogeneous and dynamic geographical region, which "invited" a radical transformation of physical and social space, from industry and infrastructure to language and literary canons. The international-minded drive of the 1920s to overcome the constraints of borders was rechannelled into a constructive effort within a clearly demarcated space. The unshackled boundary evolved into a guarded borderline.

In its first largely contextual and historical section, this chapter explores how the Bolshevik rhetoric of internationalist expansion was replaced by the trope of (re)construction within a clearly demarcated space. In the late 1920s, border-transcending internationalism (world revolution), which strongly resonated with Bakhtin's and Tynianov's conceptions of culture, became literally internalized and started to signify primarily inter-ethnic relationships within the bordered space of the Soviet Union. A similar development is reflected in the political agenda of the Comintern – from aspirations to create a worldwide Soviet Union to the recognition of national distinctiveness and the defensive policies aimed to protect the already established socialist communities from the threat of fascism. The concept of the Third Period, adopted in 1928, predicted mass working-class radicalization; however, after the rise of the Nazi Party to power in Germany in 1933, it was supplemented with the "People's Front Against Fascism and War" policy.

In the second part, the chapter reconsiders the ongoing debate on the relationship between the emancipatory 1920s and the inhibiting 1930s, or between the avant-garde and socialist realism. It replaces the rigid binary division, professed by Vladimir Paperny and other cultural historians, with an acknowledgement of an important intermediary stage during which the avant-garde and modernism in general responded to the overpowering political environment and its national-international inflections by rechannelling their transformative aesthetic energy and finding a meaningful application for this energy, both fig- uratively and literally. The passage from the avant-garde experimentation of the early period to the neoclassical socialist realism was in many ways linked to the evolution of the nationalities policy in the country. This change was largely defined by Stalin's description of proletarian culture as "national in form, socialist in content."[4] Formal experimentation was possible only in the national context, and only with the dominance of singular socialist content. That very national form was the last sanctuary of modernist "strangeness."

Finally, to illustrate the international-national tension, this chapter pre- sents a case study of Andrei Platonov – a daring experimenter of the 1920s who earnestly strove to become a socialist realist writer in the 1930s and was also concerned with the (inter)national realities of the Union of Soviet Socialist Republics (USSR). The writer's two trips to Turkmenistan in 1934 and 1935 largely defined his almost desperate urge to contribute to socialist construction. The trips also took place during the most crucial period for the Comintern: 1934 was the last year of the "Third Period," as defined by the organization's ideologues – a time of widespread economic collapse and the radicalization of the working class throughout the world. It was followed in 1935 by the Seventh (and last) Congress of the Comintern, during which the protective and anti-fascist "Popular Front" policy was announced. Platonov reflected the two trends in his own, idiosyncratic way: his staggering anti-fascist text "Garbage Wind" (1933) and his piercing Turkmen novella *Dzhan* (1934–35), both pub- lished posthumously together with the short story "Takyr" (1934), do not sim- ply explore cultural otherness and proletarian brotherhood, but also survey the limits of human existence and even create a case for unorthodox methods of nation-building. Platonov actively engages Soviet oriental cultural trends and Stalinist political conundrums in his Turkmen corpus: he deeply immerses himself in the rich and heterogeneous cultural past of the region, but, at the same time, he transplants local ethnic roots into universal proletarian soil and even elevates them to a mythological plane. Moreover, Platonov, in sync with Bakhtin's and Tynianov's conception of the border, bridges a set of different divides – not only geographic (centre versus periphery) but also a figurative division between socialist realism and modernism.

The Communist *Intra*national

The Third Communist International (or the Comintern) advocated world communism and was a major driving force of what Kris Manjapra refers to as "aspirational cosmopolitanism."[5] The Comintern's statutes proclaimed that its aim was "to fight by all available means, including armed struggle, for the over- throw of the international bourgeoisie and for the creation of an international

Soviet republic as a transitional stage to the complete abolition of the State."[6] This initial radical and annihilating drive was inspired by Marx's statement that "the working class has no country." Hence, the Comintern issued statements addressing the internal affairs of countries on every continent and made appeals to almost every working community – from the repressed "negroes" of North America to the exploited toilers of Indonesia and Egypt.

However, its emancipatory rhetoric, fully manipulated by the Soviet ideological apparatus, was quite often infused with thoroughly orientalist sentiments. In "Theses on the Eastern Question," for example, the Fourth Comintern Congress resolved that the alliance with the proletariat of the "advanced" countries was essential for the "backward" working communities of the Orient. The necessity of this alliance was dictated "by the fact that it is only from the victorious proletariat of the advanced countries that the workers of the East can get disinterested help for the development of their backward productive forces."[7]

The rhetoric of "enlightening the backward" found in Bolshevik policies designed to assist the workers of the Orient in "development" and "modernization" follows the conventions of orientalist discourse. Therefore, the Comintern ideologues exploited a key aspect of orientalism: its inherent role of mediating between unenlightened ethnic populations and the values of a "universal" civilization. Socialist construction (physical transformation of space) and comprehensive culture-building initiatives (cultivation of mental space) are those practices that help "retrograde" nations "catch up" with the flow of history and become self-sufficient builders of the communal socialist edifice. This outlook was probably why Eugene Lyons, the first Western journalist to be granted an interview with Joseph Stalin, famously referred to the latter as the "infallible Leader and master of the Russian empire and also of that empire beyond Russia represented by the Third or Communist International."[8]

However, the later periods of the Comintern became less and less infused with expansive orientalist refrains and grew increasingly defensive: the orientation of the policies was redirected towards an "internal," already "unshackled," socialist space. The change mimicked the radical shift undergone by the political structure of the Soviet Union by the end of the 1920s – the possibility and even the necessity of building "socialism in one country" became part of the political scene. The Comintern's activities were severely disrupted by internal conflicts within the Bolshevik Party in the fractional struggles of the 1920s involving Trotsky, Zinoviev, and Bukharin. As a result, Trotsky founded the International Left Opposition in 1930, which later evolved into the Fourth International with the aim of assisting the working class in reaching truly "international" communism.

The growing threat of fascism helped the Comintern justify its protective stance. The last congress of the organization, which took place in Moscow in the summer of 1935, officially endorsed the Popular Front against the threat of fascism. A few years later, the rhetoric of bordered space started to dominate the political atmosphere within the organization. The Comintern Executive Committee (ECCI) issued a manifesto on the eleventh anniversary of the Russian Revolution, which proclaimed: "[The] Stalinist word is inviolable ... The frontiers of the Soviet country are inviolable. On the borders of the USSR there stands unyielding the strongest army in the world, the Red Army of Socialism."[9] This declaration was a triumphal representation of a boldly delimited and securely guarded space, a representation that proved to be instrumental in both a cultural and a political sense. The fluid border, which Bakhtin and Tynianov conceptualized in the 1920s, solidifies and becomes a concrete and immovable entity.

The purges of the late 1930s weakened the Comintern and strengthened its awareness of its limits even further. On 15 May 1943, an ECCI resolution was sent out to all sections of the International, calling for the Comintern's dissolution. The resolution – which should be read skeptically, considering Stalin's need to appease his wartime allies – stated that "with the increasing complications in the internal and international relations of the various countries, any sort of international centre would encounter insuperable obstacles in solving the problems facing the movement in each separate country."[10] The initial striving towards the complete withering away of any kind of state found its "culmination" in the impossibility of navigating the peculiarities of labour movements in individual countries. The attempt to reach borderless proletarian homogeneity resulted in a situation in which national diversity proved to be an insurmountable political obstacle.

The Comintern's progression from the project of emancipation to the centralized mobilized state is mirrored in rhetorical shifts in Soviet nationality policy. As many historians have established, the vehement enthusiasm that existed for ethnic particularism throughout much of the 1920s dissipated and was replaced with a gradual advent of Russophile sentiments. By 1934, the comprehensive politics of indigenization throughout the Soviet Union was brought to a standstill,[11] and the country witnessed the gradual rehabilitation of the Russian nation and culture (1932–38). One of the first rhetorical moves towards this rehabilitation was the introduction of the concept "friendship of peoples."[12] It was an essential intermediary stage that divided radical expansionist internationalism from a centre-periphery model of socialism, with Russians playing the role of first among equals. The concept was introduced at a 1935 meeting with Tajik and Turkmen collective farmers – cotton shock workers. The fact that the latter were representatives of two young republics – vigorously fighting their inherited "backwardness" – is essential, because economic and cultural spheres were conceived as inherently interrelated. These former subjects of mistreatment and manipulation were presented as having already abandoned their feelings of resentment towards their former exploiter (the tsarist regime) and its cultural paradigm (Russian culture).

However, the "friendship of peoples," as a rhetorical move, gradually evolved into a patronizing relationship. The abandoned attempts to prescribe the use of native languages in government administration along with the 1938 law mandating the study of the Russian language by all non-Russian schoolchildren signalled a radical shift in Soviet nationalities politics. The centralized state required a common language, which was necessary for its executive efficiency. In Stalin's own words, "in the conditions of a multinational state such as the USSR, knowledge of the Russian language should be a powerful means for communication and contact among the peoples of the USSR, enabling their further economic and cultural growth."[13] Russian gradually evolved into a supranational language, while its bearers – the Russian people – acquired a new status of first among equals and became the fulfiller of the hopes and dreams of the international community of toilers.[14] This discursive reorientation had enormous consequences for artistic policies and practices. The change was reflected in the dominant themes of the vast majority of artistic projects that the state commissioned in the 1930s: the shift from boundless internationalism to internal diversity, and then from internal diversity to Russocentrism, which itself was further intensified by patriotic rhetoric during the Second World War.

In Medias Res

The gradual ideological shift from the emancipatory 1920s towards the confined late 1930s comprised an essential phase in Soviet ideological and cultural periodization; I argue that it deserves to be recognized as such (see table 7.1 for more details). The ongoing debate on the relationship between the liberating 1920s and the inhibiting 1930s, or the avant-garde versus socialist realism, is dominated by two narratives: one of difference and one of sameness. Vladimir Paperny's oft-cited study *Architecture in the Age of Stalin: Culture Two* (1985) forcibly presents a vision of two dominant cultural tendencies that shaped the Soviet ideological landscape after the October Revolution of 1917 and up to Stalin's death in 1953. The egalitarian, experimental, and horizontal avant-garde of Culture One (circa 1917–31) is set off against the repressive, monumentalist, and vertical "neoclassicism" of Culture Two (1932–53).[15] While Paperny presents a rigid dichotomy between the two camps, Boris Groys emphasizes socialist realism's organic "continuity with the avant-garde project."[16] More radically, the latter insists that the official aesthetic dictum of the post-1934 Soviet Union comprises the avant-garde's "culmination and in some sense its completion."[17] "Stalinist culture both radicalizes and formally overcomes the avant-garde; it is, so to speak, a laying bare of the avant-garde device and not merely a negation of it."[18] I argue that, instead of Paperny's two separate banks or Groys's continuous flow, a dam was built for the purposes of diverting the avant-garde's river of creative impulse. This dam dramatically turned the flow in the direction of the Eastern periphery of the country, where it nourished the aesthetically arid lands and contributed to the flourishing of the new Soviet subjectivity.

Paperny's structuralist binary pair not only attempts to explain the rupture that took place in the 1930s, which set the avant-garde aesthetic "anarchy" apart from stately socialist realism, but also claims that the tension between the two cultural paradigms is in fact a recurring oscillation, in a Nietzschean sense, which shapes the entire course of Russian history. An imposing set of binaries – for example, beginning-ending, movement-immobility, horizontal-vertical, uniform-hierarchical, collective-individual, mechanical-living, abstraction-name, good-evil, mutism-word, improvisation-notation, efficacious-artistic, realism-truth, business-miracle – helps Paperny to trace the effects of ideological and aesthetic tensions in the arts and particularly in early Soviet architecture. This rather narrow focus is to some extent justified by the special ideological weight architecture carries and by the fact that the art of designing and creating buildings was of utmost importance to "the First Architect and Builder of our Socialist Fatherland"[19] – Joseph Stalin.

The rupture described by Paperny resonates with the concept of the "Great Retreat" – an established historiographic term introduced by Nicholas Timasheff in his classic 1946 monograph *The Great Retreat: The Growth and Decline of Communism in Russia*.[20] Though its discursive coordinates have been adjusted in recent scholarship, the term still comprises a unique trope used to describe and conceptualize practically contemporaneous events.[21] "Great Retreat" suggests an irrevocable reversal of the communist revolutionary agenda under Stalin in 1934 and, in many ways, echoes Trotsky's thesis on the betrayal of revolutionary ideals. As Timasheff puts it, the Bolshevik ideologues had to make various concessions and "abandon part of their plan or even some position already gained, and remold the social configuration according to ideas which were not theirs."[22] However, the 1946 term reveals an inherent paradox, because "retreat" signifies not a radical "departure" from a political course and implementation of foreign ideas but also a process of "coming back" to one's own original domain. This withdrawal to the already familiar, as a deviation from the path of boundless expansion, is what characterized the "retreat" in question. To be precise, it was a return to, or a rhetorical turn towards, the alien and at the same time somewhat familiar space – the former colonies of the Russian empire. The Soviet Union's own fringe – the red Orient of Central Asia and to some extent the Caucasus and the Siberian territories – evolved into a primary *topos* for ideological manipulation and played a key role in the early and mid-1930s as a space of transition and reinforcement of the utopian hope for socialist transformation. This area was the place where, or into which, the retreat took place – a site where the aborted international expansion found its new home and built its new defensive front line.

7.1 Culture One and a Half: Between the Avant-Garde and Socialist Realism

Internationalism 1917–28	Transition	Internal Diversity 1928–38	Transition	Soviet Stalinist Civilization 1938–53
Boundless space		Periphery		Centre
Universality		Exotic but on its way to being normalized		Russian as a transparent and translucent culture
Export of the revolution	Socialism in one country (1925)	"Empire of Nations"	Gradual rehabilitation of the Russian nation (1932–38)	Etatism
Proletarian "brotherhood"	"Affirmative action"	Friendship of peoples (1935)	Internationalization of Russian language and culture	Russians – first among equals (1938)
Great power chauvinism as the greatest danger		Publication of Stalin's Marxism and the National and Colonial Question (1935) and Creative Work of the Peoples of the USSR (1937)	Local nationalism and great power chauvinism are pronounced as equally dangerous (1932)	Stalin's Short Course (1938); Anti-cosmopolitan campaign; The Molotov–Ribbentrop Pact and the annexation of the Baltic states (1939–40)
Foundation of the Comintern (1919); Establishment of the Communist University of the Toilers of the East (1921)	Trotsky's removal from the Party (1927)	The Comintern's Popular Front policy; Completion of the national delimitation of Central Asia (1924–36)	Great Terror; Execution of diaspora nationalities; The 1936 Soviet constitution	Closure of the Communist University of the Toilers of the East (1938); Trotsky's assassination (1940); Dissolution of the Comintern (1943)
New Economic Policy (1921–28)	Industrialization and collectivization	Socialist construction; First five-year plan; Great Break (1929)	Heavy industry development	Third five-year plan aborted by the war
Adoption of "The Internationale" as the Soviet national anthem (1922)			Hymn of the Bolshevik Party (1938)	Adoption of the Soviet national anthem (1944)

Latinization of alphabets; Esperanto	*The project of latinization of Russian is abandoned (1930)*	Culture-building; Canonized histories of the various Central Asian republics began to appear; Attacks on Mikhail Pokrovskii's historical school (1936)	*Mandatory learning of Russian (1938)*	Cyrillization of alphabets
Formal experimentation	*National in form, socialist in content*	Attacks on formalism; emergence of historicism	*Socialist content*	Soviet style
Diversity of artistic movements	*The Russian Association of Proletarian Writers (RAPP) dominates literary process*	RAPP disbanded (1932); Artists' Unions created; National literatures celebrated		Total bureaucratization of the cultural process
Establishment of the "World Literature" series with Gorky's assistance (1919)		Culture of "exultation"; Mass jubilee celebrations of Firdawsi (1934), Pushkin (1937), Nizami (1937), Rustaveli (1937), Dzhambul (1938)	*Stalin's criticism of Demian Bedny's Knights (Bogatyri, 1936)*	Russian culture rehabilitated
Avant-garde experimentation		"In search" of socialist realism		Verbatim socialist realism
Montage, collage	*Factography*	Epic, ode, and folklore		Complete confluence of aesthetic and political projects
Faktura		Ornament		Template

A similar adjustment to our understanding of the Soviet topographical progression and ideological course of the time can be made with the argument that Paperny presents in *Culture Two*. International versus national is a somewhat "muted" binary pair, which, though not vigorously articulated throughout his book, plays a key role in Paperny's exploration of the Soviet ideologues' spatial practices. An everlasting tension between the two was present in the history of the Soviet Union from its foundation. The largely international and even supranational avant-garde of the 1920s is contrasted with the stilted vision of "socialism in one country" of the later period. At one point, Paperny writes:

> "Workers of the world unite!" – this Marxist slogan, written in Culture One on the covers of nearly all architectural publications (and totally absent from that venue in Culture Two), indicates that the idea of the international unity of a single class clearly dominated in Culture One over the concepts of either national or state unity.[23]

The slogan to which Paperny refers indeed disappeared from the covers of architectural publications, but its persistent presence on the front page of *Pravda* – the main news outlet in the country – since its reopening on 5 March 1917 until the present day can hardly be ignored. The international aspect of Soviet politics never faded away. Its rhetorical underpinning, however, endured a drastic transformation throughout time: from the truly international expansion of socialism without borders, to internal diversity and the importance of the periphery, and finally to an established state with clear borders where the mantra of internationalism served more like a habitual incantation that was gradually losing its magic spell.

I argue that Paperny's bold binarization, however convenient in its expediency, misses a crucial aspect. The concept of two cultures – international modernist experimentation and centralized Stalinist aesthetics – ignores a vital intermediary stage, which was essential for taming the centrifugal aspirations of the avant-garde and channelling them into the centripetal flow of socialist realism. This stage, which I refer to as "Culture One and a Half," was primarily preoccupied with the racially coloured Soviet periphery, where the Bolshevik policymakers tested and refined key ideological tools that were essential for the formation of Culture Two. The rise of etatism and the formation of Soviet civilization were bolstered by a series of cultural and ideological phenomena: the concept of the friendship of peoples; the notion of socialist construction; the attack on formalism with the consequent rise of the Stalinist formula of "national in form, socialist in content"; the prominent role of the epic genre; the creation of national literary canons; and the practice of translation. The blatant orientalization of the country's periphery along such lines, in keeping with the general conventions of orientalism, played a key role in establishing the rigid boundaries of Soviet identity.[24]

Culture One and a Half is not characterized by any kind of rupture or fissure. One of its essential features is temporal scatteredness. Duration was key to the process of transference from one cultural paradigm to another. This intermediary orientalist stage helped Stalin to accomplish a relatively smooth transition from socialist internationalism to the state of largely Russified homogeneity. What Culture One and a Half established is the practice of "mediation," which gradually evolved into a tool of ideological and cultural coercion. This tool was the driving engine of the Soviet discursive machine. Mediation (from Latin *mediatio* – "a division in the middle") is understood as a practice of interference with a subsequent discursive or practical resolution. The term is inherently theological and was originally applied to Christ, who "mediates" between God and humans.[25] The vanguard of the Bolshevik Party assumed a messianic role: it cultivated mediation between the supranational goal of the communist revolution (the transcendental realm) and the necessity for local and familiar culture (the given reality). It provided assistance in transition, for the masses ostensibly lacked agency and required guidance to reach a higher and more abstract goal.

The roots of this practice go back to the Bolsheviks' old mantra – the alleged inability of the proletariat and peasantry to gain socialist consciousness without external assistance. In *What Is to Be Done* (1902), Lenin forcibly argues that the common working class is inept and incapable of bearing the standard of the proletarian revolution. Its aim is limited to having "bread and butter" on its table. Hence, "class political consciousness can be brought to the workers *only from without*," and, in order to develop potential consciousness where it is less apparent, the political movement relies exclusively on the vanguard of the proletariat.[26] In classic orientalist fashion, Lenin argues for the necessity of external interference, justified by the lack of agency in the object of transformation. The subaltern, in the Spivakian sense, has to be represented and spoken for.[27] Stalin emulates the structure of Lenin's argument in his "Reply to *Social-Democrat*," in which he exposes eight "lies" about the Bolsheviks' political agenda and reinstates one single truth: "the masses of proletarians, as long as they remain proletarians, have neither the time nor the opportunity to work out socialist consciousness."[28]

The original spatial trope "from without," which presumes a location outside of the object of transformation, acquires a hierarchical-vertical character in Stalin's later concept "revolution from above," which sought to build socialism by means of forced collectivization. *History of the All-Union Communist Party (Bolsheviks): Short Course*, a book commissioned and heavily edited by Stalin, proclaims that the elimination of the kulaks as a class was as important as the destruction of the capitalist dominance in the sphere of industry. "The distinguishing feature of this revolution," the book states, "is that it was accomplished *from above*, on the initiative of the state, and directly supported *from below* by the millions of peasants, who were fighting to throw off kulak bondage and to live in freedom in the collective farms."[29] The rhetorical spins that characterize Stalin's speech and writing patterns are distinctly enacted in this passage, and they establish a vertical axis of political hierarchy. Ordered from above but supported from below becomes a formula that establishes the dominance of the enlightened vanguard over the peasants and workers, who lack any progressive consciousness whatsoever.

However, the orientalist energy is channelled into a different direction once the collectivization and industrialization efforts recede in the mid-1930s. The main recipients of enlightenment "from without" become the developmentally "backward" nationalities of the Soviet periphery. The Soviet nations were divided, in a classic orientalist fashion, into two groups: Western and culturally advanced (the Russians, Ukrainians, Belorussians, Georgians, Armenians, Jews, and Germans) and Eastern and culturally backward (the remaining nationalities, most of which were inhabitants of Central Asia and Siberia).[30] The "backward" nationalities of the Soviet Union were able to skip the traumatic stage of capitalism and accomplish a leap from feudalism to socialism with some help from without – primarily from the already "advanced" Russian proletariat. As Stalin unambiguously put it at the Twelfth Party Congress in April 1923, a number of republics and peoples "had scarcely entered the stage of capitalism" and therefore were "incapable of rising to a higher level of development and thus catching up with the nationalities which [had] forged ahead unless they receive[d] real and prolonged assistance from *outside*."[31] Socialist construction (physical transformation of space) and comprehensive culture-building initiatives (cultivation of mental space) were the practices meant to help them "catch up" with the flow of history and become plenipotentiary builders of the communal socialist edifice. The trope of backwardness and the resulting inferiority complex generated the much-needed energy of transformation.[32]

The period between 1928 and 1938 was a vital intermediary stage for Soviet culture and politics. Of primary importance at this point was a preoccupation with the oriental fringes of the Soviet Union, where Bolshevik policymakers tested and refined key ideological tools essential for the formation of the "new Soviet man." Central Asia evolved into a key contact zone where the past met the present, and the clash between the two produced the bright socialist future. The space was an ideal pre-modern *Gemeinschaft*, ready to join the universal socialist family. However, in classic orientalist manner, the "retrograde" region was deemed unable to transcend its own borders on its own – there was a need for a "middleman," a mediator. It is notable, for instance, that envoys of the Central Committee of the Soviet Writers' Union were sent to every republic to supervise, direct, and mediate the process of consolidation that organized local writers and poets into serviceable bureaucratic entities. The list of writers included several notable modernist names: Boris Pil'niak was sent to Azerbaijan, Iurii Tynianov to Georgia, Andrei Bely and Osip Brik to the RSFSR nationalities, while Yurii Olesha, Ilya Ilf, and Evgenii Petrov travelled to Tatarstan. Colonial socialism, as a transitional stage, was born. The locals could not resist cultural subjugation and were not able to write back to the centre of the Soviet empire, because the state consolidated power in the region and closely monitored both the social and political spheres. Almost every attempt to make an autonomous local voice heard was cast as a manifestation of bourgeois nationalism.

The Soviet modernizing project faced a vast Eastern territory, inhabited by multi-ethnic, multilingual, and generally dispersed and disorganized local populations. Ethnicity and statehood simply did not coincide. This remarkable ethnic complexity was addressed discursively and politically by means of the project of national delimitation (1924–36), when the vigorous consolidation of international proletarian forces was combined with the demarcation of national territories in Central Asia. Terry Martin highlights the fact that the Bolsheviks never provided an explanation for how the promotion of minorities' particularistic identities at a sub-state level was supposed to contribute to the unity of the newly founded country.[33] The delineation of Central Asia was both a division and a unification: an attempt to transcend and to reach for communism via demarcation. The Soviet nation-building initiatives resulted, according to Yuri Slezkine, in "a spectacularly successful attempt at a state-sponsored conflation of language, 'culture,' territory and quota-fed bureaucracy."[34] However, the policies that enthusiastically affirmed diversity were implemented against the general background of "sameness" so that the universal appeal of communism could never be forgotten. Thus, the Bolsheviks "never stopped celebrating separateness along with communalism."[35] The given internal "diversity" was one of the quintessential features of the Culture One and a Half paradigm.

During and after the establishment of physical borders, the state embarked on cultural construction (*kul'turnoe stroitel'stvo*). It acted as a curator of discrete vernacular languages and their cultural canons, thus involuntarily emphasizing the constructed character of national identity. This curatorial work – accelerated by the First Congress of Soviet Writers, where the actual discussion of the dictum of socialist realism was overshadowed by the celebration of "minor" national literatures and their oral traditions – was of crucial importance. The task of defining and essentializing the idea of the nation and placing it on a pre-existing cultural map was necessary before one could use it as a solid building block for the universal proletarian cultural edifice. Cultural specificity and locality played an essential role in addressing the universal ideals of the communist project.

But it was not just cultural construction that was taking place. The first five-year plan and the proposed centralized economy, with their emphasis on industrialization and collectivization, became the key concepts and mechanisms driving the new paradigm of the country: construction on a mass scale. This paradigm played a crucial role in the creation of "socialism [and culture] in one country" in the sense that it filled a void, superseded backwardness, and incited enthusiasm. The creative legion was given its own tool to assist its constituents in the process of construction: the dictum of socialist realism, which profoundly influenced late modernist projects. Almost all canonical definitions of socialist realism contain a reference to the trope of socialist construction. Zhdanov's words serve as an important example: "Our Soviet writer derives the material for his works of art, his subject-matter, images, artistic language and speech, from the life and experience of the men and women of Dnieprostroy, of Magnitostroy ... Our Soviet literature is strong by virtue of the fact that it is serving a new cause – the cause of socialist construction."[36] In this sense, the artistic word finds its inspiration point and teleological end in the experiences of the builders of real life, and this approach, as Groys highlights, resonated with the avant-garde's radical tendency to erase the difference between real life and its artistic representation.

Maxim Gorky, in turn, asserted that being a Soviet writer was a huge responsibility, since it "places us not only in the position, traditional to realist literature, of 'judges of the world and men,' 'critics of life,' but gives us the right to participate directly in the construction of a new life, in the process of 'changing the world.'"[37] The writer's position was not that of an outside critic and contemplator; it was the position of a co-participant who leaves an imprint on the reality of life. The cultural sphere was actively engaged in the transformation of the physical landscape of the country. While Western European modernists such as Joyce and Yeats "invented nostalgic frameworks of belonging ... built out of the native, local knowledge they had left behind,"[38] their Soviet counterparts were not susceptible to any such sentimental yearning. They were concerned, first and foremost, with assisting in the construction of a new society. Hence, they helped create literary canons of the "formerly repressed" Soviet minorities, participated in the creation of artistic unions in the republics, translated their classical and contemporary literary works, and described and glorified numerous construction projects. Thus, in contrast to European modernism's fixation on the "primitivism" or "foreignness" of the other (for example, Picasso's use of African art forms or Ezra Pound's fascination with Japanese literary forms),[39] the Soviet blend of socialist orientalism was preoccupied with the other's ability to "transform." The Soviet orientalist project was not a mere "strategy of representational containment,"[40] to use Jameson's formulation; rather, it was a stratagem of radical transformation with a promise of the total erasure of difference in the future.

The process of the transformation, reimagination, and reinvention of the East was not purely discursive. Instead, the construction of nations, languages, and the new self were accompanied, and in many ways defined, by the physical transformation of the landscape. The importance of infrastructure, which established essential economic and cultural networks between various dispersed nationalities, was indisputable to the Bolsheviks. They were tireless builders of thousand-mile canals, extensive railway networks, and roads. Electrification, industrialization, and land cultivation were key refrains in the political discourse of the time, and Soviet authorities were renowned for projects that were epic in scale. The material base and the ideological superstructure were both radically transformed.

An Engineer of the Human Soul

The case of Andrei Platonov, a key modernist figure who experimented with language in the 1920s and who, by the mid-1930s, found himself in a position to contribute to socialist construction, reflects the trend discussed in the preceding section. The "a-national" proletarian character of his 1920s texts (the eternal Platonovian *prochii* – a miscellaneous other of *Chevengur* and *The Foundation Pit*) evolved into an ethnically "particular other" in the course of very few years. The latter was a product of the Culture One and a Half paradigm: an ultimately marginal figure who is "normalized" by developing a socialist mentality. The given "reformed" man or woman would substantially contribute towards the subsequent formation of the Soviet subjectivity. Moreover, Platonov's hands-on involvement with industrial and technical devices made him a perfect illustration of the Stalinist vision of writers as "engineers of the human soul." The writer oscillated between practical projects (land reclamation and engineering) and lofty artistic endeavours throughout his life. In the 1930s, his soul-engineering talents found full application in the Turkmen Soviet Socialist Republic. His novella *Dzhan* (which means "soul" in Turkmen) and short story "Takyr" depict a nation-building effort on the fringe of the Soviet Union.

The writer's discursive turn towards the East – yet within the Soviet Union's internal borders, as if mirroring the Comintern's ideological turn – was preceded by an acknowledgement of the fascist threat from without. In 1933, Platonov corresponded with Gorky regarding the possibility of publishing his short story "Garbage Wind" (*Musornyi veter*) in the almanac *The Year Seventeen* (*God semnadtsatyi*, 1934). The short story powerfully explores the threat of fascism and was written just before the writer launched his Central Asian projects. Permeated with grotesque elements, it depicts the physical metamorphosis and ultimate disintegration of the German scientist Albert Lichtenberg, who is married to Zel'da – a woman from "Russian Asia" – during the early years of Hitler's reign. Arrested, tortured, and castrated by the Nazis, the protagonist literally sacrifices his body to the impoverished mother of two dead children by preparing a meal made of his own flesh. The story's finale is staggering: Lichtenberg bleeds to death, the woman dies by the cradle before the "meal" is ready, while the cooked meat is eaten by a policeman who comes to the house in search of Lichtenberg. The repressive state literally consumes its dissident citizen.

Responding to Platonov's request, Gorky praised the force of the story's artistic expression, but famously deemed the plot utterly unrealistic and bordering on macabre delirium.[41] In further exchanges between the two, Platonov begged the chief literary authority of the country to be allowed to join one of the numerous creative brigades that were being sent by the Writers' Union to major construction sites and remote parts of the country; the outcome was Platonov's first trip to Turkmenistan in 1934. The trip was organized in conjunction with the collectively authored volume *Radiant Days: Almanac on the 10th Anniversary of Turkmenistan 1924–1934* (*Aiding-Giunler: Al'manakh k desiatiletiiu Turkmenistana, 1924–1934*) – a compilation of literary works celebrating ten years of Soviet nation-building initiatives in the region. As his involvement with the project reveals, Platonov's interest in corporeal imagery had not receded, but was blended with the tropes of nation-building: the individual body had become part of a unified national entity.

Radiant Days is an evocative nation-building artefact, which attempts to draw the geographical and cultural borders of a newly "imagined" Turkmen nation. It accomplishes its mission by fusing reality and fiction, while socialist realism, which actively reflects the process of the construction of socialist reality, provides a supervening framework. As Vsevolod Ivanov and Abolqasem Lahouti explained in the foreword, the almanac was designed according to a plan of a "comprehensive embrace of the life and socialist construction of the republic."[42] Various fictional entries – poems and stories by Turkmen and Russian writers – were framed by documentary material (political, historical, and geological). Together, they represented a total vision of the young Soviet republic. The "real" accounts, written by the leading specialists in their respective fields (such as the academician Ivan Gubkin and the geographer Moisei Nemchenko), saw Turkmenistan through the lens of its "industrial potential" and natural resources. They validate the lofty and edifying fictional narratives by imposing on these the materiality of the real. These reports continued the universal colonial tradition of treating a peripheral space as a "mere" raw material appendage (*syr'evoi pridatok*), though in the Soviet empire's case, the appendage was attached to the cause of the universal proletarian revolution. Various folkloric traditions of the Soviet republics, and those of Central Asia in particular, also served as a source of raw material for the tradition of socialist realism.

Thus, the Soviet Orient constituted a space with an abundance of raw materials and ancient traditions that gained meaning and value only through a process of assimilation and mediation initiated by the ideological centre. The natural and cultural resources of the East actively fuelled the modernizing and transformative urge of Soviet orientalism. However, this abundant "fullness" was dialectically balanced by a distinct sense of emptiness. Soviet Central Asia was a perfect "tabula rasa" on which political and artistic totalitarianism could inscribe its theoretical dogmas. Turkmenistan in particular, with over 80 per cent of its land covered by the Kara-Kum Desert, was in the most literal sense an empty space, passively waiting to be inscribed onto and into the Soviet universalizing discourse.

Platonov's application to take part in the Turkmen trip, a text expected to follow bureaucratic standards and reflect socialist realist conventions, blatantly reveals his transformative aspirations. He writes: "I would like to write a novella about the best people of Turkmenistan, those who diffuse their lives for the transformation of their desert motherland, where wretched bare feet walked on the destitute remains of their fathers, into the communist society, equipped with first-rate machines."[43] In this "bureaucratic" note, Platonov immediately enters the realm of the imagined Orient and transforms it by linguistic means. His prose seeps through the pores of normalized state language. "Diffuse their lives," "wretched bare feet," "the destitute remains of their fathers" are all examples of the super-normative broadening of the semantic capacity of Soviet bureaucratic and literary languages. These phrases do not adhere to the conventions of official language that would be appropriate for such a document. Platonov begins writing his literary text about Turkmenistan in the very application; fiction already infiltrates the restrictive reality of bureaucracy. More importantly, his dense prose reflects the main ambition of yet-to-be-written texts: archaic plain nature will be overcome by cutting-edge communist machines.

However, this binary opposition – archaic nature versus industrialized culture – fails to hold because of the inner tension present in Platonov's aesthetic project. On the one hand, some elements of his Turkmen corpus seem to subscribe to conventional orientalist clichés about backward, empty nations ripe for modernization, as the writer – in part – looks at Turkmenistan from the point of view of the Soviet "imperial" gaze. But Platonov accomplishes something altogether more original, hybrid, and idiosyncratic when he enters the fluid field of the Soviet Orient. The unequivocal political cause is replaced by an ambiguous artistic gesture.

Platonov's contributions to the project of nation-building in Turkmenistan were infused with both "fullness" and "emptiness" as refrains of socialist construction, though he never managed to achieve the ideological certitude of his peers. During his first trip to the Central Asian republic, he was supposed to officially participate in two collectives – the Academy of Sciences' Commission for Production Development (led by the geologist Mikhail Baiarunas) and the Soviet writers' brigade (led by the poet Grigorii Sannikov). The writer visited various scientific laboratories located in the Caspian Sea region and the Kara-Kum Desert and obtained the much-needed "raw material" for both his engineering and literary endeavours. As a result, Platonov-the-engineer's obsession with all kinds of tangible aspects of socialist construction in Turkmenistan

(for example, the lack of fresh water and the problem of desertification) corre-
lated with Platonov-the-writer's genuine fascination with the abstract mythological narratives that shaped the "newly constructed" Turkmen nation.
Viewed through this prism, it is no coincidence that Platonov's very first
Turkmen text was a brief documentary exposé in the local newspaper *The
Turkmen Spark* (*Turkmenskaia iskra*), published a few days after his departure.
It describes a certain comrade Dzhafarbaev, an invented inventor,[44] who was
assisted by a certain Moscow engineer in creating two technical inventions: a
high-speed three-rail track and a device for deep drilling.[45] Interestingly, two
fictional characters of Platonov's 1930s prose are concerned with precisely
these industrial spheres: the engineer Sartorius of *Happy Moscow* (*Schastlivaia
Moskva*, 1933–36) works extensively on problems of high-speed motion,[46] and
the engineer Vermo of *The Juvenile Sea* (*Iuvenil'noe more*, 1932) creates a device
for deep drilling that works by means of "electric flame."[47] These inventions
appear to be colonial in essence, for they transform "uncultivated" space by
extracting natural resources and shipping them to the metropolitan centre.
However, the inventions were never realized; in spite of their urge to transform
the realm of the real, they remained in the contemplative domain of imagination and fiction.

More generally, the real and fictional technological devices and mechanisms
that the writer designed and imagined in the 1930s present a peculiar blend of
the avant-garde notion of "life-building" and the socialist realist obsession with
construction that would bring utopian strivings to fruition. Thus, Platonov's
1930s texts reconcile the aesthetic technicality of modernism and the mantra
of socialist construction that features in socialist realism. However, they do
not perform a merely synthesizing function; by and large, Platonov's earnest
attempts to evolve into a socialist realist writer, glorifying the Soviet state's firm
strides towards the communist future, failed to achieve the semantic certitude
of truly Stalinist texts. His linguistic abnormality, though substantially subdued
after Stalin's criticism of his 1931 novella *For Future Use* (*Vprok*), did not allow
for the creation of a stable semantic field.

In "Takyr," a short story written for *Radiant Days*, Platonov builds a narrative
of overcoming spontaneity (*stikhiinost'*) and gaining socialist consciousness
(*soznatel'nost'*); the progression is depicted with national Turkmen "idiosyncra-
sies." All the metaphysical uncertainties that permeated Platonov's early works
recede into the background. They are replaced with a clear awareness of the
proletarian mission, a determined progression towards communist ideals, and
the real transformative projects of socialist construction.

Dzhumal', the main heroine of the short story, passes through every stage of
development to gain her communist mentality, evolving into an active builder
and transformer of her nation and the landscape it inhabits. The main heroine
is essentially alien to the Turkmen land. Her mother, an Iranian Kurd enslaved

by robber-warriors and forcibly relocated from Iran at age fourteen, gave birth to her in Turkmenistan. Dzhumal' is thus a descendant of the settled people of Iran and is forced to lead a nomadic way of life. One day her tribe makes a stop at an old abandoned tower in the desert that is inhabited by a mysterious Austrian man – a prisoner of the First World War. The site turns out to be contaminated by plague, which the mother eventually contracts. The tribe abandons the two women and all their belongings in fear of the deadly infection, and Dzhumal', after the death of her mother, spends a few years living with the Austrian man – until she again encounters her abusive and patriarchal stepfather and the man who had purchased her to be his wife. The men, she learns, are now fighting the Red Army. Dzhumal' decides to steal their horses and rifles after they fall asleep and hands the ammunition over to the Bolsheviks. The young woman, who takes her mother's name as surname and becomes Tadzhieva, thus emphasizing her maternal lineage, subsequently graduates from an agricultural institute. She is then sent back to the desert as part of a plant-cultivating expedition with the task of establishing in the heart of the Kara-Kum Desert an experimental laboratory-nursery for adapting plants to *takyr* soil. She finds the tower with the skeleton of the Austrian man and her mother's grave nearby and establishes the nursery. The *takyr*, poisoned by plague, becomes a site for experimental plant breeding. The abandoned sanctuary where her mother had perished becomes the site of future life.

The theme of socialist transformation is developed even further in the central text of Platonov's Turkmen corpus – the novella *Dzhan*, which was conceived during the writer's second visit to the republic in 1935. But, to counterbalance the abstract collective body of Stalinism, he presents the ailing human body of a nomad. *Dzhan*, if reduced to its narrative core, is a story about the process of building communism in one isolated desert. The novella's protagonist, Nazar Chagataev, is the child of an extramarital affair between Giul'chatai, a married Turkmen woman, and Ivan, a Russian soldier in the Khiva expeditionary force. The wretched mother, unable to provide for her son, is obliged to send him away, but the boy is saved by a shepherd and then sent to a Soviet orphanage. After receiving an education in Moscow, the adult Chagataev is sent back to the Turkmen desert to reclaim his native nation for the purposes of building communism. Before his departure from the capital, he marries a divorced and already pregnant Russian woman named Vera and adopts her adolescent daughter, Kseniia. The protagonist's return to his mother and motherland is marked by scenes of extreme physical devastation and suffering. After wandering in the open space of the desert, the people of the Dzhan nation finally settle down – with the aid of Chagataev, who merges with their collective body and shares in their misery and anguish.

This nation of outcasts, the vagabonds of Dzhan, inhabits an uninhabitable desert-like space, located in contemporary Turkmenistan. These people are not "mere" Turcophone steppe nomads of Eurasia who, according to Adeeb Khalid, "represented the outer limits of Orientalism's concerns"[48] – Platonov's subjects are outcasts from among outcast tribes. The small nation, in a rather confusing fashion, is a heterogeneous group that consists of runaway convicts, orphans, old slaves, women unfaithful to their husbands, godless people, and mockers of the world.[49] Positive complementariness – the foundation of any ethnic formation – is negated here and transformed into mutual disparity. Stalin's definition of a nation as "a historically constituted, stable community of people, formed on the basis of a common language, territory, economic life, and psychological makeup manifested in a common culture" is rendered irrelevant.[50] The people of Dzhan are "marginals" (from the Latin *margo* – border or boundary) – they dwell on the borderline of both discursive and material existence and exemplify the productive marginal essence of culture as conceived by Bakhtin and Tynianov. They are also typical Platonovian "miscellaneous others" (*prochie*), who are destined to become the surrogate for a new post-ethnic Soviet man.

There are three variations of the text's ending, and all of them problematize the straightforward incorporation of the Dzhan people into a socialist nation: the version abridged by Soviet editors in 1964, which describes the dispersal of the Dzhan people after Chagataev's failed attempt to collectivize them; the writer's original ending, which adds Chagataev's return to Moscow together with the Turkmen girl Aidym and his reunion with Kseniia, who survives her mother; and the extended third redaction, which depicts the hero setting off to bring the people together only to find out that they have reunited of their own accord – after this revelation Chagataev leaves for Moscow with Aidym. This last version can be considered a somewhat happy socialist realist ending: the people settle themselves, and the younger generation, represented by Aidym and Kseniia, continues along the road towards Soviet enlightenment. Platonov's commitment to inventing a proper ending that might satisfy the totalitarian regime reveals what is at least an attempt at being a true Soviet writer.

However, what is essential is that all three versions respect the Dzhan nation's volition and agency. The people refuse to become a homogenous corporeal entity under Chagataev's guidance. Instead, their communal body undergoes a process of dispersion in an open, non-hierarchical space. As a result, the notion of "national form" as a vessel for the socialist content undergoes a radical reconceptualization – or even an absolute discreditation. The diverse endings also reveal a tension between the peripatetic (nomadic) borderless communism and the settled "socialism in one country." Indeed, settling down the nomads of Soviet Central Asia was one of the key "socio-cultural" initiatives in the Stalinist 1930s. The process of halting the free movement of the nomadic tribes, who knew no borders, was not yet just another restrictive biopolitical procedure. The transformative passage from a "homeless" nomad into a "cultured" sedentary was considered to be equal to the transformation of a peasant into a proletarian.

It had major ideological consequences: as one of the articles in *Our Achievements* (*Nashi dostizheniia*) put it in 1931: "The cultured and semi-settled part of the East strides towards communism, bypassing the banker; the nomads are forcing their way to socialism straight from their primitive tribal communes."[51] The possibility for archaic feudal societies to reach socialism while bypassing the "painful" stage of capitalism was a discursive "coping" mechanism by means of which nomadic "backwardness" could be conceived in the Stalinist state.

Moreover, taking into consideration the region's specificity, Platonov elevates the real problem of the Soviet nation-building project to the level of mythology. The clash between nomadic and settled ways of life is reflected in the tension between Iranian Ohrmazd and Turanian Ahriman (or Ahura Mazda and Angra Mainyu), who represent the kingdoms of light and darkness respectively. According to Zurvanism, a now-extinct branch of Zoroastrianism, Ohrmazd is the highest spirit of worship, a guardian of justice and material prosperity (settled way of life), while Ahriman is a hypostasis of the "destructive spirit" that ravages cities (nomadic way of life). The two are in constant battle, but eventually Ohrmazd will prevail. Platonov, however, reverses the mythological narrative and endows Ahriman with the sympathetic qualities of a sorrowful vagrant, while Ohrmazd is depicted as an avaricious accumulator of riches. The Dzhan people are followers of Ahriman – they comprise an eternally wandering tribe, resisting Soviet sedentary policies. The nomadic tribe can be compared to the tumbleweed, a persistent motif of the novella, which appears at crucial narrative points. The plant, which "is freer and more alive than a laborer with no land,"[52] evades the Bolsheviks' grass-rooting (*korenizatsiia*) policies while clearly resonating with Bakhtin's and Tynianov's border-traversing concepts of culture. The entrance of the tribal and untamable Dzhan people into the normative framework of the Soviet state is postponed, as they continue their tumbleweed-like journey through the open and windy space of the Turkmen desert.

While the Dzhan collective body evades political incorporation, it still faces ideological or spiritual dilemmas that are manifest in the tension between the categories of "body" and "soul." In this light, it is worthwhile to consider what may be alternately termed the opposition or the amalgamation of the people as a mass body and its name, "*dzhan*" – again, "soul" in Turkmen. The collective flesh of the nation merges with the individual notion of soul, and this physical-spiritual amalgamation reverberates throughout the novella. At a certain point, Chagataev hears the sounds of "the slow pulse of his own soul"[53] inside his own body: the soul is beginning to take material form. The corporeality of the soul in Platonov's texts suggests that he sought to discern, on the basis of any spiritual abstraction, a physical experience.

The body-soul dichotomy emerges on the very first pages of the novella in Platonov's meticulous description of a mysterious diptych (figure 7.1). The painting's first panel shows a "big man" standing up on the earth and piercing

7.1 Engraving from Camille Flammarion, *L'atmosphère: Météorologie populaire*, 1888.

the sky with his head, "gazing into the strange infinity," while the second image depicts the same scene, but with the exhausted body and its dried-up head "rolling along the outer surface of a sky" in search of "a new infinity, where there really is no end and from which there is no return to the poor, flat place that is the earth."[54] Present here is the supernatural urge to pass beyond the boundaries of one's own body, an attempt at self-annihilation.

In the final text of the novella, Chagataev observes this diptych in Vera's room, but, in an alternative version of the scene, the diptych's appearance is instead inspired by a vision of the Kremlin: "Golden fog enveloped the sky; it was so thick that it resembled twilight. But that twilight was animated, as if the empty air had become overgrown with waterweeds and started flowering. The spires of the Kremlin towers were lost in the heights, in the haze of the flowering air, in the impermeable glow of the morning, and were invisible. Chagataev remembered an old painting."[55] The transformed body of the diptych, which achieves a horizontal level of infinity, thus finds its roots in the materialized and manifestly vertical ideological entity of the Kremlin spires. The destiny of the human body, which is depicted as attempting to gain a new (meta)physical home, is defined by the clash of terrestrial and celestial realms. Here, over-coming the physical boundary and reaching out to the metaphysical realm res-onates with and also provides a critique of the Soviet project's emancipatory urge, which had gradually evolved into a restrictive biopolitical paradigm.

As I have argued elsewhere, Platonov, deeply immersed in the intricacies of Soviet culture and politics, clearly understood the discursive deadlock in which human subjects could find themselves, suspended between the realms of the aesthetic and the ideological, the corporeal and the political, and the natural and the cultural.[56] His artistic and practical involvement with the Soviet Orient and its roaming inhabitants – from the meat-producing farms of Kazakhstan to the oil-extracting sites of Turkmenistan – allowed him to appreciate the "strangeness" of the region and to incorporate it into his work. The fabric of his texts of this period comprises a testimony to the complex process of the for-mation of a new Soviet subjectivity. This case represents a literally productive application of modernist border-traversing energy for constructive purposes.

As Katerina Clark suggests, the concepts of "national" and "international" or "transnational" cannot be perceived as "absolute binary opposites," especially in the context of the Soviet 1930s.[57] Indeed, rigid binarism, as a process of uncon-ditional affirmation or negation, was at the very least problematic for the way Soviet culture was defined at the time. By 1936, the internationally minded Bolsheviks, who held the universal borderless state as their ultimate ideal, had completed the radical process of national delimitation in Central Asia. Firm frontiers, which remain largely intact to this day, delineated the Soviet Orient and connected it with the ideological and epistemic centre – Moscow. This process established an immobile permanent centre with peripheral territories acknowledging its centrality, in direct contrast to Bakhtin's and Tynianov's understanding of boundary-traversing cultural dynamism. The Soviet Orient – constituted by the newly delineated Central Asian republics and the northern territories of Siberia – was on the fringe of the newly established Bolshevik state, yet, at the same time, was at the centre of that state's attention. It was here that centralizing administrative and aesthetic policies were inexplicably mixed with the emancipatory trends of the universal communist project, and it was here that tradition clashed most violently with political and cultural innovation.

The constitutive, as well as repressive, force of Stalinism, applied during the process of nation-building, permeated all aspects of Soviet life. Representatives of the radical avant-garde and modernism of the 1920s found themselves in a position where they had to revisit or even reformulate their aesthetic princi-ples. The formal demands of the doctrine of socialist realism and the political push to explore geographical liminality put pressure on the famed modernists; as a result, the formal audacities of modernism were subdued. Yet, their work found a constructive application in the East, representing a crucial aesthetic

development as Soviet society was undergoing a drastic ideological transformation. Socio-political transformation and aesthetic experimentation, then,
went hand in hand. The space where this transformation took place was of the
greatest importance. The Soviet Orient was the ultimate margin of modernity,
and this marginality proved essential for the consequent radical transfiguration
of the late-Soviet modernist project itself. Formal experiment underwent radical modification during the process of the transformation of the vast territory
of Central Asia and the establishment of its cultural core. This period was a
crucial intermediary stage – Culture One and a Half – that provided a discursive bridge between the audacious avant-garde experiment of the 1920s and the
stilted aesthetic framework of socialist realism.

Andrei Platonov's attempt to inscribe himself into the heroics of socialist construction and to serve the Stalinist state's cause was probably the most desperate
and earnest, if one compares the outcome of his work on the Soviet Orient
to other projects accomplished by other famed modernists and avant-gardists
such as Aleksandr Rodchenko, Dziga Vertov, or Viktor Shklovsky. His attempt
was most striking in its failure: the never-published texts, in spite of their general socialist orientation, disrupted socialist propriety by means of linguistic
abnormality, radical corporeal imagery, and unconventional character typol-
ogy. Platonov's Orient failed to be ideologically and aesthetically contained;
though it was forcibly delimited and comprehensively controlled, it aspired
towards international and even metaphysical transcendence. In this "failure,"
the writer appeared to share Bakhtin's and Tynianov's conceptualization of cultural process as a productive tension between centre and periphery, between
centripetal and centrifugal drives. For him, culture essentially defies borders.

NOTES

1 Mikhail Bakhtin, *Sobranie sochinenii. Tom 1. Filosofskaia estetika 1920-kh godov*
   (Moscow: Iazyki slavianskoi kul'tury, 2003), 282. Translation by Caryl Emerson.
2 This stance also echoes another concept authored by Bakhtin – "outsideness"
   (*vnenakhodimost'*). The individual is never confined within his or her boundaries
   but occupies an extraterritorial position: "To be means to be for another, and
   through the other for oneself. A person has no sovereign internal territory, he is
   wholly and always on the boundary; looking inside himself, he *looks into the eyes of
   another or with the eyes of another.*" Mikhail Bakhtin, "Toward a Reworking of the
   Dostoevsky Book," in *Problems of Dostoevsky's Poetics*, trans. Caryl Emerson (Minneapolis: University of Minnesota Press, 1984), 287, emphasis in the original.
3 Iurii Tynianov, *Poetika. Istoriia literatury. Kino* (Moscow: Nauka, 1977), 257, emphasis in the original. Translation is mine, as are subsequent translations unless
   otherwise indicated.

4   Joseph Stalin, "The Political Tasks of the University of the Peoples of the East," in *Works*, vol. 7, *1925* (Moscow: Foreign Languages Publishing, 1954), 140.

5   Sugata Bose and Kris Manjapra, eds., *Cosmopolitan Thought Zones: South Asia and the Global Circulation of Ideas* (London: Palgrave, 2010), 13.

6   Jane Degras, ed., *The Communist International, 1919–1943, Documents*, vol. 1, *1919–1922* (London: Frank Cass & Co., 1971), 163.

7   Ibid., 388.

8   Eugene Lyons, *Stalin, Czar of All the Russias* (Philadelphia, PA: J.B. Lippincott, 1940), 183.

9   Jane Degras, ed., *The Communist International, 1919–1943, Documents*, vol. 3, *1929–1943* (London: Oxford University Press, 1965), 429.

10 Ibid., 477.

11 Adrienne Lynn Edgar, *Tribal Nation: The Making of Soviet Turkmenistan* (Princeton, NJ: Princeton University Press, 2006), 97–8.

12 "Rech' tov. Stalina," *Pravda*, no. 335 (12 June 1935): 3.

13 Joseph Stalin, quoted in Peter A. Blitstein, "Cultural Diversity and the Interwar Conjuncture: Soviet Nationality Policy in Its Comparative Context," *Slavic Review* 65, no. 2 (Summer 2006): 290.

14 See Terry Martin, *The Affirmative Action Empire: Nations and Nationalism in the Soviet Union, 1923–1929* (Ithaca, NY: Cornell University Press, 2001), 453. Terry Martin observes: "By 1938, this Russian cultural priority had also increasingly grown primordial roots. Russian superiority was no longer confined to the era of socialism but extended back a millennium in time."

15 Vladimir Paperny, *Architecture in the Age of Stalin: Culture Two*, trans. John Hill and Roann Barris (Cambridge: Cambridge University Press, 2011).

16 Boris Groys, *The Total Art of Stalinism: Avant-garde, Aesthetic Dictatorship, and Beyond*, trans. Charles Rougle (Princeton, NJ: Princeton University Press, 1992), 36.

17 Boris Groys, "Stalinism as Aesthetic Phenomenon," in *Tekstura: Russian Essays on Visual Culture*, trans. Alla Efimova and Lev Manovich (Chicago, IL: University of Chicago Press, 1993), 120.

18 Groys, *The Total Art of Stalinism*, 44.

19 Hugh Hudson, *Blueprints and Blood: The Stalinization of Soviet Architecture, 1917–1937* (Princeton, NJ: Princeton University Press, 1994), 172.

20 Nicholas S. Timasheff, *The Great Retreat: The Growth and Decline of Communism in Russia* (New York: E.P. Dutton & Co., 1946).

21 See David L. Hoffmann, "Was There a 'Great Retreat' from Soviet Socialism? Stalinist Culture Reconsidered," *Kritika: Explorations in Russian and Eurasian History* 5, no. 4 (Fall 2004): 651–74; Matthew E. Lenoe, "In Defense of Timasheff's Great Retreat," *Kritika: Explorations in Russian and Eurasian History* 5, no. 4 (Fall 2004): 721–30; Martin, *The Affirmative Action Empire*, 414–30.

22 Timasheff, *The Great Retreat*, 355.

23 Paperny, *Culture Two*, 44.

24 However, one should highlight that the Soviet mould of orientalism challenged Western imperialist practices and was inherently anti-European.

25 See 1 Timothy 2:5: "For there is one God, and one mediator between God and men, the man Christ Jesus."

26 Vladimir Lenin, *What Is to Be Done? Burning Questions of Our Movement*, ed. V.J. Jerome, trans. Joe Fineberg and George Hanna (New York: International Publishers, 1969), 78, emphasis in the original.

27 See Jonathan Flatley's essay (chapter ten in this volume) for further discussion.

28 Joseph Stalin, "A Reply to *Social-Democrat*," in *Works*, vol. 1, *1901–1907* (Moscow: Foreign Languages Publishing, 1954), 164.

29 *History of the Communist Party of the Soviet Union (Bolsheviks)* (Moscow: Foreign Languages Publishing, 1945), 305, emphasis in the original. However, the position "from above" becomes detrimental when there is no engagement with the "below": "In a number of districts, preparatory work and patient explanation of the underlying principles of the Party's policy with regard to collectivization were being replaced by bureaucratic decreeing from above, by exaggerated, fictitious figures regarding the formation of collective farms, by an artificial inflation of the percentage of collectivization" (307).

30 Martin, *The Affirmative Action Empire*, 167. Martin provides an official table of ninety-seven "culturally backward" nationalities of the Soviet Union.

31 Joseph Stalin, "National Factors in Party and State Affairs," in *Works*, vol. 5, *1921–1923* (Moscow: Foreign Languages Publishing, 1953), 190–1, my emphasis.

32 Russia's backwardness, which is still an issue in the early 1930s, substantially recedes towards the end of the first five-year plan. According to Martin, Stalin makes an essential rhetorical turn while addressing a group of Soviet industrialists in February 1931: "Overcoming Russia's historic backwardness was not only a duty before the Soviet working class, but 'our duty before the world proletariat.' Thus, overt Russian nationalism became covert internationalism." Martin, *The Affirmative Action Empire*, 270–1.

33 Terry Martin, "Modernization or Neo-Traditionalism? Ascribed Nationality and Soviet Primordialism," in *Stalinism: New Directions*, ed. Sheila Fitzpatrick (London: Routledge, 2000), 354.

34 Yuri Slezkine, "The USSR as a Communal Apartment, or How a Socialist State Promoted Ethnic Particularism," *Slavic Review* 53, no. 2 (Summer 1994): 414.

35 Ibid., 415. Amartya Sen challenges the assumed rigid distinction between rootless cosmopolitanism and parochial nationalism by arguing that patriotism has played a "contingently constructive role" in mediating ethnic differences. Nation-states have always been capable of creating a provisional unity within difference, and the Bolsheviks' nationality policy of the 1930s is a clear illustration of this aptitude. Amartya Sen, "Is Nationalism a Boon or a Curse?" *Economic and Political Weekly* 43, no. 7 (16–22 February 2008): 39–44.

36 Andrei A. Zhdanov, "Soviet Literature – The Richest in Ideas, the Most Advanced Literature," in *Problems of Soviet Literature: Reports and Speeches at the First Soviet Writers' Congress*, ed. H.G. Scott (Westport, CT: Greenwood Press, 1979), 40.

37 Maxim Gorky, "Soviet Literature," in Scott, *Problems of Soviet Literature*, 67.

38 Elleke Boehmer and Steven Matthews, "Modernism and Colonialism" in Michael Levenson, ed., *The Cambridge Companion to Modernism* (Cambridge: Cambridge University Press, 2011), 288.

39 This approach partially resonated with practices of the early Russian avant-garde. Among other publications on the topic, see Boris Chukhovich, "Sub rosa: Ot mikroistorii k 'natsional'nomu iskusstvu' Uzbekistana," *Ab Imperio*, no. 4 (2016): 117–54; Michael Kunichika, *"Our Native Antiquity": Archaeology and Aesthetics in the Culture of Russian Modernism* (Boston: Academic Studies Press, 2015); Steven S. Lee, *The Ethnic Avant-Garde: Minority Cultures and World Revolution* (New York: Columbia University Press, 2015); Harsha Ram, "Spatializing the Sign: The Futurist Eurasianism of Roman Jakobson and Velimir Khlebnikov," in *Between Europe and Asia: The Origins, Theories, and Legacies of Russian Eurasianism*, ed. Mark Bassin, Sergey Glebov, and Marlène Laruelle (Pittsburgh, PA: University of Pittsburgh Press, 2015); Jane Ashton Sharp, *Russian Modernism Between East and West: Natal'ia Goncharova and the Moscow Avant-Garde* (Cambridge: Cambridge University Press, 2006).

40 Fredric Jameson, "Modernism and Imperialism," in *Nationalism, Colonialism, and Literature*, ed. Terry Eagleton, Fredric Jameson, and Edward W. Said (Minneapolis: University of Minnesota Press, 1990), 50.

41 Natal'ia Kornienko, "Istoriia teksta i biografiia A.P. Platonova (1926–1946)," *Zdes' i teper'*, no. 1 (1993): 221.

42 Grigorii Sannikov, ed., *Aiding-Giunler: Al'manakh k desiatiletiiu Turkmenistana, 1924–1934* (Moscow: Izdanie iubileinoi komissii TsIK–TSSR, 1934), 3.

43 Elena Rozhentseva, "Opyt dokumentirovanija turkmenskikh poezdok A.P. Platonova," in *Arkhiv A.P. Platonova. Kniga 1* (Moscow: IMLI, 2009), 400.

44 I would like to thank Eric Naiman for coining this phrase.

45 A.P., "Dva interesnykh proekta. Izobreteniia t. Dzhafarbaeva," *Turkmenskaia iskra* (11 May 1934): 3.

46 Andrei Platonov, *Schastlivaia Moskva*, in his *Sobranie*, vol. 4, *Schastlivaia Moskva. Ocherki i rasskazy 1930-kh godov* (Moscow: Vremia, 2010), 72.

47 Andrei Platonov, *Iuvenil'noe more*, in his *Sobranie*, vol. 3, *Efirnyi trakt. Povesti 1920-kh – nachala 1930-kh godov* (Moscow: Vremia, 2009), 392.

48 Adeeb Khalid, "Russian History and the Debate over Orientalism," *Kritika: Explorations in Russian and Eurasian History* 1, no. 4 (Fall 2000): 694.

49 Andrei Platonov, *Dzhan*, in his *Sobranie*, vol. 4, *Shchastlivaia Moskva. Ocherki i rasskazy 1930-kh godov* (Moscow: Vremia, 2010), 131.

50 Joseph Stalin, "Marxism and the National Question," in *Works*, vol. 2, *1907–1913* (Moscow: Foreign Languages Publishing, 1953), 307.

51 Adalis, "Osedaiut kochevniki," *Nashi dostizheniia*, no. 9 (1931): 50.
52 Andrei Platonov, *Soul and Other Stories*, trans. Robert Chandler et al. (New York: NYRB Classic, 2007), 105.
53 Ibid., 57.
54 Ibid., 9.
55 IMLI (Institut mirovoi literatury), f. 629, op. 1, d. 53, l. 217.
56 Nariman Skakov, "Soul Incorporated," *Slavic Review* 73, no. 4 (2014): 800.
57 Katerina Clark, *Moscow, the Fourth Rome: Stalinism, Cosmopolitanism, and the Evolution of Soviet Culture, 1931–1941* (Cambridge, MA: Harvard University Press, 2011), 9.

Chapter Eight

Street Theatre and Subject Formation in Wartime China: Origins of a New Public Art

XIAOBING TANG

The Chinese University of Hong Kong

Street theatre (*jietou ju*),[1] which comprised dramatic skits that took place in public venues and sought to rally general support for the war effort, was one of the many new art forms and practices that flourished in the early stage of the War of Resistance against Japan (1937–45). A more inclusive term for such performances was "mobile theatre" (*yidong yanju*), the idea of which was to bring dramatized presentations on current events close to the public by staging them on a street corner or in a marketplace, teahouse, village temple, or schoolyard. When the war broke out, street theatre was enthusiastically embraced as an effective means for educating and mobilizing the nation. Its passionate practitioners, most of them trained in modern Western-style drama (known as "spoken drama" in contradistinction to traditional operas) and based in urban centres, took their creations to villages and small towns across the country, bringing a new theatrical experience to, as well as rousing patriotic sentiments among, rural and culturally distant communities. In the process, the most successful street theatre opened up an interactive space in which a national public could be called forth and a collective identity openly pledged. Theatre itself was profoundly transformed as well and contributed to an emerging political culture (figure 8.1).

The significance of street theatre in the history of modern Chinese drama and, more broadly, modern Chinese culture has long been appreciated by scholars and historians. In 1947, Hong Shen (1894–1955), a leading dramatist, undertook to assess the developments in dramatic arts over the past decade and devoted much space to discussing mobile theatre. Decades later, in a general study of "popular culture forms" developed during the Sino-Japanese War, historian Chang-tai Hung observed that street theatre, by removing the boundary between art and life, or between stage and audience, "redefined the meaning of Chinese spoken drama in a time of national crisis."[2] A comprehensive history of modern Chinese drama published in 2008 describes the war period as a moment when theatrical performances moved from the indoor stage to an

8.1 This publication describes "street theatre" in four languages. *Jinri Zhongguo* (*China Today*) 1, no. 3 (September 1939): 23 (Hong Kong). Image courtesy of the Shanghai Library.

open square, and the much-desired objective of forging a "public theatre" became reality. Through theoretical debates and extensive experiments in form, the field of drama gained rich experiences and moved even closer to creating a public theatre that was also national.[3] More recently, historian Brian DeMare has demonstrated the crucial function of drama troupes in the success of the communist revolution in rural China. While he does not use the term "street theatre" or limit his scope to the war period, his study underscores the contributions of mobile theatre to a modern political culture or, indeed, to politics as theatricality.[4]

Various studies and narratives help us see different aspects of the street theatre movement. Nonetheless, some dimensions of its development and ramifications deserve further investigation. They are underexplored not so much because of a lack of attention or documentation as because of approaches that may overlook connections or complexities. In his influential study, Chang-tai

Hung insightfully observed that street plays had an enormous impact in rural areas, providing a novel experience "as important for the dramatists as for the peasants they performed for."[5] Yet, by confining street theatre to an account of modern spoken drama and to the condition ushered in by the outbreak of the war, his narrative does not fully register, in my view, the rich intellectual and institutional forces that sustained this new form of public theatre, even though he does refer to earlier efforts at popularization and education. More generally, I maintain that the movement's relation to the war and beyond calls for closer consideration, especially with regard to its impact on the formation of a new public culture.

In this chapter, I examine the multiple discourses, events, and practices – in particular the War of Resistance – that shaped and propelled the street theatre movement in China from the late 1920s to the early 1940s. My focus here is not so much on specific plays or scripts as it is on reflections and writings about street theatre as an art form, practice, and movement. In tracing this complex history, I extend my narrative to the late 1920s to acknowledge international sources for the emerging movement. By "wartime," I mean not merely the final outbreak of the war in 1937, but also the growing popular mobilization in the wake of Japanese encroachments in Manchuria in 1931. Underlying this narrative is a broader story of how concerted efforts at resisting imperialist claims and aggressions turned aspirations for a transnational political identity or alliance, such as the Comintern vision of a proletarian world revolution at this historic juncture, into energetic programs that reaffirmed and reimagined the nation as a sustaining and indispensable community. This resolute national turn answered a historical exigency but also prepared what was to be described, by the late 1930s, as a necessary nativization (or sinicization) of Marxism in the Chinese revolution.

A central goal of this study is to understand the "novel experience" brought by street theatre to its reconceptualized audiences as well as to its practitioners. A better grasp of this new experience will, I hope, help us overcome the reductive but prevalent view that sees little more than political instrumentalism in such artistic practices.[6] As an innovative form of public art, street theatre in a moment of national crisis sought to raise consciousness, disseminate fresh expressions, and inspire new imaginings. Much more effectively than print culture, it hastened the formation of a modern national imagination. At the same time, its young practitioners would often proudly compare themselves to an expedient guerrilla force in the war effort. Such a comparison underscored the self-positioning of an artistic avant-garde, distinguished by its tactical adaptability as much as by its fundamental commitment to a symbiotic, rather than antagonistic, relationship to a national community it strove to call forth. What we witness in this brief history, I argue, is a course of development with paradigmatic significance for our study of modern Chinese artistic and political culture.

Divergent Visions of a Public Theatre

In a recent study of the theatre movement in areas controlled by the governing Nationalist Party (Guomindang) in wartime China, literary scholar Fu Xuemin calls our attention to the important part played by street theatre in awakening and instilling a national consciousness in the general public. Drawing on an anthropological notion of ritual performance, she points out that street theatre functioned as a teaching session where "the bottom strata of the populace received a political baptizing,"[7] through which symbolic enactments of a national community were performed. Fu also comments on the dearth of in-depth studies of this form of political theatre and proposes that we understand the historic impact of street theatre as the result of efforts made by many constituents, from government agencies to cultural workers to the general public. According to Fu, the movement for a public theatre existed in two different branches in the early 1930s, but it was the War of Resistance that brought the movement to fruition. The first was the left-wing theatre movement pursued by cultural radicals, mostly in Shanghai; the second was the "new peasant theatre" experiment undertaken by the American-educated dramatist Xiong Foxi and his colleagues in Ding County in north China.[8]

We may trace the conceptual origin of the left-wing theatre movement in Shanghai to the heated "revolutionary literature" debate that at once energized and divided the nascent cultural left in the late 1920s, especially after the Northern Expedition ended in a bloody anti-communist purge by the right-wing Nationalist Party in 1927. The debate erupted as a generation of students, most of them trained in Japan, returned to Shanghai and called for a radical critique of existing cultural practices and institutions.[9] These spirited critics denounced the New Culture Movement of the May Fourth tradition as an outdated liberal humanist enterprise, and theorized the necessity of a revolutionary culture against the reality of a violently aborted political revolution. Between 1928 and 1930, a group of these politically committed theorists addressed the urgent need to develop a proletarian theatre. They argued that theatre was by far the most effective art (weapon, in fact) for mobilizing and organizing the proletariat and that, as the most comprehensive and socially engaged form of art, it was also the one best suited for a new collective life. To create a proletarian theatre, they proposed at once a resolute rooting out of old theatre and a jettisoning of modern bourgeois theatre.

One main source for this vision was the people's theatre movement in the Soviet Union. In elaborating on the meaning of the new theatre movement, for instance, Shen Qiyu (1903–70) referred to a 1920 manifesto issued by the Theatrical Department of the People's Commissariat of Enlightenment. He also reproduced a statement by the French dramatist Romain Rolland on the need for public holidays and spectacles. For the group of Chinese critics, the Soviet experience was an inspiration, as it illustrated how a progressive and universally resonant culture had been built in what they admired as a politically advanced nation. They called attention to agitprop performances and mobile theatre. Shen wrote especially to introduce the "transformed mélodrame [*sic*]" of agitprop skits, which would often culminate in viewers singing revolutionary songs along with the actors.[10]

For Ye Yichen (Shen Xiling, 1904–40), who studied stage design in Japan, the first step towards a proletarian theatre was to develop a "mobile theatre in the street." His discussion of the new theatre movement was particularly productive and prophetic, as he touched on several issues that were to confront subsequent efforts at creating a public theatre. On the question of how to make theatre a meaningful part of people's lives, Ye observed that it had to begin with changing the mode of theatrical production. A proletarian mode of theatrical production would require that everyone contributing to the process acquire a "proletarian ideology." Furthermore, given that its intended audience was an "uneducated, underdeveloped, and absolute proletariat," the new theatre must adopt the form of realism in order to be effective – not a classical bourgeois realism of passive representation, but an active and passionate realism informed by a proletarian consciousness.[11] Also, recognizing that dialects would present a serious challenge in "a country without linguistic unity" such as China, Ye proposed a pragmatic two-pronged approach: standard speech for developed urban areas, local dialects for the countryside.

In late 1929, this group of young theorists decided to put into practice their proposals by forming the Art Theatre Society in Shanghai. The few plays the Art Theatre Society produced in early 1930 were mostly adaptations of works by left-leaning European and American playwrights, such as Romain Rolland and Upton Sinclair. A notable exception was a one-act play, written by poet Feng Naichao (1901–83), about textile workers in Shanghai. Within a few months of opening, however, the society was shut down by the authorities. In reviewing the efforts of the youthful group, Tian Han (1898–1968), a prominent dramatist deeply sympathetic to the emerging cultural left, would see but a "wishful proletarian theatre" in what the Art Theatre Society, as well as his own Southern Drama Society, was attempting to deliver. It was a largely foreign theatre that failed to speak to ordinary urbanites, let alone factory workers.[12]

In September 1931, the newly formed League of Left-Wing Dramatists, in which Tian Han played a leading role and Ye Yichen, Shen Qiyu, and others were members, issued a program for action. (A similar mission statement would come from the more influential League of Left-Wing Writers two months later.) The first task for the left-wing dramatists, according to the program, was to go among the urban working class and actively guide a proletarian theatre movement. The program stressed the importance of winning the support of young students and city dwellers, and of approaching peasants and raising their consciousness. Most notably, the program addressed the question of form. "Besides striving to develop proletarian realism in Chinese theatre, we should make full but critical use of currently popular forms, such as variety shows."[13] In order to attract rural audiences, performances could take the form of either new theatre or traditional folk theatre. Furthermore, while forming mobile theatres with worker associations, league members were encouraged to organize itinerant entertainers for more extensive engagement with the working class.

These policy statements indicate a significant rethinking of what would constitute a theatre of and for the industrial working class. They also reflect the extended discussion among the cultural left around 1930 of issues and challenges in creating a mass-oriented literature and art. A few months after publishing its program, the League of Left-Wing Dramatists helped factory workers in Shanghai organize the Blue Shirt Theatre Group, which would incorporate into its performances songs and games familiar to fellow workers.[14]

The brief but intense movement in left-wing theatre, largely confined to the industrial and unevenly colonized city of Shanghai, drew inspiration from a politically committed and highly experimental theatre in the contemporary Soviet Union. It subscribed to the Comintern vision of a world revolution that, in transcending national boundaries, promised to usher in more fulfilling, because more universally meaningful, class identities and alliances. An imaginative expression of such international solidarity at the time was the play *Roar, China!*, written by the Soviet playwright and futurist poet Sergei Tret'iakov (1892–1939) and first produced by the Art Theatre in Moscow under the direction of Vsevolod Meyerhold (1874–1940).[15] Chinese dramatists on the left were heartened by the global resonances of *Roar, China!*, but also took to heart the imperative that the Chinese themselves must speak up as determined fighters against imperialism and capitalism. How the Chinese could speak and roar as a mobilized national collective, however, was a question that the left-wing theatre movement was to answer, not so much through repeated attempts to adapt and produce Tret'iakov's technically complex play in Chinese cities, which did culminate in the successful staging of *Roar, China!* in Shanghai in September 1933, as through the exploration of street theatre as a new public art.

In the meantime, on New Year's Day 1932, dramatist Xiong Foxi (1900–65) arrived in Ding County in Hebei (north of Shanghai) to start his experiment of bringing modern theatre to the rural population. This "new peasant theatre" experiment had the support of the National Association of Mass Education Movement, founded in 1923 by the Yale-educated Y.C. James Yen (Yan Yangchu, 1890–1990) with the goal of improving the daily life of the nation through literacy campaigns and elementary education. The experiment also reflected Xiong Foxi's own dissatisfaction with the then-trendy slogan of a "public theatre."

Five years later, in 1937, Xiong Foxi wrote and published a detailed report on his experiment. He observed that traditional theatre, ranging from various local operas to folk songs and dances, had failed to respond to the rapidly changing times of the twentieth century. However, new theatre, which to him included the crude and often burlesque "civilized play" of the 1900s, an amateur-based "student theatre" of the May Fourth era, and an elitist "art theatre" of the late 1920s, had failed to establish any meaningful connection with the general public. (In terms of audience preferences, the crowd-pleasing "civilized play" was far more popular than its more serious successors, but, to Xiong, such popularity was unfortunate and detrimental.[16]) To the key question "Who is the general public in China today?" he had a clear answer: the peasants, who constituted over 85 per cent of the Chinese population. A truly public theatre would therefore mean a theatre responsive to peasant needs and preferences. To achieve his goal of creating such a theatre, Xiong and his colleagues adopted two basic principles: no holding on to tradition and no mimicking the West.[17]

Given the context, Xiong's experiment was a revolutionary one, as he resolutely shifted the attention from better educated city dwellers to the vast rural population. Yet, unlike his contemporary left-wing dramatists, Xiong did not seek to radically alter the social system or power structure of the countryside. On the contrary, he and his colleagues took a pragmatic approach to all aspects of promoting a new theatre in a village setting. They began by performing for the villagers but ended with encouraging villagers to act and perform for themselves. Based on their experience, they found an open-air theatre to be the most conducive venue; they also came to regard the entire theatre ground as a stage open to communal participation. One way to turn spectators into participants, remarked Xiong in his 1937 report, was to make theatre a mobile event, one that audiences could follow and take part in on the street or in the village square, just as with itinerant opera troupes during fairs and festivals.[18]

It is important to note at this point that the proponents of a proletarian theatre and those of a new peasant theatre all spoke of a "public theatre" (*dazhong xiju*) in the early 1930s. The "public" in the first case was an explicitly political concept and pointed to a class alliance yet to be forged; in the second, it acknowledged a cultural and sociological condition to be ameliorated through general enlightenment. Evoked in twentieth-century China by many an art and literature movement in its claim to social relevance and cultural modernity, if also political legitimacy, the concept of the "public" (*dazhong*) has generated a cluster of cognate variations such as *minzhong, gongnong dazhong*, and eventually *qunzhong*. Sorting out what this concept implies and how it functions is a useful way to assess and compare the self-positioning of a given conception of art or literature. The street theatre movement is significant in this regard because its unfolding in one short decade illustrates how different projections of the public emerged, overlapped, and then converged.

It so happened that, in 1932, government officials in charge of cultural policies also turned their attention to popular cultural forms as a means of disseminating the Nationalist Party agenda of social reconstruction and modernization. Guidelines for a "popular literature and art campaign" were widely distributed to local Party offices, requesting that greater efforts be made to improve cultural life in rural areas. "Popular literature and art" (*tongsu wenyi*) in this context meant readily accessible and familiar forms, grouped into two categories: literary (novels, spoken drama, song lyrics, and the like) and pictorial (painting and photography).[19] One objective of the campaign was to counteract the cultural left and the communist movement, but its broader agenda was to cultivate a national consciousness and morality among the populace. In their interest in using popular culture to advocate their respective political ideologies, as literary scholar Ni Wei observes in an informative study, the nationalists and the communists had much in common. They shared the same enlightenment desire to reform and update indigenous cultural practices that they regarded as backward, even medieval.[20]

Yet, the Nationalist Party–sponsored campaign was less than successful in generating results. One reason for its ineffectiveness was that the forms it promoted were still too literary or too highbrow for the rural population. Traditional theatre, for instance, was widely disparaged and not regarded as salvageable until two years after the campaign had been launched.[21] The campaign was ultimately a top-down initiative that had little interest in turning villagers into active participants or creators of a new culture. Its organizers did not see the need to interact with audiences in the same way as Xiong Foxi and his colleagues did with their peasants. Nor was the campaign motivated by a desire to recognize and speak for an emerging social group, as was theorized by the advocates of a political theatre. For promoters of a "popular literature and art," the goal was to disseminate modern values through familiar forms or to package new wine into old bottles, as the process came to be known.

Each of these programs unfolding around the same time harboured a distinct understanding of the nation in its pursuit. Each entailed a separate political vision as well and led to various experimentations. The outbreak of the Sino-Japanese War in 1937 brought an extraordinary moment of unity among these different camps. The widespread appeal of street theatre in the early years of the war had been prepared, in both theory and practice, by the spirited cultural left in particular. As Tian Han saw it, the proletarian theatre movement was revitalized, even justified, as a truly public theatre movement amid growing agitation for resistance after the Manchurian Incident of 1931, in which Japan seized control of northeast China (1932).

Moving from Stage to Street

In the few short years before the final outbreak of the war, the cultural left undertook to develop a public theatre for the cause of resistance, often in alliance with an increasingly vocal student movement in major cities that demanded a more assertive government policy against an expansionist Japan. However, as the Nanjing government took measures to suppress agitation by the left and to promote its idea of a nationalist literature and art, open discussions of a public theatre were increasingly curtailed.[22] Modern spoken drama, nonetheless, flourished in cities such as Shanghai and Nanjing, in part because it was perceived as embodying a modern and cosmopolitan culture.

As large-scale productions of spoken drama grew technically more sophisticated and attracted attention, street theatre with a resistance theme, largely a preoccupation of left-wing dramatists, persisted and reached beyond an urban audience. A good example of this latter development is the street play *Put Down Your Whip*. In 1928, Tian Han wrote a one-act play, *Miss Mei (Meiniang)*, for his Southern Drama Society, drawing on an episode from Goethe's *Wilhelm Meister's Apprenticeship*.[23] The short play climaxes when a compassionate young man stands up to protect a girl named Mei (Mignon) from her abusive father. Three years later, the aspiring playwright Chen Liting (1910–2013) rewrote Tian Han's play and made it about the suffering of flood victims in the contemporary period. He also gave the new play a more provocative title: *Put Down Your Whip*.

In 1936, Cui Wei (1912–79), a drama student who in 1932 had joined a group to take new-style theatre to rural villages, updated the script of *Put Down Your Whip* again, turning it into a street play about resisting Japanese aggression. He also became best known for playing the role of the father, who, as a refugee from occupied Manchuria, is reduced to collecting alms while his daughter sings as a street performer. The young man who stops the father from venting his frustration on the daughter is now a young worker who tells everyone present that they should unite and turn their weapons against the invaders.[24] The transformation of the play, which Tian Han described as a continual process of making the plot speak to the Chinese people,[25] encapsulates the evolution of the left-wing theatre movement, especially in terms of its changing thematic concerns – from humanist compassion to social criticism to national resistance.

Central to the continuing appeal of *Put Down Your Whip* are the different moments of recognition that it dramatizes. In the 1936 version, when the girl tells the intervening young man that the ill-tempered old man is in fact her loving father, the audience, along with the young man, learns that she and her father have lost their family and home in occupied Manchuria. The knowledge of them being a loving family is followed by the realization that their grievous fate is tied with their being Chinese, or members of the nation as an extended family. It is this assumption of an injured but shared national identity that the play works towards and that would bring an audience in the 1930s together as an awakened collective. Watching the play on the street or in a village square, therefore, was never meant to be a solitary or entertaining experience. On the contrary, the audience was to become part of the action and, in joining the impassioned singing or chanting at the end, to publicly perform its national allegiance.

This audience involvement is apparently what happened in the spring of 1937 when Cui Wei and his travelling troupe took the play to north China, where the Japanese army, already in control of Manchuria in the northeast, had asserted its presence. On 4 April, the group performed for hundreds of college students west of the city of Beiping (as Beijing was then known). The event, organized by a multi-college student union, took place under close police supervision. By the time the performance began in a square in mid-afternoon, students had gathered in a circle, watched several skits, and done much singing. To forestall likely police intervention, organizers did not announce the play as part of the program and led the police to think the actors, when they made their entrance, were local entertainers trying to earn a living. For an eyewitness to the scene, the most powerful moment was when everyone watching the play joined the action and shouted in unison, "Put down your whip!"[26] Even the police chief could not help being moved.[27] When the play came to an end, students burst out singing. This time it was "March of the Volunteers," the bestirring theme song of the popular 1935 film *A Poem of the Great Wall*.[28]

Thanks to events like this, *Put Down Your Whip* became the best-known street play in the country by early 1937.[29] Many mainstream journals and pictorials, such as *Eastern Miscellany* and the *Shenbao Weekly Supplement*, published photographs of troupes performing for soldiers in north China (figure 8.2). Chen Boer (1910–51), a rising film star in Shanghai and erstwhile member of the Art Theatre Society, attracted much media attention for her performance as the daughter. She embodied, according to a report in *Shenbao*, a new femininity in fulfilling her responsibility as a national citizen.[30]

In July 1937, *Illumination*, a major left-leaning cultural journal in Shanghai with Hong Shen and Shen Qiyu as its chief editors, devoted a special issue to "the mobile theatre movement," thereby putting the topic of public theatre back on the agenda for left-wing drama theorists and practitioners. Earlier, the journal had endorsed a new theatre movement spearheaded by college students in Beiping. Student performances of the street play *Fight Our Way Back Home* in rural villages in 1936, according to a commentator, marked the true beginning of a "national defence theatre."[31]

Among dramatists active in Shanghai, there were widespread expectations that 1937 was going to be a remarkable "year of the theatre." Some took note of the unprecedented number of theatre companies producing technically demanding multi-act plays on diverse subjects; some anticipated the bustling field to continue transitioning from amateurism to professionalization; some were

8.2 Cover of the *Shenbao Weekly Supplement*, 7 March 1937. The caption reads: "'Let's unite and fight our way back home!' A scene from *Put Down Your Whip* performed by the Shanghai Women and Children Supporting Our Troops Group at the Hundred-Spirit Temple." Image courtesy of the University of Michigan Library.

heartened by the growing popularity of spoken drama, with the Carlton Theatre in downtown Shanghai becoming a regular venue. There was also talk about organizing a first-ever national theatre festival.

This general excitement was captured in *The Age of Theatre*, a journal launched in May 1937 and intended as a forum for theatre practitioners of all political persuasions. First among the pressing issues the editorial board wished to address, against the "increasingly dangerous storm gathering over the Pacific," was how to create a national resistance theatre and to search for new forms for it.[32] For several contributors to the inaugural issue, the imminent danger of Japanese aggression called for further action in taking theatre to the public. One specific form of public theatre should be street plays, because, as one commentator put it, when (not if!) the "war of self-defence" breaks out, "the plays that the general public needs are not necessarily what is staged in a palatial theatre, but in every desolate square and every dark trench."[33]

In light of these discussions, the July 1937 issue of *Illumination* was organized less for presenting further justifications than for addressing concrete challenges to the practice of street theatre. Contributors found it lamentable that spoken drama could hardly compete with itinerant folk performers in attracting peasant viewers. (Earlier in May, the journal had featured a report on the theatre scene in the Communist Party–controlled Yan'an, giving special attention to "living newspaper" performances. The reporter explained that the staging of a "living newspaper" had first developed in the Soviet Union but seemed to be an ideal form for the peasant theatre that Xiong Foxi had been promoting in China.³⁴)

At the centre of the special issue was a round-table discussion in which Cui Wei and others shared their experiences of performing for peasants, soldiers, factory workers, and students. Discussants emphasized the importance of developing scripts in tune with different audience expectations and local settings. They discussed how accepted gestures in traditional opera could be incorporated to indicate movements and spatial configurations in a street performance. Such techniques, remarked Cui Wei, would help relocate theatre to an open space and break down the presumed fourth wall in modern drama. Other issues brought up in the discussion included the difficulty of speaking different dialects in order to be intelligible to regional audiences and the need to respect local customs. (A recent performance of *Put Down Your Whip* outside Shanghai had to be interpreted for villagers so they could understand the northern accent–based "national tongue" spoken by the actors.³⁵) Finally, as a practical guide, the discussants offered an organizational chart that would enable a travelling troupe to operate efficiently.

Concrete suggestions aside, the special issue underscored the need to take the mobile theatre movement to the countryside, raising several points that would have far-reaching implications. First, there was a conscious shift towards regarding street performances as an effective means to inform the public and to boost national unity and willpower. This shift was a notable reorientation, as most of those involved in street theatre had been associated with the cultural left. It reflected the growing consensus for a national defence theatre and, more generally, the idea of forming a popular front against fascism. An essay in the special issue even attributed the enthusiasm demonstrated by young organizers of village-bound theatre troupes to Chiang Kai-shek's teaching that the best way to defend the nation was to offer one's service in the countryside.³⁶

A second point was the need to continue searching for a theatrical language that rural viewers could understand and appreciate. A rural village was obviously far less adequately equipped to support modern theatre than a city, but it had "the material conditions needed for rural theatre." A "rural theatre worker" therefore should know what forms the local audience would be receptive to, how to produce a "rural script," which methods of production to adopt, and also how to overcome the "toxic elements" of old theatre.[37] This recognition of underdeveloped and yet self-perpetuating cultural conditions in the Chinese countryside had underlain the "new peasant theatre" experiment pursued by Xiong Foxi, albeit for a different cultural and social agenda.[38]

The growing appreciation of traditional theatre as a useful resource prompted further thinking over how best to synthesize old forms and new contents. As one contributor, Liu Feizhang (1909–2006), pointed out in his article for the special *Illumination* issue, "the adoption from old theatre of certain forms and methods for staging a show, along with the infusion of new, meaningful contents, is an effective, necessary approach during the transitional period for spoken drama to go to the rural area."[39] In a separate article, Xu Qing further distinguished "old theatre" (*jiuxi*) from "native theatre" (*tuxi*) and called on rural theatre workers to integrate both with modern spoken drama for the purpose of "changing the contents of native theatre, keeping the good and discarding the bad."[40]

Finally, a third topic in the discussion that was to gain increasing relevance was the status, or subject position, of mobile theatre practitioners in the countryside. Those engaged in rural theatre, according to Xu Qing, should not form a separate and isolated group as their counterparts in urban centres had done. "Ideal rural theatre workers are not people dispatched from the city, but rather 'natives' [*tuzhu*] of the villages."[41] This expectation echoed closely Xiong Foxi's aspiration of enabling peasants to change themselves from spectators into participants and eventually into performers. It reflected the wish to see not only theatre as an integral part of an enriched communal life but also theatre practitioners as organic culture makers in a rural community. Such rooted practitioners, observed Xu Qing in 1937, were urgently needed in the rural theatre movement.[42]

The Nation as Stage and Spectacle

The special issue of *Illumination* on a mobile theatre movement was prepared on the eve of the 7 July 1937 Marco Polo Bridge Incident outside Beiping, in which Chinese and Japanese troops exchanged fire and a seemingly accidental skirmish led to the outbreak of the Second Sino-Japanese War. When news of fighting broke out, public opinion in China was resolutely supportive of the troops that put up a fight; the public also welcomed the event as a long-awaited historical turning point. Like their counterparts at scores of similar publications across the country, the editors of *Illumination* issued two manifestos in the 25 July issue of the journal and called on the entire nation to unite and participate in a revolutionary war. They pointed out that, against a much better equipped and financed enemy, "our most powerful weapon in resistance" as well as "our most reliable strategy for victory" was a well-organized people.[43]

The sudden onset of the war brought the already vociferous resistance move-ment to an even higher pitch. It also meant that mobilization efforts, until now not openly endorsed by the Nationalist government, could be coordinated more systematically. Patriotic passion, or what the literary theorist Hu Feng (1902–86) would describe as a "primitive excitement,"[44] electrified the nation as the war suddenly threw everything into painfully sharp relief. A "comprehensive war-time mobilization of literature and art," declared the poet and playwright Guang Weiran (1903–2002), was in order. Guang saw the national War of Resistance as a time when "realistic, robust, and combative" works of art were needed. The war demanded expedient and uplifting reportage, just as it called for catchy and heartening songs in the battlefield. Of the greatest impact and reach, asserted Guang, was theatre, especially mobile troupes that operated like guerrilla forces.[45]

It is also true that, as the critic Zheng Boqi (1895–1979) observed later, the cultural field – in particular its left wing – had long been dedicated to the cause of resistance and was at the ready when the war finally came.[46] Within days of the Marco Polo Bridge Incident, dramatists in Shanghai formed a new or-ganization to better coordinate contributions to the war effort. On 7 August, efforts by some sixteen scriptwriters, nineteen directors, and over a hundred actors resulted in the rousing premiere of *Defend the Marco Polo Bridge*, a spo-ken drama containing three independent one-act plays. Coincidentally, soon after in Nanjing, Tian Han finished a script called *Marco Polo Bridge*, a four-act play about a student theatre troupe trying to rally Chinese soldiers and vil-lagers with speeches and songs. As Liang Luo points out, its self-referential play-about-a-play structure renders this work "a model of guerrilla drama war-fare in the style of a Brechtian *Lehrstücke*, or 'teaching play.'"[47]

By the end of August 1937, the newly formed Shanghai Dramatist Associa-tion for National Resistance had organized thirteen performance groups to be dispatched to the interior. Ten such teams eventually left Shanghai before the Japanese occupation of that city in November, taking mobile theatre as well as many key participants in the modern theatre movement onto a far broader national stage.[48]

Most of the ten Shanghai-originated theatre troupes were active in cities across the east and southeast parts of the country, and many would soon find their way to the historic tri-city of Wuhan in central China, which, writes histo-rian Stephen MacKinnon, served from January to October 1938 as "the staging ground and logistics base for two million Chinese troops defending the central Yangzi region against Japanese attacks."[49] Wuhan was where most of China's prominent artists and intellectuals converged as well. By the end of 1937, with the fall of the capital city of Nanjing, almost all the groups engaged in modern theatre across the country had arrived in Wuhan.[50]

It was in Wuhan that an All-China Theatre Association for Resistance was cre-ated to promote a united front. The organization was the first of its kind to have a truly national reach, as it included representatives from a broad range of theatrical traditions and genres from different regions, in addition to modern spoken drama. It also brought together dramatists of different political affiliations, such as Tian Han, Hong Shen, Xiong Foxi, and Zhang Daofan (1897–1968), the last a major figure overseeing the cultural policies of the Nationalist government. For the common cause of resistance, the entrenched rift between left and right was temporarily put aside, and "the most divisive field of spoken drama," as one contemporary commentator saw it, had finally formed a unified force.[51]

On 1 January 1938, the newly formed national theatre association published its manifesto in *War of Resistance Theatre*, a biweekly that Tian Han and others had started two months earlier. Convinced that theatre was the most effective instrument for mobilizing the nation, the new collective saw the war as ushering in a new condition for the development of theatre. It saw the need for dedicated formal innovations as well:

With regard to form, we have resolutely departed the grey stage in the city and moved into the sunshine, to the countryside, and onto the national battleground of fierce fighting; this change in stage, combined with the demands of audiences engaged in the War of Resistance, will necessarily bring a new life to our theatre art.[52]

This historic transition from city to countryside and battleground also meant redoubled efforts to engage in street theatre. Over its short existence of several months, *War of Resistance Theatre* devoted many pages to reporting on performances or activities by various troupes in different locations. It published scripts of one-act plays and carried discussions of how best to stage mobile theatre. In the meantime, the Nationalist government had officially endorsed many theatre troupes, thereby securing them support from local Nationalist Party branches as well as government offices. As a result, interest in and coverage of mobile theatre was no longer limited to left-leaning journals and newspapers (figure 8.3). By May 1938, even *The Central Daily*, the organ of the Nationalist Party, began promoting street plays as an indispensable component of the war efforts.[53]

Gaining ever-wider currency in general discourse, as troupes were formed and dispatched across the country, was the idea that mobile theatre would function as an expedient guerrilla force. Just as prevalent was the idea of a street play serving as a "living newspaper" explaining current events to the largely illiterate rural population. This standpoint was how actor Liu Baoluo (1907–41), for instance, approached extemporaneous script writing when he led a twenty-member team in conducting, in his words, a "guerrilla war by means of theatre" in Zhejiang Province in late 1937.[54]

The fact was that mobile theatre remained the best and only reliable means of mass communication when radio broadcast and cinema, although available

8.3   Pictorial insert in *Zhonghua huabao* (*The China Pictorial*) 67 (July 1938): 20 (Hong Kong). The lower Chinese caption reads: "Theatre workers in Guangzhou perform a resistance play *Put Down Your Whip* in street." Image courtesy of Shanghai Library.

technically, were confined to urban areas and severely constrained by the war conditions. It would be hopeless, as Chen Boer remarked, to wait for the screening of a newsreel about the current war, given the time and technology it took to make it happen.[55] Yet, the travelling theatre troupes delivered more than just news updates. As dedicated agents of a national cause, these dramatists, most of them in their early twenties, brought to rural villagers new ideas, songs, and languages, as well as new emotions, expressions, and world views. They embodied a refreshing set of modern values, while they also came into direct contact with many social strata of Chinese society, encountering complex, uneven, and perplexing realities that tested their resolve and extended their understanding of art as well as of their nation.

For instance, when Hong Shen and his fourteen-member troupe left Shanghai in August 1937, their primary objective was to facilitate communication between the front and the hinterland, while providing support to wounded soldiers. They would also perform songs and plays to inspire patriotism among the general public.[56] In early September, they reached Xuzhou (a city hundreds of kilometres northwest of Shanghai) and were invited to a nearby village. There, the spirited young actors found themselves warmly welcomed by a regiment of Chinese soldiers as well as wide-eyed schoolchildren. Amid applause, singing, and speeches, they performed on a makeshift stage flanked by machine guns. The final play was an updated version of *Put Down Your Whip*, adapted to the new locale.[57] Many years later, one of the team members recalled fondly how they would, in subsequent stops, recruit local residents as extras for the play *Defend the Marco Polo Bridge* and how the composer Xian Xinghai (1905–45) would go in front of the curtains between plays and teach the audience new songs.[58]

Yet, when the team went farther northwest and arrived in Luoyang in Henan Province, they found a sleepy town hardly touched by the ongoing war or recent history. At their next stop, they became even more disappointed because their local hosts turned out to be deceitful and corrupt, treating the theatre troupe as upscale entertainment for their relatives. This unpleasant experience reminded the group from Shanghai that, "besides resisting an external enemy, there are many more struggles we cannot give up."[59] An even more thought-provoking report came from the team that was active mostly in rural Anhui from September 1937 to early 1938. In reviewing the group's experience over five months, Cheng Mo was forthright about issues that needed attention. One central problem, in his view, was that the team had set out with inadequate theories and expectations:

> As soon as we reached the hinterland and began to work under altered circumstances, those theoretical principles ran into new realities. We began to understand the complexity of the rural situation deep inside China, and the differences in living conditions, customs, and mores from one place to another ... Such discoveries made us realize that we need to adapt theatre creatively to different environments, and employ different methods accordingly.[60]

The reason for the inadequacy of those earlier theories, Cheng suggested, was because they were based either on partial evidence or a lack of actual experience. In the remote countryside, even a street play could be too novel and too demanding a spectacle for local residents. The most serious challenge, however, was that theatre alone was not sufficient. A play might rally a community and stoke its patriotic pride, but to organize and educate the public there had to be local centres. Cheng considered the phase for mobile theatre to be practically over, as a new stage in the War of Resistance had already set in. The time had come to send theatre workers to every corner of the country to foster a broader wartime theatre.

The idea of theatre playing a role in organizing a national public, of theatre troupes acting as a task force in wartime mobilization, was, as we have seen, far from new. Editors of the Shanghai-based journal *Illumination* had advocated such an approach since the outbreak of the war. For editors of the Wuhan-based *War of Resistance Theatre*, one important explicit mission of theatre during the war was to organize the public into effective units of resistance. They believed the success of a public-oriented theatre should be measured by the extent of the action undertaken by its audience.[61] In short, street theatre had to go beyond theatre and theatricality in order to be truly meaningful.

In January 1938, Wang Pingling (1898–1964), an influential editor of *The Central Daily* and a board member of the All-China Theatre Association for Resistance, wrote to stress the importance of theatre workers going one step further in creating local organizations and providing practical guidance *after* staging a performance. Only then, he argued, would it be possible to sustain the impact of mobile theatre and enable the public to take action on its own. For this reason, Wang stated, it was imperative for those committed to resistance theatre to prepare themselves through a systematic self-critique and study.[62]

The expectation of theatre, or specifically mobile theatre, to deliver more than rousing feelings and to participate directly in cultural and social organization would soon receive a significant institutional boost when an emergency national congress of the Nationalist Party convened in Wuhan and adopted, on 1 April 1938, the twin agenda of "armed resistance and national reconstruction" as the basic policy of the wartime government.[63] On the same day, also in Wuhan, the Ministry of Political Affairs under the National Military Council established a Third Department to oversee public education and international communication. The new department, just like the ministry itself, was formed with cooperation between the nationalists and the communists. Guo Moruo (1892–1978), a prominent communist writer who had at one point been hunted by the Nationalist government, was appointed its head, and Tian Han, a much-respected figure in the field of theatre, was put in charge of its arts section.

In the following months, the arts section organized ten theatre troupes, along with four public education teams and four film projection teams. (The theatre troupes were largely based on the teams that had arrived from Shanghai.) In September, after a brief military training, the ten troupes left Wuhan for different combat zones.[64] On seeing the teams off, Tian Han penned a poem to express his vision for the wartime theatre movement: "With four hundred million actors/ Across a ten-thousand-mile battle front/ A grand epic drama we create/ As the entire globe beholds the spectacle" (figure 8.4).[65]

Conclusion: A Paradigmatic Course of Action

The dispatching of ten theatre troupes to the battleground in September 1938 was a high point of the campaign, coordinated by the All-China Association

8.4 Photograph showing a public performance of *Put Down Your Whip*. *Jinri Zhongguo* (*China Today*) 1, no. 3 (September 1939): 24 (Hong Kong). Image courtesy of Shanghai Library.

of Writers and Artists for Resistance (formed in March 1938), to take literature and theatre to the countryside and among the soldiers. Within weeks, however, the tri-city of Wuhan fell to the advancing Japanese army. By then, the Nationalist government had moved its wartime capital farther inland to the city of Chongqing. The relocation not only brought government agencies, personnel, and resources deep into southwest China, but also exposed many cultural figures and institutions to an interior hardly touched by the modernization drive in the coastal regions during the previous decade. As the sobering prospect of a bitter and protracted war sank in, the mobile theatre movement also gradually lost its momentum.

The passing of what a playwright would in late 1940 describe as an "excessive excitement and excessive optimism" in the early stage of the war led to critical reflections on the impact and achievements of street theatre.[66] While hardly anyone questioned the sincerity and dedication of the troupes, or the patriotic passion aroused during many of the public performances, critics as well as practitioners began to observe a formulaic approach, vacuous sloganeering, and stunted creativity. "The more cultured segment of the audience," as

Chang-tai Hung sees it, would find less satisfaction and might even feel "an implicit yet unmistakable hostility toward literature and words" in street theatre.[67]

Complicating the familiar issue of how to make theatre accessible and engaging to the public was the question of what would constitute a desirable national form for the new theatre. The question was not easy to answer, as it was predicated on how the nation itself was imagined under the conditions of war. Furthermore, as emergency turned into routine, it became increasingly clear to writers and commentators that the reality of war was far more complex and exasperating than first anticipated, and that fresh forms of engagement had to be developed. Routinization of war steadily led the unity and heroism evident at the beginning to give way to inertia and factionalism. The year 1941, according to one postwar account, marked a turning point for the mobile theatre movement because it saw a notable reduction in battlefield performances, the rise of commercial theatre in the interior, as well as more severe censorship imposed by the Nationalist government.[68] Also in that year, the nationalist-communist coalition began to unravel as hostilities broke out between troops controlled by the two political parties vying for power and control.

The turning point reached in the early 1940s did not mean an end to street performances, however, or an abandonment of the long-cherished goal of creating a public theatre. On the contrary, mobile theatrical performances as a versatile, politically charged art form would continue and thrive in the border regions administered by the communists. There, many dramatists active in Shanghai in the first half of the 1930s joined forces with communist theatre workers who had survived the Long March and developed their own troupes and repertoire.[69] Together, they would carry on a concerted search for public theatre in markedly different circumstances. Soon, they would turn street plays, along with other expressive forms such as street poetry, *yangge* dance, and collective singing, into a significant aspect of a resolutely public-oriented social life in what were called "liberated areas," especially in Yan'an. They would also help develop a set of techniques for implementing radical social programs through theatrical performances and spectacles. Revolution as public theatre was to become a powerful and well-practiced technology. The most salient example of such political theatricality would be the peasant population's acquisition of a new public role and self-consciousness through speeches and actions during the communist-led land reform from the late 1940s to the early 1950s.[70] The Cultural Revolution that persisted into the 1970s also saw continued efforts, first by the radical Red Guard movement and then by state cultural organizations, to keep alive the practice of street theatre and performances as a revolutionary heritage.

For this long and eventful historical process, through which public theatre emerged as an integral part of modern Chinese political culture, the street theatre movement at once provided a steady impetus and served as a forerunner. It spearheaded an effective way of rallying and organizing a local community. Always an artistic practice seeking public engagement and social impact, street theatre can hardly be understood or appreciated in isolation from the collective experience of war and revolution in twentieth-century China. At the same time, the street theatre movement illustrates concretely why the creation of a new art form in modern China has always had to address the need to posit and engage the public, the imperative for artists to understand and relate to their audience, and the desire for an eclectic national form at once new and familiar.

One particularly significant dimension of the street theatre movement, in hindsight, is the growing realization among its practitioners that, in order to speak to and for their rural audience, they had to adapt, organize, and educate themselves. An integral part of Hong Shen's 1948 assessment of the achievements of wartime theatre, for instance, is a rich literature on the "self-education of theatre workers."[71] Just like the peasant spectators they wished to awaken as self-conscious members of a national community, the artists themselves needed to undergo self-transformation so as to acquire and articulate, along with their audience, a new voice and subject position. A street performance could be viewed as a teaching session, a modern-day ritual, or even a conversion process, but it was ultimately a communal experience affecting and bringing together both performer and spectator. A fundamental commitment to the nation in crisis thus underlay the street theatre movement and many other artistic activities during this historical period. This commitment also determined that a genuine artistic avant-garde in modern China must aspire to transform its audience as well as its practitioners through the same dynamic creative process.

ABBREVIATIONS

CZYK:	*Chuangzao yuekan* (Creation Monthly)
GM:	*Guangming* (Illuminations)
KZXJ:	*Kangzhan xiju* (War of Resistance Theatre)
XJSD:	*Xiju shidai* (The Age of Theatre)
ZGHJ:	*Zhongguo huaju yundong wushinian shiliao ji* (Historical documents from the fifty years of the spoken drama movement in China)
ZHMGS:	*Zhonghua minguoshi dang'an ziliao huibian* (Compendium of archival materials from the history of the Republic of China)
ZSWH:	*Zhong Su wenhua: Kagnzha sanzhounian jinian tekan* (Sino–Soviet Cultures: Special commemorative issue on the third anniversary of the War of Resistance)

NOTES

1 All translations of Chinese texts and terms, unless otherwise noted, are by the author.
2 Chang-tai Hung, *War and Popular Culture: Resistance in Modern China, 1937–1945* (Berkeley: University of California Press, 1994), 57.
3 Tian Benxiang, Hu Zhiyi, et al., *Zhongguo huaju yishu tongshi* [Comprehensive History of the Art of Spoken Drama in China] (Taiyuan: Shanxi jiaoyu, 2008), 279–90.
4 Brian James DeMare, *Mao's Cultural Army: Drama Troupes in China's Rural Revolution* (Cambridge: Cambridge University Press, 2015).
5 Hung, *War and Popular Culture*, 62.
6 DeMare's approach in *Mao's Cultural Army*, for instance, reinforces this instrumentalist understanding: "The Chinese revolution is an opportune forum for investigation into the relationship between drama and politics, as propaganda teams and drama troupes staged dramas from the late 1920s to the Cultural Revolution and beyond in the hope of influencing their audiences" (14).
7 Fu Xuemin, *1937–1945: guojia yishi xingtai yu guotongqu xiju yundong* [1937–1945: State Ideology and the Theatre Movement in the Guomindang-Controlled Areas] (Beijing: Zhongguo shehui kexue, 2010), 36.
8 Ibid., 19. The 2010 study by Fu Xuemin does not address the active promotion of theatre in the communist Red Army in the Jiangxi Soviet from the late 1920s until 1934. There, drama troupes, following the Soviet example, were organized to educate and entertain a mostly military audience. This chapter will not delve into that lively but contained scene either, except to note towards the end that a historic convergence between communist theatre workers and practitioners of street theatre would occur in Yan'an and other regions in the late 1930s.
9 Xiaobing Tang, *Origins of the Chinese Avant-Garde: The Modern Woodcut Movement* (Berkeley: University of California Press, 2008), 43–72.
10 Shen Qiyu, "Yanju yundong zhi yiyi [The Meaning of the Theatre Movement]," *CZYK* 2, no. 1 (2008): 29.
11 Ye Yichen, "Yanju yundong de jiantao [Examination of the Theatre Movement]," *CZYK* 2, no. 6 (1929): 33.
12 Tian Han, "Xiju dazhong hua he dazhong hua xiju [Making Theatre Public and a Public Theatre]," *Beidou [The Big Dipper]* 2, no. 4 (1932): 83–5.
13 "Zhongguo zuoyi xijujia lianmeng zuijin xingdong gangling [The Most Recent Program for Action of the Chinese Left-Wing League of Dramatists]," in *ZSWH* 1 (Beijing: Zhongguo xiju, 1958), 305.
14 Tian Han, "Xiju dazhong hua he dazhong hua xiju," 84.
15 See Tang, *Origins of the Chinese Avant-Garde*, 213–27, for a discussion of *Roar, China!* and its ramifications in the 1920s and 1930s in China. For a more extensive study of the history of Tret'iakov's play in East Asia, see Kun-liang Chiu, "Theatre's

Performance, Circulation and Political Struggle: Focusing on the History of the Performance of *Roar China!* in East Asia," *Xiju yanjiu* [*Theatre Studies*] (January 2011): 107–50. For recent accounts of the many transformations of Tret'iakov's play, see Mark Gamsa, "Sergei Tret'iakov's *Roar, China!* between Moscow and China," *Itinerario* 36, no. 2 (2012): 91–108; and Steven S. Lee, *The Ethnic Avant-Garde: Minority Cultures and World Revolution* (New York: Columbia University Press, 2015), 83–118.

16 For a more recent scholarly reassessment of this new-fangled theatrical form, see Siyuan Liu, *Performing Hybridity in Colonial-Modern China* (New York: Palgrave Macmillan, 2013).

17 Xiong Foxi, *Xiju dazhong hua zhi shiyan* [The Experiment of Creating a Public Theatre] (Nanjing: Zhongzheng shuju, 1937), 16–18.

18 Ibid., 95–9.

19 "Tongsu wenyi yundong jihua shu [Proposal for a Popular Literature and Art Campaign]," in *ZHMGS* 5, no. 22 (Nanjing: Jiangsu guji, 1994), 321.

20 Ni Wei, *"Minzu" xiangxiang yu guojia tongzhi: 1920–1948 nian Nanjing zhengfu de wenyi zhengce ji wenxue yundong* [Imagination of the "Nation" and State Control: The Cultural Policies of the Nanjing Government in 1928–48 and Literary Movements] (Shanghai: Shanghai jiaoyu, 2003), 198–218.

21 The Nationalist government in the early 1930s continued to view traditional or old theatre with the same suspicion that prominent figures from the turn of the twentieth century through the late 1920s expressed on numerous occasions. Zhou Zuoren, for instance, argued that "Chinese old theatre has no value" and should be discarded: "Lun Zhongguo jiu xi zhi ying fei [On the Reason to Discard Chinese Old Theatre]," *Xin qingnian* [*New Youth*] 5, no. 5 (1918): 526–7.

22 Ma Zhaoyan, "Xiju dazhong hua de wenti [Issues in Making a Public Theatre]," *Juxue yuekan* [*Theatre Studies Monthly*] 3, no. 4 (1934): 1–16.

23 See Barbara Kaulbach, "Street Theater in China in the 1930s," *Asian and African Studies* 10, no. 2 (2001): 148–59; and Hung, *War and Popular Culture*, 57–61, for more information on the play and its transformations.

24 See "Fangxia ni de bianzi: dumu ju [Put Down Your Whip: One-Act Play]," *Shenghuo zhishi* [*Life Knowledge*] 2, no. 9 (1936): 520–6. "A group of dramatists" is credited as author of this version. A note at the end says that the play had been produced many times, each time leading to further revisions. Two years later, in 1938, *Zhanshi qingnian* (*Wartime Youth*) published another version, with Chen Liting credited as the author. In this version, the young intervener becomes a farmer. *Zhanshi qingnian*, no. 9 (1938): 11–18.

25 Tian Han, "Zhongguo huaju yishu fazhan de jinglu he zhanwang [The Path and Prospect of the Development of the Art of Chinese Spoken Drama]," in *ZGHJ* 1 (Beijing: Zhongguo xiju, 1958), 7.

26 Pucheng nüshi, "Dao Xiangshan qu! [To the Fragrant Hill!]," *GM* 2, no. 10 (1937): 1407–13.

27 You Jing, "Yidong yanju zuotanhui jilu [Transcript of Roundtable Discussion of Mobile Theatre]," *GM* 3, no. 3 (1937): 190.

28 For an account of the popularity of this song and its rich history, see Liang Luo, *The Avant-Garde and the Popular in Modern China: Tian Han and the Intersection of Performance and Politics* (Ann Arbor: University of Michigan Press, 2014), 145–76. *A Poem of the Great Wall* was the English title given to the historic 1935 film *Fengyun ernü* by the Denton Film Studio that produced it.

29 According to one contemporary account, the play attracted tens of thousands, if not hundreds of thousands, of viewers. Liu Feizhang, "Ruhe jiejue juben kong-huang yu kefu yanchu shang de kunnan [How to Solve the Shortage of Scripts and Overcome Difficulties in Performance]," *GM* 3, no. 3 (1937): 195–8.

30 "Chen Boer huilai la [Chen Boer Returns]," *Shenbao* [*The Shun Pao*], 8 March 1937: 21.

31 Zhang Geng, "Yijiu sanliu nian de xiju: huo shidai de huo jilu [Theatre in 1936: Living Records of a Living Time]," *GM* 2, no. 2 (1936): 871–3.

32 "Xiju shidai [The Age of Theatre]," *XJSD* 1, no. 1 (1937): 1–2.

33 Yi Lei, "Yijiu sanqi nian Zhongguo xiju yundong zhi zhanwang [The Prospect of the Theatre Movement in China in 1937]," *XJSD* 1, no. 1 (1937): 30.

34 Ren Tianma, "Fushi (Yan'an) de huaju yu 'huobao' [Spoken Drama and "Living Newspapers" in Fushi (Yan'an)]," *GM* 2, no. 12 (1937): 1514–18.

35 Jiang Julin, "Xiju zai Wusong [Theatre in Wusong]," *XJSD* 1, no. 2 (1937): 400–2. The same event is also recounted in *GM* 3, no. 3 (June 1937): 62–6.

36 Liu, "Ruhe jiejue juben konghuang."

37 Xu Qing, "Xiju dazhong hua [The Making of a Public Theatre]," *GM* 3, no. 3 (1937): 198–202.

38 Xiong's account of his experiment was promptly reviewed in *The Age of Theatre*. The reviewer warmly applauded the playwright's commitment but questioned his reformist beliefs (Yin 1937). Yin Yang, "Du *Xiju dazhong hua zhi shiyan* [Reading *The Experiment of Creating a Public Theatre*]," *XJSD* 1, no. 2 (1937): 407–14.

39 Liu, "Ruhe jiejue juben konghuang,"197.

40 Xu, "Xiju dazhong hua," 199.

41 Ibid.

42 Xu, "Xiju dazhong hua."

43 "Women de xuanyan (1) [Our Manifesto (1)]," *GM* 3, no. 4 (1937): 213–14.

44 Hu Feng, "Minzu zhanzheng yu women: Lüelun sannian lai wenyi yundong di xingshi [National War and Us: A Brief Essay on the Development of Literature and Art in the Past Three Years]," *ZSWH* (1940): 236–8.

45 Guang Weiran, "Lun zhanshi wenyi zong dongyuan [On Wartime Comprehensive Mobilization of Literature and Art],"*GM* 3, no. 4 (1937): 275–9.

46 Zheng Boqi, "Lüetan sannian lai de kangzhan wenyi [A Brief Essay on Resistance Literature and Art over the Past Three Years]," *ZSWH* 1 (1940): 193–8.

47 Luo, *The Avant-Garde and the Popular*, 123.

48 Hong Shen, *Kangzhan shinian lai Zhongguo de xiju yundong yu jiaoyu* [The Theatre Movement and Education in China over the Decade since the War of Resistance] (Shanghai: China Books, 1948), 5–6.

49 Stephen R. MacKinnon, *Wuhan, 1938: War, Refugees, and the Making of Modern China* (Berkeley: University of California Press, 2008), 11.

50 According to a contemporary report, eighteen theatre groups, or over 95 per cent of those involved in the theatre profession, gathered in Wuhan. Qiu Tao, "Zhonghua quanguo xijujie kangdi xiehui chengli jingguo [The Formation of the All-China Theatre Association for Resistance]," *KZXJ* 1, no. 4 (1938): 152–3.

51 Yang Hansheng, "Wo de zhuci [My Congratulations]," *KZXJ* 1, no. 4 (1938): 154.

52 "Zhonghua quanguo xijujie kangdi xiehui chengli xuanyan [Manifesto on the Formation of the All-China Theatre Association for Resistance]," *KZXJ* 1, no. 4 (1938): 151.

53 Wu Ling, "Zhanshi de jietouju [Wartime Street Theatre]," *The Central Daily*, 11 May 1938.

54 According to Liu Baoluo, his theatre troupe put on fifty-seven performances in fifteen locations over a forty-four day period in Zhejiang in September–October 1937, for a total of 30,150 viewers. They staged over 140 one-act plays. Liu Baoluo, "Zhankai xiju de youjizhan [Undertake a Guerrilla War through Theatre]," *KZXJ* 1, no. 1 (1937): 6–9.

55 Chen Boer, "Dui jiuwang yidong jutuan de jianyi [Suggestions to National Salvation Mobile Theatre Troupes]," *KZXJ* 1, no. 1 (1937): 9–10.

56 "Yidong yanju chufa [Mobile Theatre Performance Sets Out]," *Kangzhan sanri kan* [*War of Resistance Publication Once Every Three Days*] 2 (1937): 9.

57 Bai Lu, "Xiju de lieche: zhanshi yidong yanjudui dier dui zai Xuzhou [The Train of Theatre: The Second Team of Wartime Mobile Theatre Troupes in Xuzhou]," *Fengyu* [*Wind and Rain*] 5 (1937): 13.

58 Yan Yiyan, "Zai jiuwang yanju erdui de rizi li [During the Days of Being with the Second Team of the National Salvation Theatre Troupes]," in *ZGHJ* 3 (Beijing: Zhongguo xiju, 1985) 176–92.S

59 Zhang Jichun, "Women yao he fengjian shiSli zuo douzheng: jiuwang yanjudui dier dui tongxin [We Should Fight Feudal Forces: Letter from the Second Team of the National Salvation Theatre Troupes]," *KZXJ* 1, no. 2 (1937): 47.

60 Cheng Mo, "Liudong yanju de wuge yue jian: Shanghai jiuwang yanju diba Dui Gongzuo Baogao Zhiyi [Five Months with a Theatre Troupe: First Report of the Eighth Team of the Shanghai National Salvation Theatre Troupes]," *KZXJ* 1 nos. 6–7 (1938): 249.

61 "Chuangkan ci: kangzhan xiju de lingyi shiming [Mission Statements: The Other Mission of Theatre during the War of Resistance]," *KZXJ* 1, no. 1 (1937): 3–4.

62 Wang Pingling, "Zhanshi de yidong yanju [On Wartime Mobile Theatre]," *KZXJ* 1, no. 5 (1938): 180–1.

63 "Zhongguo Guomindang kangzhan jianguo gangling [The Program of Armed Resistance and National Reconstruction Adopted by the Chinese Nationalist Party]," *ZHMGS* 5, no. 1 (1994): 386–89.

64 Tian Han, "Kangdi yanjudui de zucheng jiqi gongzuo [The Formation of Resistance Theatre Troupes and Their Work]," *Xiju chunqiu [Theatre Annals]* 2, no. 2 (1942): 1–12.

65 Song Baozhen, *Zhongguo huaju shi* [History of Chinese Spoken Drama] (Beijing: Sanlian shudian, 2013), 211.

66 "Yijiu siyi nian wenxue quxiang de zhanwang [The Prospect of Literary Developments in 1941]," *Kangzhan wenyi* 7, no. 1 (1941): 4–6.S

67 Hung, *War and Popular Culture*, 62.

68 Tian Jin, "Kangzhan banian lai de xiju chuangzuo [Theatre Works during the Eight Years of the War of Resistance]," *Xinhua ribao [New China Daily]*, 16 January 1946. Collected in Hong Sheng, *Kangzhan shinian lai Zhongguo de xiju yundong yu jiaoyu* [The Theatre Movement and Education in China over the Decade since the War of Resistance] (Shanghai: China Books, 1948), 134–41.

69 In May 1938, Zhang Jichun, a member of the second troupe led by Hong Shen, joined an impromptu performance at a temple fair in Yan'an. Zhang Jichun, "Qingliang shan jintian bu qingliang [The Qingliang Hill Is Not Quiet Today]," in *Wuyue de Yan'an* [Yan'an in May] (Chongqing: Dushu shenghuo, 1939), 159–64. For a contemporary account of the "Red Theatre" in the communist-controlled area, see Edgar Snow, *Red Star over China* (New York: Grove Press, 1968), 119–25.

70 Xiaobing Tang, *Visual Culture in Contemporary China: Paradigms and Shifts* (Cambridge: Cambridge University Press, 2015), 61–101; DeMare, *Mao's Cultural Army*, 113–43.

71 Hung, *War and Popular Culture*, 81–124.

Chapter Nine

In the Shadow of the Inquisition:
The Spanish Civil War in Yiddish Poetry

AMELIA M. GLASER

UC San Diego

Introduction: Spain – Past, Present, and Future

W.H. Auden donated the proceeds of his 1937 Spanish Civil War poem-pamphlet "Spain 1937" to the Spanish Medical Aid Committee. The widely circulated poem synthesizes "Yesterday," "To-day," and "To-morrow" into a vision of a democratic Spain:

> Yesterday the theological feuds in the taverns
> And the miraculous cure at the fountain;
> Yesterday the Sabbath of witches; but to-day the struggle

Auden, who based his work on a brief visit to Spain at the beginning of the war, was one of many poets describing the war from afar in a multitude of languages. His poem struck a chord: two months after the first printing, the publisher released an additional 2,000 copies.[1] For Auden when he wrote this poem, as for other left-leaning European poets, the "trial of heretics" was one marker of the medieval exotic, a politically horrifying yet poetically compelling history still haunting present-day Europe. Auden employs images of a superstitious past, together with the realities of the current war in Spain, to suggest the coming of a future rational, secular enlightenment.

The imperative of offering a teleological narrative that rejects antiquated religious practices was all the more urgent for Jewish writers for whom the Spanish Inquisition and expulsion from Spain – a near-biblical episode in collective memory – echoed everywhere in the emergence of fascism. Yiddish poets around the world, particularly those aligned with the Communist Party, hastened to depict Spain as the epicentre of current and past pain. The Soviet Yiddish poet Peretz Markish wrote: "I am once again your guest; the honour makes me sad!"[2] The Mexican Yiddish poet Jacobo Glantz described the "Hebrews" of Spain's past rising from their graves to fight together "with the bricklayers against the Inquisition." The American Yiddish poet Aaron Kurtz described the descendent of Marranos fighting in the trenches with the International Brigades and replacing Hebrew prayers with the communist credo "No Pasarán." Jewish writers who identified ideologically with the Comintern-sponsored International Brigades found in the war a theme not only for their progressive rationalist worldview but also a reason to address via communist revolution a history of trauma dating back to the fifteenth century. With this poetic return to Spain came a Comintern-inspired Jewish aesthetics that merged past, present, and future. These three Party-aligned poets, Peretz Markish, Aaron Kurtz, and Jacobo Glantz, each of whom devoted an entire book to Spain during the Spanish Civil War, offer key case studies in how the war affected a Jewish poetics of internationalism.

Yiddish writers offer an ideal case study in the aesthetics of the Communist International. By the 1930s, Party-identified Yiddish writers spanned multiple continents, from the Soviet Union to the United States, Latin America, and Europe. The leftist Jewish writers who eschewed Zionism, religion, and capitalism in favour of revolutionary utopianism had cast their lots with an international project. The rise of Hitler confirmed, for many leftist Jewish writers, the importance of communism as a viable alternative to a fascist trend that threatened the lives of Jews among other ethnic groups. For Jewish communists and communist sympathizers, the fascist rebels who rose up against the Spanish Republic in 1936 confirmed the inextricability of Jewish survival and the Soviet-led challenge to fascism worldwide. The journalist Melech Epstein later wrote: "No ethnic group in Europe or the United States was so deeply touched by the Spanish civil war as was the Jewish ... [who] felt, by and large, that the struggle among the barren hills of north and central Spain was a proving ground for Hitler and Mussolini."[3] Thousands of Jewish volunteers fought with the International Brigades, totalling about one fifth of the volunteers. The Naftali Botwin Company, a unit of the International Brigades, used Yiddish as its official language.[4] Others fought on a literary front. Cary Nelson writes in his study of American poetry of the Spanish Civil War: "Just how quickly poetry took a significant place in the war remains startling even today."[5] Markish, Glantz, and Kurtz, all affiliates of the Communist Party, present the past, present, and future in a way that corresponds both to thematic historical movement and to changes in poetic form.

The triadic past-present-future structure of Auden's poem can be traced in all three of the cycles I shall examine, all of which synthesize the Inquisition and news reports about the Spanish Civil War to yield a collective, utopian future. This triadic structure bears a useful resemblance to Marx and Engels's adaptation of Fichte's thesis-antithesis-synthesis model of social change.[6] The aesthetic structure that tends to emerge in long Yiddish poems about the Spanish Civil War depends on three symbiotic modes – the lachrymose motif of

Jewish liturgical tradition, the documentary spotlighting of a Spanish other in need, and the glimpse of a rational, communist, new order as envisioned through experimental, agitprop-inspired genres, including placard poems and revolutionary prophesy.[7] Yiddish poetic cycles dedicated to Spain, by embedding themselves in a historical process, fulfil a similar function to historical novels which, according to Georg Lukács, are significant because "their authors have tried to show artistically the concrete *historical genesis* of their time." Furthermore, as with the historical novel, "only a real understanding of these [social historical and human moral] forces in all their complexity and intricacy can show their present disposition and the paths which they can take towards the revolutionary overthrow of Fascism."[8] The cycles of poems that follow this structure thus simultaneously experiment with diverse poetic forms and motifs, and strive to be historically self-conscious. The darkness-to-light arc of the past-present-future themes, moreover, gives the cycles a religious structure, even as the content of the poems remain strictly anti-clerical.

If, in hindsight, fascist Spain appears strikingly similar to the increasing totalitarianism of the Stalinist administration that supported the International Brigades, for Jews the two could not be compared, and a great many volunteers cast their lots with the Comintern-sponsored International Brigades.[9] Still, we could not do justice to the political nature of the Yiddish Spanish Civil War poetry without acknowledging the controversies surrounding Party-aligned art, even among the like-minded. Many pro-Republican memoirs of Spain, including George Orwell's 1938 *Homage to Catalonia*, cast doubt upon the virtues of the Soviet forces in Spain. Auden, who revised his "Spain" multiple times, ultimately deemed it too ideological in tone, called it "trash," and removed it from his collected works.[10] Hannah Arendt criticized Bertolt Brecht for writing in praise of the Communist Party, even "during the Spanish Civil War, when he must have known that the Russians did everything they could to the detriment of the Spanish Republic, using the misfortunes of the Spanish to get even with anti-Stalinists inside and outside the Party."[11] Marc Chagall rejected appeals to portray the Spanish Civil War on canvas and wrote disdainfully that his rival "Picasso may spit on Spain, even on Paris; but my colors come from Pokrova Street in Vitebsk. And are indeed Jewish."[12] However, though the singular influence the Soviet Union exerted on discourse around the Spanish Civil War may have been overly partisan for some, it challenged others to reconcile group affinity with internationalist politics and to find suitable forms to do so. As Harsha Ram writes in chapter one in this volume, "Soviet literature at once reified the nation and relativized its importance by inserting it into a federal structure that reconfigured relations between local, regional, and central actors."[13] Jewish communists and fellow travellers, regardless of whether they were in the Soviet Union, sought ways of integrating national concerns into an internationalist structure.

Chagall may be an exception that proves the rule: his public refusal to depict the Spanish Civil War surprised readers, including some on the Spanish front. Leftist Yiddish writers, even those outside the Soviet sphere, tended to link Spain to the rise of Nazism in Germany. The Yiddish poet Kadia Molodowsky ends her 1937 poem "To the Volunteers in Spain" (*Tsu di volontiorn in Shpanye*) with the cautious fantasy of joining the war effort.

Kh'vel nokh oykh efsher nemen a biks oyf di aksl.	I too will still maybe take a rifle on my shoulder.
Un oyb kh'bin alt shoyn dertsu, vel ikh onton a vaysn khalat un vern a shvester –[14]	And if I'm too old for it, I'll put on a white coat and become a nurse –

Civil War Spain was a space for virility, for fantasy. And it was a place that allowed leftist and left-leaning Jews to reshape the image of what it meant to be a Jew without abandoning a broader struggle.

That Yiddish poetic portrayals of Spain synthesized Jewish, Spanish, and Communist Party interests was possible due in part to changing literary policy within the Communist International. The rise of fascism in the 1930s led the Party to abandon the hard-line anti-socialist doctrine of the Third Period and seek a more inclusive policy. This decision came about alongside the rise of the Popular Front in Western Europe – an alliance that united the communists, socialists, and radical parties.[15] The policy of promoting more Popular Front writers, adopted at the 1935 Seventh World Congress of the Comintern, reflected this desire for political inclusivity.[16] This more liberal literary atmosphere encouraged Party-aligned poets to marry internationalism with national interests in their anti-fascist verse. Not only did the outbreak of the Spanish Civil War align anti-fascist ideology with the specific case of Spain, but by 1936 Jews were also aware that fascism presented as great a threat to Jewish life in Europe as to Spanish democracy. Communist Yiddish poets of the interwar years like Aaron Kurtz who had previously avoided Jewish topics began integrating themes of Jewish memory into their work. This Judaizing of communist themes, which would become essential to Soviet and Soviet-aligned poetry during the Second World War, began for all practical purposes with Spain.

Since none of the three poets I shall address here – Peretz Markish, Aaron Kurtz, and Jacobo Glantz – visited Spain, their books attest to the ideology surrounding the Spanish Civil War rather than personal experience. In all three poets' Spanish Civil War cycles, the distant past is represented through Jewish collective memory. Nonetheless, references to the Inquisition demonstrate how the Spanish Civil War was crucial to combating both anti-Semitism and anti-communism. Yiddish poets' indulgence in a lachrymose treatment of the Jewish past simultaneously served as a Jewish call to arms to fight the fascist rebels and as one example of the dangers of Christian conservatism. All of the poems' present tense is in Spain, and, as we shall see, the poets tend to adopt a documentary tone when describing current events. The Spanish soil, described from a distance in all three volumes, is exoticized and even sexualized. Therefore, if the "past" segments of these books offer a temporal exoticizing and distancing, the "present" segments, often framed by letters, news reports, photos, or other documentary genres, represent a geographical distancing. All three Spain cycles culminate in poems that present the future utopian ideals that drew many of the International Brigaders to Spain. The content of these future-oriented sections is a collectively imagined utopian future. These are often the most formally innovative poems in the volumes, for they present new populist forms inspired by agitational slogans, popular songs, and the placard poems that began emerging shortly after the Bolshevik Revolution. Taken together, these three elements of the Spain poems suggest a compatibility between Jewish tradition and communism.

The Yiddish poetry of the Spanish Civil War has been all but completely forgotten, obscured in short order by the poetry of the Second World War.[17] This loss has kept scholars from appreciating the connection between these poets' early years amidst the high modernism of the 1910s and 20s and their Second World War poetry. However blind Kurtz's, Markish's, or Glantz's adherence to communism was, outrage that a poet dare link aesthetics to politics can deter scholars from assessing the outcome. As Alan Wald has warned, "too often a preoccupation with Communist affiliations leads to the deductive fallacy of making presumptions about the artistic process according to supposed political loyalties of authors."[18] Arendt acknowledges, after all, that the Party brought Brecht "into daily contact with what his compassion had already told him was reality: the darkness and the great cold in this valley of tears."[19] In the following pages, therefore, I will set out to describe how the war in Spain allowed poets to integrate a crucial national concern for many Jews at the time – the threat of Nazism in Europe – into existing concerns of the Comintern.

Past

Peretz Markish's representations of Jewish suffering made him the Yiddish poet laureate of the Russian Revolution. Born in 1895 in the Ukrainian shtetl of Polonnoye, he completed a traditional Jewish elementary education (*heder*) and even worked for a cantor before serving in the Russian army during the First World War. A member of the triad that made up the Kiev-Grupe in revolutionary Kiev, he went on to co-edit the Warsaw-based *Literarishe Bleter*. Those who knew him in his youth often remarked on his striking good looks, his strong voice, and his shocking poetry of revolution.[20] In the years following his 1926 return from Warsaw and Berlin to the Soviet Union, he wrote increasingly

Party-aligned poetry; the Spanish cycle, referencing the most pressing international topic of the time, bolstered his credentials as a Soviet poet whose topics were of international concern. Nonetheless, he opens his long poem, "Spain," by placing the war on a continuum of historical Jewish suffering. "Mounds of ash from my past" are piled in cemeteries beside the fresh corpses. For Markish, the war is a modern Inquisition that has targeted communists as well as Jews as its heretics.

Kh'bin nokhamol dayn gast!	I'm once again your guest!
Der shtolts iz mir fartroyt!	The honour makes me sad!
Ikh hob di shvue nit farhit.	I haven't kept the oath.
Dem neyder nit getsaytikt;	The ancient ban hasn't been lifted;
af dayn besalmen fun di lesterer, baym ployt,	in your graveyards for transgressors, by the fence
tliyen nokh berglekh ash fun mayn amol, fartsaytns! [21]	still smolder ash-heaps from my past, from long ago!

Through this figurative return to Spain, Markish simultaneously upholds the memory of his ancestors and breaks with traditional religious practice.[22] Markish's reference to the desecrated oath recalls an edict, allegedly in place since the expulsion, forbidding Jews from visiting Spain.

Spain may have been a site of Jewish collective suffering, but it also spawned its own diaspora, and the legacy of Jewish suffering has been viewed, paradoxically, as a source of Jewish strength. Jewish memory writing on the European diasporic experience, as Yosef Hayim Yerushalmi showed in his seminal work *Zakhor*, can be traced to the expulsion from Spain, which engendered a large body of liturgical and even historical literature in the subsequent century. The expulsion from Spain, which, Yerushalmi reminds us, emptied Western Europe of its Jews, "altered the face of Jewry and of history itself."[23] Moreover, even for those Ashkenazi Jews who had no direct tie to Sephardic Jewry, Spain stood as an example of Jewish heroism through suffering. Ismar Schorsch has written of the "myth of Sephardic Supremacy" in Western European Jewish culture. By evoking the Inquisition, Markish also proudly evoked his own possible Sephardic family background. According to family lore, an ancestor, Lorenzo Markish, was an admiral with Portuguese roots.[24]

By opening his poem with past moments of violence, Markish employs what Maurice Halbwachs has called "external" or "social" memories as well as the "internal" or "personal" memories of his own experience.[25] The "external" memories are of the Inquisition. As for the "internal" memories, readers would immediately recognize in "Spain" the modernist pogrom poems Markish had published a decade and a half earlier. In particular, the piles of ash (*berglekh ash*) recall his 1921 *The Mound* (*Di Kupe*), in which he described a mound of bodies after a pogrom during the Ukrainian Civil War. In the poem "*Di Kupe*" (The Mound), piles of corpses after a pogrom are compared to "filthy wash":

A kupe koytek gret – fun untn biz aruf iz!	A mound of dirty laundry – from the bottom up!
Na! Vos dir vilt zikh, dul-vint, krats aroys un nem dir!	Here! Take what you want, crazy wind, dig in and take it!
Antkegn zitst der kloyster,	Sitting opposite is the church,
vi a tkhoyr, bay kupe oysgeshtikte oyfes.[26]	like a skunk by a heap of strangled fowl.[27]

In both poems, the dead, piled into mounds, have been humiliated. The "filthy wash" that is up for grabs in the 1921 poem gives way to "bones of my grandfathers" that are "mocked" in "Spain." Whereas in "*Di Kupe*," the mound itself speaks, presumably to God, in "Spain," the voice of the poet describes the piles:

S'zaynen nokh berglakh ash fun mayn amol tsezayt do	Mounds of ash from my past are still scattered here
mit kvarim fun gefalene in shlakht banand;[28]	side by side with the graves of those fallen in battle;

With these mounds of history, Markish views memory in strikingly similar terms to Halbwachs, for whom "history indeed resembles a crowded cemetery, where room must constantly be made for new tombstones."[29] Markish's external and internal cemetery of history is, like Halbwachs's, crowded by the dead.

The image of the humiliated mound was one that Markish returned to time and again throughout his career, including in his 1929 "Brothers," where he described the many who succumbed to typhus.[30] Markish's perpetual return to his death mounds undermines his simultaneous allegiance to the rhetoric of progress. His many mounds, intriguingly, also recall the romantic Marxism of Walter Benjamin, who, in his critique of Stalinist dialectical materialism, "Theses on the Philosophy of History," portrays an angel of history who "would like to stay, awaken the dead, and make whole what has been smashed."[31] Markish, like Benjamin's angel, may have had his wings caught in the storm "called progress," but he continues to gaze steadily at the wreckage of the past. That the Spanish Civil War occasioned a return to Markish's mounds of Jewish history attests to the Comintern's new encouragement of Jewish national solidarity in the face of the fascist threat. Markish viewed the outbreak of the Spanish Civil War as a catastrophe on the level of the revolutionary pogroms sixteen years earlier – a catastrophe shared by Jews, Spaniards, and other leftists across Europe. "Spain" thus offers an internationalist message, while weaving into it two lachrymose Jewish strands – the rise of Nazism and the Inquisition.

Markish would return to his mound again during the Second World War when, in a 1941 speech to the Jewish Anti-fascist Committee shortly after Hitler's invasion of the Soviet Union, he spoke of the Nazi desecration of Jewish villages: "Mountains of corpses and ashes are all that remains of towns in which Jews had lived for almost a thousand years." Writing of this 1941 speech, David Shneer suggests: "By referencing his own famous poem and the long history of Jewish responses to destruction, Markish was placing the current Nazi wave of violence against Jews on the backdrop of this history."[32] The Soviet critic Sergei Narovchatov later called the Spanish poems the beginning of a "new period of Peretz Markish's creativity":[33] the Spain cycle opens a period when Markish would deal specifically with the rise of fascism, save for the brief period after the Hitler-Stalin non-aggression treaty.[34] Although Narovchatov downplays the increasing presence of religious themes in Markish's works, he astutely links the Spain cycle to Markish's later Second World War poems.[35] Indeed, Gennady Estraikh has explored how, a few years later, Markish "created in his post-Holocaust writing a space in which to explore a thematics of rebellion in a way that combined his understanding of Communism and Jewishness."[36] Markish is clearly already working to describe a coexistence of Judaism and communism in the Spain cycle.

The cycle has received little attention from Markish scholars, no doubt in part because, during the brief Hitler-Stalin alliance (1939–41) that followed the Spanish Civil War, overtly anti-fascist poems were outlawed in the Soviet Union. Devoted communists after 1939 had to place their trust in Stalin's policy, and, as Lisa Kirschenbaum has aptly noted, "the memory of the war in Spain potentially complicated such determination to follow the party line."[37] Yet, when Markish first published "Spain" in the *Naye Folkstsaytung* in 1936, it very much reflected the Soviet zeitgeist. Karl Schlögel reminds us: "From 16 July 1936, the first day of the revolt of the officers around General Franco against the Spanish Republic, to the capitulation of Republican Spain at the end of April 1938, Spain was a central topic of all reporting."[38] Esther Markish would later recall noticing a newspaper clipping of her husband's "Spain" in the study of the Party chief of Abkhazia during a writer's convention over New Year's 1937–38.[39] Markish includes in his poem the ironic suggestion that art itself becomes irrelevant during war: "A shining sword in your hand/ should be three times lighter than the castanets' song (*Zol in dayn hant a blitsndike zayn di shverd/ Un dray mol laykhter vi di lid fun kastanietn!*)."[40] Markish's appeal to the struggle against fascism in Spain did not hurt his public recognition. He received the Lenin prize and became a candidate for Party membership in 1939, which he finally received in 1942.[41]

Markish purportedly said, in the 1930s: "We look to the past ... not to strengthen our bond to it, but so the future might enter us more quickly."[42] With "Spain," Markish managed to place national collective memory in service to a current struggle against fascism. In the second half of "Spain," Markish writes of the "blood-enraged storm/ Of Swastika and Inquisition (*Blut-tsebushevetn tsug/ Fun haknkreyts un inkvizitsie*)."[43] Markish, however, shifts continuously between dangers confronting Jews in particular (the swastika and the Inquisition) and dangers confronting all people, especially Spaniards. The next line begins, "For every murdered child – pay! (*Far yedn umgebrakhtn kind – batsolt!*)"[44] The international concern about Spanish civilians shifts the conversation from the local to the universal, moving the literary work out of the past into the present and towards the future.

Markish was not alone in merging a poetics of Jewish memory with communist internationalism. The American poet Aaron Kurtz (1891–1964), in his poem "Kol Nidre," depicts a Jew, Dovid Rom of Lemberg – who we learn has Marrano ancestry – in the trenches outside Cordoba with non-Jewish comrades. The poem begins with a Yiddish translation of the Kol Nidre prayer for the Day of Atonement:

... ale nidris	... All vows
un ale asuris	and all prohibitions
vos mir hobn genumen af zikh – zaynen	that we have taken on ourselves – are
botl.[45]	null.

Dovid goes on to commune with his Spanish ancestor:

Herst di elterzeydes reyd	Hear great-grandfather's speech
fun 1481, –[46]	from 1481, –

By referencing 1481 – the beginning of the Inquisition – Kurtz, like Markish, links historical Spanish anti-Jewish violence to contemporary anti-Jewish and anti-communist violence.[47] Moreover, in Kurtz's "Kol Nidre," the power of Jewish prayer yields to the power of collective worship. Dovid from Lemberg is joined in reciting the Kol Nidre not by a traditional minyan of ten Jewish men but by his Spanish and German comrades in arms, Pedro and Johannes.

Un Pedro fun Madrid,	And Pedro of Madrid,
un Yohanes fun Hamburg,	and Johannes of Hamburg,
helfn zingen di tfileh fun shpanishn id,	help sing the Spanish Jew's prayer,
gezungen fun eynikl Dovid	sung by his grandson Dovid
fun Lemberg.[48]	of Lemberg.

The traditional prayer of atonement bonds the three soldiers and admits Dovid's ancestor into the circle of comrades.

Kurtz, like Markish, distanced himself as a teenager from the religious milieu of his childhood. He was raised in a Lubavitcher Hasidic family outside Vitebsk (now Belarus), left home at the age of thirteen, worked as a hairdresser for circuses and theatre troops, and emigrated to the United States in 1911. He began publishing Yiddish poetry, often experimenting with avant-garde forms, in the early 1920s. Although Kurtz emphasizes the international collective in his poem – especially after joining the American Communist Party (CPUSA) in 1926 – he shared with Markish a desire to connect Jewish distant memory, recent experiences of the pogroms, and the anti-fascist effort in Spain. In another poem, Kurtz's "Yosl, the Polish Jew" (*Yosl, der poylisher yid*) has escaped death in Poland "to come – to death and to mould life (*tsu kumen – af toyt un af lebn zikh meldn*)."[49] Jewish voices heard throughout Kurtz's book suggest that a long Jewish history of trauma in the diaspora is precisely what has prompted Jews to volunteer to fight in Spain. Kurtz opens his poem "The Last Funeral" (*Di letste levaye*), for example, with the command, "Die, Feudal Spain/ corpse," followed by the promise: "We will blow you up to the highest heaven/ in your Medieval Cathedrals."[50] For Jewish communists, religion was part of the past, but past religious persecution helped to justify a collective future. By linking fascism to the medieval persecution of Jews and Protestants, the Yiddish poet made a strong argument for fighting the political conservatives who touted Spain's Catholic legacy.

The most grotesque combinations of feudal and modern Spain come from Jacobo (Yakov) Glantz (1902–82), who emigrated to Mexico from Novovitebsk in Soviet Ukraine in 1925. Like Markish and Kurtz, Glantz received enough religious education to integrate Jewish themes into his avowedly secularist verse. He began writing poetry in Russian, but shifted to Yiddish in Mexico, where, in addition to writing, editing, and painting, he worked as a dentist and later owned a restaurant.[51] Mexico, impoverished as it was after its own revolution, was the only foreign country to offer the Spanish Republic badly needed financial assistance, sending, according to Adam Hochschild, "a gift of 20,000 rifles, ammunition, and food."[52] The coalescence of Mexican interests in the Spanish Republic and Jewish concerns about the rise of fascism coincided with Glantz's long-held agenda: "a Jewish need to enter and be part of Latin American culture," according to Adina Cimet.[53] Glantz's belief in integration may have motived him to write his 1936 *Flags in Blood* (*Fonen in Blut*), a book illustrated by the radical American visual artist William Gropper, which, like the works of Markish and Kurtz, places Jewish collective memory of the Inquisition in service to leftist internationalism. In the poem "In the Wide Wanderings of My People" (*In vandervaytkayt fun mayn folk*), resurrected Jewish corpses from the Inquisition fight alongside the Loyalists. Streams of blood awaken corpses, and they begin to agitate for the fight for a "new Spain (*far Shpanye a banayter*)."

Hearing the cry of their ancestors, "the Hebrews arose from their graves (*Zenen oyfgeshtanen fun di kvorim di Hebreyer*)"

Un ineynem mitn moyrer kegn inkvizitsie,	And with the bricklayers against the Inquisition,
zikh ayngeshribn in di reyen fun militsie –[54]	registered in the ranks of the militia –

Glantz allows a felicitous rhyme to set the "ranks of the militia (*reyen fun militsie*)" directly against the "Inquisition (*inkvizitsie*)" itself, and visually highlights the couplet by printing it in boldface. The Republican cause is thus presented as a unique opportunity to correct a past moment of Jewish martyrdom and not only to fight a modern insurrection.

"Blood is always blood," Glantz writes in his introduction, explaining the book's political emphasis. "I, hearing the cry of a people in a bloody tragedy day and night, squeezed 'between the walls' of neutrality and snobbish diplomacy, – can't dream, but become feverish."[55] Todd Presner has discussed the paradoxical intellectual origins of twentieth-century "muscular Judaism": "It epitomized the rebirth of the strong Jew as drawn from Jewish history and mythology; but, at the same time, many of the anti-Semitic stereotypes of Jewish degeneracy were internalized in its conceptualization."[56] The notion that the Jew had to reform him or herself depends on a stereotype of past Jewish passivity. So too, the leftist Yiddish poets who wrote about Spain had to reconcile this history of anti-Jewish violence in Europe with a current willingness to fight, and possibly kill, peaceful victims.

The history of anti-Semitic violence in Spain led the Canadian Yiddish poet Esther Shumyatsher to question the relationship between bearing arms and Jewish identity. She begins her poem "I Am a Jew" with a rousing call to a Yugoslav, a Russian, a Yankee, and a Jew to "Arise, and come defend Madrid!" She then undercuts her cry by citing historical Jewish pacifism: "I can't hold a gun:/ My grandfather was a poor Jew./ My grandmother read the Tsene Urene/ And translated it literally."[57] Shumyatsher concludes, however, that Jewishness offers its own reason to fight in Spain. She goes on to recall the history of forced conversion through an imagined encounter, in which

Es tselemnt zikh a frumer Katolik,	A devout Catholic crosses himself,
un zogt dem Yidn tsu	and promises the Jew
dos getlekhe glik.	eternal happiness.

Shumyatsher's reference to forced conversion, like Kurtz's secularized "Kol Nidre," illustrates the extent to which Jews viewed the Spanish Civil War as a return to the Inquisition. After all, the allegory of medieval Spain appealed to conservatives and republicans alike. As Paul Preston has shown, in response to the Republic's anti-clerical legislation, anti-Semitic sentiments, present to some degree since the Middle Ages even with Spain's miniscule Jewish population, returned, and "the bilious rhetoric of the Jewish-Masonic-Bolshevik conspiracy was immediately pressed into service."[58] For Jews, however, the Inquisition had been the defining anti-Semitic episode in European history, and, for those who accepted the Comintern's secularist ideology around Spain, anti-Catholic actions were carried out in the interest of eradicating religious bigotry. Moreover, acceptance of violence helped to combat the stereotype of Jewish passivity. Speaking to Jewish volunteers on the Aragon front, the journalist Melech Epstein suggested as much: "Four and a half centuries ago, Jews were driven from Spain to many lands, and the country was boycotted by them. Now young Jews from many lands are hurrying to Spain to rescue her, and perhaps the whole of Europe, from fascist domination."[59] The utopian poets who wrote Spanish Civil War cycles sought a reconciliation of the historical interests of Spain's persecuted Jewish community with contemporary anti-clerical communist interests. Past trauma, that is, was only worth evoking if it could serve a progressive future.

This juncture in time was, let us remember, a moment when Jewish thinkers from across the political spectrum, from Zionism to Bolshevism, sought antecedents for a new vision of Jewish military power. Jacobo Glantz's book, published by the "Gezbir" society, which was formed to support the Soviet autonomous Jewish region of Birobidjan, might be read as offering an alternative, like Birobidjan itself, to Zionism. Glantz reminds his readers that it is "the grandchildren of Jewish martyrs/ from Toledo and Madrid" who join the struggle. The image of ethnic Jews fighting side by side with non-Jews, like Kurtz's collective Kol Nidre prayer, not only expresses an internationalist hope for the future but also expands a key moment in Jewish collective trauma to include the non-Jews of contemporary Spain.[60] In this Comintern revision of the lachrymose motif in Jewish memory, the past, rather than serving "competitive victimology" (to use Dominick LaCapra's term), can be redeemed through its comparison to other groups' historical and current tragedies.[61]

Un s'hobn eyniklekh fun Yidishe martirer	And the grandchildren of the Jewish martyrs
fun Toledo un Madrid	of Toledo and Madrid
geshafn batalionen – [62]	formed battalions –

The relationship between the prodigal Jewish "grandchild" and the ancestral martyrs of the Inquisition is here, as in Kurtz's "Kol Nidre" and Markish's

"Spain," a crucial part of the Jewish poetics of Spain. The Inquisition evoked a tradition of Jewish memory, but one that has been revised to suggest a multi-ethnic collective.

The Jewish historian Salo Wittmayer Baron began criticizing what he called the "lachrymose" tendency in Jewish history in 1928.[63] Like Baron, the poets Glantz, Kurtz, and Markish all reject the notion that suffering should set Jews apart from other nations and embrace the idea of Jews' intimate connection and integration into a multi-ethnic world. However, all three poets harness a lachrymose tradition to draw attention to a contemporary tragedy of universal concern. Markish challenges a community of Europe's Jews to view the Spanish Civil War as equal to the tragic story of the past. For Kurtz, the task of collectively remembering transfers from the Jews to the International Brigades. And for Glantz, the war folds history towards the present, reincarnating medieval victims as soldiers. For the communist Yiddish writers, group memory added Jewish historical meaning to the collective struggle against the fascists. However, this historical meaning only held value if they could demonstrate that Jewish collective concern could be transferred from Jewish memory to the present conditions of Spain. We shall now turn to how this present is represented in the same cycles.

Present

"I've seen your picture./ Azure eyes – sharp and mild (*Kh'hob gezen dayn bild/ Aziere oygn – sharf un mild*)."[64] Jacobo Glantz opens his poem "Lina Odena's Eyes" (*Di Oygn fun Lina Odena*) with a description of a photograph, widely published in Popular Front newspapers in 1936. Lina Odena, a twenty-five-year-old communist, found herself behind nationalist lines and shot herself to prevent capture. With this reference to the contemporary media, Glantz employs visual documentary evidence – a form of communist factography – to create a present tense in his cycle. As Steven S. Lee has noted elsewhere, factography, which sought the "precise fixation of fact," tended to "cast the non-European Other in a radical, experimental light."[65] The same might be said of Spanish subjects who, in all three Yiddish cycles, serve as a means of overcoming the past. The documentary image of Odena offers a stagnant, fleeting vision of a present tense – one that links medieval Spain with a dawning, revolutionary future:

Oygn – vos farmogn	Eyes – that possess
letstn goysesdikn likht	the last dying light
fun kloysterdike mnoyres,	of church candelabras,
un oygn vos balaykhtn veln dos gezikht	and eyes that will light the face
fun tsukunftike doyres.[66]	of future generations.

Odena's immortalized gaze bears witness to an irretrievable past at the dawn of a new era. The present itself is a means to an end.

In popular culture, Odena symbolized a young Republican Spain that chooses death over captivity. As Tabea Alexa Linhard has demonstrated, this narrative was both gendered and racialized, for poems and romanceros of the time often cast Odena's suicide as an act preventing inevitable rape by North African soldiers in Franco's army.[67] Glantz's poem does not mention rape. In fact, he dedicates the poem to the "Revolutionary woman, who fell in battle outside Talavera," suggesting uncertainty about the nature of her demise. However, Glantz does employ the common image of a feminized Spain as a counterpart to the male revolutionary, a role often symbolized by the communist activist Dolores Ibárruri (better known as La Pasionaria) who famously stated: "It is better to be the widows of heroes than the wives of cowards." Foreign writers often cast Spanish characters – whether male or female – as exotic bodies, which, as Edward Said has observed of orientalized women, "are usually the creatures of a male power-fantasy."[68] Even the most progressive poetic tributes to Republican Spain often use either female or servile metaphors to suggest a country awaiting its hero, pregnant with a new society, mourning a beloved soldier, or defying its master.

Figures emblematic of Spanish culture emerge throughout Glantz's book to symbolize a renewal of an ancient landscape. In "On the Evening Steppe of La Mancha" (*Oyf farnakhtikn step fun La Mancha*), Sancho is suddenly loath to follow Quixote's dreams:

S'hot shtolener trot fun geshikhte	The steel tread of history
di alte khaloymes tsetrotn ...	has trampled old dreams ...
Es sheylt zikh durkh khmares gedikhte	It peels itself through thick clouds
der tavl fun naye gebotn ...[69]	the tablet of new commandments ...

The Marxist-Hegelian march of history replaces the quixotic fictions of old Spain with a new order, and, Glantz suggests, this new order will be more realistic, more rational. This new secularist faith, of course, borrowed liberally from religious form, even as it waged war on religious content. Igal Halfin has written of Russia: "Imbuing time with a historical teleology that gave meaning to events, Marxist eschatology described history as moral progression from the darkness of class society to the light of Communism."[70] This communist teleology led all three poets to firmly place their Jewish images and associations in the past, while their depictions of Spain could remain in the fleeting present, and depictions of a Soviet-style utopia were reserved for the future.

The merging of a Marxist eschatology with the reality of widespread Spanish Catholicism is especially apparent in "Red Christ" (*Royter kristus*), where Glantz depicts a revolutionary Christ who "shows soldiers the way/ through church ruins (*un er vayzt dem veg soldatn/ durkh di kloystershe ruinen*)."[71] This figure is the Christ of revolution, akin to the Christ of Alexander Blok's 1918 "The Twelve," who leads a motley group of Red Army soldiers through a Petersburg snowstorm. With his revolutionary Christ, Glantz offers an antidote to Franco's Catholic collaborators: "Today Christ is a red leader/ at the Somosierra front (*Haynt iz Kristus – royter firer/ Oyfn front fun Somesiera*)." The poem is dated 11 October 1936, several weeks after the republican fighters surrendered to the fascists at the Somosierra mountain pass, north of Madrid. Glantz, writing in the first months of the war, describes what he assumed would be a transitional, revolutionary moment. His Loyalist heroes are martyrs – saints of a new revolutionary religion who are bound only to the present moment.

Peretz Markish had been using reportage to bridge past and future since the Russian Revolution.[72] As in his earlier writing on the Russian Revolution and in Glantz's cycle, Markish employs elements of factography to ground utopian ideals and past trauma. As Seth Wolitz has written of Markish's 1922 *Radyo*, "Markish carefully angles his appeal to the Jewish reader by attacking the old ways and insisting that the ruins left by the [Russian] Civil War must be left behind in the past."[73] Markish's Spanish characters are similarly rooted in the kind of fleeting present he described in 1917, when he wrote "My Name Is Now" (*Mayn nomen iz atsind*). And indeed, Markish frequently compares the "now" of Spain to the Russian Revolution. In "Ballad of a Delegate" (*Balade vegn delegate*), the speaker asks:

– *az vi vayt iz den funanden bizn lebn?*	– so how far is it from there to life?
– *az vi vayt iz den biz Moskve fun Madrid?*[74]	– so how far is it to Moscow from Madrid?

The idea that Moscow is both life and the spiritual centre of revolution reflects the geographical power balance of Comintern poetics and distinguishes this volume from Markish's revolutionary verse of nearly two decades earlier. By the late 1930s, Markish's allegiances were with the Party, centred in Moscow – his home since 1926.

The ultimate Spanish stereotype appears in Markish's "Toreador," who has exchanged his bull for the combined spectre of fascism and the Inquisition. Like Glantz's Lina Odena, Markish's toreador is both anachronistic and revolutionary:

Nu, fokher uf dayn roytn tukh, toreador,	Well, fan up your red cloth, toreador,
es vart dos folk, der umgeduld farzidt dort,	a people waits, impatience boiled over there,
nit keyn buhay vet haynt aroys dir tsu der por,	no bull will today come out to be your match,
es geyt dos fintstere geshpenst fun inkvizitors![75]	the dark spectre of the inquisitors is coming!

The toreador's red cape becomes a red flag – a visual and tangible fabric connecting Spain's cultural icon of violence to Bolshevik iconography: "And like a flag it should float to the heights! (*Un vi a fon zol er a shveb ton in di haykhn!*)."[76] This poem was likely a response to news coming from Spain's republican fighters. The former bullfighter Melchor Rodríguez, an anarchist, was, paradoxically, an important voice for pacifism.[77]

For many, the most moving stories from Spain involved children. Eleanor Roosevelt, despite her husband's non-interventionist policy, worked to raise money to feed Spanish children.[78] The Introspectivist poet Aaron Glants-Leyeles, in his "Ballad of Spain," conjured "Pepito" – a boy of four forced to flee Spain for France.

Pepito falt un heybt zikh, Pepito heybt zikh, falt –	Pepito falls and gets up, gets up and falls again –
Pepito iz shoyn gantse, shoyn gantse fir yor alt.[79]	Pepito is already a four-year-old young man.[80]

Portrayals in the Yiddish press of the youngest and most vulnerable victims of the war were inextricable from Jews' fear for the broader implications of Nazism. Leyeles wrote in an *Inzikh* editorial about the threat of fascism to Spaniards and Jews alike: "Is there no mercy? No, not these days. A small, old culture, maybe the oldest in Europe, is attacked and plundered – there isn't a peep, there isn't a rousing of conscience ... So, beloved humankind, look at the Basques. This is your mirror nowadays." Leyeles maintained hope that the Basques, who survived the "cruel pirates" of the past, "will similarly overcome their contemporary enemies ... As we will overcome ours, which are the same."[81] A Trotskyite, Leyeles was openly disdainful of colleagues – notably including Aaron Kurtz – devoted to Stalin; yet, news from Spain bridged left-wing political divides.[82]

Both Kurtz and Glantz composed Spanish lullabies about children whose parents were dead or fighting the fascists. Several Spanish characters in Aaron Kurtz's *No Pasarán* are parents awaiting their children. The old, blind Karmelita waits for her children "to return her Spain to her (*zoln ir tsurikbrengen*

ir Shpanye)." Karmensita, a woman about to give birth, lies feverish in a hospital. It is unclear whether the future holds life or death:

Arum, af tishlekh, blien kvaytn,	Around, on little tables, bloom flowers,
ershtn mame-shmeykhl vekn-oyf di	their scent should awaken the first ma-
duftn.	ternal smile.
Neyn. Dos glien vundn af halb-toyte,	No. These are wounds that blossom on
	the half-dead,
dos flien toyt-buketn funderluftn.[83]	these are death-bouquets that fly from
	the sky.

These parental figures personify the revolutionary moment of anticipation.
The conceit is not unique to poetry, or to Yiddish: Bertolt Brecht and Mar-
garete Steffin build their 1937 one-act play, *Señora Carrar's Rifles*, around a
mother figure who, having lost a son, becomes convinced she must join the
Republican forces.[84] The emphasis on parents and children envisions Spain
as both effeminate and immature – an old nation rendered inexperienced by
revolution.

The Spanish landscape itself also symbolizes the embattled present. Kurtz's
"Andalusian Landscape" (*Andaluzier Landshaft*) is labelled parenthetically
"from a painter's letter." The artist describes natural beauty ("Spain: splendor/
of a thousand Colorados"), which gives way to the pathetic fallacy of war.

A hayntikn moler in Shpanye	A contemporary painter in Spain
geyt nit on dos amolike moln.	doesn't care to depict the past.
Antikn	Antiques
zaynen mer nit keyn teme:	are no longer a theme.
In kharuve templen ligt ashik tseshosn	In temples, shot to ash
di altertum-manie,	is obsession with old times,
di teme iz – toyt af di berg, toyt in di	the theme is death on mountains, death
toln,	in valleys,
brenendike brikn,	burning bridges
vos himl-fayern tsenemen	that heaven's fires consume
un lebns gerangl in di feld-shpitoln.[85]	and life's struggle in field hospitals.[86]

The painter is only able to depict the present in the midst of its destruction – the
temples, shot to ash, the burning bridges. The past, significantly, no longer has
a place.

Kurtz's choice of the letter-poem is important to his documentation of
contemporary Spain. Kurtz writes in his introduction to *No Pasarán* that the
book's contents are based largely on documentary material, including "letters

from the Spanish front, correspondences, and conversations with returned
brigaders. The names of the heroes in this book are not fictitious."[87] Kurtz's
letters reflect the fascination with the documentary among poets, across languages, during the Popular Front period. The letter-poem lent writers like
Langston Hughes and Muriel Rukeyser a diversity of dialects and perspectives.[88] Leftist Yiddish poets, too, used letters to channel the voices of the politically disenfranchised, be they the Scottsboro defendants and their mothers
or the convicted Italian anarchists Sacco and Vanzetti.[89]

To include Spain in a decades-long international struggle for revolution,
the Yiddish poets, writing from afar, carefully draw their descriptions from
current reportage. Crucial to all three cycles, however, is the sense that Spain
is prepared to lose its national particularity to a new internationalism. Thus,
Glantz's Odena witnesses a change in world order; Markish mentions Madrid
and Moscow in the same breath; Kurtz's Andalusian landscape must dismantle the old to make way for the new. For the revolutionary poet, of course,
the present moment cannot hold, and must usher in a utopian future. In the
final section of this chapter, let us turn to the "future" elements in the Yiddish
Spain cycles.

Future

The protagonist in Aaron Kurtz's "A Letter from a Nurse" (*A briv fun a kranknshvester*) writes: "it smells/ of poplar and death/ in my hospital (*es shmekht/
mit toppol un mit toyt/ in mayn shpitol*)."[90] She describes four men who died
that night: an Austrian miner, a Moorish hunter, a Sigter Hasid, and a German poet. Each dying man glimpses a version of the future, and each makes
a statement before death. The Moor, presumably one of the many North
Africans forced to fight in Franco's army, cries: "The Moors, all the Moors,/
Must cross sides (*Di Murn*, ale *Murn,/ muzn dezertirn*)." This sentiment likens
Kurtz's poem to Langston Hughes's 1937 "Letter from Spain," a poem written
in the voice of an African American volunteer who receives a Moorish prisoner's last breath:

> We captured a wounded Moor today.
> He was just as dark as me.
> I said, Boy, what you been doin' here
> Fightin' against the free?[91]

Hughes's semi-fictional narrator urges the North African to see the connection
to Spanish colonialism and slavery and, through this connection, to reject the
Francoist rebels.[92] Kurtz's North African comes to the same conclusion, bless-
ing a freer future with words that merge instruction and prophesy.

If Hughes's African American protagonist recognizes himself in the still-enslaved dying Moor ("Then something wonderful'll happen/ To them Moors as dark as me"), then Kurtz, who was raised in a Hasidic milieu, presents his own twin in his Hasidic figure, who realizes that fighting the fascists in Spain is an extension of his religious beliefs:

O, ikh bentsh di groyse tsayt	Oh, I bless this great time
vos hot gelernt mir vi zikh tsu shlogn	that has taught me how to fight
far ofene tir un toyer tsum erdishn	for open doors and gates to an earthly
gan-edn.[93]	garden of Eden

A few years earlier, the fusion of religious prophesy with communism would have bordered on heresy for religious Jews and communists alike, but the overt anti-Semitism expressed by the fascist rebels and their Nazi allies allowed for a new framing of Jewish tradition that could, at least in the realm of poetry, coexist with revolutionary ideals. This proposed coexistence often took the form of utopian slogans that, repeated, can be likened to internationalist prayers. These prayer-like slogans form the third component of the Comintern-aligned Yiddish Spain cycles. The future-oriented poems in all three volumes are the clearest in their communist ideology. They are also the most formally inventive, with internationalist mantras appearing as refrains and poems written in the form of Republican placards. The future poems, as well, find the poets experimenting with the dissolution of subjectivity to evoke a diversity of voices.

Jacobo Glantz and Peretz Markish, like Kurtz, indulge in visions and dreams through prophetic figures, often at the moment of death. In a poem dedicated to the memory of the poet Federico García Lorca, assassinated early in the war in his hometown of Granada, Glantz writes of future generations:

O, dayn vort,	Oh, your word,
dos vort fun vorn,	the word of warning,
vort fun dor	word of a generation
vos vert geborn	being born
in yamen blut fun dayn Granade.[94]	in seas of blood from your Granada.

By turning the poet into a prophet, Glantz also turns him into a warrior.

Markish creates a more explicit prophet-warrior with "Pancho Video," a sniper who rises from the grave to shout Republican agitational propaganda (agitprop) to enemy soldiers. The refrain, "Pancho Video isn't only a sniper,/ Pancho Video is agitprop! (*Pantsho Video iz nit bloyz a snayper,/ Pantsho Video iz oykh agitprop!*)" envisions Pancho as a poet, prophet, and warrior.

Words, Markish implies, are as important to the war as bullets. During the Spanish Civil War, poems were disseminated in much the same way as pamphlets and placards, which blurred the boundaries between art and agitprop.[95] Loyalist posters presented easily digestible images and caricatures. A poster for the Syndicalist Party depicts the many arms of the Popular Front threatening a caricatured businessman with a top hat. He stands atop a swastika, indicating the fascist-capitalist connection in Europe (figure 9.1). Pro-Republican poems often recapitulated the slogans and visual symbolism found in poster art, binding more tightly the poetic message with a popular signifier.

Many of Kurtz's letter-poems in *No Pasarán* are polyphonic in the Bakhtinian sense, where multiple autonomous voices form a collective dialogue. In a poem titled "The Orchestra" (*Der orkester*), labelled "A Letter from Dave," Kurtz describes a musical ensemble, which functions as a harmonious international collective:

Unzer orkester shpilt, in shpiln herstu	Our orchestra plays, in playing you hear
di harmonie	the harmony
fun hundert felker in eyn brigade:	of a hundred peoples in one brigade:
der gitarist – a romantisher Venetsianer,	the guitarist is a romantic Venetian,
der karnetist – a zakhlekher Belgrader,	the cornettist – a matter-of-fact Belgrader,
fidl shpilt a Yid	a Jew plays the violin
un af vos du vilst –	you name it –
Daytshn Shvedn Yenkis, Indianer! [96]	Germans Swedes Yankees, Indians!

Kurtz's international symphony evokes the spirit of the dream future – a utopia not yet attained, but one that might be akin to the International Brigades. The orchestra, "in the hinterlands not far from the trenches," plays "the Spanish anthem/ and the Internationale," thus producing a collective of nations.

Kurtz had long sought new forms for poems that could inspire the working Yiddish-speaking masses. His 1927 *Placards* (*Plakatn*), which he wrote a year after joining the CPUSA, adopts the genre of revolutionary street placards. The poems in *Plakatn* are shapely, waving across the page like flags with alternating very short and very long lines of blank verse. They are Mayakovskian, emphatic, occasionally punctuated with English phrases. The short lines, meant to conjure placards at a rally, appreciate mass movements as an integral form of poetry. In one poem, "Union Square," Kurtz writes:

9.1 A poster for the left-wing Syndicalist Party during the Spanish Civil War. The poster was created by Manuel Monleón for the Workers' Committee of Control (UGT). Translation: Discipline. Unified Command. Syndicalist Party. Lithograph, UC San Diego Special Collections.

Di fete shtiftates fun shtot, di kalte
   balebatim dayne,
hobn nit keyn nakhes fun dayn haver-
   shaft mit mikh,
dem nar,
vos kumt aher fun ale vilde vinklen
fun der velt un putst dikh oys
in bender un
fonen.[97]

The city's fat stepfathers, your cold
   masters,
take no pride in your friendship with
   me,
the idiot,
who comes here from all the world's
wild corners and dresses you up
in books and
flags.

L. Khanukov, writing for the communist *Freiheit*, appreciated Kurtz's tireless quest for usable poetic forms and called *Plakatn* "already a book of a ripe poet, who has found his way in life."[98] He remarks further on Kurtz's ability to feel "the power of the awakened masses. He is their tribunal."

With the letter-poems in *No Pasarán*, Kurtz again experimented with a new formal mode gaining prominence in leftist poetry. The letter form, like the placards, allowed Kurtz to loosen his grip on the individual voice, opting instead for the voice of a collective. However, whereas the placard poem suggests voices in unison, verbally capturing the exclamatory atmosphere of a protest, the letters that populate *No Pasarán* salvage the individual experiences that comprise that collective. Kurtz's inclusion of Civil War slogans, often in Spanish ("*¡No pasarán!*," "*¡Salud!*," "*¡Viva la Espagña!*") and at the end of a poem, merges the individual voice with a collective spirit, binding his diverse cast of characters more tightly together and reinforcing the discourse of collectivity. In his discussion of poetry and discourse, Anthony Easthope observes poetry's potential "to bring the signifier into a reinforcing relation with the signified, so giving the poetic message a quality of 'reification' able to convert it into an 'enduring thing.'"[99] Hannah Arendt makes a similar, but far more sinister, observation to Easthope's, viewing slogans as signifiers "designed to translate the propaganda lies of the movement, woven around a central fiction ... into a functioning reality."[100] Although agitation around Spain cannot be completely uncoupled from the strictures of the Soviet 1930s, to dismiss the poetry of Comintern sympathizers on the grounds of politics would be to miss the aesthetic innovation involved in their particular exaltation of the signifier.[101] Indeed, Arendt's discomfort with slogans demonstrates the power of political literature in the Popular Front poetry. As Cary Nelson has noted, "for a moment in the 1930s, verbal creativity and political slogans were considered poetic partners."[102]

Glantz's volume, like Kurtz's, emphasizes revolutionary optimism even as it memorializes the war's early casualties. In a brief preface, the Soviet-aligned editorial team expresses hope that the poems "should serve the broad Jewish masses in their struggle against bloody fascism."[103] Towards the end of the collection, Glantz shifts from poems about individuals towards collectivist slogans. He employs the same "placard (*plakat*)" form that Kurtz used in his 1925 *Plakatn* – evoking proletarian poetry of the 1920s. One poem, titled simply "Placard" (*Plakat*) responds to the September 1936 battle at Talavera de la Reina by heralding a new era:

A naye era	A new era
heybt zikh on in Eyrope.	is beginning in Europe.
Sopet	Sopet
der tsaytungs-farkoyfer.	the newspaper-vender.
Zayn kol vi a shoyfer	His voice like a shofar
ruft un vornt un gornt	calls and warns and yearns
in luft.	to the sky.
– Di luft iz ful mit dinamit[104]	– The sky is full of dynamite

Although the battle at Talavera devastated the Republican army, the defeat led to an international call to defend Madrid. As Antony Beevor puts it, "the communist slogan that 'Madrid will be the grave of fascism' was powerfully emotive and the battle for the capital was to help the party to power."[105] Glantz's newspaper vendor, a modern town crier, announces the headlines, which would be posted on the streets alongside placards. Like Kurtz's Hassid in the "Letter from a Nurse," Glantz's Sopet also reinscribes Jewish tradition onto an internationalist message: the shofar, rather than heralding a new Jewish year, heralds a new era for all workers.

"A Poem about Gide the Banker in a Sleepless Madrid Night" (*A lid vegn banker Khid in a shloflozer nakht fun Madrid*) is parenthetically labelled "in the style of a placard (*Plakatish*)." The eponymous banker, Gilberto Gide, is plagued by visions of Christ and an image of "a bloody banknote." But, rather than saving Gide,

Got tut on	God puts on
a shvartsn kapushon	a black cape
un geyt fun shtub aroys ...[106]	and walks out of the house ...

True to the placard form, the poem is comprised of fragmented images: short stanzas recall the visually compelling posters that were ubiquitous at the time – visual works of agitprop flaunting clear, readily digestible messages. The image of Jesus donning a soldier's black cape can be likened to war posters that, despite the Republic's anti-clerical actions, accuse the nationalists of Christian hypocrisy.[107] In one Popular Front poster, an International Brigader stands before a female symbol of international peace, whose cruciform posture and dove suggests a true understanding of Christianity (figure 9.2).

Glantz's meandering poem ends with a reminder that the Loyalist forces are watching (and punishing) the actions of the fascists and their allies:

Bavakht iz yeder trot	Guarded is every step
un shpan! –	and stride! –
NO PASARÁN![108]	NO PASARÁN!

The "guarded step" simultaneously evokes war propaganda and the biblical lines from Isaiah 21:6, "Go set up a sentry." Like the biblical watchman, Glantz's implied Loyalist guards are prophet-soldiers, watching for the enemy and for the dawn of a new era.

Peretz Markish, the only poet of the three to have made his home in Soviet Russia, used more Soviet reference points in his Spain cycle than Kurtz or Glantz. In the poem "Commander Diestro," which closes Markish's volume, the eponymous character, a philosophy student who takes up arms after a bishop shoots his father,

9.2 Poster advertising the International Brigades. Translation: The Madrid Popular Front to the World Popular Front. Homage to the International Brigades. Courtesy of Getty Images.

is a Spanish Vasily Chapaev, the decorated Red Army commander from the Russian Civil War who had died in battle: "Just like that Chapaev once fought! (*Ot azoy z'amol geshlogn zikh Tshapaiev!*)"[109] Whereas "Spain" begins with sadness, Diestro leads a group to successfully occupy a church. Evoking Chapaev, Markish once again contributes to the view of Spain as a new theatre for world revolution. The poem ends with a vision of victory. Diestro, his arms wounded, is taken to the hospital, where the battle continues to play out in the commander's mind.

On bavustzayn z'er gelegn a mesles dort,	He lay there unrecognized for twenty-four hours,
vi a kholem iz adurkhgegan di shlakht,	like a dream he went back through the battle,

un gekumen, vi a vunder, iz der zig, –	and it came, like a wonder, victory, –
s'hot farlangt azoy dos folk, di	the people have so longed for the
Republik![110]	Republic!

Like the dying Robert Jordan in Hemingway's *For Whom the Bell Tolls*, Diestro does not see victory, but dreams victory. His anonymity, by the end of the poem, emphasizes the unimportance of the individual in the face of a collective future, but his role within that collective is that of the dying prophet.

Comintern-aligned Jews, faced with the foreboding rise of fascism across Europe, placed their hope in the Spanish Republic. Ilya Ehrenburg, who travelled to Spain as a Soviet newspaper correspondent, felt optimistic in 1936 when France voted in the Popular Front candidate, Leon Blum. "I rejoiced with the others: after Spain – France! It was clear now that Hitler would not succeed in beating Europe to her knees ... I think back to the spring of 1936 as to the last happy spring of my life."[111] The desire to see an end to the fascist threat helps to explain the tenacity with which supporters of the Republic clung to the hope of victory. The future-oriented poems in Markish, Glantz, and Kurtz's Spain cycles express the same collective will.

Epilogue: Spain to the Second World War

From the moment Stalin and Hitler signed a non-aggression treaty in 1939, the prospect of the Second World War overshadowed the defeat in Spain for Jewish leftists in and outside the Soviet Union. When, following the Nazi invasion of the Soviet Union, anti-German literature was again published, Markish wrote several Second World War works that placed Jewish history in the context of Nazism, much in the same way he had placed the Inquisition in the context of the rise of fascism in 1936.

The Spanish Civil War eventually became a paradigm for martyrdom during the Second World War.[112] Markish's *Footsteps of a Generation* (*Trot fun Doyres*) finds a young widower, Metek, searching for the words to discuss his wife's death in the Spanish Civil War with his father-in-law. Metek thinks of the biblical Joseph's brothers as he prepares to show his father-in-law "the bloody party card of his daughter, who gave her life for freedom in Spain." The return to the motif of Spain in this story of a Jewish family during the Second World War universalizes the fight against Hitler from a Jewish concern to a long war against fascism. It also shows the role of the Spanish Civil War, and the Comintern, in the development of Jewish literature. Metek hopes to convince his father-in-law "that with his daughter's blood too would be written the history of the freedom-movement not only in Spain but ... in the whole world."[113] Spain, even during the Second World War, remained a heroic moment, a moment when Jews stood up to fight the injuries and injustices of history.

"Everybody knows how the war ended," Muriel Rukeyser wrote, in the opening to her posthumously published novel, *Savage Coast*.[114] In hindsight, the Spanish Civil War devastated the liberal ideals of freedom and justice that inspired not only the leftists who joined forces with the Loyalists but also moderate democracies that remained strategically neutral. However, Jewish ideological investment in the International Brigades offers a crucial context for understanding much of the literature of trauma associated with the Holocaust.[115] So, too, the Yiddish poetry of the Spanish Civil War introduced a modern poetics of anti-fascism in Europe, one that aped the fascist uses of history and met violence with violence. The cycles we have considered here, each in its own way, integrate a traumatic past, current documentary accounts of Spain, and collective slogans that prophesied a progressive future. That all three poets merge national memory, their current internationalist commitment, and Marxist eschatology demonstrates the ubiquitous artistic devices that Comintern-aligned poets deployed in Spain.

NOTES

I am grateful to the following colleagues for their comments and suggestions on this chapter: Marc Caplan, Michael Davidson, Alma Heckman, Steven Lee, Harriet Murav, Pamela Radcliff, Sarika Talve-Goodman, and Alan Wald. I thank Margo Glantz and David Markish for their permission to publish their fathers' work.

1 Humphrey Carpenter, *W.H. Auden: A Biography* (London: Faber & Faber, 1981), 219; W.H. Auden, *Spain* (London: Faber & Faber, 1937).
2 All translations, unless otherwise noted, are my own. AMG.
3 Melech Epstein, *Pages from the Colorful Life: An Autobiographical Sketch* (Detroit, MI: Wayne State University Press, 1971), 123.
4 On the Botwin Company, see Gerben Zaagsma, "Propaganda or Fighting the Myth of *Pakhdones*? *Naye Prese*, the Popular Front, and the Spanish Civil War," in *Choosing Yiddish: New Frontiers of Language and Culture*, ed. Lara Rabinowich, Shiri Goren, and Hanna S. Pressman (Detroit, MI: Wayne State University Press, 2013), 88–101.
5 Cary Nelson, ed., *The Wound and the Dream: Sixty Years of American Poems about the Spanish Civil War* (Urbana: University of Illinois Press, 2002), 23.
6 See Harry Ritter, *Dictionary of Concepts in History* (Westport, CT: Greenwood Publishing Group, 1986), 114. On Marx's interpretation of Hegelian dialectics, see H.P. Kainz, *Hegel's Philosophy of Right, with Marx's Commentary: A Handbook for Students* (The Hague: Martinus Nijhoff, 1974).
7 Salo Wittmayer Baron is considered the first to observe, and critique, what he called the "lachrymose" motif in Jewish history in his treatment of pre-modern Europe.

Baron, "Ghetto and Emancipation: Shall We Revise the Traditional View?" *The Menorah Journal* 14 (1928): 515–26.

8 Georg Lukács, "The Historical Novel of Democratic Humanism," in *The Historical Novel*, trans. Hannah Mitchell and Stanley Mitchell (Lincoln: University of Nebraska Press, 1983), 342–3, emphasis in the original.

9 The Comintern's financial and organizational support of the International Brigades in Spain alienated democratic governments, including the United States, whose non-interventionist policy may well have cost the Republic its victory. Helen Graham has noted, for example: "The haemorrhaging of time and money that Non-Intervention inflicted at the start of the war, solely upon the Republic, was absolutely devastating." Helen Graham, *The Spanish Republic at War, 1936–1939* (Cambridge: Cambridge University Press, 2002), 158.

10 Tim Kendall, *Modern English War Poetry* (Oxford: Oxford University Press, 2006), 108.

11 Hannah Arendt, *Men in Dark Times* (San Diego, CA: Harvest Books, 1970), 216.

12 Marc Chagall, letter (1948) to Leo Kenig. Cited in Benjamin Harshav, *Marc Chagall and His Times: A Documentary Narrative* (Stanford, CA: Stanford University Press, 2004), 641. Chagall published his correspondence with Lisner, a Jewish fighter in Spain who suggested themes for Chagall to take up "with your artistic rifle, your brush." Quoted in Harshav, *Chagall*, 473–5.

13 Harsha Ram, "World Literature as World Revolution: Velimir Khlebnikov's *Zangezi* and the Utopian Geopoetics of the Russian Avant-Garde," in chapter one, page XX of this volume.

14 Kadia Molodowsky, "Tsu di Volontiorn in Shpanye," in *In land fun mayn gebeyn* (Chicago: Shtayn, 1937), 17. Much of the 1937 collection *In land fun mayn gebeyn*, in which the poem appears, documents the rising anxiety over Nazism in Europe. For a good discussion of this book, see Allison Schachter, *Diasporic Modernisms: Hebrew and Yiddish Literature in the Twentieth Century* (Oxford: Oxford University Press, 2011), 178.

15 See Andrea Orzoff, "Interwar Democracy and the League of Nations," in *The Oxford Handbook of European History, 1914–1945*, ed. Nicolas Doumanis, (Oxford: Oxford University Press, 2016), 261–81. Key Soviet literary figures debated ways of broadening literary policy to match the united political front. Ilya Ehrenburg, in a 1934 letter to Stalin, argued that a MORP (International Organization of Revolutionary Writers) too closely aligned with Bolshevism would discredit the Soviet cause in the eyes of the West. Ilya Ehrenburg, quoted in Anson Rabinbach, "Paris, Capital of Anti-Fascism," in *The Modernist Imagination: Intellectual History and Critical Theory*, ed. Warren Breckman et al. (New York: Berghahn Books, 2009), 199.

16 Nonetheless, as Pamela Radcliff and others have suggested, the Soviet focus of Comintern policy probably ultimately weakened the interwar left. Pamela Radcliff, "The Political Left in Interwar Europe," in Doumanis, *Oxford Handbook of European History*, 282–300, 294.

17 Arendt, *Men in Dark Times*, 213

18 Alan M. Wald, *Trinity of Passion: The Literary Left and the Antifascist Crusade* (Chapel Hill: University of North Carolina Press, 2007), 14.

19 Arendt, *Men in Dark Times*, 239.

20 Edward Stankiewicz, remembering his meeting with Markish, would later compare him to a movie actor. Edward Stankiewicz, *My War: Memoir of a Young Jewish Poet* (Syracuse, NY: Syracuse University Press, 2002), 27.

21 Peretz Markish, *Lider vegn Shpanye* (Moscow: Farlag "Emes," 1938), 3.

22 See Yosef Haim Yerushalmi, "In the Wake of the Spanish Expulsion," in *Zakhor: Jewish History and Jewish Memory* (Seattle: University of Washington Press, 1982), 53–75.

23 Yerushalmi, "In the Wake of the Spanish Expulsion," 59–60.

24 David Markish, personal correspondence, 2016.

25 Maurice Halbwachs, *On Collective Memory*, ed. and trans. Lewis A. Coser (Chicago, IL: University of Chicago Press, 1992).

26 Peretz Markish, *Di Kupe* (Kiev: "Kultur Lige," 1922). The poem was published twice – in 1921 and 1922.

27 My translation is based on David Roskies, *Against the Apocalypse: Responses to Catastrophe in Modern Jewish Culture* (Syracuse, NY: Syracuse University Press, 1984), 100.

28 Peretz Markish, *Lider vegn Shpanye*, 7.

29 Maurice Halbwachs, *The Collective Memory* (New York: Harper & Row, 1980), 52.

30 Harriet Murav has observed the similarity between Markish's 1921 "Di Kupe" and his depiction of the spread of typhus in his 1929 "Brothers." Harriet Murav, *Music from a Speeding Train: Jewish Literature in Post-Revolution Russia* (Stanford, CA: Stanford University Press, 2011), 33.

31 Walter Benjamin, *Illuminations*, trans. Harry Zohn (New York: Schocken, 1968), 257. For a good discussion of Benjamin's approach to Marxism, see Michael Lowy, *Fire Alarm: Reading Walter Benjamin's 'On the Concept of History'* (Brooklyn: Verso, 2016).

32 David Shneer, "Rivers of Blood: Peretz Markish, the Holocaust, and Jewish Vengeance," in *Peretz Markish: A Captive of the Dawn*, ed. Joseph Sherman, Gennady Estraikh, Jordan Finkin, and David Shneer (Cambridge: Legenda, 2011), 139–56, 142.

33 Sergei Narovchatov, "Peretz Markish," in Peretz Markish, *Stikhotvoreniia i poemy* (Leningrad: Sovetskii pisatel', 1969), 29.

34 David Lederman writes, for example, that it was forbidden in the Soviet Union to play anti-Nazi repertoire following the Hitler-Stalin pact. See Lederman, *Fun yener zayt forgang* (Buenos-Ayres: Tsentral-farband fun Poylishe yidn in Argentine, 1960), 101–2. One of Markish's earliest poems about the Second World War, "The Dancer from the Ghetto," remained unpublished until after the war due to censorship. See Esther Markish, *The Long Return* (New York: Ballantine Books, 1978), 102–3.

35 Harriet Murav has written of Markish's Second World War works: "Perets Markish's poem 'Ho Lakhmo' (The bread of affliction) and his epic *Milkhome* (War) all respond to the killings of Jews." Murav, *Music from a Speeding Train*, 154.

36 As an example, Estraikh cites the observation of Markish's fictionalized portrayal of the Vilna poet Hirsh Glik in the play *Ghetto Uprising* that the ghetto fighters "recite

'Sh'ma Yisroel', 'Hear, O Israel' (rather than, say, the much more conventional 'For Motherland, for Stalin!') as part of their affirmation of faith upon dying." Cited in Gennady Estraikh, "Anti-Nazi Rebellion in Peretz Markish's Drama and Prose," in Sherman et al., *A Captive of the Dawn*, 172–85, 177.

37 Lisa Kirschenbaum, *International Communism and the Spanish Civil War* (Cambridge: Cambridge University Press, 2015), 185.

38 Karl Schlögel, *Moscow 1937*, trans. Rodney Livingstone (Cambridge: Polity Press, 2013), 95.

39 Esther Markish, *The Long Return*, 84–5.

40 Peretz Markish, *Lider vegn Shpanye*, 4.

41 Estraikh sees the Spain cycle, along with Markish's 1935 *Dem balegufs toyt* (*The Kulak's Death*) and his 1940 *Poeme vegn Stalinen* (*Poem about Stalin*), as evidence of "Markish's readiness to be in effect an amanuensis for the regime." Gennady Estraikh, "Anti-Nazi Rebellion," 170. Including the Spain cycle in this list of Stalinist poems, however, denies its place in the continuity of Markish's anti-fascist writings.

42 Sergei Narovchatov, "Peretz Markish," in Peretz Markish, *Stikhotvoreniia i poemy* (Leningrad: Sovetskii pisatel', 1969), 27.

43 Peretz Markish, *Lider vegn Shpanye*, 6.

44 Ibid.

45 Aaron Kurtz, "Kol Nidre," in *"No Pasarán": Lider, Balades un Poemes fun Shapnishn Folk in zayn Kamf kegn Fashizm* [*"No Pasarán": Songs, Ballads, and Poems of the Spanish People in Their Struggle against Fascism*] (New York: Yiddish Cooperative Book League of the Jewish Section of the International Workers Order, 1938), 56. (Hereafter, this book will be referred to as *NP!*)

46 Kurtz, "Kol Nidre," *NP!*, 56.

47 The first auto-da-fé is said to have taken place in 1481, leading to a mass exodus of Jews even before the expulsion in 1492. See Manuel Da Costa Fontes, *The Art of Subversion in Inquisitorial Spain: Rojas and Delicado* (West Lafayette, IN: Purdue University Press, 2005) 39.

48 Kurtz, "Kol Nidre," *NP!*, 58.

49 Kurtz, "Yosl," *NP!*, 73.

50 Kurtz, "Di letste levaya," *NP!*, 92.

51 Adina Cimet, *Ashkenazi Jews in Mexico* (Albany, NY: SUNY Press, 1997), 79.

52 Adam Hochschild, *Spain in Our Hearts: Americans in the Spanish Civil War, 1936–1939* (Boston: Houghton Mifflin Harcourt, 2017), 45.

53 Cimet, *Ashkenazi Jews in Mexico*, 80.

54 Jacobo Glantz, *Fonen in blut* (Mexico City: "Gezbir," 1936), 18.

55 Ibid., 7.

56 Todd Presner, *Muscular Judaism: The Jewish Body and the Politics of Regeneration* (Abingdon, UK: Routledge Jewish Studies Series, 304), 4.

57 Esther Shumyatsher, "Ikh bin a yid," in *Ale tog: Lider un poemes* (New York: Erd un heym, 1939), 109.

58 Paul Preston, *The Spanish Holocaust: Inquisition and Extermination in Twentieth-Century Spain* (New York: W.W. Norton & Co., 2012), 10.

59 Epstein, *Pages from the Colorful Life*, 123.

60 Glantz, *Fonen in blut*, 18.

61 Kurtz's seamless shift from trauma to politics falls into the trappings of what LaCapra has identified as "competitive victimology." Dominick LaCapra, *Writing History, Writing Trauma* (Baltimore, MD: John Hopkins University Press, 2014), 217.

62 Glantz, *Fonen in blut*, 17.

63 For a good discussion of Baron and the "lachrymose conception" of history, see Robert Liberles, *Salo Wittmayer Baron: Architect of Jewish History* (New York: New York University Press, 1995), 338–59.

64 Glantz, *Fonen in blut*, 52.

65 Steven S. Lee, *The Ethnic Avant-Garde: Minority Cultures and World Revolution* (New York: Columbia University Press, 2015), 84. For his definition of "factography," Lee cites Sergei Tret'iakov, "Happy New Year! Happy *New Left!*" in *Russian Futurism through Its Manifestoes: 1912–1928*, trans. and ed. Anna Lawton and Herbert Eagle (Ithaca, NY: Cornell University Press, 1988), 267.

66 Glantz, *Fonen in blut*, 52.

67 Cited in Tabea Alexa Linhard, *Fearless Women in the Mexican Revolution and the Spanish Civil War* (Columbia: University of Missouri Press, 2005), 125.

68 Edward Said, *Orientalism* (New York: Vintage Books, 1974), 207.

69 Glantz, *Fonen in blut*, 26.

70 Igal Halfin, *From Darkness to Light: Class, Consciousness, and Salvation in Revolutionary Russia* (Pittsburgh, PA: University of Pittsburgh Press, 2000), 40.

71 Glantz, *Fonen in blut*, 27.

72 Seth Wolitz has discussed Markish's three long poems of the early 1920s, a triptych comprised of *Volin* (*Volhynia*) as the past, *Di kupe* (*The Mound*) as the present, and *Radyo* (*Radio*) as the future. Seth Wolitz, "Markish's *Radyo* (1922): Yiddish Modernism as Agitprop," in Seth Wolitz, *Yiddish Modernism: Studies in Twentieth-Century Eastern European Jewish Culture* (Bloomington, IN: Slavica Publishers, 2014), 253–64, esp. 255.

73 Ibid., 253–64; quote at 263.

74 Peretz Markish, *Lider vegn Shpanye*, 9–10.

75 Peretz Markish, "Toreador," in *Lider vegn Shpanye*, 28.

76 Ibid., 29.

77 Hochschild, *Spain in Our Hearts*, 85.

78 Ibid., 205.

79 Aaron Glants-Leyeles, "Shpanishe balade," in *Opklayb Lider Poemes Drames* (New York: Congress for Jewish Culture, 1968), 170.

80 Translation: Aaron Kramer, *A Century of Yiddish Poetry* (Cranbury, NJ: Cornwall Books, 1989), 151.

81 A L-s (Aaron Glants-Leyeles), "Oyfn Spanishn front," in *Inzikh*, no. 36 (June 1937): 191.

82 In a review of the fifteenth anniversary issue of the *Freiheit*, the editors of the Intro-spectivist journal *Inzikh*, which had published some of Kurtz's early experimental poems, accuse Kurtz of "conformism and Stalinist inertia." Citing Kurtz's open appreciation of Stalin, the *Inzikh* editors write, of Kurtz, that "when the soul must answer to politics, to the Party-Cheka – this is already a great danger, death in the literal sense of the word, for the tiniest spark of artistry." "Reflektsies: Signal – epitaf oyf a bankrot," *Inzikh*, no. 34 (April 1937): 126.

83 Kurtz, "Karmensita," *NP!*, 65.

84 Bertolt Brecht, *Die Gewehre der Frau Carrar: Text, Auffuhrung, Anmerkungen* (Dresden: Verlag der Kunst, 1952).

85 Kurtz, "Andaluzier landshaft," *NP!*, 40.

86 Aaron Kurtz, "Andalusian Landscape," trans. Amelia Glaser, in *Proletpen: America's Rebel Yiddish Poets*, ed. Amelia Glaser and David Weintraub, trans. Amelia Glaser (Madison: University of Wisconsin Press, 2005), 325. (Translation has been edited.)

87 Kurtz, Author's note, *NP!*, 3.

88 See, for example, Muriel Rukeyser, "Mediterranean: The Signs and Sounds of the First Days of the Spanish War Stamp on the Poet's Mind More Than a Visual-Aural Impression," *The New Masses*, 14 September 1937, 18–20; esp. 18. Rukeyser was evacuated from Spain, where she had been reporting on the 1936 anti-fascist Olympics, and the poem is written in the form of a report from one of the first Loyalists.

89 For examples of letter-poems on Scottsboro, see Amelia Glaser, "From Jewish Jesus to Black Christ: Race Violence in Leftist Yiddish Poetry," *Studies in American Jewish Literature*, 34, no. 1 (2015): 44–69.

90 Kurtz, "A briv fun a kranknshvester," *NP!*, 36.

91 Langston Hughes, "Letter from Spain," in *The Collected Poems of Langston Hughes*, ed. Arnold Rampersad (New York: Vintage Classics, 1994), 201–2.

92 Hughes later described visiting field hospitals where he met dark-skinned Moroccans fighting in Franco's army. Arnold Rampersad notes this detail in *Collected Poems of Langston Hughes*, 647n201.

93 Kurtz, "A briv fun a kranknshvester," *NP!*, 36.

94 Glantz, *Fonen in Blut*, 33.

95 Nelson, *The Wound and the Dream*, 12.

96 Kurtz, "Der orkester," *NP!*, 59.

97 Aaron Kurtz, "Yunyon Skver," *Plakatn* (New York: Yidish lebn, 1927), 10–19, 10.

98 L. Khanukov, "Aaron Kurtz: Dikhter fun kreftikn vort," *Freiheit*, 20 March 1938, 3.

99 Anthony Easthope, *Poetry as Discourse* (New York: Routledge, 1983), 15. Easthope cites Roman Jacobson, "The Dominant," in *Readings in Russian Poetics*, ed. L. Matejka and K. Pomorska (Cambridge, MA: MIT Press, 1960), 371.

100 Hannah Arendt, *Totalitarianism, Part Three of the Origins of Totalitarianism* (Orlando: Houghton, Mifflin, Harcourt, 1968), 62.

101 Schlögel, *Moscow 1937*, 101. A purge of Trotskyites took place in Spain as well as in the Soviet Union. See Kirschenbaum, *International Communism and the Spanish Civil War*, 138.

102 Nelson, *The Wound and the Dream*, 30–1.

103 Glantz, *Fonen in Blut*, 5.

104 Ibid., 44.

105 Anthony Beevor, *The Battle for Spain: The Spanish Civil War 1936–1939* (New York: Penguin, 2006), 150.

106 Glantz, *Fonen in blut*, 47.

107 According to a description of winter campaign dress during the Spanish Civil War, "the *capote-manta*, a large, loose cape for winter, was used very widely by both Republicans and Nationalists." See Patrick Turnbull, *The Spanish Civil War, 1936–39* (Oxford: Osprey, 1978), 32–3.

108 Glantz, *Fonen in blut*, 49.

109 Peretz Markish, "Kommandir Diestro," in *Lider vegn Shpanye*, 36. The Vasilyev Brothers' immensely popular 1934 film *Chapaev* was screened across Spain. Ilya Ehrenburg remarks that the Spanish anarchists were so upset by the death of the hero that the committee began cutting the end of the film: "They said: 'What's the point of fighting if the best men get killed?'" See Ilya Ehrenburg, *Memoirs 1921–1941*, trans. Tatania Shebunina in collaboration with Yvonne Kapp (Cleveland, OH: The World Publishing Company, 1964), 370. As Lisa Kirschenbaum has put it, "whereas in Spain Chapaev provided a model of Bolshevik masculinity, in the Soviet Union, coverage of the Spanish civil war offered influential and to some degree competing models of militarized and maternal communist womanhood." Kirschenbaum, *International Communism and the Spanish Civil War*, 127.

110 Peretz Markish, "Kommandir Diestro," *Lider vegn Shpanye*, 37. Markish began publishing his Spain poems in journals in 1936. See, for example, "Shpanye," in *Naye folkstsaytung*, 28 November 1936, 4.

111 Ehrenburg, *Memoirs 1921–1941*, 336.

112 See, for example, Estraikh, "Anti-Nazi Rebellion," 168–81; and Murav, *Music from a Speeding Train*, in particular chapter five: "*Yeder zeyger a yortsayt*: The Past as Memory in Postwar Literature."

113 An excerpt of the novel was published in *Yidishe kultur*. Peretz Markish, "In der varshever geto," *Yidishe kultur*, no. 4 (1957): 2.

114 Muriel Rukeyser, *Savage Coast* (New York: The Feminist Press, 2013), 7.

115 Allison Schachter has written of Molodowsky that "her Yiddish poems in the 1930s had a decidedly brash style, referencing the Spanish Civil War and the Popular Front alongside New York City skyscrapers and Eastern European landscapes." Schachter, *Diasporic Modernisms*, 178.

Chapter Ten

"Beaten, but Unbeatable": On Langston Hughes's Black Leninism

JONATHAN FLATLEY
Wayne State University

When one feels subject to a controlling, unfriendly, and abusive power, as so many people in the United States and around the world do now, what is to be done? Recognized genres of political activity – such as voting or marching in the streets – can seem radically inadequate as a response to a government's manifold and murderous hostility towards its people.[1] In the search for forms of collective resistance, it can be useful to examine those moments in the past when otherwise discouraged, cynical, or alienated people have come together in solidarity to form energetic, hopeful, and demanding collectives, which then engage in transformative political action. How did they produce this way of being with each other in the world? What practices or genres helped to bring a new mood into being? In the effort to understand how such groups and such moods are made, the black radical tradition offers a formidable set of lessons, since that tradition is constituted by the ongoing need to invent or improvise genres for opposing and surviving white supremacy. An examination of this tradition reminds us first of all that, in order to come together in solidarity, there needs to be a way for a collective to become aware of itself as a collective and to find a way of being together.

This task, we might remember, was also the task that Vladimir Lenin assigned to the revolutionary party whose function, he argued in *What Is to Be Done?*, is to represent the revolutionary class to itself so that it can move from being a class "in itself" (a group that shares interests but whose members are not aware of being a group) to a class "for itself," a self-conscious group ready to act in solidarity.[2] Lenin's pursuit of this project by way of the revolutionary party, along with his particular interest in the liberation of black people, meant that, as Robin Kelley put it, for black radicals looking for alternatives to an often racist American socialist movement, "Lenin turned out to be something of a friend."[3]

While Langston Hughes did not start writing poems about Lenin until the 1930s, he had long been interested in an anti-racist, globally minded social-ism.[4] From the very beginning of his career as writer, he was centrally engaged with the political and poetic problem of representing a black collectivity and representing it first of all to itself rather than to a white or "general" public. As he explained in *I Wonder as I Wander*, "I wrote about Negroes, and primarily for Negroes."[5] In so doing, Hughes experimented with what poetry is and what it can do, as he searched for genres to represent black people to black people as a group in a way that might create and sustain optimism about fighting white supremacy and the poverty it created. In what Fred Moten might call the ongoing "improvisational discovery" of his black studies,[6] Hughes confronted basic questions about the very possibility of poetry and politics, and affirmed the necessity of a political poetry and a poetic politics. Hughes looked for ways to give voice to "whole groups of people's problems" by making poetry that defied what people expected of poetry, borrowing from the blues and other "low-down" forms, and then, later, by creating a blues-inflected black communist voice, a Leninist blues.[7] Throughout it all, despite the failures and the mishaps and the relentlessness of the violence and humiliations of a white supremacist capitalism, Hughes never gave up on finding ways to "think about feeling good, to make disparate aspects of feeling good thinkable," as Michael Snediker puts it.[8] Hughes's optimism was, in this sense, a queer optimism, one that was not based on a belief in progress or other given normative modes of attachment to the world like the family, but on ways of finding, creating, and valuing moments of group joy in the present, even if it was the modest, ambivalent joy of laughing to keep from crying.

"What Kind of Poem"

Hughes began his career with the publication of "The Negro Speaks of Rivers," which charts an itinerary for the speaker ("the Negro" of the title) by rivers in Southwest Asia, Africa, and North America. Here, already, we can see Hughes's sense of "blackness as an object of knowledge beyond the nation-state," to borrow from Brent Edwards.[9] When that poem was published in 1921 (when Hughes was nineteen) in *The Crisis*, edited by W.E.B. Du Bois (to whom Hughes's poem was dedicated), Du Bois had already made an influential case for the importance, for the black writer, of representing a black collectivity. Indeed, such a representation was one of the chief achievements of Du Bois's *The Souls of Black Folk* (1903), where the figure of the veil and the concept of double consciousness provided the basis for a theory of black feeling and experience in the white supremacist United States. In so doing, even though the book was apparently addressed to a white, "general" readership, Du Bois's book of "sketches and essays" seems to have provided for many African American readers what one critic described as the "special exhilarating feeling any reader gets when an author names things that the reader has felt very deeply but could not articulate."[10] Du Bois articulated African American feelings not only in the sense of putting them into language but also in the connective sense stressed by Stuart Hall.[11] He created a constellation of relations, linking the critical historical analysis of social, economic, and political structures with phenomenologically rich, personal accounts of the emotional effects of being a black person in the United States, allowing his readers to recognize their own subjectivities as examples of broader social formations and thus also to see their commonality with others.[12] In so doing, Du Bois turned the experience of "being a problem" from a despair-inducing one into a way to feel connected to other persons, indeed to see that one is part of a collectivity that could engage in a potentially victorious political struggle. Not only did Du Bois provide a vocabulary that allowed for "black folk" to be aware of themselves as a group formed by a set of shared structures of feelings and experiences – not skin or blood but "soul." He also made a case for the significance of the sorrow songs – the "articulate message of the slave to the world" – as a collectively composed, performed, and experienced musical form that dwells on loss and disappointment but does so in a form which returns insistently to the promise of justice and the righteous overthrow of an oppressive order. Thus, in *Souls*, the problem of collective self-representation and resistance is presented as a political and aesthetic problem, one that is most compellingly addressed by black music.

Furthermore, Du Bois showed that the creation of a collective black consciousness which might lead to collective action is not only a question of reasoned persuasion, but of shifting a collective mood. By "mood" here, I mean the overall atmosphere in or through which thinking, feeling, and acting occurs, a way of "being with" and "being in" the world that shapes our thoughts, our will, and our particular affective attachments to particular objects.[13] A concept I borrow from Heidegger, *Stimmung* may also be rendered as attunement. As what shapes our apprehension of the world prior to cognition and volition, a mood directs our attention and makes it possible to care about something. In so doing, the shifting attunements of mood constitute one basic way that "bodies are continuously busy judging the environments and responding to the atmospheres in which they find themselves," as Lauren Berlant puts it.[14] Yet, mood in Du Bois, as in Heidegger, is not a psychological concept, not some interior condition that reaches out to colour the world. Even as we "feel" them on a subjective, emotional level, moods belong to a shared, public world.[15] They are, in essence, ways of being "with," fundamentally collective. Moods arise from and also are the way we encounter the historical situation into which we have been "thrown" or "set." We live in the moods that are already in the world, shared by others, and specific to our historical moment. Inasmuch as moods are a fundamental mode of being, we are never not in a mood. Moods do, however, shift and change by way of "counter-moods." But one cannot simply decide to be in another mood. One needs techniques and practices to bring counter-moods into being.

If the souls of black folk are shaped by a deep disappointment, by a necessary relation to loss, as Du Bois suggested – losses produced by the murderous hostility to black life, but also by the lack of economic and political opportunity, and the social and personal rejections that exclude black persons from putatively common but in fact "white only" spaces of commerce, sociality, conviviality, and citizenship – then the task of the black writer is to find a way to make those losses a locus for the awakening of a counter-mood shaped by collective self-awareness and political striving instead of depression or despair. Black music, the sorrow songs in particular, are a crucial practice for making this shift happen. If all (black) art must be propaganda so long as Jim Crow is the law of the land, as Du Bois memorably asserted, then the propagandistic task requires compelling recognition from the nation by way of "the art of the black folk" so that they will be treated as fully and equally human.[16] But it also involves attuning a black collectivity to its own power as a collective, transforming what might otherwise be individual experiences of resentment and alienation into a common, powerful, political determination. This transformation was one of the key continuing effects achieved by *The Souls of Black Folk*, and it was a project that Hughes energetically embraced.

But, unlike Du Bois who in *Souls* at least was preoccupied (though by no means exclusively) with the black intellectual and the "advance guard," Hughes aimed to address and represent the "the low-down folks, the so-called common element."[17] Having such an audience in mind directly affected how he thought about poetic form, as he explained later in his essay "My Adventures as a Social Poet" (1947), where he offered a pointed critique of the "beauty and lyricism" one finds in poetry about "love, roses and moonlight, sunsets and snow."[18] That kind of poetry is "really related to another world, to ivory towers, to your head in the clouds, feet floating off the earth." The experience of culture as something that separates itself out from and rises above the suffering and injustice of everyday life could, in principle, be attractive to one who was "born poor – and also colored – in Missouri."[19] But the fact is, Hughes noted: "Try as I might to float off into the clouds, poverty and Jim Crow would grab me by the heels, and right back on earth I would land." Hughes could not dwell in that space of "autonomous" art, which is not just an imaginative or spiritual place but also a material and institutional one. The "quiet life" of other poets can only be lived in places where one has a room of one's own and the time and freedom to write.

"Beauty and lyricism" are not just unattainable for Hughes; they are also complicit in the maintenance of poverty and white supremacy. To spend one's efforts trying to dwell in that space of spiritual or imaginative freedom is not just a "rejection of a bad historical form of existence, but also its exoneration," as Herbert Marcuse argued in 1937.[20] It encourages one to ignore the problems that may have made beauty attractive in the first place, even though those problems – Jim Crow and poverty – will not disappear on their own. Moreover, the scene of natural beauty is in no way neutral or universally available. "Almost all the prettiest roses I have seen have been in rich white people's yards – not in mine," Hughes wrote. Like the leafy suburban streets that viewers see at the beginning of Jordan Peele's 2017 film *Get Out*, such spaces are hostile to black life. Hughes reminded his readers that "sometimes in the moonlight my brothers see a fiery cross and a circle of Klansmen's hoods. Sometimes in the moonlight a dark body swings from a lynching tree – but for his funeral there are no roses." Poems about the lyrical experience of the beauty of moonlight therefore are at the same time documents of barbarism, affirmations of the white supremacist order of things.

But, unlike the Dadaists and Surrealists who had a similar suspicion of beauty and lyricism as fundamentally compensatory and thus affirmative of the current order of things, Hughes did not give up on poetry as such; he thought that poetry could be a genre for bringing people together to oppose the conjunction of poverty and white supremacy. Thus, in "Call to Creation" (1930), he urged "Futile beauty-makers –/ Work for a while with the pattern-breakers!" In an effort to "march with the new-world-makers," Hughes aimed to write "a new song."

How exactly one should march with the new-world-makers and address the experiences of poor, oppressed, and exploited non-white workers of the world was not exactly clear, however. The absence of a model for this project is directly addressed by Hughes's early (1924) short poem "Johannesburg Mines."

> In the Johannesburg mines
> There are 240,000
> Native Africans working.
> What kind of poem
> Would you
> make out of that?
> 240,000 natives
> working in the
> Johannesburg mines.

The poem was first published in 1925 in the leftist literary magazine *The Messenger*, which was edited by prominent black socialist A. Philip Randolph. Then, in 1928, it appeared, in a slightly different version, in *The Crisis*, the monthly journal of the National Association for the Advancement of Colored People (NAACP) edited by Du Bois, whose literary editor was Jessie Fauset.[21] Later, another slightly different version appeared in *Good Morning Revolution*, which seems to be based on a typescript in Hughes's papers (at the Beinecke Library), to which I will return later.

The poem begins with an apparently neutral assertion: "In the Johannesburg mines/ There are 240,000/ Native Africans working." The term "native" (a term in wide journalistic usage at the time) indicates, by way of negation, the foreign, colonial presence.[22] At the same time (within a poem published by an African American poet in a socialist journal), the term invites a comparison between native African workers in the Johannesburg mines – famous for the gold found there – and black workers in the United States, who live in a similarly racist society but are exiled rather than native Africans.[23] What kind of a common existence might this group of native and non-native – diasporic – Africans constitute?

The poem's first lines represent this group of "natives" primarily with the number 240,000. The specific (if probably not precise) number seems less at home in a poem than in a newspaper or magazine article about the South African economy and labour conditions. It is the kind of number that would be of interest to investors, perhaps, and also to the Comintern and the Communist Party of South Africa (CPSA), which, when Hughes wrote this poem in 1924, had been directed by the Comintern to shift its emphasis from the white workers who had sought to maintain a hierarchical colour line in the mines towards black workers, eventually adopting a "native" republican anti-imperialist position.[24] These 240,000 workers constitute the class that could lead a revolution, and, in this sense, the number – the magnitude – is an indication of potential force, akin in significance to the number of troops massing at a border.

But the number is also essentially abstract; its numerals, which do not signify like letters, seem oddly neutral amidst the enjambed lines promising a lyric voice and poetic figuration. In focusing on the number, Hughes seems to challenge his readers to ask how one could represent or imagine in any concrete or affectively powerful way this multitude of workers. The problem concerns not only the difficulty of representing 240,000 anything, but the question of how this particular collectivity – working underground, in mines, out of sight, and across the ocean – might be represented. And, if this still relatively small number is beyond concrete imagining, the representational problem is further complicated when we think about how this figure of 240,000 workers is itself a metonym of even greater numbers of miners and other African workers, native and exiled, and indeed of the "workers of the world," whom Marx and Engels exhorted to unite.[25]

Thus, when Hughes asks, in the centre of the poem, what kind of a poem you would "make out of that," he seems to be asking not only how one represents this collectivity of 240,000 "Native Africans working" but also how one represents the collectivities produced by a transnational, imperial, racial capitalism. In this, Hughes offers a distinct response to what Fredric Jameson argued was a fundamental representational problem of modernism and one of the chief motives for its formal innovations: the impossibility of representing, from the

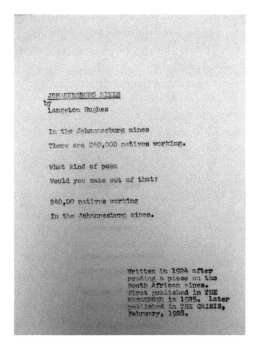

10.1 Langston Hughes, "Johannesburg Mines" (typescript). Courtesy of Random House. From the Langston Hughes Papers, James Weldon Johnson Collection in the Yale Collection of American Literature, Beinecke Rare Book and Manuscript Library.

point of view of life in the metropole, the realities of the colonies, which were the conditions of possibility for that lifeworld but also constitutively absent from it.[26] These native workers, whose labour brings gold, the very "standard" of value, out of the earth, are not only necessary to life in London or New York but also to the basic operations of imperial capital as such. Yet, they are just as foundationally excluded, erased even, from the worlds that this capital animates.

In the abovementioned typescript of the poem, Hughes wrote that the poem was "written in 1924 after reading a piece on the South African mines (figure 10.1)."[27]

As Hughes presents it, a reading experience here motivates the writing of this poem, which itself records the sense of "not knowing" how to respond to the existence of these workers and their oppression. In *What Is to Be Done?* Lenin had emphasized that reading newspaper stories about the experiences of similarly abused and oppressed persons could spark a feeling of revolutionary solidarity and a radical shift in the political mood of the reader.[28] By contrast, Hughes describes the experience of reading the news and feeling "frustrated" by the absence of available models for intervening, for being in solidarity, for doing something in response. Without such a model or genre (in Berlant's sense), without a collective mood already in circulation to shift into, one may experience a sense of being affected and wanting to act but not knowing how. As we know, this frustration is not an outdated feeling.

Hughes's question – "What kind of poem would you make out of that?" – is not only ironic and rhetorical. It is a real poetic and political problem centring on the question of "poetry" and "voice": through what form could these 240,000 workers acquire a voice? Can others – a poet living on another continent, for instance – help such a group acquire a voice? In other words, Hughes seems to be asking: "Can the subaltern speak?"

In her influential essay, Gayatri Spivak emphasizes the distinction between two senses of "representation" that may be easily conflated – "representation as 'speaking for,' as in politics, and representation as 're-presentation,' as in art or philosophy."[29] Where English has one word, German has two: *vertreten* ("to represent" in the first, political sense of a proxy or "representative") and *darstellen* (to "re-present" in the second, aesthetic or tropological sense). Spivak argues that an examination of the complex interaction between these distinct senses of representation is of direct relevance to the question of political organization and revolution, of how a class in itself can become a class for itself.[30] Spivak returns to the classic formulation of the problem in *The Eighteenth Brumaire*, where Marx lamented that, while a class (in this case the small peasants) may be formed by groups of persons who live in similar conditions and share a set of economic interests – interests opposed to those of other groups from whom they are isolated – these persons may nonetheless have no way of communicating among themselves and representing (in the *vertreten* sense) themselves in the political process. In such cases, as Marx famously remarks, "they cannot represent themselves, they must be represented."[31]

Spivak draws attention to the ways that the two different senses of "represent," while distinct, tend towards intertwining. For instance, it may be because the peasants have no way to represent themselves to themselves (in the *darstellen* sense) – they do not have a picture of themselves as a group – that they cannot come together to speak for themselves in the political arena. In such a situation, they may, as Marx explains, be especially susceptible to manipulation, allowing themselves to be spoken for by a political figure who can provide a narrative or image of their interests and promise to provide for them. ("I see and understand your problems, and I alone can fix them.") On the one hand, Spivak, following Marx, draws attention to this dangerous moment where the "hero" or "leader" may step into this gap between the class in itself and the class for itself as a representative of the class. She is particularly attentive – as is Hughes – of the way that "speaking for" somebody else can effectively silence them. But, on the other hand, Spivak also cautions us not to treat "the oppressed" as if they somehow have an innate capacity to "speak for themselves" outside the thickets of representation.[32] As I noted, Lenin proposes to address this problem with the revolutionary party, which would represent (in the *darstellen* sense, in a Party newspaper first of all) the working class to itself in a way that brings the class into the activities of representation (in the *vertreten* sense), allowing it to recognize itself as a class with its own capacity for representing itself and acting in the political sphere.

"Johannesburg Mines" seems to ask if poetry might function like a Leninist party. How is it possible to represent (*darstellen*) a collective in a poem without "speaking for" it, and thereby replacing or silencing it, but also without presenting it as somehow not needing representation in both the political and aesthetic senses? Hughes's poem certainly makes no effort to speak for the "natives working" nor to give a picture of the workers or their experience. At first, this absence appears to answer the poem's question – "What kind of poem would you make out of that?" – by saying that there is no poem to be "made out of that," except for one that is self-ironizingly about that impossibility itself.

But, in a way that suits the complexity of the problem here, the poem does have a notable "poetic" device, a chiasmus that may itself give an "image" of the workers, even as it represents the problem of representation itself. You can see that the poem's final sentence reverses the order of the clauses in the first (with only "there are" subtracted).[33]

In the Johannesburg mines	There are 240,000 natives working
X
240,000 natives working	in the Johannesburg mines

The descent into the middle of the poem's chiasmus, where the question about making a poem "out of that" is posed, is the only moment where the poem comes out of the mines. It is also where the poem's central "poetic" device is mined, since it is the question at the poem's centre that serves as the pivot leading to the reversal of the poem's opening assertion. This reversal, however, is unlike Frederick Douglass's famous statement, "You have seen how a man was made a slave; you shall see how a slave was made a man," where the meaning is reversed along with the words.[34] The chiasmus in Hughes's poem reverses the order of the clauses in the sentence without changing its meaning. The reversal is strictly formal. The speaker and the reader begin and end in the mines, reproducing for the reader (in miniature) the repetitive, never-ending nature of the work and the enclosed quality of the situation structuring it. In this way, the chiasmus that is the poem's central poetic device points to a collectivity of black workers and their situation while emphasizing the poem's failure to do anything to change that situation.

Yet, at the same time, by highlighting an unaccomplished reversal, the poem raises the possibility of a successful one. This poem may be powerless to reverse the situation of the multitude of workers whose existence it points to from across the Atlantic Ocean, but that powerlessness itself also indicates the power that lies elsewhere – in the workers (and readers) themselves. What is needed, the poem suggests, is not a poem to render the experience of the workers movingly compelling, sympathetic, or (worse yet) beautiful, but some form of representation (*darstellen*) that would allow the "natives working" to represent (*vertreten*) themselves in the political struggle for liberation in their own name.

In other words, how can a writer represent that group constituted by racial and economic oppression so that its members are empowered, so that they may themselves speak and act? Hughes stayed alert to the poetic and political complexities of any attempt to represent, to speak of or speak for a group of oppressed persons, but he remained committed to the project of doing so. Hughes found a resource for this project in the form and feeling of the blues.

"Black, Beaten, but Unbeatable Throats"

In Langston Hughes's first volume of poetry, *The Weary Blues* (1926), the title poem's speaker sees and hears the blues being sung, and describes and cites the "Weary Blues" he hears. That poem presents the blues as a form and a feeling, and considers its reception. Yet, even as the poem's speaker imitates the blues singer and appears to become more intimately connected to him as the poem moves on, the difference between the poem's speaker and the blues singer remains one of the poem's chief topics, as if Hughes is trying to work through what relation he as a poet wants to have to the blues.[35] But, in his second book, *Fine Clothes to the Jews* (1927), Hughes eliminates the mediating frame of a speaker encountering the blues singer; instead, as Hughes explained in the preface to the volume, the first eight and last nine poems of the book are themselves "written after the manner of the Negro folk-songs known as *Blues*." These poems follow the "strict poetic pattern" of the blues: "one long line repeated and a third line to rhyme with the first two. Sometimes the second line in repetition is slightly changed and sometimes, but very seldom, it is omitted."[36] In other words, Hughes was not just borrowing from the blues; he was composing them and bringing them under the aegis of "poetry."

Even if they did not immediately appear to be so, these poems were "social poems," Hughes later wrote, in the sense that "they were about people's problems – whole groups of people's problems."[37] The poems represent a collective by way of single voices that stand in for a broader group. "The *I* pictured in many of my blues poems," Hughes wrote, "is the poor and uneducated negro of the south – and not myself who grew up in Kansas."[38] In his use of this "I," Hughes expands upon the "I" in poems such as "The Negro Speaks of Rivers" (among other early poems), where his "I" represents a global, diasporic "Negro" people brought together by and through a long history, figured by the rivers "known" by the "I" of the poem. He also borrows from Whitman's "I," about which Hughes wrote: "One of the greatest 'I' poets of all time, Whitman's 'I' is not the 'I' of the introspective versifiers who write always and only about themselves. Rather it is the cosmic 'I' of all peoples who seek freedom, decency, and dignity, friendship and equality between individuals and races all over the world."[39]

If Whitman's is a cosmic "I," Hughes's is "low-down;" he seeks to represent the specificity of a collectivity comprised of the black, the poor, and the queer, as Martin Ponce, Shane Vogel, and Sam See have argued.[40] How can the lyric "I" represent that low-down existence? Throughout his career, Hughes constantly played with the nature and function of his speaker, trying to find means to indicate the ways in which this "I" was also necessarily situated, thrown into various situations where agency was limited, situations that had to be survived or escaped. At the same time, he wanted this "I" to indicate the black group of which this single subjectivity is a part, the others that enable this "I" to speak.

The distinct "I" of the blues is one of several resources Hughes found in the "old-time basic anonymous 12-bar, 3-line lyric, deep South blues that nobody knows who made up, nobody knows who added what line where."[41] As Hughes indicates here, the form of the blues brings with it a history of the voices that have made the blues up; the blues voice contains multitudes. Notably (even scandalously) capacious in terms of the particular experiences it could give voice to, there are, as Hughes notes, many blues: family blues, loveless blues, left-lonesome blues, broke-and-hungry blues, and desperate going-to-the-river blues. The experiences of women speaking openly of sex and desire, in particular, are central to the blues; indeed, when Hughes wrote *Fine Clothes*, the blues had been made famous by female singers like Ma Rainey and Bessie Smith. And Hughes's blues poems feature a female voice more often than not.[42] Not infrequently, the blues are related to pleasures and troubles with same sex objects of love or gender non-conformity. As Eric Garber argued, the blues represented gay and lesbian sexual practices and feelings as "a natural part of life."[43] As we know, the collective composition and multitudinous experiences given voice within the form were met with a broad, popular reception. How did Hughes understand their aesthetic force, their capacity to address and represent a black collectivity?

Hughes spoke to the particular aesthetic force of the blues in several places, including "Songs Called the Blues" (1941). There, Hughes explained that the blues spring from and give voice to the material reality of black poverty: they are "of the poor streets and back alleys of Memphis and Birmingham, Atlanta and Galveston, out of black, beaten, but unbeatable throats, from the strings of pawn-shop guitars, and the chords of pianos with no ivory on the keys."[44] The instruments that produce the sounds of the blues – the voice, the guitar, the piano – have been shaped by privation. The guitar has been pawned; the piano has lost its white keys; the throats are beaten. In becoming the blues, the voices from the "black, beaten" throats are shown to be "unbeatable."

It is worth taking a moment to reflect on this reversal (beaten – unbeatable) that occurs in the throats that sing the blues. Although one does not often think of a throat as "beaten," the word here seems to mean worn down, worn out, and weary: "overcome by hard work, exhausted" (as the *Oxford English Dictionary* defines it). More frequently, the word refers to the experience of being struck with repeated blows, as described in the Bible passage that Frederick Douglass said his master would recite when whipping his Aunt Hester: "He that knoweth his master's will, and doeth it not, shall be beaten with many stripes."[45] With this word, Hughes also references the violence inherent to white supremacy, a violence that did not cease with the abolition of chattel slavery.

But then, a rhythm may also be beaten on a drum or other instrument, as Hughes indicates in this same essay a few sentences later, noting that the blues are city songs "beating against the lonely walls of hall bed-rooms where you can't sleep at night" (213). This beating, making the walls sound with rhythm, is a protest against weariness, an effort to find rest and to populate a lonely space with reverberations. In that movement into sound, the meaning of "beat" changes, indicating now the rhythm of what Hughes elsewhere calls a "marching-on syncopation."[46]

Precisely to the extent that the throats that sing the blues belong to bodies that have survived being beaten and are still here, still singing and moaning, they have shown themselves to be unbeatable, undefeatable. They constitute a formidable power, one that poses a threat to racial capitalism, because these voices are made in bodies that know, have felt, and have survived the violence necessary to keep racial capitalism going.[47] In the blues, these voices are sharing that sense of unbeatability with others, providing a rallying point, a site where other voices can meet and find a new way of being together.

In the blues, togetherness comes into being at a moment of laughter. Although "the Blues are songs you sing alone" and the "mood of the Blues is almost always despondency," Hughes wrote, "when they are sung people laugh."[48] There is a fundamental disjuncture or reversal in the music between the mood or tone of the music and the way that the song affects its audiences.[49] How can we understand this reversal?

The conversion of feeling, the shift into a different mood, happens at the moment when the blues yoke together the feeling of depressive loneliness with the sense of sharing this feeling with others "like me," as in Hughes's "Misery":

Black gal like me,
Black gal like me
'S got to hear a blues
For her misery.

The blues "'ll ease ma misery" precisely inasmuch as they address an audience that shares the feeling. In that moment of feeling alike, the laughter – one that "keeps you company" – arrives. As Hughes put it years later in 1966, "humor is laughing at what you haven't got when you ought to have it," like money for rent, or a man to love you, or a home to return to. But, Hughes added, "of course, you laugh by proxy."[50] The singer of the blues thus does "represent" (in the *vertreten*, proxy sense noted by Spivak) the group of listeners, but not in order to then speak or act "for" them. Instead this representation changes the way the group exists with and for each other, because they are now experiencing a feeling in common with each other, by way of the singer. One laughs at the singer and their troubles because those troubles are yours too, as if the feelings need to be plural, need to find other feelings "like them," to know that somebody else knows the troubles I see.[51]

Thus, blues laughter is not a cathartic laughter so much as an ironizing, long historical perspective, "loud-mouthed" laughter "in the hands of Fate" (to borrow from Hughes's poem "Laughers").[52] It is a laughter that can see the ridiculousness of this misery, the humour in history's cunning, miserable ruses. As Sam See points out, this humour is like camp (in Esther Newton's understanding); it is about laughing at one's incongruous position instead of crying.[53] If not curative, blues laughter is nonetheless capable of producing a counter-mood, a shift into a different way of being attuned, because, in establishing a way of being with others who know what it is like to feel this way, it affirms a "love of life too precious to let it go."[54] It is joyous in the sense emphasized by Spinoza (and Gilles Deleuze following him) inasmuch as it increases what Spinoza calls the "power of acting or force of existing."[55] The blues increase this power in part by offering a way of being or becoming attuned to others in relation to a given historical problem – poverty, state racism – while still keeping this problem in view as a problem experienced in common. To borrow the title of Jonathan Scott's book, it is a "socialist joy."[56]

The sense of joining together with others who are "like me" that characterizes the aesthetic experience of the blues is amplified in *Fine Clothes to the Jew* by the very plurality of the lyrics themselves. Hughes's blues lyrics are a concrete presentation of a collection of distinct voices and distinct situations, a multitude of "black, beaten, but unbeatable" voices that come together in Hughes's collection of them. As Shane Vogel has noted, this collection also thereby creates what Ann Cvetkovich has called an "archive of feeling," an archive that attends to feelings and the situations that produce them and stands in a "queer (that is oblique and askew) relationship to official archives."[57]

What, we are invited to wonder, is the relationship of the poet to this archive of feelings, and how does it address an audience? From one perspective, as Brent Edwards has suggested, Hughes's blues look like transcriptions of songs heard by the poet, who is recording "an individual listener's affective connection to the music" as well as pointing to "the collectivity of listeners the music allows, the connections it fosters."[58] That such a practice was attractive to Hughes is indicated by the transcriptions of blues lyrics one can see in his papers. These lyrics are transcribed from records in his collection, which he seemed to have had the habit of cataloguing in sometimes elaborate lists. In fact, Hughes's affective connection was powerful enough that he brought his Victrola and some records – Bessie Smith, Louis Armstrong, and Ethel Waters – with him to the Soviet Union, which occasionally made his luggage a little heavier on his journey than it might have been, but also made his room a "kind of social center."[59]

I recognize here the behaviour of a fan: one who wants to be close to his music and who copies the voices he hears, repeating the words with his hands so that, when he listens, he can amplify his feeling by reading the words too. As transcriptions, Hughes's blues poems are not representing a collectivity that he stands in for "as poet" so much as they are representing a group, made up mostly of female voices, which he wishes to join. As Edwards observes, the blues poems in *Fine Clothes* are also a song book from which readers may sing and in which readers may find a collective voice by joining the voices on the page.[60] In a collection that is both archive and score, Hughes's promiscuous inhabitation of a series of mostly female, distinct but similarly bluesy, voices models a mimetic participation in a collectivity, which he invites his readers to copy.[61]

Although the idiom and genre changes, this feeling of participation, of joining together with others "like me," is precisely the aim of the explicitly political poetry Hughes increasingly wrote in the 1930s. But there, as he shifted and experimented with the genre, the poetry was joined with explicit political demands and expectations, ones capable of sustaining collective affective attachment to a political goal, at least for a time.[62]

"Like a Flag"

Inasmuch as "the deep South blues that nobody knows who made up" spoke directly to African Americans about their lives, addressing "whole groups of people's problems," and yet appealed to "to the ear and heart of people everywhere,"[63] Hughes found in the blues a form for representing black Americans to themselves in a way that could link those experiences to oppressed people elsewhere.[64] Thus, in his blues poems, Hughes was already engaged in a problem that concerned the Comintern during the same period.

Through the 1920s, as we know, the Comintern had undertaken the task of encouraging revolutionary communist movements around the world. Through a series of debates over several congresses, the Comintern emphasized the important work that national communist parties could do in organizing and representing a potentially revolutionary class to itself, working along lines established by Lenin in *What Is to Be Done?* (1902).[65] To this project was added an increasingly impressive commitment to anti-racist, anti-imperialist politics, a Comintern position that had become, as Robin Kelley, Mark Solomon, Kate Baldwin, Minkah Makalani, and others have reminded us, "more sympathetic and sensitive to the racial nature of American class struggle" because black radicals like Claude McKay, Otto Huiswoud, and Harry Haywood had made it so.[66]

In 1928, the Comintern's anti-racist internationalism took the form of the controversial "Black Belt" thesis, which held that black people in the United States constituted an oppressed nation across a continuous geographical area where they were in the majority, akin to an internal colony, with the right to self-determination.[67] Although the idea that black people in the South should fight for secession from the United States seemed unrealistic to many black communists, especially at first, the Black Belt thesis articulated a complex and canny nationalist internationalism that did important work. As Kate Baldwin observes, it was part of an approach that "encouraged both the self-determination of peoples united by culture and yet oppressed by a national unit that excluded them, and the transnational alliance of peoples similarly excluded by ethnic absolutism – under the mantle of world internationalism."[68] Importantly, as Kelley points out, the thesis recognized that "African Americans had their own unique revolutionary tradition and their interests were not identical to those of white workers."[69] Moreover, on a practical level, the thesis created a motive for the Communist Party USA (CPUSA) to engage in energetic organizing in the South, and not only in the South, as Mark Naison observes in his book on the Party's activities in Harlem.[70] Timothy Johnson and others have shown how these efforts sensibly focused on concrete grievances at the local level, ones that would bring workers or sharecroppers into conflict with the owner class and towards their own commitment to self-determination, while, at the same time, the propaganda also made the case for "Lenin as the leader of the oppressed nations" and the idea that "in the Black Belt of the South, the Negro majority must be allowed to decide for itself what form of government it wants."[71] By elevating the status of the African American struggle against racist oppression into a geopolitically significant one, the Black Belt thesis created a way for black people to come together locally with a sense of national and even global political expectations and alliances that might anchor optimism about the possibility of victorious political struggle.

When the CPUSA began its organizing in the South, the correspondence between the Comintern's project and the blues was not missed by the Party itself. In its organizing efforts, the Party began to make use of the blues along with spirituals, sometimes replacing the lyrics of familiar songs with communist lyrics. Robin Kelley notes that "readers of the *Southern Worker* and party members sent in transcriptions of blues they may have heard or wrote themselves," which the newspaper would sometimes print.[72] While the blues offered a way for black people to feel recognized and to recognize their own unbeatability, when linked to the infrastructure of a revolutionary party those feelings could be articulated with an explicit political project, one that established collective political action – in solidarity with friends and against enemies who had now been identified – as part of a horizon of expectations. This project and its potential is one reason, I think, that the propagandistic genres of the Party were attractive to Hughes.[73] Such a genre could participate in the formation of the "potential power" of the "black millions," in whose name Hughes now spoke with increasing confidence.[74]

Hughes's project and the Party's tasks converged around the Scottsboro case, where the Party's support for black people against white supremacy was at its most public. Because the CPUSA had already been involved in the battle against lynching, when nine black youths were falsely charged and wrongly convicted of raping two white women on a train in Alabama, the legal defence arm of the Party, the International Labor Defense, was ready to appeal the verdict and start the effort to mobilize global public opinion in support of the defendants.[75] The NAACP, by contrast, vacillated. "They shall not die!" became the rallying cry in the massive propaganda campaign in the Soviet Union as well as in the United States. As one element of his energetic support for the youths and their defence, Hughes wrote several poems about the case, which were published together with his agitational play *Scottsboro, Limited* in a special volume to raise funds for the defence.

Hughes's interest in the representational function of the Communist Party is evident in the play, which draws on a range of agitational techniques.[76] The play opens with "the eight Black Boys" chained together, walking "slowly down the center aisle from the back of the auditorium," where they are confronted by a "White Man" who emerges from the audience. In response to his challenge to their right to be there, the "1st Boy" answers: "We come in our chains/ To show our pain." The clearly racist man continues his threatening behaviour, suggesting that the boys just want to "show off." Defiantly correcting him, the "8th Boy" says: "We come tonight/ To lift our troubles high./ Like a Flag against the sky."[77] The flag here is less a symbol of something than it is a technology for attracting attention and publicizing a position. By lifting their troubles high, the boys make something that may have been obscured or hidden visible from afar. While the language of "troubles" and "lifting high" recalls the sorrow songs, the flag is an unmistakable reference to a dominant trope in Soviet propaganda of the moment, which made frequent reference to "marching under the banner" of Lenin or the October Revolution (figure 10.2).[78]

As Hughes presents it, the play is itself like the flag in doing the representational work of making these troubles public, while also locating them in a specific place: "look here – here is where the trouble is."

10.2 Viktor Koretsky, "Men and Women Workers of All Countries and Oppressed Colonies Raise the Banner of Lenin," 1932. Poster RU/SU 1032, Poster collection, Hoover Institution Archives, http://digitalcollections.hoover.org/objects/22484.

After the opening, the short play depicts the Scottsboro boys riding on the train, being unjustly accused, arrested, tried, and sentenced to death. In the "death house," the 8th Boy voices his resistance, addressing the prison keeper (played by the same white man as the Sheriff and Judge) who has just told them to "shut up in there:"

> 8TH BOY: I won't shut up.
> I've nobody to talk for me,
> So I'll talk for myself, see.
> RED VOICES: And the Red flag, too, will talk for you.
> 1ST BOY: Listen, boys! That's true – they've sent a lawyer
> to talk for me and you.

In a reversal of Marx's observation that the French peasants "cannot represent themselves, they must be represented," here the 8th Boy is not represented – he represents himself. Then, in talking for himself, he finds that "the Red flag, too, will talk for you." The Red Voices find him and join with him, amplifying and "talking for" him and his fellow defendants in the legal process as well, sending lawyers to represent them in court. Like a flag, the CPUSA also brought attention to the trial, while amplifying the voices of the Scottsboro defendants and powerfully focusing international attention on the fact that black persons in the United States, especially in the South, were not in fact protected (represented) by the state.[79]

In comparing this "talking for" to the flag, which is now identified as "Red," the Red Voices indicate the nature of their representational mode. The flag is neither proxy nor picture, but it does "stand for" the Communist Party, conjuring up a political position and set of ideals, an anti-capitalist, anti-racist political force and a nation-state, fighting for black self-determination.[80] It also marks a position: "We are *here* and we stand for these things: Join us!" For Lenin, Lars Lih notes, "to appear in public under a banner with a revolutionary slogan was the essential militant act" because it "announced to the world who you were and what you were fighting for."[81] As such, it "inspired your own fighters and rallied others to the cause." In fact, by proclaiming its commitment to fighting white supremacy in the Scottsboro trial, the CPUSA did attract other similarly committed persons like Hughes to the cause. In attracting people to a position to join with others, the Party encouraged people to choose a side in a battle they might have otherwise ignored, thereby "concentrating and harnessing inchoate political emotion," as Jodi Dean pointed out, directing it towards a group of friends with a specific goal and identifying enemies who must be opposed to achieve that goal.[82]

By speaking for himself, the 8th Boy comes to recognize that the Red Voices are speaking for him and the other boys, which in turn leads them all to feel that "the voice of the red world is our voice, too," as the 8th Boy says. To which the Red Voices respond: "The voice of the red world *is* you!/ The hands of the red world are our hands too."[83] In the model Hughes presents here, the function of the Party is first to listen and answer to people already talking (not to "lead"), and then to "talk for" them by amplifying their voices and bringing them together with others in solidarity. The Party thereby itself grows, is in an ongoing state of becoming bigger, not as a "leader" but as a kind of representational device allowing emerging collectives to see themselves as if from outside and to thereby recognize themselves and each other: "the voice of the red world is you!"

Such an amplifying "withness" is one goal of Hughes's 1930s communist poems. It is achieved through the creation of a voice that lifts certain troubles high while marking out a political position.[84] Like Aretha Franklin demanding R-E-S-P-E-C-T, Hughes models a voice that joins with others and can be joined. When the Queen of Soul warns "you better think/ think about what you're trying to do to me," the "me" is at once her voice and all the people singing "me" with her, finding their own group voice by joining in with hers. Such voices can be essential for the formation and circulation of counter-moods that replace political depression or cynicism with active demands for liberation: "Oh, freedom (freedom), freedom (freedom)."[85] In his ongoing poetic improvisation, Hughes was looking for and finding such voices, voices that could create a space – a gap, Jodi Dean would say – where a collective can enter in.[86]

Hughes's play literalizes this gap in *Scottsboro, Limited*, as the Red Voices join the Scottsboro defendants on stage. "Comrades!" they call to each other and proclaim their will to "Fight! Fight! Fight! Fight!" They will fight – "Black and white together" – "To put greed and pain/ And the color line's blight/ Out of the world into time's old night." Here, Hughes's stage notes say, "the 'Internationale' may be sung and the red flag raised above the heads of the black and white workers together."[87]

"Marx Communist Lenin Peasant Stalin Worker ME!"

A strong case can be made that the formal innovations in Hughes's poetry of the 1930s were motivated by his efforts to create new genres for the work of representing black collectivities to themselves in order to bring them into solidarity. The shift in his writing, in any case, is apparent even at first glance, not only because of the frequent reference to revolution, the Soviet Union, Lenin, comrades, and red flags. There are also more capital letters, exclamation points, and unusual layouts and orthography. These poems, as James Smethurst has shown, are also among Hughes's most formally innovative and "modernist" in form.[88]

Although Hughes had begun the shift before his trip to the Soviet Union in 1932 and 1933, his experiences there clearly expanded his sense of the possible, both politically and poetically. The Soviet Union, Hughes wrote, presented "a clear example in the world to prove to our American 'experts' in race relations that it DOES NOT TAKE A HUNDRED YEARS, it does NOT take generations to get rid of ugly, evil, antiquated, stupid Jim Crow practices – if a country really wants to get rid of them."[89] He later elaborated: "Meagre as the resources of the country were, white and black, Asiatic and European, Jew and Gentile stood alike as citizens on an equal footing protected from racial inequalities by the law. There were no pogroms, no lynchings, no Jim Crow cars as there had once been in Tzarist Asia, nor were the newspapers or movies permitted to ridicule or malign any people because of race. I was deeply impressed by these things."[90] Moreover, as he noted in *I Wonder as I Wander*, for the first time in his life, he was also able to earn a comfortable wage as a writer. The Soviet opposition to racism and poverty was highlighted by its juxtaposition with the long Southern reading tour he had just conducted, where the violently, damagingly oppressive effects of racism and its intersection with exploitative capitalism were on abundant display.[91]

The Soviet Union was a place where the beaten had, literally, become unbeatable. In *I Wonder as I Wander*, Hughes tells the story of an old Uzbek man he met in Bokhara, Haji Mir Baba, who had been badly beaten and whipped by the Emir's jailers before the revolution. He had met Lenin in Moscow in the early days of the Soviets. "When Lenin asked him how he had happened to become a Communist, Haji turned around, slipped out of the upper part of his robe, so that his back was bare, and Lenin saw his scars."[92] The Soviet Union, created in a revolution won by those who had been beaten, stood as an undeniable example of the possibility of radical anti-racist, anti-capitalist change from below.

Hughes's Soviet-inspired enthusiasm for communist ideals is apparent in "Goodbye Christ," one of the poems he wrote while he was in the Soviet Union, which also turned out to be one his most controversial. Otto Huiswoud, a leading black communist from Dutch Guiana who was in Moscow at the time and befriended Hughes and some of his companions, secured the poem for the November–December 1932 issue of *The Negro Worker*, the journal of the International Trade Union Committee of Negro Workers (a Comintern organ), where he was a contributing editor. The journal – which itself represents a fascinating instance of the black Leninism of the period – was based in Hamburg and edited by Trinidadian George Padmore.[93] The poem appeared alongside articles such as "New Slave Law in South Africa," "The Land of Socialist Construction: Fifteen Years of the Soviet Union," and "Under the Banner of the Red Aid – the Scottsboro Case."

The five stanza poem is addressed directly to "Christ." The financial and moral corruption and hypocrisy of the church is front and centre: "Listen

Christ/ You did alright in your day, I reckon –/ But, that day's gone now/ ... The popes and preachers've/ ... sold you to too many." It is now time for a "new guy" who can't be sold.

> Goodbye,
> Christ Jesus Lord God Jehova,
> Beat it on away from here now.
> Make way for a new guy with no religion at all –
> A real guy named
> Marx Communist Lenin Peasant Stalin Worker ME –
> I said, ME!

Hughes here announces the arrival of a "new guy" who is "real" and who has "no religion at all." Recalling Soviet anti-religious propaganda and campaigns for the "new Soviet man," the poem directly advocates replacing the reverence for Christianity and the church with a newly energetic attention to Marx, Lenin, and Stalin (better to study their writings, their teachings) and to the groups they represent: workers, peasants, and communists.

This turn away from God and towards communism, these lines seem to suggest, will enable a new self-possession, an exuberant "ME!" Yet, the assertion that "Marx Communist Lenin Peasant Stalin Worker ME" is the "name" of this new person complicates this reading: What kind of a name is this? And what does it tell us about "ME"?

Where "Christ Jesus Lord God Jehova" comprise a series of names for something "unrepresentable," which might be substituted for each other, depending on your beliefs or disposition, the "new guy" has a name comprised of different kinds of subjects indicating different modes of representation. Although the line is structured paratactically, the absence of commas distinguishes it from the long lists we find in Whitman. Instead, we have a compound name, made up of a chain of references that together aim to tell us something about the subject named. We have the recognizable holy (Stalinist) Soviet trio of Marx, Lenin, and Stalin, sometimes joined by Engels to make four, which traces out an implicit narrative: the arguments made by Marx against capitalism and for communism were put into revolutionary action by Lenin, whose vision of communism is perpetuated in state form by Stalin. Interspersed with the proper names are the generic subjects – communist, peasant, worker – which also suggest a progressive narrative, with the communist as the goal or beacon towards which the peasant and worker strive.

The "communist" names a kind of ideal, but, inasmuch as it is not a class identity, it also refers to a different kind of subject. On the one hand, in a capitalist country like the United States, it indicates an oppositional future-oriented political position publicly taken. On the other hand, in the Soviet Union the communist is what the peasant and worker have become, a new person – or at least the aspiration towards one – with distinct values and habits and feelings. This communist subject comes into being after the revolution.

Combining these different modes of naming and representing together into a single name – a name whose last component is "ME" – indicates the multitudinousness of this new subject, the fact that this subject is singularly plural. Hughes explained it in the following way: "The *I* which I pictured was the newly liberated peasant of the state collectives I had seen in Russia merged with those American negro workers of the depression period who believed in the Soviet dream and the hope that it held out for a solution of their racial and economic difficulties."[94] While Hughes does not resist or problematize the effort to bring together these different populations across the globe here, as he did in "Johannesburg Mines," the oddness of the compound name still communicates the difficulty of the representational work he is proposing. As this subject moves across continents, the temporality of this "ME" is disjointed too: rooted in the specific experience of Jim Crow but also looking towards a future that can be imagined because it exists now in the Soviet Union.

In this "name," Hughes places the "representers" (Marx, Lenin, Stalin) and the "represented" (communist, peasant, worker) together.[95] Akin to the 8th Boy in *Scottsboro, Limited* who speaks "for himself" because nobody speaks for him, which then prompts the Communist Party to speak for him (like a flag), this "new guy" is both representer and represented. The "ME" here is like the collectivity that is "for" itself, aware of itself, and can join together in solidarity – as a single plural "ME."

This "ME" is collective not only in the sense that it means to metonymically represent a large, international group. I also take it to indicate a group at the level of reading, a red chorus of ME's speaking together with the poet. The plurality of this "ME" – and the "ME!" that follows it – is indicated typographically by its capital letters, which Hughes had been using for some time to indicate different kinds of voices. For example, in his 1926 "Cat and the Saxophone (2AM)," capital letters indicate the voice of the music in the background of a cabaret singing "Everybody Loves My Baby But My Baby Don't Love Nobody But Me," written by Jack Palmer and Spencer Williams, which trades lines with people talking.[96] The capital letters here indicate that this voice is the voice of the atmosphere, the setting itself.[97] In the thirties, Hughes appeared to borrow his use of capital letters from agitational writing, where it often indicated increased volume or group voices.[98] (Several good examples include Hughes's "Air Raid over Harlem," "Tom Mooney," and "Advertisement for the Waldorf Astoria.") In some of Hughes's poems written in the 1930s, including "Goodbye Christ," capital letters retain something of the insurgency of the voice entering into the poem from the shared situation, like music being performed in a cabaret – as if they signify the voice not only of a concrete group but of the collective mood as such.[99]

In "Goodbye Christ," the "ME!" directs our attention to the limits and potential of the lyric voice. Where "I" is a subject, grammatically speaking, "me" is a direct or indirect object. In his blues lyrics, the frequency of "me" in lines like "Ma man left me," "Nobody to love me," "That man that done me wrong" refers to the feelings of having things happen to one, of being an object of events one does not control, and the sense of loneliness this experience can produce, the very loneliness that the blues reverses through performance. By way of the "ME," "Goodbye Christ" performs a move analogous to the one made in the blues poems. Where the reversal in the blues happens at the moment of reception by way of laughter, "Goodbye Christ" works by holding out this "ME" as a place where a red chorus of readers might locate their own collective voice. That a multitudinous "me" is in Hughes's poetic lexicon can be observed in "Air Raid over Harlem," where the "me" is Harlem itself.

Where Theodor Adorno argues that "the lyric work hopes to attain universality through unrestrained individuation," we might say that Hughes instead gives voice to the restraining quality of black individuation.[100] In emphasizing the "me," Hughes references the way being a black person in a white supremacist society is to be objectified but that this very process of being treated as object is also the locus of a great "potential power," one that could overturn racial capitalism from below, on the low-down frequencies. Hughes discloses here, to borrow from Fred Moten, "the objectional and ontological sociality of the black voice, where being black is only being black in groups."[101] Hughes's call to raise troubles high is not the lyric escape into the realm of roses and moonlight – which anyway, Hughes knows, is a site of black death. Instead, his lyric voice seeks to function like a flag, a red flag, a Leninist flag, marking out a position, making the position and the group visible so that others can join in, so they know where to go, where to gather. Hughes knows how important it is to "move as a team/ never move alone," as Chuck D once put it.[102]

In this way, Hughes returns to the poetic and political problems raised by "Johannesburg Mines," where the poem's avowal of its own powerlessness, its distance from absent workers, indicates by way of negation the potential power of workers and readers who must both represent and be represented if the colonial exploitation of workers is to be ended. In that poem, the potentially powerful collective, capable of consequentially reversing the subjection of African natives working in the mines, is clearly at a remove from the poem and from poetics as such. In "Goodbye Christ," however, the audience collective and its potential power emerges from within the poem, which models a new voice with a new name. As if to underscore the replacement of the lyrical "I" with a collective "ME," the poem compactly narrates it in a separate, short stanza: "I said, ME!"

The Party between Darkness and the Dawn

Hughes continued to publish leftist poems through the Second World War, including one simply titled "Lenin" (1946). At the beginning of each of its three stanzas, the speaker repeats the observation that "Lenin walks around the world." This walking, the speaker observes, surpasses all manner of barriers: physical, national, linguistic, and racial. Then, as the sun sets and the red star of communism rises "between the darkness and the dawn," we realize we have shifted from a spatial to a temporal register. The overall message of the poem seems clear enough: Lenin walking around the world leads to a communist revolution.

The image of Lenin walking around the world recalls a Soviet poster with a giant Lenin sweeping the world of its capitalist and religious filth or propagandistic images featuring a revolutionary figure, as big as the earth itself (as in the image used on the masthead of *The Negro Worker*), breaking or tearing the chains of capitalism and imperialism binding the earth. But walking is also ordinary, even slow, the everyday mobility of a body moving through space from one place to another, going to work, to the store or the bar, to meet people and talk with them. If his means of transport is humble, more fantastic is the fact that neither frontiers nor barricades nor barracks impede Lenin. "Nor does barbed wire scar him." He is unbeatable. Perhaps this Lenin is something like the "spirit of revolution," the very urge to resist or rebel. This combination of feeling and idea (which I've been calling a revolutionary mood) translates across all manner of boundaries. Thus, "black, brown and white receive him." Language, too, is no barrier. "The strangest tongues believe him," Hughes writes, suggesting that what makes Lenin powerful is the way that his words find their way onto the tongues of others. Like the other figures Hughes lists with Lenin in his poem "Scottsboro" – Nat Turner, Dessalines, John Brown, and Moses – this Lenin is a ghost who haunts the present, inspiring the walkers and speakers who find their words in his mouth to redeem the injustices from the past.

As in the blues, where a final twist often shifts the feeling of the poem, here too the last lines veer in another direction. Lenin is still walking around the world, but now we have a sense of the world turning, a day ending: "The sun sets like a scar." In a simile both visual and conceptual, the sunset is a red mark between earth and sky, as if the day itself has been a wound of which the sunset is a visible trace, a sign of the damage done, but survived. We are still in the realm of the global, but now it is the world that is turning (rather than being walked around), and the world's revolution is also a communist revolution: "Between the darkness and the dawn/ There rises a red star."

In Hughes's writing, the temporal mode that occurs between sunset and the dawn gets its rhythm from the blues, something that Hughes had indicated when he framed the entirety of *Fine Clothes to the Jew* with two blues poems, the first singing of the setting sun and wondering what "de blues'll bring," the last asserting that the "sun's a risin'" is gonna be his song. "I could be blue but/ I been blue all night long." The time "between the darkness and dawn" is even more specific, however. That moment after closing time but before the day begins is, as Shane Vogel has pointed out, in the time and space of the "afterhours." Away from the clock time that sets the tempo of the work day, the afterhours is a "mode of temporality that reorganizes the normative temporal order upon which logics of familial reproduction and capitalist productivity are constituted and maintained."[103] The afterhours is a "queer temporal register" that "unfolds in defiance of city and moral law to create fugitive spaces like the afterhours club" or the rent party, which charges money for admission in order to raise the funds to pay the rent for somebody who needs it, and where late night music and dancing are promised. In such a space, in those last hours before dawn, various deviant, illegal, or otherwise unexpected and unofficial activities, affinities, and intimacies could come into being.

The afterhours is also the temporal register in which Hughes imagines the red star rising. In this, Hughes's Leninist revolution may borrow the time signature of rent party.[104] The rent party, like the Communist Party, takes the threat of dispossession as an occasion for coming together. And, like the red collectivity of revolution, the rent party comes together in the afterhours: "the dancing and singing and impromptu entertaining went on until dawn came in at the windows," Hughes remembers in *The Big Sea*.[105] These parties were "more amusing than any night club," not only because there were no white tourists but also because of the black working class joy that could be found there: "I met ladies' maids and truck drivers, laundry workers and shoe shine boys, seamstresses and porters. I can still hear their laughter in my ears, hear the soft slow music, and feel the floor shaking as the dancers danced" (233).

Hughes knows there is a particular feel to that moment when it's not really night anymore but the day has not yet broken. If the situation is right, it can feel like the world is filled with so much possibility that it is as if "tomorrow may be/ a thousand years off," as he wrote in his poem "Tomorrow." That is how revolution would feel, how it should feel. Clocks stop, laughter fills the air, the floors shake, and now stretches out forever: "*Some dawns/ wait.*"[106]

History, of course, had more cunning, miserable ruses up its long sleeve. Not only would another "S" (for Soviet) not be added to "USA," but the Comintern would dissolve; Stalinist terrors would get worse and become more widely known; and Jim Crow and the systematic devaluing of black life in the United States would continue unabated. On a personal level, Hughes would be viciously attacked for "Goodbye Christ" and then, later, called before the House Un-American Activities Committee. Although he publicly dissociated himself from the Soviet Union and from communism in response to the anti-communist environment of the Cold War 1950s, he kept up his social ties with his old communist friends and continued to receive invitations and communications from the Soviet Union up until the end of his life. And he never abandoned the project that had attracted him to the Soviet Union and to the Communist Party in the first place: representing black people as a collective to black people, with the aim of shifting his own and his readers' way of being attuned to each other and to the world, creating group moods that opened up a way of being in solidarity in the battle against institutionalized racism and poverty.[107] His first major resource in this project, the blues – and then the jazz that grew out of the blues – would remain a constant in his poetics, as we can see in his ambitious portrait of multitudinous Harlem, *Montage of a Dream Deferred* and his late *Ask Your Mama: 12 Moods for Jazz*.[108]

Thus, although Soviet propaganda became less of a formal model for him and the explicit allusions to the Soviet Union and to Lenin mostly receded, Hughes's work remained animated by his commitment to attuning black people to their own collective power, transforming what might otherwise be individual experiences of loss and trauma into a powerful political determination. My proposition is that Hughes's bluesy, black Leninism, which places "black, beaten, but unbeatable" voices at the centre of a poetics that works like a flag to make a place for readers to find a collective voice, remains relevant and vital at this moment. As the #blacklivesmatter movement has so vividly dramatized in their powerful representation of black lives, in a world where state-supported murderous hostility to black life continues, the invention of new genres of collective opposition remains essential for the end of white supremacy to feel and be possible.

NOTES

1   I am borrowing from Lauren Berlant here in thinking about genre as a particular way of being in and with others in the world, a genre with narrative expectations about how that way of being will develop. Berlant writes that she understands genre as "an aesthetic structure of affective expectation, an institution or formation that absorbs all kinds of small variations or modifications while promising that the persons transacting with it will experience the pleasure of encountering what they expected, with details varying the theme." Lauren Berlant, *The Female Complaint: The Unfinished Business of Sentimentality in American Culture* (Durham, NC: Duke University Press, 2008), 3–4. See also Lauren Berlant, "Austerity, Precarity, Awkwardness," (paper presented at the panel, "Sensing Precarity," held at the American Anthropological Association, 25 November 2011), https://supervalentthought.files.wordpress.com/2011/12/berlant-aaa-2011final.pdf; and Lauren Berlant, "Genre Flailing," *Capacious:*

Journal for Emerging Affect Inquiry 1, no. 2 (2018): 156–62, https://doi.
org/10.22387/CAP2018.16.

2 On the class for itself, see Karl Marx, *The Poverty of Philosophy*: "Economic conditions
first transformed the mass of the people into workers. The combination of capital has
created for this mass a common situation, common interests. This mass is thus already
a class as against capital, but not yet for itself. In the struggle ... the mass becomes
united, and constitutes itself as a class for itself. The interests it defends become class
interests." *The Marx Engels Reader*, 2nd ed., edited by Robert C. Tucker (New York:
W.W. Norton, 1978), 218.

3 Robin D.G. Kelley, *Freedom Dreams: The Black Radical Imagination* (Boston: Beacon
Press, 2002), 44. Kelley's chapter on "'The Negro Question': Red Dreams of Black
Liberation" (36–59) is one of the best surveys of black engagement with the Soviet
Union and the Communist Party.

4 Hughes's grandmother had been married to one of the members of John Brown's
party, so he had been raised in a familial setting that valued strong opposition to
white supremacy. Arnold Rampersad notes that Hughes "had been a socialist sympathizer ever since high school in Cleveland, when delirious kids at Central High,
most of them of East European immigrant stock, had celebrated the 1917 Bolshevik
Revolution in Russia by parading a red flag around the grounds." Arnold Rampersad,
"Introduction," *Selected Letters of Langston Hughes*, ed. Arnold Rampersad and David
Roessel with Christa Fratantoro (New York: Knopf, 2015), xxiii.

5 Langston Hughes, *I Wonder as I Wander: An Autobiographical Journey* (New York:
Hill and Wang, 1956); this quotation is taken from the 1986 reprint by Thunder's
Mouth Press, 42.

6 Fred Moten, *Stolen Life* (Durham, NC: Duke University Press, 2018). Moten is here
speaking of Du Bois: "What is given in Du Bois's composed and scholarly production
of the question of the Negro is the possibility of an improvisational discovery: of a politics of the black ordinary and of everything that is both enabled and endangered by
such a politics, which is to say by the anthropological and/or sociological attitude that
the discovery of the concept of the object of the black ordinary demands" (115).

7 Langston Hughes, "My Adventures as a Social Poet" (1947), in *Collected Works
of Langston Hughes*, vol. 9, *Essays on Art, Race, Politics, and World Affairs*, ed.
Christopher De Santis (Columbia: University of Missouri Press, 2002), 269–77, quote
at 270.

8 Michael Snediker, *Queer Optimism: Lyric Personhood and other Felicitous Persuasions*
(Minneapolis: University of Minnesota Press, 2009), 3.

9 Brent Edwards, *The Practice of Diaspora: Literature, Translation and the Rise of Black
Internationalism* (Cambridge, MA: Harvard University Press 2003), 67. On the
transnationality of "The Negro Speaks of Rivers" and its "I" in relation to Whitman's,
see Jahan Ramazani, *Transnational Poetics* (Chicago: University of Chicago Press,
2009), 60–3. Hughes was a committed and complex internationalist in his personal
and professional travels, his political commitments, and his far-reaching writing in

several genres, as critics such as Brent Edwards, William Maxwell, Kate Baldwin, John Patrick Leary, Steven S. Lee, and others have demonstrated. See William J. Maxwell, *New Negro, Old Left: African American Writing and Communists Between the Wars* (New York: Columbia University Press, 1999); Kate A. Baldwin, *Beyond the Color Line and the Iron Curtain: Reading Encounters Between Black and Red, 1922–1963* (Durham, NC: Duke University Press, 2002); Brent Edwards, *Practice of Diaspora*; Brent Edwards, "Langston Hughes and the Futures of Diaspora," *American Literary History* 19, no. 3 (Fall 2007): 689–711; John Patrick Leary, "Havana Reads the Harlem Renaissance: Langston Hughes, Nicolás Guillén, and the Dialectics of Transnational American Literature," *Comparative Literature Studies* 47, no. 2 (2010): 133–58; Steven S. Lee, *The Ethnic Avant-Garde* (New York: Columbia University Press, 2015).

10 Henry Louis Gates, Jr., introduction to *The Souls of Black Folk*, by W.E.B. Du Bois (New York: Bantam Books, 1989), xxii.

11 See Stuart Hall's comments on his use of the term "articulation" (which he borrows from Ernesto Laclau's *Politics and Ideology in Marxist Theory*) in "On Postmodernism and Articulation: An Interview with Stuart Hall," ed. Lawrence Grossberg, in *Stuart Hall: Critical Dialogues in Cultural Studies*, ed. David Morley and Kuan-Hsing Chen (New York: Routledge, 1996): "It is the articulation, the non-necessary link, between a social force which is making itself, and the ideology or conceptions of the world which makes intelligible a process they are going through, which begins to bring onto the historical stage a new social position and political position, a new set of social and political subjects" (143–4). See also Jennifer Slack, "The Theory and Method of Articulation in Cultural Studies," in the same volume, 112–27.

12 I'm borrowing here from my "'What a Mourning': Propaganda and Loss in W.E.B. Du Bois's *Souls of Black Folk*," in *Affective Mapping: Melancholia and the Politics of Modernism* (Cambridge, MA: Harvard University Press, 2008), 105–57.

13 Heidegger quotes from *Being and Time*, trans. John Macquarrie and Edward Robinson (San Francisco: Harper and Row, 1962). For an explication of Heidegger's understanding of mood, placed within the context of his philosophical project, see Charles Guignon, "Moods in Heidegger's Being and Time," in *What Is an Emotion? Classic Readings in Philosophical Psychology*, ed. Cheshire Calhoun and Robert C. Solomon (New York: Oxford University Press, 1984), 230–43.

14 Lauren Berlant, *Cruel Optimism* (Durham, NC: Duke University Press, 2011), 15. To be clear, "mood" is not Berlant's key term here; she is working with a distinct set of terms – affective atmosphere, style, and genre.

15 On mood's essentially public, historical character, see also Ben Highmore and Jenny Bourne Taylor," Introducing Mood Work," *New Formations* 82 (2014): 5–12, quote at 8; Ben Highmore's *Cultural Feelings: Mood, Mediation and Cultural Politics* (London: Routledge, 2017), and my "Reading for Mood," *Representations* 140, (Fall 2017): 137–58.

16 Du Bois writes that "until the art of the black folk compels recognition they will not be rated as human." "Criteria of Negro Art" (1926), reprinted in *W.E.B. Du Bois: A Reader*, ed. David Levering Lewis (New York: Henry Holt, 1995), 509–15; these

quotes at 514, 515. Du Bois's strategy is one that had been obligatory for the African American cultural worker since Phillis Wheatley. The achievements of black persons must bear the burden of representing "the race," demonstrating that black people are equally smart (and thus equally human) to white people.

17 Langston Hughes, "The Negro Artist and the Racial Mountain," *Nation* 122 (23 June 1926): 692–4, reprinted in *Collected Works of Langston Hughes*, vol. 9, 31–6, 32.

18 Hughes, "Social Poet," 269.

19 Du Bois, for instance, references the appeal of the "kingdom of culture" at various moments in *The Souls of Black Folk*, especially at the end of "Of the Training of Black Men," where he dreams of dwelling "above the veil" with Shakespeare, Balzac, Dumas, Aristotle, and Aurelius (88–9) or in "Of the Coming of John," where the African American hero of the story is overwhelmed by "the infinite beauty of the wail" of Lohengrin's swan (186).

20 Herbert Marcuse, "The Affirmative Character of Culture" (1937), in *Negations: Essays in Critical Theory* (Boston: Beacon Press, 1968), 88–133, quote at 92.

21 The later versions play with the enjambment, lengthening the lines, subtracting the word "out" (in *The Crisis* version) and the word "Africans" (in the last version).

> *The Crisis* version (as printed) is as follows:
> – In the Johannesburg mines
> – There are 240,000 native Africans working.
> – What kind of poem would you make of that?
> – 240,000 natives working in the Johannes-burg mines.
>
> Compare the *Good Morning Revolution* and typescript version:
> – In the Johannesburg Mines
> – There are 240,000 natives working.
> – What kind of poem
> – Would you make out of that?
> – 240,000 natives working
> – in the Johannesburg mines.

22 In its reference to "native," this sentence also implicitly connects the colonialism of Africa to the settler colonialism and "Native Americans" of North America, although it should be noted that, in the 1920s, "American Indian" was in much wider usage than "Native American," which only surpassed the former phrase in the 1990s.

23 South Africa was, along with the United States and Nazi Germany, the other major paradigm of racist state formation in the twentieth century. See George M. Fredrickson, *Racism: A Short History* (Princeton, NJ: Princeton University Press, 2003). I am borrowing the term "racial capitalism" from Cedric Robinson, *Black Marxism* (Chapel Hill: University of North Carolina Press, 2000).

24 On the South African Communist party, see Apollon Davidson, Irina Filatova, Valentin Gordonov, and Sheridan Johns, *South Africa and the Communist*

International: A Documentary History (London: Frank Cass, 2003); Sheridan Johns, "The Comintern, South Africa, and the Black Diaspora," *The Review of Politics* 37, no. 2 (April 1975): 200–34; Allison Drew, "Bolshevizing Communist Parties: The Algerian and South African Experiences," *International Review of Social History* 48, no. 2 (August 2003): 167–202.

25   In this regard, Hughes's use of number is distinct from Vladimir Mayakovsky's long poem "150,000,000" (1919–20). Although that poem also makes showy use of a number to represent a large collectivity, its poetics is otherwise distinct. A comparison of the two poems deserves its own substantial treatment; here I can offer just a few preliminary thoughts. Inasmuch as Mayakovsky's number 150,000,000 refers to the population of the Soviet Union, it means to represent and celebrate the collectivity that has already accomplished a revolution, not a potentially revolutionary class of currently oppressed workers. Thus, it is not a class in itself that still needs to become a class for itself, but a collectivity that has already represented itself to itself and acted on the historical stage. The issues about subaltern representation that I discuss later do not apply here in the same way. Instead, the poem appears to seek to celebrate and glorify this collectivity. Although Mayakovsky claims that this 150,000,000 is the "name of the craftsman of this poem," the poem itself does not problematize the representation of a collectivity in the way Hughes does. Indeed, the poem confidently represents this large collectivity, first by claiming that "150,000,000 now speak through my lips," and then by centring the poem around the allegorical "Ivan," who stands in for the masses who fought and won the revolution. In Ivan's battle against Woodrow Wilson, who stands for the bourgeois world, the poem may be seen to veer from the epic to the mock epic (as Mayakovsky's translator, James H. McGavran III, notes); this apparent lack of seriousness reportedly irritated Lenin. A reading of the poem and its use of number becomes more complex when we consider it as a response to Aleksandr Blok's famous 1918 poem, "The Twelve." See *Aleksandr Blok: Selected Poems*, trans. Jon Stallworthy and Peter France (Manchester, UK: Carcanet Press, 2000), 94–110. For an English translation of "150,000,000," see Vladimir Mayakovsky, *Selected Poems*, trans. James H. McGavran III (Evanston, IL: Northwestern Press, 2013), 196–247, and the helpful note, 363–4. For the Russian, see the Soviet Academy of Sciences edition of the complete works, *Polnoe Sobranie sochinenii v trinadtsati tomakh*, 13 vols., (Moscow: Gosudarstvennoe izdatel'stvo khudozhesvennoi literatury, 1955–1961). See also "One Hundred Fifty Million," in *The Life of Mayakovsky*, by Wiktor Woroszylski, trans. Boleslaw Taborski (New York: Orion, 1970), 261–83.

26   See Fredric Jameson, "Modernism and Imperialism," in *Nationalism, Colonialism and Literature*, by Terry Eagleton, Fredric Jameson, and Edward W. Said, with an introduction by Seamus Deane (Minneapolis: University of Minnesota Press, 1990), 50–1.

27   I was unable to locate the piece in question, though I did find reference in newspapers and magazines to the gold and diamond output of the mines, the description of a horrible mining accident, the enforcement of the colour line, and South African efforts

to encourage (white) American tourism. South Africa was also a regular topic in the various leftist publications Hughes had been reading since high school.

28 I wrote about this passage in "How a Revolutionary Counter-Mood Is Made," *New Literary History* 43 (2012): 503–25.

29 Gayatri Chakravorty Spivak, "Can the Subaltern Speak?" in *Marxism and the Interpretation of Culture*, ed. Cary Nelson and Lawrence Grossberg (Urbana: University of Illinois Press, 1988), 271–313, quote at 275. A revised version of the essay appears in the "History" chapter of Spivak's *The Critique of Postcolonial Reason: Towards a History of the Vanishing Present* (Cambridge, MA: Harvard University Press, 1999), 198–311.

30 See also Hanna Pitkin's *The Concept of Representation* (Los Angeles: University of California Press, 1967), which makes an effort to bring together the various meanings of the word, partly by way of ordinary language philosophy.

31 Karl Marx, *The Eighteenth Brumaire of Louis Bonaparte* (New York: International Publishers, 1963). The famous passage reads, in part: "The small-holding peasants form a vast mass, the members of which live in similar conditions but without entering into manifold relations with one another ... In so far as millions of families live under economic conditions of existence that separate their mode of life, their interests and their culture from those of the other classes, and put them in hostile opposition to the latter, they form a class. In so far as there is merely a local interconnection among these small-holding peasants, and the identity of their interest begets no community, no national bond and no political organization among them, they do not form a class. They are consequently incapable of enforcing their class interest in their own name, whether though a parliament or through a convention. They cannot represent themselves, they must be represented" (123–4).

32 Spivak: "My point is that Marx is not working to create an undivided subject where desire and interest coincide. Class consciousness does not operate towards that goal. Both in the economic area (capitalist) and in the political (world-historical agent), Marx is obliged to construct models of a divided and dislocated subject whose parts are not continuous or coherent with each other" (Spivak, "Can the Subaltern Speak?," 276).

33 In the various typescripts of the poem in Hughes's papers, you can see him playing around with the enjambment.

34 Frederick Douglass, *Narrative of the Life of Frederick Douglass, An American Slave. Written by Himself* (1845) (Cambridge, MA: Harvard University Press, 2009), 72. See also Henry Louis Gates, Jr., *The Signifying Monkey* (New York: Oxford, 1989), 128, on chiasmus as one of the most common tropes in slave narratives. Thanks to Lara Cohen for sharing her insights on chiasmus in this poem.

35 Jahan Ramazani, *Poetry of Mourning: The Modern Elegy from Hardy to Heaney* (Chicago: University of Chicago Press, 1994), 143–7.

36 *The Collected Works of Langston Hughes*, vol. 1, *The Poems: 1921–1940*, ed. Arnold Rampersad (Columbia: University of Missouri Press, 2001), 73. See also Edwards on this shift in *Practice of Diaspora*, 59–62.

37 Hughes, "Social Poet," 270.

38 Langston Hughes, "Concerning 'Goodbye Christ,'" in *Essays on Art, Race, Politics*, 208.

39 Langston Hughes, "The Ceaseless Rings of Walt Whitman," introduction to *I Hear the People Singing: Selected Poems of Walt Whitman* (New York: International Publishers, 1946), reprinted in *Essays on Art, Race, Politics*, 482–5, quote at 484.

40 See Martin Ponce, "Langston Hughes's Queer Blues," *Modern Language Quarterly* 66, no. 4 (December 2005): 505–37; Shane Vogel, "Closing Time: Langston Hughes and the Queer Poetics of Harlem Nightlife," *Criticism* 48, no. 3 (Summer 2006): 397–425; Sam See, "'Spectacles in Color': The Primitive Drag of Langston Hughes," *PMLA* 124, no. 3 (2009): 798–816.

41 Langston Hughes, "I Remember the Blues," in *Good Morning Revolution*, ed. Faith Berry (New York: Citadel, 1992/1973), 164–7, quote at 167. (Hereafter, *Good Morning Revolution* will be referred to as *GMR*.)

42 By my count, of the seventeen blues lyrics in *Fine Clothes to the Jew* (New York: Alfred A Knopf, 1927), in nine the speaker is explicitly female ("Misery," "Suicide," "Gypsy Man," "Lament Over Love," "Gal's Cry for a Dying Lover," "Young Gal's Blues," "Midwinter Blues," "Listen Here Blues," and "Hard Daddy"); in two the speaker is explicitly male ("Bad Man" and "Po' Boy Blues"); and in six ("Hey!," "Hard Luck," "Homesick Blues," "Bound No'th Blues," "Ma Man," and "Hey! Hey!") the gender of the speaker is not clearly identified, with one of those speakers expressing desire for a man ("Ma Man").

43 Eric Garber, "A Spectacle in Color: The Lesbian and Gay Subculture of Jazz Era Harlem," in *Hidden from History*, ed. Martin Duberman, Martha Vicinus, and George Chauncey Jr. (New York: NAL Books, 1989), 318–31, quote at 320; also quoted by Sam See, "'Spectacles in Color,'" 800, who argues that Hughes's blues perform the instability of identity as a natural, but not normative, feeling. "When low-down race and down-low gender intersect," See compellingly writes, "their center is queer feeling, an affect that rejects identity and claims nonnormative experience (racial or sexual) as natural" (802). In addition, See provocatively connects racial crossing and gender crossing (in drag) with Hughes's frequent use of chiasmus.

44 Langston Hughes, "Songs Called the Blues," *Phylon* 2 (Summer 1941), reprinted in *Essays on Art, Race, Politics*, 212–13.

45 Douglass, *Narrative of the Life*, 64.

46 Hughes, "I Remember the Blues," 167.

47 Georg Lukács, *History and Class Consciousness* (Cambridge, MA: MIT Press, 1971), esp. 168–9. Lukács makes a similar point about the workers who have experienced their own reification and thus have a singular insight into the operations and nature of capital, making them the revolutionary class.

48 Langston Hughes, "A Note on Blues," in *Fine Clothes*, xiii.

49 In his *Narrative of the Life*, Frederick Douglass described a related disjuncture between the tone of a song and the feeling it is representing when he wrote that the slaves "would sometimes sing the most pathetic sentiment in the most rapturous tone,

and the most rapturous sentiment in the most pathetic tone" (25). See Sianne Ngai's
important work on tone in *Ugly Feelings* (Cambridge, MA: Harvard University Press,
2005), 38–88.

50 Langston Hughes, "A Note on Humor," in *The Book of Negro Humor*, ed. Langston
Hughes (New York: Dodd, Mead and Co., 1966), reprinted in *Essays on Art, Race,
Politics*, 525.

51 I make a similar point about Plato's understanding of tragedy in "Reading for Mood,"
143–4.

52 Langston Hughes, "Laughers," in *The Poems: 1921–1940*, 107–8.

53 Sam See argues that the humour of the blues is akin to the humour of camp: "As
Esther Newton records, such feeling was also central to drag performance, which
often relies on a camp aesthetic, a 'system of humor' that Newton defines just as
Hughes defines the blues: 'Camp humor is a system of laughing at one's incongruous
position instead of crying. That is, the humor does not cover up, it transforms.'" See
Newton, *Mother Camp* (Chicago: University of Chicago Press, 1972), 109; and Sam
See, "'Spectacles in Color,'" 805.

54 Hughes, "I Remember the Blues," 167.

55 Baruch Spinoza, *Ethics*, ed. and trans. Edwin Curley (New York: Penguin, 1996), 113
(II, 204). See Gilles Deleuze, "L'affect et l'idée" (course lecture at the Université de Paris
VIII, Vincennes, 24 January 1978), available at https://www.webdeleuze.com/cours/
spinoza (in the original French and in English translation). See also Gilles Deleuze,
Expressionism in Philosophy: Spinoza, trans. Martin Joughin (New York: Zone Books,
1992), esp. chap. 14, "What Can the Body Do?"

56 Jonathan Scott, *Socialist Joy in the Writing of Langston Hughes* (Columbia: University
of Missouri, 2006).

57 Vogel, "Closing Time," 400. Ann Cvetkovich understands an "archive of feelings" as
a collection of cultural texts that are "repositories of feelings and emotions, which
are encoded not only in the content of the texts themselves but in the practices that
surround their production and reception." Ann Cvetkovich, *An Archive of Feelings:
Trauma, Sexuality, and Lesbian Public Cultures* (Durham, NC: Duke University Press,
2003), 7.

58 Edwards, *Practice of Diaspora*, 67.

59 Remembering his time in Ashkhabad, Hughes writes that "perhaps it was because of
music that my room became a kind of social center. Everywhere, around the world,
folks are attracted by American jazz. A good old Dixieland stomp can break down
almost any language barriers, and there is something about Louis Armstrong's horn
that creates spontaneous friendships" (*I Wonder as I Wander*, 114). He also recalls
socializing with other travellers on the Moscow-Tashkent express: "I had brought
along my victrola with Louis Armstrong and Ethel Waters, so I contributed some lusty
canned music to the long ride through the Ural Mountains and the Kizyl Kum desert"
(104–5). A few days later, however, as he had to move his luggage along, he also
remembers that "my records seemed heavier than usual" (108). Later, in Tashkent,

he recalls sitting with friends with "my Harlem victrola playing Bessie Smith, Louis Armstrong and Ethel Waters" (150).

60 In this sense, as Edwards notes in *Practice of Diaspora*, Hughes's blues bear a similarity to "a musical score: a writing that precedes and structures a performance rather than follows and records it" (61).

61 Hughes's poetic identification with femininity here resonates interestingly with his writings on the lives of Muslim Central Asian women, examined by Kate Baldwin in "Between Harem and Harlem: Hughes and the Ways of the Veil," in *Beyond the Color Line and the Iron Curtain*, 86–148.

62 I am leaning on Lauren Berlant's understanding of genre here: "A genre is an aesthetic structure of affective expectation, an institution or formation that absorbs all kinds of small variations or modifications while promising that the persons transacting it will experience the pleasures of encountering what they expected, with details varying the theme." See Lauren Berlant, "Introduction: Intimacy, Publicity and Femininity," in *The Female Complaint*, 1–31, quote at 4.

63 The quotes here, in order, are from "I Remember the Blues," *GMR*, 167; "Social Poet," in *Essays on Art, Race, Politics*, 270; and "Songs Called the Blues," in *Essays on Art, Race, Politics*, 215. See also Brent Edwards, who writes that if the blues circulate globally, offering to speak "to everyone," the music also always "speaks for the place it 'comes from.'" Edwards, *Practice of Diaspora*, 66.

64 In "I Remember the Blues," Hughes writes: "I have heard the 'St. Louis Blues' on Japanese jukeboxes sung in Japanese, in Russia sung in Russian, and in the various languages of Europe. In French provincial cafes with their little orchestras, almost every time a party of American tourists walks in, they play 'The St. Louis Blues,' evidently under the impression that is the American National Anthem" (166, *GMR*). Along similar lines, in "Songs Called the Blues," Hughes writes that "the Blues have something that goes beyond race or sectional limits, that appeals to the ear and heart of people everywhere – otherwise, how could it be that in a Tokio restaurant one night I head a Louis Armstrong record of the *St. Louis Blues* played over and over for a crowd of Japanese diners there? You don't have to understand the words to know the meaning of the Blues, or to feel their sadness, or to hope their hopes" (215, *Essays on Art, Race, Politics*). See also Brent Edwards, *Practice of Diaspora*, 59–68, for a discussion of Hughes on the blues. Of particular relevance is Edwards's brilliant reading of "Jazz Band in a Parisian Café" from *Fine Clothes to the Jew*, which connects Paris to "the Georgia roads" by showing that "the possibility of black internationalism is heard to be a matter of music" (68). For a more detailed analysis of Hughes's blues lyrics (and engagement with the blues more generally), see Steven Tracy's impressively thorough *Langston Hughes and the Blues* (Urbana: University of Illinois, 1988). I also learned much from Angela Davis's *Blues Legacies and Black Feminism* (New York: Vintage Books, 1999); and Emily Lordi, *Black Resonance: Iconic Women Singers and African American Literature* (New Brunswick, NJ: Rutgers University Press, 2013).

65 On the history of the Comintern and its interaction with American communists,
    see Jacob Zumoff's thoroughly researched *The Communist International and US
    Communism 1919–1929* (Chicago: Haymarket, 2014), especially chapters 14–16,
    which traces the Comintern's evolving position on the "Negro Question" and the
    influence of black radicals on that evolution. See also Mark Solomon's indispensa-
    ble *The Cry Was Unity: Communists and African Americans* (Jackson: University
    of Mississippi Press, 1998), in particular, "The Comintern's Vision," 38–51, on the
    Comintern; and Meredith Roman, *Opposing Jim Crow: African Americans and the
    Soviet Indictment of U.S. Racism, 1928–1937* (Lincoln: University of Nebraska Press,
    2012).

66 Kelley, *Freedom Dreams*, 45. This commitment was signalled by Lenin at the Second
    Comintern Congress in 1920, when he noted that "all Communist parties should render
    direct aid to the revolutionary movements among the dependent and underprivileged
    nations (for example, Ireland, the American Negroes, etc.) and in the colonies." See V.I.
    Lenin, "Draft Theses on National and Colonial Questions for the Second Congress of
    the Communist International," in *Collected Works*, 2nd English ed. (Moscow: Progress
    Publishers, 1965), 31:144–51, also available at https://www.marxists.org/archive/lenin/
    works/1920/jun/05.htm. The position was debated and revised throughout the twenties
    through the active influence of black radicals such as McKay and Huiswoud (at the
    Fourth Congress of the Third International in 1922), whose input was *sought* by the
    Comintern, distinguishing it from the communist parties in the United States and
    South Africa. See the works of Mark Solomon, Kate Baldwin, Minkah Makalani, and
    Jacob Zumoff on the extensive, impressive, complex interactions between black radicals
    such as Cyril Briggs, James Jackson, Harry Haywood, and others with the Communist
    Party and with the Comintern.

67 As Timothy V. Johnson put it, the right to self-determination meant that African
    Americans could "determine whether they wished to remain as part of the United
    States, separate as an independent nation, or create another category of political/eco-
    nomic relationship. This was an extension of the Comintern's worldwide demand for
    self-determination for colonial peoples." Timothy V. Johnson, "'We Are Illegal Here':
    The Communist Party, Self-Determination and the Alabama Share Croppers Union,"
    Science & Society 75, no. 4 (October 2011): 454–79, quote at 454.

68 Baldwin, *Beyond the Color Line and the Iron Curtain*, 10.

69 Kelley, *Freedom Dreams*, 49.

70 On the effects of the Black Belt thesis on the CPUSA's activities, see Mark Solomon, *The
    Cry Was Unity*; and Timothy Johnson, "'We Are Illegal Here.'" Johnson points out that,
    although the thesis took the form of an emphasis on the "right of self-determination," it
    is not as if local organizers went around making the argument for self-determination.
    Rather, they sensibly focused on "concrete grievances that would lead the sharecroppers
    into confrontation with the Landowners" (458), which would eventually lead them to
    the recognition that self-determination would help them solve their local problems. See

also Mark Naison, *Communists in Harlem during the Depression* (Urbana: University of Illinois Press, 1983), 18.

71 These quotations are from a Communist Party directive, "Outline for Speakers at Lenin Memorial Meetings," 1933 (Files of the Communist Party, 255:3310), cited by Johnson in "'We Are Illegal Here,'" 460–1. As Johnson notes, black communists in the South at the time were "perfectly capable of understanding that African Americans should rule politically in that area of the country where they were the majority" (469). It is also worth noting that the focus on self-determination did not deter the Party from organizing in urban centres such as Harlem, as Mark Naison details in *Communists in Harlem*.

72 Robin D.G. Kelley, "'Comrades, Praise Gawd for Lenin and Them!': Ideology and Culture among Black Communists in Alabama, 1930–1935," *Science & Society* 52, no. 1 (Spring 1988): 59–82, quote at 75. For the Party's interest in and use of black music, see also Kelley's, "'Afric's Sons with Banner Red': African American Communists and the Politics of Culture, 1919–1934," in *Race Rebels: Culture, Politics and the Black Working Class* (New York: The Free Press, 1994), 103–21.

73 Lauren Berlant's work on intimate public spheres and genre in *The Female Complaint* influenced my thinking here, as did Jodi Dean's arguments for the affective power of the Party in *Crowds and Party* (New York/London: Verso, 2016).

74 "We can reveal to the Negro masses from which we come, our potential power to transform the now ugly face of the Southland into a region of peace and plenty." Langston Hughes, "To Negro Writers," *American Writers Congress*, ed. Henry Holt (New York: International Publishers, 1935), 139–141. Reprinted in *GMR*, 135–7; and *Essays on Art, Race, Politics*, 131–3, quote at 131. Hughes proposes to speak in the name of the "black millions" in the opening lines of "A New Song" (1933).

75 In his biography of Hughes, Rampersad notes that this "vastly increased the organization's prestige in Harlem." See Arnold Rampersad, *The Life of Langston Hughes*, vol. 1, *1902–1941: I, Too, Sing America* (New York: Oxford University Press, 1986), 216.

76 As Susan Duffy points out in her helpful introductory text, these techniques were later made famous by Bertolt Brecht, but they were already in fairly wide use in a number of communist theatre productions in the United States. See Susan Duffy, "Hughes's Move to the Left: *Scottsboro, Limited*," in *The Political Plays of Langston Hughes* (Carbondale: Southern Illinois University Press, 2000), 24–36. The play, *Scottsboro, Limited*, is printed on pages 37–49.

77 Hughes, *Scottsboro, Limited*, 39.

78 Also, where "Nobody Knows the Trouble I See" pluralizes and thus changes the sense of isolation described in the song through the act of collective singing itself – nobody knows the trouble I see except all these other people singing these words with me – the flag "against the sky" is public and outward-facing. Everybody can see these troubles.

79 For more on this extremely interesting play, and on the emergent figure of the "New Red Negro" therein, see James Smethurst's *The New Red Negro: The Literary Left and*

African American Poetry (New York: Oxford University Press, 1999); and Maxwell, *New Negro Old Left*, 125–51.

Also, see the following scene, later in the play (*Scottsboro, Limited*, 46–7):

8TH BOY: Burn *me* in the chair?
　NO!
　(*He breaks his bonds and rises, tall and strong.*)
　NO! For me not so!
　Let the meek and humble turn the other cheek—
　I am not humble!
　I am not meek!
　From the mouth of the death house
　Hear me speak!
RED VOICES: Hear him speak! Hear him speak!
MOB VOICES: Shut up, you God-damn nigger!
RED VOICES: Hear him speak!
BOYS: Hear us speak!
8TH BOY: All the world, listen!
　Beneath the wide sky
　In all the black lands
　Will echo this cry:
　I will not die!
BOYS: We will NOT DIE!
MOB VOICES (*Snarling*): Quick! Quick! Death there!
　The chair! The electric chair!
8TH BOY: No chair!
　Too long have my hands been idle
　Too long have my brains been dumb.
　Now out of the darkness
　The new Red Negro will come:
　That's me!
　No death in the chair!

80　On symbolic representation, and the example of the flag, see Pitkin, *Concept of Representation*, 92–111.
81　Lars Lih, *Lenin* (London: Reaktion Books, 2011), 45–6.
82　Dean, *Crowds and Party*, 242.
83　Hughes, *Scottsboro, Limited*, 47.
84　Hughes makes the connection between his poetic voice and the flag or banner in a number of his poems from this period, including poems that are not explicitly communist, such as "The Negro Mother," where the speaker asks her "dark children in the world out there" to "lift high my banner out of the dust." *The Collected Poems of Langston Hughes*, ed. Arnold Rampersad (New York: Vintage Books, 1995), 155.

85 As Daphne Brooks put it, Franklin turns vocal runs into "a thousand miles of free-dom." Daphne Brooks, "Drenched in Glory: How Aretha Franklin Gave Voice to Embattled Black Women – and Transformed a Nation," *The Guardian*, 17 August 2018, https://www.theguardian.com/music/2018/aug/17/drenched-in-glory-how-aretha-gave-voice-to-embattled-black-women-and-transformed-a-nation.

86 Dean, *Crowds and Party*, 28. "The communist party holds open the gap through which the people appear as the political subject."

87 Hughes, *Scottsboro, Limited*, 49.

88 See Smethurst, *New Red Negro*, 101–15.

89 Langston Hughes, "The Soviet Union and Color," *Chicago Defender*, 15 June 1946, reprinted in *GMR*, 88–90, quote at 90.

90 Hughes, "Concerning 'Goodbye Christ,'" *Essays on Art, Race, Politics*, 207–8.

91 Hughes describes this trip in "Poetry to the People," in *I Wonder as I Wander*, 39–67, and, more compactly and to more devastating political effect, in "Concerning 'Goodbye Christ,'" *Essays on Art, Race, Politics*, 207.

92 Hughes, *I Wonder as I Wander*, 134–5.

93 On this poem's publication, see Rampersad, *The Life of Langston Hughes*, vol. 1, 252–3. On *The Negro Worker*, see Brent Edwards, "Inventing the Black International: George Padmore and Timoko Gouran Kouyaté," in *Practice of Diaspora*, 241–305; Minkah Makalani, "The Rise of a Black International: George Padmore and the International Trade Union Committee of Negro Workers," in *In the Cause of Freedom: Radical Black Internationalism from Harlem to London, 1917–1939* (Chapel Hill: University of North Carolina Press, 2011), 165–94; and Holger Weiss's exhaustive and detailed, *Framing a Radical African Atlantic: African American Agency, West African Intellectuals and the International Trade Union Committee of Negro Workers* (Leiden/Boston: Brill, 2014).

94 Hughes, "Concerning 'Goodbye Christ,'" *Essays on Art, Race, Politics*, 208.

95 Marx, Lenin, and Stalin variously represent the worker, peasant, and communist (in the *vertreten* and the *darstellen* sense), but each in different ways. Marx, for instance, could be said to represent (in the sense of depicting, theorizing, describing) the con-dition of the worker under capitalism in texts from the *Economic and Philosophic Manuscripts* to *Capital* itself and to speak for the worker and the communist in the *Communist Manifesto*. Lenin, too, in the Communist Party, represented the work-ing class to itself, enabling it to come together as a revolutionary collective. At the moment when Hughes composed the poem, Stalin's authoritarian violence was not fully apparent (at least not to Hughes), and Hughes was probably most concerned with the way that Stalin "spoke for" the communist, worker, and peasant (including in the silencing way described by Spivak) in leading the Soviet state, but also by directing the Comintern to support and defend the interests of black people in the United States and elsewhere.

96 See Shane Vogel's brilliant reading of this poem in "Closing Time." See also Brent Edwards's discussion in *Practice of Diaspora*, 65–6.

97 This technique is a topic for another essay, but it is worth thinking through Hughes's use of capital letters in poems – some of his most interesting poems – such as "Advertisement for the Waldorf Astoria," "Air Raid over Harlem," "Wait," and "Broadcast on Ethiopia."

98 See Marcy Dinius on agitational punctuation in "Look!! Look!!! at This!!!!": The Radical Typography of David Walker's Appeal," *PMLA* 126, no. 1 (2011): 55–72.

99 This latter was something Hughes also experimented with more explicitly in poems such as "The Colored Soldier," "The Black Clown," and "The Big-Timer" (all from 1932), which he also called dramatic recitations or monologues, where "the mood" is described or narrated in a separate column to the left of the poem "itself."

100 Theodor Adorno, "On Lyric Poetry and Society," in *Notes to Literature*, vol. 1 (New York: Columbia University Press, 1991), 37–54, quote at 38. Jonathan Culler's *Theory of the Lyric* (Cambridge, MA: Harvard University Press, 2015) was also helpful in thinking about Hughes's mode of poetic address and his ambivalence about the lyric tradition.

101 Fred Moten, *Black and Blur* (Durham, NC: Duke University Press, 2017), 133.

102 Public Enemy, "Welcome to the Terrordome," in *Fear of a Black Planet*, Def Jam Recordings and Columbia Records, 1990.

103 Shane Vogel, "Closing Time," 402n40.

104 I was inspired by Fred Moten to think about the connection between the political party and the rent party: Fred Moten, "Air Shaft, Rent Party," in *Stolen Life* (Durham, NC: Duke University Press, 2018), 188–90.

105 Langston Hughes, *The Big Sea: An Autobiography*, American Century Series, 2nd ed. (New York: Hill and Wang, 1993), 229.

106 Langston Hughes, "Tomorrow," originally published in *Montage of a Dream Deferred*, 1951, reprinted in *Collected Poems*, 405.

107 On the controversy around "Goodbye Christ," see Arnold Rampersad, *The Life of Langston Hughes*, vol. 2, *1941–1967: I Dream a World* (New York: Oxford University Press, 1988), 4–5; on his testimony before Senator McCarthy and Roy Cohn, see 208–25. See also Baldwin, *Beyond the Color Line and the Iron Curtain*, 87–8; and Lee, *Ethnic Avant-Garde*, 143–4.

108 See Sarah Ruddy's argument about *Montage of a Dream Deferred* as a factographic work committed to both representing and transforming multitudinous black Harlem. Sara Ruddy, "This Fact Which Is Not One: Differential Poetics in Transatlantic American Modernism" (PhD diss., Wayne State University, 2012), *Wayne State University Dissertations*, 473, https://digitalcommons.wayne.edu/oa_dissertations/473/.

Chapter Eleven

A Comintern Aesthetics of Anti-racism in the Animated Short Film *Blek end uait*

CHRISTINA KIAER
Northwestern University

The best-known aesthetic project of Comintern anti-racism is the feature-length fiction film *Black and White* (*Chernye i belye*)[1] about black and white labour struggles in the American South, planned by the German-Russian film studio Mezhrabpomfil'm (International Workers' Aid Film) in 1932. It has gained both its fame and its communist internationalist credentials from the spectacular visit of a group of twenty-two African Americans to Moscow – under the initial auspices of an invitation arranged by the Communist Party of the United States of America (CPUSA) – to participate in the film's production. The group included Harlem Renaissance poet Langston Hughes, who was meant to serve as script consultant; he and the other members of the group wrote vividly about their experiences as African Americans in the communist Union of Soviet Socialist Republics (USSR), and the project was widely publicized in the United States as well. Even though the film was never made, as a social and literary event the project remains one of the most closely studied episodes in the history of the relations between black and red.[2]

Steven S. Lee has recently returned us to the aesthetic side of this project by offering for the first time a close reading of the original script of *Black and White*, written by Georgii Grebner, to argue that it was not the "pathetic hodge-podge" about racism in America that Hughes would accuse it of being in his 1956 memoir, *I Wonder as I Wander*. Rather, Lee proposes that, if it had been made, the film might have mobilized avant-garde aesthetic practices such as factography, montage, and estrangement, as well as dramatic narrative, to produce a programmatic but also aesthetic indictment of American racism – a tantalizing if unprovable proposition.[3] The lost promise of the film, made all the more poignant by Lee's optimistic reconstruction, is that this project might have been an aesthetic production in which Soviet socialist aesthetics would have worked in collaboration with the African American aesthetics of the Harlem Renaissance, allowing African American voices and agency to shape the Comintern narrative on race – contravening the common assumption that

11.1 Ivan Ivanov-Vano and Leonid Amal'rik, directors, *Blek end uait*, 1932. Still from Episode 3. Courtesy of Gosfil'mofond.

the Comintern was always in the position of imposing Marxist dogmas and agendas onto people of colour around the globe.

This chapter examines a related film project of a similar title, but one that was actually produced: the short animated sound film *Blek end uait*, directed by Ivan Ivanov-Vano and Leonid Amal'rik and released by the same studio, Mezhrabpomfil'm, on the occasion of the fifteenth anniversary of the Russian Revolution in November 1932 (figure 11.1). Based on futurist poet Vladimir Mayakovsky's 1925 poem of the same name (which is the Russian translitera-tion of the English words "black and white") about the poet's encounter with colonial racism in Cuba, the animated film, like the poem, tells the story of an Afro-Cuban man named Willie (Villi) who shines the shoes of the white bosses and ultimately confronts them with questions about black versus white labour. Although the film was made without the collaboration of African Americans like Hughes, by localizing the larger Comintern analysis of the structures of race and class in the character of Willie, and by making the affective depic-tion of his coming to consciousness into an aesthetic task, the film makes a space – modest but pronounced – for the black socialist agency promised by its aborted big brother, *Black and White*.

Both films are lost to us in different ways: for *Black and White*, only the script remains; for *Blek end uait*, no script and only the final six and a half minutes of the original twenty minutes of running time have been preserved.[4] Yet, it is in this final section that the short film builds to its coming-to-consciousness crescendo. It combines the shorthand, geometric forms of its overall avant-garde aesthetic with a dramatic musical score and searing images of racist violence drawn from the contemporary Comintern campaign protesting the Scottsboro verdicts, stemming from the trials of nine black teenage boys falsely accused of raping two white women in the American South in 1931. In so doing, the end of the film shifts the weight of the action from Cuba to the United States (which was not a setting in Mayakovsky's poem) and integrates visual models derived from the many newspaper illustrations, posters, and other mass images of American racism that were appearing at the moment of the film's making. This mix of factography and avant-garde form from the 1920s – which Lee has also identified in the script for the feature-length *Black and White* – with the emerging socialist realist concern about the affective depiction of the "socialist emotions" of the individual subject, suggests what a Comintern aesthetic of anti-racism might have looked like in 1932.[5]

The mixing of visual aesthetic models in *Blek end uait* was authorized by the unusual circumstance of a topical film based on a significantly earlier text. Not only had the visual imagery of Mayakovsky's constructivist colleagues in 1925 been superseded by 1932, but the conventions of the depiction of racial difference had also undergone a sea change in the same period. When Mayakovsky penned "Blek end uait" in 1925, an official Comintern policy of anti-racism had already been in place for three years, but it had not yet penetrated into cultural production. The "Theses on the Negro Question" that emerged from the Fourth Congress of the Comintern in Moscow in 1922 specifically acknowledged the leading role of African Americans in communist struggle. Responding to Claude McKay, the Jamaican-born poet of the Harlem Renaissance who had addressed the congress, the "Theses" took up his claim that African Americans, especially those who had come to an advanced proletarian class consciousness through their industrial labour in the American North, would be a vanguard in the struggle for worldwide communist revolution.[6] Mayakovsky's trenchant critique of the racism against Afro-Cubans and African Americans that he witnessed on his travels, both in the poem "Blek end uait" and in his pamphlet *Moe otkrytie Ameriki* (*My Discovery of America*, 1926), reflects the anti-racism of the Comintern and the Soviet state, as well as his own personal repugnance towards racism and his interest in African American culture.[7] Yet, in the 1920s, exoticizing and denigrating depictions of Africans and African Americans, including images of blackface, still appeared frequently in Soviet culture, persisting from the pre-revolutionary period or imported from the West, and were not perceived to be in conflict with official proclamations of racial enlightenment. Aspects of Mayakovsky's own primitivizing characterization of his black hero Willie, such as his description of Willie's limited brain power ("*V mozgu u Villi/ malo izvilin/ malo vskhodov/ malo poseva*" [In Willie's brain/ the coils are few/ little is grown/ little is sown]) and the simplistic patterns of speech that he bestows on him, betray the as yet superficial and unreflective Soviet embrace of anti-racism.[8]

This outlook would change dramatically after the Sixth Congress of the Comintern in 1928, which adopted the "Resolution on the Negro Question in the United States" that was far more binding and wider reaching than the "Theses" of the Fourth Congress. The "Resolution" declared that African Americans should be supported not only as oppressed workers and potential leaders in the struggle for communism in the United States, but also as part of a distinct nation in the American South (the so-called "Black Belt" or *chernyi poias* thesis) with the right to self-determination. It also sternly reprimanded "white chauvinism" in the CPUSA. With this extensive resolution of twenty-five points – concluding with the ringing declaration: "Henceforth the Workers (Communist) Party must consider the struggle on behalf of the Negro masses, the task of organizing the Negro workers and peasants and the drawing of these oppressed masses into the proletarian revolutionary struggle, as one of its major tasks" – the Comintern suddenly placed African Americans at the centre of international communist policy. Although the resolution did not specifically mention cultural production, point fourteen is explicit about the need to mobilize education:

> An aggressive fight against all forms of white chauvinism must be accompanied by a widespread and thorough educational campaign in the spirit of internationalism within the Party, utilizing for this purpose to the fullest possible extent the Party schools, the Party press and the public platform, to stamp out all forms of antagonism, or even indifference among our white comrades.[9]

The evidence of Soviet visual and literary culture in the years immediately following suggests that the resolution was indeed perceived as a call to create works about African Americans and to abolish the traditional racial stereotypes that had lingered through most of the 1920s.

The filmmakers Ivan Ivanov-Vano and Leonid Amal'rik, then, were tasked with transforming Mayakovsky's brief, focused account of the experience of a destitute, aging, and openly dim-witted black man in colonial Cuba – with his inchoate questions about why the white man eats ripe pineapple, while the black man has to eat a rotten one; or why the white man does white work, and the black man does black work – into a film that would be adequate to the more

directed rhetoric of Comintern anti-racism in 1932, with its particular emphasis on politically conscious African Americans and their leading proletarian
class status within the economic structures of the United States.

Mobilizing Mayakovsky

Even though Mayakovsky's poem had been published at an earlier, very different moment in Comintern views on race, his stature as a public literary figure
was such that any statement he had made on race would have authority. Even
if his poem was set in Cuba – which is to say, not the United States, which was
the contemporary focus of Soviet anti-racism – and even though it featured a
protagonist who was obviously less "conscious" in the Marxist sense than the
image of highly conscious black leftist agitators favoured by the Soviet press in
1932, the very facts of the name "Mayakovsky" and the title "black and white"
made it a go-to text for cultural production at this moment of orchestrated
public focus on anti-racism.

   Already in 1930, for example, erstwhile futurist Osip Brik wrote a theatrical sketch and film director Nikolai Ekk (also at the studio Mezhrabpomfil'm)
wrote a script for a "sound cinema-poem [*Zvukovaia kino-poema*]" based on
Mayakovsky's poem.[10] Brik's theatrical script was a relatively straightforward
presentation of the poem, involving a narrator/reader and the characters of
Willie, an "old negro," and Mister Bragg, the "sugar king," to speak the lines of
dialogue from their violent confrontation at the end of the poem. (The directions do not specify where an actor to play an "old negro" would be found; at
this point, the common technique of using blackface on white actors was falling out of favour, as its associations with American racism began to be understood.) The sketch is set in Havana, but Brik specifies that jazz music should be
played while a silent young man and woman dance in the background, which
would have "Americanized" the proceedings for Soviet audiences who associated jazz with African Americans.

   Ekk's script for his "sound cinema-poem" made the connection between
Mayakovsky's poem and racism in the United States even more pronounced.
Laid out in vivid photomontages of images from American magazines combined with handwritten dialogue and directions in red pen, the script frequently combines images of palm trees invoking the tropical Cuban setting
of Mayakovsky's poem with images of American skyscrapers and advertisements for modern American products (figure 11.2), and includes photographic
images and verbal descriptions of characters such as a fat, self-satisfied "typical" American capitalist with gold teeth, a pretty white "Miss," a little boy
who is "100% white," and a fat white pastor, deliberately directing the Cuban
story to the United States. Filling an entire notebook with scrawled red text,
frequently crossed out and amended, the script is a highly personal, almost

11.2 Nikolai Ekk, script for a film based on Mayakovsky's poem "Blek end uait," 1930.
Courtesy of the Russian State Archive of Literature and Art.

feverish meditation on racism, primitivism (images of African huts), and love lost to conditions of racist oppression (the addition of the character of a sad black woman or *negritianka*) – a textbook demonstration of an artist struggling to psychically work through this "new" problem of racism with the analytical tools provided by Mayakovsky and the Soviet press.

Ekk seems to have conceptualized the film according to the structure of silent cinema, writing down lines that he imagined as intertitles, but accompanied by a special score of sounds and music that would complement the affective power of the hallucinatory visual images he planned: for the opening, "sharp, dry, broken sounds, in some kind of distinctive rhythm"; later, like Brik, he calls for the "syncopated rhythms of jazz"; and at another point in the script, accompanying a cut-out photographic image of a tribal African woman, "the plaintive, touching motif of a negro song."[11] By including this "negro song" – presumably a reference to the spirituals that many Soviet critics considered to be a more authentic form of African American music than commercialized jazz – Ekk both takes an appropriately Marxist position on African American music and inserts an additional emotional and exoticizing element into his version of Mayakovsky's poem.

Ekk's script also includes a more sober page consisting solely of an article about lynching clipped from a Soviet newspaper with the title "Black Hatred," which is labelled in Ekk's insistent red pen: "The facts that are the basis for this script" (figure 11.3). The clipping is undated, and the source is not given, but in 1930 articles about lynching in America began to appear with sudden frequency in the Soviet press in conjunction with the first major event to put the new Comintern resolution into effect: the orchestrated public outcry around the August 1930 trial of two white American workers at the Stalingrad tractor

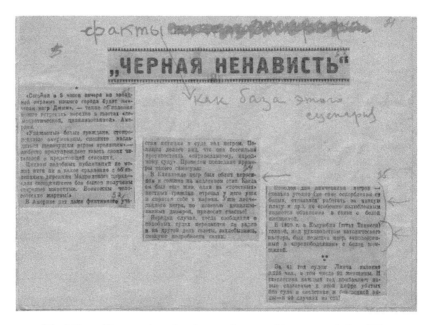

11.3 "Black Hatred," an article on lynching in the United States, in Nikolai Ekk's script for a film based on Mayakovsky's poem "Blek end uait,"1930. Courtesy of the Russian State Archive of Literature and Art.

factory who had assaulted an African American worker, Robert Robinson.[12] The trial received extensive coverage in the press, bringing sustained public attention to American racism against African Americans for the first time. The racist attitudes of the visiting white American workers in Stalingrad, Lemuel Lewis and George Brown, were consistently linked to the existence of lynch law in the United States.

The article clipped by Ekk is lurid in its evocation of racist violence. While the kinds of events it described are historically accurate, it provides no dates, exact locations, or citations for its claims, producing a generalized spectacle of horror rather than precise analysis.[13] It opens with a suspiciously non-specific "quotation" from an unnamed American newspaper: "Today at 5 o'clock in the evening on the western edge of our town the negro Jim will be lynched. Dear white citizens, 100% Americans, hurry to enjoy a nerve-tingling spectacle." While newspaper announcements of coming lynchings certainly existed, especially earlier in the century, the generalized "our town" and the stereotypical name "Jim," with no surname, betray that this particular announcement was made up by the Soviet journalist. Ekk's energetic red arrows, however, point to other sections of the article: a monstrous undated lynching "in Cleveland" in which a black man was burned to death and had his ears cut off, as good luck trophies, while he was still alive; and mentions of relations with white women as the justification for lynching black men. This latter detail was never elaborated upon in the press, given the firmly G-rated nature of Soviet public culture, but the sexual aspect of American racism seems to have interested Ekk, as demonstrated by his inclusion of the characters of the white "Miss" and the sad *negritianka* in his script.[14] The insertion of a sexual narrative into Mayakovsky's chaste, fully masculine story of a confrontation between men, in addition to the sensuous, stream-of-consciousness nature of the script, may help to explain why Ekk's "sound cinema-poem" was never produced.

The film that was in fact produced on the basis of the story of Lewis, Brown, and Robinson at the Stalingrad tractor factory, *Black Skin* (*Chernaia kozha*, dir. Pavel Kolomoitsev, Ukrainfil'm, 1931), steered clear of sexuality and experimental sound and imagery, focusing instead on how Soviet class solidarity can eradicate the inappropriate racist attitudes of visiting white American proletarians and on the representation of African Americans as conscious political actors. A full-length silent feature film, *Black Skin* tells the story of three American autoworkers who lose their jobs in the Depression and decide to go to the Soviet Union to work at a car factory there. Just as in Stalingrad, two of the workers are white and one is black, although in the film, one of the white workers is a woman, Mary, and she displays no racism against Tom, the black worker. But when the three of them arrive at the Soviet factory, the other white worker, Sam, refuses to share a dormitory room with Tom, and the two men almost come to blows. The Soviet workers let Sam know that such racism is unacceptable in the USSR and resolve to help Tom, who has declared that he wants to become a shock worker. The film ends with Tom, who has led the way in exceeding production norms, being congratulated by Sam and his fellow Soviet workers and appearing on the cover of the factory magazine (figure 11.4). Collaborative proletarian labour has empowered Tom and allowed him to attain purposeful consciousness as a worker and potential leader, and has successfully combatted Sam's "white chauvinism." As expected in the standard narrative of Soviet-style Marxism, the universal category of class solves the local problem of race.

In line with the Comintern directive for an educational campaign, *Black Skin* was meant to be shown in various public contexts accompanied by lectures and debates, as specified in the booklet published along with the film (*Chernaia kozha*, published by Ukrainfil'm, 1931). Extending the educational reach of the project, the booklet includes an anonymous historical essay about racism in America, which heavily cites Lenin's texts on the nationalities question as well as excerpts from the Trinidadian-British communist writer George Padmore's

11.4   Actor Kador Ben-Salim in the role of the American worker Tom in *Black Skin*, directed by Pavel Kolomoitsev, 1931 (Ukrainfil'm). Courtesy of Gosfil'mofond.

book *Kak zhivut amerikanskie negry* (*How American Negroes Live*, 1931) on the continued conditions of near-slavery in which African Americans worked and lived in the American South.[15] The role of the African American character Tom was played by the African actor Kador Ben-Salim. The measure of this film's distance from earlier Soviet representations of African Americans can be taken in comparison to Ben-Salim's role in the earliest Soviet "hit" film, the Civil War–themed silent film *Krasnye d"iavoliata* (*Little Red Devils*) of 1923, in which he played the character of another American Tom, Tom Jackson – a circus performer who joined the two main characters in their adventures as Red partisans against the Whites.[16] From the role of a sidekick who provides exotic interest and a visual – if no other – guarantee of Bolshevism's anti-racism, the black actor now plays a role that becomes the central pivot of the story and imagery in the film *Black Skin*.[17] The black character Tom's development into a conscious industrial shock worker who can stand up to racism with the support of his Soviet comrades modelled a new way of representing African Americans in Soviet film in the wake of the Comintern resolution.[18]

Against the backdrop of a film like *Black Skin*, two young writers at the Mezhrabpomfil'm studio's animation section proposed returning to Mayakovsky's poem "Blek end uait" to make it into an animated sound film.[19] It would be only the second animated film in Russia to be made with sound, after Mikhail Tsekhanovskii's *The Post* (Pochta, 1929), and the first with its own specially written musical score. Drawn animation was underdeveloped in Russia, where the first cartoon was produced in 1924 (by Dziga Vertov), a decade later than in the United States, and comparatively few were produced overall.[20] The cartoons were also different: most early Soviet drawn animation efforts were agitational or satirical films promoting aspects of socialist life, rather than the entertaining cartoons emerging from vaudeville and minstrelsy that dominated American offerings. It is not difficult to imagine why a film project based on Mayakovsky's poem, even one involving expensive animation, would have been so readily approved by the Mezhrabpomfil'm studio. Given the strong satirical focus of Soviet cartoons, the medium would have seemed ideal for a filmic version of Mayakovsky's biting critique of racism. According to the censor's notes, production on the film began in January 1932, at a moment of extreme awareness of race in the USSR in response to the publicity around the Scottsboro trials, and the same moment that Mezhrabpomfil'm was initiating planning on the live-action film *Black and White*, including issuing invitations to African Americans in the United States to travel to Russia to act in it.[21] A smaller, animated film based on a Soviet classic of anti-racism by the venerated revolutionary poet, and coming out of the more modest animation department, must have seemed like an appropriate companion piece to the studio's ambitious feature-length live-action project: the studio would be producing not one but two films on the extremely topical theme of racism in America.

The studio brought the project to Ivanov-Vano, a graduate of the famous post-revolutionary Moscow art school (VKhUTEMAS, *Vysshie Khudozhestvenno-Tekhnicheskie Masterskie* [Higher Art and Technical Studios]) where Mayakovsky had been influential and avant-garde artists such as Aleksandr Rodchenko taught. Ivanov-Vano was already one of the leading Soviet animators at age thirty-two. Overwhelmed by having recently been made head of the animation studio at Mezhrabpomfil'm and by the challenge of making his first sound film, he brought in his younger colleague, Leonid Amal'rik, to co-direct. Ivanov-Vano had previously made a highly successful, partially animated film based on the children's story *Krokodil* by the popular writer Kornei Chukovskii: *Sen'ka Afrikanets* (*Sen'ka the African*, 1927), which followed earlier Soviet conventions of exoticizing Africans. It tells the story of a young Russian boy, Sen'ka, who dreams himself to Africa, where he meets exotic wild animals and escapes a cannibal. The film is lost, and the drawings by Daniil Cherkes and the few stills that remain do not depict the cannibal, but it is possible that the cannibal exhibited the stereotypical primitivized features of the African "savage." *Blek end uait* shows us the transformation of the director himself, who went, in the space of a few short years, from unselfconsciously making an exoticizing film like *Sen'ka Afrikanets* to producing a structural depiction of race as its own critical category, related to but not exclusively determined by class, through the mediation of Mayakovsky and the contemporary Comintern-derived discourse of anti-racism.

Black Labour

The film's shift towards a more structural depiction of racism was partly the result of the script itself, with its tripartite division of the film into three contrasting "episodes" of which only the third, and shortest, would directly act out scenes from the poem with Willie as a protagonist. According to Ivanov-Vano's memoirs, the first of the three episodes, from which no stills or film fragments or even written accounts survive, was meant to evoke Mayakovsky's opening line describing Cuba as a "paradise country [*rai strana*]." In this section, Ivanov-Vano writes, they strived to create beautiful, fairy-tale–like images of the "paradise" of the tropical island as a deliberate contrast to the depictions of the hard labour of black workers that formed the subject of the second episode, which contrasted the "white" world with the "black" world, especially through depictions of white leisure versus black labour. Finally, the third episode of the film, "The Question of Questions [*Zakoriuka iz zakoriuk*]," localized the experience of racism through the character of Willie and his questions for the white bosses.[22] It is possible that the first episode of the film contained representations of women as part of the exoticizing vision of Cuba as a "paradise country." Otherwise, images of black female labour or even of any women at all seem to have been absent from the rest of the film, underscoring the masculine bias of the Comintern narrative of black labour and activism, and of Mayakovsky's poem.

In the typical language of Soviet self-criticism (his memoirs were published in 1980), Ivanov-Vano claimed that the entire first episode on the "paradise country" was a failure, resulting in "exotic" images that departed from the rest of the film – perhaps reminding him of the exoticizing images in his own and other earlier Soviet animation work or, possibly, in Ekk's script. But he was pleased with the results in the second episode on black labour:

> We didn't want in this episode to show the individual fate of the hero Willie, for which some critics later reproached us. It wasn't in the script. It seemed to us then that it was much more important to generalize the presentation of the unbearable forced labour of the blacks.[23]

This passage suggests that both the scriptwriters and the directors aimed to bring the project in line with contemporary Comintern anti-racist rhetoric by emphasizing the centrality of blacks to the plantation labour that was only alluded to in Mayakovsky's poem – focused, as it was, on Willie's individual,

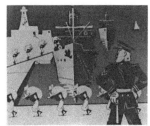

11.5 Ivan Ivanov-Vano and Leonid Amal'rik, directors, *Blek end uait*, 1932. Stills from Episode 2. Left and middle panels from I.P. Ivanov-Vano, *Kadr za kadrom* (Moscow: Iskusstvo, 1980); right panel from I. Vano, *Risovannyi fil'm* (Moscow: Goskinoizdat, 1950).

small-scale and sub-proletarian labour as a shiner of shoes. The three stills that remain from this mostly lost second episode represent male labour on a massive scale of multiple workers engaged in identical and seemingly endless, burdensome tasks (figure 11.5). The stills also demonstrate how closely Ivanov-Vano and Amal'rik followed their plan to construct a visual language for the film that would come closest to the outraged, anti-racist spirit of Mayakovsky as well as, more generally, to the "poster-satirical form [*plakatno-satiricheskii*]" that they associated with his aesthetic.[24] "Poster-like [*plakatno*]" was a standard synonym, or euphemism, for the shorthand, graphic, geometric or even abstract visual language of the avant-garde of the 1920s.

Ivanov-Vano felt that they had been especially successful in those shots "where the action is arranged along diagonals (towards the right and towards the left), and where long single line formations [*sherengi*] of blacks performed their mechanistic labour."[25] Ivanov-Vano and Amal'rik could have called on any number of images from the 1920s and the early 1930s, by Mikhail Cheremnykh, Aleksandr Deineka, and many others, for the diagonal compositions and shorthand visual language of Soviet agitational art. Mayakovsky himself was a visual artist who had gone to art school, deriving his deliberately primitivizing visual style from the traditional Russian *lubok* or wood-block print. The stencilled posters that he made for the windows of the state telegraph agency ROSTA during the Civil War (figure 11.6) were an inspiration for the extreme shorthand depictions of worker's bodies in solid-coloured silhouette, the caricatured faces of self-satisfied capitalists, and the insistent contrast between grotesquely fat capitalists and trim or emaciated workers that would dominate Soviet visual culture over the next decade.[26]

In the drawings for the film, the class and racial divisions between Afro-Cuban workers and their white capitalist overlords were figured through an insistent contrast of black and white forms – not only of black and white bodies, but also

11.6 Vladimir Mayakovsky, ROSTA poster, number 858, 1921. "Every truant is a joy for the enemy. But a hero of labour is a blow to the bourgeois." Courtesy of the Russian State Archive of Literature and Art.

of diagonally and geometrically divided blocks of objects, landscape, and space. In a still from the film showing workers carrying huge baskets on their backs, for example, the black skin of the bodies is contrasted with the white of pants and hats, and the single line formation of silhouetted black workers in front marches along a line of black ground, carrying white baskets, while the second line of workers marches along an uphill diagonal of grey ground, carrying black baskets, in a rhythmic, trudging, ever-upward repetition (see figure 11.5, left). In another still of similar lines of workers loading sacks of sugar onto ships in the harbour, the sharp diagonal of the gang plank carries the background line of workers up to the ship, and the imposing ships are themselves neatly divided into white and black halves, right down to the ripples in the water below them (see figure 11.5, middle). The repetition of marching columns of black workers is broken only by the figure of the looming white policeman dressed in black, with an evil, block-like face straight out of a caricature, who stands immobile, a colonial overseer as well as an enforcer of racist law. A third still literalizes the slavery metaphor for plantation labour through the large black chain that cuts across the surface of the shot (see figure 11.5, right). It also includes a line of white workers trudging identically to the two lines of black workers behind them as a way to emphasize the solidarity between black and white workers facing the same enemy of capitalist oppression. This class solidarity was the ultimate goal of Comintern policy towards African American workers, even if, in the 1928 resolution, it recognized white chauvinism and neglect as a continuing barrier. The barriers to this solidarity lay in representation as well as social relations: even here, in this self-consciously anti-racist film, the white workers are presented as more advanced proletarians. They are dressed in industrial work clothes in the form of one-piece coveralls and wear heavy black work shoes, while the black workers are barefoot and bare chested, wearing short white "tropical" pants.

When Ivanov-Vano wrote about his satisfaction with his diagonal compositions and marching formations of workers, he added: "these shots called up the sensation of the inescapability of the slave labour of the blacks."[27] The labour was technically not slavery, but the Comintern regarded plantation labour as being in some ways a continuation of slavery, especially in the American South. George Padmore's influential Russian book *How American Negroes Live* (1931), which, as we saw earlier, was cited in the educational booklet published along with the film *Black Skin*, contained a section on "Southern Oppression" and named the main forms of oppression against African Americans as "(a) peonage, (b) slavery, (c) lynching, (d) Jim Crowism," describing in detail the laws and practices that continued systems of enslavement.[28] Labour practices in the American South would also, we recall, have been the subject of the cancelled live-action film *Black and White*. While the black labour portrayed in the animated *Blek end uait* is clearly set in Cuba, with images of palm trees,

Spanish colonial architecture, and sugar cane farming, the poem and film both contain references to white bosses with Anglo names, which evoke the US companies that dominated the sugar, tobacco, and other industries in Cuba at that time – and so, by association, the slave-like conditions of labour in the American South. In Mayakovsky's poem, Willie sets up his shoeshine stand in front of the business of "Энри Клей энд Бок, лимитейд [*Enri Klei end Bok, limiteid*]" – which, in the film, results in the building being labelled with a sign, in a mix of capitals and lowercase Latin letters, "HENrY KLAY and BOCK LtD." Mayakovsky personifies Henry Clay as a "cigar king," but the historical cigar company Henry Clay and Bock & Company Ltd. had been named after the long-dead American politician, not an actual cigar maker named Henry Clay; it was founded as a British company in 1888, taking over from an earlier Cuban company called Henry Clay. The company moved their cigar factory to Trenton, New Jersey, in 1932, suggesting an especially strong American connection towards the end of the company's time in Cuba. The poem and film also contain the character of a "sugar king" with the name "мистер Брэгг [Mister Bregg]," presumably the common Anglo-American name Mr. Bragg – again invoking the many American sugar corporations in Cuba that harvested, processed, and shipped sugar to the United States.[29]

The aesthetic structure of *Blek end uait*, however, exceeds programmatic Comintern images of the structural class exploitation of black plantation labour in former colonies like Cuba and in the United States. In the two or so minutes of footage from the second episode that survive, these kinds of images are rendered sensuous and emotional by the film's use of sound, music, and montage. In one sequence that remains, an exaggeratedly corpulent black priest in a cassock promenades – or more properly sashays, swishing his backside from side to side like a showgirl on a stage – along a straight line from left to right through a colonial country landscape (figure 11.7, top left). He stops to raise his cross and bless, first a lean, shirtless white male worker and then a lean, shirtless black male worker. There is a cut to a pair of identical, faceless workers standing bent at slight diagonals in the same landscape a bit further along the road, the black one with white pants and hat, the white one with dark pants and hat, who repeatedly lift their hoes and strike the earth in unison, while behind them, climbing up a hill in a diagonal line from lower right to upper left and partially hidden behind a stand of sugar cane, black workers carry heavy white sacks on their backs (figure 11.7, top right), as in the stills examined earlier. A series of cuts move between the pair of workers and a thuggish white overseer lounging on a blanket under a parasol nearby (figure 11.7, bottom left); he stands up and swings a whip at them. The workers stiffen and look ready to object, but then the priest enters the frame and blesses them with his cross, his huge belly silhouetted against the white background, until, heads bowed, the two workers again pick up their hoes (figure 11.7, bottom right).

11.7 Ivan Ivanov-Vano and Leonid Amal'rik, directors. *Blek end uait*, 1932. Stills from Episode 2. Courtesy of Gosfil'mofond.

These limited actions are rendered in simple, not to say primitive animation technique with, in most cases, only one section of the image in motion at any one time.[30] But the music of the original score by Grigorii Gamburg works so closely with each movement and cut that the entire sequence is rendered dramatic and rhythmic. The string section moves the action along with an energetic march, following the priest's swaying backside; wind instruments strike low notes to underscore the heavy fall of the blows of the hoes and to warn of the imminent whipping; percussion crashes as the overseer stands up to swing his whip like a lasso. The music is punctuated by theatrical silences as well as diegetic sounds like the whistle of the whip or, later in the scene, a satisfied growl exchanged by the overseer and the priest when the overseer gives him a big pineapple as a reward for his services in quieting the workers with religion (figure 11.8).

11.8 Ivan Ivanov-Vano and Leonid Amal'rik, directors. *Blek end uait*, 1932. Still from Episode 2. Courtesy of Gosfil'mofond.

Ivanov-Vano was stunned by the effectiveness of the music and sound – with which he was working for the first time – for rendering "the rhythmic plasticity of the movement of the drawings in a more emotional key."[31] This emotional key was augmented by the aesthetic richness of the simply drawn images, compared with other examples of early Soviet animation. The artists used gradated grey paper for the drawings, rather than plain white, to add depth and tone, and a Molar lens and different gauzes to achieve a softness of the image; Ivanov-Vano wrote that they wanted to produce an effect of heat and languor, or "southern steaminess [*iuzhnaia znoinost'*]." Through these pioneering techniques, and in the face of a lack of technical know-how and material, *Blek end uait* transformed an "agitational" cartoon with subject matter stemming from Mayakovsky's famously stark verse – "*V Gavane/ vse/ razgranicheno chetko:/ u belykh dollar,/ u chernykh – net* [In Havana/ everything/ is delimited/ distinctly/ the whites have dollars/ the blacks don't]" – and from Comintern directives, into an affective filmic experience comparable to live-action drama or, perhaps, to the stream of sound and images in Nikolai Ekk's delirious, unrealized script for a "sound cinema-poem" about *Blek end uait*.

11.9 Ivan Ivanov-Vano and Leonid Amal'rik, directors. *Blek end uait*, 1932. Final stills from Episode 2. Courtesy of Gosfil'mofond.

Black Consciousness

The film's affective "emotional key" was raised to its most intense level in the third and final episode, where the larger racist structures are finally localized in the individual story of Willie himself and his coming to consciousness. In the final frames of the second episode, after the black priest receives the pineapple from the white overseer, he sits down at a table and greedily slices it up, revealing a close-up of his face rendered in unabashed blackface caricature (figure 11.9, left). The depiction of his face and body, combining Mayakovsky's most vicious caricatures of fat capitalists with the traditional pictorial stereotype of the African face, might seem out of place within the new Comintern directives for combating white chauvinism, except for one fact: he is a priest and therefore represents a black person who is a class traitor to his labouring black brothers, joining forces with capitalism and religion against atheist, working class solidarity. He deserves, presumably, to be caricatured as harshly as the white overseers with their nasty square jaws and tiny mean eyes. The priest's contented slicing of the pineapple brings us directly to the character of Willie, who wonders why "the white/ eats/ ripe pineapple/ the black –/ one soaked with rot." The priest in fact dissolves into an image of Willie's black hands shining a pair of shoes while the voice of the dramatic narrator, the actor Konstantin Eggert, intones the lines from Mayakovsky's poem about "the question of questions" emerging in Willie's mind. In this transition to the third episode, Willie's shoe-shining hands dissolve into an image of a white man in a suit and top hat seated at a table with an enormous pineapple before him (figure 11.9, middle), which in turn dissolves into an image of a black man who appears to be Willie at a cruder table with only a tiny, dried-out pineapple, a crucifix on the wall behind him (figure 11.9, right).

A white question mark emerges in front of Willie's face, filling the screen (figure 11.10, left), which then transforms into twisting, abstract lines (figure 11.10, middle) and a spinning line that eventually forms the wheel of the white man's car (figure 11.10, right). This formally daring and openly modernist sequence recalls

11.10 Ivan Ivanov-Vano and Leonid Amal'rik, directors, *Blek end uait*, 1932. Stills from Episode 3. Courtesy of Gosfil'mofond.

the dancing white geometric lines and shapes of Viking Eggeling's abstract film *Diagonal Symphony* of 1924, which Ivanov-Vano saw for the first time in 1928 when it reached the USSR from Germany. Ivanov-Vano was impressed by the novelty of Eggeling's technical experimentation, but wondered about the film's lack of subject matter, asking, "What is all this for?"[32] In *Blek end uait*, the white lines on black are harnessed for the didactic function of alerting us to a shift in the film from Willie's silent suffering to the episode of his internal questioning, emblematized by the floating question mark, from which he emerges as a more conscious subject with greater agency than Mayakovsky had allowed.

The white man's car speeds along a palm tree–lined road and then past modern white buildings in a deserted cityscape until it reaches Willie, who sits in front of a building with a large sign announcing Henry Klay and Bock Ltd. Willie stands up and confronts the white man with his question, declaimed in ringing voice-over by Eggert (see figure 11.1):

Ai beg ior pardon,	I beg your pardon,
mister Bregg!	Mister Bragg!
Pochemu i sakhar,	Why should sugar,
belyi-belyi,	white-white,
dolzhen delat'	be made
chernyi negr?	by a black Negro?
A esli vy	And if you
liubite	love
kofii s sakharom,	coffee with sugar,
to sakhar	then please
izvol'te	make the sugar
delat' sami.	yourself.

The question, simple and disarming as it is, gets right to the heart of the Marxist interpretation of alienated labour that the viewer has just seen laid out in all the images of labouring black bodies zigzagging the landscape in the second episode. Why should black workers contribute their labour power to making white sugar, which capitalist relations of production ensure that they will neither eat nor profit from? But in this episode of the film, the outrage is personalized, aimed directly at the ridiculously posturing Mr. Bragg with his big body and tiny calves and pointy feet. The caricature is partly derived from Mayakovsky, particularly his gaping-mouthed capitalist with a hat hopping off his head in his ROSTA design (see figure 11.6), but in this sequence the film also approaches the antics of American animation from this time, as Mr. Bragg screws up his face, wiggles the cigar in his black hole of a mouth interspersed with a few teeth, and makes surprised and outraged "ohhh" sounds as he listens incredulously to Willie's insolence.

In both the poem and the film, Willie's moment of speaking revolt is short lived. Mr. Bragg growls (like the priest and overseer before him) and groans until he curls his fist and swings at Willie, leading to shots of bursting clouds and floating stars in a familiar evocation of "cartoonish" violence. In the poem, there are six lines from the punch – about Willie getting back up, dusting himself off, picking up his shoeshine brush again – until the climactic, manifesto-like closing lines:

Otkuda znat' emu,	How could he know
chto s takim voprosom	that such a question
nado obrashchat'sia	must be addressed
v Komintern,	to the Comintern
v Moskvu?	to Moscow?

Mayakovsky here abruptly departs the "paradise land" of Cuba, where we have spent the entire poem, for the bracing shores of Moscow, where the Comintern provides the only solution to racist oppression. He holds out the Comintern like a gift – a shining vision of collective salvation – that will be more effective than Willie's confused and questioning voice. Even if the spirit of the poem is one of anti-racism, it constructs the black labouring subject as ultimately passive and incapable of resistance without the guidance of the Comintern. This viewpoint was characteristic of the early period of Soviet anti-racism, when holdovers of exoticizing racial stereotypes still dominated cultural production.

In the film, however, Willy's question and the violence it engenders do not lead directly to the lines about the Comintern. Instead, the film takes a visual excursus into specifically American imagery of even greater violence. The amusing and openly Disneyesque sequence of the confrontation with Mr. Bragg comes to an abrupt end as he drives away, leaving Willie crumpled motionless on the ground. The music starts up again as Mr. Bragg drives past the Havana harbour and then back along the same palm tree–lined highway (figure 11.11, first row, left). The shot zooms in on the stereotypical blackface doll hanging from its neck in the rear window (figure 11.11, first row, right), a nasty little commodity reminding us that Mr. Bragg comes from the land of lynch law, as Soviets referred to the United States. As if instigated by the appearance of this material reminder of US racism, the palm trees along the highway transform into electrical poles with lynching victims hanging from them, stretching towards a vanishing point in the distance (figure 11.11, second row, left). The image then cuts to a still of Willie's face, seemingly observing this horror, while the music stops and the narrator begins to recite the final lines of Mayakovsky's poem about Willie picking himself back up and not knowing that he should turn to the Comintern. During this recitation, we see black prisoners marching in a chain gang (figure 11.11, second row, right), black inmates alone in prison cells (figure 11.11, third row, left), and, finally, black prisoners being placed in electric chairs (figure 11.11, third row, right) and the switch being thrown by a large white hand (figure 11.11, fourth row, left). The recitation completed, the music starts up again as we see an image of Lenin's tomb at the Kremlin (figure 11.11, fourth row, right), followed by communist slogans and images of billowing, presumably red flags held aloft by black hands (figure 11.12).

Lynching was not a Cuban practice, and the electric chair was exclusive to its country of invention, the United States of America. The black lynching doll that swings gaily from the back windscreen of the white man's car offers a malevolent introduction to the serialization of capitalist violence to follow in the endless lines of lynched black bodies suspended from the electrical posts, culminating in rows of electric chairs. The insertion of these images of specifically American racism picks up on the American names of the bosses in Mayakovsky's poem to take the problem of American racism centre stage. The appearance of this repellent, hyperbolic violence in the film *Blek end uait* – completely absent from the source poem – stemmed from the Soviet obsession at this moment with US racism as the ultimate instructive case: Willie would not be able to come to full consciousness as a black socialist subject without a detour through the United States.

There is a factographic element in the film's insertion of precisely lynching and electric chair images, which appeared frequently in Soviet mass visual culture at this time. As we have seen, press coverage of the August 1930 trial of two white American workers at the Stalingrad tractor factory for assault on an African American worker occasioned the wide publication of articles on lynching in America, such as the one clipped by Nikolai Ekk for his screenplay for *Blek end uait*. For example, on 28 August two major newspapers, *Komsomol'skaia pravda* (*Komsomol Truth*) and *Trud* (*Labour*), published photographs of the same American lynching on their front covers (figure 11.13, left and middle): that of Thomas Shipp and Abram Smith, accused of robbing and murdering a white man and raping his white girlfriend, who were killed by a lynch mob on 7 August 1930 in Marion, Indiana. (The woman later

11.11 Ivan Ivanov-Vano and Leonid Amal'rik, directors, *Blek end uait*, 1932. Stills from Episode 3. Courtesy of Gosfil'mofond.

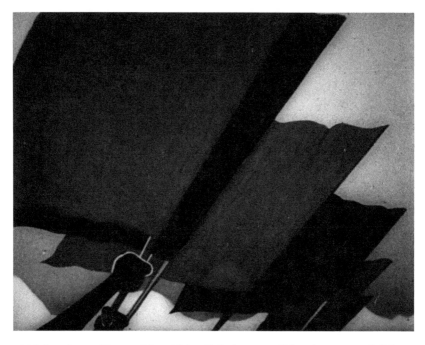

11.12 Ivan Ivanov-Vano and Leonid Amal'rik, directors, *Blek end uait*, 1932. Still from closing credits. Courtesy of Gosfil'mofond.

recanted the rape charges; the photograph would go on to become one of the most famous lynching photographs of the time.[33]) Yet, in spite of how recent and internationally well-documented the Marion lynching was, neither caption identifies the time or place or victims; they state simply "*Sud lincha*" or "*Sudom lincha*" (trial by lynching). The caption in *Komsomol'skaia pravda* even provided the misinformation that the two negroes had been accused of murdering a white woman. Two days later on 30 August, *Komsomol'skaia pravda* published another lynching photograph on its front page (figure 11.13, right), captioned "In Lewis's Motherland," this time identifying the location as "Marion (America)." The photograph is taken from behind and tightly cropped, revealing no details of the setting or participants, but it is clearly not from the Marion lynching: this victim is naked and appears to have been burned, and is not hanging from anything like the same tree.[34] As we saw in the article on lynching clipped by Ekk, the aim of these vague and generalized reports was to suggest the terrifying ubiquity of lynchings in the United States as a way to distance the Soviet Union, with its Comintern racial enlightenment, from its capitalist rival.[35] Ivanov-Vano and Amal'rik's haunting image of the lynching

11.13 From left to right: front pages of *Komsomol'skaia pravda*, 28 August 1930; *Trud*, 28 August 1930; and *Komsomol'skaia pravda*, 30 August 1930.

highway takes these anonymous images of American lynchings in the Soviet mass press to their logical conclusion.

The event in the history of Comintern anti-racism that left the most traces in visual culture was the international campaign against the Scottsboro trials. Nine black teenage boys were falsely accused of raping two white women on a train in Tennessee in March 1931 and were subsequently tried in Scottsboro, Alabama. Eight of the nine boys were immediately sentenced to death. The CPUSA took up their case, providing support for their numerous appeals and turning the trials into an occasion for international opprobrium against the American legal system.[36] The case was widely reported in the Soviet press, along with photographs and cartoons, starting in May 1931 when the news of the trial condemning the young men to death first broke; there was another upsurge in late June–early July 1931 during the lead-up to the original 10 July execution date; and again in April 1932, when the death sentences were upheld in yet another trial. This sustained attention in the press, as well as in mass-produced posters, formed the visual atmosphere of anti-racism in the months leading up to, and during, the production of *Blek end uait*. Any viewer seeing the lynching imagery, and the sequence of black prisoners being placed in the electric chair one after another, would immediately recognize their connection to the mass images of the Scottsboro case.

The electric chair dominated most press accounts and images as an especially malevolent object of American mass production and execution. The caption below the photograph of the group of Scottsboro prisoners in *Komsomol'skaia pravda* on 16 May 1931 stated: "They face the electric chair!" (figure 11.14, left), and the electric chair was a fixture of press accounts as well as cartoons and political posters. A fanciful drawing published in the same newspaper on 4 July 1931, just six days before the original execution date, essentially took the underfed, unemployed teenage Scottsboro prisoners from the by-then-well-known group photograph and turned them into a brawny, defiant crew of workers in production uniforms, menaced from above by electrical caps, albeit without the chairs (figure 11.14, middle). *Blek end uait* includes shots not only of the electric chairs but also of the hand throwing the switch that was another repeated trope of Scottsboro imagery. A histrionic newspaper cartoon, also from the weeks leading up to the execution date, shows a typical caricatured fat capitalist in a top hat with his hand about to throw the switch outside the Scottsboro prison house. The long arm of the Comintern reaches down from the proletarian sky and quite literally stops his hand in mid-motion (figure 11.14, right).

Critical historians have pointed out that the Comintern campaign to save the "Scottsboro Boys" was paternalistic: the boys could only be saved through the exemplary anti-racism of the Comintern, just as negroes more generally should look to the Comintern for their emancipation rather than to their own local forms of resistance. This argument fits with the critique that Mayakovsky's closing lines rendered the black subject passive: "How could he know/ that such

11.14 Imagery of the Scottsboro trials in the Soviet press. From left to right: *Komsomol'skaia pravda*, 16 May 1931; *Komsomol'skaia pravda*, 4 July 1931; and *Komsomol'skaia pravda*, 29 June 1931.

a question/ must be addressed/ to the Comintern/ to Moscow?" Willie doesn't have access to knowledge of the Comintern ("How could he know?") and therefore cannot be conscious of the fact that he could be emancipated through communism. The film, then, in its veneration for Mayakovsky and its insertion of dutiful visual references to the signature images of the various Comintern anti-racist campaigns would seem open to similar criticisms of paternalism coupled with self-congratulation. The argument of this chapter, however, is that the film belies this familiar critical approach. Through its very aesthetic form, it confronts precisely that paternalistic model of the ever-passive black subject awaiting enlightenment from the Comintern.

The film may draw on the familiar photographs and satirical cartoons from the mass press, but they lose their caustic, demagogic tone when they are subsumed within the rhythmic aesthetic flow of the film. Their essential outlines remain – lynching victims, prison cells, electric chairs, switches thrown – but their affective register is transformed from one of public ideological outrage to what Ivanov-Vano had referred to as a "more emotional key."[37] He uses this phrase to refer to the effects of the music on the animation, but it can be extended to the structuring of the images in the film as a whole. The filmmakers used music and montage to render the repeated images of oppressed labourers in the second episode sensuous and affective as well as analytical and political. The endless diagonal lines of plantation workers moving across the screen, images of the mundane suffering of heavy labour, were dramatized by the sensuous techniques for rendering the drawings "steamy" and by the vivifying orchestral music – by turns dirge-like and portentous, ominous and anticipatory. Similarly, in the third episode, the grisly press images are transformed into lushly rendered figures arranged in rhythmic, repetitive lines – even when the figures are hanged from poles, chained in prison cells, or strapped into electric chairs – with the emotional key shifting to the libidinal power of violence and abjection. In the film's most searing sequence, when the avenue of palm trees gives way to the lynching highway, the music quiets to a melancholy oboe as we speed along. Then the resonant timbres of Eggert's commanding voice accompany us as the camera pans upward along multiple prison cells, examining prisoners with hands bound or outstretched in supplication, and then pans sideways as iron bars slide closed across the electric chairs. This "emotional" rendering has the effect of de-sensationalizing the press images and making them available for an empathetic, rather than scripted political, response. Most importantly, this response is modelled for us by Willie himself – by the black subject who must, in the end, be the author of any emancipatory narrative.

The film delivers this modelling – and in so doing makes its most transformative aesthetic intervention into Mayakovsky's poem and into the paternalistic Comintern rhetoric – through its insertion of close-up images of Willie's face into the final "American" sequence. A single, still shot of his grizzled head fills the frame, his eyes staring directly out at us (figure 11.15, left). The drawing is

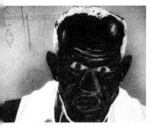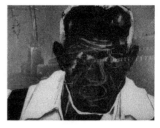

11.15 Ivan Ivanov-Vano and Leonid Amal'rik, directors, *Blek end uait*, 1932. Stills from Episode 3. Courtesy of Gosfil'mofond.

somewhat crude and shorthand, but it is not satirical. This portrayal is neither a caricature nor a stereotype of a black face. The receding hairline, white hair, and deep lines are individualizing, but the open mouth and wide eyes suggest a generalized horror, as if, despite all his hard experience of the world, he is confronting something that is finally opening his eyes. The word "KLAY" appears vertically on the wall behind him, emphasizing that he is occupying a specifically American space as he confronts these images: this shot of his face first appears after the sequence where the (Cuban) palm trees turn into (American) lynching poles. First, there is a black screen, and then his face appears along with a voice-over intoning the next to last set of lines from Mayakovsky's poem: "the negro/ breathed/ through his bashed-up nose." His face then dissolves into the image of a chain gang trudging behind the bars of a massive prison gate. The dissolve into these bars causes Willie's face to appear momentarily to be behind bars (figure 11.15, middle), underscoring his vulnerability to the racist application of the law. As Eggert begins to recite the final lines about the Comintern ("How could he know?"), the camera moves slowly upward from one dark, solitary prison cell to another, followed by shots of the electric chairs and a white hand throwing the switch. There is another chilling dissolve from the white hand throwing the switch into Willie's face, as the narrator reads the final line, "To Moscow." As the plaintive notes of the wind instruments start up again, Willie's face dissolves into the image of Lenin's mausoleum in front of the Kremlin wall (figure 11.15, right).

This sequence of dissolves between images of American racial violence and Willie's horrified face insert a space – absent in the poem – for him to come to consciousness about the larger structural problems of racism, rather than simply subordinating himself to the external will of the Comintern and its certainty that class solidarity will overcome racism. The Comintern is helping him come to this consciousness, certainly, through its mission of educating the world about lynching and lynch law in the United States. But the appearance and reappearance of the struggling intensity and emotion on that face insist on the internal process he undergoes before finally choosing the revolutionary path to the Comintern in Moscow. In its affective aesthetics, and its concomitant attention to Willie's coming to consciousness, *Blek end uait* exceeds reductive notions of how Soviet Marxism only approached race through the category of class.

The film's insertion of these images of an individual subject's emotions – and indeed the "emotional key" of the film itself – represents a shift in Soviet film and artistic production more broadly around 1932 towards the lyrical or, as the critic Nikolai Iezuitov put it, towards "a style of *socialist feelings*" that would complement the existing, more directly political "style of socialist concepts."[38] The film vividly embodies the key transitional moment around the Party's infamous April 1932 decree dissolving all artistic factions, which was meant to curb the power of the most militant proletarian arts organizations across media. *Blek end uait* took form before the decree, in the context of a film industry that produced (mostly silent) "agitational" films, but was released in the "post-April" (*posleaprel'skii*) – a much-used adjective at the time – period during which the film production system began to call for more nuanced and audience-pleasing films involving complex narratives and emotions. Perhaps unexpectedly, given the film's origins in a polemical Mayakovsky poem, its topical and agitational subject matter of racism, its almost factographic use of contemporary press images, and the fact that it was a cartoon – an as yet underdeveloped, and also primarily agitational, Soviet medium – it offers an unusually precise demonstration of how feeling and emotion are just as integral to communist consciousness as analyses of social processes.

Blek end uait was made at the same time that communist literary theorist Georg Lukács, who was actively involved in Moscow artistic debates at this time, wrote his essay "Reportage or Portrayal?" (*Reportage oder Gestaltung?*, 1932) – which can also be translated more literally as "reporting or shaping" – to challenge the factographic model of literature as pure reportage, or letting the facts speak for themselves. He argued that true proletarian literature should portray or shape reality, rather than merely report on it, through the psychological and emotional narrative techniques pioneered in nineteenth-century realism. We might see *Blek end uait*'s sublation of contemporary reportage on racial violence into more emotional images as a resistant response to factography and the recently dominant documentary and agitational mode in Soviet cinema. In Lukács's concept of portrayal, the author speaks for the subject portrayed, precisely as a way to present the motive forces underlying reality more cogently than simply reporting the subject's unreflected speech. The reality leading towards socialism would speak through the author, who can function as a kind of medium of history precisely because of his or her socialist partisanship. In his related essay of the same year, "Propaganda or Partisanship" (*Tendenz oder Parteilichkeit?*, 1932), Lukács writes: "Correct dialectical portrayal and literary re-creation of reality presuppose partisanship on the writer's part."[39] In this model of literary portrayal, Lukács imagines that partisan authors have unrestricted access to the historical forces that shape their proletarian protagonists, as if history were not also structured around racial, gender, and other difference.

In the case of *Blek end uait*, the black subject is portrayed as coming into consciousness through the partisanship of white filmmakers, exacerbating the distance between the author and the proletarian subject that is already presupposed in Lukács's model of the partisan author. The partisan white filmmakers, with their good intentions of "shaping" an account of racist reality, do not have access to the experience of actual black subjects; Willie is not speaking for himself, but being spoken for. Had Mezhrabpomfil'm made the aborted live-action film *Black and White*, with Langston Hughes as script consultant and twenty-one African American actors, the result might have offered a possibility for black subjects to speak for themselves by contributing to the partisan narrative portrayal of their experiences. Hughes thematized this problem of voice in his 1931 short play about the Scottsboro trials, *Scottsboro, Limited*. There the character named 8th Boy says: "I won't shut up. I've nobody to talk for me, So I'll talk for myself, see."[40] This model of the "black boy" talking for himself is not a possibility within the configuration of Mayakovsky's poem and Ivanov-Vano and Amal'rik's film. Yet, the script for Hughes's play continues, after the declaration made by 8th Boy that "I'll talk for myself," with an interjection from the chorus called the Red Voices: "And the red flag, too, will talk for you." Here, as Jonathan Flatley argues, something visual is being inserted into the question of voice: the boy will speak for himself, and then, not the Communist Party or some communist writer but the red flag as a visual symbol of collectivity will also speak.[41] The proposal of this chapter is to leave open the possibility that the repeated images of Willie's face as he comes to consciousness, combined with the billowing red flags held aloft in the film's conclusion as the music rises to an orchestral swell – the only positive images to appear in what we have left of the film – might begin to gesture towards the portrayal, in Lukács's sense, of the voice and agency of the oppressed.

Blek end uait's evocation of black agency could, then, be seen as a potent aesthetic response to the Comintern resolution that – in its most generous interpretation – called for an educational campaign to promote self-directed black political consciousness and white self-interrogation. Yet, the fullest critical response that we have from the time, penned by the censor assigned to the film before its release, was firm in its derision of the film's "formalist," "poster-like," and "mechanistic" style – all code words at that time for avant-garde or modernist – as well as of the film's political content, including its depiction of the Comintern. He was incensed by how the ending showed an image of the Kremlin when the lines "to the Comintern/ to Moscow" were read by Eggert: "Politically this is unacceptable. In this ending, the Comintern is personified by the Kremlin, which in no way corresponds to reality."[42] The censor is right enough: the Comintern was nominally an international organization, not a Soviet one, and its headquarters were separate from the Soviet government located in the Kremlin. But this critique is itself mechanistic: Lenin was, after all, the founder of the Comintern, and the image from the film is of his mausoleum in front of the Kremlin wall, rather than the Kremlin per se. It also brings a charge against the film that should more properly have been brought against Mayakovsky: the poet is the one who says that Willie should have addressed his question to Moscow. Similarly, and more consequentially, the censor derided the negro character for being obsequious and helpless (*smiren i bespomoshchen*): "His question sounds passive. In this question there is none of the curiosity that awakens consciousness." Once again, the charge is unfairly brought against the filmmakers, when Willie's questions were demonstrably taken, word for word, from Mayakovsky. This criticism also indicates that the censor was not looking closely at the film and its aesthetic choices, beyond identifying them as modernist in form; he mentions neither the mesmerizing violence of the concluding American images through which the filmmakers expanded upon Mayakovsky's limited dialogue, nor the curiosity – and possibly awakening consciousness – evinced by Willie's anguished response to them. When the censor slightly expanded his handwritten comments for a brief account of the film in *Kinorepertuar*, the publication of the film censors, he added critical commentary on the film's sound, going so far as to oppose the affective nature of the sound film to his idea of the political, claiming that the sound and musical score "erased political thought from the film."[43] This censor was not, as yet, convinced by the political efficacy of Iezuitov's turn to the "style of socialist feelings" in Soviet cinema.

Other than the censor's report, there is little information about the film's distribution or reception. The files on most films in the Gosfil'mofond archive contain any published reviews, but none are included in the folder on *Blek end uait*. A search of the Soviet national and film press yielded only a couple of other contemporary mentions of the film beyond brief advertisements and announcements confined to October–November 1932: the filmmaker Lev Kuleshov, in a brief article on Soviet animation in *Kino gazeta* in 1933, claimed that *Blek end uait* was the best animated film yet made in the Soviet Union, but offered no specific analysis; and V. Blium, in a brief article on sound in recent animated shorts in *Sovetskoe iskusstvo*, noted the film's achievements in sound design and its expression of "a great and entirely serious idea."[44] The otherwise quite deafening silence on this film, which was so timely and such an aesthetic achievement within animation at the time, is likely the result of the very same forces that cancelled the live-action *Black and White* film: in 1932, the USSR was attempting to gain diplomatic recognition by the United States and did not want to risk offending Americans with depictions of violent American racism. Archival documents prove that this issue led to the cancellation of the live-action film: a major American businessman and engineer leading construction on the Dnieper Hydroelectric Station, Colonel Hugh Cooper, got wind of the planned film from the many press accounts of the arrival of the African Americans in Moscow and took offence. He gained an audience with Politburo members and got the film cancelled in the summer of 1932, before filming even began; and indeed, the United States would go on to officially recognize the USSR in 1933.[45] The short animated film *Blek end uait* proceeded to get made, under the radar as it were, throughout the summer and fall of 1932, but, upon its initial and apparently limited release in November, it immediately became clear that it could be equally problematic for the Americans, and it appears that it was soon pulled from theatrical distribution and further reviews were not published.

Yet, there was one review, published, ironically enough, in America, that comprehended precisely the film's lyrical achievement. The *New York Times* Moscow film correspondent Bella Kashin, writing in an article on Soviet animation in 1934, referred to the film obliquely as a two-reel sound film based on a poem dealing with "the sociological problem of racial discrimination." The article admiringly contrasted the topicality of Soviet animation, as well as its quality, drama, and lyricism, with the shallow "comic antics" of Mickey Mouse in the United States.[46] To expand on Kashin's comparison, we can conclude that if Mickey Mouse's shallow antics = bourgeois aesthetics, then *Blek end uait*'s lyrical anti-racism = Comintern aesthetics.

NOTES

Many thanks to Amelia Glaser and Steven Lee for their vision of Comintern aesthetics and their dedication to bringing this volume to completion. I also thank audiences at the annual conference of the Association for Slavic, East European and Eurasian Studies (2015) and of the Society for Media and Cinema Studies (2016), as well as at the Faculty Colloquium in the Department of Art History, Northwestern University (2015) for their comments on earlier versions of this paper, and Robert Bird for his response and assistance at every stage.

1 The literal translation of the Russian title of the script, *Chernye i belye*, is "Blacks and Whites," emphasizing the actual black and white protagonists over the ontology of blackness and whiteness. Unless otherwise noted, translations from the Russian are my own.

2 See Steven S. Lee, *The Ethnic Avant-Garde: Minority Cultures and World Revolution* (New York: Columbia University Press, 2015); Ani Mukherji, "The Anti-Colonial Imagination: The Exilic Productions of American Radicalism in Interwar Moscow" (PhD diss., Brown University, 2011); Joy Gleason Carew, *Blacks, Reds, and Russians: Sojourners in Search of the Soviet Promise* (New Brunswick, NJ: Rutgers University Press, 2008); Glenda Elizabeth Gilmore, *Defying Dixie: The Radical Roots of Civil Rights, 1919–1950* (New York: W.W. Norton & Co., 2008); Kate A. Baldwin, *Beyond the Color Line and the Iron Curtain: Reading Encounters between Black and Red, 1922–1963* (Durham, NC: Duke University Press, 2002); William Maxwell, *New Negro, Old Left: African-American Writing and Communism Between the Wars* (New York: Columbia University Press, 1999); Allison Blakely, *Russia and the Negro: Blacks in Russian History and Thought* (Washington, DC: Howard University Press, 1986).

3 See Lee, *Ethnic Avant-Garde*, chap. 3, "From Avant-Garde to Authentic: Revisiting Langston Hughes's "Moscow Movie.""

4 The censor's one-page typed "*Udostoverenie*" (certificate) approving the release of the film states that it consisted of two reels totalling 540 metres, with a running time of twenty minutes. See the file folder on *Blek end uait* at Gosudarstvennyi fond kino-fil'mov RF (Gosfil'mofond Rossii/GFF); unpaginated. Only the final part of the second, shorter reel, which is 6:32 in length, remains at Gosfil'mofond. Digital versions currently available of this remaining footage are more or less incomplete or out of order.

5 On this shift towards the depiction of feelings or emotions in Soviet artistic production, see Christina Kiaer, "Lyrical Socialist Realism," *October 147* (Winter 2014): 56–77; and Emma Widdis, *Socialist Senses: Film, Feeling, and the Soviet Subject, 1917–1940* (Bloomington, IN: Indiana University Press, 2017). The only scholarly publication on *Blek end uait* is "*Black and White*: Race in Soviet Animation," chapter 2 in Maya Balakirsky Katz, *Drawing the Iron Curtain: Jews and the Golden Age of Soviet Animation* (New Brunswick, NJ, and London: Rutgers University Press, 2016), 56–74, which came to my attention after the present essay was in production. There are some overlaps in our analyses, such as the context of the Scottsboro trials. Katz's chapter is, however, marred by inaccuracies, misquotations, and unsupported conjecture that make it an unreliable source. For instance, she characterizes *Blek end uait* as a "simplification of the plot and characters" (63) of the cancelled live-action *Black and White* and as possibly even produced as a replacement for it; she also says it is five minutes long. But the plot and characters of the cancelled film were not reflected in *Blek end uait*; the two films were conceived concurrently, and the running time of the animated short was twenty minutes (see note 4).

6 Unlike McKay, the "Theses" emphasized the leadership role of African Americans only within the limited sphere of the African struggle against oppression. Kate Baldwin argues that the Comintern lacked commitment to actual anti-racist practices at that time, citing its refusal to call out CPUSA delegates to the congress for their racism. See Kate Baldwin, "'Not at All God's White People': McKay and the Negro in Red," in *Beyond the Color Line*, chap. 1.

7 The publication of *Moe otkrytie Ameriki* made Mayakovsky a public authority on America, despite the book's occasional inaccuracies. On his critique of US racial violence, see Meredith L. Roman, "Forging Soviet Racial Enlightenment: Soviet Writers Condemn American Racial Mores, 1926, 1936, 1946," *The Historian 74*, no. 3 (Fall 2012): 530.

8 Steven S. Lee argues, "Not only does Mayakovsky deny his character a distinctive voice and a developed mind, but he also denies Willie any means of local resistance." Lee also notes the disempowerment of Willie at the very level of his speech: rather than giving him any local specificity (as an Afro-Cuban, presumably Spanish-speaking subject), he speaks at first in stilted English ("Ai beg yor pardon, mister Bregg!") and then in the rhyming, alliterative, staccato voice of Mayakovsky himself. See Steven S. Lee, "Translating the Ethnic Avant-Garde,"

in *Ethnic Avant-Garde*, chap. 1, 23–4. On the contradictions in Mayakovsky's anti-racist intentions, see also Roman, "Forging Soviet Racial Enlightenment."

9   See "The 1928 Comintern Resolution on the Negro Question in the United States," *The Daily Worker*, 12 February 1929.

10 Both of these documents exist in manuscript form at the Russian State Archive of Literature and Art (RGALI); for Brik's *intsenirovka*, see 2324.1.221 (*Bykov Anatolii Vladimirovich, Levshina Anastasiia Aleksandrovna*); for Ekk's scenario, see 2794.1.58 N.V. Ekk. The first Soviet feature film with synchronous sound would not be produced until 1931: Ekk's own *Putevka v zhizn'* (*A Ticket to Life*) from Mezhrabpomfil'm.

11 See RGALI, 2794.1.58: 1, 33, and 16, respectively.

12 On this trial and the publicity surrounding it, see chapter one of Meredith L. Roman, *Opposing Jim Crow: African Americans and the Soviet Indictment of U.S. Racism, 1928–1937*, Justice and Social Inquiry (Lincoln: University of Nebraska Press, 2012). I am indebted to Roman's detailed research, especially in the contemporary periodical press.

13 This article clipped by Ekk corroborates Roman's claim that a general tendency in Soviet reporting on lynching was to elide dates and locations, in order to create a more frightening picture of the illogical terror of lynching.

14 On the libidinal economy of lynching, see Baldwin, "'Not at All God's White People.'"

15 *Kak zhivut amerikanskie negry* was a translation into Russian of the American section of Padmore's much larger English-language work on Africans and the African diaspora across the globe: George Padmore, *The Life and Struggles of Negro Toilers* (London: R.I.L.U. Magazine for the International Trade Union Committee of Negro Workers, 1931), https://www.marxists.org/archive/padmore/1931/negro-toilers/index.htm. The booklet on *Chernaia kozha* is held in the file folder on the film at Gosfil'mofond and states explicitly that the film was based on the Stalingrad trial (6).

16 According to J. Hoberman, Kador Ben Salim was a Senegalese deserter from the French interventionist forces in Odessa during the Civil War, who made himself indispensable to Soviet film. After his appearance in *Little Red Devils* in 1923, he would play almost all the blacks of any nationality to appear on screen for more than a decade. See J. Hoberman, *The Red Atlantis: Communist Culture in the Absence of Communism* (Philadelphia, PA: Temple University Press, 1998), 281.

17 Although Ben-Salim's Tom was nominally the central character in *Black Skin*, it can be argued that the true star was the white racist Sam: the camera lingers on him more closely as he is transformed from a racist into a Soviet internationalist. At least aesthetically in this case, the campaign against "white chauvinism," which was all about white people, took precedence over the campaign for the liberation of black people themselves.

18 Another Soviet film from this moment also featured Kador Ben-Salim as an African American worker who has decided to move to the Soviet Union: *Vozvrashenie Neitana Bekkera* (*The Return of Nathan Becker*, 1932), a Yiddish-language sound

film from the Belorussian film company Belgosfil'm. The bricklayer Nathan Becker returns to the Jewish shtetl he left years before for the United States, bringing his wife and his African American friend Jim with him. Jim's role is largely ornamental, however: as a visual sign of the promise of Soviet anti-racism, he is present in many scenes, but he doesn't speak and his character is not developed beyond his stated status as a skilful bricklayer. (Tom and Jim were favourite names for African American characters in the Soviet imagination.)

19 Ivanov-Vano writes in his memoirs that the script was proposed by a young poet, Aleksandr Kovalenko, and a scriptwriter, Iosif Skliut. See I.P. Ivanov-Vano, *Kadr za kadrom* (Moscow: Iskusstvo, 1980), 67. He noted that the script "was not dramatically developed" and that he felt hampered by having to follow the structure of the three distinct episodes that it specified (69). Ivanov-Vano also reveals that *Blek end uait* has been lost for a long time: while preparing to show a selection of early Soviet animation at the International Exposition in Montreal in 1967, he was disappointed to find that *Blek end uait* was already missing from the State Film Archive in Moscow, Gosfil'mofond (81).

20 On early Soviet animation, see Laura Pontieri, *Soviet Animation and the Thaw of the 1960s: Not Only for Children* (New Barnet, UK: John Libbey Publishing, 2012), chap. 1, "From Propaganda to Children's Films." The first animated films in the United States were part of vaudeville acts, rather than mass distributed films.

21 See the handwritten censor's notes in the file folder on *Blek end uait* at Gosfil'mofond, 1932, unpaginated.

22 See Ivanov-Vano, *Kadr za kadrom*, 69–70, on the sections of the film.

23 Ibid., 70.

24 Ibid., 68.

25 Ibid., 70.

26 The film's depiction of the colonial landscape was also indebted to Mayakovsky's travel sketches of Cuba, as published, for example, in *Krasnaia niva* no. 35 (1926): 11 (illustrated in Lee, *Ethnic Avant-Garde*, 57).

27 Ivanov-Vano, *Kadr za kadrom*, 70.

28 Padmore, *Life and Struggles of Negro Toilers*. See part 1, chapter 2, "Black Slaves in the New World," section I, "The United States of America," subheading "Southern Oppression." Section I on the United States also contains a subheading on "White Chauvinism and the Labour Movement," like the Comintern resolution of 1928.

29 Edward Stuyvesant Bragg was US consul general in Havana in 1902. It is conceivable that Mayakovsky came across his name on his visit to Cuba.

30 Soviet animators did not yet have access to the cel animation technique used in the United States in which animators could draw moving figures on the surface plane of an image on celluloid, allowing background images to be reused in multiple frames. On cel animation technique, see Donald Crafton, *Shadow of a Mouse: Performance, Belief and World-Making in Animation* (Berkeley: University of California Press, 2013), 160–80; on early Soviet animation techniques, see Pontieri, *Soviet Animation*.

31 Ivanov-Vano, *Kadr za kadrom*, 70.
32 See Ivanov-Vano, *Kadr za kadrom*, 59–60. The abstract spinning line that transforms into a wheel also had a Soviet predecessor: the scene of an abstract spi-
ralling vortex in Mikhail Tsekhanovskii's 1929 animated sound film *Pochta* (*The
Post*), based on Samuil Marshak's children's book.
33 The photograph of the Marion, Indiana, lynching that was used and misidentified
in both the *Komsomol'skaia pravda* and *Trud* illustrations of 28 August 1930 was
a cropped version of a "Souvenir Portrait" taken by a local studio photographer,
Lawrence Beitler.
34 The caption for the illustration in *Komsomol'skaia pravda* from 30 August 1930
calls the victim a "worker-negro" and states that he was lynched because he
"actively participated in preparations for a strike." Neither the Marion victims nor,
indeed, most lynching victims were communist activists, but, as Roman points
out, black victims of white racial violence were consistently identified as such
in the Soviet press in order to suggest that lynchings were a method not only of
racial oppression but of anti-revolutionary violence. See Roman, *Opposing Jim
Crow*, chap. 1. Two short related articles appear to the right of the photograph:
one asserting Lewis and Brown's guilt, entitled "*Posledovateli lincha v Stalingrade*"
(Followers of Lynch Law in Stalingrad); and another "*SSSR unichtozhaet rasovuiu
rozn*" (The USSR Eradicates Racial Strife), announcing that the Italian fascist
newspaper *Popolo d'Italia* saw the trial against Lewis and Brown as demonstrating
the "*iskrennee zhelanie SSSR unichtozhit' vsiakie rasovye otlichiia mezhdu rabo-
chimi* (the genuine desire of the USSR to eradicate all racial distinctions between
workers)."
35 The self-serving nature of Soviet outrage at American lynch law, especially in light
of the Soviets' own problematic human rights record, is captured by the phrase
that arose in political anecdotes of the Khrushchev era, "*A u vas negrov linchuiut*"
(But in America you lynch negroes) – referring to the stock response of Soviet
demagogues to any criticism of the Soviet Union by the United States.
36 See James A. Miller, Susan D. Pennybacker, and Eve Rosenhaft, "Mother Ada
Wright and the International Campaign to Free the Scottsboro Boys, 1931–1934,"
The American Historical Review 106, no. 2 (April 2001): 387–430.
37 Ivanov-Vano, *Kadr za kadrom*, 70.
38 See N. Iezuitov, "O stiliakh sovetskogo kino," [On the Styles of Soviet Cinema],
Sovetskoe kino 5–6 (1933): 31–47; italics in the original. See also Widdis, *Socialist
Senses*; and Christina Kiaer, "Lyrical Socialist Realism."
39 Georg Lukács, "Propaganda or Partisanship?" trans. Leonard E. Mins, *Partisan
Review* 1 (April–May 1934): 44.
40 See Jonathan Flatley's citation and discussion of this play in chapter ten of this
volume, "'Beaten, but Unbeatable': On Langston Hughes's Black Leninism,"
313–51.
41 Ibid.

42 Censor's notes on *Blek end uait*, Gosfil'mofond, unpaginated. The censor's signature is illegible, but grammatical indicators suggest a male writer. He finds the film simplistic in its "petty bourgeois" depictions of the horrors of capitalism, which call forth pity from the viewer, demonstrating that he is not impressed with the film's "emotional key."

43 See the anonymous entry on *Blek end uait* in *Kinorepertuar*, nos. 11–12 (1932): 2–3; citation from 3. In a further, tantalizing note on sound in the film, the censor writes that the film is not without exoticism "in the character of the negro, playing and singing little songs, without any relation to the subject matter" in a section whose sole purpose is "awakening in the viewer feelings of pity for negroes" (3). Since the part of the film that might have contained these songs, presumably spirituals, has so far been lost, it is impossible to say where they might have appeared within the three episodes or how they were used. It suggests another connection to Ekk's script for a "sound cinema-poem" of *Blek end uait*, with its inclusion of a "plaintive, touching motif of a negro song" (see note 10).

44 See L. Kuleshov, "*Ochen' vazhnoe iskusstvo*" [A Very Important Art] *Kino gazeta*, 10 February 1933; and V. Blium, "Opyt zvukovoi mul'tiplikatsii," *Sovetskoe iskusstvo*, 27 November 1932, 4. Blium was responding to a special showing of recent sound animation that he had attended, suggesting that the film may not have been released in regular theatres. Katz claims that the film received "high accolades" from critics (61), but the only contemporary source she cites is Blium. Later, in 1940, the leading children's book author Kornei Chukovskii would look back on *Blek end uait* as an exception to what he saw as the norm of derivative Soviet animation, but he offered no specific discussion of its merits. See *Komsomol'skaia pravda*, 15 February 1940, 6.

45 See G.L. Bondareva, ed., *Kremlevskii kinoteatr 1928–1953: Dokumenty. Seriia Kul'tura i vlast' ot Stalina do Gorbacheva* (ROSSPEN: Moscow, 2005), 190–1n3. Mukherji and other authors on the *Black and White* group offer detailed accounts of the documentation surrounding the cancellation, with Lee concluding that the evidence is by now definitive that it was American interference that got the film cancelled, rather than the poor script quality, as Hughes would claim in his memoir (see note 2).

46 Bella Kashin, "In the Moscow Screen World: 'Animated Graphic Art' in the Land of the Soviets," *New York Times*, 21 January 1934: X4. The comparison to Mickey Mouse is particularly pertinent, because of his origins in the conventions of blackface minstrelsy. See Nicholas Sammond, *Birth of an Industry: Blackface Minstrelsy and the Rise of American Animation* (Durham, NC: Duke University Press, 2015). Ivanov-Vano wrote extensively and critically about Disney in his memoir.

PART THREE

History: Beyond the Interwar Years –
Afterlives of Comintern Aesthetics

Chapter Twelve

The Revolutionary Romanticism of Alice Childress's "Conversations from Life"

KATE BALDWIN

Tulane University

When Paul Robeson declared in 1934 that the Soviet Union was where he "walked in human dignity for the first time," he marked a distinctive turn away from his prior life as a popular Hollywood icon best known for his rendition of "Ol' Man River" in Jerome Kern and Oscar Hammerstein's *Show Boat* (1927). In so doing, he moved away from the generally demeaning and reductive popular representations of American blacks that circulated in the 1930s and, in particular, from the film *Sanders of the River*, which was to be one of his last Hollywood appearances. So condescending was the final edited footage of *Sanders* (released in 1935) that the *Harlem Liberator* declared: "The producers of the film have the nerve to create the disgraceful impression that the African natives *like* the way the English robber barons exploit, brutalize, and mercilessly terrorize them ... A picket line should be thrown around every theater showing this picture."[1]

In aligning himself with the Soviet Union, Robeson not only rebuked Hollywood's tendencies towards white supremacy, he also embraced the attraction of black leftists to Soviet Russia in the 1930s. Like the well-known writers Claude McKay and Langston Hughes before him, Robeson lauded the Soviet claim to abolish racism along with the vestiges of class distinctions. But lesser-known figures also warmed to the promise of the Soviet project. The editorial board of the *Harlem Liberator* quickly pointed to the imperialist overtones of *Sanders*; it likewise took up the Soviet cause with unparalleled gusto. Alongside editor Cyril Briggs, others such as Otto Hall, Otto Huiswoud, and James Ford championed the Soviet Union unapologetically in the paper's pages, documenting, among other things, a disdain for black passivity to white chauvinism. Instead, they sought to fire up the revolutionary tendencies of decades of black dissent.

Named for William Garrison's abolitionist paper *The Liberator* (1831–65), the *Harlem Liberator* boasted a dynamic mix of race pride, interracial solidarity, and internationalism, wrapped in a cultural politics that wedded aesthetic innovation, anti-imperialism, and class unity across racial lines. According to critic Cathy Bergin, the *Harlem Liberator* was the first paper to "promote and produce a discursive black communist subject."[2] Like Mark Solomon, Mark Naison, and others before her, Bergin links the rise of black communism to the financial fragility of the period and the deepening chasm between white business owners and black moderates who were rightly suspicious of racism within the bourgeois ranks. Naming the fiction of cross-racial solidarity as a middle-class myth, the *Harlem Liberator* sought to find a balance between modes of address to a black readership and a commitment to interracialism as a cornerstone of communist praxis. The paper addressed this tension by documenting the way in which the black world was at the centre of international, communist-supported anti-capitalist protest.

Although short-lived, the *Harlem Liberator* became a model for Robeson's own commitment to generate a new black communism in journalistic form some twenty years later. Like the *Harlem Liberator*, Robeson's *Freedom* offered a vibrant mix of black-centred news coverage, global headlines documenting strands of anti-capitalism, and interracial projects dedicated to fighting imperialism and racism alike. Unlike the *Harlem Liberator*, however, *Freedom* highlighted women's contributions to the black radical cause, placing women at the centre of international, anti-imperial protest. Women were not only featured as the "Face of Africa" on the paper's front page (June 1953), but women journalists were featured throughout *Freedom*'s pages. Alice Citron, Vicky Garvin, Claudia Jones, Eslanda Robeson, Lorraine Hansberry, Alice Childress – to name only the best known – were regular contributors. (In fact, in any given issue, the women reporters might outnumber the men.) If the *Harlem Liberator* sought to discursively shape an early black communist who was representatively male, *Freedom* took up that project decades later with an added eclecticism best represented by its female contributors, in particular Alice Childress. The postwar work of Alice Childress, whose column "A Conversation from Life" appeared in Robeson's *Freedom* from November 1950 to August 1955 (figure 12.1), offers a prime source for scrutinizing how black internationalists imagined and proposed to create a black collectivity in the years when popular support for communism had waned, and women, in particular black women, were deprived of civic rights as the postwar turn to a domesticated femininity positioned women on the periphery of political agency. In an era historically typified by the iconicity of the "housewife," Childress's column offered a means to dislodge the enduring centrality of this figure to feminist work. The *Harlem Liberator* may have documented the centrality of interracialism to international communism, but what might it mean to put a black female domestic at the centre of anti-capitalist protest?

To be sure, a lot had changed in the twenty years between the *Harlem Liberator*'s demise and *Freedom*'s first issue: the Second World War had proclaimed the twentieth century to be that of fascism and totalitarianism, a claim that was

12.1 "A Conversation from Life: Two Can Play the Game," *Freedom*, May 1953.

being roundly challenged by thinkers such as Henry Luce, who were more eager to name an American century. McCarthyism had stepped in to attenuate the battle. In 1929, communism was a project as yet untested – the headiness of its animating claims against class-based injustices and racism was still exhilarating and seductive, particularly for American blacks who were Depression weary and confined by government-sanctioned Jim Crow. But, by 1951, no one could utter pro-Soviet Russia comments and not be accused of treason (figure 12.2). For example, in January 1954 Childress's *Freedom* column "A Conversation from Life" lamented the fraught state of public affairs: "Every word you read is Communist this and Communist that and McCarthy, McCarthy, McCarthyism. Everybody is being investigated to see if they think anything Communist. Air raid sirens are blowing all over the land and the whole populace is stirring and tossing with troubled dreams every night and the little children are crawling under their desks in school and holdin' their little hands over their heads – to protect them from **atomic blasts**."[3] As Childress noted, ubiquitous systems of surveillance and fear-mongering investigations sought to occupy every nook and cranny, while the government insisted upon public performance of ritual helplessness in the face of atomic annihilation. Childress's column openly railed against this tyranny: "We are all going to suffer much more until we wake up and defend the rights of the Communists – defend their right to speak and be heard, to write and be read, to vote and to run for public office."[4] Childress's appeal to "we" positioned her at the centre of a black public for whom she was both trying to speak and prompt into action by stressing everyday vulnerabilities to the terrors of McCarthyism. Moreover, these vulnerabilities revealed the connectedness between black publics in the United States and those abroad by implicitly connecting the violence of intra-state structures and those of European colonialism.

Indeed, Childress's complexly voiced column may offer the best means of understanding the way that, in the early 1950s, *Freedom* reimagined black collectivity, the status of what we might call a black groupness. "A Conversation from Life" provided a space in which reader identification could become a means for opening to an imagined political grouping through a communicative technique that hearkens back to the African American tradition of call and response.[5] But it also intervened in those predominantly male antecedents to suggest a new audience of meaning-makers – those previously unaddressed and, as such, unheard. In pursuing a feminist transnationalism, "A Conversation from Life" raised questions about ideology and form, gender and language, and the relationship between the vernacular and the political. From what became their more or less regular back page location, Childress's columns framed the dilemmas of a newspaper created to prod leftist and black publics to action (figure 12.3). "A Conversation from Life" helps to answer the question about how it might be possible to use one voice to reflect and move many to action.

12.2 *Freedom*, January 1954.

Reading Childress's columns in this way offers an opportunity to challenge the idea of a pre-formed, unified subject or national people allegedly called into being by the paper. The form of the paper – its artistry – reveals how subjectivity can be fragmented within a venue that claims "my people" as a self-understood and self-affirming entity. In this way, "A Conversation from Life" recast some of the tenets of an international revolutionary aesthetics heralded by Lenin and suited them for engagement in a post–Second World War world.

Freedom began as a project spearheaded by Paul Robeson and editor Louis Burnham to expose the radical hypocrisies of an era in which the United States claimed to be the leader of the free world and yet Jim Crow laws prevailed. Moreover, Robeson and his staff (including W.E.B. Du Bois and Alphaeus Hunton) sought to underscore the links between the multiple infringements on black freedom in the United States and those of people of colour throughout the world. These connections were systemic and institutional, linked to legacies of colonialism and slavery and the routes of capitalist accumulation. *Freedom*'s aim was to replace the dominant and allegedly objective news about black and brown people in the United States and abroad with an objectivity that took black subjectivity into account. Headlines such as "Labor Council Links Fight

4 FREEDOM   January, 1954

A Conversation from Life

By ALICE CHILDRESS

MARGE, there's an awful lot of upsets going on today. You can't pick up the newspaper without getting the tremors. Everybody is going around with a worried hang-dog expression. Too many people are frightened and fearful and worried and just plain heartsick.

Every word you read is Communist this and Communist that and McCarthy, McCarthy, McCarthyism. Everybody is being investigated to see if they think anything Communist. Air raid sirens are blowing all over the land and the whole populace is stirring and tossing with troubled dreams every night and the little children are crawling under their desks in school and holdin' their little hands over their heads—to protect them from **atomic blasts.**

The church is being investigated, the school is bein' investigated, the library shelves is bein' investigated, the Army is bein' investigated, the unions is bein' investigated, social clubs, political clubs, scientists, actors, writers, business people, housewives, the post office, the fire department, social workers, factory workers, store keepers, aunts, cousins, sisters, grandmothers, daughters, sons, brothers and husbands—all bein' investigated!

And for what? . . . Yes that's what they say—to see if they are Communists, or sympathize with Communists, or have ever belonged to any organization that had Communists in it, or if they have ever entertained a Communist or spoken to a Communist, or read a Communist paper or thought any thoughts that a Communist might also think.

Why, Marge, WHY? . . . Yes, they say that too—that Communism is wicked or keeps people from being free and is just outright awful . . . But the particulars are so skimpy. . . . Why is it awful? "Because you'll lose your freedom," they say! The freedoms we prize so much, like—reading what you want, saying what you want, choosing your friends like you want, publishing any book or paper you want to publish, reading what you like, going to whatever church you want . . . every citizen in the land having equal rights to vote, serve on juries and all the rest of the equal rights that citizens are supposed to have. . . .

NOW, MARGE, you just turn on your television set at almost any time and you will be sure to find some discussion ragin' about, "How we can stop Communism"—and it will be called some kind of "forum," and you will see that they have p[illegible] three or four or more f[illegible] who **hate** Communism—to tell you what it is; and if by chance there is one person who is not too sure whether it's all that bad, he will sure wish he hadn't been there by the time the others finish ruining his reputation or his business or both.

But one thing you never see is a Communist sittin' in on it and explaining what he thinks Communism is—and defending it. That's not allowed! No, mam!

Now if the object of McCarthy is to stop Communism and convince all the American people that it's bad, it seems to me it would be a shortcut for him to get a well-known Communist on television and rip into him in a open debate and show the people what a Communist thinks about . . . and if McCarthy is right he could pick his arguments to shreds. Why doesn't he do that? I ask you, **why?**

No. . . . Instead there's a whole lot of hullabaloo about not allowin' Communist books on the library shelves, not allowin' Communists to write on newspapers or teach in schools, or act in plays, or speak their piece anywhere. In other words, they are tellin' the American public, "You just might believe every word you hear."

. . . That's very true, Marge. There are folks that are speakin' out against terrorizin' the public, but most of 'em use the strangest reasonin'. They will say, "We must not be questioning and terrorizing **innocent people.**" Now who in the devil can decide who is innocent beforehand? What they are sayin' really is: "Let's terrorize the Communists by fair means or foul and at the same time try not to bedevil folks who are not Communists."

Now I contend that terrifying and bedeviling are not fit methods to use on any citizen and we are all going to suffer much more until we wake up and defend the rights of Communists—defend their right to speak and be heard, to write and be read, to vote and to run for public office, to have the full benefits of trial by jury.

It is laughable, Marge, but I hear people everywhere beginning their sentences . . . "I am not a Communist, **but** . . . ." Why does someone have to announce that they are not a Communist before they can tell me what they are thinking?

WELL, the upshot of it all is just this . . . There is one thing in which I am agreein' with McCarthy . . . **If we are going to persecute people for what they read or think** there is nothing else for the persecutors to do but to keep the readin' and thinkin' matter out of sight and sound. Then we must raid the libraries and remove all books that the ruling body in this land deems unfit for our minds . . . we must suppress all movies that they think unfit . . . we must close all schools that they think unfit . . . we must close off every avenue that they think unfit and put away or do away with all people who have such ideas, close all churches and social groups that hold such ideas and purge every home in the land to root out such ideas—that is if we are ready to trade **Justice** in exchange for **Persecution.**

That's right, Marge. The question today is **not** McCarthyism or Communism. It is—American Justice.

. . . What is its definition? You see, Marge, to me peace means a lot more than not bein' in a war. It means peace in your heart and mind; it means my n e i g h b o r s and friends and all mankind growing in wisdom and love and understanding; it means finding a cure for cancer; it means feeding the hungry, making garden apartments out of the slums, stopping polio, opening up every school in the land to all races; it means friendship and laughter and freedom from fear; it means grownup folks not bein' ashamed to go to school and learn to read and write and enjoy this big, beautiful world; it means making it the social rage to belong to the millions rather than the "four hundred."

That's right, Marge, there are two doors in front of us: Persecution or Justice, and it's up to the American people to decide which one it will be. . . . I've made up my mind, Marge. How about you?

HUGH BRYSON

This Man Is On Trial . . . WHY?

HUGH BRYSON is the President of the National Union of Marine Cooks & Stewards, one of the oldest maritime unions on the West Coast.

THE TECHNICAL CHARGE on which he is being brought to trial claims that he falsified an oath required by the anti-labor Taft-Hartley Board.

OVER 230,000 other union members have signed this oath, which is required by the law, to the effect that they "are not now" members of the Communist Party, or "affiliated" with that party.

BRYSON WAS the first leader of a national union to be indicted on such a charge. (Several others have since been indicted and similarly face trial.)

THE PURPOSE of Taft-Hartley is to smash unions; the "anti-communist" affidavit is one of the weapons of the law. It is designed to take away from union men and women the right to elect their own officers, and to replace those officers with others who will conform to what the employers—not the workers—want.

What Negro Leaders Think of MCS!

Wide support for what MCS had done for its members exists in the Negro community from coast to coast. Most recently, a resolution passed unanimously in San Francisco at a meeting sponsored by Negro community leaders, had this to say:

"We . . . recognize that those elements most vocal in condemnation of this union's policies have violated and are still violating the laws of our land rather than following the democratic hiring practices of the union they condemn, as far as Negro citizens are concerned. . . .

"The officers and leadership of this union have helped bring into real practice in their union affairs the Constitution and Bill of Rights of our country. Those who attack this union for its contribution to racial democracy attack the economic and social aspirations of this community."

The meeting at which this resolution was passed was sponsored by Dr. and Mrs. Carlton Goodlet, community leaders, Messers Albert James and William Chester, (leaders of the Intl. Longshoremen's & Warehousemen's Union), Messers Cecil L. Finley and Samuel Coleman (undertakers), Drs. Legrand L. Coleman and Washington E. Garner and the Rev. F. D. Haynes, a leader of the National Baptist Church.

WIDESPREAD SUPPORT

The late beloved pastor of the Pleasant Hill Baptist Church (San Francisco) and president of the Baptist Ministers' Union, the Rev. R. L. Turner, had this to say at the 1951 convention of MCS:

"I find it very encouraging to find myself associating with people like yourselves, who dedicate their time and energies to uplifting humanity. . . . I have much sympathy for the MCS. . . . I disdain discrimination from any source. . . . Anything in life that is worth doing must be built in struggle."

At the same convention, the internationally celebrated artist Paul Robeson, who is an honorary member of MCS, spoke and said, "I have never been so proud to be a member of a union. I have experienced no prouder moment than being here and taking part in this discussion as a working member of this union. I can tell you, I challenge any other union to match what I heard tonight. . . ."

In January, 1954, the "Baptist Ministerial Alliance," of San Francisco representing the Negro Baptist Churches of the Community, passed a resolution pledging full support to Mr. Bryson and his Cooks & Stewards. Thousands of individuals, organizations and unions, have gone on record in support of Hugh Bryson. Won't you join us?

EQUALITY IN THE UNION—A union with such principles must carry them into its internal affairs or be found guilty of hypocrisy. Here is President Hugh Bryson (at head of table) with the members of the general council of MCS. Typical leaders are Al Thibodeaux, port agent, and Joe Johnson, national secretary-treasurer, seen to the right of Bryson.

What YOU Can Do to Help:

- Send for the record of Hugh Bryson and his union, the MCS, from the MCS Defense Committee, 148 Liberty St., N. Y. C.
- Bring these facts to your fellow citizens—in your church, your fraternal organization, your union, your neighborhood.
- Contribute as generously as you can to the defense of this outstanding fighter for Negro-white unity.
- Ask Attorney-General Herbert J. Brownell (Dept. of Justice, Washington, D.C.) to drop the indictment of Bryson.

I am willing to help and have checked the things that I can do.

NAME ....

ADDRESS ....

ORGANIZATION ....

CITY .... STATE ....

'Big Truth' is the Answer

(Continued from page 1)

Terra Haute Jim Crow jail, then we concede McCarthy's right and Brownell's right to jail you and me and Harry Truman, and to dig up Franklin D. Roosevelt and put him in jail too!

The defense of Davis and his colleagues, the demand for their immediate amnesty, is the very foundation of any claim we have to basic civil liberties. Certainly we of the Negro people, bombed and lynched and falsely jailed for decades understand this.

We must counterpose to the Big Lie the Big Truth of our times—that any kind of general war will destroy all the peoples of the world, that different social systems must live together in peaceful cooperation and competition, that the American people will not be abreast of the rest of the world until we choose a government really dedicated to the needs and welfare of the working people, the poor farmers, the Negro millions and all the oppressed of this land.

12.3 "A Conversation from Life," *Freedom*, January 1954.

of Negro People and Unions," "'Peace' Treaty Reduces Japan to Colonial Status," "We Licked Jim Crow at Stuyvesant Town," "Memo to NAACP Leaders: It's Time to Fight – Not Fawn," and "Egyptian People Fight for Freedom" exhibited the paper's focus on international racial justice. To this end, *Freedom* showcased black writers and covered news stories about international class warfare and sexual subordination. *Freedom* created a polyphonic discursive space in which news articles were juxtaposed with photographs, pictures by such artists as Charles White, literary pieces by well-known authors such as Langston Hughes, cartoons, op-eds, and a letter to the editor section titled "Get It Off Your Chest."

On the face of it, *Freedom* sought to connect its readers to the world by moving between the singular story of its founder and the larger stories of his people. Once Robeson's passport was revoked in 1951, his appeals to the links between mobility and African American enfranchisement were all the more candid. By opening each issue with Robeson's column, titled "My Story," *Freedom* not only borrowed the tactic of storytelling to connect with workers, but in so doing highlighted the critical links between storytelling, community, and the international.

While *Freedom* has been classified as a vestige of the black popular front, it highlights the dilemmas and questions about just what that front entailed, politically and aesthetically. In particular, a doctrinaire politics of affiliation and form as espoused by Soviet principles in the 1930s is resituated by Childress's postwar black feminist transnationalism.[6] This chapter addresses both the continuities and ruptures between interwar polemics about Soviet "socialist realism" and *Freedom*'s interpretive "social realism." I turn to these aesthetic markers as a means of getting to the discontinuities between Leninist internationalism and Childress's postwar feminist transnationalism. Of central importance to both considerations is the role of the newspaper.[7]

On the one hand, the newspaper as the venue for Childress's work can be read with an eye to Lenin's proclamations about the newspaper's usefulness in fomenting working-class consciousness. On the other hand, *Freedom* veers from Leninist dogma about the way news is reported. Housed within a platform that proclaimed, "Where one is enslaved, all are in chains," Childress's columns participated in the production of a realist aesthetic that drew on popular front methods. As Michael Denning has elaborated, these methods were themselves indebted to and in conversation with early Soviet aesthetic claims about the connections between social progress and artistic practice.[8] In this sense, I am investigating two categories – "cultural politics" and "aesthetic ideologies" – that Denning convincingly disentwines in his landmark study *The Cultural Front*.[9] Doing so enables me to bring together at the site of her "Conversation" both Childress's affiliations within the *Freedom* milieu and the symbolisms wrought by her engagement with the newspaper as an aesthetic form. This shift also enables us to move beyond a Cold War heritage of reading realism as a stale aesthetic method devoid of the vibrant complexities of modernism. As the critic C. Vaughn James has noted, "'socialist realism' tends to be taken almost automatically as referring to something wholly negative ... and socialist realism is similarly taken to mean the total negation of artistic experimentation."[10] Pitting realism against modernism, and likewise public culture against aesthetics, is a legacy of Cold War paradigms for understanding the varied cultural fronts of mid-century radicalism.[11]

Although Childress later removed herself from any prior association with the left, her column amplified her connections to mid-century black radicalism. As William Maxwell and Mary Helen Washington have taught us, Childress's FBI file is a testament to her leftist past and to the links between these leftist affiliations and the fine arts.[12] Ironically, it is from this file more so than from Childress's own memoir that we learn of her early links to such communist-influenced organizations as the Jefferson School of Social Science, the movement to repeal the Smith Act, the Committee for the Negro in the Arts (CNA), the America Negro Theatre (ANT), the Committee to Restore Paul Robeson's Passport, and, perhaps most importantly, the Sojourners for Truth and Justice, of which she was a founding member.[13] The extensive links between black radicalism and communism, the Communist Party of the United States of America (CPUSA), and the Soviet Union have been richly documented by scholars such as Mark Naison, Bill Mullen, Mark Solomon, William J. Maxwell, Robin D.G. Kelley, Steven Lee, Dayo Gore, Mary Helen Washington, and others. In the 1920s, racism within the ranks of American socialists and union leadership created well-warranted suspicion about the aims of the left amidst black intellectuals and workers. However, recruiting efforts by the CPUSA to attract black membership in Harlem, Chicago, Philadelphia, and elsewhere were more successful as the decades dragged on; by the mid-1930s, black communism was a mood if not a movement. The media circus created by the Yokinen trial (a CPUSA trial in which a white man was tried for acts of racism) and the trials of the Scottsboro boys (whose defence was funded by the CPUSA with Soviet support) helped to establish communist legitimacy among the black public. Amidst this activism, Childress acquired what Washington calls her leftist "credentials" by carving her own kind of radical activism. In "A Conversation from Life," we see the possibilities of this theatrical vision etched most clearly. Childress's column was the product of an important moment when black radicalism, cultural progressivism, Soviet communism, popular front aesthetics, and an anti-colonial internationalist vision all collided in the thinking and cultural milieu surrounding *Freedom* (figure 12.4). Although Childress did not travel to the Soviet Union until nearly twenty years later, in 1971, her column must be considered in the framework of these robustly interwoven analytics.[14] For it is here, on a stage composed from these various platforms, that the gaps and continuities between these discourses become most audible.

12.4 *Freedom*, December 1952.

While *Freedom* cannot be termed socialist realism per se, the aspects of experimentation described by James can be connected to the social/collective project of the paper as community building across artistic and methodological lines. Cracking open questions of affiliation and genre, *Freedom* brought together the work of activists, poets, artists, authors, singers, actors, social workers, and politicians. In this way, *Freedom* broke down reality as much as it reflected it, reconstructing radical subjectivity through an eclectic mix of genres.

Key to *Freedom*'s novelty was its headlining of female writers and reporters. Alongside articles by Eslanda Robeson, Lorraine Hansberry, Shirley Graham, Vicky Garvin, Thelma Dale, Claudia Jones, and others, Childress's column helped to shape *Freedom* as a magazine that made an expressed space for black women. As highly stylized fictional pieces, Childress's contributions shifted attention from the information offered by a news-oriented publication to the powerful imaginary of a black female domestic worker. Her columns, among the magazine's most popular pieces, also undercut the dominance of news about men that the publication showcased, and thus moderated attention to a representative black masculinity as the face of radical blackness.[15] In intervening in the presentation of what constituted the news in this way, the columns also helped to establish the rhetorical investments of the newspaper as a source of agitational agency.

When V.I. Lenin penned his thoughts about the newspaper as a genre in his 1901 essay "Where to Begin?," he had in mind the creation of an all-Russian newspaper that would transform diverse local movements into a unified revolutionary one. As the Party's political organ, Lenin's paper would both reflect political discontent and incite action: the newspaper's purpose was not simply exposure and arousal but also collective organization. As Lenin famously wrote, "the role of a newspaper, however, is not limited solely to the dissemination of ideas, to political education, and to the enlistment of political allies. A newspaper is not only a collective propagandist and a collective agitator, it is also a collective organizer."[16] Because revolutionary parties were banned in Russia, the production and dissemination of the Party newspaper became a backbone for surreptitiously building networks and membership. In this sense, Lenin likened the paper to a scaffolding around which a building is built, imagining it as connective tissue and a facilitator for the emergence of a permanent political organization.

Although not typically read in an aesthetic framework, Lenin's version of the newspaper parallels basic components of socialist realism: a focus on ordinary people and on contemporary events and their social significance; and, of course, the use of a form that does not call attention to its properties of signification. Moreover, the newspaper deploys a realist-based epistemology; it is pedagogical in its purpose with the aim of providing a new "common sense." An editorial desire to produce this kind of shift in attention can be witnessed quite starkly in the case of *Freedom* as a reaction to US journalism's own realism and its epistemologies around who could and could not be seen and heard in the United States. At the same time, *Freedom* did not strictly follow a realist rulebook. Alongside journalistic reports, the paper shared "Stories for Children," written by Elsie Robbins, that featured tales of black heroism during slavery such as "A Slave Ship Revolts and Steers Its Way to Freedom"[17] and "Frederick Douglass Lived a Hard Life as Slave,"[18] as well as large doses of sentiment called upon to expose the outrages of white supremacy. For example, the August 1952 issue featured a section on the way white supremacy dominated prisons filled with black inmates. Headlines such as "Prisoner Tells Court of Horror of Georgia Camp; Fights Return," "Killings? Who – Us?," and "Southern Prison Farms Practice Feudal Torture Daily" (alongside a sketch of a tortuous machine used to stretch the human body) were sure to provoke ire. In this sense, *Freedom*'s mid-century recuperation of Lenin's call to journalistic action proved to be in continuum not only with Lenin and with what Andrei Zhdanov called socialist realism's "revolutionary romanticism," but also with popular front tenets about the creation of an oppositional aesthetic.[19] Like Lenin's paper, *Freedom* can be seen as a collective organizer, working the margins of the politically acceptable, but its pages also reveal the ways in which communication, especially about the particularities of the people, was differently facilitated between builders after the vanguard revolutionary moment of the early 1900s had passed.

Lenin's invocation of the newspaper as a revolutionary mouthpiece requires a reconsideration of the genre's basic assumptions. As a form, the newspaper is both ostensibly objective (concerned with relaying information) and deeply aesthetic (indebted to expressive culture). Journalism proposes to present facts and information as a literal repository of recorded events. At the same time, the act of reporting is equally indebted to the representation of these same facts. A conglomeration of narrative truths and historical ones, a newspaper is a prime example of the unstable binary between the literal and the literary, or between information and story.

Childress's work addressed this false division directly. As Mary Helen Washington has noted, "throughout the column, Childress/Mildred puts the major ideas of the paper in the language of an ordinary person in the community."[20] The movement noted by Washington between "ideas" and "language" reflects the vacillation suggested earlier between information and story. It is a movement that has as its aim an arousal of the reader and the shaping of an audience. Herein lies the understanding of an aesthetic based in bodily sensation, the link between reaction and group identity.

In fact, the newspaper is an instrumental genre (in Lenin's formulation) because it brings together these two poles of relay (information and narrative) at the site of the reader or subject.[21] For Lenin, the subject was the working class, although admittedly many of his imagined proletarians could not read. And it was this working class that he sought to prod to political action through straightforward reporting, or an accurate depiction of events as they happened. But *Freedom*'s iteration of the newspaper, particularly in light of Childress's contributions to it, enables us, indeed compels us, to ask: Who is the subject? Who are the people? How do we move between them?

Written as conversations between women, each column is an elocutionary missive. Each opens as Mildred Johnson, a black domestic, greets her good friend and neighbour Marge in the space of an urban kitchen and then goes on to discuss her day and/or a topic from *Freedom*'s headlines. To read Mildred's addresses to Marge is, as the title implies, to engage in their conversations. These are conversations from life in which that life is expressively formulated as on the precipice between real and imagined. (Many of Mildred's stories are clearly tall tales.) At the same time, these exchanges indicate a wider horizon of exchange.[22] The truth of the conversations is less the point than the connections they foster. What would it mean, then, to take these conversations as a kind of mis-en-scene, a feminist model for staging or imagining the engagement of a wider, international community of interlocutors?

In order to get back to the Mildred–Marge dyad previously described and, likewise, my initial question about how *Freedom*, in centring the black domestic, helps to move the reader from subject to group, from first to plural personhood, I want to turn to Kenneth Burke's pivotal essay "Revolutionary Symbolism in America" in which he calls for an idiomatic shift from "the workers" to "the people."[23] Burke writes that "the people" are a "more reliable symbol for *propaganda by inclusion* than [is] the strictly proletarian symbol [of the worker] ... which makes naturally for a *propaganda by exclusion*, a tendency to eliminate from one's work all that does not deal specifically with the realities of the workers' oppression – and which, by my thesis, cannot for this reason engage even the full allegiance of the workers themselves." Substituting "the people" for "the worker," Burke elaborates: "I am suggesting that an approach based on the positive symbol of 'the people,' rather than upon the negative symbol of 'the worker,' makes more naturally for this kind of identification whereby one's political alignment is fused with broader cultural elements."[24] Burke is important here for two reasons: first, for his invocation of "the people" as the targets of arousal through inclusion in an enunciated community; second, for his introduction of identification as the cornerstone for political alignment with "broader cultural elements." As it turns out, "people" and "identification" lead us down two different paths in critical thinking and, in particular, black critical thinking. Some scholars have maintained that for Childress, as for the collective staff of *Freedom*, "'*the* people' was a racialized '*my* people,' a phrase that, in the more doctrinaire period of the 1930s, might have earned her a reprimand for putting race before class solidarity."[25] In this understanding, racism is the deepest scourge, and Childress's work departs from Lenin's doctrinaire notion of class, pitching race as equally significant to one's sense of selfhood. But, in reclaiming "the people" through Childress's invocation of "my people," I also want to trouble the interpretation of this black-oriented public as explicitly raced. Instead, I would propose to see this "people" as a broader and more flexible grouping based in "people of colour" in which any link to black ancestry places one in proximity to the group. In turn, following Childress, the links become further problematized when she proposes to see this female community across visible racial lines. This point brings us to the question of identification: for it is through identification, and the unstable poles of cohesion and fragmentation these poles reflect, that these people are reachable. Identification leads us away from cohesion. Childress's columns break from Leninist class-based doctrine to a more flexible Western Marxist notion of identification that summons Stuart Hall's idea of articulation, which he describes as

> the form of the connection that can make a unity of two different elements, under certain conditions. It is a linkage which is not necessary, determined, absolute and essential for all time. You have to ask under what circumstances can a connection be forged or made? The so-called "unity" of a discourse is really the articulation of different, distinct elements which can be rearticulated in different ways because they have no necessary "belongingness." The "unity" which matters is a linkage

between the articulated discourse and the social forces with which it can, under certain historical conditions, but need not necessarily, be connected.[26]

In this regard, it is important to situate Childress's work in the context of black cultural producers on the left who were influenced by the Comintern's Black Belt thesis of 1928, the notion that African America constituted a community of culture linked by language, territory, economics, and psychology, and positioned in the black South as an oppressed nation. Although the notion of a self-determined black American nation was never a viable political reality, the yoking of political enfranchisement to cultural autonomy carried a certain purchase with many of the leading African American intellectuals of the 1930s and 1940s, including Langston Hughes, Richard Wright, Ann Petry, Chester Himes, and Ralph Ellison. In this period, these figures (and others) were captivated by the notion of linking self-determination to the notion of a unique black cultural production concentrated within vernacular traditions and capitalizing on this affiliation as key to black advancement and political action. In her columns, we can certainly see Childress aligned with traditions of social protest, but hers is hardly a formulaic social realism as defined by Richard Wright in the 1930s and 40s.[27] Mildred Johnson embodies a fusion of black vernacular culture and political struggle, but she puts women's issues front and centre, and many of her tales are fantasies more in line with what critic Richard Iton calls "the black fantastic" than a determined future. She remains ambivalent about the notion of a unified "collective black consciousness," and she sees class and race consciousness not as a soundtrack for political dogma like the Black Belt thesis but rather as the result of fragmented and discontinuous racial subjectivities.[28]

For example, the edition of the paper in which Childress's second column appeared in 1951 opened with Robeson's "Here's My Story" column, which proclaimed: "We Negro people are very mature in our political understanding." This invocation of "my people" is juxtaposed with the charcoal etching of an oversized dark hand emerging from the ground at the centre of a city skyline beneath the headline, "National Negro Labor Council Calls Founding Convention." Below the etching, we read "Jamaica's People Hold Out Their Hands," the headline to an article about the devastation caused by a hurricane near Kingston (figure 12.5).[29] The intermixture of people and hands on the front page can be adduced further by opening the paper to page two. Here the reader would find an editorial about Chinese women "speaking bitterness" in the People's Republic of China as a suggestive framing for a gathering of the black feminist group Sojourners for Truth and Justice in Washington, DC, where they "poured forth an acid condemnation of the[ir] barbarous subjection." The reader would also see a letter praising *Freedom* from a self-identified "so-called white person."[30] But the terms of radical collectivity are most starkly outlined by Childress in her column on the facing page.

DEC 4 '51

Here's My Story
By PAUL ROBESON

Vol. I—No. 10   ITH   OCTOBER, 1951   10c A Copy

Freedom

Where one is enslaved, all are in chains

ON THE INSIDE

The Meaning of the Labor Convention
by William R. Hood and Vicky Garvin . . . pp. 4-5
•
The Sojourn for Truth and Justice
by Lorraine Hansberry
p. 6
•
Happenings in Harlem . p. 3

WE NEGRO PEOPLE are very mature in our political understanding. We may not act at once upon all we sense and know—but we know.

Our forefathers and mothers before us sensed and correctly evaluated the tremendous crisis facing this land in the pre-Emancipation years.

Finally this nation was torn apart. It had to decide, and it did, in fratricidal combat. The answer was crystal clear as it resounded across the land —this nation "conceived in liberty and dedicated to the proposition that all men are created equal!" -- cannot live half slave and half free.

Unfortunately, the enemies of the American people still range the country, free, wide and handsome. The Rankins, Lanhams, DuPonts, Reynolds, Morgans, are still with us—apostles of Jim Crow and wage slavery, advocates of a return of our folks and poor white folks as well to modern agricultural and industrial serfdom. . . . . any . . . . among the rank and file of our people. Talk to the Negro people, the thousands and millions of us, Brother, we're bitter. We haven't been fooled. We know we don't have basic opportunities, do not enjoy our basic freedom—as in fact do no other Americans. We sense and see the real enemies of our land for what they are, sitting as they do in lofty and powerful places.

BUT WE KNOW that history is at the crossroads. We see people like ourselves pressing toward and gaining freedom in the tens of millions. Truman, McCarthy, Wallace, McCarran, Budenz, can argue and distort among themselves, but the Chinese people have their freedom and they're going to keep it. The Indian people, the Indian masses, watch and weigh their chances. The peoples of
(Continued on Page 7)

Douglass on Labor:
"We invite your earnest attention (b) the condition of the laboring classes all over the South. Their cause is one with the laboring classes all over the world. The labor unions of the country should not throw away this colored element of strength . . . In what we have to say for our laboring class we expect to have and ought to have the sympathy and support of laboring men of every color."
—*Frederick Douglass, from speech at 1883 Convention of Colored Men.*

National Negro Labor Council Calls Founding Convention

All Roads to Cincinnati

'To the Good People of the World'
Jamaica's People Hold Out Their Hands
By FORTUNATE

KINGSTON, Jamaica.—One reads with alarm about the typhoons of China and the earthquakes of Chile, but to read about the hurricane that struck Jamaica on Aug. 17, 1951 is not only to be alarmed but to be shocked out of one's wits. It was a bleak day and the warning of the hurricane was being flashed throughout the island all day. The day was comparatively fair, with several showers of rain falling at intervals of one hour.

At 7 p.m. on that memorable day, the winds started to blow. The night came and the showers became more intense. The radio flashed more hurricane warnings. The governor of the island came on the air and made a stunning appeal and warning to the people to remain indoors and all the men to remain at home with their families. He informed the citizens of the many places of shelter and the arrangements made by the Red Cross and the government for people in distress.

At 8 p.m. the wind intensified
(Continued on Page 8)

As soon as FREEDOM learned of the disastrous hurricane which swept the island of Jamaica, we wrote to His Worship the Mayor, Mr. Ken Hill, offering our help. At the direction of the Mayor, a leading Jamaican journalist, Fortunate, sent the moving description and appeal which appears here.

Negro working men and women from all parts of the country are responding to the founding convention of the National Negro Labor Council which will be held in Cincinnati, Ohio, Oct. 27 and 28.

Declaring that "American foreign policy cannot advance freedom for Asians and Africans until American domestic policy advances freedom for American Negroes as a people," the call states that "the time has come to establish a permanent national organization in order to mobilize the greatest organized strength of Negro workers."

The Convention committee will be the outgrowth of a year's labor by the continuations committee of the Chicago Conference for Negro Rights held in June, 1950. Officers of the continuations committee are president, William R. Hood, secretary of Ford Local 600, UAW-CIO; vice-president, Cleveland Robinson, who is also a vice-president of the Distributive, Processing and Office Workers Union (Ind.); and executive secretary, Coleman Young, veteran labor leader of Detroit and former director of organization of the Wayne County CIO Council.

During the past year the continuations committee has established 23 Negro Labor Councils in major industrial centers throughout the country and these Councils have joined in initiating the National founding convention.

Convention officers, in an exclusive interview with FREEDOM, pointed out that special efforts are being made to guarantee a large and representative delegation from the South and that the convention will pay particular attention to the problems of Negro sharecroppers as well as industrial workers.

In inviting delegates from local unions, departments, shops, rank and file committees and non-union organizations, the convention sponsors promise a kind of leadership that "will be content with nothing less than full freedom for the Negro people and an end to the era of second-class citizenship."

Join Our 4-in-4 for FREEDOM Drive — See Page 8

12.5 *Freedom*, October 1951.

The column opens, "Well, Marge I started a new job today.... Just wait girl. Don't laugh yet. Just wait 'til I tell you.... The woman seems real nice.... Well, you know what I mean.... She was pretty nice anyway."[31] For many readers, the exchanges between Mildred and Marge would have been recognizable, common threads taken from everyday life. At the same time, the columns understand that a Mildred or a Marge is not typically the one who is publically addressed. So, while they are enunciating Mildred through Marge (and vice versa), they are at the same time addressing a gap in public address, which returns us to the point about the epistemological project of *Freedom*: its basic understanding of its audience as having been marginally recognized, represented only by under-representation ... and ellipses.[32] Instead, Childress's column transforms black working-class women, the audience, the hearers, and the heard. Taking the isolated vantage point of the female domestic worker as its pivot, the columns turn isolation into camaraderie, conversations between women that entreat others to join in. "A Conversation from Life" thus created a new audience of meaning-makers outside of the usual (white) media's forms of address.

What such a new audience portends is well crafted in a column titled "The 'Many Others' in History"[33] (figure 12.6). The column opens, "Good evenin', Marge. I am so sorry I woke you up... Yes, I know it's 12 o'clock...Well, I got to work tomorrow too but I just have to tell you about your friend Mildred...." The column goes on to describe a "Negro History meeting," presumably run by Freedom Associates, during which the fictional Mildred heard lectures about famous African Americans including Harriet Tubman, Sojourner Truth, John Brown, Frederick Douglass, Frances Harper, "and many others." Stuck on this seemingly throw-away phrase often repeated by the speakers, Mildred took it upon herself to enquire why, "you folks kept talking about 'many others'.... But you didn't tell much about them." Recapping her lesson to the lecturers for Marge, Mildred describes how she proceeded to recount the "many others" in her family, "Well, the way they took it you could tell that I was talkin' about their grandmas too.... So I told 'em, 'I bet Miss Tubman and Miss Truth would like us to remember and give some time to the **many others**....'" Seamlessly moving between third person "your friend Mildred," first person "I," and the ellipses of Marge, Mildred then all but retracts the story, "Stop that, Marge.... If I'd of known you would cry, I wouldn't of told it." The conversation here is pedagogical, directly instructing the teachers about what they should already know, and, in so doing, inviting the audience, via Marge, to take up the place of the student, listener, overhearer in the conversation. In this way, the "many others" are the open-ended audience recognizing themselves, and their ancestors, in this previously untold blank black history. At the same time, the conversation is structured to connect, to move its audience – perhaps even, like Marge, to tears. The connection is through the unnamed past, the "many others" that implicate and enunciate the blank space left bare by a "greatest hits" approach to black

12.6 "A Conversation from Life: The 'Many Others' of History," *Freedom*, February 1952.

history, but also through a shared mood of exclusion, sadness, and, perhaps most importantly, a refusal to rest on that note. A retraction of the story promised after the fact proves the teller to be somewhat duplicitous in her intentions: the line, "If I'd of known you'd cry, I wouldn't of told it," is disingenuous, a wink at the rhetorical strategies of telling and un-telling. The shared story here is told to provoke the reader to critical cognition through sensory reaction. Having been scolded, a reader cannot retract bitterness; she can only seek to redirect her acrimony elsewhere.

And where should that be? The column is nested within pages that open with a striking portrait of Robeson by distinguished artist Charles White, an article by W.E.B. Du Bois proclaiming that Negro unity "can help change the world," the inauguration of William V.S. Tubman as president of Liberia, and the poem "The Negro Mother" by Langston Hughes. To see Robeson proclaiming, as he and William Patterson did that year before the United Nations, "We Charge Genocide" in the brushstrokes of White's drawing (figure 12.7), alongside the incantation of Hughes's stark lines, "Dark ones of today, my dreams must come true:/ All you dark children in the world out there,/ Remember my sweat, my

DEC 4 '53

Here's My Story

By PAUL ROBESON

SIX MONTHS AGO the truce negotiations began in Korea. But today the bloodshed continues, and American diplomats and top brass persist in carrying on the most shameful war in which our country has ever been engaged.

A hundred thousand American dead, wounded and missing have been listed in this war which nobody—not even the most cynical politician—bothers to call a "police action" any more. And more than that, we have killed, maimed and rendered homeless a million Koreans, all in the name of preserving western civilization. U. S. troops have acted like beasts, as do all aggressive, invading, imperialist armies. North and south of the 38th parallel, they have looked upon the Korean people with contempt, called them filthy names, raped their women, lorded it over old women and children, and shot prisoners in the back.

Is it any wonder that Rev. Adam Powell, N. Y. Congressman, returns from a lengthy tour of Britain, Europe, the Near East and Africa to report that the United States is "the most hated nation in the world."

Yes, our government is well hated because it has forced on the people a policy which places this nation in deadly opposition to the liberation movements of hundreds of millions of people in all parts of the globe.

WHEN THE IRANIANS took back their rich oil fields from the British exploiters, whose side were we on? Now that the Egyptian masses are calling for John Bull to get out of Egypt and the Suez Canal, [illegible] Kai-shek's mercenary troops violating the borders of Burma to achieve a springboard for attack upon the Chinese mainland, do we rush to protect the sovereignty of Burmese soil or do we lend covert and open support to Chiang's marauders?

In Indo-China, Indonesia, Malaya—which side are we on? The question almost answers

(Continued on Page 6)

Freedom

Where one is enslaved, all are in chains

Vol. II—No. 1 FEBRUARY, 1952 10c a Copy

The Charge IS Genocide

Drawing of Paul Robeson by the distinguished artist, Charles White

Make the Rulers of This Nation Heed!

ON DEC. 18 PAUL ROBESON led a delegation in New York and William L. Patterson strode into Paris' Palais Chaillot to present the historic petition, "We Charge Genocide," to members of the United Nations secretariat. The petition charged the government of the United States with the mass murder of the Negro people.

One week later, on Christmas night, 1951, the lynchers gave their answer: Mr. and Mrs. Harry T. Moore were bombed to death as they lay in their bed at Mims, Florida.

They thought by this bestiality to cut off the current of our protest. They meant to silence the Southern clamor for votes and freedom. They sought to discourage us from waving our grievances before the eyes of the world.

How they miscalculated!

On Jan. 19 at Jacksonville, not many miles from where the Moores lie buried, James M. Hinton, South Carolina president of the NAACP, exhorted delegates from 12 Southern states to a renewed dedication in the struggle to bring Moore's killers to justice and to win the unhindered right to vote.

Hinton had himself escaped from a South Carolina mob. He had himself recently received a warning note from the cowardly Klan. But he stood erect and thundered: **"Be not deceived, God is not mocked. Whatsoever a man soweth, that shall he also reap."**

And throughout the land, the thunder of the people's wrath was heard.

In Miami a thousand citizens, black and white, marched through the streets to a memorial service for the martyred dead.

In North Carolina a banker, editor, minister, lawyer and labor spokesman shared a church pulpit and merged their voices in the cry for justice.

Negro fishermen and white fur trappers—union brothers in Louisiana's gulf and bayous—demanded that the President act.

Woodsmen from the State of Washington, seamen on both coasts, housewifes, domestics, auto men and steel workers, men and women of all denominations and every walk of life transformed their initial dismay into spirited protest and accusation.

But our voice has not yet been loud enough!

More than a month has passed since Christmas. The killers are still at large. The government has set its apologists to work and has failed to place the murderers behind bars and on the gallows where they belong. It has failed in 10,000 lynchings since 1882.

The charge of genocide is true!

We must heed Paul Robeson's call for the all-embracing unity of the Negro people together with the multi-million forces of labor and progressive Americans. The NAACP civil rights mobilization in Washington on Feb. 17 must become a fighting expression of the popular demand for an end to the crime of lynching. A million copies of the Civil Rights Congress historic document, "We Charge Genocide," should be put into the hands of the people.

In united voice we must roar until the heavens quake and the rulers of this nation heed: Avenge the murder of the Moores! Stop the crime of genocide!

STACK 3

12.7 A drawing of Paul Robeson by Charles White on the front page of *Freedom*, February 1952.

pain my despair./ Remember my years, heavy with sorrow –/ And make of those years a torch for tomorrow" is to situate Mildred's story in the context of a vivid aesthetics rooted in links between private feeling and publicly oriented emotion. What Mildred offers are fantasies of partial connection and agency that rely on the affective objects of identification – genocide, dreams, memory, and the overheard conversation.

To reach what we can only now problematically term "my people," Childress's columns summon strategies of identification that work by connecting personal feeling with public emotion. These conversational vignettes are based on imagined exchanges in which a female other, Marge, is called into being in order to consolidate the speaker, Mildred. Marge is summoned as Mildred's interlocutor, but she is also Mildred's limit, her margin. (The alliteration between "Marge" and "margin" is, to my thinking, not incidental.) By posing Marge in the indexed, elliptical spaces between Mildred's utterances, the column also invites the reader to take up the position of Marge. Marge reminds us that identity is a falsely closed concept and that identities emerge through a constitutive outside (a margin). As Stuart Hall reminds us, "they emerge within the play of specific modalities of power, and thus are more the product of the marking of difference and exclusion, than they are the sign of identical, naturally-constituted unity."[34] The dyad between domestics in "A Conversation from Life" reminds us that every identity has its excess, that the very notion of Mildred as a unified whole unto herself is a fiction. Rather, she is a mark, a rhetorical sign of suturing; in Hall's words, she is a "performance of the temporary attachment to a subject position that discursive practices construct for us."[35] As such, she/ they mark an opening more than a closure – an opening, an enjoinment to the reader to "come on in." The coffee is usually on, and Mildred is ready to get down to serious elocutionary business. Mildred makes use of the elliptical Marge to rehearse a quotidian indignity or a popular news item. In the course of these elocutions, Mildred confronts racism, advocates for civil rights, and champions collective resistance. Her language draws from the criticism of racial liberalism in the 1950s forwarded by the left and thus shapes this portrait of black radicalism as one that forwards feminist consciousness as key to societal change. In advocating for the centrality of domestic labourers to the sustenance of the black community, Mildred notes, "After freedom came, it was domestics that kept us from perishin' by the wayside."[36] This comment suggests Childress's indebtedness to her *Freedom* colleague Claudia Jones, whose essay "An End to the Neglect of the Problems of Negro Women" (1949) analysed black women through a Marxist lens and proclaimed the centrality of black women – as the most oppressed of the oppressed – to the radical movement. In particular, Jones underscored the position of the black domestic worker as that of "unbearable misery," part of what she termed the "super exploitation" of the Negro woman worker; and Jones claimed that "the continued relegation of Negro women to domestic work has helped to perpetuate and intensify chauvinism directed against all Negro women."[37] If black domestics could be seen as representative of the exploitation of all black women, then their day-to-day interactions with white employers, who were for the most part women, indicated the location of a critical ontology of racism within female interactions. In other words, women were at the centre of racism as a structure and as a lived experience. Childress's comment about post-emancipation suggests the centrality of the black domestic not only to the sustenance of the black community – but to the future of black globality.

If we follow Hall's notion of the suturing of identities across difference, we can see in Mildred and Marge a prefiguration of Hall's insight that "all identifications are imaginary, the sedimentation of the 'we' in the constitution of any 'I.'"[38] It is the articulation of this "we" that Mildred, as radically open to interlocutors, frames as an unstable "I." This manner of speaking is a kind of calling into being that also asks for imitation, a kind of injunction to "feel with me" at the site of a black domestic worker. This structure of address encourages us to ask about how art works to summon arousal *and* create connection, which returns us to aesthetic theory. As Steven Lee notes in his introduction to this volume, "the aesthetic here refers to inner and outer sensations mediated by the body's surface ... a radical aesthetic that foregrounds the sensory rather than any particular form – an aesthetic bound not to art or realism but to 'corporeal, material nature.'" The resulting "critical cognition" facilitates the revolutionary potential of the newspaper, creating links between aesthetic arousal and political action. In Childress's columns, the link is routed through Mildred, and, like Marge, we are all potential overhearers of this conversation. There is a lack of uniformity in Mildred's audience, evidenced by the placement of her column in the midst of "speaking bitterness," the "so-called white person," and the Jamaican hand. In this way, Childress's columns use the shape of the dyad to open up to a collective and the mood of shared response.

Mildred connects the unstable "I" of the domestic to the international "we." As a representative figure for the maid, she is situated at the centre of international news. But she also links domestic labour to international struggles for enfranchisement. First, Mildred places women at the centre of racial dynamics and illuminates the way gender is constitutive of the divisions between blacks and whites. In particular, the column offers a radical critique of white globality by placing women's interactions at the centre of the material and psychic structures of racism. This move is not just about admitting "others" into a white paradigm, but using a coloured paradigm to shift the centrality of "we the people" to a "we the feminist people of colour."

For example, *Freedom*'s first issue of 1953 proclaimed the momentous changes to US immigration law wrought by the unprecedented McCarran Act. This law not only directly limited immigration from the "Asia-Pacific triangle" (two-thirds of the world's population), but also gave preference for substantial migration to people from Western Europe who willingly allied themselves with the United States against socialism. Especially targeting the West Indies, the origin of nearly 25 per cent of the New York metropolitan area's 750,000 blacks, the McCarran Act was eventually used to deport *Freedom* writer Claudia Jones from the United States. Jones was not only West Indian; she was also an elected official of the CPUSA and a staunch advocate of black domestics' rights.[39] As mentioned earlier, she is credited with inspiring the point of view, if not the character, of Mildred as the cornerstone of black radicality. Of the thousands of black domestics who worked in the New York area, a large portion of them were from the West Indies. Mildred's columns repeatedly call attention to this fact.[40]

The January 1953 issue of *Freedom* offers a robust example of the way Childress threaded the topic of her column through the month's pressing news and yet torqued the emphasis or unitary notion of "my people" via a black feminist transnationalism. Sandwiched in the midst of second anniversary greetings from hundreds of *Freedom* readers, "A Conversation from Life" (figure 12.8) opens, "Sit down Marge and act like you got nothin' to do.... No, don't make no coffee, just sit ..." Mildred tells Marge a story about running into another domestic doing laundry in the basement of her boss's building. After inadvertently brushing against the other white maid's dirty laundry and being demonstrably reprimanded, Mildred is not really surprised to find herself ready to "pop" the maid in the mouth: "You are right!... My hand was just itchin' to pop her in the mouth, but I remembered how my niece Jean has been tellin' me that poppin' people is not the way to solve problems." Instead, Mildred approaches her sensibly and asks the maid why she snatched the laundry out of Mildred's reach. Not satisfied with the maid's desultory answer, Mildred launches in: "Sister, you are a houseworker and I am a houseworker – now will you favor me by answering some questions?" In the course of her question and answer seminar, Mildred learns that she earns more than the white domestic; that the white houseworker is also required to "do extra things that ain't in the bargain," to "cram eight hours of work into five and call it part time." Having established a kind of uneasy parallel as women workers, Mildred "gets personal": "'I notice you speak with an accent ... Tell me do you have to register as a foreigner under the new McCarran Act?' She nods yes again ..." But, when Mildred presses her on their proximity, the white woman balks. Mildred continues to emphasize their relatedness ("Now when you got to plunge your hands in all them dirty clothes.... how come you can't see that it's a whole lot safer and makes more sense to put your hand in mine and be friends?") until the white domestic takes Mildred's outstretched hand and declares Mildred her friend.[41] This example of interracialism between working women not only foregrounds alliances based on gender and class across race, but uses the background of the McCarran

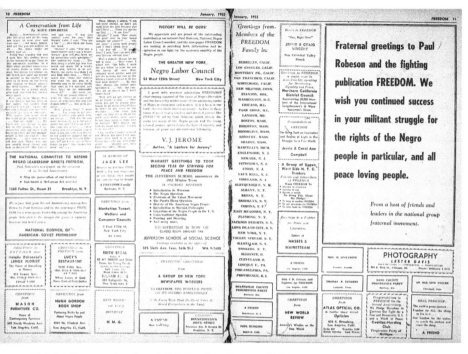

12.8 "A Conversation from Life," *Freedom*, January 1953.

terror to expose the way international connections could be used to harden the more fluid lines of internationalism into material obstacles. The McCarran Act put citizens in jeopardy based on their connections to a nationalized elsewhere. It said that, if you are a particular kind of foreigner, you do not belong; it built a wall. As this column shows, *Freedom* was attempting to do the opposite: to make international connections into multiracial bridges of resistance. Delineating in a material way who was not of the people, the McCarran Act made international connections into barriers. "A Conversation from Life" addresses and reimagines the international camaraderie of marginalized, disenfranchised people through a conversation between women.

In this post–popular front era, just who was included in the people was vitally critical. I will close this chapter by looking at another dynamic space in *Freedom*, the "Anniversary Greetings from Readers," from January 1953 (figure 12.9). Each year, the paper published wishes of good tidings it received from its readers. In this issue, the editors also published a list of 350 readers who sent their greetings, a list broken down by state and, in New York, broken down by borough. While New York boasted the most readers, subscribers hailed from as far away as Canada and Washington, with California the second

12.9 "Anniversary Greetings from Readers," *Freedom*, January 1953.

most represented state. This aggregation of readers and their greetings offers a critical moment to reflect on the dynamics of shared feeling emphasized in Childress's column. While the structure of anniversary greetings is, to be sure, more general and frequently fraternal (as in "Fraternal greetings to Paul Robeson and the fighting publication FREEDOM"), it also offers a way of giving the addressee a voice: as in "Here's to FREEDOM 'Now, Right Now!' Jenny & Craig Vincent, San Cristobal Ranch"; or the more quiet, "A Friend, Bayside, N.Y." and "A Well Wisher, Brooklyn, N.Y." In open defiance of the Smith Act and the fear of association with Paul Robeson, these pages not only name names, they name lists of names. They are one version of the people categorized not by race, class, gender, or nation but through asymmetrical affiliations of support for *Freedom*.

In spite of the best efforts of its organizers and writers, *Freedom*'s circulation numbers began to dwindle in the mid-1950s. Childress's column of January 1954, with which I opened my discussion, pointed to the suppression wrought by McCarthyism. But Childress's columns also move in less predictable directions. For example, one column bares the stakes of the radical newspaper's discursive tactics. In a revealing moment, Mildred announces: "Marge, I wish I was a poet.... Now that's no cause for you to stop stringing the beans and lookin' at me like you was struck by lightnin'... No, I don't wish it on account of I want to be famous, but I do wish it because sometimes there are poetry things that I see and I'd like to tell people about them in a poetry way; only I don't know how and when I tell it, it's just a plain flat story."[42] Coming after three years of a feminist vernacularized recapping of the ideas of *Freedom*, this statement is at first surprising. Upon closer examination, however, Mildred's desire to relate "poetry things I see" in a "poetry way" reveals more about the newspaper's investment in aesthetic transparency. In *What Is to Be Done*, Lenin famously announced that "art may be genuinely free only when it is released from all hindrance in the fulfilment of its true social function, which is to serve the interests of the masses. Freedom of the arts [is] related to their *narodnost'* ... Bourgeois freedom is in fact illusory, depending ultimately on the purse."[43] In fact, Mildred's column here partly refutes Lenin, suggesting that there is no "literal" outside the literary – only the emotion or feeling attached to an experience, captured in a sensate realm of the aesthetic. In the column, Mildred subsequently describes the scene of an elderly white couple checking into a hotel room for a night. She pens it as an example of starry-eyed, geriatric love persisting in spite of obvious penury. Even though she paints a vivid picture, Mildred condemns her discourse as insufficient to the scene: in her account the story attempts to grasp the moment, but it falls flat – or into what she calls "plain flat story." Mildred comments:

> That's all there is to the story and it sure don't sound like much the way I tell it but if I was poet I would sing a song of praise for the love in their eyes and I would make you see the sight of a lifetime when that ragged lady bent over those roses, and I would tell how awful it is to be old and broke in the midst of plenty.... And that's what I mean when I say – sometimes I wish I was a poet.[44]

In Mildred's estimation, poetry is more effective than straightforward reporting at reaching the "it" of conveyable experience, because poetry aims not for verisimilitude but for aesthetic engagement. Poetry offers a perhaps more honest artifice in that it can call attention to its strategies of representation, to its form as intrinsic to its meaning. What Mildred offers us here, then, is a window to the way her use of journalistic form sought to occupy that space of conveyed experience, the "we" sedimented within the articulation of the "I." Through Mildred, we are encouraged to feel and experience the first person of our interiority differently after an encounter and engagement with the plurality of her conversations. Poetry here is a word for a feeling summoned by experience that wants to be translated – not necessarily through direct transmission but through artifice – so Childress is calling for a more honest summoning of attachment to an experience or event: "I see poetry things," she says.

The dilemma is how to translate these "poetry things" for a world that will be moved by that translation. As Jonathan Flatley has elegantly demonstrated for us, Lenin proclaimed that the link between journalism and action was feeling. In his analysis, feeling depends on the iteration of events through straightforward journalistic accounts that connect to a past thought-image.[45] In "A Conversation," Mildred conveys another routing of emotion and attachment that beckons beyond the literal, indeed undresses the literal as quite literary. What makes her column so interesting is that it brings her performance background to the newspaper and orients it so that we have to see the entire paper as theatrical. From Eslanda Robeson's review of the movie *Blackboard Jungle*, to Shirley Graham's review of her husband's *The Souls of Black Folks*, to Lorraine Hansberry's assessment of the Japanese film *Hiroshima*, the layout itself of *Freedom* was set up as a kind of conversation, one that is, following Mildred's example, summoning its addressee. To be sure, these conversations are meant to be agitational, but a closer consideration helps us to see how these juxtaposed voices are also asking for imitation, how they are invested in creating a community of shared feelings, suturing subjects together through the articulation of a feminist black transnationalism. The lesson of Mildred (and likewise of the radical newspaper) is that she accomplished this goal on a monthly basis by moving her readers through performative, feminist conversation rather than through orthodox repetition of information.

What becomes clear upon reading *Freedom* in its entirety is that Childress's column offers a means to underscore the point that what is being said may not be as important as how the story is told. The issue here seems to be almost counterintuitive: the possibilities of a politics of dissent may not be determined by its authentic translation but rather by interruption and, at times, manipulation, exaggeration, and inaccuracy. Rather than a broad, sweeping, exacting gesture of "I" to "you" to "we," what is foregrounded throughout these columns are quotidian, mundane, heartfelt connections. However fleeting and seemingly superficial – a black domestic's hand extended to that of a white domestic's – these moments of camaraderie are summoned and shared.

Childress's work helps us to see that, as a point of entry, black internationalism, especially a feminist transnationalism, does not offer a straightforward route out of domestic domination and oppression, nor does it unfold along the identical terms of oppression within a nation state. But Childress's columns offer us a directional out of this quandary if we understand them to be enunciating a resistant black groupness, not a tale of heroic individualism, with women's contributions at the helm. There is certainly a lesson here for the twenty-first century, one that juxtaposes bourgeois women's deep entrenchment in norms of domesticity with the appeal of the black domestic as a siren for a global feminist resistance.

NOTES

1 *Negro Liberator*, 15 July 1935, 5; emphasis in the original.
2 Cathy Bergin, *"Bitter with the Past but Sweet with the Dream": Communism in the African American Imaginary* (London: Brill, 2016), 51. See also Eric Naison, *Communists in Harlem during the Depression* (New York: Grove Press, 1983); Mark Solomon, *The Cry Was Unity: Communists and African Americans, 1917–1936* (Jackson: University of Mississippi Press, 1998).
3 Alice Childress, "A Conversation from Life," *Freedom* 4, no. 1 (January 1954): 4.
4 Ibid.
5 Call and response is a widely recognized pattern in African American cultural tradition: a speaker lays out a "call" to which a listener responds in kind. In the twentieth century, scholars of African American literature identified this pattern as a distinctly black literary and cultural aesthetic. For example, the *Riverside Anthology of African American Literature* traces this pattern through black fiction, poetry, drama, essays, sermons, speeches, criticism, journals, and song lyrics, from spirituals to rap. Patricia Liggins Hill, ed., *Call and Response: The Riverside Anthology of the African American Literary Tradition* (New York: Houghton Mifflin, 1997). Childress is not included in this anthology.
6 In delineating a difference between internationalism and transnationalism, I am following on my earlier work in *Beyond the Color Line and the Iron Curtain*, as well as the work of Michelle Stephens, who helpfully distinguishes a difference between these two modes of imagining solidarity across nations. Internationalism, in this sense, is about a recognized statehood from within, which peoples themselves recognize as nationally oriented first and then externally connected to peoples of other nation-states. Transnationalism, in distinction and in the way I see Childress's invoking it, suggests connections across nation-state divides, but these connections importantly also apply to the stateless, the nationally disenfranchised. In this way, black transnationalism is the reconfiguration of a Leninist vision of the merging of self-determination and internationalism. This vision was abandoned by the Sixth Comintern Congress in 1928, when a focus on domestic issues foreclosed those of the international. See Kate Baldwin, *Beyond the Color Line and the Iron Curtain: Reading Encounters between Black and Red, 1922–1963* (Durham, NC: Duke University Press, 2002), 210–11.
7 C. Vaughn James, *Soviet Socialist Realism: Origins and Theory* (New York: St. Martin's Press, 1973), 14. From C. Vaughn James, Susan Platt, David Shapiro, and Andrew Hemingway, warnings against reading "socialist realism" alongside "social realism" abound. As James puts it, socialist realism was a "method," whereas social realism was about ideals and values: "Socialist realism, it must be stressed in conclusion is the 'artistic method' whereby the artist fulfils the demands put upon him by the Communist Party. It should therefore be carefully distinguished from the social realism, which in the parlance of Western critics may be taken to refer

to the artist's concern with social themes, not with a political programme." James's caution notwithstanding, many critics have, at the same time, noted that debates within international Marxist and communist circles describe a socialist realism that was wide ranging and flexible in its exact definition, at times strictly adhering to socialist principles and at other times permitting artistic interpretation.

8 These conversations were taken up with especial vibrancy at the 1934 All-Union Writer's Congress, when Andrei Zhdanov announced the new aesthetic platform of "socialist realism." In addition to the well-known Russian writers, Gorky, Babel, Olesha, Pasternak, Chukovskii, and Tret'iakov, an international audience and roster of speakers in Moscow included Andre Malraux, Louis Aragon, Rafael Alberti, Ernst Toller, Robert Gessner, and Lloyd Brown. See also Barbara Foley, *Radical Representations: Politics and Form in U.S. Proletarian Fiction, 1929–1941* (Durham, NC: Duke University Press, 1991).

9 Michael Denning, *The Cultural Front* (London: Verso, 1998), xix.

10 James, *Soviet Socialist Realism*, xii. C.V. James continues to state that socialist realism "is itself an artistic experiment on an unprecedented scale. For not only is it an attempt to enlist the poet as philosopher, the writer as tribune and the artist as teacher in the translation of the socialist dream into reality, but it explores the almost unknown interstices between artistic genres by uniting poet, painter, sculptor, singer, actor, dancer, and director in one common socio-aesthetic system."

11 In various ways Alan Wald, Barbara Foley, and James Smethurst are exceptions to this rule. They argue that cultural production of the US communist left reflected modernist techniques and formal experimentation, and I have learned much from their examples. For an insightful argument about realism's persistence across the mid-century through popular culture, see Chris Vials, *Realism for the Masses: Aesthetics, Popular Front Pluralism and U.S. Culture, 1935–1947* (Jackson: University Press of Mississippi, 2009).

12 See William J. Maxwell, *F.B. Eyes: How J. Edgar Hoover's Ghostreaders Framed African American Literature* (Princeton, NJ: Princeton University Press, 2014).

13 Mary Helen Washington, *The Other Blacklist: The African American Literary and Cultural Left of the 1950s* (New York: Columbia University Press, 2014), 126.

14 In this sense, whether or not Childress was a member of the Communist Party is not the point; indeed, such summations of left-oriented writers have frequently led to an easy dissociation of cultural producers from their political alliances and affiliations, the institutions as well as the cultural fields, in which they worked. It is precisely this centre-periphery bias that Michael Denning undoes so brilliantly in *The Cultural Front*, where he writes that this kind of narrative "leads to a remarkably inadequate understanding of the depth and breadth of the social movement, as well as a disproportionate emphasis on central Party leaders, an over-reading of the significance of pronouncements in Communist Party journals, and, in some cases, a search for the Moscow gold that kept it all running" (xviii). Alan Wald makes a similar point in his discussion of the black literary left, noting that "what

is more memorable than formal membership in the Party is that, for Black writers, the publications, clubs, and committees that were at least in part created by Party members, and with Party support, constituted principal venues in which many Black writers came together to formulate ideas, share writings, make contacts, and develop perspectives that sustained their future creative work." Alan Wald, *Exiles from a Future Time: The Forging of the Mid-Twentieth-Century Left* (Chapel Hill: University of North Carolina Press, 2002), 267.

15 *Freedom* was an experimental paper, different from the leftist publications also headquartered in New York with which *Freedom's* editorial ideology was partially aligned, such as *The Daily Worker*, *Masses and Mainstream*, Alan Clayton Powell's *People's Voice*, and *The Sunday World*. Other important New York–based left-wing organizations included the Council on African Affairs (CAA), the Civil Rights Congress (CRC), and the Committee for the Negro in the Arts (CNA). The first page of *Freedom* featured Paul Robeson's column "My Story," and various follow-up stories often connected back to Robeson's story. Childress gathered over fifty of these "Conversations" and, with a few edits and additions, collected them into the novel that became *Like One of the Family: Conversations from a Domestic's Life*, published in 1956 by Independence Publishers.

16 "Where to Begin?" (1901) *Iskra*, no. 4 (May 1901), rpt. *Lenin's Collected Works*, vol. 5 (Moscow: Foreign Languages Publishing House, 1961), 13–24.

17 Elsie Robbins, "A Slave Ship Revolts and Steers Its Way to Freedom," *Freedom* 2, no. 2 (February 1952): 7.

18 Elsie Robbins, "Frederick Douglass Lived a Hard Life as Slave," *Freedom* 2, no. 3 (March 1952): 7.

19 Andrei Zhdanov, "Extracts from Contributions to the First All-Union Congress of Soviet Writers, 1934," in *Russian Art of the Avant-Garde: Theory and Criticism 1902–1934*, ed. John E. Bowlt (New York: Viking, 1976), 293.

20 Washington, *The Other Blacklist*, 142.

21 Lenin writes, "We must blame ourselves, our lagging behind the mass movement, for still being unable to organize sufficiently wide, striking, and rapid exposures of all the shameful outrages. When we do that (and we must and can do it), the most backward worker will understand, *or will feel*, that the students and religious sects, the peasants and the authors are being abused and outraged by those same dark forces that are oppressing and crushing him at every step of his life. Feeling that, he himself will be filled with an irresistible desire to react, and he will know how to hoot the censors one day, on another day to doing the work of the Holy Inquisition, etc." *Lenin's Collected Works*, 5:414.

22 My thinking here is influenced by a variety of theories of the public sphere, particularly the relationship between discursive spaces such as newspapers or magazines and their various reading publics. See especially Jürgen Habermas, *The Structural Transformation of the Public Sphere*, trans. Thomas Burger with Frederick Lawrence (Cambridge, MA: MIT Press, 1991); Benedict Anderson, *Imagined*

Communities (London: Verso, 1991); Nancy Fraser, "Rethinking the Public Sphere," *Social Text* 25/26 (1990): 56–80; C. Squires, "Rethinking the Black Public Sphere: An Alternative Vocabulary for Multiple Public Spheres," *Communication Theory* 12, no. 4 (November 2002): 446–68; Michael Warner, "Publics and Counterpublics," *Public Culture* 14, no. 1 (Winter 2002): 49–90.

23 Denning, *The Cultural Front*, 443–5. Denning describes Burke as the "major cultural theorist of the Popular Front."

24 Kenneth Burke, "Revolutionary Symbolism in America," in *The Legacy of Kenneth Burke*, eds. Herbert Simons and Trevor Melia (Madison: University of Wisconsin Press, 1989), 271–2.

25 Washington, *The Other Blacklist*, 130; emphasis in the original.

26 S. Hall, D. Morley, and K.-H Chen, *Stuart Hall: Critical Dialogues in Cultural Studies* (London: Routledge, 1996), 115.

27 Richard Wright, *African American Literary Theory*, ed. Winston Napier (New York: New York University Press, 2000), 50. Wright published his seminal "Blueprint for Negro Writing" in 1937, in which he expanded upon the idea that Marxism could "create a picture which, when placed before the eyes of the writer, should unify his personality, organize his emotions, buttress him with a tense and obdurate will to change the world … In turn this changed world will dialectically change the writer." Wright placed Negro folklore at the centre of this vision of what he called a "complex simplicity."

28 Richard Iton, *In Search of the Black Fantastic: Politics and Popular Culture in the Post–Civil Rights Era* (New York: Oxford, 2010).

29 *Freedom* 1, no. 10 (October 1951): 1.

30 Ibid., 2.

31 Alice Childress, "Conversation from Life," *Freedom* 1, no. 10 (October 1951): 3.

32 This observation is not, of course, to take away from the strong tradition of the black press. It is, rather, to acknowledge that mainstream media was still largely coded as white and as addressed to white audiences.

33 Alice Childress, "Conversations from Life: The 'Many Others' in History," *Freedom* 2, no. 2 (February 1952): 2.

34 Stuart Hall, "Introduction: Who Needs 'Identity'?" in *Questions of Cultural Identity*, ed. Stuart Hall and Paul du Gay (London: Sage Publishers, 1996), 1–17.

35 Ibid.

36 This statement is from Childress's column titled "All About My Job," collected in *Like One of the Family: Conversations from a Domestic's Life* (New York: Independence Publishers, 1956; Boston: Beacon Press, 1986), 37.

37 Claudia Jones, "An End to the Neglect of the Problems of Negro Women," rpt. in *Claudia Jones: Beyond Containment*, ed. Carol Boyce Davies (London: Ayebia Clarke Publishing, 2011), 74–86, quotations at 75–6.

38 Hall, "Who Needs 'Identity'?" quotation at 3.

39 Claudia Jones was arrested twice, first under the Smith Act (for being a member of the CPUSA) and then deported in 1955 under the McCarran Act. After a short stint in jail at Ellis Island, Jones was incarcerated for over a year in the notorious Federal Women's Prison in Alderson, West Virginia, where later Angela Davis and Assata Shakur would be imprisoned. The authoritative literary biography of Jones is called *Left of Karl Marx*, by Carol Boyce Davies, to whose work I am indebted. To underscore the transatlantic context of black liberation in the United States and to highlight McCarthyism's ultimate inability to prevent anti-colonial intellectuals from constructing their politics upon an analysis of the intersections between capitalism, racism, and empire, see the anti-colonial themes of the *West Indian Gazette* (1958–65). Edited by Jones, this journal picked up across the Atlantic from where *Freedom* left off and provided a point of continuity between the anti-colonialist politics of the Second World War and the 1960s generation. Carol Boyce Davies, *Left of Karl Marx: The Political Life of Black Communist Claudia Jones* (Durham, NC: Duke University Press, 2007).

40 See, for example, Childress's "Conversations from Life" column in *Freedom* 2, no. 3 (March 1952): 8.

41 Alice Childress, "A Conversation from Life," *Freedom* 3, no. 1 (January 1953): 10.

42 Alice Childress, "Conversation from Life," *Freedom* 4, no. 2 (February 1954): 4.

43 Quoted in James, *Soviet Socialist Realism*, 12.

44 Alice Childress, "Conversation from Life," *Freedom* 4, no. 2 (February 1954): 4.

45 Jonathan Flatley, "How a Revolutionary Counter-Mood Is Made," *New Literary History* 43, no. 3 (Summer 2012), 503–25.

Chapter Thirteen

When Comintern and Cominform Aesthetics Meet: Socialist Realism in Eastern Europe, 1956 and Beyond

EVGENY DOBRENKO
University of Sheffield

The cultural history of the twentieth century – a century of revolutions and mass societies – has been written primarily as a history of the avant-garde being defeated by mass culture and, in the Soviet case, by socialist realism, which at a certain point won the upper hand as an instrument of political control, mobilization, and manipulation. To paraphrase Walter Benjamin, aestheticized politics scored a victory over politicized aesthetics. The political revolutionary art of the Comintern was buried under the avalanche of socialist realism, and the story of its demise became the history of twentieth-century Eastern European aesthetics. In this chapter, we suggest a change of perspective, looking at the year 1956 as a point in history when the path of revolutionary aesthetics and ideology, which had long seemed dead, and that of the dying socialist realist aesthetics crossed against the backdrop of far-reaching political and cultural transformations of Eastern and Central European societies.[1] These pages are reflections on how the story in question is not really that of revolutionary culture being defeated by nationalized culture but, on the contrary, of how the former came back to life as the latter was surrendering its position.

The avant-garde aesthetics that arose with the Comintern was political in its essence, a product of revolutionary struggle whose dynamics were determined by its adherents' revolutionary views on politics and the arts. At the same time, state socialism gave birth to an aesthetics of a completely different kind. Aesthetics turned into an instrument of political "control," devoid of any political "content," since independent political thought (not to mention action) became a sign of dangerous dissidence. Politics was completely monopolized by the Communist Party and the state bureaucracy, thus giving rise to depoliticized art. Artists were no longer ideologists but "engineers of human souls," as Stalin called them in 1932, essentially Party functionaries,[2] while revolutionary art itself was ostracized and replaced with totalitarian kitsch, which was "accessible to the people."[3]

Boris Groys insists that revolutionary culture itself, the culture of the Comintern, contained a seed of its future transformation into socialist realism – the potential for self-negation.[4] Vladimir Paperny, on the contrary, claims that, in Russia, these two trajectories of progress and reaction have been alternating throughout history, the development being not progressive but cyclical ("Culture Two" follows "Culture One" and vice versa).[5] Here, the reference to "Russia" is intentional; throughout the period of Soviet occupation, Eastern Europe was included in the orbit of a Russian historical paradigm. If we detect the fundamental difference between the Comintern-aligned avant-garde and the aesthetics of socialist realism in the role and status of the artist as either a politically responsible agent (in the former case) or a Party functionary voicing a pre-formulated political position (in the latter one), we will see that both theories of the development of political aesthetics are justifiable. On one hand, for all its revolutionary impetus, political aesthetics was rigorous in its rigidity, thus paving the way to Party aesthetics, which one can, following Groys, associate with the establishment of socialist realism. On the other hand, this evolution does not exclude a certain cyclicity in the alteration of political and aesthetic paradigms of Soviet history for which Paperny pleads. The analysis offered below presents a model of interpretation that would accommodate both these theories.

The Cominform's Institutional Aesthetics

Socialist realism carries the traits of its creator. Stalin was first and foremost a politician, whose doctrinarianism was rather specious. His thinking and the institutions he created were evidence of his pragmatism and his awareness of a particular political moment's needs. Socialist realism has traditionally been seen as a political and aesthetic doctrine, a practice as well as a result of Soviet aesthetic production. At the same time, socialist realism itself lacked definition. Or, rather, all its definitions were consistently vague – and for good reason, since its functions were those of a political institution whose needs were best served by vague rather than precise definitions.

First, the vagueness made it possible to "control" arts and literature by changing the course of action, depending on the demands of the moment. For example, today conflictlessness is all the buzz, but tomorrow it will be declared a pernicious "varnishing of reality"; today historicism is celebrated, but tomorrow it will become a shameful "escape from the present day," and so on. Deciding on "the right kind of dogma" on an ad hoc basis was the way to regulate the whole sphere of artistic production.

Second, the vagueness allowed for "normalization" insofar as it was at the core of the newly acceptable conventions. Authors were supposed to follow conventions that remained consistently vague, which made it possible not only to change the conventions themselves at any given moment, but also to control the authors' "compliance" with these (constantly changing) points of reference and requirements. Nobody can know for sure what forms and conventions are acceptable today, which is why everybody must be ready to use a whole range of such forms and conventions at any time, if needed.

Third, the vagueness was the source of terror, as nobody can know what the next step on the minefield will bring: whatever was propagated and celebrated yesterday is to be condemned and eradicated today, and vice versa. Anyone can become the target of the next campaign.

Of the three dimensions of socialist realism (doctrine, practice, institution), the latter is the most important: socialist realism is, first and foremost, an institution; attempts to hide this fact are the basis of its permanent doctrinal fixation. Endless discussions, extensive theorization around the doctrine of socialist realism (whereby these discussions were themselves part of the institution) were supposed to conceal the reality that socialist realism was not a doctrine served by various institutions. Rather, the opposite was true: socialist realism was itself an institution. It was an institution of control, normalization, and terror; as such, it was served by a doctrine whose main feature was maximum vagueness and main function was to conceal its real political functions. In other words, the institution did not serve the doctrine, but, rather, the doctrine served the institution. Socialist realism was exactly such an institution, one that covered the whole range of the production and consumption of aesthetic works – from the Writers' Union to censorship. Understandably, as soon as this institutional conveyor belt was disrupted, socialist realism fell apart. In other words, contrary to the prevalent view, socialist realism was not the fuel for the functioning of institutions but, rather, the very engine itself. Insofar as writers and artists worked within the constraints of socialist realism, they were just its agents.

It is from this perspective that we will look at what was happening in Central and Eastern Europe and in the Soviet Union during the Cominform period, especially after Stalin's death. The Cominform was a postwar reincarnation of the Comintern.[6] Because the very same Andrey Zhdanov, who declared the introduction of socialist realism in 1934 and supervised the development of Soviet culture to the end of his days (hence the designation of the whole epoch as *zhdanovshchina*), played a central role in the creation of the Cominform, a closer comparison of these two projects is called for, especially since the Cominform was dissolved right after the Twentieth Party Congress. The termination of the Cominform's activity in April 1956 practically marked the beginning of the disintegration of the Eastern European imperial project – a disintegration that was only stopped at the end of 1956 by tanks in the streets of Budapest.

Following Stalin's death, it became apparent that the ideas forming the basis of avant-garde aesthetics in the early Comintern period of the 1920s had not only survived the long Stalinist winter,[7] but were ready to blossom in Khrushchev's thaw with an even greater force, set off against the horrific experience of Stalinism. Having now found their way back as "socialism with a human face," these principles were now perceived as less utopian and rapidly acquired popularity among the intelligentsia that emerged from the era of Stalinism, whose members had never relinquished revolutionary ideals. Key ideological slogans of the day, both in the Soviet Union and in Eastern Europe, were "Back to the Leninist norms of Party life," "Back to the humanist ideals of the Revolution," and "Back to a broad democratization of public life." In the same spirit, the revolutionary "Culture One," the avant-gardism of the 1920s, was rehabilitated. Stalinist literary politics had grown out of the anti-formalist campaigns and was intent on completely expelling the avant-garde from the history of literature and culture (the relevant campaigns took place in the 1930s in the Soviet Union and after the Second World War in Eastern Europe). Now, this art was enjoying a triumphant comeback. The trajectories of the avant-garde and state socialism crossed paths again, but, this time, the roles were distributed the other way around. The former was no longer receding under the assault of the latter; the avant-garde was back, and it was stronger and more popular than before.

The events of 1956 brought about reform of the socialist realist doctrine (on the face of it) and of socialist realism as an institution (in its essence). The basis for socialist realism's transformation was increasing institutional liberalization, which was obvious, even though it may not have been openly declared. There no longer loomed the threat of a labour camp or a death sentence, which had been in store for just about anybody in Stalin's time. Under Khrushchev, it was almost exclusively dissidents who had something to fear, and, even in their cases, punishment was mostly limited to campaigns of intimidation (for example, the Pasternak affair in 1958, when the state-sponsored bullying of Pasternak was initiated following the awarding of the Nobel Prize for *Doctor Zhivago*; and the avant-garde Manege exhibition in 1962, when Khrushchev poured insults and threats upon modernist artists exhibiting their works in the centre of Moscow). Granted, in those years and even later, in the 1960s, the possibility of repression (arrests, camps) was never too far away – suffice it to remember Iosif Brodsky (1963–64) or the Sinyavsky–Daniel affair (1965–66). But, for the most part, the range of "means of controlling artistic matters" at the disposal of the authorities was now limited to campaigns of intimidation and forced exile (Solzhenitsyn, 1974; Voinovich and Aksenov, both 1980; the "Metropol affair," 1979; and others).

This liberalization was also reflected in the status of socialist realism after 1956. In just a few years, socialist realism no longer resembled its original version. In order to understand why this process was so rapid and, in fact, irreversible, we must remember that, unlike the 1920s avant-garde, which had cosmopolitan roots and developed as an international phenomenon, socialist realism, in its original version, was not an export product. It was only after 1948 that socialist realism expanded beyond the borders of the Soviet Union and became part of a new model of culture in all Eastern European countries. Having been created "for one country," socialist realism became an international phenomenon. Its rapid transformation or, rather, crisis was partly because a moment came when the very foundations of socialism began to be questioned in these countries. This questioning could never have happened in the Soviet Union in the mid-1950s, but it was the price that had to be paid for socialist realism's internationalization. As we will see, the price turned out to be too high.

The Yugoslav Factor

The year 1956 was the turning point in the history of socialism that marked the beginning of its decline. The usual reference is the Twentieth Party Congress in the Soviet Union and the beginning of de-Stalinization. But it is unlikely that these events would have brought about the demise of socialist realism if it had been strictly an internal Soviet affair. De-Stalinization destabilized the regimes in the countries of the Soviet bloc; consequently, those countries refuted the cultural models that had been introduced after the war, which had little connection with their history and culture. The stronger the local literary tradition and the more solid the local literary culture, the less organic these countries found the Soviet model and the less inclined they were to accept it – good examples are Poland, Hungary, and Czechoslovakia, which all had strong literary traditions. These countries openly challenged the proposed status quo. At the same time, in countries with weaker or younger national traditions (Romania, Bulgaria, Albania), the situation remained under the control of the regime. One exception to the rule, however, was Yugoslavia. As a consequence of the conflict between Stalin and Tito, Yugoslavia found itself literally pushed out of the Soviet bloc and was forced to find its own way into socialism, different from the Stalinist model. As a result, Yugoslavia quickly acquired maturity, both politically and culturally.

By engaging in a conflict with Tito, Stalin created a somewhat alternative model of socialism, which, with both the Stalinist model in crisis and the Eastern European tradition often resistant to the Stalinist influence, became an early prototype of "socialism with a human face," displaying features that ranged from workers' councils at factories to relative freedom in aesthetic matters. These ideals were advocated by the leaders of Hungary in 1956 and Czechoslovakia in 1968, as well as by reformers in Poland in 1981 and the Soviet Union in 1987. In a certain sense, after the break with the Soviet Union in 1948, Yugoslavia became a real laboratory of "reformism," which all post-Stalinist reformers aspired to – from Imre Nagy and Alexander Dubček to Mikhail Gorbachev.

Like other practices of Stalinism, socialist realism in its pre-1948 version had been introduced in Yugoslavia using the same methods as were used in all the other countries of "the Soviet zone of influence." But the break of 1948 made the leaders of Yugoslavia position themselves as representatives of a regime that was both socialist and anti-Stalinist. In other words, the foundation was set to create a "non-Stalinist" version of socialism. This new version had no room for particularly infamous Stalinist inventions, such as socialist realism. The refutation of socialist realism in Yugoslavia found its most famous expression in Miroslav Krleža's speech at the Third Congress of Yugoslav Writers in Ljubljana in 1952, where he claimed that the main task of Yugoslav socialist literature was to defend the Yugoslav socialist status quo and thus to ensure the national and cultural survival of Yugoslavia.[8] Krleža declared that there was nothing socialist about socialist realism, that it was just a slogan whose only purpose was to propagate the rule of the Communist Party of the Soviet Union (CPSU), which itself had turned into an imperialist state institution.

Krleža mocked Zhdanov's primitive understanding of the arts and compared "the engineers of human souls" with the medieval Inquisition's burning of heretics. "Directives and ultimatums are good when it comes to chopping off heads, but not when it comes to creating art," he said, calling the advocates of socialist realism "aesthetic Jesuits" led by vulgar taste and political utilitarianism.[9] He accused socialist realism of being anti-revolutionary and aesthetically retrograde. He spoke up against primitive anti-modernism, claiming that art of this kind did nothing but cultivate backward thinking. Krleža, who had been expelled from the Party for his objections to Stalinist socialist realism, called for "a third way" in the arts, an aesthetic paraphrase of the political "third way" that Tito proposed as the right choice for Yugoslavia. If literature followed this "third way," Krleža assumed, it would continue to fight for creative freedom, for a variety of styles and forms of expression, for freedom of speech, and for independence of moral and political convictions. Krleža's criticisms were especially painful because, even before the war, he had been the most prominent left-wing Yugoslav intellectual and had also been an open sympathizer of the Russian Revolution.

Although the first step towards re-establishing cultural ties between the Soviet Union and Yugoslavia took place at the Second Congress of the Soviet Writers in December 1954, the Yugoslav approach to the Soviet artistic practices did not really change. Rather, as we will see, Soviet aesthetic theory itself began to change. Marko Ristić's article "On Cultural Ties and Co-existence," which appeared as an editorial in the June 1955 issue of the magazine *Delo*,[10] spoke about the possibility of restoring the lost cultural ties "under the new conditions." But the article also emphasized that Yugoslavia's position on cultural matters was not going to change:

> Yugoslavia does not form part of any bloc, which makes it easier for it to be open
> to multilateral exchanges and cultural contacts. Being open to a diversity does not

presuppose eclecticism. Diversity is freedom, richness, life. And in the sphere of arts it means, for example, the possibility of a fruitful cooperation at the highest level of various approaches and concepts. Unlike in Eastern European countries, in Yugoslavia there is no official, programmatic, leading, state- or Party-managed aesthetics.[11]

The transparent hints at a direct juxtaposition of Yugoslavia's stance to that of the "Soviet bloc" became a justification for the country's policy in matters of cultural contacts, which were to be determined exclusively based on the following principle:

In some cases, our cultural exchanges with certain countries will be limited. It [limitations] will happen if, in these countries, self-willed and administrative guidelines on aesthetic matters make the presence, and the example, of our free art appear as a corrosive influence and if this presence and example are deemed to be in disagreement with the prescriptions and restrictions in force in these countries.[12]

Ristić expressed satisfaction that "our contacts with the West have never been severed, as happened in Russia."[13] At the same time, Soviet literature continued to be published in Yugoslavia, but its promotion and popularity was grounded in the general conviction that "the pinnacle of Soviet literature" was "post-October prose" and nothing worthy of interest had appeared there from the mid-1930s onward (that is, during the Stalinist period, which the Yugoslav publishers ignored completely). The 1920s, too, were represented by a narrow selection of works, which included Leonid Leonov's *Thief*, Isaac Babel's *Red Cavalry*, Boris Pil'niak's *Naked Year*, Yury Olesha's *Envy*, and Zamiatin's *We*. The works being promoted in the Soviet Union as examples of socialist realism (Alexander Fadeev's *Rout*, Dmitry Furmanov's *Chapaev*) were disregarded. As a result, Soviet literature was represented in Yugoslavia, just like in the West, mostly by the modernism of the 1920s, and the available works hardly extended to socialist realism, which emerged after the defeat of modernism.

Unsurprisingly, the Yugoslav position on the arts was seen in the Soviet Union as "revisionist corrosion." A further complication was that, unlike writers and officials from the "Soviet bloc" countries, Yugoslav writers did not restrain themselves, even when they addressed the public at the highest possible level. For example, when Milan Bogdanović, vice-president of the Union of Yugoslav Writers, presented his report "Ten Years of Yugoslav Literature" at the Union's Fourth Congress, which took place in Ohrid, Makedonia, on 15–17 September 1955 and was attended by 130 delegates, he spoke about socialist realism, claiming it had become a dogma. The newspaper *Borba* published a summary of the report on 17 September 1955, quoting Bogdanović, who had made it clear that, even before 1948, "we had not completely fallen victim to the revolutionary-utilitarian directives and tried not to restrain literary inspiration and literary form by any strict supervision." Even before 1948 in Yugoslavia, he reiterated, "this theory had not been really realized," not even when "all our social, political and cultural life was governed by the propagation of a foreign experience, by an attempt to force directive methods upon us." And, from 1948 on, he pointed out, "our life has been driven by the deep impulse of increasing independence."[14] The periodical *Politics* reprinted Bogdanović's report under a lengthy title, which was a quotation from the report itself: "The literary word is not to be subject to any censorship except for the judgment of the public, of readers and critics." Since censorship was one of the cornerstones of social-ist realist aesthetics, this statement must have been a thorn in the flesh of the authorities, not only in the Soviet Union but also in other Soviet bloc countries.

As the atmosphere became tenser, the Yugoslav rhetoric became more and more militant. In his report "Individual Freedom and Creative Freedom in Socialism,"[15] Natasii Mladenovic called socialist realism "a theory of eunuchs, not that of real, authentic artists."[16] The report was originally written for the Congress of Polish Writers, but had been presented at a literary evening in the Foreign Journalists' Club in Warsaw because the congress was postponed at the very last minute, after the delegates had arrived. As the congress had been planned for November 1956, it seems safe to conclude that it was post-poned because of the 1956 revolution in Hungary, commonly referred to at the time as "the Hungarian events" (23 October–5 November).[17] Even before 1948, Mladenovic said, "Our cultural traditions, our tradition of resistance, the personal resistance of a great number of Yugoslav communist artists who were raised in completely different historical, social and political conditions – all of this has played a role in the fight against the narrow template and schematiza-tion of Socialist Realism."[18] And, from 1948 onwards, he noted, "a steady for-ward movement of the struggle for socialist democracy in culture and the arts" has taken place. In "detecting and disclosing various forms of *Zhdanovism*, we could see all the more clearly … how useless the administrative management of life, of culture, of the arts is." Mladenovic argued that the Writers' Union was a purely professional organization, with no right to influence the aesthetic views of its members, and that journals, newspapers, publishing houses, and theatres must be allowed to work without being subject to censorship. He particularly focused on unmasking four supposedly "Marxist" myths that had been pro-moted in the spirit of Zhdanovism and Stalinism: the subjection of the arts to politics; the belief that socialist realism was the only artistic method possible in socialism; the promotion of cultural autarchy; and the assumption that a Marxist artist had to obey a uniform, simplified, and one-sided point of view in matters of aesthetics, style, and taste. In conclusion, Mladenovic declared that "the state of Soviet literature will improve not as a result of moving it out from fancy villas and palaces to factories, but only when the atmosphere of free debate has been created, an atmosphere of pluralism conducive to the development of socialist democracy in the sphere of aesthetics."[19] Clearly, all of this discussion had not so much to do with aesthetics as with politics.

In order to understand how such public proclamations by "Yugoslav comrades" are likely to have been received in, for instance, Poland, as Soviet tanks fired at protesters in the streets of Budapest, let us turn to just one exemplary episode: Jan Kott's famous 1956 speech, which revolutionized the debates.

The Polish Challenge

Socialist realism as the new method for Polish literature was declared at the Congress of Polish Writers in Szczecin in January 1949. The adoption of socialist realism became possible after the events of autumn–winter 1948. At that time, Jan Kott was considered to be the leading Marxist literary scholar in Poland. Stefan Żółkiewski, a Party functionary and the major official literary critic of the country, said in his talk on contemporary Polish literature given in Moscow in June 1950 that Kott's book on the history of Polish literature was "one of the few critical studies published in Poland that offers a Marxist understanding of literary developments, that helps understand the class essence of literary struggles and of the transformations that aesthetic norms undergo."[20] The collection of Kott's essays, written during the war and published in part in 1945 and then again in 1948 under the title *Mythology and Realism*, was seen as the best example of the genre. Kott was one of the most authoritative voices on classical literature, but he also wrote on contemporary literature and social issues. Being a serious Marxist theoretician, he advocated a socially engaged literature and stood against the understanding of poetry as a "maddening phenomenon of the spirit," against formalist experiments, against André Gide's "antisocial and amoral" concept of man, and against the "pessimistically tragic" characters of Joseph Conrad and André Malraux.

Kott gave his speech, "Mythology and the Truth," at the Nineteenth Session of the Council for Culture and the Arts in the Ministry of Culture and the Arts of Poland on 24–25 March 1956. The topic of the session was "Modernity and Revolutionary Art."[21] The effect of his talk was akin to that of an explosion: Kott openly criticized the Stalinist model of culture. He said that the time had come, finally, to renounce the mythologization of reality, which is based on the conviction that whatever happens, happens in accordance with the demands of historical progress. Such incantations and liturgical formulas were supposed to transform objective reality, to ensure a victory over enemies, and to raise the standard of life of the people, but none of these goals had proved reachable. It was, hence, necessary to go back to realism, because it was there that true Marxism was rooted.[22]

The Soviet literature of the 1920s had been truthful, according to Kott. It "reflected the real social process; it showed the historical and the personal drama of the people of October, their dreams and hopes, their pain, their struggle and suffering; it did not seek to avoid the brutality of tragedy; and it knew how to fight persistently for the future of the revolution." Even the works written somewhat later, during the first five-year plan and collectivization, reflected people's life truthfully.[23] Kott placed the beginning of the period of stagnation in the mid-1930s, when literature and the arts "stopped telling the truth, stopped understanding the historical process, stopped being the conscience and the mind of the revolution." For Kott, "*Zhdanovshchina* goes back to the moment socialist realism was announced – and its mythology canonized." But he did not limit himself to criticizing the doctrine. While he had no doubt that "both the aesthetics of socialist realism and the selection of particular works from the nineteenth century canon were false, the implied understanding of the historical process reflected in this literature and in this art was even more false. Creative activity became a justification not of the regime but of the system, turning into an art of glorification, a grandiose genre of solemn celebrations, an ever-present piece of stage design."

Kott gave the discussion a political twist the moment he said that Soviet literature was the kind of literature "which is not allowed to speak about crimes, which is expected to remain silent about show trials that shocked one's conscience and have been everyday reality for years, a literature whose lips are sealed and which has been sucked deeper and deeper into the thickness of lies, creating an increasingly distorted phantom of reality. The only reason why, through all these years, it has retained some features of literature is because the light of the Great October [Revolution] has still been shining on it, however weakly, and because it has always spoken on behalf of the future on issues that matter most to humankind."[24] Obviously, this view was by no means an anti-socialist position, but it was orthodox in the 1960s sense of the word: Kott was speaking "against" socialist realism because he was "for" socialism.

But Kott did not limit his criticism to socialist realism. He also said that, in the 1930s, Marxist thought "became vulgar, fixed, often swaying towards idealist positions or else feverishly clinging to outdated formulations, eager to avoid facing new questions and new problems," labelling as anti-democratic, anti-revolutionary, and anti-humanist everything that "in the Western art went beyond nineteenth-century conventions, any search for new forms of expression."[25] In this sense, Kott reconsidered the importance of the "breaking point" that had been caused by the introduction of socialist realism in Poland: "It was a breaking point of sorts. It marked the beginning of a slow but unstoppable process of the death of conscience, of an ever-increasing moral blindness. Literature ceased to be a reflection of contemporary life in Poland. It turned into an illustration of a scheme, removed from the truth of life."[26]

Kott shared the position of most of his fellow reformers in that for him, too, Marxism remained the ideal to strive for, which was exactly the reason why the practices of socialist realism were a move away from Marxism: "Literature and the arts to which we later started to apply the adjective 'schematic' were not only about schematic poetics. It is not about poetics, stylistics or other forms of expression. We are talking here about a massively distorted depiction of life, about a lack of common sense and courage, about cowardice and sycophancy, about myth-making that came to replace Marxism."[27]

The doctrine and the practice of socialist realism were not the only targets of Kott's criticism. He also spoke about institutions such as artistic unions, which, he claimed, "have contributed to the process of the degeneration of literature and the arts," having turned into "educational organizations, monitoring and leading their members by the hand. More and more often, writers, scientists and artists came to be regarded as pupils whose homework needed to be checked to make sure they kept up with their assignments." For this, everybody must be held accountable: "We've given our moral consent to the insults to be spoken, to the crimes to be committed. And for this we will, of course, have to bear responsibility."[28]

Whatever started to happen after Stalin's death was, for Kott, evidence of an "ideological, intellectual and moral awakening. It was as if the people who had spent the winter in hibernation started to open their eyes, to think, to stand up for their opinions. Gradually, we were going back to being revolutionaries and Marxists." Kott was unequivocal in his unmasking of the official position about allegedly "fighting on two fronts: on the one hand, against schematism; and on the other, against those who see reality through blue glasses. In practice, what happens is that all the criticism, all the bullets came to be directed exclusively at those who were searching for historical truth, for a way to return to revolutionary morality – because they were, of course, making mistakes, as one does when crawling out of darkness, after a prolonged night."[29] This was the state at which Soviet culture would remain frozen until perestroika.

Kott, however, remained faithful to his Marxist convictions. He pleaded for a politically responsible art: "We are condemned to politics, which means that we are condemned to take a conscious part in our history, with our hearts and our minds. We demand from literature, from painting, from all the arts the whole truth about the fate of the revolution and a ruthless struggle for the future of socialism."[30]

Kott insisted his position was true to the spirit of the Party: "Writers are not separate from the Party and from the people who live in modern day Poland. They only gave voice to their anxiety and to their doubts, and signalled an awakening of their revolutionary consciousness. Writers who are Party members played a significant part in this awakening. And this was, I think, the best way in which they could have fulfilled their Party duty."[31] Accordingly, the art these people were creating was to become "a great political art and literature, to be perceived not as an execution of a social order, not as an illustration of some thesis declared and then changed, month after month or every six months. No – this would be a truly political literature and art, which will do revolutionary justice by people and by history, which will never stop fighting for the revolution, for keeping the revolution pure up until its final victory."[32] Clearly, Kott brushed away the attempts of some critics with high positions in the Party hierarchy to present contemporary literature as "maligning." From his point of view, the opposite was true: "Over the last months, our literature has made the first steps into forbidden territory, has started asking questions which are most vital for our whole generation, and especially for the communists. These are questions about revolutionary dignity, about fate, about the future of the revolution. It must be said clearly: we are living by these questions. And the only claim to the greatness of our literature and art can come from answering these questions."[33]

Kott's report lifted invisible barriers, and the press was flooded with expressions of dissatisfaction, which had until then remained unspoken.[34] For example, the poet, playwright, and literary critic Antoni Słonimski, who in 1956 would become chairman of the Union of Polish Writers, said: "Our main problem is not that we are true to Marxism, but rather that we have abandoned the teachings of Marx and Engels." An example of how this shift happened was the First Congress of Soviet Writers in 1934, when, according to Słonimski, "following Gorky's light-minded ideas, using his authority as a writer, Zhdanov set the foundations of the socialist realist teaching, and this special weapon for annihilating the arts was distributed among officials who spent the next twenty years, led by sentiments of subservience and extreme fear, destroying with great pleasure everything they could."[35]

Without mincing his words, Słonimski continued: "At the Twentieth Congress, they talked about decentralization and about sending writers to peripheral regions as a way to save literature. I would happily send some of our writers to hell, but I doubt that upon their return they will be able to produce masterpieces like those of Dante."[36] He concluded by calling for political transformation:

> The changes for the better that we have been observing since literature came out of the dark times of fear and cynicism are not to everyone's liking. Sad, orphaned supporters of Beria can still be encountered here and there, as can those who had supported the murderers, people whose very existence and whose power were only possible at a time when political and literary blackmail reigned. One of the most immediate tasks we are facing is the management of the Union's literary activities. The Red Salvation Army must finally stop beating the drums; it must put an end to public confessions, to happy, non-obliging self-criticism, to preaching.

While welcoming "our coming out of the medieval darkness," however, Słonimski was aware that "an improvement of the conditions of our cultural life and literature depends not on some managing bodies and institutions, but on restoring civil freedoms. The freedom of expression, which is guaranteed by the [Polish] Constitution, cannot be a toy in the hands of anonymous officials."[37]

Some other participants also sharply criticized the bureaucratic management of the arts, in which the poet Julian Przyboś detected a renunciation of Marxism, supporting Kott's claim that "historical materialism ended once socialism had been constructed." Like Kott, Przyboś did not doubt the validity of Marxism. He spoke as a determined communist when he said that "one must trust in the greatness of the communist idea, one must trust in the greatness of the events that are taking place. I believe, I am deeply convinced, that after the eleven years of existence of the People's Poland there is not a single thinking person who does not think that the future belongs to communism. If somebody does not think this way, he is not a thinking person, and creative people are thinking people."[38] He suggested that "we return, not in words but in deeds, to the Leninist traditions when various groups and artistic movements were active," because "the rebellious spirit of the European avant-garde was directed not only against frozen artistic forms, but also against bourgeois social relations," and socialist realism "was only a stick created by Zhdanov to beat the arts to death, a stick only of use to officials in the propaganda bureau, to acolytes and eulogists."[39]

The appeal for a renunciation of socialist realism was accompanied by an appeal for "artistic freedom" and a rejection of censorship, that is, against the very institutional foundations of Stalinist art. Przyboś suggested that "in our arts, a variety of movements and traditions should be allowed to coexist. Spontaneously emerging innovative artistic groups should be able to publish magazines; they should be offered opportunities to address the public; they should be granted access to theatre halls and to organizations in charge of project-making, architectural planning and industrial production." On the other hand, he claimed that the socialist realist visual artist Alexander Gerasimov and such "elephantine giraffes of buildings as the Palace of Culture and Science" in Warsaw are "not socialist art, but a caricature of it."[40]

The artist Isaac Celniker, who himself had been accused of formalism, joined in the appeal to rehabilitate the 1920s, the "Leninist period in the Soviet arts." "If we say that the Twentieth Party Congress is the first Leninist congress in the past twenty years and are not afraid of it being anti-Soviet propaganda, then we shouldn't be afraid of saying the same about the arts, and we must acknowledge that 'Gerasimovism' as a type of culture, as an artistic phenomenon is counter-revolutionary with respect to Mayakovsky and Eisenstein."[41] He reminded the public of how the enforcement of this kind of art involved a kind of moral blackmail: "Tell me what your attitude to Soviet art is, and I will tell you what your attitude to the Soviet Union is."[42]

The pressure of criticism was so strong that even those Polish socialist realist writers who had been most supportive of the socialist realist line had to plead their allegiance to the proposed course. For example, the vice chairman of the Union of Polish Writers and a member of the Central Committee of the Polish United Workers' Party (PUWP), Jerzy Putrament, pointed out the moral responsibility of Stalinists, of those who, under Stalin, "did not think twice about accusing, torturing and who are, hence, guilty, regardless of whether or not they believed in doing this for the benefit of the revolution."[43]

The Hungarian Explosion

Such was the context in which the Yugoslav literati in Warsaw appealed to a "free discussion" and "socialist democracy." As Philippe Ben wrote in the Parisian *Le Monde*, "Poland did not know the triumph of a Polish Tito, but it is on its way to a Polish Titoism without Tito."[44] The tanks in the streets of Budapest were supposed to block this way. The tragedy that followed was not so much a result of the Soviets' desire to stop "counter-revolution," but rather of their inability to offer a program for reforming Stalinist socialism that would be able to compete with the Yugoslav example. The "socialist democracy" in Eastern Europe was a threat not only to Stalinist socialism but also to the Soviet regime itself, which was busy renovating the façade of Stalinism. In fact, by creating an empire of Eastern European satellites, Stalin created a mirror in which the Soviet Union saw its reflection. Until Stalin's death, this mirror had been covered, but once the cover was removed, it became clear that Stalinist socialism was facing an existential challenge of the kind it had not faced since the days of fighting the Trotskyist opposition in the 1920s. It was much easier to oppose the bourgeois West during the Cold War than to oppose Marxism, with which, by the early 1950s, the Stalinist regime had but a rhetorical connection. The meeting between Stalinism and Marxism posed an existential threat for the former, triggered by Khrushchev's secret speech at the Twentieth Party Congress – and that threat is why the seeds of socialist reforms in Hungary were erased so mercilessly.

The situation in Hungary was significantly different from that in Poland. Under Mátáyas Rákosi, Hungary had followed the way of accelerated industrialization and collectivization, which had been rather unpopular in the predominantly agrarian country. Poland, on the other hand, had chosen the path of reducing investments into heavy industry, placing an emphasis on improving the workers' standard of living, and achieving compromises with the peasantry. The government had even taken steps towards reviving smaller forms of private property. Polish agriculture had been the least collectivized in the

communist camp (only about 9 per cent of all agriculture had been collectivized). In 1956, the majority of cooperatives dissolved themselves. By making
Władysław Gomułka, who had been branded as a "right deviationist" just a
short time previously, head of the state in October 1956, the Soviet government saved "Polish socialism" and managed to keep Poland in the Soviet orbit
without major intervention. But saving "the foundations of socialism" had its
price: it meant removing from the management of the country not only staunch
Stalinists but also liberals and Jews. Poland remained in the Soviet camp, but
it was becoming increasingly self-sufficient and nationalistic. The same thing
was now happening in Hungary, but this time a military intervention became
necessary because the change of power had not taken place early enough.

The situation in Hungary was heating up so quickly that one could trace
almost weekly changes in how writers who had been quite loyal to the regime
just a short time ago suddenly were at the very centre of the uprising. It is
not by chance that, after the events of 1956, the Union of Hungarian Writers
was dissolved. The Petőfi Circle, created in 1954 and transferred under the
management of the Democratic Union of Youth (a Hungarian version of the
Komsomol) in 1955, turned into the country's main political club, with writers
playing a leading role. When, on 27 June 1956, the club hosted a discussion on
the role of the press in society, it was broadcast for some 7,000 people to hear –
such was its popularity. In 1956, the club became the ideological and political
centre of the uprising. On 30 June, a Plenum of the Central Committee of the
Hungarian Communist Party issued an order for the circle to cease its activities,
and those Party members who tried to oppose the decision were expelled from
the Party. The circle members actively participated in preparing the ground for
the events of October 1956, in particular by promoting demands for reforms.
Naturally, they were not talking about reforming the doctrine itself, but only
about reforming the institutions. As an illustration of the connection of political demands with literature and the arts, let us look at a writers' conference that
took place in mid-September 1956, on the eve of the Hungarian uprising.

After the defeat of the Hungarian revolution of 1919, nearly all leftist politicians, intellectuals, and writers left the country, emigrating primarily to the
Soviet Union. Many returned from Moscow after the war, but they were strangers
to Hungarian literature, where the more talented populist writers dominated. As
Hungary was an agrarian country, a characteristic feature of its national literature was its populism. Both the populist writers, on the one hand, and leftist
reformers inside the Party, on the other, were opposed to "leftist sectarianism," a
euphemism used at that time to designate Stalinism.

One can get a pretty good idea of the atmosphere in the weeks preceding the
conference from reading an editorial article written by the playwright and scholar
of aesthetics Gyula Háy and published in the most oppositional publication of the
country – the literary newspaper *Irodalmi Újság*.[45] The article openly called for

"free literature" and the abolishment of censorship. One should only be allowed to prohibit what the law prohibited, the author argued, that is, instigation to murder, arson, robbery, "overturning the people's democracy" [!!], and so on. Everything else should be allowed. "The freedom of literature," Háy wrote, "is constrained by the existence of some special institutions that were created for keeping literature under control." The authorities in charge of book publishing and theatres should no longer have the right to censor books and theatre programs. Their task should be limited to dealing with administrative and financial issues. "The truth is that, in matters of book publishing and staging plays, the constraints have been significantly relaxed, but they are still there, it is not yet freedom ... Any sort of control, open or veiled, over the publishing of books and theatre performances, any form of censorship should be abolished by a state decree."[46]

Even though the Hungarian uprising was suppressed as counter-revolutionary, in its spirit, it was orthodox in its adherence to communist ideals. Suffice it to say that Háy accompanied his appeals for an annihilation of censorship and unrestrained artistic freedom with a reminder that "there is no absolute freedom" (even when walking down the street, one must obey signs and traffic lights).[47] He also stressed his high opinion of the Union of Hungarian Writers, which "over the last year and a half ... has turned into a real political centre, into a source of progressive politics, Leninist in its spirit."[48] But, even though (or because) Gyula Háy called for a "purification" and strengthening of the system, on 17 September 1956, at a general meeting of Hungarian writers, his position received no support.

Reporting to Mikhail Suslov on the meeting, Georgy Gulia, the special correspondent of *Literaturnaia Gazeta* in Hungary, gave full expression to his shock and amazement at what had happened: "Some writers talked about how it's the first time since the revolution of 1848 that the writers' community has been so united, that the Union of Hungarian Writers is the second political centre of the country, where schematists and dogmatists have been expelled from all the leading positions." Gulia was particularly worried that Hungarian communists were telling him "there was the spirit of the Twentieth Party Congress at the writers' meeting," and "the communist writers stress that their speeches there were inspired by the Twentieth Party Congress and by the spirit of Leninism," even though "what they say and what they demand contradicts these statements." What Gulia heard at the meeting seemed to him unthinkable, but what was particularly frightening was that these developments found support beyond the writers' milieu: when "all the most radical talks were reprinted in *Irodalmi Újság*, all the copies of the newspaper were sold out literally within half an hour" (that newspaper would be shut down following the events of 1956). Gulia was in a true panic: "The situation in the literary milieu is even more problematic than that with the infamous discussions in the Petőfi Circle. I find it very serious and potentially likely to cause complications of a non-literary character, unless Hungarian authorities get the situation under control."[49]

Trying "to get the situation under control" and seeing how unpopular Rákosi's regime was and how strong the intellectuals' role in the political events was becoming, the authorities tried to make certain concessions. For example, just a month after they closed down the Petőfi Circle in June 1956, the Central Committee of the Hungarian Workers' Party removed Rákosi. This move was supposed to calm down the intellectuals. It was also a bribe of a kind: the circulation of *Irodalmi Újság* was increased, the publication of three new journals – *Nagyvilág, Életképek*, and a magazine on aesthetics edited by György Lukács – was allowed. A new regulation on the payment of royalties was introduced from 1 October 1956. These measures, however, did not help release the tension among the writers' community. The September meeting was preceded, accompanied, and followed by discussions on socialist realism.

The 1956 events in Hungary – the intense growth of national self-awareness and formation of civil society – were institutionally incompatible with socialist realism. This situation explains why the poet Lajos Konya, when speaking at the Conference of Hungarian Writers attended by over 200 members of the Writers' Union,[50] proposed to "examine in all details the connection between Zhdanovist aesthetics, Stalinist dogmatism and the personality cult. We must gradually start setting the fundamentals of new aesthetics. But first of all we must acknowledge that our literature can be only realist; what makes it socialist is a particular writer's world view."[51] These remarks were followed by observations on what was happening at the institutional level, as the speaker protested against manipulations that resulted in "some members of the top management of the Union, who had either been asked to leave or else resigned of their own will, being replaced with people who have mostly been recruited from a narrow circle of sectarians resistant to the interests and convictions of the majority of writers ... No collective can be obliged to appoint as their leaders those who are opposed to the will of the collective and who have proven more than once that they are unsuitable for the leadership."[52]

The conference gave a very hard time to the so-called "communist writers," primarily ex-emigrants returned from Moscow, who had been isolated from Hungarian literature for decades and whose status was guaranteed by their loyalty to the regime. *Irodalmi Újság*'s editorial titled "Following the Conference of Hungarian Writers," which saw light on 29 September 1956, just a month before the beginning of the bloodshed, spoke about the responsibility of these writers for the situation:

Public opinion has the right to demand from us an explanation of why those very writers who showed themselves in the political and literary-political conflicts of the recent time to be the most passionate and partisan supporters of Stalinist dogmatism, demagogues and champions of the personality cult as a blindly celebrated, anti-democratic authority – why those very writers have remained silent or else have been conspicuous through their absence in the most recent debates. In the past, they stooped more than once to ad hominem insults and libel. So why are they silent now? Why is it that, at the session of the writers' parliament that convened after the July decree, they failed to find a single word of self-criticism, even though they had more than enough reasons (on the basis of that very July decree) for acknowledging that their views had been wrong, that they had fallen victim to personal prejudice? ... Their demonstrative absence and silence just confirm that those who criticized them and did not support them in the elections of the leadership of the Writers' Union were right. And it is strange that *Szabad Nép* in its report about the writers' conference is being squeamish about how this small group of people has been "offended," instead of subjecting their unworthy – especially for communists – behaviour to justified criticism.[53]

Aesthetics had given way to the main, institutional dimension of socialist realism. Now, in discussions of the socialist model of culture, questions of morality were at the top of the list. This moralization was the reverse side of the return of politics, as the political discourse was still restrained by numerous taboos. In this sense, Ottó Major's article in *Irodalmi Újság*, "The Unity of the Party and the Morality of the Writer: Thoughts Following the Writers' Conference,"[54] is symptomatic. Major reminded his readers:

> As the united front of writers was being formed in October 1954, when it became obvious that the accusations against László Rajk had been fabricated and the sacred war against Yugoslavia was grounded in slander and lies, at that moment, something broke. This break in literature and, ultimately, in our whole spiritual life was a moral break. We suddenly realized that our art had been serving criminal political aims, that the moral foundations of everything we had been doing for years were, to say the least, arguable. The burden of responsibility on our shoulders could not make any less true the fact that, as it turned out, we had been victims of a deception ... Spiritual perturbation, bitterness, suppressed anger – this is what has kept our literature going.[55]

It was in acknowledging the "moral" responsibility of literature that the author saw an opportunity to overcome Stalinism. Having rejected the claims of Stalinism as revolutionary, Major formulated a dilemma that communist writers were facing: "Those who set up a juxtaposition between the writers' struggle for restoring morality, on the one hand, and the unity of the Party, on the other, are doing a disservice to the very cause of unity they are pleading for ... Unity cannot be in contradiction to justified moral requirements."[56]

What is moral is communist. And the fact that socialist realist institutions stop functioning in an environment based on moral values means that socialist realism itself is quite distanced from "Leninist ideals." Institutionally, socialist realism in Hungary collapsed in 1956 when the participants of the writers' conference refused to include in the managing body of the Union the writers

who had been vehement supporters of Rákosi's regime in the late 1940s to early
1950s. "What is the reason that none of the sectarians, including those of our
colleagues who had come back from emigration, has been re-elected to the
managing board?" Major asked. "It has nothing to do with the popularity of the
former emigrants, the proof of which is the respect with which Sarolta Lányi
is treated." Major did not doubt that many of the "emigrants" were wonderful
writers, interesting people who had many friends and helped many others, like,
for example, Béla Illés.[57] "How, then," he asked, "can one explain the fact that
the writers refused to place trust in him or in the other 'emigrants'?" Major
offered the following explanation:

> The majority of the writers who had been forced by the counter-revolutionary
> groups to leave the country had themselves experienced decades of Stalinist rule
> and witnessed the horrors that were mentioned in Khrushchev's speech ... A wrong
> understanding of the interests of the communist movement and – one must say this
> openly – fear has made it impossible for them to speak the truth. But nobody asked
> them, they who knew the facts, to support by their artistic activity the commit-
> ment of similar crimes in their own country. After the Twentieth Party Congress,
> these writers – former emigrants – had (and still have) an opportunity to join the
> majority of Hungarian writers. Instead of this, however, they chose the way of sec-
> tarian opposition. Which is why they have lost our trust, which is why they did not
> become members of the democratically elected management board of the Union.[58]

Socialist realism collapses when it collapses as an institution. Theoretical
debates are only important insofar as they signal institutional transformations.
As is well known, the decree of the CPSU Central Committee from 23 April
1932, "On Restructuring Literary-Artistic Organizations," which marked the
beginning of the socialist realist project, gave a clear outline of the project's
institutional foundation: it presupposed the creation of a "single union of Soviet
writers with a communist fraction in it." Once this "fraction" was expelled from
the union, the union itself stopped being an institutional foundation of socialist
realism. Now, nothing remained but the doctrine itself, and the outlines of this
doctrine became somewhat blurred.

In the discussion about socialist realism taking place in *Irodalmi Újság* just
before the uprising, these changes were more than obvious. A characteristic
example is an article by the critic Imre Keszi titled "Socialist Realism or Socialist
Literature?,"[59] in which the author tried to take a broader look at socialist realism
in the more general historical and literary perspective of twentieth-century progressive literature. What he saw was that "the very concept of Socialist Realism
is too narrow for outlining the whole potential, or the whole highest potential,
of socialist literature." He asked: "What kind of realism is this that can include, if
needed, the beautiful fairy tale about the knight János but that will have no place

for Zola's portraits of society? What kind of realism is this that can allow for all kinds of ridiculous pomposities and for idealistic subversions of schematic literature in all countries, but that rejects the best works created in Soviet literature in the fiery 1920s or in German literature in the Weimar period?"[60] A martyrology of socialist realism followed: Pil'niak, Babel, early Ehrenburg, Kataev, and Esenin, as well as Brecht and Friedrich Wolf of the cyanide period. Then, there were Upton Sinclair and Dos Passos. "Today it is clear," the author concluded, "that this literature, which for a long time was dismissed with just this one empty general label 'cosmopolitan' ... plays no less a role in the history of socialism than those works that are recognized as the best examples of socialist realism. It is worth a thousand times more than all the works by the Azhaevs, the Popovs, the Babayevskys and all their Hungarian and other followers taken together." And, calling for his audience to fight the "Party-minded and state-sponsored narrow-mindedness,"[61] Keszi concluded: "Socialist Realism is a form and a method, but one cannot force a form or a method onto literature, not even the best form and the best method, because who can know that tomorrow will not bring with it something even better? Which is why writers must be encouraged to aspire not to follow a particular form, a particular method, not to obey socialist realism, but rather to subscribe to a particular view, a particular understanding of the world: socialist literature."[62]

So, for Imre Keszi, it was not about realism, but about the socialist character of literature. What is particularly interesting in this connection is that Lukács, for whom realism had always been the primary value, reached the same conclusions from the opposite starting point, as becomes evident from the interview with him that appeared in *Irodalmi Újság* on 13 October 1956 and in *Szabad Nép* on 14 October 1956. In *Irodalmi Újság*, the interview was published under the title "Young People Ask – György Lukács Replies." One of the most influential Marxist philosophers and critics and, at the time, a leading literary functionary, Lukács (at that time doing his best to avoid making any political declarations) was asked to respond to questions from the students at the literary and historical faculty of Budapest University.[63] Among other things, he said that socialist realism "could not be narrowed down to a few average works which appeared in Hungary between 1949 and 1953. We can, of course, talk about the history of socialist realism, which features the names of Gorky, Nexø, Sholokhov, Tibor Déry ... The mark of any progressive literature is realism. Any history of literature is a cemetery of anti-realist tendencies and works."[64]

Szabad Nép quoted Lukács's confirmation of his pan-realist views when he was asked a question about socialist realism. He responded:

The necessity to fight for realism is a result of the fact that a significant number of our writers and artists fell under the influence of anti-realist tendencies during the reign of Horthy. After the liberation of the country, the process of purifying, strengthening, affirming realism began. But because of the sudden break that occurred in 1949 [when communists seized power and the Hungarian People's Republic was proclaimed], this process never came to completion. Socialist realism was introduced not as a result of discussions about realism, but primarily as a result of administrative interference, which firmly established the sectarian rule of formalism ... What we must now do is unbutton the badly fitting jacket and button it up properly, that is, welcome broad, explanatory discussions of realism and other literary movements. In the course of these discussions, we must completely renounce the sectarian worldview according to which there is a deep abyss, possibly even irreconcilable differences, between socialist realism and earlier realistic movements.[65]

Clearly, Lukács's pan-realism was so comprehensive that, faced with the danger of modernism being rehabilitated, he was even prepared to declare his solidarity with socialist realism and, still a captive of Stalinist vocabulary, he proposed to study "the national form" of socialist realism. But still – though from the realist perspective – Lukács was, in fact, promoting the same "socialist literature" as the supporters of modernism like Imre Keszi.

These discussions of the aesthetics of socialist realism revealed its political essence. Considering that this exposure of the device was accompanied by removing from literary institutions writers who were transmitters of governmental policy, we can say that these events marked the end of the socialist realist epoch. Hungarian writers found themselves at the centre of the national uprising of 1956, which was, essentially, an explosion of national versions of socialism. It may have been suppressed in a military and political sense, but it did score an ideological victory. There was no going back to socialist realist dogma. The era of Cominform aesthetics was over. The only aesthetics possible for the East European socialist regimes themselves was interwar modernism, putting them back in touch with the revolutionary Marxist tradition, progressive ideas of modernization, and thus granting them legitimacy.

The Soviet Response

In the Soviet Union after 1956, the term "Petőfi Circle" became absolutely odious. But the Eastern European storm of 1956, which forced the Soviet Union to use direct military force in order to retain its control over the countries of the "Eastern bloc," had direct consequences both for Eastern Europe and for the Soviet Union. It became obvious that serious changes were in order. In nearly all the "countries of people's democracy" government officials were replaced, Stalin's most odious supporters were made to leave, radical Soviet methods of industrialization and collectivization were abandoned, and "national socialisms" became an option again, after they had been silenced by Stalin's quick and total Sovietization in 1948–49. Now, there were Hungarian, Polish, Romanian, and other "ways to socialism." A shift in the ideology occurred that, despite the permanent fight with "bourgeois revisionism," was exactly such a revision of Stalinism, which made it possible to retain "the countries of people's democracy" under the Soviet influence for the next thirty-five years.

But it would be a mistake to assume that these changes were only needed for Eastern Europe. In order to exercise efficient control over Eastern European countries, the gap between the Soviet model and the Eastern European one had to be overcome, at least in part. Thus, in parallel with the developments in Eastern Europe, the Soviet Union also had to undergo some transformations so that its internal models would be compatible with those followed by "the fraternal socialist countries."

The crisis of socialist realism became so obvious and so deep that, in 1956, the Moscow Institute of World Literature started planning a major conference on realism with the participation of twenty prominent scholars, including scholars from France, Yugoslavia, the United States, Italy, England, and, of course, socialist countries.[66] Then, the list of proposed participants was reduced to those from China, the German Democratic Republic, Poland, Czechoslovakia (Jan Mukařovský), Hungary (György Lukács), Bulgaria (Todor Pavlov), Romania, France (Louis Aragon), and some others.[67] But, even in this reduced format, the project was never realized. Such was the decision of Dmitrii Polikarpov, head of the Department of Culture in the CPSU's Central Committee: "Considering there is much in this matter that is unclear and complicated, which must first be worked through by Soviet literary scholars, the Department of Culture considers it more appropriate to first organize a discussion without the participation of any foreign guests."[68] The top Party officials preferred not to take any risks and to keep the discussion under control.

Such was the background to the discussion on realism that took place on 12–18 April 1957 in the Institute of World Literature. It was the first discussion on realism since the mid-1930s where serious questions were at least raised, if not resolved. Back then, serious theoretical discussions had been held in the pages of the journal *Literaturnyi kritik*. But there was a difference: in the 1930s, participants in the discussion included György Lukács and Mikhail Lifschitz, while in the 1950s, the participants were Mikhail Khrapchenko and Iakov El'sberg. The Stalinist epoch took its toll on Soviet intellectual history: discussions became rather less profound, much more politicized, while the general cultural level of the participants was sometimes simply dismal. In 1956–63, Soviet literary scholarship was never free of incessant vehement discussions about realism and socialist realism, realism and modernism, realism in connection with other artistic methods, the relationship between socialist realism and the classical heritage, and so on.[69] Everything was questioned: the monopoly of realism, the history that had been invented to serve as its basis (Soviet scholars of aesthetics seriously talked about the realism of folklore, the realism of antiquity, the realism of the Enlightenment, and other such "realisms"), the very concept of "an artistic method," and, of course, the concept of "socialist realism." The validity of this latter term was not really doubted, but it was losing its foundations, its roots, and, most importantly, its exclusivity. Suddenly romanticism, modernism, and other movements and schools were mentioned, which, though criticized, could now be studied for comparison.

The theoretical debates and doctrinal liberalization were supposed to prevent deep – institutional – transformations and to attribute ideological legitimacy to said institutions, which is not to say that doctrinal changes had no significance. On the contrary, they were indicative of changes in the logic of the institutions and their political content. It was now clear that socialist realism, once it had been removed from the pedestal, would no longer be able to claim back its status. "Socialist literature" was a new concept introduced for Eastern European and Western literatures, which could not fit into the Procrustean bed of the socialist realist dogma. It was an infinitely stretchable term, created in order to claim everything that could not be covered by socialist realism but that, for some reason, could not be considered part of "bourgeois modernism" either (for example, leftist artists).

The idea of a "socialist literature" was like a magnet. It called back from oblivion the kind of literature that had become simply unmentionable earlier, which included, first of all, authors from national canons whose way to publishing houses had previously been impeded by restrictions of Stalinist doctrine. Socialist literature was cosmopolitan, pluralist, connected with the revolutionary Marxist tradition, socially involved, and critical of the existing social order. It was politically engaged and appealed to themes of class struggle, while being aesthetically connected with modernism, progressivism, and technicism. In other words, socialist literature was everything that the literature of the Cominform in its Zhdanovist version was not, appealing as it did to nationalism, romanticism, and popular taste, glorifying the existing social and political order, persisting in remaining disengaged from the artist's individual political opinions, and aesthetically backward. In essence, these were two generically related, but opposite aesthetic programs, one of which was a culture of anti-bourgeois rebellion and the other, a culture of state socialism. The former relied on free political and aesthetic activity, while the latter catered to the propagandistic demands of the ruling political regime – and it was this latter culture whose rapid collapse was set in motion after 1956.

As the re-emergence of "socialist literature" happened under the conditions of a political monopoly of communist regimes, socialist realism itself was becoming eroded. Previously acceptable interpretations of socialist realism were no longer possible, not even when they were coming from its most orthodox supporters, not even in a country like Bulgaria, however far it may have been from liberal reforms. Sometime later, the leading Soviet historian of

Bulgarian literature, Dmitrii Markov, proposed a theory of "socialist realism as a historically open aesthetic system," which became a new stage in the "curing" of the method.[70] Markov did not have to invent anything new. His theory was brought to life by writers themselves in 1953–57, who turned socialist realism from a tool of repressive Party control, censorship, and surveillance into an aesthetic theory that was benevolent, liberal, broadly defined, open to anything that showed talent, as well as new, inventive, and truly special, and, most importantly, constantly changing and serving noble socialist (if not social-democratic) goals. It was as if writers had not just lived through a whole decade of socialist realism manifesting its presence in a completely different way.

Nevertheless, the idea of "socialist literature" became a serious challenge for socialist realism. Not only did the new theory deprive the state-sponsored theory of its monopoly over being right, but it also made defining the strict parameters of socialist realism even harder. The lack of a clear definition was especially challenging, as just at that time Soviet proponents of socialist realist aesthetics were involved in an endless debate with "revisionist" Western Marxists, such as Roger Garaudy with his theory of "realism without shores" and Ernst Fischer, a former Comintern activist who developed the principle of co-existence and cultural convergence. Socialist realism was rapidly losing whatever doctrinal specificity it may have possessed.

Once it lost its exclusivity, socialist realism started to melt like a candle. What followed was its slow death or, rather, a half-life in the state of an induced coma, a process that would take more than three decades. Of course, this institutionalized aesthetics, whose defining feature was its totality, could not just vanish overnight. But, once the institutional support was no longer strong enough, this totality was becoming less comprehensive, and it had to give way to other aesthetic movements. This process had started after Stalin's death. Figuratively speaking, if, in 1949, socialist realism occupied something like 95 per cent of the public cultural space, in 1959 it was only 70 per cent; in 1969, it went down to 50 per cent; in 1979, to 30 per cent; and in 1989, it was only 5 per cent. Proponents of political aesthetics, including those who had a strong socialist orientation and whose sympathies could thus be traced back directly to inter-war modernism, were claiming more and more cultural territory.

Paradoxically, when Comintern aesthetics, represented by the Eastern European reformers of socialism, confronted its Stalinist – Cominformist – socialist realist reincarnation, it refused to recognize its own reflection, denouncing it in rage. Back then, in 1956, socialist realism survived that frontal collision. But, starting in the 1960s, it was becoming more and more just a "historical episode" in the recent past of the Soviet bloc countries, an episode that retained but loose ties with the literature and art of the time. It may have still enjoyed the status of a master narrative, of an ideological frame, a pattern for modelling the histories of national literatures, but it had almost completely lost the connection with the living artistic process and many of its former institutional privileges and features. By the end of the 1980s, socialist realism remained a peripheral ritual code, "a page in the history books," until it perished under the ruins of the Berlin Wall together with Soviet socialism.

In the Soviet Union, the tendency was the same, but its dynamics were slightly different. There, unlike in "the countries of the people's democracy," socialist realism had developed deep roots in literature and culture – at the ideological, institutional, and, to a significant extent, professional levels. By 1956, more than one generation of writers had been working according to its guidelines: there were those who had started writing before the revolution and had been fellow travellers in the 1920s, as well as two subsequent generations – the 1930s generation and the first postwar generation. These deep roots guaranteed a certain margin of safety for socialist realism within the Soviet Union itself. But not too much.

The year 1956 triggered the unstoppable process of separation between literature and socialist realist discourse. In Stalin's time, socialist realism had been an operational category, an instrumental concept that loyally served the critics, the censors, and the Party managers of Soviet literature. After 1956, that same socialist realism started to move more and more into the sphere of theoretical discussions and counter-propaganda. Its institutional existence was pretty much guaranteed but, at the same time, deprived of its instrumental status; this existence had only symbolic value and belonged to a category of an almost epic past, losing its legitimizing role. The discussions of the early 1960s still bore traces of attempts to restore a connection between the living literary process and the demands of socialist realism. For example, in the debates on new war prose in the early 1960s, orthodox critics still tried to appeal to the demands of socialist realism. But in the 1970s a complete break between socialist realist theory and the living artistic practice occurred, with the former fully retreating into the sphere of theory and history of literature. At about the same time, literary criticism stopped appealing to socialist realism, and the debates about the new wave of war prose, village prose, lyric poetry, or city prose were taking place with no reference to socialist realism whatsoever. The participants in the debates now turned for support not to socialist realist theory but to the national past and the "morally ethical quest." By the beginning of perestroika, socialist realism in the Soviet Union had been firmly relegated to the history of literature, and even ritualistic incantations from the highest levels of power about loyalty to its ideals became quite rare. The death of socialist realism in the Soviet Union did not attract much attention – it simply did not regain consciousness, drifting into non-being in the endless chain of academic debates. At a certain point the comatose patient was, finally, disconnected from the artificial life-support system, as were all the other Soviet political and cultural institutions.

One could say that, after 1956, the marriage contract between literature and socialist realism, even though it was not officially dissolved, became completely void. In the satellite countries, the married partners started living separately, having lost any contact with each other, so that when socialist realism died, literature did not even notice. Literature had already been living its own independent life for quite some time, maybe keeping the family name of the former spouse, with both partners sharing access to the same artistic centres, top-class apartments, and literary funds. The arrangement resulted in certain inconveniences, but also guaranteed significant privileges to literary officials who had been responsible for keeping "the most advanced artistic method" in a state of suspended animation for decades. In the Soviet Union, the comatose spouse, living for decades in the intensive-care unit, was dressed up and made presentable for anniversaries and special occasions, after which the patient was brought back to the life-supporting environment of academic conferences and connected to the artificial breathing equipment supplied by "collected volumes of academic articles" on "topical problems of Socialist Realism." Only the grandchildren of the heroes of socialist realism – conceptualists and masters of Sots-art – remembered the once "deadly weapon" and were inspired by its aesthetics. They were the only ones who brought the wreath of irony to the gravestone of socialist realism. Here, we can now return to Boris Groys's point introduced at the beginning of this chapter: late- and post-Soviet conceptualism, as it turned socialist realism into a target of irony and ridicule, detected in avant-gardist political aesthetics (Culture One) the main origin of socialist realism (Culture Two). In doing so, conceptualism positioned itself beyond the previously valid paradigm of the alternating Culture One and Culture Two. This demonstrative refusal to adopt either position in the continuous conflict of the two cultures gives hope that one day the spiral will be broken.

NOTES

This chapter is part of an Arts and Humanities Research Council (AHRC)–funded project on the Sovietization of Eastern European cultures after the Second World War.

1 The year 1956 was one of the most remarkable years of the twentieth century, a year that changed the world and one that – like 1789 and 1848 – brought unprecedented challenges to those in power and was a subject of numerous studies from different perspectives. See recent works: Francis Beckett and Tony Russell, *1956: The Year That Changed Britain* (London: Biteback Publishing, 2015); Simon Hall, *1956, The World in Revolt* (New York: Pegasus Books, 2016); Kathleen E. Smith, *Moscow 1956: The Silenced Spring* (Cambridge, MA: Harvard University Press, 2017).
2 See Evgeny Dobrenko, *The Making of the State Writer: Social and Aesthetic Origins of Soviet Literary Culture* (Stanford, CA: Stanford University Press, 2001).
3 Ibid.

4 See Boris Groys, *The Total Art of Stalinism* (Princeton, NJ: Princeton University Press, 1988).

5 See Vladimir Paperny, *Architecture in the Age of Stalin: Culture Two* (Cambridge: Cambridge University Press, 2011).

6 On the Cominform, the Information Bureau of the Communist and Workers' Parties, the first official forum of the international communist movement since the dissolution of the Comintern, which confirmed the new realities after the Second World War including the creation of an Eastern bloc, see Fernando Claudin, *Communist Movement: From Comintern to Cominform*, trans. Brian Pearce (London: Penguin Books, 1975); *The Cominform: Minutes of the Three Conferences 1947/1948/1949*, ed. G. Procacci et al. (Milan: Feltrinelli, 1994).

7 See Katerina Clark, *Moscow, the Fourth Rome: Stalinism, Cosmopolitanism, and the Evolution of Soviet Culture* (Cambridge, MA: Harvard University Press, 2011).

8 Miroslav Krleža, Govor na Kongresu književnika u Ljubljani // *Republika* 10–11 (1952), Цит по: M Krleža, "Govor na kongresu književnika u Ljubljani" in *Svjedočanstva vremena*, Književno-estetske varijacije (Sarajevo: Oslobodjenje, 1988). This tradition has its roots in the Comintern era, when the genre of so-called "social literature" became common in Yugoslav letters largely thanks to writers of a socialist orientation. Krleža, a member of the Communist Party of Yugoslavia since 1918, was one of them.

9 Ibid., 34.

10 *Delo*, no. 4 (1955).

11 Russian State Archive of Literature and Art (RGALI), fond 631, opis' 26, delo 3584, l. 47. Note that all translations into English are by Evgeny Dobrenko and Natalia Jonsson-Skradol.

12 Ibid.

13 Ibid.

14 RGALI, fond 631, opis' 26, delo 3588, ll. 11–12.

15 *Knizhevne noviny*, 9 December 1956.

16 RGALI, fond 631, opis' 26, delo 3596, l. 63.

17 On the 1956 Hungarian Revolution, see Csaba Békés, Malcolm Byrne, and János M. Rainer, *The 1956 Hungarian Revolution: A History in Documents* (Budapest: Central European University Press, 2000); John Matthews, *Explosion: The Hungarian Revolution of 1956* (New York: Hippocrene Books, 2006); Victor Sebestyen, *Twelve Days: Revolution 1956. How the Hungarians Tried to Topple Their Soviet Masters* (London: Weidenfeld & Nicolson, 2007); Paul Lendvai, *One Day That Shook the Communist World: The 1956 Hungarian Uprising and Its Legacy* (Princeton, NJ: Princeton University Press, 2008).

18 RGALI, fond 631, opis' 26, delo 3596, l. 64.

19 RGALI, fond 631, opis' 26, delo 3596, l. 67.

20 RGALI, fond 631, opis' 14, delo 670, l. 40.

21 *Przegląd kulturalny*, no. 14 (5 April 1956).

22 For an erudite discussion of two leading trends within the Marxist critical tradi-
    tion, the dogmatic trend exemplified by Stalin, Zhdanov, and Gorky, and a more
    liberal trend represented by such leading Marxist aestheticians as Georg Lukács,
    Roger Garaudy, and Erns Fisher, see George Bisztray, *Marxist Models of Literary
    Realism* (New York: Columbia University Press, 1978).
23 RGALI, fond 631, opis' 26, delo 2246, l. 5.
24 RGALI, fond 631, opis' 26, delo 2246, ll. 5–7.
25 RGALI, fond 631, opis' 26, delo 2246, l. 7.
26 RGALI, fond 631, opis' 26, delo 2246, l. 9.
27 Ibid.
28 RGALI, fond 631, opis' 26, delo 2246, l. 10.
29 Ibid.
30 RGALI, fond 631, opis' 26, delo 2246, l. 11.
31 RGALI, fond 631, opis' 26, delo 2246, l. 12.
32 RGALI, fond 631, opis' 26, delo 2246, l. 13.
33 Russian State Archive of Contemporary History (RGANI), fond 5, opis' 36, delo
    13, l. 32.
34 See discussion in *Przegląd kulturalny*, no. 14 (5 April 1956) and the report:
    RGALI, 631/26/2246.
35 RGALI, fond 631, opis' 26, delo 2246, l. 13.
36 RGALI, fond 631, opis' 26, delo 2246, l. 15.
37 RGALI, fond 631, opis' 26, delo 2246, l. 16.
38 RGANI, fond 5, opis' 36, delo 13, l. 42.
39 RGANI, fond 5, opis' 36, delo 13, l. 43.
40 RGALI, fond 631, opis' 26, delo 2246, l. 18. Alexander Gerasimov was a leading
    proponent of socialist realism in Soviet visual arts and one of the most prolific
    Soviet "court painters" who painted Stalin and other Soviet leaders. He was also a
    prominent functionary, head of the Union of Artists of the Soviet Union and the
    Soviet Academy of Arts, and at the forefront of the attacks against cosmopolitan-
    ism and formalism during the Zhdanov era.
41 RGANI, fond 5, opis' 36, delo 13, l. 46.
42 RGALI, fond 631, opis' 26, delo 2246, l. 20.
43 RGANI, fond 5, opis' 36, delo 13, l. 44.
44 Philippe Ben's words from his article in the French *Le Monde* of 9 August 1956
    were quoted with understandable indignation by Boris Ponomarev, head of the
    Section for Ties with Foreign Communist Parties at the Central Committee of
    the CPSU, in his "information note" of 30 August 1946 to members of the Central
    Committee, which addressed "Some Points on the Internal Political Situation
    in the Polish People's Republic after the 7th Plenum of the PUWP's Central
    Committee" (RGANI, fond 5, opis' 28, delo 398, l. 179).
45 Gyula *Háy* [Before Writers' Conference] // *Irodalmi Újság*, no. 36 (8 September 1956).
46 RGALI, fond 631, opis' 26, delo 1209, l. 45.
47 RGANI, fond 5, opis' 36, delo 13, l. 86.

48 RGALI, fond 631, opis' 26, delo 1209, l. 45.

49 RGANI, fond 5, opis' 36, delo 13, ll. 97–8.

50 *Irodalmi Újság*, no. 38 (17 September 1956).

51 RGALI, fond 631, opis' 26, delo 1209, l. 57.

52 RGALI, fond 631, opis' 26, delo 1209, l. 56.

53 RGALI, fond 631, opis' 26, delo 1209, l. 63.

54 *Irodalmi Újság* (29 September 1956).

55 RGALI, fond 631, opis' 26, delo 1209, l. 65.

56 Ibid., 66.

57 It should be noted that the attitudes to émigré writers varied a lot, as did the behaviour of these writers. Some of them occupied high positions and were staunch Stalinists in conflict with their colleagues (for example, Sándor Gergely), while others, despite their association with the regime, were well regarded (for example, Lukács).

58 RGALI, fond 631, opis' 26, delo 1209, l. 67.

59 *Irodalmi Újság* (6 October 1956).

60 RGALI, fond 631, opis' 26, delo 1209, l. 71.

61 Ibid.

62 RGALI, fond 631, opis' 26, delo 1209, l. 73.

63 Lukács's most influential writings of the time are best presented in György Lukács, *The Culture of People's Democracy: Hungarian Essays on Literature, Art, and Democratic Transition, 1945–1948*, ed. and trans. Tyrus Miller (Leiden, NL: Brill, 2013).

64 RGALI, fond 631, opis' 26, delo 1209, l. 73.

65 Ibid.

66 RGANI, fond 5, opis' 36, delo 17, l. 53.

67 RGANI, fond 5, opis' 36, delo 17, ll. 59–60.

68 RGANI, fond 5, opis' 36, delo 17, l. 62.

69 Materials from these discussions were published in *Problemy realizma v mirovoi literature* (Moscow: GIKhL, 1959); *Sotsialisticheskii realizm i klassicheskoe nasledie* (Moscow: GIKhL, 1960); *Problemy sotsialisticheskogo realizma* (Moscow: Sovetskii pisatel'*, 1961); *Realizm i ego sootnosheniia s drugimi tvorcheskimi metodami* (Moscow: Izdatel'stvo AN SSSR, 1962); *Sovremennye problemy realizma i modernizm* (Moscow: Nauka, 1965).

70 Dmitrii Markov's theory of socialist realism was considered in the Soviet Union and in the Eastern bloc countries to be the last word of literary scholarship. His book *Genesis of Socialist Realism: From the Experience of Southern and West Slavic Literatures* [Генезис социалистического реализма. Из опыта южнославянских и западнославянских литератур] (Moscow, 1970) was translated and published in Bulgaria (1972), Slovenia (1972), Czechoslovakia (1973), GDR (1975), and China (1981). It was also published in English by a central publishing house in Moscow (1978).

Chapter Fourteen

Visions of the Future: Soviet Art, Architecture, and Film during and after the Comintern Years

VLADIMIR PAPERNY
UCLA

MARINA KHRUSTALEVA
Independent Scholar

This chapter builds on *Culture Two*, Vladimir Paperny's dissertation on architecture and culture under Stalin, which he wrote in 1979 while living in the Soviet Union.[1] The radical juxtaposition of two incompatible cultural mechanisms, "Culture One" and "Culture Two," which he argued alternated across Russia history, was, to some degree, a polemical reaction to official Soviet historiography, which insisted on the linear continuity of Soviet history. Boris Groys's *Gesamtkunstwerk Stalin*,[2] written in the 1980s, contained elements of veiled polemics with Paperny's manuscript, which Groys had read in the early 1980s. If Paperny exaggerated the incompatibility between the avant-garde and socialist realism, Groys exaggerated continuity. Subsequently, there have been a few academic attempts to soften Paperny's rigid structuralism and to concentrate on the transition from one period to another.[3] Later, looking for ways to escape what he perceived as a Russian never-ending oscillation between two cultures, Paperny published a short book titled *Culture Three*, where he offers a survey of theories (including his own) that might help Russian culture to escape "the eternal return of Stalinism."[4]

We think that the relationships between internationalism and nationalism, between the avant-garde and socialist realism are more complex than they appeared to an observer trapped in the Soviet 1970s. Nonetheless, as we shall attempt to show, the abruptness and perceived unpredictability of both the collapse of the Union of Soviet Socialist Republics (USSR) and the resurrection of many features of Stalinism a decade later demonstrate that the 1979 Paperny model has preserved some utility.

The Third Communist International was created to replace the previous two in dramatically changed circumstances – it followed the success of the Bolshevik Revolution of 1917. However, the meaning of the word "International" was constantly changing. Initially, the Bolsheviks saw their victory in an international context. The Revolution for them was not so much about Russia and not even about Soviet power. "We are no longer Muscovy and not just the Soviets," wrote Karl Radek in October 1918, "but the vanguard of the world revolution."[5] The Bolsheviks were hoping that the first anniversary of their coming to power would result in a world revolution. Despite food scarcity during the Civil War, Lenin insisted on creating, at every large granary, a special reserve intended for feeding German workers. *Pravda*, the official Party newspaper, enthusiastically supported the idea: "We will move it to Germany the day after their revolution."[6] At the closing of the First Congress of the Comintern in Moscow on 6 March 1919, Lenin euphorically (and without his usual sobriety) proclaimed: "The ice has started to melt. The Soviets have won in the whole world."[7]

In the mid-1920s, the "International" component of the Comintern started to wane. A growing number of communists in various countries became disappointed by the handling of the Comintern in the USSR. "I will feel utterly alone and inappropriate in this organization," wrote German Marxist Clara Zetkin, "which has transformed from a living political organism into a dead mechanism that swallows orders in Russian at one end and spews them out in different languages at the other end, a mechanism that has turned the huge world-historical significance and content of the Russian Revolution into the rules of the Pickwick Club."[8] At about the same time, Angelo Tasca, a founding member of the Italian Communist Party, sent a letter to his Party Secretariat, giving the following assessment of the situation: "The responsibility lies with Stalin. The Comintern does not exist; the Communist Party of the USSR does not exist. Stalin is a 'teacher and master' who controls everything."[9]

In the early 1920s, while politicians were busy with practical matters, artists and designers, those who accepted the Soviet power (willingly or, sometimes, as a practical necessity[10]), started to generate their visions of the future. In 1921, at the end of the bloody Civil War, which practically destroyed the country, and in the early days of the New Economic Policy, which restored some elements of capitalism, artist Lyubov Popova and architect Aleksandr Vesnin made a sketch for a military parade titled "Struggle and Victory" in honour of the Third Congress of the Comintern (figure 14.1). This unrealized performance was supposed to take place in the summer of 1921 on the Khodynka Field on the outskirts of Moscow. The idea was to build two temporary structures representing two cities – one capitalist, one socialist. The "citadel of capitalism" was a cubist composition comprised of solid geometric volumes of various shapes. The socialist "city of the future" combined both solid and dynamic elements. A system of cables, supported by dirigibles, connected the two cities and carried banners endorsing the Third Comintern and world revolution.

No explanations of this sketch by Popova or Vesnin have been found. The only description of the performance is in an article by theatre critic Samuil Margolin.[11] He points out that the script for this mass action was developed with the participation of theatre director Vsevolod Meyerhold. According to Margolin, detachments of infantry, cavalry, motorcyclists, and athletes with

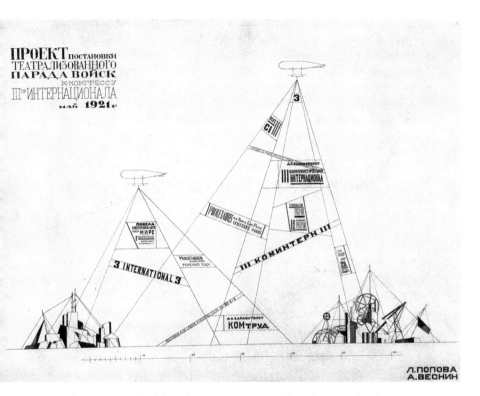

14.1 Lyubov Popova and Aleksandr Vesnin, a proposal for a dramatized military parade "Struggle and Victory" in honour of the Third Congress of the Comintern, 1921. State Tretyakov Gallery.

the support of airplanes, artillery, and military bands had to smash the city of capitalism and then march into the city of the future. A model of the set was approved, and the construction of the buildings started, with Popova personally in charge; but a few weeks before the celebration, "the production was cancelled due to a general resolution prohibiting the expenditure of sums and materials for Comintern celebrations, taking into account the extremely difficult economic conditions of the country."[12]

At the same time, another mass action dedicated to the Third Congress of the Comintern was in a planning stage, in this case, to take place in Red Square in Moscow. The situation is the opposite of Popova and Vesnin's Khodynka project: no sketches have been found, but a detailed scenario has survived. Written by People's Commissar of Education Anatoly Lunacharsky, the script consisted of five acts representing five stages of socio-economic development: primitive society, slave-owning Egypt, the European feudal era, capitalism, and the future socialism. Anticipating a lack of funds, Lunacharsky suggested that the production could be limited to the last two stages – capitalism and socialism.

There is a striking similarity between these two unrealized performances. Lunacharsky's fourth act starts with erecting a set looking like a heap of buildings. Next comes a popular uprising, its suppression by the troops, fraternization of soldiers and rebellious workers; they dismantle the capitalist city and march into the city of the future.[13] It is tempting to suggest that Popova and Vesnin were familiar with Lunacharsky's script, although no proof of that has been found.

Describing the future socialist city, Lunacharsky wrote that it was to be "a group of wonderful, fantastic buildings, shining with iridescent colours (I would recommend the predominance of light, airy buildings)." "The main task," he continued, "is to create a truly charming image, which would give a hint of *seeking the city that is to come*."[14] In the original, the word "seeking" was given in the old Russian form (*grad vzyskuemyi*) taken from Saint Paul's letter to the Hebrews (13:14). In the context of Lunacharsky's biography, the biblical reference was not surprising – for a long time, he had been trying to reconcile religion and socialism.[15] But in the context of the Communist International, the "heavenly" vocabulary (shining, iridescent, light, airy), as well as the biblical references, may suggest a quasi-religious, messianic understanding of communism by the early Soviet Comintern supporters.[16]

Another vague image of the future appeared in the very first issue of the avant-garde magazine *LEF* (an abbreviation of *Left Front*) in 1923. A prominent place in this issue was occupied by constructivist Anton Lavinsky's schematic drawings representing the city of the future (figure 14.2).

In his commentary, art theorist Boris Arvatov attempted to rationalize Lavinsky's graphic exercises: "City in the air. City of glass, of asbestos. City on springs. What is this – eccentricity, a fad, a gimmick? No, just maximum expediency. In the air – to free the ground. Made of glass – to fill with light. Asbestos – to facilitate construction. On springs – to create balance."[17] It's easy to imagine the bafflement of any engineer reading these lines, which sound more like poetry than any practical description.

Forty pages later in the same issue we find Aleksandr Rodchenko's book covers and mobile billboards (figure 14.3). They are drawn in the same graphic style as Lavinsky's city of the future.

Looking at both sets of drawings created by an artist, an architect, and a designer, all of them affiliated with constructivism, it appears that the graphic style of presenting ideas is more important to them than the ideas themselves. The graphic style of Russian constructivists is unique and recognizable; still, it belongs to what later will be called the "international style," which includes De Stijl, Bauhaus, Le Corbusier, and the like. While Lavinsky's and Rodchenko's drawings did not represent anything specifically communist, they were clearly

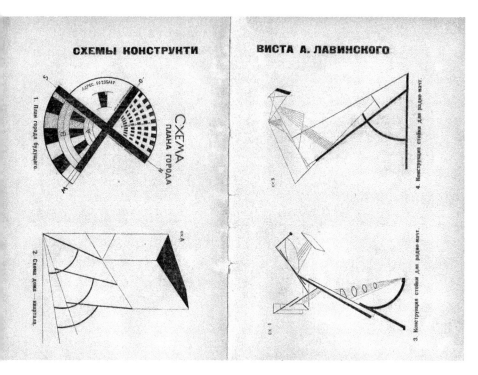

14.2 Anton Lavinsky, schematic drawings representing the city of the future. *LEF*, no. 1 (1923): 62–3.

international. The revolution in visual arts, in which Lavinsky and Rodchenko were participating, was closely connected with the "world revolution," which Karl Radek had in mind in 1918 when he said, "We are no longer Muscovy and not just the Soviets."

The revolution in Germany, eagerly awaited by the Bolsheviks in 1918, never happened. Mies van der Rohe's monument to the murdered co-founders of the German Communist Party, Karl Liebknecht and Rosa Luxemburg (figure 14.4), erected in 1926, was demolished by the Nazis in 1935. The style of the monument was very close to the Bauhaus (where Mies would serve as the last director from 1930 to 1933), to Soviet constructivism, as well as to Kazimir Malevich's *arkhitektons* – rectangular plaster blocks arranged in complex combinations.[18]

Two years later, in July 1938, the infamous *Entartete Kunst* (*Degenerate Art*) exhibition opened in Munich and later travelled to other German cities. Modernism was presented there as a conspiracy by artists identified as "Jewish-Bolshevist." Not all of the "degenerate" artists were Jewish and not all of them were Bolshevist. This Nazi formula would apply to the victims of the 1936–38

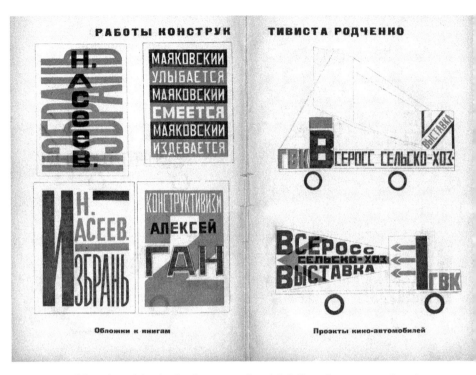

14.3 Aleksandr Rodchenko, book covers and mobile billboards. *LEF*, no. 1 (1923): 106–7.

Moscow Trials – Zinoviev, Kamenev, Trotsky, and Radek – an indication that, at that moment, Stalin and Hitler were fighting with the same international group of people. The trials created a split among the Western left-wing groups of artists and intellectuals. A hundred and fifty American artists signed a letter published in the *New Masses* in support of "the verdicts in the recent Moscow trials of the trotskyite buckarinite [*sic*] traitors."[19] For other members of the Western left, these trials caused a feeling of deep pessimism. American literary critic and essayist Philip Rahv published in *Partisan Review*, which he had co-founded, an essay titled "Trials of the Mind," where he wrote: "The failure of capitalism had long been assumed, but the failure of communism was a chilling shock and left the intellectual stripped of hope and belief in progress, with only himself and his own talents to rely upon."[20] The process that Serge Guilbaut called "the de-Marxization of the American intelligentsia" had already started.[21]

The "communist" component was also waning in the USSR. The slogan "Workers of the World Unite," which in the 1920s was printed on practically all newspapers' mastheads and on many book and magazine covers, disappeared

14.4 Mies van der Rohe, monument to Karl Liebknecht and Rosa Luxemburg, 1926.
Deutsches Bundesarchiv.

from everywhere except the official Party publications and the works of the
Moscow Marx-Engels-Lenin Institute. This exception was, of course, significant, and it demonstrated, as Nariman Skakov argues in chapter seven of this
volume, that the shift between cultural modes was never instantaneous and
complete.

The goal of building communism remained, but its fulfilment was moved to
an undefined future. The state prosecutor, Andrei Vyshinsky, ended his speech
in one of the infamous show trials of the 1930s with the following words: "Time
will pass, and above us, above our happy land, our sun will shine as brightly and
as happily as before, with its rays of light. We, our people, will still be striding
along a road, cleansed of the last traces of filth and vileness of the past, following our beloved leader and teacher – the great Stalin – *forward, ever forward*
towards Communism."[22]

The gradual shift from Marxism to a traditional worldview was evident in
the 1934 decree, signed by Stalin and Molotov, denouncing the way history
was taught in schools: "Instead of civil history taught in a lively, absorbing

way, pupils were presented with abstract definitions of social-economic forma-tions."[23] In light of this shift, it's not surprising that the Comintern was liqui-dated nine years later.

The Seventh and last Comintern Congress took place in Moscow in 1935. The nationalist trend of the previous few years (making the "defense of the Soviet Union" the key goal of the Comintern) and hostility towards Western social democrats suddenly gave way to some level of internationalism. The res-olutions included demands "to establish a united front on a national as well as international scale."[24] This about-face was so blatant that Dmitry Manuilsky, secretary of the Comintern's Executive Committee, had some explaining to do: "Many people believe that by our attitude to the united front with social-dem-ocrats we are deviating from Stalin's theory that fascism and social-democ-racy are not antipodes but twins."[25] According to Manuilsky, it was precisely "the interest of the defense of the Soviet Union" that required "taking part in a united front or Popular Front governments, on an anti-fascist platform."[26]

The year 1935 was a seminal year for the Soviet Union. Stalin's 1931 slogan "Technology Determines Everything"[27] was replaced by his new one: "Cadres Determine Everything."[28] The immediate implications of that change are obvi-ous, considering that the first chairman of the Comintern's Executive Committee from 1919 to 1926, Grigory Zinoviev, was already serving a ten-year prison sen-tence.[29] On 15 May 1935, Stalin made a short, congratulatory speech at the open-ing of the first Moscow subway line. Constructivism by that time was already denounced as a "Trotskyist theory," and no constructivist architect participated in designing the stations. The shock labour construction of the underground tunnels was officially performed by the enthusiastic Komsomol youth but, actu-ally, performed by GULAG prisoners. The fact that many engineers and almost all heavy equipment came from the United States was never publicized. Thus, international cooperation continued but secretly from the "masses."[30]

By 1935, the competition for designing the Palace of the Soviets, which had begun in 1931, was over. The three winning entries were ordered to be merged into one, and the architects Boris Iofan, Vladimir Gelfreikh, and Vladimir Shchuko were busy producing endless renderings and models of the building, which was expected to be the greatest architectural creation in history. There was a peculiar requirement for the building. G.B. Krasin, deputy chairman of the Palace of the Soviets building team, described it this way: "The structure must not only be durable for a certain period of time, but must last forever, as the whole idea of our society is forever."[31] Anticipating the shock this require-ment would produce, he added: "Engineers are not accustomed to building such structures."[32] Just like with Lavinsky's "asbestos city on springs," it is easy to imagine the bewilderment of the engineers tasked with inserting the concept of "eternity" into their calculations. The future still seemed vague but, in con-trast to the constructivist vision, immutable. This future, of course, had nothing to do with the hectic and frightening Soviet reality where nobody, from a janitor to a member of the Politburo, could be sure about their fate in the next days.

In 1935, the planning for two major exhibitions was set in motion, one, national – the All-Union Agricultural Exhibition in Moscow; the other, international – the Soviet pavilion for the 1937 Paris Exposition Internationale. Comparing the two exhibitions will allow us to see the difference between architectural messages aimed at internal and external audiences.

The forced collectivization of agriculture in the USSR, which started in 1928 and lasted, by some estimates, to the end of the 1930s,[33] resulted in the death or displacement of millions of peasants and an unprecedented famine. The first measure for overcoming food shortages was the creation of an elite class of collective farm shock workers (*kolkhozniki-udarniki*), analogous to Stakhanovites[34] in the cities. The Second All-Union Congress of Collective Farm Shock Workers took place in Moscow in February 1935. Grigory Shegal's painting *Stalin at the Second Congress of Collective Farm Shock Workers* (figure 14.5) should be viewed together with the official pass to the congress (figure 14.6). The pass had a number, a stamp, an embossed emblem of the USSR, and a warning: "transferring of the pass will be prosecuted." Obviously, the pass holders were not regular farmers.

One of the resolutions of the congress was to open the All-Union Agricultural Exhibition (VSKhV) in 1937, for 100 days, to "reflect the growth of people's *well-being and the flourishing of collective farm culture*" and in this way to tap the "enormous reserves of collective farms."[35] Following the idea of "building socialism in one country," problems of agricultural production were to be solved within the gated territory of the VSKhV, almost as a parody of the gospel story of feeding five thousand people with five loaves of bread and two fish.[36]

The religious connotations we saw in the pre-Revolutionary and early Soviet periods gave way, in the 1920s, to an aggressive anti-clerical campaign, which included demolition of churches and execution of priests. However, some religious practices and symbols were repurposed to represent the new social order. Thus, the Easter processions with icons and gonfalons re-emerged as the official 1 May and 7 November "demonstrations." Achievements of Soviet "heroes" were often presented as miracles. The miner Aleksei Stakhanov was alleged to be able to produce fourteen times his quota of coal; the creators of the Palace of the Soviets were required to make it stand literally forever; and the painted blue skies with airplanes on ceilings of the underground metro stations represented the Soviet version of paradise. In general, the periods of Culture One (1920s and 1960s) were the most hostile to Christianity, while the periods of Culture Two came closer to accepting or imitating Christian symbols and practices.

The Agricultural Exhibition was supposed to open on 1 August 1937, just a few months after the opening of the Soviet pavilion at the Paris Exposition Internationale. However, construction works in Moscow were proceeding

14.5 Grigory Shegal, *Stalin at the Second Congress of Collective Farm Shock Workers*, 1935. State Russian Museum.

14.6 The official pass to the Second Congress of Collective Farm Shock Workers, 1935. Pavel Nefedov's archive.

slowly and in a very "low-tech" mode. The opening date had to be moved to 1 August 1938. The new date also turned out to be unrealistic, mostly as a result of the Great Purge. On 15 March 1938, the People's Commissar of Agriculture, Mikhail Chernov, was executed as an "enemy of the people." He was replaced by Robert Eikhe, who in a few months was also arrested and eventually executed. The chief architect of the VSKhV, Viacheslav Oltarzhevsky, was arrested[37] and replaced by Sergei Chernyshov and later by Anatoly Zhukov. The key word of the time became *bditel'nost'* (vigilance). Vigilance required finding traces of subversive activity in the pavilions designed and built under the "enemies of the people" and, predictably, such traces were found. First, the pavilions were not durable enough. The fact that the original requirement to keep the exhibition open for just 100 days was only later extended to five years did not matter. In a sense, the concept of "eternity" replaced the concept of "time." The retroactive application of new laws and decisions became standard judicial and administrative practice.

Accusations against "enemies of the people" invariably included spying for foreign intelligence services. The accused were subjected to psychological and physical torture in order to force them, prior to execution, to publicly admit to these non-existing foreign connections. By that time, the official propaganda successfully planted the idea (which fell on fertile soil) that the state borders of the Soviet Union were in fact synonymous with the border between good and evil. Any notion that a "good Soviet person" could naturally become corrupt, would contradict this worldview. Corrupting force must come from the outside, which again suggests the quasi-religious nature of this worldview, which, in the 1930s, started to grow simultaneously from the top and from the bottom. In this worldview, the possession of "wrong" ideas was tantamount to "possession" by agents of evil.

Viacheslav Oltarzhevsky's fate is illuminating. In 1924, he emigrated to the United States. He graduated from New York University (NYU) Extension and joined a prominent architectural firm Helmle, Corbett and Harrison (later Corbett, Harrison and MacMurray). In 1935, frustrated by the Great Depression, he accepted an invitation to return to the USSR and was appointed chief architect of the VSKhV. Sergei Alekseev, chief engineer of VSKhV, recalled in his memoir some circumstances that had led to the architect's arrest: "Oltarzhevsky's secretary, Irina Gleizler, often in the presence of staff, talked with Oltarzhevsky in English, and Korostashevsky's secretary spoke with him in Yiddish. Some co-workers were outraged."[38] This xenophobic attitude towards non-Russian languages is corroborated by many foreigners living in the USSR in the 1930s – they did not dare speak their language in public.

The VSKhV actually opened on 1 August 1939, two years after the opening of the Soviet pavilion at the Paris Exposition Internationale of 1937 and a few months after another Soviet pavilion at the 1939 New York World's Fair. By 1939, any specific lifespan was dropped from the VSKhV narrative. The shift from temporary to durable was happening in other monumental projects, beginning with Lenin's Mausoleum, which was rebuilt twice, from a temporary wooden structure of 1924 into a more durable wooden structure in the same year and, finally, into an "eternal" granite and marble monument of 1930. Clearly, concepts of "eternity" and "immutability" were in conflict with the officially professed Marxism.

Immediately after the opening, the VSKhV became a favourite location for film shooting. The first film with a scene shot there was *Podkidysh* (*Foundling*, 1939). The plot had nothing to do with agriculture, but the director, Tatiana Lukashevich, apparently could not resist the temptation to take a car chase scene into the new public attraction. In 1940, Grigory Aleksandrov released *The Shining Path* (figure 14.7), a film that could be considered a remake of his and Sergei Eisenstein's 1929 *The General Line*.[39] The 1929 film had shown the difficult path to collectivized agriculture and the resistance of some peasants. In 1940, the path became "shining." Even though the film, just like *Foundling*, was not about agriculture, the final sequence took place at the recently opened

14.7 Frame from Grigory Aleksandrov's 1940 film *The Shining Path*.

VSKhV. In this scene, the painted backdrop represented the Palace of the Soviets. The set designer[40] created a backdrop showing a future, which was false on more than one level – the Palace of the Soviets was never built,[41] and, in any case, its planned location was far away from the exhibition. Since the film was a Soviet version of Cinderella, however, such fairytale elements were somewhat justified.

The 1937 Soviet pavilion in Paris was designed by one of the co-authors of the Palace of the Soviets, Boris Iofan, possibly the most privileged Soviet architect, whose office was near the Kremlin. From 1916 to 1924, he studied architecture in Italy. In 1921, under the influence of Palmiro Togliatti and Antonio Gramsci (both active participants of the Comintern), he became a member of the Italian Communist Party. Two year after his repatriation to Russia, he changed his party affiliation to the Communist Party of the Soviet Union (CPSU).

Iofan was the winner of competitions for pavilion design for both the 1937 Paris and 1939 New York exhibitions. In both cases, his winning design not only was clearly modernist but also had an uncanny resemblance to Malevich's *arkhitektons* (figure 14.8).

14.8 Left: Kazimir Malevich, *Arkhitekton Gota*. State Russian Museum. Right: Boris Iofan, proposal for the Soviet pavilion at the 1937 International Exhibition of Arts and Technology in Modern Life in Paris. Shchusev State Museum of Architecture.

The authors of the losing entries to both competitions (they included several ex-constructivists) were trying to follow the anti-modernist Party line, not realizing that there were two Party lines, one for the internal audience, the other for the external. The use of Malevich, in some sense, was an architectural equivalent to support for the Popular Front in the face of the German threat. It was not surprising that Jacques Gréber, the master architect of the Paris exhibition, placed Boris Iofan's pavilion directly opposite Albert Speer's German pavilion decorated with a swastika. This architectural confrontation was not lost on the French press (figure 14.9). ·

In fact, both teams tried hard to present their country as a victim rather than an aggressor. "Awkwardness arose," wrote Soviet structural engineer Pavel Lvov, "from the fact that our sculptural group *Worker and Collective Farm Woman* looked as if it was flying like a tornado directly at the Nazis. It was impossible to turn the sculpture, as it was lined up with the axis of the building."[42] Albert Speer had a similar concern: "I designed a cubic mass, which seemed to be checking this onslaught."[43]

14.9 Cartoon from the French newspaper *Candid*, 15 July 1937.

14.10 Mural in the Soviet pavilion at the 1939 New York World's Fair (photo). State Russian Museum.

The 1939 Soviet pavilion in New York presented yet another vision of the future, which again involved the Palace of the Soviets. Ekaterina Zernova, a former modernist artist, was a member of the group working on the main mural to be installed in the Soviet pavilion (figure 14.10). Unlike *The Shining Path*, where the Palace of the Soviets was used as a backdrop, this mural was to be a backdrop to a huge model of the palace. In her memoir, Zernova leaves a vivid description of how the "vague shining future" came into being in a dialogue between artists and the authorities:

A government commission, which included architects, came to approve the mural. The commission found that people on the mural were unobjectionable, but that the architecture was not ... The city of the future should look different. And what was the architecture of the future? On this matter, there were different opinions. We did not receive any clear instructions, although most architects were in favour of the classics. We had to cover very large areas with white paint and build new columns and high-rise buildings, and the main thing was to build an architecture that no one had ever seen ... A government commission came for the second time and again said they could accept the people but the architecture required radical reworking ... The buildings in the middle should disappear into the background, get lost in the haze, and become barely distinguishable. It took many kilograms of white paint and a week of hard work. Finally, it was done and the government commission accepted the mural. It was rolled up in a huge coil and sent to New York.[44]

The 1939 Molotov-Ribbentrop Pact, the division of Poland, the Soviet invasion of Finland, and the subsequent annexation of the Baltic states presented even more serious problems for the Western intellectual left-wing than the 1936–38 trials had. The American Artists' Congress, with its strong ties to the American Communist Party, refrained from any direct condemnation of the USSR. In 1940, a dissident group within the congress, which, among others, included Mark Rothko, Lewis Mumford, Stuart Davis, and Marxist art critic Meyer Schapiro as their unofficial leader, published a declaration of their secession from the congress in which they stated bluntly: "The American Artists' Congress ... endorsed the Russian invasion of Finland and implicitly defended Hitler's position by assigning the responsibility for the war to England and France."[45]

The German invasion of the USSR in June 1941 made life for Western left-wing intellectuals somewhat easier – now it was okay to support Stalin, who no longer was allied with Hitler. Surprisingly, many Soviet intellectuals also breathed a sigh of relief because of this invasion – it had been very hard for them to reconcile pre-1939 anti-Nazi rhetoric with photos of smiling Stalin, Molotov, and von Ribbentrop on the front page of the official *Pravda* newspaper (24 August 1939). They would have been shocked were they privy to the sight of the flags with swastikas adorning the Moscow airport in honour of Ribbentrop's arrival in 1939,[46] as well as the sound of the Red Army band playing the Nazi Party anthem "Horst Wessel Lied," whose lyrics included lines like "*Kam'raden die Rotfront und Reaktion erschossen Marschier'n im Geist in unsern Reihen mit* [Our comrades shot by the Red Front and Reaction are marching in spirit in our ranks]."[47]

During the war, some of the Soviet architects working on the Palace of the Soviets, as well as prominent stage designers, were recruited to camouflage Moscow by covering the Kremlin, Lenin's Mausoleum, and other important structures under huge canvases with fake buildings painted on them.[48] A different kind of artistic disinformation was used by the US Army during the Normandy invasion. The Ghost Army, officially known as the 23rd Headquarters Special Troops, put on a "travelling road show" utilizing inflatable tanks, sound trucks, fake radio transmissions, and the like.[49] Many of the participants were artists and designers, including Bill Blass, later a famous fashion designer, and Jack Masey, the future producer of the 1959 American Exhibition in Moscow.

In 1943, Marxism was pushed even further back when the status of the Orthodox Church was unexpectedly upgraded. Since 1917, Russian churches had been consistently raided for anything that could be a source of hard currency, which, among other things, was used to support foreign communist parties and Comintern activities. Churches and monasteries were demolished or converted into warehouses, workers' clubs, prisons, or just abandoned to decay. Unexpectedly, on 4 September 1943, Stalin invited Metropolitans Sergius, Alexy, and Nikolay to his office and gave them permission to convene a Council, which, on 8 September 1943, elected Sergius Patriarch of Moscow and all of Russia. Consequently, thousands of churches began to function, theological schools opened, and the Moscow Theological Academy Seminary, which had been closed since 1918, re-opened.

The new role of the church was immediately observable in architecture. The ceiling in the underground subway station Komsomol'skaia on Moscow's Circle Line, designed by Aleksei Shchusev, included mosaics featuring icons and other religious symbols (figure 14.11). Shchusev, whose career started long before the Revolution, in his youth restored and designed many churches – the Trinity Cathedral in Pochayiv Lavra, memorial church on the Kulikovo Field, cathedral for the Marfo-Mariinsky Convent in Moscow. His last creation, the cathedral-like Komsomol'skaia station (1952), showed that his career had made a complete circle – with a brief sidestep into constructivism in the 1920s.

Was legitimizing and recruiting the Orthodox Church simply a wartime strategy to foster popular support? That would have been the case in 1941, but in 1943, after the battles of Stalingrad and Kursk, victory for the Allies was expected. We rather see it as part of the overall shift from Marxism to cultural traditions of old Russia with its official triad of "Orthodoxy, Autocracy, and Nationality,"[50] or, in other words, from future to past, from internationalism to nationalism, from Culture One to Culture Two.

The Comintern is no more, but its aesthetics have survived – though not in its original form. Many well-known contemporary architects name the Russian avant-garde as a source of their inspiration. When, in 2003, Vladimir Paperny asked American architect Richard Meier what attracted him to Russian constructivism, Meier replied: "The relationship of line, surface, color, movement and space. Tatlin's Tower, for instance, excites me by its understanding of abstraction and space." When reminded that Russian constructivists attached a very strong social program to their work and basically wanted to change the world through architecture," Meier replied: "And they showed it was impossible. If you want to change the world you become a politician."[51] With a few exceptions, this position is shared by today's architects, for which they are frequently criticized.[52]

Today, the aesthetics of the early Soviet period has survived mostly as a style (fashionable at times), an empty shell, with the social content removed. This lack of content equally applies to Russia and to the rest of the world. In Russia,

14.11 Aleksei Shchusev, Komsomol'skaia underground subway station, 1952, and fragment of the ceiling. Photo © Alexei Narodizkiy.

14.12 Dan Flavin, *1964*, 1964. Dia Art Foundation.

activists involved in the preservation of crumbling constructivist buildings do it for historical and aesthetical reasons. Practically no one in today's Russia is interested in reviving experiments in collectivist living.

Outside of Russia, the fate of Tatlin's Monument to the Third International is telling. For Richard Meier, it is only "abstraction and space." An even more formal interpretation of the monument was presented by American minimalist artist Dan Flavin (1933–96). Flavin was influenced by abstract expressionism as well as the Russian avant-garde. Between 1964 and 1990, he created thirty-nine "monuments" to Vladimir Tatlin, all made of fluorescent tubes (figure 14.12).

Most of these artistic interpretations ignore the fact that Tatlin's monument was designed as the headquarters of the Comintern, where rotating geometric shapes made of glass represented legislative and executive branches of the world government. One exception is, perhaps, the floating chandelier replica of the monument by Ai Weiwei, discussed by Steven S. Lee in the introduction to this volume. Ai's work seems to address the political aspects of Tatlin's Tower, albeit in a form of soft satire.

Tatlin's monument was never built – not because of any political or financial restrains; it simply could not be erected. Contemporary calculations have shown that the structure could not support itself and would have collapsed;[53] therefore, all spectacular three-dimensional renderings of the tower as standing in St. Petersburg are gravely misleading. Vladimir Tatlin was not an engineer. His background was in icon painting. His romantic vision of a tower reaching the heavens is yet more proof of the quasi-religious nature of early Comintern aesthetics. Perhaps, it's not a coincidence that both Flavin and Ai use light to represent Tatlin's utopian dream.

Despite their different and changing attitudes towards Orthodox Christianity, both Culture One and Culture Two demonstrate almost unbreakable ties with it. The "matricide" attacks on the church in the 1920s and 1960s gave way to a truce in the late 1940s and, nowadays, have come to a type of caesaropapism that Russia had under the tsars.

NOTES

1 Vladimir Paperny, "*Kul'tura Dva: Sovetskaia arkhitektura 1932–1954. Popytka kul'turologicheskoj interpretacii*" (manuscript, Vladimir Paperny's archive). The English translation: Vladimir Paperny, *Architecture in the Age of Stalin: Culture Two*, trans. John Hill and Roann Barris (New York: Cambridge University Press, 2002). Also translated into Czech (Arbor Vitae) and Italian (Artemide).

2 The English translation: Boris Groys, *The Total Art of Stalinism: Avant-Garde, Aesthetic Dictatorship, and Beyond*, ed. and trans. Charles Rougle (Princeton, NJ: Princeton University Press, 1992).

3 For instance, Katerina Clark has argued that "the two concepts [national and international] cannot be seen as absolute binary opposites." See Katerina Clark, *Moscow, the Fourth Rome: Stalinism, Cosmopolitanism and the Evolution of Soviet Culture, 1931–1941* (Cambridge, MA: Harvard University Press, 2011), 9. The transition between the two cultural periods is the subject of Nariman Skakov's chapter seven in this volume. This transitional period, which he calls "Culture One and a Half," is described as "a vital intermediary stage, which was essential for taming the centrifugal aspirations of the avant-garde and channelling them into the centripetal flow of socialist realism." It should be noted that *Architecture in the Age of Stalin* itself concedes the simplified nature of the Culture One/ Culture Two model, noting, for instance, that "although between cultures there is always a certain temporal boundary, this does not mean that the boundary can be marked by one point on the timeline. It is rather a stretch of time over which the two cultures coexist and conflict with each other until one devours the other. This stretch of coexistence and conflict is the most interesting to the researcher because both cultures, as they struggle for survival, blurt out many things about which they would have preferred, in more settled times, to remain silent" (xxv).

4 "I do not believe," writes Paperny, "that Russia is forever doomed to spin in the Merry-go-round of melting and hardening, internationalism and xenophobia, chaos and totalitarianism. Although cyclical changes exist in almost all cultures, civilization is precisely what does not let these changes to slide into the extremes of both phases." See Vladimir Paperny, *Kul'tura Tri. Kak ostanovit' maiaynik?* (Moscow: *Strelka Press*, 2012), Kindle Locations 620–4. All translations are ours, unless indicated otherwise.

5 Speech by Karl Radek at a rally at the Michelson plant in Moscow, *Pravda*, 6 October 1918, quoted in Aleksandr Vatlin, *Komintern: Idei, Resheniia, Sud'by* (Moscow: ROSSPEN, 2009), 32.

6 N. Osinsky, "Vse na mesta!" *Pravda*, 6 October 1918, quoted in Vatlin, *Komintern*, 32.

7 V.I. Lenin, "Closing Address to the First Congress of the Comintern," V.I. Lenin, *Polnoe Sobranie Sohinenij* (Moscow: Politizdat), 37:513, quoted in Vatlin, *Komintern*, 62.

8 Clara Zetkin in a letter to Jules Humbert-Droz, 25 March 1929, quoted in Vatlin, *Komintern*, 244.

9 The letter is dated 20 January 1929; quoted in Vatlin, *Komintern*, 244. Tasca was expelled from the Party later the same year.

10 Vladimir Mayakovsky, for instance, who in February 1917 was advocating "art free from politics" and was against the Bolshevik government, later, in November, changed his mind: "We need to welcome the new power and get in touch with it." In his 1922 autobiography, he in fact completely rewrote history: "To accept or not to accept? There was no such question for me (and for other Moscow futurists). My revolution." V.V. Mayakovsky, "Ia sam" [diary, entry of

October 1917], *Izbrannye sochineniia* (Moscow: Khudozhestvennaia Literatura, 1981), 1:47.

11 S.A. Margolin, "Massovoe deistvo 'Bor'ba i pobeda' (Massovoe deistvo Vs. Meierkhol'da). Iz tsikla 'Neosushchestvlennyi teatr,'" *Ekho*, no. 13 (1923): 11.

12 *Vestnik teatra*, nos. 91–92 (15 June 1921): 16.

13 A.V. Lunacharsky, "Stsenarii dlia massovogo deistva na prazdnike Tret'ego Internatsionala (1921)," in *Literaturnoe Nasledstvo*, t. 80 (Moscow: *Nauka*, 1971), 664.

14 Ibid.; emphasis added.

15 See Lunacharsky's *Religiia i Sotsializm* (St. Peterburg: *Shipovnik*, 1908–1911).

16 It's also worth mentioning that some of the Russian avant-garde participants (Vladimir Tatlin, Ivan Leonidov) came from icon painting.

17 Boris Arvatov, "Oveshcestvlennaia utopiia" *LEF*, No. 1 (1923): 106–8.

18 Malevich saw the future of visual arts in three-dimensional objects. "The painting is long gone," he wrote in 1920. "The further development of suprematism I entrust to young architects." Kazimir Malevich, *Chernyi kvadrat* (Moscow: Direkt-Media, 2014), 42.

19 Serge Guilbaut, *How New York Stole the Idea of Modem Art: Abstract Expressionism, Freedom, and the Cold War* (Chicago: University of Chicago Press, 1983), 27.

20 Ibid., 28.

21 Ibid., 36.

22 Andrei Vyshinsky, "Pravo-trotskistskaia banda shpionov i diversantov smetena s litsa zemli," *Arkhitektura SSSR*, no. 3 (1938): 2; emphasis added.

23 *Sobranie zakonov i rasporiazhenii raboche-krestianskogo pravitel'stva SSSR, 1924–1937* [Collection of laws and resolutions of the workers' and peasants' government of the USSR, 1924–1937], no. 26 (1934): 206.

24 *The Communist International, 1919–1943: Documents*, selected and edited by Jane Degras, vol. III, *1929–1943* (The Royal Institute of International Affairs, PDF), 353, https://www.marxists.org/history/international/comintern/documents/volume3-1929-1943.pdf.

25 Ibid., 347.

26 Ibid., 356.

27 I.V. Stalin, "Speech in the Kremlin Palace at the Graduation of the Academicians of the Red Army, 4 May 1935, *Pravda*, 6 May 1935.

28 Ibid., 60.

29 The "Moscow Centre" trial, January 1935. Zinoviev was executed after the second trial, "Trial of the Sixteen," in 1936.

30 Even the "Trotskyist" constructivism was secretly preserved. "It's OK to criticize constructivists," said Lazar Kaganovich, the second most powerful man in the country, in a private meeting with a group of architects, "but not too harshly, please, they are building some important objects for us." For the exact quotation,

see Daniel Udovički-Selb, *Soviet Architectural Avant-Gardes: Architecture and Stalin's Revolution from Above, 1928–1938* (London: Bloomsbury, 2019).

31 This "forever" is analogous to Vyshinky's "forward, ever forward" that he will utter a few years later.

32 G. Krasin, deputy chairman of the Palace of the Soviets building team, speaking at the First Congress of Soviet Architects in 1937. Russian State Archive of Literature and Art (RGALI), fond 674, opis' 2, ed. khr. 33, 127.

33 Collectivization continued from 1932 on a gradually diminishing scale.

34 The Stakhanovites were named after Aleksei Stakhanov who, on 31 August 1935, allegedly mined the improbable 102 tons of coal in less than six hours (fourteen times his quota).

35 Resolutions of the Second All-Union Congress of Collective Farm Shock Workers, *Sobranie zakonov i rasporiqzhenij raboche-krest'iamskogo prvitel'stva SSSR, 1924–1937*, 1935, no. 11, 8, 3; emphasis added.

36 Stalin, who at the age of ten attended a theological school and at fifteen, an orthodox seminary in Georgia, was well familiar with the four Gospels. He could have been conscious of this connection.

37 His name is sometimes spelled Oltarzhevski or Oltarzewski. His story had a happy ending. In the labour camps, he was in a privileged position, recruited to work as an architect. In 1943, he was released and soon was able to return to architectural practice. Among other buildings, he was a co-author with Arkady Mordvinov of one of the seven Moscow high-rises, the Hotel Ukraine. For this building, Mordvinov received Stalin's Prize; Oltarzhevsky, as a former "enemy of the people," did not.

38 Sergei Alekseev, "Istoriia stroitel'stva i proektirovaniia Vsesoiuznoj sel'skokho-ziajstvennoj vystavki 1939 goda (VSKhV)" (unpublished manuscript [copy with present authors]), 2. This memoir, probably written in the late 1970s, showed that Alekseev's understanding of the events was formed somewhere between the late 1930s and the early 1950s. He believed in the guilt of "enemies of the people" and dropped hints of Jewish conspiracy.

39 *The General Line* was released in 1929, then, by Stalin's directive, renamed *The Old and the New* and heavily edited, and, in 1930, banned.

40 Boris Knoblok, who graduated from the Russian avant-garde school VKhUTEMAS in 1926.

41 The first several stories of the steel frame were dismantled during the Second World War.

42 P.N. Lvov, "Kak delalas' statuia," *Arkhitektura SSSR*, no. 5 (1937): 13–14.

43 Albert Speer, *Inside the Third Reich* (New York: Touchstone, 1970), 81.

44 Ekaterina Zernova, "Iz istorii sovetskoj monumental'noj zhivopisi," quoted in *Vystavochnye ansambli SSSR: 1920s–1930s. Materialy i dokumenty* (Moscow: Galart, 2006), 419–20.

45 *New York Times*, 17 April 1940. Quoted in Guilbaut, *How New York Stole the Idea*, 40.

46 Michael Bloch, *Ribbentrop* (New York: Crown Publishers, 1992), 247.

47 Arthur Koestler describes his disillusion with Soviet communism after watching von Ribbentrop's arrival in Moscow on 27 September 1939 in his chapter in *The God That Failed: Six Studies in Communism*, ed. Richard Crossman (London: Hamish Hamilton, 1950), 81.

48 Jean-Louis Cohen, *Architecture in Uniform: Designing and Building for the Second World War* (Montreal: Canadian Centre for Architecture, 2011), 209.

49 For information about this elaborate disinformation "show," watch the *The Ghost Army* trailer at https://vimeo.com/224400725.

50 Another possible translation of *Pravoslavie, Samoderzhavie, Narodnost'*: Orthodoxy, Autocracy, Populism.

51 Vladimir Paperny, *Fuck Context* (Ekaterinburg: *TATLIN*, 2011), 20.

52 See, for example, Nicolai Ouroussoff, "It Was Fun Till the Money Ran Out," *New York Times*, 19 December 2008.

53 See, for example, the video on the Tatlin Tower from Cambridge Architectural Research Ltd (published on 1 September 2012) at https://youtu.be/7AbglRpxXWo.

Chapter Fifteen

Comintern Media Experiments, Leftist Exile, and World Literature from East Berlin

KATIE TRUMPENER
Yale University

"To My Little Radio"
You little box I carried on my flight
Anxious lest the fragile valves should break
From house to train, from train to house to boat
So that my enemies might always speak
Beside my bed and to my agony
The last I hear at night, the first by day
Of all their victories and my dismay:
Give me your word you won't give up on me!

– Bertolt Brecht (written 1940–41
in Scandinavian exile, trans. Tom Kuhn)

When Vladimir Tatlin designed his Monument to the Third International (1919–21), the top tier of his three-level, differentially rotating building was to house communications equipment, revolutionary radio continuously broadcasting to the world. Although never realized, his monument design inspired Soviet and worldwide communist aesthetics, while Soviet revolutionary film amplified the tower's emphasis on media as political network. Esfir Schub's 1932 meta-documentary *Komsomol – Sponsor of Electrification* (USSR, 1932) shows young Soviet activists organizing and transmitting multilingual communist radio broadcasts across Europe; Dziga Vertov's *Enthusiasm* (USSR, 1931) and *Three Songs of Lenin* (USSR, 1934) celebrate film and radio for linking the newly constituted Soviet Union, creating a transnational communist public sphere.

In 1920s Berlin, Willi Münzenberg's communist media empire made Berlin the Comintern's most important operations centre beyond the Soviet Union.[1] Münzenberg's organizations spearheaded German and world distribution for Soviet political films; surmounting government censorship, the films' wild popularity convoked a new political film public and catalyzed the creation of new kinds of cinematic institutions (committed studios, distribution companies, and film clubs) in Germany and across Europe.

Comintern media aesthetics shaped several generations of German leftist filmmakers and writers. This chapter begins by considering how Münzenberg's Comintern-funded media operations shaped Weimar Republic political identity; how the Nazis countered, appropriated, and eventually dismantled these institutions; and how German leftist refugees in the Soviet Union tried to reassemble them, before they themselves were targeted and often "purged" during the late 1930s Stalinist terror. The chapter's final sections explore the complex media aesthetics of the postwar German Democratic Republic (GDR), whose official resurrection and institutionalization of Münzenbergian institutions were countered, in the 1960s and 70s, by growing intellectual and aesthetic resistance to the GDR's still-Stalinist conceptions of the public sphere, in the name of a revitalized communist avant-garde. The chapter initially focuses on film (key to 1920s and 30s consciousness-raising), then on radio (emerging in the 1930s as a weaponized medium for state and resistance forces), and, finally, on literature (itself in increasingly intense dialogue with mass media theory and practice). The chapter's exploration of continuities and divergences between literary conceptions dominant in Western and Eastern Europe, Moscow and Berlin, as between German communist, émigré, and dissident writers, culminates with a cluster of 1960s media-themed poems and songs by East Berlin dissidents Reiner Kunze and Wolf Biermann.

Throughout, the chapter considers the ways specific media and media practices shaped successive forms of internationalist cosmopolitanism, feeding a particular, communist conception of world cultural networks – and world literature. In 1773, Johann Gottfried Herder's pioneering world song anthology, *Voices of the Peoples in their Songs*, promulgated cross-cultural translation and reading to cultivate empathetic solidarity with small, oppressed nations.[2] In subsequent decades, Herder's former protégé Goethe repeatedly evoked "world literature."[3] At intervals over the last two centuries, Goethe's cosmopolitan ideal has underwritten attempts at international literary relations, the gradual institutionalization of comparative literature as a discipline, and world literature's current reincarnation as a pedagogical initiative.[4]

However, Herder's more politicized notion of world literature – imagining a meshed global literary and hence political system – also shaped a rather different sphere, the cultural imagination of international socialism. Karl Marx and Friedrich Engel's *Communist Manifesto* (1848), Martin Puchner argues, influentially inaugurated a new mode of world literature, not least in its implicit claim to be written simultaneously in multiple languages, negating a single language of origin.[5] In 1932, the Comintern began publishing *International Literature*, a multilingual, multi-site literary journal to put into practice Marxist ideas about world literature. Throughout the 1930s, the Comintern also promulgated new literary and media models. In Cold War East Berlin, this chapter will show, their revival and intertwinement fed multiple, site-specific conceptions of world literature.

During the 1920s, Berlin emerged as the Western capital of Comintern operations, a sister city to Moscow. The first country to grant diplomatic recognition to the nascent Soviet Union, Germany quickly evolved into a major economic and cultural partner. Given the simultaneous success of the Russian Revolution and failure of Germany's own 1918–19 revolutions, the German left looked to Moscow, riveted by cultural developments there. During the Russian Civil War, moreover, Berlin became the initial Western gathering point for some 400,000 Russian refugees, including dozens of major writers and painters. In the 1900s, Russian and German artists' groups (Jack of Diamonds, Blue Rider, Die Brücke) had influenced one another, sometimes clustering in German artists' colonies (like Murnau, Bavaria).[6] Now Berlin's courtly Charlottenburg district (promptly nicknamed "Charlottengrad") housed émigré theatres, journals, and presses; although literary activity remained largely based in Russian, artists' circles participated in informal but intense German-Russian dialogue across ideological and linguistic lines. (Filmmaker Hans Richter and artist Kazimir Malevich, for instance, discussed a collaborative animated film.)

In 1923, Germany's runaway inflation rendered Berlin unaffordable for most émigrés, who moved on to Paris or back to the Soviet Union. By then, however, Berlin had become the base for Comintern-funded media and cultural activity. A co-founder of the German Communist Party (KPD), Münzenberg had been the international secretary of the Young Communist International, in 1919 convoking its first – covert – international congress in Berlin and in 1920 representing it at the Second Comintern World Congress in Petrograd and Moscow. In 1921, he founded a Berlin-based Comintern relief organization, International Workers' Aid (IWA), to help drought-stricken Volga Russians, then striking German workers, and worldwide disaster victims. IWA speakers soliciting donations were routinely accompanied by documentaries about the fledgling Soviet Union.[7] In 1922, the IWA began organizing stand-alone Soviet film screenings, establishing a new organizational branch to promote worldwide proletarian film distribution, support Soviet and German agitational filmmaking, and foster Soviet-German cinematic exchange.[8] It bought portable projection equipment to show films after political speeches and hosted film evenings in rented halls and the IWA's dedicated Berlin cinema. By 1924, thousands gathered in Leipzig for a filmic wake for Lenin; 3,000 attended a Berlin screening; and, in the provinces, so many thousands of young viewers gathered for a free Soviet documentary screening that hundreds had to be turned away.[9]

By 1930, Party media organizations published a popular workers' illustrated newspaper, distributed agitational short films, and planned a regular "proletarian newsreel."[10] Substantial Moscow funding gave these Berlin front organizations leeway to experiment, without requiring immediate popularity with German viewers (however ideologically desirable that remained).[11] They established a Soviet-German publishing and bookstore network and two key Soviet-German film companies: Mezhrabpom film studio (named for the Russian IWA acronym, founded in 1923 as a Soviet/KPD joint venture) and its spin-off Prometheus (founded in 1926, jointly Mezhrabpom and KPD–owned), a German and international distributor for revolutionary "Russian" films.

Initially envisioned for Soviet theatre and film people to develop experimental work (under a transnational structure offering some shelter from Soviet state control), Mezhrabpom began providing foreign financial backing for Soviet filmmaking and brought Soviet films and filmmakers (including Sergei Eisenstein, Vertov, and Schub) to Germany.[12] Over its thirteen years of operation, Mezhrabpom produced 600 films. Its Soviet productions spanned classic agitation and experimental genre films; in Berlin's very different political context, the studio produced an important series of experimental communist films about Germany's turbulent political situation.

During the mid-1920s, German films – expressionist films, genre and costume films – dominated the Soviet film market.[13] The influence became reciprocal after Eisenstein's *Battleship Potemkin* (USSR, 1925) galvanized German viewers – despite being censored six times during its first six months of German distribution and twice (as elsewhere in Europe) banned outright. These protracted censorship battles only intensified German leftists' belief in cinema's potential importance; *Potemkin*'s critical and commercial success fueled popular interest in left-wing film. In 1928, communist playwright Friedrich Wolf headed a new Stuttgart film society that drew hundreds of left-wing workers to "private" *Potemkin* and other "Russian film" screenings, complete with political discussion and dissemination of pro-Soviet brochures.[14]

Potemkin's success abroad also prompted its renewed domestic Soviet distribution – and Germans' ecstatic reception of further "Russian films" proved vital for Soviet filmmakers, offsetting often withering initial receptions by Soviet newspapers and functionaries. Throughout the 1920s, Berlin's artistic sphere remained more plural and contradictory than Moscow's, and by the 1930s, leftism and modernism became increasingly, thrillingly intertwined there, forging an aesthetic with surprisingly broad resonances.

Prometheus, crucially, reinvested its "Russian film" profits to produce an ambitious series of militant German "workers'" films. Long-standing Prometheus employee Piel Jutzi synchronized a *Potemkin* sound version, and his agitational melodrama for Prometheus, *Mother Krause's Journey to Happiness* (*Mutter Krausens Fahrt ins Glück*, Germany, 1929), drew stylistically on Soviet montage. Even more experimentally, Slatan Dudow's 1932 *Kuhle Wampe, or To Whom Does the World Belong* (co-written by Bertolt Brecht and Ernst Ottwalt, music by Hanns Eisler) showcased communist cultural institutions as alternatives to traditional family structures; triumphantly, the film's very making involved over 4,000 Berliners.[15]

By the early 1930s, Party-affiliated newspapers, newsreels, theatre companies, discussion circles, and continuing education classes kept young leftists politically informed and urged their participation in Party-sponsored leisure activities: athletic games, parades, festivals, and film clubs. Radio, too, played an increasingly important role in political education; Free German Listeners Association groups gathered to listen to Radio Moscow's documentary and educational programs.[16] Together, *Kuhle Wampe* underscored, such organizations provided occasions for political discussion and strengthened participants' ties to the Party and the collective, constituting an ideological lifeworld.

But leftist film culture's success and influence also drew the attention of Germany's far right. By the early 1930s, Nazis routinely gathered to disrupt screenings of left-wing productions, Hollywood pacifist, and black-themed films; the German government responded with intensified film censorship and repression. The Nazi boycott of "Bolshevik" films helped precipitate Prometheus's 1931 bankruptcy. *Kuhle Wampe* proved Prometheus's final production. Like *Potemkin*, it was initially banned, over liberal and left-wing protests. In 1932, its premiere (a single Moscow screening attended by Brecht and Ottwalt) confused Moscow viewers and journalists, alienated by its coolly ironic account of social life.[17] In Berlin, by contrast, its subsequent reception was ecstatic, and it indelibly impressed many leftists.[18]

In 1932, Berlin police stormed Mezhrabpom's German office, confiscating prints and archives, arresting and trying Mezhrabpom leaders, and abruptly ending Mezhrabpom's work in Germany. The 1933 Reichstag arson attack gave the Nazis an opening to seize power. They immediately pushed Jewish and leftist directors out of filmmaking (and other arts), dissolved leftist institutions, systematically arrested prominent Jews and leftists, or forced them into exile. Berlin's Comintern office moved to Copenhagen. Münzenberg fled to Paris, opened a new Mezhrabpom branch, and promptly convoked a large pan-European anti-fascist conference (whose participants organized many subsequent German boycotts, including film boycotts).[19] In Germany, meanwhile, the Nazis rapidly seized full control of all media. Within weeks, *Kuhle Wampe* was banned anew, alongside other leftist films, books, and music. Its intermittent international runs – in Amsterdam, Paris, London, New York, Zurich – were framed by worldwide concern over German developments: the 1934 New York screenings were "prefaced by screen talks" by Norman Thomas and Henrik Van Loon, "denouncing Hitlerism and the persecution of the Jews."[20]

In Germany, the Nazis produced ideological newsreels and features, and took full advantage of their government airwave monopoly. By subsidizing inexpensive radio sets (so-called *Volksempfänger*, people's receivers), they enabled nationwide reception of Nazi speeches, broadcast programming, and eventually

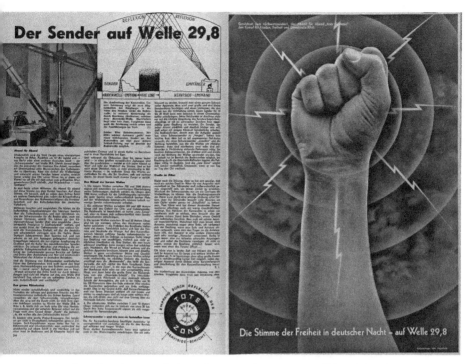

15.1 Duels in the ether: E.L., "The Radio Network on Wave 29.8" (article); and John Heartfield, *The Voice of Freedom in the German Night on Radio Wave 29.8* (photo-montage), *Die Volks-Illustrierte* (The People's Illustrated, pub. Prague), no. 16 (21 April 1937): 244–5. © 2006 Artists Rights Society (ARS), New York; John Heartfield Estate. Image: Beinecke Library, Yale.

news of military victories. They interpolated the ethnically redefined "German people" as a national audience; eventually, anyone caught listening to "enemy" radio was threatened with execution.

From exile, some leftists nonetheless extolled the continuing reach of communist media. From Prague, for instance, John Heartfield regularly published anti-fascist collages in a German-language communist picture-post magazine, *Die Volks-Illustrierte*. A 1937 article about a communist-affiliated Czech underground radio station was thus illustrated with Heartfield's iconic collage *The Voice of Freedom in the German Night on Radio Wave 29.8*, celebrating its nightly broadcasts into Nazi Germany, "evening for evening, 'despite the Gestapo,' fighting for peace, freedom and democracy" (figure 15.1). A communist fist radiates concentric radio signals, sending lightning bolts across the sky.

Radio Days

Heartfield memorialized the undying power of the communist message, broadcast through the ether. Brecht's 1940 poem "To My Little Radio" (quoted at the beginning of this chapter) presents radio very differently, apostrophizing a personal portable radio set, anxiously carried into emigration. Composed during Brecht's exile years in Scandinavia, set by Hanns Eisler in 1942–43 during their overlapping Los Angeles émigré sojourns, and anthologized in their *Hollywood Songbook*, it became the German émigrés' most celebrated art song. It metonymically transposes the anxieties of exile – and the world-historical forces necessitating exile – onto the "*Kofferradio*" (literally "suitcase" radio) itself: fragile, easily misplaced, or irreplaceably broken. Its owner, too, is fragile enough to be damaged in transit. As Theodor Adorno insisted from Los Angeles: "Every intellectual in emigration is, without exception, mutilated."[21]

The *Volksempfänger* broadcasts Nazi messages into every German household. Brecht's portable radio, a relic of consumer-oriented Weimar Republic media culture, emblematizes a new, diasporic dispensation: smaller, quieter, individualistic. Yet, even several countries away, it broadcasts the same bad news as German radios, news of Nazi victories, conquests, apparent unstoppability. Such news, and the political worries it ignites, haunts the radio owner even in sleep – and frames every new day. Nonetheless, the radio remains indispensable, a perverse link to a vanished point of origin, an emblem of subjectivity, held close to the ear and, even in exilic isolation, a communicative link to a broader world. The news is public, but the little radio creates a zone of intimacy, privacy, perhaps even talismanic protection. Because its lyric apostrophizes a machine, because its Eislerian melody is understated, hesitant, abruptly falling silent, Brecht's song escapes sentimentality, even self-pity. Still, in its abbreviated, quiet way, it celebrates the survival of the lyric self, an interiority safeguarded at once in, through, and despite mass media.

Throughout the 1920s, Brecht engaged in self-conscious "media experiments," publishing a communist breviary, pioneering radio plays, and framing a public censorship trial as a new form of media pedagogy.[22] This poem, relatedly, explores the interface between radio propaganda and the fragile but still-armoured self. Unlike *Kuhle Wampe*, *Komsomol*, or Heartfield's collage, Brecht's poem expresses no faith in the long reach, or inevitable triumph, of Comintern media initiatives and aesthetics. It neither celebrates communist broadcasts as a countervailing political force nor registers international cultural and military resistance to Nazism. Brecht stresses not alternative channels of information but the imperative to keep tuning into Nazi stations, to monitor his enemies' doings, their latest plans to annihilate him. Brecht's pragmatic wartime writings work for, but do not assume, leftist victory, finding comfort only in the ongoing sardonic whispers of a not-yet-defunct interior(ized) voice.

At the end of the Weimar Republic, German leftists forced into worldwide diaspora worked to spread Comintern cultural templates and media initiatives. Leftists who survived the war (and the USSR's Stalinist purges) eventually brought these models back with them to postwar Eastern Europe. The rest of this chapter explores their long posterity in the GDR (where they became enshrined as key templates for cultural institutions), but also the posterity of Brecht's hounded sardonic voice, echoed not only in his personal scepticism towards GDR cultural initiatives but also by 1960s dissident poets, self-conscious Brechtian inheritors determined to resist Stalinist incursions.

Polish dissident poet Adam Zagajewski offers an especially trenchant gloss on Brecht's émigré poem – and postwar communist media. Brecht yearned for a leftist victory. But when it came, Nazi-occupied Europe was liberated only to be partially re-subjugated under Soviet occupiers. In 1945, during Zagajewski's infancy, his own family was thus forcibly resettled, part of Poland's post-Yalta mass population transfer from Lvov (formerly Polish Galicia, now claimed by the Soviet Union) to Upper Silesia (one of the eastern German provinces reassigned to Poland, its ethnically German population deported en masse). Zagajewski's 1991 essay "Two Cities" evokes his upbringing in an uprooted family and a ghostly, newly Polish city, whose entirely displaced and resettled population inhabited the forcibly abandoned houses of their German predecessors.[23]

Zagajewski's 1991 poem "Electric Elegy" apostrophizes this inheritance as a now-defunct 1930s German radio. Unlike Brecht's portable radio, carried into exile, Zagajewski's "bulky" radio was presumably an old *Volksempfänger*, too heavy to move and thus left behind in Upper Silesia in 1945 by its expelled German owners.

Farewell, German radio with your green eye
and your bulky box,
together almost composing a body and soul. (Your lamps glowed
with a pink, salmony light, like Bergson's
deep self.)
        Through the thick fabric
of the speaker (my ear glued to you as
to the lattice of a confessional), Mussolini once whispered,
Hitler shouted, Stalin calmly explained,
Bierut hissed, Gomułka held endlessly forth.
But no one, radio, will accuse you of treason:
no, your only sin was obedience: absolute,
tender faithfulness to the megahertz;
whoever came was welcomed, whoever was sent
was received.[24]

Despite its change of ownership, and the poem's protestations, the radio never achieves political neutrality. Its sympathies remain both pro-German (more joyously transmitting Schubert than Chopin) and adapted to the postwar period's new political threats. When tuned, illicitly, to Radio Free Europe or the BBC, "your eye would grow nervous,/ the green pupil widen and shrink/ as though its atropine dose had been altered."

Brecht's more portable radio travels from continent to continent in his keeping, channelling world news as it ominously unfolds; that radio remains a source of talismanic protection only insofar as it activates Brecht's own angry, anxious interior voice. Zagajewski's radio remains an ominous relic of Nazism and German domination, surviving into a different dispensation of communist domination. The political oratory cumulatively transmitted through the radio includes the voices not only of Mussolini and Hitler, but also of Stalin, of Comintern-schooled former Soviet secret police (NKVD) agent Bolesław Bierut, and of Comintern-schooled Władysław Gomułka, together instrumental in establishing communist Poland. Bierut remained a hard-line Stalinist; after Stalin's and Bierut's deaths and the 1956 Polish October, Gomułka functioned as an anti-Stalinist reformer. Yet, during the 1960s, he retained power by enabling the anti-Semitic campaign that drove most of Poland's surviving Jews into emigration, persecuted protesting students, and mandated Poland's participation in the 1968 Soviet invasion of Czechoslovakia.

Like Zagajewski's German/Polish city, his German/Polish radio functions as a historical echo chamber and a confessional, channelling political obedience, expedience, fear, and passivity. The radio eroticizes the listener's relationship to the world, while inducing political complicity during a succession of occupations and dictatorships. The radio's content may switch languages and ideologies along with its owners, but the listener's receptive passivity remains constant. The radio's transmission taints music itself: even Chopin (that quintessential nineteenth-century political émigré, whose melancholy music expressed Poland's frustrated national aspirations and inspired resistance during Poland's Tsarist, Prussian, Austro-Hungarian, and Nazi occupations) has his music co-opted by the postwar communist government (often functioning as a Soviet puppet state and, under Stalinism, persecuting Polish nationalism).

In 1975, after Zagajewski signed the *Letter of 59*, protesting Poland's continued Sovietization, his works were banned in Poland. In 1982, Zagajewski went into exile in Paris, later teaching in the United States. Still, at least in spirit, the bulky German radio accompanied him, its signal fading only as Eastern Europe's communist states lost legitimacy, then power. "At night, forlorn signals found shelter in your rooms";[25] as the radio dies, its voice becomes cracked, attended by rattling, coughing, "and finally blindness/ (your eye faded), and total silence." The poem ends with an envoi, not an apotheosis – the German radio is to "sleep peacefully ... dream Schumann" and most emphatically stay asleep, stay dead, even "when the next dictator-rooster crows."[26]

Radio initially penetrated Eastern Europe by way of Nazi-subsidized *Volksempfänger*, with their diet of German music, anti-Slavic and anti-Semitic oratory. But Zagajewski's title, "Electric Elegy," also implicitly eulogizes the longer-term legacy of communist modernism, emblematized by Lenin's famous 1920 electrification campaign, celebrated by Vertov and Schub. As Johannes R. Becher insisted in a 1929 poem (set to music in 1953 by Eisler and performed by mass choirs in still-Stalinist East Germany), Lenin thereby "shook the world from sleep, with words of lightening ... with words that became machines ... became electricity ... remain permanently written in every heart."[27] For Zagajewski, too, the electricity of radio is linked to the powerful, if hazardous, electricity of twentieth-century political speech. Radio in his poem "is" modernism, potentially converting even nineteenth-century instrumental music into a potent political weapon. Brecht's portable radio allowed the émigré listener to find his own subjectivity, anger, and agency. Zagajewski's *Volksempfänger*, with its odd Cyclops eye and survival across the twentieth century, has a life of its own. It electrifies its listeners, but sometimes risks electrocuting them or draining them of vitality and will. Early twentieth-century avant-gardes used radio, electrified sound, and noise to deliver new existential shocks to European listeners.[28] Yet, such shocks, Zagajewski insists, have a complex and contradictory politics.

Émigré Media Culture: Mezhrabpom and After

From 1930 onward, Mezhrabpom dedicated itself to international and anti-fascist filmmaking, trying to achieve better Western market saturation and intensifying its push against capitalist and fascist cinema. Unofficially, moreover, the studio attempted to extend a tradition of left avant-garde filmmaking increasingly under attack in the Soviet Union itself. After 1933, as the Soviet Union became a crucial – if often fatal – "refuge" for German and European communists fleeing Third Reich persecution and expansionism, Mezhrabpom's reconstituted "Red Front" unit gave many German émigrés the hope of continuing the Weimar workers' film tradition. However, their efforts foundered in the increasingly volatile Soviet political climate. Only three of their films were actually finished, under increasingly difficult conditions: Vsevolod Pudovkin's avant-garde *Deserter* (USSR, 1932, about a young German communist's Soviet political education); Erwin Piscator's *The Revolt of the Fisherman* (USSR, 1934, based on a strike novel by German communist Anna Seghers); and Gustav von Wangenheim's *Fighters* (USSR, 1936, chronicling a German worker's communist awakening after the Reichstag fire).

Although Mezhrabpom's multinational statutes, location, and funding gave it more financial and artistic autonomy than other Soviet studios, it reported directly to the Comintern, and its productions were subjected to the normal Soviet censorship process.[29] From the mid-1920s onward, the Soviet state film industry viewed – and consistently undermined – Mezhrabpom as unwelcome, unfair competition. Mezhrabpom paid its workers better wages than its state counterparts, employing them irrespective of Party membership.[30] Hence, it was criticized for its apparent lack of commitment to "political mass work" necessary to develop their consciousness.[31] In a political climate of escalating paranoia and denunciation (and the official "campaign against formalism"), Mezhrabpom's defiant avant-gardism often had political consequences (although the many attacks on the studio hardly mentioned formal or stylistic questions).[32]

In the early 1930s, Mezhrabpom began inviting prominent German and other leftists to the Soviet Union to make films in a new "foreigners' section," intended to boost Soviet audiences' insight into "the political and social situation in other countries."[33] Most of the projects ended in disaster. Hans Richter and Friedrich Wolf's Soviet-German strike docudrama *Metal* foundered on political grounds after a German-Soviet trade agreement made Soviet officials loath to offend the German government; fearing arrest, Richter eventually fled the Soviet Union. So did Piscator, after von Wangenheim and other émigrés denounced him. Film luminaries including Max Ophüls, Joris Ivens, Willi Bredel, and Béla Balázs were similarly mistreated or disillusioned.[34]

Fighters was released only after stormy censorship discussions.[35] It had employed large numbers of émigrés as actors and technicians (including cameos by *Kuhle Wampe* star Ernst Busch and Friedrich Wolf's eleven-year-old son, Konrad, later the GDR's most prominent film director). As the émigrés' most important collective achievement, *Fighters* also became an inadvertent memorial to an exile community soon to be decimated. In 1936, at the height of the purges, the Soviet government abruptly dissolved Mezhrabpom itself. German émigrés associated with the studio were left unemployed. Some fled the Soviet Union. Others were arrested; many eventually died in Soviet penal and labour camps.[36]

During the 1920s, Moscow's Hotel Lux became known as the "headquarters of the world revolution," as the Comintern's premiere lodgings for prominent international guests. In the early 1930s, it offered refuge to many famous German leftist artists and political leaders fleeing Nazi Germany. By the mid-1930s, however, it had been redubbed "the golden cage of the Comintern," a potential death trap where German émigrés knew themselves watched and were anxiously awaiting arrest.

Émigrés began "disappearing" from von Wangenheim's directorial team already during the filming of *Fighters*; several were arrested on set. Many others eventually died in the Gulag: only a third of *Fighters*'s workers, Günther Agde estimates, survived both the purges and the war.[37] Von Wangenheim became the only member of his anti-fascist theatre troupe to outlive the purges – in part by denouncing other émigrés, from Piscator and Balázs (publicly accusing them of Trotskyism) to well-known Brechtian actress and fellow troupe member Carole Neher (who died in 1942 in a Stalinist labour camp).[38]

In the postwar GDR, this grisly history was never openly discussed, remaining largely unknown. In the late 1940s, most American, French, or British occupation officials initially suspected German intellectuals of Nazi collaborationism. Soviet officials, by contrast, offered them material support, based on leftists' interwar history of cross-cultural collaboration; some occupation officers had previously worked at Mezhrabpom or other Comintern initiatives and tacitly hoped to revive their spirit.

Nonetheless Mezhrabpom itself remained a repressed memory; virtually no earlier German-Soviet co-production was (re)released.[39] Only in the 1960s did young GDR and West German curators became interested in Weimar leftist films, ensuring the recirculation of films like *Mother Krause's Journey* and *Kuhle Wampe* and cultivating a new veneration for Mezhrabpom as the life-saving "sanctuary" of German exiles.[40] In 1963, the premiere of East Berlin's first cinematheque, Filmkunst-Theater Camera, thus showcased a restored print of *Fighters*.

Émigrés, understandably, saw such revivals with mixed feelings. In 1945, as survivors began returning to Berlin and re-establishing cultural institutions in the Soviet occupation sector, von Wangenheim helped co-found DEFA, the GDR state film studio. Yet, he had also brought back from Moscow a grisly relic of émigré travails: an album of *Fighters's* production photographs. During the purges, he had scratched out the faces of fellow émigrés who had been "disappeared," lest he be incriminated by association.[41] Decades later, he sometimes wept openly while showing GDR colleagues the album or recounting his Moscow sojourn.[42]

Until the Berlin Wall's erection in 1961, Berlin still felt cosmopolitan; cultural life involved not only Berliners but also members of the Soviet, American, British, and French occupation forces and, in the early postwar years, a huge refugee population from across Europe. Cultural offerings and audiences were correspondingly diverse – and initially involved cooperation among the occupation forces. After the onset of the Cold War and Germany's formal partition, however, even German-German cultural exchange became strained and intermittent. Until 1972, West Germany refused the GDR diplomatic recognition, trying to force other nations to acknowledge itself as the sole legitimate German state. East Berlin's own efforts to present itself as a world capital depended structurally on its Warsaw Pact allies, whose respective cultural centres brought progressive Eastern European and Third World music, film, and literature to Berlin audiences.[43]

In the 1960s GDR, officially sanctioned cultural exchanges with fellow Eastern European countries created a new, expiatory sense of cultural history and geography, resituating German history in relationship to Eastern rather than Western Europe. This reorientation necessitated intense, ongoing expiation for Germany's long history of internal colonialism and Third Reich expansionism's genocidal effects. Such efforts were partly strategic – a cultural equivalent of the Warsaw Pact – but also self-consciously postcolonial, occurring against the backdrop of Soviet military and Eastern bloc political support for ongoing African, Asian, and Latin-American decolonization efforts. They also created a very particular GDR framing of the Holocaust, locating it primarily in Eastern Europe and understood as an extension of long-standing colonial racism.

For GDR citizens severely restricted in their movement and travel, cultural and mass media experiences became crucial, reassuring them that a larger world was still present. East Berlin was heavily militarized. With the building of the Berlin Wall in 1961, it also became physically surrounded by massive concrete barriers, minefields, and watchtowers. Yet, East Berlin's airwaves involuntarily transmitted West German alongside GDR government stations as well as American and British Armed Forces radio. As we will see, this Cold War battle of the airwaves (like the long-term enlistment of GDR writers to work with GDR government film, television, and radio studios) shaped a literary culture unusually attentive to media issues – not least because they raised questions of the public sphere, "propaganda," and the political agency of media producers and consumers in a state media monopoly.[44]

International Literature, Communist Diaspora, and World Literature as Decolonization

Literature knows no frontiers, and must remain common currency among people in spite of political or international upheavals.

– Charter of the PEN Club
(founded 1921, London)

From 1932 onward, the Comintern-sponsored periodical *International Literature* informed an international audience about progressive literature worldwide. Although Moscow-based, the journal appeared simultaneously in variant foreign-language editions, edited from different parts of the world.[45] In early nineteenth-century Britain, radical corresponding societies had enshrined a decentred political process, establishing a network of like-minded radicals.[46] *International Literature* worked on a global scale, finding worldwide resonances of contemporary socialist aesthetic doctrines, especially in emerging Third World countries, and implicitly promoting Soviet-centred internationalism. Yet, at times it explored a genuinely plural aesthetic universe, encompassing divergent literary traditions and traditional literatures (including those grounded in aristocratic or sacral authority).

In 1933, as many German writers were forced into exile, some relied heavily on the international leftist cultural network to secure visas, work, and new audiences. Others expanded this network, organizing international literary conferences, émigré presses, salons, theatre troupes, and periodicals in Amsterdam,

New York, Mexico City, and Shanghai.[47] Moscow nonetheless understood itself as the capital city of the international leftist intelligentsia: a new world literary centre and dissemination point for avant-garde literary practice and institutions, summoning intellectuals from many countries to participate in international congresses and new cultural initiatives, and a privileged platform from which to survey the world situation.[48] Moscow's 1934 All-Union Congress of Soviet Writers thus included speeches by German émigrés in Western as well as Soviet exile; Karl Radek's address, "Contemporary World Literature and the Tasks of Proletarian Art," like Georg Lukács's subsequent *The Historical Novel* (written in 1937 from Moscow exile), weighed aesthetic strategies and political tendencies of an international array of contemporary novels, written in a wide range of languages.[49]

Some émigrés, including communist playwright Friedrich Wolf, found a crucial literary home in *International Literature*, founded in socialist counterpoint to Western European internationalist initiatives. From the early 1920s onward, Soviet and German communist literary culture had diverged sharply from Western European models. Berlin Dadaist manifestos like Georg Grosz and John Heartfield's "The Art Scab" (Der Kunstlump, 1920) and Alexei Gan's Moscow manifesto "Constructivism" (1922) had urged the death of art, the destruction of traditional cultural institutions.[50] For Grosz and Heartfield, the German revolution's potential to transform lives far outweighed any collateral damage to art works sustained by revolutionary violence.

In London, by contrast, PEN International's 1921 charter implicitly reflected the new League of Nation's pacifist aims. Although PEN was a pioneering human rights organization, its charter also championed "works of art" as "the patrimony of humanity at large [that] should be left untouched by national or political passion," calling on writers to uphold "mutual respect between nations and people" and "to champion the ideal of one humanity living in peace and equality in one world." A further article, adopted in 1947, underscored a progressive view of history: "the necessary advance of the world towards a more highly organised political and economic order renders a free criticism of governments, administrations and institutions imperative." Most influentially, the 1947 addendum defended both freedom of expression – "the principle of unhampered transmission of thought within each nation and between all nations" – and individual writers facing political persecution.[51] In this capacity, during the 1960s and 70s, PEN became a crucial defender and champion of dissident Eastern European writers, publicizing their travails and framing their work for Western literary audiences.

Such activity inevitably ran the risk of simplifying Eastern Europe's own complex literary politics and literary traditions. Interwar Soviet and German leftist writers, after all, had understood themselves as quasi-journalistic "producers" or vanguard figures able to transcend class positions, articulate Party values, and effect mass political conversions. From the outset, PEN's self-conception was very different. Although its first president, John Galsworthy, and early members (including Joseph Conrad, George Bernard Shaw, H.G. Wells) were social and political critics, in some cases outspoken socialists, PEN's programmatic emphasis on the unimpeded circulation of ideas and texts, as on the right to personal expression and conscience, reflected British liberal notions of free markets and free trade, a vision of literature where poets spoke not only (pace Percy Bysshe Shelley's ringing 1821 *A Defence of Poetry*) as "the unacknowledged legislators of the world" but as individuals and free agents.

German communists in the 1930s envisioned an engaged art. Yet, once loosed into a range of exilic situations, they were forced to adapt themselves to local aesthetic ideas. Take the case of three key Berlin Marxist writers, who grasped their exiles in strikingly different terms – predictive of their post-1945 responses to East Berlin's promise to become a new gathering point and homeland for German communists. In 1933, Friedrich Wolf fled Berlin for Moscow. His family remained in Moscow until 1945, witnessing radical shifts in Soviet cultural and émigré policy and the Stalinist purges. Wolf's young sons later played foundational roles in GDR political and cultural life. Markus Wolf, trained by the Comintern for undercover work, returned to Germany in 1945 to work as a radio journalist; he eventually became the GDR's famous "spy-master" and, later, its most influential perestroika advocate. In 1945, as a nineteen-year-old Red Army soldier, Konrad Wolf helped conquer Berlin, stayed on as an occupation film censor, and eventually became the GDR's most incisive filmmaker. In 1988, the brothers arguably inaugurated belated GDR public discussion of the purges with the publication of Markus's book about their Moscow boyhood, based on a film project Konrad had not lived to realize.[52]

Far more than either son, Friedrich Wolf retained an orthodox relationship to Party culture. (He died in 1953, a few months before the Soviet suppression of the East Berlin workers' uprising and before Khrushchev's 1956 Secret Speech alerted the Party to the extent of Stalin's misdeeds.) Friedrich Wolf's 1930s Moscow sojourn was nonetheless strangely temporary. He adapted several of his anti-fascist plays into Soviet films. Yet, he spent much of the decade on the move – serving as a doctor during the Spanish Civil War, enduring French internment at its end; travelling to New York, Paris, Copenhagen, Stockholm to literary congresses and to oversee local productions of his anti-fascist plays. During his years as a roving anti-fascist, Friedrich used *International Literature* as a literary and ideological home, repeatedly publishing reviews comparing far-flung theatre, film, literary, and cultural scenes, measured implicitly against Soviet literature and film as a political (if not linguistic) base for communists like himself, while reflecting on cinema and theatre as transnational forms.[53] Wolf's travels not only enabled broad-based cultural reporting, but also intensified his sense of the systemic contradictions of capitalist cultural life and of participating in a truly international socialist film/theatrical circuit.

Bertolt Brecht pointedly did *not* emigrate to Moscow, and his relationship to Party culture remained ambivalent. While Friedrich Wolf moved to East Berlin in 1945 to help found new theatrical and film institutions and shape GDR cultural politics, Brecht remained in the United States until 1947, his departure propelled by his forced appearance before the House Committee on Un-American Activities. Yet, only in 1949 did he return to (East) Berlin, and only after being promised his own theatre. His Berliner Ensemble promptly became a major institution. Still, Brecht remained cautious and (at least privately) sardonic about the GDR's Stalinist cultural politics.

Like Wolf, Peter Weiss was threatened during the Third Reich as a Jew and a leftist. During adolescence, he thus fled Berlin for London, Prague, Switzerland, and finally Stockholm, which remained his base for the rest of his life. He never re-immigrated to Germany. Yet, he continued to write in German: autobiographical novels about his émigré childhood, a history of European avant-garde cinema, alongside celebrated plays – about French revolutionary libertinism; Portuguese colonial policies in Angola, Mozambique, and Guinea; and Vietnam's long anti-feudal, anti-colonial history. His magisterial novel trilogy, *The Aesthetics of Resistance*, published in installments during the 1970s, commemorates the emergence of émigré internationalism, reconstructing the German left's aesthetic debates and paths of emigration. Yet, *Aesthetics* glorified neither Scandinavian social democracy nor Sweden's wartime neutrality. Like its long account of leftist aesthetic debates and factionalism during the 1930s and the Spanish Civil War, *Aesthetics* fictionalizes Brecht's wartime sojourn in Denmark, Sweden, and Finland to chronicle a regional history of leftist internecine fighting and political betrayal.

Weiss's ongoing Swedish expatriate life, and consequently extraterritorial participation in postwar German letters, made him one of very few able to circumvent Cold War divides, collaborating closely with both East and West German literary establishments. In 1965, as a Brechtian "media-experiment," Weiss premiered *The Investigation*, his docudrama/oratorio based on the 1963 Frankfurt Auschwitz Trial transcripts, simultaneously in seventeen theatres: in London (directed by Peter Brook), both Germanys, and both Berlins. These synchronized premieres represented important cross-system dialogue between two otherwise hostile Europes (by way of Scandinavia as a third, social democratic quadrant). In West Berlin, the play opened in Piscator's *Freie Volksbühne*. Yet, the play's most extraordinary instantiation was a staged reading in East Berlin's Academy of Arts, enlisting the GDR's most famous intellectuals, performers, directors, and writers, including returned émigrés Ernst Busch, Konrad Wolf, and Brecht's widow Helene Weigel.[54]

In 1970, during a state visit to Poland, West German Chancellor Willi Brandt knelt at the Monument for the Warsaw Ghetto Uprising. Unlike most of his generation, Brandt had spent the Third Reich as an anti-fascist resistance fighter (in Norwegian and Swedish exile, and undercover in Germany). Nonetheless, he humbled himself in an official, religious gesture of national contrition – immediately impressed on world consciousness in an iconic photograph. Five years before, by co-directing and acting in Weiss's Auschwitz trial docudrama, the GDR's most prominent intellectuals had made a comparable gesture of self-implication, expiation, and admonition. Many were former anti-fascists, émigrés, or concentration camp survivors; now they assumed the roles not only of survivors but Nazi perpetrators.

Current Western accounts of the "German memory problem" remain fore-shortened. Its consensus – that the GDR was even farther behind than West Germany in problematizing the Nazi era or anti-Semitism – occludes early GDR literature and films' sustained focus on the Holocaust as key to everyday fascism. By the 1960s, moreover, GDR intellectuals had taken up a memory problem running parallel to that left by the Holocaust. Working backwards from Nazi racial policies' devastating, often genocidal impact on Polish, Soviet, and Czech civilian populations, GDR intellectuals attempted to think through German history as one of intra-European imperialism. In postwar West Germany, by contrast, a particular configuration of political events and forces prevented any large-scale working through of Germany's history of eastern expansionism. The Cold War barred most intellectual or touristic contact between West Germany and Poland, Czechoslovakia, the Baltics, or the Soviet Union, even as post-1945 German ethnic expellee pressure groups framed West German public discourse about Eastern Europe.

The postwar period, then, saw an implicit – perhaps pernicious – division of labour in anti-fascist memory work between the two Germanies: the West focused almost exclusively on the Holocaust as deterritorialized genocide; the East, primarily on fascism as imperialist expansionism, on slave labour as cultural subordination and obliteration. This focus remained, for better or worse, the GDR's primary framework for addressing the Holocaust as genocide, implying that the Nazis' particular fears of Eastern European Jewish life were rooted as much in phobic anti-Slavic racism as in anti-Semitism. If West Germany came to emphasize anti-Semitism as the heart of Nazism, the GDR emphasized imperialism as the heart of fascism, understood as a striking conjuncture between expansionist atrocities, mass murders of those under occupation, and industrialized genocides of putatively parasitic or homeless populations.

From the Enlightenment onward, virtually every European country strained to imagine itself further north and west, hence more central to and in Europe: Hungary's most influential modernist journal *Nyugat* (1908–41) bore the simple but weighty title *West*. Throughout the 1960s and 70s, for the first time in German history, GDR cultural policy urged the opposite trajectory, imagining the future of German culture as part of the history of an Eastern, rather than a Western, European cultural axis. This approach built implicitly on the cooperative, transnational work of Münzenberg, Mezhrabpom, and the Comintern schools in Moscow and wartime Kushnarenkovo, where German and Eastern European émigré cadres were trained side by side to lead a future communist Europe.[55]

Globally, the 1960s became a period of decolonization – the breakup of Europe's last overseas empires and the founding of new postcolonial states. GDR intellectuals embraced their own decolonization model. The Nazis had denied Poland, Czechoslovakia, and the Soviet Union the status of civilized or "cultural nations." Now, GDR intellectuals attempted to link their own culture with the East, taking Germany out of Western Europe and relocating it among the Eastern European nations it had wronged in a permanently expiatory relationship to them. Throughout the 1960s, leading GDR intellectuals produced heartfelt conversion novels, stories, memoirs, and films: having occupied Eastern Europe as soldiers, been mentored intellectually by their Soviet captors, having met, visited, and translated their Eastern European counterparts and confronted the devastating effects of Nazi occupation, they found themselves forced to re-examine their family backgrounds, inherited values, and childhood racial indoctrination. These texts promised to mould the mass experience of ordinary GDR citizens, permitted to vacation only in Eastern Europe and thus positioned geographically (if artistic narratives and films had prepared them) to undergo cathartic conversions of their own.[56]

Seen cynically, official GDR cultural programs and policies intended to cement strategically important ties between GDR intellectuals and Eastern European counterparts, in the process reinforcing popular acceptance of the Oder-Neiße line, the Warsaw Pact, and even ongoing Soviet occupation as national salvation. Yet, cultural programs called into being under official auspices could nonetheless end up, at particular moments of crisis, influencing GDR political or aesthetic thinking in ways that challenged or destabilized government control. The GDR film studio decentralized in the late 1950s following Polish precedent; film students were sent to study in Moscow, Prague, or Łódź; writers were encouraged to meet and translate one another: all this interaction developed bonds and alliances, intermeshed aesthetic models that could not be so easily abandoned when government policy shifted. In 1956, in the wake of the suppressed Hungarian Uprising, after leading GDR intellectuals sent Walter Janka to Budapest to rescue theoretician Georg Lukács, Janka himself was arrested, tried, and imprisoned in the GDR.[57] In 1968, after the Soviet invasion of Czechoslovakia, GDR poets like Kunze became dissidents, unyielding in their solidarity with Czech intellectuals. In the early 1980s, when Poland declared martial law and eventually closed mass border-traffic with the GDR, many GDR intellectuals mourned the plight of their Polish interlocutors, feeling impoverished by severed communication. And in 1956, 1968, 1981, as again in the late 1980s glasnost period, university film clubs were censured, even banned

for their ongoing attempts to screen the most daring films from neighbouring Eastern European countries.[58] Such challenges to government censorship
practices – and attempts to follow what was going on elsewhere in Eastern Europe –
implicitly demanded a more open, cosmopolitan public sphere.

And how, it might be asked, did Polish, Hungarian, Czech, or Soviet intellectuals view GDR solidarity and philo-slavism? With interest, often, but also with
light scepticism and ongoing astonishment that GDR intellectuals still embraced
the socialist project so whole-heartedly, fought so ardently for its salvation.

The Aerial: Media Discourse and Discontents

They fear books and poems They fear plays and films They fear records and tapes They
fear writers and poets They fear journalists ... They fear radio stations They fear television satellites They fear the free flow of information They fear foreign literature and
newspapers They fear technological advancement They fear publications, printings
presses and copiers They fear typewriters ... They fear the truth They fear freedom They
fear democracy They fear the Human Rights Charter They fear socialism So why do we
fear them?

> – František Vaněček, "One Hundred Points" (1973–74),
> adapted by Czech experimental rock group Plastic People
> of the Universe, whose ban and imprisonment galvanized
> human rights manifesto Charta 77

The worldwide political upheavals of 1989 were fundamentally media events:
Tiananmen Square's televised massacre of protesters; the GDR's mass protest
marches; the Ceauşescus' televised execution. Arguably, the 1980s information
revolution sealed the demise of Soviet-style states, as advances in cybernetics
galvanized major, rapid, worldwide economic changes to which few centrally
planned economies were flexible or capitalized enough to adjust. Meanwhile,
the proliferation and privatization of digital technology increasingly challenged
government media and information monopolies. By the 1980s, Czech dissidents used video cameras to document civil disobedience and conduct video
interviews, dubbed their "Original Video Journal" into multiple copies, and
smuggled them out of the country for distribution to an international émigré
network.[59] Meanwhile, the GDR airwaves inadvertently transmitted not only
left-wing West Berlin punk and pirate stations, but also a monthly West Berlin
radio show, hosted by left-wing GDR political exiles, addressing East Berlin
compatriots with forbidden political news and critical analyses.

The GDR stringently controlled access to photocopiers along with film processing, radio licensing, and publication; most citizens had no access to VCRs
or computers, no easy means of duplicating, exchanging, or disseminating information. The 1980s' fledgling dissident social movements (environmental,

peace, gay rights, electoral reform, and democratization activists) took shape under Protestant church protection – not least because the church was officially permitted to duplicate texts and operate copiers. Meanwhile, a belated underground art scene (including super-8 experimental film screenings) flourished in large cities, persisting despite huge material obstacles: little access to cameras or film stock, Stasi (GDR secret police) oversight of all film developing, and lack of access to copying (unique copies sometimes destroyed accidentally in projection or during government raids).[60]

The GDR's protest groups and experimental film scene remained politically vulnerable, watched and infiltrated by the Stasi. Yet, in both contexts, media – in an artisanal, counter-cultural sense – played a crucial role in articulating GDR intellectuals' growing hopelessness, disillusionment, and disengagement. This function, as the rest of this chapter will argue, was a role media had played since the 1960s. The Cold War was not least a media war, a face-off between competing media notions. The 1960s and 70s dissident literature and song were correspondingly media obsessed. Kunze's poems and Biermann's home-made audio recordings (eventually distributed only as *tamizdat*, via West Germany) underscored media's centrality in the preservation of subjectivity and inwardness under socialism. Yet, their work is fully intelligible only in light of communist media politics.

In 1953, when East Berlin workers protesting unrealistic norms ignited a spontaneous uprising, unrest spread briefly to other GDR regions as listeners heard the news on RIAS, West Berlin's popular music and investigative journalism station. Founded in 1949, RIAS (short for Radio in the American Sector) was partly American government funded, operating under the motto "the free voice of a free world."[61] On this occasion, the station's in-depth coverage included live interviews with East Berlin protesters about their complaints and aspirations, alongside dramatic live coverage of Soviet firing on demonstrators. In retaliation, the GDR government attempted to jam Eastern reception of RIAS's signals.[62]

In 1961, the GDR government erected the Berlin Wall to staunch the westward flow of refugees, justifying its erection as a means of curbing Western media's pernicious effects. The wall immediately halted the pervasive practice of cross-sector cinema-going – and, in the GDR, the Party's Central Committee again discussed erecting an additional "electronic wall" to jam all television signals from the West. Instead, national initiatives tried to modify viewing habits. Citizens found watching Western television were humiliated. Antennae still facing West, GDR novelist Brigitte Reimann recorded in her diary, "are thrown down from the roofs and trampled on."[63] GDR public television sets had locks on their channel selectors to ensure they remained tuned to Eastern stations; GDR schoolchildren, and adults buying television sets, had to sign pledges not to watch Western stations.

But the GDR obsession with the West continued, despite the Berlin Wall, Stasi surveillance, and reprisals. For another thirty years, many citizens illicitly continued to tune into Western radio and television, some specifically to watch commercials. Physically, they lived in one Germany; psychically, in an imagined, alternative world uncircumscribed by Cold War borders and polarities.

Kunze's 1965 poem "The Antenna" celebrated unbounded viewing. After "the street threatened it:/ I'll saw you off," an aerial flees to the roof, then into the house, then into the room. But each place of refuge threateningly "pointed fingers at it." In the end, the antenna "fled into a brain"; only it can "offer safety ... For the time being."[64]

A technology intended to boost reception comes under acute political and existential threat, hounded from the public into the domestic sphere and finally into the head. For the moment, GDR heads still harbour and safeguard aerials, pointed in various directions, capable of tuning in many different stations. Those internalizing such aerials defy political threat – and the state's insistent right to media monopoly, to regulate and control all communication. When GDR citizens had sought out West Berlin's pre-wall "border cinemas" or illicitly tuned into Western radio or television stations, they entered an interior, extraterritorial world neither defined by sector borders nor circumscribed by Cold War polarities.

When GDR writers like Kunze and Biermann evoked media, they did so as a barometer of social conditions and political attitudes, and as a catalyst for collective fantasy life. Issues of media raised central questions of public, audience, consciousness, political, and social control. As their titles suggest, Kunze's poetry collections, *Low Volume* (*Zimmerlautstärke*, 1972, published only in West Germany) and *Letter with a Blue Seal* (1973), increasingly explored metaphors of (failed or muffled) communication. Several poems explore epistolary exchanges, implicitly raising the question of how to write in the knowledge of postal censors, standing to intercept and disrupt the communicative circuit.

The short poems and prose pieces of Kunze's *The Wonderful Years* (published in 1976 in West Germany) drew on hundreds of conversations with GDR teenagers, students, apprentices, and soldiers, chronicling embittering experiences with personal censorship and media control. As one soldier recalls in "Heros," GDR troops mobilized in 1968 to support the Soviet invasion of Czechoslovakia had their radio dials taped over, preventing them from hearing Western newscasts and political analysis. Their commanders led them in long media analysis sessions of Beatles' lyrics and The Doors' *Light My Fire* – punctuated, ironically, by screenings of Western movies, including Swedish soft-porn films (a genre otherwise unknown to the GDR public), clearly intended to "excite" them for battle. Having learned from the 1953 uprising, the GDR leadership remained determined to shield soldiers from competing media accounts of current developments. But their distrust of "foreign" media, Kunze suggests, did not forestall cynical deployment of Western films to produce in its soldier-viewers precisely those negative effects – pornographic arousal, sexually laden militarist aggression – which communists had long condemned.

From 1964 until his 1976 expulsion, Wolf Biermann endured a mode of artistic house arrest. As East Berlin's most famous and most-spied-upon dissident poet, he lived under twenty-four–hour Stasi surveillance so relentless it generated a 150,000 page file.[65] Although officially banned from performing or recording, Biermann transformed his downtown apartment into a makeshift recording studio; his recordings were smuggled to West Berlin, released on record, and played on West Berlin radio, where they reached GDR listeners (and tape recorders).

His first record, released in West Germany in 1968, took its title, *Chausseestraße 131*, from Biermann's East Berlin address (a venerable literary neighbourhood, since Brecht had lived at Chausseestraße 125). The cover photo (as on Biermann's following albums) featured Biermann's living room. His apartment had long functioned as a bohemian salon, where East Berlin poets, actors, painters, and West Berlin visitors gathered for impromptu music-making and political conversation. Part of Biermann's principled stance towards the Stasi and the GDR government was to accept his involuntary relinquishment of privacy. His apartment was bugged? All the more reason to entertain friends, rehearse new songs, have sex with the windows open, for anyone to hear.

Chausseestraße itself provided the record's unforgettable sound. Taped on improvised equipment, with open windows, the album features Biermann's lively performances (in the spirit of Weimar cabaret and post-thaw Russian guitar-poets) against intermittent birdsong and streetcar noises, brakes squealing, on the boulevard below.[66]

Chausseestraße's most famous track thematized and championed this raw sound. "Barlach Song" was originally commissioned for Ralf Kirsten's *The Lost Angel*, an ambitious GDR Brechtian/expressionist film about pacifist expressionist artist/poet Ernst Barlach, forced into inner emigration during the Third Reich, his plays banned, his sculptures removed from public exhibition. The GDR's official prohibition against Biermann led the song to be cut – and in 1966 the film was banned, pre-release, for five years, because it implicitly allegorized the situation of GDR artists, caught by shifting, often hostile cultural policies. Biermann's lyrics described increasingly hallucinatory fears of the outside world, as a child urges its mother to shut the window, shut out apocalyptic external threats. Yet, when Biermann recorded this song, his recording mode implicitly fought paranoia and claustrophobia by opening his own windows wide, capturing ambient sounds as the tape recorder ran.

In *Low Volume*, in turn, Kunze's poem "Wolf Biermann Is Singing" commemorated the distinctiveness and meaning of Biermann's sound. When Biermann sings of "Barlach's dire straits," listeners also hear "the streetcar screeching in the room."[67] For Kunze, and other GDR auditors, the streetcar unforgettably frames the record – the sound simultaneously of censorship, poetic defiance, and everyday life.

Biermann's subsequent records were made under equally improvised conditions. "Enfant perdu" (on *Don't Wait for Better Times*, 1973) eulogizes schoolboy Florian Havemann (son of dissident scientist Robert Havemann, Biermann's close friend), arrested after protesting the Soviet invasion of Czechoslovakia and hounded out of the GDR. Biermann's title echoes Heinrich Heine's sardonic 1849 lament about the long, seemingly hopeless struggle for German democracy – and its toll on loyal fighters. Biermann's protest song lamented forced emigration "from East to West" against the backdrop of a sound collage, recorded from GDR, West Berlin, and British Armed Forces radio. In an early instance of "sampling," the song overlaps celebratory coverage of GDR military parades honouring a Czech government delegation (and the post-invasion renormalization of GDR-Czech military relations), Vietnam War newscasts, disc jockey patter, and Christian and Jewish religious services.[68]

Chausseestraße 131 used the auditory equivalent of a camera obscura, letting in and recording the world as the background to songs about inner emigration and insistently staying put. In "Enfant perdu," Biermann breaks out of virtual house arrest by traversing the dial, noting the political ironies on (and between) frequencies. The ensuing aural collage effectively counters one-sided GDR media pedagogy. State power rests partly on an information monopoly and a willingness, in a crisis, to jam radio and television signals, tape over the radio dial. Yet, it cannot entirely prevent citizens from hearing, seeing, and comparing media for themselves. Those with a radio can dial themselves outside GDR bounds, gaining perspective and context. And those with a tape recorder can dub, even make their own records, whether or not the state sanctions them.

In turn, Swedish poet Tomas Tranströmer's 1973 poem "To Friends behind a Border" eulogizes Eastern European fellow poets, caught in political snares. Although "I wrote to you cautiously ... what I couldn't say/ filled and grew like a hot air balloon/ and finally floated away through the night sky." The letter is read by the censor, under his lamp, its words leaping "like monkeys at a wire mesh." In the poem's final stanza, Tranströmer exhorts his interlocutor: "Read between the lines. We will meet in two hundred years/ when the microphones in the hotel walls are forgotten–/ when they can sleep at last," becoming ammonites.[69]

Like Kunze, Tranströmer is interested in airspace, a zone above borders (maybe beyond language itself) where thoughts circulate. Kunze's "Aerial" implicitly echoes "Thoughts Are Free" (the famous German political song printed anonymously in 1790, popular around the 1848 revolution but banned after its failure, and played on occasion during the Third Reich by regime resisters, including Sophie Scholl of The White Rose).

Thoughts are free,
No one can guess them.
They flit by like night shadows.

No one can guess them, no hunter shoot them
with bullets and lead ... thoughts are free ...
Even if they imprison me in a dark prison ...
my thoughts will tear down the bars
and cleave the walls: Thoughts are free.

Ideas move through the air like shadows, move through walls, cannot be pre-dicted, hunted, caught, or contained. But Tranströmer goes further, imagining not only thoughts as a private realm of freedom but the mind as a medium for receiving or sending broadcasts, for a silent, invisible means of communication with others, of thinking with others, at a distance, across apparently unbridge-able state defences.

For Tranströmer, the act of writing "to friends beyond borders" seems com-promised; afraid to say too much, incriminate his correspondent, the poet says too little. The censors are waiting to steam open the mail. Written words strain, captive. Even spoken words are threatened, for the hotel walls contain hidden microphones, intended to record, trap, incriminate. But (unwritten) thoughts are still free, float into the sky like dirigibles; and correspondents, reading be-tween the lines as if decoding invisible ink, can hope for better times ahead, a future century when the microphones are obsolete, petrified, fossilized.

"To Friends" appeared during the Watergate crisis. With his potent image of the electronic bug, hidden in the hotel wall, Tranströmer implicitly indicts not only Eastern Europe, with its secret police and notoriously bugged Intourist Hotels, but the Watergate Hotel and the "free world" itself. Sweden, in this con-text, appears as a place of really existing social democracy, an extraterritorial space between Cold War fronts, between the First and Second worlds.

Literature, the PEN Club charter insists, "knows no frontiers, and must re-main common currency among people in spite of political or international up-heavals." During the Cold War, this chapter has argued, East Berlin intellectuals developed two distinct but potentially overlapping ways of understanding their place in the world. The first was implicitly a Comintern legacy, a Moscow-based notion of official internationalism that circulated through organs like Mezhrab-pom and *International Literature*; the second identified more closely with the émigré cosmopolitanism of the wartime communist diaspora. One under-standing involved readjusting literary tectonic plates, moving their literature's tradition and trajectory into new alignment – with their former enemies, with their newly liberated East-Central European political or cultural colonies. This adjustment was an implicitly expiatory, perhaps explicitly postcolonial move, which awoke and fed a growing curiosity about large parts of Europe that Ger-mans had been raised to ignore or mock. What intellectuals had discovered was Europe's literary plenitude, the aggregate richness of apparently minor literatures.

The second move involved a different kind of cosmopolitanism, as intellectuals came to see themselves not only as citizens of the literary world (à la PEN Club) but as lucky enough to stand at nodal or overlap points of the world media system. Their own focus on media – on the free passage of sound and telecommunication waves over otherwise impenetrable borders – could make their worldview seem deterritorialized, abstract, moving off the ground into the airspace above Europe. But, in the process, they also came to see themselves as irreducibly free agents, engaged in new conversations – however cautious, coded, or sotto voce – with peers in Eastern, Western, and Northern Europe. Crucially, their view was shared by key European literary figures. In this vision, the only impediments to a world literature were external political circumstances: a geopolitical world divided by walls, wires, jammers, bugs. But these remained powerless to contain or even record the swooping freedom of thought, let alone topple the indestructible antennae inside every head.[70]

NOTES

1 Karl Schlögel, *Berlin Ostbahnhof Europas. Russen und Deutsche in ihrem Jahrhundert* (Berlin: Siedler Verlag, 1998).

2 On Herder as framer/founder of world literature, see my "World Music, World Literature: A Geopolitical View," in *Comparative Literature in the Age of Globalization*, ed. Haun Saussy (Baltimore: Johns Hopkins University Press, 2006), 185–202.

3 For Goethe on world literature, see David Damrosch, Natalie Melas, and Mbongiseni Buthelezi, eds. *The Princeton Sourcebook in Comparative Literature: From the European Enlightenment to the Global Present* (Princeton, NJ: Princeton University Press, 2009), 185–202.

4 Franco Moretti, "Conjectures on World Literature" (2000), in *Distant Reading* (London: Verso, 2013), 43–62; Pascale Casanova, *The World Republic of Letters*, trans. Malcolm DeBevoise (Cambridge, MA: Harvard University Press, 2004); David Damrosch, *What Is World Literature?* (Princeton, NJ: Princeton University Press, 2003); Aamir Mufti, "Orientalism and the Institution of World Literatures," *Critical Inquiry* 36 (2010): 458–93; Emily Apter, *Against World Literature: On the Politics of Untranslatability* (London: Verso, 2013).

5 Martin Puchner, *Poetry of the Revolution: Marx, Manifestos, and the Avant-Gardes* (Princeton, NJ: Princeton University Press, 2005).

6 Konstantin Akinsha, ed., *Russian Modernism: Cross-Currents of German and Russian Art, 1907–1917* (Munich: Prestel, 2015).

7 Bruce Murray, *Film and the German Left in the Weimar Republic: From Caligari to Kuhle Wampe* (Austin: University of Texas, 1990), 52; Dobrin Michev, *Mezhrabpom-organizatsiia proletarskoĭ solidarnosti, 1921–1935* (Moscow: Mysl, 1971); on Münzenberg's interwar media work, see Jean-Michel Palmier, *Weimar*

in Exile: The Antifascist Emigration in Europe and America, trans. David Fernbach (London: Verso, 2006), 308–23.

8 Münzenberg's "Erobert den Film" enumerates IWA offices promoting film culture in the United States, France, Czechoslovakia, and Germany; IWA distributed proletarian films in thirteen European countries, Canada, Argentina, Australia, South Africa, and Japan. *Propaganda als Waffe* (Frankfurt: März Verlag, 1972), 46–66.

9 Willi Lüdecke, *Der Film in Agitation und Propaganda der revolutionären deutschen Arbeiterbewegung (1919–1933)* (Berlin: Oberbaumverlag, 1973), 34.

10 Ibid., 47–9.

11 Corey Ross, *Media and the Making of Modern Germany: Mass Communications, Society, and Politics from the Empire to the Third Reich* (Oxford: Oxford University Press, 2008), 237.

12 Günther Agde, "Mit dem Blick nach Westen," in *Die rote Traumfabrik. Meschrabpom-Film und Prometheus 1921–1936*, ed. Günther Agde and Alexander Schwarz (Berlin: Bertz + Fischer, 2012), 146.

13 Alexander Schwarz, "Von der Hungerhilfe zum roten Medienkonzern," in Agde and Schwarz, *Die rote*, 28.

14 Friedrich Wolf, "Was verdanken wir dem Sowjettheater und dem Sowjetfilm?" (1942), rpt. *Kunst ist Waffe* (Leipzig: Philipp Reclam, 1969), 93. The Russian films equally galvanized Austria. Christian Dewald, ed., *Arbeiterkino: Linke Filmkultur der Ersten Republikl*; Brigitte Mayr and Michael Omasta, eds., *Fritz Rosenfeld: Filmkritiker* (both Vienna: Filmarchiv Austria, 2007).

15 Murray, *Film and the German Left*, 223. On the films' initial reception, see Gertraude Kühn et al., eds., *Film und revolutionäre Arbeiterbewegung in Deutschland 1918–1932*, 2 vols. (Berlin: Henschelverlag, 1975).

16 Schlögel, *Berlin Ostbahnhof Europas*, 141.

17 Bertolt Brecht, *Texte für Filme. Drehbücher. Protokoll "Kühle Wampe." Exposés. Szenaried*, ed. Wolfgang Gersch and Werner Hecht (Frankfurt: Suhrkamp, 1969), 185.

18 Murray, *Film and the German Left*, 223.

19 Michev, *Mezhrabpom*, 249–55.

20 H.T.S., "The Screen: German Unemployed," *New York Times*, 24 April 1933, 11.

21 Theodor Adorno, *Minima Moralia. Reflections from Damaged Life*, trans. E.F.N. Jephcott (London: Verso, 1974), 33.

22 Dieter Wöhrle, *Bertolt Brechts medienästhetische Versuche* (Cologne: Prometh Verlag, 1988); Roswitha Mueller, *Bertolt Brecht and the Theory of Media* (Lincoln: University of Nebraska Press, 1989).

23 Adam Zagajewski, "Two Cities," in *Two Cities: On Exile, History and Imagination*, (Athens: University of Georgia, 2002), 1–68.

24 Adam Zagajewski, "Electric Elegy," in *Without End: New and Selected Poems*, trans. Renata Gorcyzinski, Benjamin Ivry, and C.K. Williams (New York: Farrar, Straus and Giroux, 2001), 173–4.

25 Ibid., 172.

26 Ibid., 173.

27 Johannes R. Becher, "Der an den Schlaf der Welt rührte (Lenin)," in *Gesammelte Werke*, vol. 3, *Gedichte 1926–1935* (Berlin: Johannes R. Becher Archiv der Akademie der Künste, 1966), 147. By the early 1980s, young dissident East German samizdat poets including Rüdiger Rosenthal and Stefan Döring rewrote or parodied canonical GDR literary texts, including Becher's poem. As Rosenthal's "question" (1984) reframed it, "he shook the sleep of the world,/ with words/ that tired made us, you me/ I could sleep the whole day if I didn't/ have to write/ lenin, what does it feel like to sleep with stalin/ things are terrible for you as they always are for me." Cited in Carola Hähnel-Mesnard, "Distinctionsstrategien im literarischen Feld und Aktualisierung tabuister Traditionen in der selbst verlegten Literatur der DDR in den 1980er Jahre," in *Edinburgh German Yearbook 3: Contested Legacies: Constructions of Cultural Heritage in the GDR*, ed. Matthew Philpotts and Sabine Rolle (Rochester: Camden House, 2009), 233–59, here 239.

28 Douglas Kahn and Gregory Whitehead, eds., *Wireless Imagination. Sound, Radio and the Avant-Garde* (Cambridge, MA: MIT Press, 1992), see esp. Mark E. Cory, "Soundplay: The Polyphonous Tradition of German Radio Art," 331–72.

29 Günther Agde, *Kämpfer. Biographie eines Films und seiner Macher* (Berlin: Das neue Berlin, 2001), 172.

30 Agde and Schwarz, *Die rote*, esp. Jekaterina Chochlowa, "Das Studio der Meister: Filme und Schicksale," 68–9; and Alexander Schwarz, "Von der Hungerhilfe zum roten Medienkonzern," 32.

31 Schubin and Morosow, "Schlußfolgerungen der Reinigungskommission der Zelle der WKP/B Der Tonfilmfabrik von Meschrabpom-Film, namens 'Rotfront,'" (1933), in Agde and Schwarz, *Die rote*, 177.

32 Günter Agde, "Im Widerstreit der Bilder: Utopien und Topoi," in Agde and Schwarz, *Die rote*, 80–1.

33 Valérie Pozner, "Ein Filmprojekt scheitert. Belá Balázs' Drehbuch *Hochzeit im Wien* zum Februar 1934," in Dewald, *Arbeiterkino*, 334. Initial plans included seven films to be made inside Germany with Germans directors and technicians. Oksana Bulgakowa, "Les rapports avec l'Allemagne," in *Le studio Merabpom ou l'aventure du cinéma privé au pays des bolcheviks*, ed. Aïcha Kherroubi and Valérie Posener (Paris: Réunion des Musées Nationaux, 1996), 111.

34 Hans Schoots, *Living Dangerously: A Biography of Joris Ivens* (Amsterdam: Amsterdam University Press, 2000), 100; Malte Hagener, *Moving Forward, Looking Back: The European Avant-Garde and the Invention of Film Culture, 1919–1939* (Amsterdam: Amsterdam University Press, 2007), chap. 5.

35 Agde, *Kämpfer*, 176–8.

36 Ibid., 62, 195.

37 Agde, *Kämpfer*; Simone Schofer, "'Sowjetunion' und sowjetische Realität: Ausschnitte aus dem gesellschaftlichen Leben in den 30er Jahren," in *Filme für die*

Volksfront. Erwin Piscator, Gustav von Wangenheim, Friedrich Wolf. Antifaschistiche Filmemacher im sowjetischen Exil, ed. Rainhard May and Hendrik Jackson (Berlin: Stattkino, 2001), 25.

38 Thomas Heimann, *DEFA, Künstler und SED-Kulturpolitik: Zum Verhältniß von Kulturpolitik und Filmproduktion in der SBZ/DDR 1945 bis 1959* (Berlin: Vistas Verlag, 1994), esp. 17–33, 48–50; Maria Hilchenbach, *Kino im Exil. Die Emigration deutsche Filmkünstler 1933–1945* (Munich: K.G. Sauer, 1982); Wolfgang Schivelbusch, *In a Cold Crater: Cultural and Intellectual Life in Berlin, 1945–1948*, trans. Kelly Barry (Berkeley: University of California Press, 1998), 65; Hanno Loewy, *Béla Balázs – Märchen, Ritual und Film* (Berlin: Vorwerk 8, 2003), 382.

39 Günther Agde, "Zwischen Verlust, Tabu und Vergessen. Filmkünstler und Filme der Moskauer Filmproduktion Meshrabpom-Film in Deutschland nach 1945," in *Apropos, Film: das Jahrbuch der DEFA-Stiftung/herausgegeben von der DEFA-Stiftung* (Berlin: Verlag Das Neue Berlin, 2002), 185–8.

40 Vance Kepley, Jr., "The Workers' International Relief and the Cinema of the Left 1921–1935," *Cinema Journal* 23, no. 1 (Fall 1983): 19; see also Lüdecke, *Der Film*, 73: "The Soviet Union offered a series of German comrades the opportunity to use the resources of domestic film production to continue the anti-fascist struggle."

41 Agde, *Kämpfer*, 180, 197.

42 Günter Reisch, cited in Agde, *Kämpfer*, 32.

43 On Eastern European prototypes for GDR film culture, see my "DEFA: Moving Germany into Eastern Europe," in *Moving Images of East Germany: Past and Future of DEFA Film*, ed. Barton Byg and Bethany Moore (Washington, DC: American Institute for Contemporary German Studies, 2002), 85–104. For GDR participation in the international socialist music circuit, see Jürgen Böttcher's *Song International* (GDR, 1971), documenting East Berlin's second Festival of the Political Song.

44 See my "Old Movies: Cinema as Palimpsest in GDR Fiction," *New German Critique* 82 (Winter 2001): 39–76.

45 On *International Literature*, see Glyn Salton-Cox, "Polemics Pertinent at the Time of Publication: Georg Lukács, *International Literature*, and the Popular Front," *Twentieth-Century Communism* 12, no. 12 (April 2017): 143–68; Rossen Djagalov, "The Red Apostles: Imagining Revolution in the Global Proletariat Novel," *Slavic and Eastern European Studies Journal* 62, no. 3 (Spring 2017): 396–422. *International Literature*'s historical precedents included Victorian multilingual monthly *Cosmopolis* (1896–98), published in London, Paris, Berlin, and St. Petersburg. See Tanya Agathocleos, *Urban Realism and the Cosmopolitan Imagination in the Nineteenth Century: Visible City, Invisible World* (Cambridge: Cambridge University Press, 2013), chap. 1. In 1920, Tvetan Tzara solicited art and writing from ten countries for a (never published) multilingual *Dadaglobe* anthology. See Adrian Sudhalter et al., eds., *Dadaglobe Reconstructed* (Zurich: Kunsthaus Zürich, 2016). In 1984, a Czech émigré launched *Lettre international* in Paris; parallel language editions followed in Rome, Madrid, Berlin, Copenhagen, and, after 1989, in

Czechoslovakia, Bulgaria, Poland, Croatia, Serbia, Hungary, Rumania, Russia, and Macedonia (although some failed financially). At moments, *Lettre* saw itself extending Western European cosmopolitanism to a formerly benighted, isolated Eastern European imperium. Such narratives bypass the more complicated history on the ground.

46 E.P. Thompson, *The Making of the English Working Class* (London: Victor Gollancz, 1963).

47 See *Kunst und Literatur im antifaschistischen Exil 1933–1945* (Leipzig: Philipps Reclam, 1979?–1989), 7 vols.; Marcus G. Patke, *Zu nah der Sonne. Deutsche Schrift-steller im Exil in Mexiko* (Berlin: Aufbau, 1999). After emigrating from Berlin to Paris, critic Alfred Kantorowicz founded a Library of Burned Books (German Freedom Library), opened on the first anniversary of the Nazi book burnings.

48 Katerina Clark, *Moscow, the Fourth Rome: Stalinism, Cosmopolitanism and the Evolution of Soviet Culture, 1931–1941* (Cambridge, MA: Harvard University Press, 2011).

49 Karl Radek, "Contemporary World Literature and the Tasks of Proletarian Art," in *Problems of Soviet Literature: Reports and Speeches at the First Soviet Writers' Conference*, ed. H.G. Scott (New York: International Publishers, 1934), 73–162; Georg Lukács, *The Historical Novel*, trans. Hannah and Stanley Mitchell (Lincoln: University of Nebraska Press, 1983).

50 For translated excerpts, see John Heartfield and Georg Grosz, "The Art Scab," in *The Weimar Sourcebook*, ed. Anton Kaes et al. (Berkeley: University of California Press, 1994), 483–6; Alexei Gan, "Constructivism" (1922), in *The Tradition of Constructivism*, ed. Stephen Bann (New York: Da Capo, 1974), 32–42.

51 "The PEN Charter," *pen-international.org*, https://pen-international.org/who-we-are/the-pen-charter.

52 Markus Wolf, *Die Troika. Geschichte eines nichtgedrehten Films. Nach einer Idee von Konrad Wolf* (1989; rev. ed. Berlin: Aufbau, 2000).

53 Friedrich Wolf's essays thus noted double bills of Film and Photo League and Soviet revolutionary films at New York's New School for Social Research and tracked the triumphant New York, Copenhagen, and Paris receptions of socialist realist breakthrough film *Chapayev* (Georgii and Sergei Vasil'ev, USSR, 1934) and Popular Front films like *La Marseillaise* (Jean Renoir, France, 1938). Friedrich Wolf, *Aufsätze 1919–1944* (Berlin: Aufbau, 1967).

54 *Auschwitz auf der Bühne. Peter Weiss "Die Ermittlung" in Ost und West* (DVD) (Bonn: Bundeszentrale für politische Bildung, 2008).

55 Wolfgang Leonhard, *Child of the Revolution* (1955), trans. C.M. Woodhouse (London: Ink Links, 1979).

56 See Christa Wolf's "Moscow Novella" (1961) and *Patterns of Childhood* (1976); Franz Fühmann's *The Jewish Car* (1962) and *22 Days, or Half of Life* (1973); Rolf Schneider's *The Journey to Jaroslaw* (1975); and Helge Schubert's *Anna Knows*

German (1984); films include Egon Günther's *The Keys* (1974), Konrad Wolf's *Mamma, I'm Alive* (1977), and Frank Beyer's *The Turning Point* (1982).

57 Janka's accusatory memoir *Schwierigkeiten mit der Wahrheit* (Hamburg: Rowohlt, 1989) recounted his long imprisonment and reproached revered GDR writer Anna Seghers for her reluctance to defend him. *Schwierigkeiten*'s publication caused a sensation; when the Berlin Wall fell a month later, it helped set the initial agenda for GDR intellectual de-Stalinization.

58 Wieland Becker and Volker Petzold, *Tarkowski trifft King Kong. Geschichte der Filmklubbewegung der DDR* (Berlin: Vistas, 2001).

59 Alice Lovejoy, "'Video Knows No Borders': Samizdat Television and the Unofficial Public Sphere in 'Normalized' Czechoslovakia," in *Samizdat, Tamizdat & Beyond: Transnational Media During and After Socialism*, ed. Friderike Kind-Kovács and Jessie Labov (New York: Berghahn Books, 2013), 206–20.

60 Karin Fritzsche and Claus Löser, eds., *Gegenbilder: Filmische Subversion in der DDR 1976–1989. Texte, Bilder, Daten* (Berlin: Gerhard Wolf Janus Press, 1996); Uta Grundmann et al., eds., *Die Einübung der Aussenspur: Die andere Kultur in Leipzig 1971–1990* (Leipzig: THOM Verlag, 1996).

61 RIAS read the "Freedom Oath" weekly on-air: "I believe in the sacredness and dignity of the individual. I believe that all men derive the right to freedom equally from God. I pledge to resist aggression and tyranny wherever they appear on earth."

62 Joachim Kallinich and Sylvia de Pasquale, eds., *Ein offenes Geheimnis. Post- und Telefonkontrolle in der DDR* (Berlin: Edition Branz, 2002).

63 Brigitte Reimann, 2 October 1961 entry, *Ich bedaure nichts. Tagebücher 1955–1963*, 2nd ed., ed. Angela Drescher (Berlin: Aufbau, 2001), 215.

64 Rainer Kunze, "The Antenna," *Rich Catch in an Empty Creel*, trans. Richard Dove (Copenhagen and Los Angeles: Green Integer, 2013), 83.

65 Kunze's surveillance file was smaller (approximately 3,500 pages). In 1990, the Stasi tried to burn portions, but the archived original survived; Kunze published selections as *Deckname "Lyrik." Dokumentation* (Frankfurt: Fischer, 1990).

66 Wolf Biermann, *Chausseestraße 131* (LP) (West Germany: Wagenbachs Quartplatte, 1969).

67 Rainer Kunze, "Wolf Biermann Is Singing," trans. Richard Dove, in *Rich Catch*, 128.

68 Wolf Biermann, *Warte nicht auf bessre Zeiten* (LP) (West Germany: CBS, 1973). Yet, see Florian Havemann's *Havemann* (Frankfurt: Suhrkamp, 2007) and my "Fall 1968: Expulsion of Thomas Brasch from GDR Film School Signals Fate of East German '68ers," in *New History of German Cinema*, ed. Jennifer M. Kapczynski and Michael Richardson (Rochester, NY: Camden House, 2012), 423–430.

69 Tomas Tranströmer, "To Friends behind a Border," trans. Robin Robertson, in *New York Review of Books*, 10 November 2011, 41.

70 My thanks to Ursula Deist, Annette Deist, Russell Berman, my late father Ulrich Trumpener and the late Tony Judt, Loren Kruger, Julia Hell, Anke Pinkert, John Urang, Hunter Bivens, Katerina Clark, Alice Lovejoy, Rossen Djagalov, Glyn Salton-Cox, John MacKay, Marijeta Bozovic, and Marta Figlerowicz for generative exchanges about communist aesthetics; to interlocutors at the University of Alberta, University of Minnesota, Columbia, University of Chicago, and Yale; to Robyn Creswell as to fellow world literature teachers Barry McCrea, Ben Conisbee Baer, and the late Richard Maxwell.

Chapter Sixteen

Workers of the World, Unite!

BO ZHENG
City University of Hong Kong

In contrast to most of the preceding pieces, this final chapter will place the 1920s and 30s in the background, instead foregrounding contemporary Chinese cultural practices. I work on contemporary Chinese art, in particular socially engaged art – art that is activist minded and explicitly addresses social issues. Chinese artists and critics often regard this burgeoning field as a new phenomenon, an import from the West. However, for the purposes of this volume, I will seek out echoes of 1920s leftist Chinese culture – an extension of Comintern aesthetics – in contemporary Chinese socially engaged art. I will focus in particular on two contemporary Chinese art groups, the Beijing-based music collective New Worker Art Troupe and the Shanghai-based theatre collective Grass Stage, and compare their cultural productions with 1920s workers' music and theatre. With only two sample pairs from the present and the interwar years, this chapter does not constitute a comprehensive study of the expansive history of leftist cultural practices in post-imperial China. I am less interested in celebrating the continuity of leftist cultures than revealing contemporary shortcomings – that is, the lessons that Comintern aesthetics has to offer contemporary socially engaged art.

New Worker Art Troupe

In 1995, Wang Dezhi[1] left his horse farm in Inner Mongolia for Beijing. He had been practising crosstalk (*xiangsheng*), a traditional form of stage comedy, and was hoping that he could perform in the Spring Festival Gala on Chinese national television (CCTV). He was flatly rejected. He rented a tiny room in the basement of a building and kept practising crosstalk. In order to survive in the metropolis, he picked up odd jobs: washing dishes, distributing flyers, and delivering bottled water.

In 1998, Sun Heng[2] left his job as a music teacher at a secondary school in Henan province and wandered throughout China in search of "real life."

Everywhere he went, the situation of migrant workers pained him: why were they working so hard, but still could not live a decent life? Eventually, he settled down in Beijing and started to volunteer in a school, teaching music to children of migrant workers.

In 1999, Xu Duo[3] ran away from his "boring hometown" in Zhejiang province to attend the Midi School of Music[4] in Beijing. Like his classmates, he dreamed of becoming a rock star. After graduation, however, he ended up a street singer and moved into a migrant workers' community.

Wang Dezhi, Sun Heng, and Xu Duo met in Beijing, and on 1 May 2002 they formed the New Worker Art Troupe (NWAT).[5] They started writing songs for migrant workers and performing these songs on construction sites where migrant workers were employed. Since then, they have written more than a hundred songs, released nine albums, and performed on hundreds of construction sites (figure 16.1). Their first CD, released in 2004, sold more than 100,000 copies. They received 75,000 yuan in royalty fees and used the money to set up a school for children of migrant workers in Picun,[6] a village in the far northeast suburb of Beijing. They gradually expanded their base in Picun, establishing a migrant workers' museum, a tent theatre (inspired by Japanese director Sakurai Daizo), a library, and a training centre. In 2012, they initiated the Migrant Workers' Spring Festival Gala, two hours of songs, dances, and skits performed by workers from Beijing and other provinces. The annual gala is recorded and then uploaded to popular Chinese websites, reaching a large number of viewers across the country.

NWAT is one of the most successful cultural activist groups in China today. They have a stable core of members, a set of solid institutions built up over a decade, a physical base, and a large network of supporters (academics, journalists, art professionals, and student volunteers). Unlike other socially engaged artists and collectives, NWAT members are not cultural elites; they did not attend prestigious art schools or universities, nor have they studied or lived abroad. Despite their growing reputation, they continue to regard themselves as migrant workers, representing their own people.

The working class in China today consists mainly of *nongmin-gong* (peasant labour). According to the 2013 *National Peasant-Labour Monitoring Survey Report*, published by the Chinese National Bureau of Statistics,[7] there were 269 million peasant labourers in 2013. Of these, 166 million were migrant labourers, meaning that they had left their home to work in a different town or city. Of the 166 million, 35 million brought their families with them, and the rest (131 million) left their families behind. The report states that 35 per cent of these migrant labourers (58 million) worked in manufacturing and 24 per cent (39 million) in construction. Their average monthly income, excluding accommodation and meals provided by some employers, was 2,609 yuan per month (approximately US$420). Most of the migrant labourers (85 per cent)

16.1 New Worker Art Troupe performing next to a construction site in Beijing, 1 May 2004.

worked over forty-four hours per week, the limit set by China's Labour Law. Only 29 per cent of them had work injury insurance, and 18 per cent had health insurance.

The title track of NWAT's first album, *Under Heaven All Migrant Workers Are One Family*,[8] is one of their most frequently performed songs:

You come from Sichuan
I come from Henan
You come from the Northeast
He comes from Anhui
No matter where we are from
We all labour to live
You work in construction
I work in housekeeping
You run a small business

He is a service boy
No matter which line of work we are in
It is only to survive that we come together
Migrant worker brothers hand in hand
No more worry in the labour journey
Not afraid of rain or wind
Under heaven all migrant worker
brothers and sisters are one family[9]

The title, "Under Heaven All Migrant Workers Are One Family (*tianxia dagong shi yijia*)" is a slight change from the historical slogan "Under Heaven All Workers Are One Family (*tianxia gongren shi yijia*)."[10] According to historian S.A. Smith, the original slogan was created by labour organizers Zhu Baoting[11] (1880–1947) and Dong Chuping[12] (1894–1969) during the 1922 seamen's strikes in Hong Kong and Shanghai "as a way of trying to overcome the ingrained mistrust between different regional *bang* [native associations]."[13] The unifying intention is the same in the NWAT song. The four regions mentioned at the beginning of the song are main areas where migrant workers come from. The four lines of work mentioned in the second section – construction, housekeeping, small businesses, and service – are among the top industries that employ migrant workers. Manufacturing is conspicuously missing from this list, perhaps because large factories employing migrant workers are concentrated in the south, while NWAT has been mainly performing for migrant workers in the north. This small omission is significant. It means that NWAT is not targeting migrant workers employed in large factories, who might more easily develop into organized labour. Migrant workers in construction, housekeeping, small businesses, and service are highly mobile and less homogeneous than factory workers in terms of age, gender, education, and, indeed, hometown. By contrast, the 1920s slogan "Under Heaven All Workers Are One Family" addressed organized labour. Its goal was to shift the organizing factor from different hometowns to a shared class identity. Migrant workers in contemporary China, however, are no longer organized. They may still seek help from *laoxiang* (hometown fellows), but neither *bang* nor real labour unions are there to bind them together.

In this song, "under heaven" seems to refer only to China – Sichuan, Henan, the Northeast, and Anhui – not the entire world. By contrast, labour songs in the 1920s championed an international vision. In 1924, before the 1 May International Workers' Day, Chen Tanqiu[14] (1896–1943), a communist leader in Wuhan, wrote the following song:

May 1 Festival, so heroic
World workers in unity
Initiated in Chicago
Resonated around the world

Western Europe, East Asia, and the Americas
Spilled with labour's blood every year
Never stop till we succeed
May we all strive together
Never let down the May 1 Festival[15]

The image of "the world (*shijie*)" was prominent. In another song celebrating 1 May, written in 1921 by Beijing University students teaching at Changxindian Workers' School,[16] "the world" also featured prominently in the first line:

How beautiful is freedom, the world's bright star
Fight with my blood, sacrifice for him
We shall sweep away all abusive power
Remember May 1, the auspicious day[17]

The famous "Anyuan Workers' Club Song,"[18] with lyrics written by young communist leader Li Lisan (1899–1967),[19] also emphasized "the world," repeating it three times:

We workers are insulted
We workers are oppressed
It is we who will build the world
It is we who will end oppression
Building a new world and ending oppression
We'll show our mighty strength
Workers, let's unite
Workers, let's join together
Workers, workers
Must be masters of the world[20]

In these songs from the 1920s, the idea was clear: workers in China – whether they were in Wuhan, Changxindian, or Anyuan – were part of the international proletariat. No such imagery can be found in NWAT's songs. Today's Chinese migrant workers, numbering 166 million, seem to stand alone, not shoulder-to-shoulder with Filipino workers in Hong Kong, Indonesian workers in Korea, or Mexican workers in the United States.

"The Internationale" was translated into Chinese in 1923, via two separate routes. Qu Qiubai[21] (1899–1935) first heard the song in 1920 in Harbin at a Russian party celebrating the third anniversary of the October Revolution. He later translated the lyrics from French and published them in the relaunched *New Youth* magazine. Xiao San[22] (1896–1983) first heard the song in France in 1920 and then translated it into Chinese in 1923 in Moscow. Though some words varied, both translations adhered closely to the original song.[23]

In recent years, a Korean song has become the so-called "Asian Internationale." The Korean version, titled "March for My Beloved," was first performed on 20 February 1982 at the Mangwol-dong Cemetery in Gwangju during the post-mortem wedding for Yoon Sang-won, who was killed in the 1980 Gwangju Uprising, and Park Gi-sun, a labour activist who died in 1978 due to carbon monoxide poisoning.[24] The lyrics are highly emotional but not politically specific ("Awakening, we call out, a fervent battle cry/ I'll go on ahead, and you, the living, follow!"), and the song quickly gained popularity at mass demonstrations, including labour protests. It also spread to other Asian countries. But, unlike "The Internationale," which functioned as one song in many languages, the "Asian Internationale" was appropriated into different Asian languages and adapted for various local agendas. When localized in Taiwan by the workers' band Black Hand Nakasi,[25] it became the "Workers' Battle Song."[26] In China, NWAT made it the "Workers' Glory Song."[27] International translations sharing the same utopian dream have been superseded by local adaptations for varying pragmatic demands.

The 1920s songs portrayed workers as historical agents who would "sweep away all abusive power," "build a new world," and become its "masters." By contrast, NWAT songs carry no such radical message. At best, migrant workers will enjoy "no more worry in the labour journey." Whereas songs in the 1920s called for revolution, NWAT songs advocate workers' rights. In fact, NWAT's motto is "to shout with music, to defend rights with art."[28] One song in the first album demonstrates this approach. Titled "Joining Together to Fight for Wages," it paints a vivid picture in which a group of workers have occupied the construction site to demand payment from their boss, a cunning Mr. Zhou, so they can go home after a year's hard work to reunite with their families for Chinese New Year. The song tells the story through the eyes of a young migrant worker. Boss Zhou has called in some fake "police" who try to scare the workers away, saying they will all be arrested. The narrator becomes "a bit nervous." At this moment, Old Fellow Wang, who has experienced "hundreds of battles," stands up. He exposes the shams and leads the shouting: "One condition! Pay us! One condition! Pay us!" At daybreak, Boss Zhou finally caves in and pays the workers. Sun Heng has performed this song frequently on construction sites. On one occasion, the workers in the audience were so aroused that they started to shout together. The site manager was frightened and ended the performance.

Ethnomusicologist Frederick Lau observes that "the musical style, vocal timbre, audience reception, performance setting, and quality of [NWAT's] music remind one of American folk music and concerts of the 1960s," and with Sun Heng carrying a guitar and a harmonica, "the reference of Bob Dylan is hard to miss."[29] Members of NWAT have not only been influenced by American music, they have also picked up American politics – identity politics: Sun Heng frequently argues that migrant workers need their own culture. The songs, plays, films, and spring festival galas produced by NWAT are meant for migrant workers themselves, for them to strengthen their identity and develop a new culture. It seems that the possibility for migrant workers to organize themselves into a political class is so remote that the best NWAT can hope for in the current political climate is advocacy for a unique cultural identity.

This shift from class struggle to identity politics should not surprise us. For the past four decades, the politically charged idea of "class (*jieji*)" has been replaced by the seemingly neutral concept of "stratum (*jieceng*)." Few people believe in revolution; most strive for "rational" reform and self-improvement. The only viable model out there for collective social struggle seems to be identity politics. Political scientist Lin Chun argues that "the weakness, if not the complete absence, of an independent working-class movement in China cannot be explained by repression alone."[30] There has been no ideology like Marxism to forge a theoretical foundation, no foreign threat like the Japanese invasion to galvanize a nationalist spirit, no institutional structure like the Comintern to provide valuable resources, and no Comintern aesthetics to nurture a world revolutionary culture.

World Factory by Grass Stage

Shenzhen, 22 November 2014. It was a beautiful autumn night in this subtropical city on the southern coast of China. Young and fashionable people could be seen everywhere enjoying coffee and conversation in this hip part of town called OCT LOFT,[31] two blocks of old factory buildings transformed into art galleries and design studios, cafés and restaurants. Inside OCT Contemporary Art Terminal,[32] two hundred people sat down to watch a play, *World Factory*,[33] by Shanghai-based theatre collective Grass Stage.[34]

The stage was barren, without any stage set except for a large piece of blue cloth hanging vertically to the left and three working desks in the far corner of upstage right. The cloth was a particular blue, the blue of workers' uniforms. Three unironed blue sheets were sewn together, soiled with what seemed to be oil stains. A man in his thirties with puffy permed hair came and sat on the floor, and started to play guitar and harmonica and sing (figure 16.2). It was Xu Duo of the New Worker Art Troupe. He sang "Loving This World,"[35] adapted by him from a Hani folk song:

> How beautiful, how beautiful
> This world so beautiful
> Just like goods in shop windows
> That you can never reach
> How come, how come

16.2 Xu Duo singing in Grass Stage's *World Factory* in Shenzhen, 22 November 2014.

Some despair and depart
We have given up the world
Or it has betrayed us all
Must endure, must endure
So many years we have endured
We got no time to grieve
Must continue loving this world[36]

A female clown ran onto the stage. A string was hanging around her neck, with cut-out paper dolls clipped onto it. She addressed us, the audience: "Before the show formally starts, how about I entertain you with a skit? It's called Fuyoukang Eight Consecutive Jumps." Clearly, she was referring to the series of suicides committed by workers at Foxconn's Shenzhen factories in 2010. (Foxconn's Chinese name is "*Fushikang*.") According to a 2010 *South China Morning Post* article, fourteen Foxconn workers, aged between eighteen and twenty-five, jumped off buildings and died in that year.[37] The clown invited a Mr. Lu, a mental health counsellor, to help her cut the paper dolls on the string. Mr. Lu happily obliged and made up various explanations for why these workers were psychologically weak (figure 16.3, top). No structural reasons for the deaths were mentioned. As each paper doll drifted weightlessly onto the floor, the clown and Mr. Lu expressed pity and excitement. They shrieked and laughed at the same time, their hysteria reverberating in this factory-turned-exhibition-hall.

16.3 Grass Stage's *World Factory* in Shenzhen, 22 November 2014.

The play *World Factory*, structured into eight scenes, was a combination of lectures and physical theatre. A character described as the "New Industrialist" in the script, played by Yu Kai, first appeared in scene three. "A few years ago," she said, "I went abroad to study labour protection in foreign factories. I went to Manchester, an important city in the early years of the English Industrial Revolution." The actor stood perfectly straight, delivering her monologue without any accent in a style reminding me of CCTV news anchors (figure 16.3, bottom). Machine noise started to rumble in the background. A video of the Quarry Bank Mill in Manchester (built in 1784, now a museum) was projected onto the blue cloth. "Before 1847," continued New Industrialist, "a shift at Quarry Bank Mill would last fifteen hours, from 5:30 at dawn until 8:00 in the evening, plus overtime if needed. Interestingly, information in the museum claimed that 'the working condition then was far different from modern standards.' But where is the modern standard? There are so many factories and construction sites in China not even counting overtime, so many are working ten plus hours every day." She went on to describe the kind of physical punishment workers suffered at Quarry Bank, and then her lecture was taken over by a male voice off stage, described as the "Director" in the script. The video on the screen cut to Chetham's Library in Manchester, while the Director informed us that Marx and Engels studied there in the 1840s and changed their focus from philosophy to political economy. A drumbeat was heard. Another voice gave a brief history of the Peterloo Massacre in 1819. A group of actors started to sing "*Warszawianka* (The Warsaw Song)," a popular tune in international workers' movements in the first half of the twentieth century:

> To battle bloody,
> Holy and righteous
> March, forward march,
> Workers, all[38]

Two actors dressed in workers' uniforms marched on stage. With keywords like "Strike," "Union," and "NGO" (non-governmental organization) written on pieces of cardboard, they rehearsed the forms of proletarian struggle in different stages of capitalism (figure 16.4). Then New Industrialist came back on and concluded the history lesson: "Having been to Manchester, I now know that it was the earliest World Factory. Afterwards, financial capital expanded around the globe, and factories kept moving to places with even cheaper labour. Finally they arrived in China ... On what conditions are we continuing the history of World Factory?"

This scene, and much of the play, was pedagogical. Various actors assumed teaching roles and informed us about the history of industrialization and workers' struggles, gave scientific details on the harm of industrial pollutants to the human body, and revealed the magnitude of the problem of children left behind in villages (61 million of them, of whom 40 million are under fourteen years old). Their speeches were supplemented with video footages and sound recordings, much like a TED Talk.

Sitting in the audience, I wondered – if Theodor Adorno were here, what would he say? He would label *World Factory* "propagandist," like those "earlier propagandist (tendency) plays against syphilis, duels, abortion laws or borstals," or "didactic," like the works of Brecht.[39] In "Commitment," an essay written in 1962, Adorno argues that committed art like Brecht's epic theatre is problematic: "the more preoccupied Brecht becomes with information, and the

16.4 Actors marching in Grass Stage's *World Factory* in Shenzhen, 22 November 2014.

less he looks for images, the more he misses the essence of capitalism which the parable is supposed to present."[40] Adorno holds that autonomous works of art, those that sustain a distance between form and reality like Kafka's prose and Beckett's plays, are truly political because they "firmly negate empirical reality" and "compel the change of attitude which committed works merely demand."[41] In other words, as Lambert Zuidervaart interprets Adorno, autonomous art "so thoroughly works out its own internal contradictions that the hidden contradictions in society can no longer be ignored."[42]

If Mao Zedong were here, he would disagree with Adorno sharply. As an empiricist, Mao would state that autonomous art, which in theory could lead to a fundamental negation of reality, in practice has little to offer to the revolutionary cause because such art places an extremely stringent demand on the audience, who has to be able to perceive "both the artwork's complex internal dynamics and the dynamics of the sociohistorical totality to which the artwork belongs."[43] For Mao, propagandist works, like *World Factory*, are needed to educate the masses and to awaken them. Indeed, *World Factory* would seem very familiar to Mao.

In the fall of 1921, right after the founding of the Chinese Communist Party (CCP), twenty-seven-year-old Mao visited Anyuan, the centre of Pingxiang coal mining region situated between Jiangxi province and Hunan province. The coal mine was established in 1898. By 1911, the Pingxiang Railway and

Mining Company was producing over 2,200 tons of high-quality coal per day, making it the largest Chinese-owned coal mine in the country. It employed a labour force of over 10,000 miners and over 1,000 railway workers, the majority of whom were migrant workers recruited from neighbouring Hunan province.[44] Mao made contact with the miners, and then sent twenty-two-year-old Li Lisan (1899–1967), a fellow Hunanese who had just returned from France, to Anyuan to establish a school for the workers. Li's animated spirit and down-to-earth personality endeared him to the workers. In the following May, he was able to found the Anyuan Workers' Club, which functioned as a de facto workers' union. In September, a general strike was orchestrated by Li Lisan and Liu Shaoqi (1898–1969), another Hunanese CCP member sent to Anyuan upon his return from studies in the Soviet Union. The strike was highly organized and effective. After five days, the strike ended with nearly all of the workers' demands satisfied by the company. Wages were immediately raised by as much as 50 per cent.[45] More importantly, the Pingxiang Railway and Mining Company agreed to provide a monthly subsidy of 1,100 yuan to the workers' club, a significant amount given that a miner's salary at the time was 5 yuan per month and a skilled railway worker's salary 15 yuan per month.[46] The workers' club moved into a newly renovated four-storey building. The main hall, modelled on the Bolshoi Theatre in Moscow, could seat more than 2,000 people.[47] Between 1922 and 1925, an impressive array of educational and cultural activities was organized by the club to impress upon the workers basic tenets of Marxism and cultivate a collective class consciousness.

One form of activity – known as a "costume lecture (*huazhuang yanjiang*)"[48] – was especially popular. According to Elizabeth Perry,

> the workers' club oversaw the writing and staging of thirty-one "costume lectures" ... a hybrid form of didactic entertainment that was part drama and part lecture. With moralistic titles such as "The Road to Awakening," "The Evils of Prostitution and Gambling," "The Patriotic Bandit," and "Our Victory," the costume lectures were presented in evening performances in the workers' club auditorium to enthusiastic audiences numbering a thousand or more.[49]

An article on the Pingxiang Communist Party's website, titled "Costume Lectures Showing Magical Results," details one performance vividly:

> One day, after learning that lectures were going to be delivered at the club, workers gathered in the auditorium excitedly, packing all three floors. Silence filled the hall as the workers waited for the lecture to begin. Comrade Xiao Jinguang was supposed to be the speaker, but at this critical moment, he was nowhere to be seen. Comrades in the lecture department tried to locate him anxiously. Workers in the auditorium became agitated. Suddenly, a man wearing a warlord uniform

appeared on the stage, chasing and beating a worker. The auditorium instantly exploded, like water dropped in hot oil.

Workers were infuriated. Many raised their fists and started to curse the warlord. At this moment, the "warlord" took off his hat and addressed the audience in a heroic voice: "Comrades, brothers, the warlords have brought us so much pain: endless wars, battles everywhere, pillages and rapes, exorbitant taxes and levies. We are suffering, and they are revelling."

Hearing this, workers wondered, "How come the warlord is speaking for us?"

The man on stage continued: "Now some warlords are butchering our fellow workers, cracking down on them without mercy. What should we do? Should we fight for freedom, even if death awaits? Or kneel down before their terror, begging for life?"

All the workers raised their angry fists, shouting:

"Down with the Warlords!"

"Long Live the Proletariat!"

"Fight for freedom! Never beg to live!"

The lecture ended with these thunderous slogans. When the speaker took off his costume, people realized that he was actually Xiao Jinguang! The director of the workers' club, Liu Shaoqi, came up with a hearty smile, "Fortunately you started to speak for the workers; otherwise, workers would have come onstage to thrash you."

People burst into laughter.[50]

Xiao Jinguang (1903–89), the head of the entertainment department of the workers' club, was also a young communist returnee from the Soviet Union. Later, he would become one of the leaders of the Red Army and, after 1949, the Commander of the Chinese Navy.

To gain wider support for the communist agenda, the workers also went to nearby villages to perform for the peasants. One worker recalled of the costume lectures:

Whenever we arrived someplace, the band members would beat drums and play trumpets and flutes to attract a crowd. Then we would perform a program, after which there would be a lecture on how the capitalists exploited the workers, how the landlords exploited the peasants, how we should strike down imperialism and militarism, and so on. It was warmly welcomed by the peasants.[51]

Even the Nationalists acknowledged the effectiveness of "red education" conducted by the workers' club:

Every week for the workers they prepared political reports, popular lectures, costume lectures, debate sessions, research meetings and so on. Communism was

propagated through these opportunities for the workers. So their form of education for Anyuan workers was completely inspirational, like colourful and exotic
magic, educating common workers so as to trap them, poison them, without their
noticing![52]

It is important to note that the costume lectures were produced in Anyuan
by members of the workers' club – who had no professional training in theatre – for workers and peasants in the region, whose previous exposure to
theatre was limited to traditional operas produced by local troupes. The symmetry of amateurism was sustained by a shared cultural language and class
identification.

Grass Stage, the theatre group that produced *World Factory*, also organ-
izes itself as an amateur group and takes pride in its amateurism. The name
"Grass Stage," a phrase already in circulation during the Qing Dynasty, refers
to informal troupes that travelled in the countryside and performed regional
opera on makeshift stages. Founded in 2005 by writer Zhao Chuan,[53] who had
lived in Australia during the 1990s, Grass Stage is a loose collective, based in
Shanghai, open to anyone interested in what Zhao calls "social theatre (*shehui
juchang*)."[54] Yu Lingna and Lu Lu, who played the clown and counsellor Mr.
Lu, respectively, in the opening scene of *World Factory*, both work as mental
health counsellors in real life. Ding Bo, who played the Director and various
other roles, runs a contemporary art consultancy in Shanghai and used to work
at OCAT, the art centre where the play was performed. Although much of the
preparatory research was conducted by Zhao, the play was developed by the
group collectively.

World Factory, like the costume lectures developed in Anyuan in the 1920s,
aimed to make visible the real life conditions of the working class and to
present to the audience an alternative social imaginary. However, one major
difference between *World Factory* and the costume lectures in the early twentieth century lies in how the causes of workers' sufferings are characterized
and how audiences' emotions are summoned. Whereas the costume lectures
in Anyuan always featured characters from two opposing social classes in
confrontation – workers against capitalists, peasants against landlords – and
performed explicit scenes of exploitation and physical abuse, *World Factory*
lacked any character who could be described as inherently evil. Scene four,
titled "Hands in the Assembly Line," began with the New Industrialist delivering a monologue: "I have seen many hands, many startling hands, incomplete hands, handless hands ... not in Manchester, but in Guangdong, China."
She recalled, in a solemn tone, the conversation she had with a young man
whose hand was severely injured. Then seven actors wearing workers' uniforms re-enacted body movements required of assembly-line workers, while
chanting the moves (figure 16.5).

16.5 Actors as assembly-line workers in Grass Stage's *World Factory* in Shenzhen, 22 November 2014.

> WORKER A: Knock on three connectors; place it in lathe; press button. Thread red string through three covered wires; push button. Thread copper wire through plastic tube; put on plastic connector. Put on three plastic connectors in different colours. Turn on power; check reading; check noise level; stick on compliance label.
>
> ...
>
> GROUP: Our hands, ten hours repeating the same thing ... every move precisely measured by stopwatch. No smile, no sigh, no break, no breath.

Who should be blamed for causing this misery? Terry Guo,[55] who founded Foxconn in 1974 and now claims a net worth of US$6.5 billion,[56] more than a million years of a worker's salary? Or the factory managers who practice Taylorism and enforce a military culture every day? Or those of us who buy iPhones, iPads, Kindles, PlayStations, all manufactured by Foxconn? We have moved from condemning capitalism and capitalists to condemning capitalism only. It is the "system" that enslaves us; it is uncool to name names.[57]

The fundamental impetus for the Anyuan workers' movement in the early 1920s was a claim to human dignity. The slogan of the 1922 general strike – "Once beasts of burden, now we will be men!"[58] – continued to serve as the central theme of subsequent cultural activism. The desire for dignity was translated into indignation, outpourings of collective anger. As we saw

earlier in the costume lectures, rousing the workers was as important as educating them. Xiao Jinguang first tricked the workers into believing they were
watching a real situation where a warlord was beating a worker. Witnessing
a physical attack is far more likely to activate immediate physiological and
emotional responses than listening to a verbal description of an attack. Next,
Xiao appealed to reason through speech. He then gave the audience another
opportunity to express their anger collectively by calling for a ritualized
performance of shouting slogans. Anger served "as an instrument of truth,
pointing out injustices, betrayals, and false state of affairs, and seeking to even
scores" and "promised to undermine false structures of power and reveal the
true nature of humanity."[59]

Frustration, despair, and sadness – instead of anger – was the dominant
mood in *World Factory*. In scene five, "A Shriek, Bodily Pain," a female worker,
played by Wu Meng, kept jumping rope to the point of exhaustion, while
recounting her nightmare:

> Every night I had the same dream: I saw myself walking towards the harbour,
> wanting to get on a ferry to cross a river. It was this river that had separated me
> from my child ... I helplessly watched the boat leaving shore. But my body couldn't
> move, pain and enervation.

In scene seven, "Cities Not Near, Homes But Far," Wu Jiamin, playing a child
of migrant worker parents, gave the most passionate performance in the entire
play. With a noticeable accent, he recalled how he was shuttled between different homes, taken care of by different relatives, and invariably laughed at by
schoolmates. He became increasingly agitated and began to march on stage
and sing the "Military Anthem of the People's Liberation Army." Four actors
entered in silence, gradually enclosing Wu, who continued to march and sing.
He sang to his utmost capacity for a torturously long while, eventually giving
up in desperation. For the finale, all the actors came onto the stage. As countless
blue paper dolls rained down, they danced and sang:

> Your anger has nowhere to hide
> Done with being a grain of dirt
> Done with floating nowhere
> Done with seeing them high up there
> Done with their bullshit
> Done with powerless desperation
> Done with careless existence
> Done with drawing cakes to stave off hunger
> Done with life as a dream
> Quit! Quit! Quit![60]

They sang to us, the audience, who sat there clapping. Despite the word "anger" in the lyric, no one seemed to be enraged. No collective shouting. No roaring.

In *The Vehement Passions*, Philip Fisher notes that "in anger an outward-streaming energy, active, fully engaging the will and demonstrating the most explosive self-centred claims on the world and on others, makes clear the relation of the passion to spiritedness ... to motion, to confidence, and to self-expression in the world."[61] Revolutions would not be possible without sufficient rage. Katerina Clark's chapter two in this volume shows that, during the interwar period, the "unstoppable revolutionary 'roar'" was a defining theme in literature, theatre, and film in the entire Comintern sphere, from Shanghai to Moscow to Berlin. Xiaobing Tang's chapter eight demonstrates that the pedagogical and affective form central to "costume lectures" in Anyuan in the 1920s was also crucial to the street theatre movement in the 1930s. As he describes vividly, often the audience "shouted in unison" and "burst out singing," joining with the performers to "publicly perform [their] national allegiance." As Clark summarizes, the "deafening roar" was a symbol of "massive revolutionary resistance." Collective, defiant anger literally functioned as a powerful weapon.

But the mood after revolution may completely change. As Andrew Stauffer suggests, after the onset of Terror (1793–94), the discourse that equated anger to justice during the French Revolution collapsed, "making way for a Romantic-era world in which 'virtue was regarded as an outgrowth of the exercise of the will, guided by reason, aimed at disciplining passions' rather than encouraging them."[62] Perhaps we could identify a similar pattern in twentieth-century China. After communist revolution succeeded there in 1949, Mao and the Party elite repeatedly manipulated revolutionary zeal for their utopian agenda and for power struggles. After over two and a half decades of unfulfilled passion, anger gradually lost its association with seeking justice and became synonymous with unjustifiable violence. When Deng Xiaoping gained power after the Cultural Revolution, he dramatically revamped not only the Party's economic and political policy but also its emotional pitch. Calm, calculative managers replaced passionate, fearless soldiers as heroes in both official propaganda and popular media. "Scientific development" and "harmonious society" were enshrined into the official canon. The state has become extremely vigilant against any collective emotional expression.[63] It would be too risky for Grass Stage to invite the audience to a session of slogan shouting, such as Xiao Jinguang did in Anyuan a century ago.

The lack of anger is not unique to contemporary Chinese culture. Brian Holmes recently remarked that "there has been a real decline in the capacity of artists to arouse outrage at both alienation and exploitation. The ideological force of neoliberal culture has been amazingly effective."[64] A key question is how collective affect-making – a vital element of Comintern aesthetics – can be revived as an essential strategy in contemporary socially engaged art.

Answers to this question will not emerge through theoretical investigation alone. As several authors in this volume have articulated, the social forms of cultural activism – whether theatre is enacted in a playhouse or on a street corner, whether artists work alone or shoulder-to-shoulder with other revolutionary agents – matter. The difference between autonomous art and committed art lies not so much in the ontological qualities of the artworks – as Adorno framed it – but in the social processes of cultural production and reception. Furthermore, autonomous art seems to be structurally congruent with the bourgeois form of publicness (rational-critical debate, as Habermas theorized), while committed art seems to be linked to antagonistic forms of publicness practiced by the proletariat, feminists, and queers.[65] While the bourgeois form of publicness hinges on detached, critical judgment of the free individual, counterpublic forms materialize as collective, performative, and affective modes of expression. Therefore, in order to discover strategies of collective affect-making, we need to practice in a counterpublic and "committed" mode.

In 1920s Anyuan, Xiao Jinguang and his comrades demonstrated a much higher level of commitment to their revolutionary cause – and a higher level of skillfulness in creating affective situations – than we socially engaged artists today. As mentioned earlier, more than thirty costume lectures were produced in Anyuan over a period of three years. Performances were staged regularly to crowds in the thousands, in both the workers' club and neighbouring villages. The practitioners were concerned not about creating artworks that could withstand the critic's judgment, but about cultivating a new class consciousness among the workers in the audience. It was critical that the costume lectures and other cultural events were thoroughly integrated with the club's political and economic endeavours; in other words, they were situated in a revolutionary movement. Much of today's socially engaged art occurs in the so-called "art world." Most artists aspire to create unique, one-off projects. Few are capable of working with other activists to produce extensive campaigns. These art projects might be congruent with the vision of a certain social movement; nevertheless, they remain detached organizationally. While we want to effect real change, we are afraid of being swallowed by movements, afraid of losing autonomy. Is it possible to harvest social change without sustained, intense, and iterative cultural labour that is fundamentally oppositional to art as intellectual and financial property? Could our paranoia about situatedness be a historical over-reaction to authoritarianism?

Practising situatedness, without degenerating into assimilation, is extremely difficult. The fear of artists being made servants to instrumental politics is not unfounded. A fundamental problem in Mao Zedong's 1942 Yan'an talk, which continues to govern the Chinese Party-state's cultural policy, is a hierarchical outlook concerning the revolutionary alliance. Even though intellectuals and urban petit bourgeois are part of "the people," they are considered inferior to workers, peasants, and soldiers. Rather than welcoming the tension between intellectuals and other revolutionary bodies as a healthy and even necessary force for liberation, Mao commanded that art be "subordinated to the revolutionary tasks set by the Party in a given revolutionary period."[66]

World Factory was able to bring the urban middle class, intellectuals, and migrant workers under one roof. The inclusion of Xu Duo (of New Workers Art Troupe) in the cast symbolized the alliance between blue-collar and white-collar workers. Sitting in the audience that evening were art enthusiasts (the usual visitors to the art centre), intellectuals (including Wang Hui, a renowned New Left scholar from Beijing), and migrant workers (invited by a number of labour NGOs). After the performance, Zhao Chuan, the founder of Grass Stage, facilitated a discussion that lasted for more than an hour. Among those who spoke, many were workers and labour activists. They were eager to confirm the play's truth value, testifying to workers' sufferings with personal stories. One worker from Foxconn proposed that international laws be written to ensure workers around the world are paid standard salaries, so that factories cannot keep moving to places with cheaper labour. By contrast, a few non-worker speakers questioned the play's theoretical framing (the exclusion of other forms of labour) and its artistic power (the failure to connect with the audience emotionally). The workers and non-workers focused on different aspects of the play and did not bond easily into a brotherly community. But this to me was fortunate. While we should forge an alliance between different sections of the working people, we should not suppress disagreement as Mao did, and as the Party-state continues to do. One historical lesson we should extract from twentieth-century Chinese revolution and Comintern aesthetics more broadly is that artists and intellectuals should not become workers, but work "with" workers to discover a new political consciousness and a new aesthetic practice.[67]

Much of Chinese contemporary art, since its emergence in the late 1970s, has indulged in reprocessing revolutionary iconography and rhetoric, devoid of revolutionary practice. How did Mao become the most lucrative icon and the vehicle for excessive capital? One reason is the Chinese state's practice of *mingzuo shiyou*: nominally left and pragmatically right. It clings onto socialist imagery and speech monopoly while pushing forward state capitalism. Revolutionary iconography was severed from revolutionary practice. It flows into the air, acquiring a nostalgic and orientalist chic. Only when the language of revolution finds a new social body that possesses the potential for revolutionary practice can it regain vitality and threaten the political-financial-military elite.

Zhao Chuan, Xu Duo, and their colleagues took considerable risks to make public the underbelly of the Chinese miracle and initiate a cross-class conversation. We were afforded a glimpse of the potential for a renewed revolutionary alliance. While we celebrate the resurgence of socially engaged art in China, we have to consider the following questions carefully in light of twentieth-century revolutionary practice: Can socially engaged art bring about significant social change without being situated in a sustained, intense, and widespread cultural-social movement? Can a cultural-social movement come into being without anger? How can we move beyond the question of committed art versus autonomous art and focus on the pressing task of building a new world culture for a new alliance of all working people, in opposition to the aesthetic regime of the global political-financial-military elite?

NOTES

This chapter was partially supported by a grant from the Research Grants Council of the Hong Kong Special Administrative Region, China [Project No 21403014]. Translation from Chinese to English is done by the author, unless otherwise noted.

1 王德志 (*Wang Dezhi*).
2 孙恒 (*Sun Heng*).
3 许多 (*Xu Duo*).
4 迷笛音乐学校 (*Midi yinyue xuexiao*).
5 The group first called themselves "Young Migrant Worker Art Troupe" (打工青年艺术团) and later changed their name to "New Worker Art Troupe" (新工人艺术团).
6 One Heart Experimental School (同心实验学校).
7 2013 年全国农民工监测调查报告. The Chinese National Bureau of Statistics report can be found online at http://www.stats.gov.cn/tjsj/zxfb/201405/t20140512_551585.html (accessed 13 March 2015).
8 天下打工是一家 (*tianxia dagong shi yijia*).
9 Original: 你来自四川，我来自河南 / 你来自东北，他来自安徽 / 无论我们来自何方 / 都一样的要靠打工为生 / 你来搞建筑，我来做家政 / 你来做小买卖，他来做服务生 / 无论我们从事着哪一行啊 / 只为了求生存走到一起来 / 打工的兄弟们手牵着手 / 打工的旅途中不再有烦忧/ 雨打风吹都不怕 / 天下打工兄弟姐妹们是一家. The first twelve lines are based on Frederick Lau's translation, with some revisions. See Frederick Lau, "Rise Up and Dream: New Work Songs for the New China," in *This Thing Called Music: Essays in Honor of Bruno Nettl*, ed. Victoria Lindsay Levine and Philip Bohlman (Lanham, MD: Rowman & Littlefield, 2015), 427.
10 天下工人是一家 (*tianxia gongren shi yijia*).
11 朱宝庭 (*Zhu Baoting*).
12 董锄平 (*Dong Chuping*).
13 S.A. Smith, *A Road Is Made: Communism in Shanghai, 1920–1927* (Honolulu: University of Hawaii Press, 2000), 38.

14 陈潭秋 (*Chen Tanqiu*).

15 Original: 五一节，真壮烈 / 世界工人大团结 / 发起芝加哥 / 响应遍各国 / 西欧东亚与美洲 / 年年溅满劳工血 / 不达成功誓不休 / 望大家，齐努力 / 切莫辜负五一节.

16 长辛店劳动补习学校 (*Changxindian laodong buxi xuexiao*).

17 Original: 美哉自由，世界明星 / 拼吾热血，为他牺牲 / 要把强权制度一切扫除净 / 记取五月一日之良辰 / 红旗飞舞，走光明路 / 各尽所能，各取所需 / 不分贫富贵贱，责任唯互助 / 愿大家努力齐进取.

18 安源路矿工人俱乐部之歌 (*Anyuan lukuang gongren julebu zhi ge*).

19 The Anyuan Workers' Club was founded in 1922. "Anyuan Workers' Club Song" was included in the 1964 musical *The East Is Red*, thus gaining its status as part of the communist canon.

20 Original: 被污辱的是我劳工 / 被压迫的是我劳工 / 世界啊，我们来创造 / 压迫啊，我们来解除 / 创造世界除压迫 / 显出我们的威风 / 联合我劳工，团结我劳工 / 劳工，劳工，应做世界主人翁 / 应做世界主人翁.

21 瞿秋白 (*Qu Qiubai*).

22 萧三 (*Xiao San*).

23 Qu Qiubai's translation: 起来，受人污辱咒骂的！起来，天下饥寒的奴隶！满腔热血沸腾，拼死一战决矣。旧社会破坏得彻底，新社会创造得光华。莫道我们一钱不值，从今要普有天下。这是我们的，最后决死争，同英德纳雄纳尔，人类方重兴！这是我们的，最后决死争，同英德纳雄纳尔，人类方重兴！不论是英雄，不论是天皇老帝，谁也解放不得我们，只靠我们自己。要扫尽万重的压迫，争取自己的权利。趁这洪炉火热，正好发愤锤砺。只有伟大的劳动军，只有我世界的劳工，有这权利享用大地；那里容得寄生虫！霹雳声巨雷忽震，残暴贼灭迹销声。看！光华万丈，照耀我红日一轮。

    Xiao San's translation: 起来，饥寒交迫的奴隶！起来，全世界受苦的人！满腔的热血已经沸腾，要为真理而斗争！旧世界打个落花流水，奴隶们起来，起来！不要说我们一无所有，我们要做天下的主人！这是最后的斗争，团结起来到明天，英特纳雄耐尔，就一定要实现！这是最后的斗争，团结起来到明天，英特纳雄耐尔，就一定要实现！从来就没有什么救世主，也不靠神仙皇帝。要创造人类的幸福，全靠我们自己！我们要夺回劳动果实，让思想冲破牢笼！快把那炉火烧得通红，趁热打铁才会成功！是谁创造了人类世界？是我们劳动群众！一切归劳动者所有，哪能容得寄生虫！最可恨那些毒蛇猛兽，吃尽了我们的血肉！一旦把它们消灭干净，鲜红的太阳照遍全球！

24 "March for My Beloved" lyrics: 임을 위한 행진곡 / 사랑도 명예도 이름도 남김없이 / 한평생 나가자던 뜨거운 맹세 / 동지는 간데없고 깃발만 나부껴 / 새 날이 올때까지 흔들리지 말자 / 세월은 흘러가도 산천은 안다 / 깨어나서 외치는 뜨거운 함성 / 앞서서 나가니 산자여 따르라 / 앞서서 나가니 산자여 따르라. English translation: March for My Beloved/ Without love, or honour, or even a name to pass on/ One's whole life to push forward, a fervent

pledge/ Our comrades are gone, and only a banner waves/ Until a new day dawns, let's never sway/ Although time goes, mountains and streams know/ Awakening, we call out, a fervent battle cry/ I'll go on ahead, and you, the living, follow!/ I'll go on ahead, and you, the living, follow!

25   黑手那卡西 (*heishou nakaxi*).

26   "Workers' Battle Song" (劳动者战歌) lyrics: 全国的劳动者啊，勇敢地站出来。为了我们的权益，不怕任何牺牲。反剥削争平等，我的同志们。为了明天的胜利，誓死战斗到底。杀杀！English translation: Workers of the entire country, come forward with courage/ For our rights, fear no sacrifice/ Against exploitation and strive for equality, my comrades/ For tomorrow's victory, swear to fight to the end/ Fight, fight!

27   "Workers' Glory Song" (劳动者赞歌) lyrics: 离开了亲人和朋友，踏上了征战的路途，为了生活而奔波，为了理想而奋斗。我们不是一无所有，我们有智慧和双手，我们用智慧和双手，建起大街桥梁和高楼。风里来雨里走，一刻不停留，汗也撒泪也流，昂起头向前走。我们的幸福和权利，要靠我们自己去争取。劳动创造了这个世界，劳动者最光荣！从昨天到今天到永远 – – 劳动者最光荣！English translation: Farewell relatives and friends, embark on the road of battle/ For life we hurry, for ideals we struggle/ We are not broken; we have wisdom and hands/ We use wisdom and hands to erect bridges and buildings/ Coming in wind and going in rain, not stopping for a moment/ Sweat breaking and tears flowing, charging forward with head high/ Our rights and our happiness to obtain on our own/ Labour created this world; labourers are the most glorious!/ From yesterday to today and forever, labourers are the most glorious!

28   用歌声呐喊 以文艺维权 (*yong gesheng nahn, yi wenyi weiquan*).

29   Lau, "Rise Up and Dream," 426.

30   Lin Chun, "The Language of Class in China," in *Transforming Classes: Socialist Register 2015*, ed. Leo Panitch and Greg Albo (New York: Monthly Review Press, 2014), 24.

31   华侨城创意文化园 (*Huaqiaocheng chuangyi wenhuayuan*).

32   OCT当代艺术中心 (*dangdai yishu zhongxin*). OCT stands for Overseas Chinese Town (华侨城 *Huaqiaocheng*). OCT is a state-owned conglomerate headquartered in Shenzhen, with annual revenue over 50 billion RMB (US$8 billion). OCT Contemporary Art Terminal (OCAT) was set up by OCT in 2005.

33   世界工厂 (*shijie gongchang*).

34   草台班 (*Caotaiban*).

35   和这世界谈恋爱 (*he zheshijie tanlian'ai*).

36   Original: 多美丽，多美丽/ 这个世界真美丽/ 就像橱窗里的商品/ 但你无法触摸到/ 为什么，为什么/ 有人绝望地离去/ 是我们放弃了世界/ 还是世界背叛了我们/ 要忍耐，要忍耐/ 这么多年一直在忍耐/ 我们没有时间去悲伤/ 我们要继续和这世界谈恋爱.

37 Mimi Lau, "Struggle for Foxconn Girl Who Wanted to Die," *South China Morning Post*, 15 December 2010, https://www.scmp.com/article/733389/struggle-fox-conn-girl-who-wanted-die (accessed 13 March 2015).

38 Original: 我们的斗争神圣而正义／ 前进向前进工人兄弟. English lyrics are available at http://www.dhr.history.vt.edu/modules/eu/mod03_1917/evidence_detail_35.html (accessed 29 March 2015).

39 Theodor Adorno, "Commitment," in Theodor Adorno et al., *Aesthetics and Politics* (London: Verso, 1980), 180.

40 Ibid., 183.

41 Ibid., 190, 191.

42 Lambert Zuidervaart, "Theodor W. Adorno," in *The Stanford Encyclopedia of Philosophy, ed.* Edward N. Zalta (Winter 2015 edition), http://plato.stanford.edu/archives/win2015/entries/adorno/ (accessed on 9 May 2016); quote in section 4, "Aesthetic Theory."

43 Ibid.

44 Elizabeth Perry, *Anyuan: Mining China's Revolutionary Tradition* (Berkeley: University of California Press, 2012), 19–20.

45 Ibid., 75.

46 Ibid., 79.

47 Ibid., 82–3.

48 化妆演讲 (*huazhuang yanjiang*).

49 Perry, *Anyuan*, 96.

50 The description of this "costume lecture" at the Anyuan Workers' Club in the 1920s can be found online at http://www.pxdj.gov.cn/List.asp?C-1-264.html (accessed 20 March 2015).

51 Pingxiang Municipal Party Committee, ed., *Anyuan lukuang gongren yundong* [Anyuan railway and mine workers' movement] (Beijing: Communist Party Historical Materials Press, 1990), 2:941, quoted in Perry, *Anyuan*, 96–7.

52 共党在安源教育概况 (*Gongdang zai Anyuan jiaoyu zhuangkuang*) [Summary of the Communist Party's education in Anyuan], cited in 安源团 [Anyuan Youth League], online at http://www.baike.com/wiki/%E5%AE%89%E6%BA%90%E5%9B%A2 (accessed 29 March 2015).

53 赵川 (*Zhao Chuan*).

54 社会剧场 (*shehui juchang*).

55 郭台铭 (*Guo Taiming*).

56 "#257: Terry Gou: CEO Hon Hai Precision," *Forbes*, https://www.forbes.com/profile/terry-gou/#50768ac55fbc (accessed 4 April 2015).

57 The only exception I have encountered in recent years is artist Andrea Fraser's 2011 essay "L'1%, C'est Moi," in which she goes through *ARTnews* magazine's list of top collectors in the world and lists their crimes and shady behaviours one by one. Her essay was first published in *Texte zur Kunst* in August 2011 and then

made available online for the 2012 Whitney Biennial, https://whitney.org/exhibitions/2012-biennial/andrea-fraser (accessed 1 September 2014).

58 Original: 从前是牛马，现在要做人！

59 Andrew Stauffer, *Anger, Revolution, and Romanticism* (Cambridge: Cambridge University Press, 2005), 6, 8.

60 Original: 。。。你的愤怒已无处可逃 /习惯像一颗尘埃了吗？ /习惯被飘来荡去了吗？ /习惯他们高高在上吗？ /习惯他们在那扯淡吗？ /习惯无力改变的茫然吗？ /习惯无所谓存不存在吗？ /习惯被画饼充饥了吗？ /习惯人生如梦了吗？ /不干了－－不干了－－不干了！。。。

61 Philip Fisher, *The Vehement Passions* (Princeton, NJ: Princeton University Press, 2009), 13–14.

62 Stauffer, *Anger*, 11–12.

63 See, for example, Gary King, Jennifer Pan, and Margaret Roberts, "How Censorship in China Allows Government Criticism but Silences Collective Expression," *American Political Science Review* 107, no. 2 (2013): 1–18, https://gking.harvard.edu/publications/how-censorship-china-allows-government-criticism-silences-collective-expression.

64 Marco Deseriis and Brian Holmes, "Concerning Art and Social Change," *Mute*, 4 February 2009, http://www.metamute.org/editorial/articles/concerning-art-and-social-change.

65 Jürgen Habermas, *The Structural Transformation of the Public Sphere: An Inquiry into a Category of Bourgeois Society*, trans. Thomas Burger (Cambridge, MA: MIT Press, 1989). For publicness practised by the proletariat, see Oskar Negt and Alexander Kluge, Public Sphere and Experience: Toward an Analysis of the Bourgeois and Proletarian Public Sphere, trans. Peter Labanyi et al. (Minneapolis: University of Minnesota Press, 1993). For feminist practice, see Nancy Fraser, "Rethinking the Public Sphere: A Contribution to the Critique of Actually Existing Democracy," Social Text 25 (1990): 56–80. For queer practice, see Michael Warner, Publics and Counterpublics (New York: Zone Books, 2005).

66 Mao Zedong, "Talks at the Yenan [Yan'an] Forum on Literature and Art" (1942) in *Mao Zedong Xuanji*, vol. 3 [Selected works of Mao Zedong, vol. 3, 2nd ed.] (Beijing: People's Literature Publishing House, 1991). English available online at https://www.marxists.org/reference/archive/mao/selected-works/volume-3/mswv3_08.htm.

67 Would we be able to build enough commitment without an impending crisis? Colonial invasions and the potential demise of China compelled the formation of a people's alliance in the first half of the twentieth century. Perhaps this time around we will be galvanized by ecological crises.

Coda

STEVEN S. LEE
UC Berkeley

AMELIA M. GLASER
UC San Diego

In April 2015, most of the volume's contributors convened at the University of California, Berkeley to discuss their first drafts. At the time, "Comintern aesthetics" implied for us a broad network of radical writers and artists inspired by the promise of a Soviet-led world revolution. From the outset, as the introduction indicates, we defined the term vis-à-vis existing models of world literature and culture, most notably Pascale Casanova's *World Republic of Letters*. Casanova posits Paris as the centre of this republic due to the city's unrivalled literary resources, but also to "the exceptional nature of the French Revolution" and its association with both political and cultural blossoming.[1] At the Berkeley conference, we discussed the Soviet Union and the Bolshevik Revolution as grounds for a more radical world republic; and here we followed the lead of scholars of the internationalist left, including Katerina Clark, Michael Denning, and Rossen Djagalov, whose work has helped to situate twentieth-century communism beyond Cold War divides. However, the sheer variety of contexts covered by our contributors quickly made clear the pitfalls of simply replacing a Parisian centre with a Muscovite one. As scholars working between Slavic and other literary traditions, we quickly recognized that a large part of our task in editing this volume involved bridging persistent disciplinary lines separating the largely Cold War–grounded discipline of Russian literary studies from the broader field of leftist literary studies. We viewed this project as transnational and translocal, for the overarching Marxist ideology that united the Comintern applied both to established nations and to stateless groups residing in a variety of spaces and places.[2]

Several questions arose at the conference. What did we mean by "Comintern" – the organization launched under Lenin, the collaborative United Front period of 1922–27, the hard-line Third Period of 1928–33, the renewed collaboration of the Popular Front? And what aesthetics – modernism, avant-garde, realism, socialist realism? Our guiding principle has been to keep the term as ecumenical as possible: the aesthetics under consideration arose during the early years of the Communist International but have remained influential long after the organization's formal dissolution in 1943. Moreover, we have attempted to assemble a large variety of artistic forms, including works centring on and works breaking free from the Soviet Union. As a whole, then, much of the work of this volume has involved questioning the binaries that typically come to mind when discussing aesthetics alongside communism: most prominently modernism versus (socialist) realism, but also the ostensibly corresponding divides between experimentation and dogmatism, internationalism and autarchy, ecumenicism and sectarianism. These divides, especially when considered together, do not withstand sustained scrutiny. For instance, the 1934 Soviet Writers' Congress witnessed not just the inauguration of socialist realism, but also the thorough celebration of national literatures and cultures, a fact that complicates com-mon-sense associations of socialist realism with dogmatism and autarchy. This interest in difference forces us to expand our understanding of socialist real-ism itself and consider its inclusive, ecumenical potential, particularly at its inception. Likewise, historians have shown how the Comintern of the Third Period (the Comintern at its most sectarian) witnessed the organization's most sustained appeal among anti-imperialist and anti-racist activists around the world. That is, the Comintern embraced colonized peoples as part of the global proletariat at the same time that it turned against the anti-Stalinist left both in and outside the Soviet Union. Sectarianism here coincides simultaneously with autarchy and heightened internationalism, underscoring how the Comintern could mean different things in different contexts. In turn, the fact that, for example, African Americans localized and altered communism for their own specific needs opens the possibility that something similar could occur not only beyond but also within the Soviet Union, particularly in the peripheries far from Moscow.[3] To be sure, Soviet-centred celebrations of nationhood were, on the one hand, a means of exerting control. However, Soviet nationalities pol-icy and the Comintern's outreach to the world's colonized and oppressed also initiated conversations about how to align nation and class within a Marxist framework – conversations that arguably laid the groundwork for postwar postcolonialism. The lines between interwar and postwar, world revolution and local struggle here fall away.

Having thus disrupted such time-worn binaries, we are left with a wide-ranging "communist ecumene" and the problems of scale and translation that this implies.[4] If the Soviet-centred Comintern itself only lasted as a bureaucratic entity between 1919 and 1943, the utopian art that the organization fostered would continue to thrive, inform, inspire. At the core of the Comintern was a translocal proletarian movement that used art and literature to imagine and spread communist ideology, aiming to consolidate a worldwide revolutionary class. Individual practitioners simultaneously sought new forms and borrowed existing forms, from realism to the avant-garde to documentary accounts, to convey messages that were broadly construed as revolutionary. If rallying established artists to convey a revolutionary message using techniques honed in the avant-garde – the storage of new wine in old bottles – was itself paradoxical, then all the more paradoxical was the central mission of exalting core political principles of anti-imperialism and the empowerment of the worker while making room for a diversity of national and ethnic voices – including members of religious groups that had, at various points, participated in reinforcing oppressive social hierarchies. As the vanguard of a revolutionary organization, Comintern-aligned artists and writers had no choice but to contend with disruptions and paradoxes that separated established linguistic and artistic traditions on the ground from utopian visions of a proletarian, anti-colonialist world order.

What we have concluded from the process of assembling this exemplary (if far from exhaustive) set of case studies is that, if there is a mode that can be stably identified with Comintern aesthetics, it is one that centres on sharing local genres of proletarian and anti-colonialist art through cultural translation and localization. What unites the different expressions of Comintern aesthetics is the necessity of forging a unified revolutionary class from vastly disparate material and cultural experiences so that it could overthrow capitalism across various localities. The writers and artists who attempted to visualize and spread the aesthetics of communist internationalism were thus negotiating the kind of cultural translational choice that Homi Bhabha has identified as a product of migration and globalization. Indeed, the Comintern represented its own urge towards globalization, and one that prompts us to consider global networks outside those traditionally associated with capitalist modernity. For artists and writers during the period of the Comintern, this choice presented itself as one between adapting the messages of the Party to their own cultures or adapting their own cultural needs to Party concerns.[5] In most instances of Comintern aesthetics, as in translation, the practitioner had to do a bit of both. If the Comintern's organizational and symbolic centre was Moscow and the Soviet Union, then the literature and art that supported, radiated from, and interacted with this centre necessitated the practice of literary translation, as well as localized adaptations of texts and other artistic products.[6] Thus, Marxism could be adapted to the specific needs and goals of the peoples it served, and the Party itself could adapt to the needs of individual nations with a common ideology. For instance, writers in India and China translated key ideas from the workers' revolution to create connections between the Bolshevik Revolution and the struggles against imperialism taking place far from Europe. African American writers in postwar America addressed the issues facing domestic workers in terms translatable from proletarian ones. Yiddish communists likened discrimination against religious Jews during the Spanish Inquisition to the discrimination against communists in the Spanish Civil War. And, of course, literary translation was itself an important mode of spreading a burgeoning world revolutionary movement.[7]

An aspirational movement committed to reconciling the fissures of past and future is, by nature, confined to the process of becoming. This "becoming" is not unlike what Walter Benjamin referred to in his "The Task of the Translator" as the impossibility of a perfect translation, as well as what Giorgio Agamben would later identify as the paradox of pure language, by which "what is meant is permanently unsaid."[8] The Comintern, in its attempt to bridge a doctrinaire Leninist anti-nationalism with the national struggles inherent in anti-colonialism, is best approached as a project in constant change – as a moving target. Accordingly, Pheng Cheah has recently argued that both Marxism and world literature need to be understood vis-à-vis temporal becoming, as opposed to simply spatial dispersion. Cheah discerns through the "sheer persistence of time" teleologies and worldings that open alternatives to capitalist globalization and, thus, restore to world literature (specifically the postcolonial novel in this case) its normative force, its ability to transform rather than merely reflect world systems.[9] This opening of alternatives has been precisely the aim of *Comintern Aesthetics*: to reclaim world literature and culture's transformative potential via the creative shockwaves generated by an incomplete but still resonant world revolution – the Comintern's decades-long disruption (both actual and symbolic) of capitalism and colonialism.

Many of the questions – aesthetic and identitarian – that the volume poses remain quite relevant to practitioners of radical and socially engaged art. Even as new media has given rise to experimental art forms not in circulation during the period of the Comintern, contemporary artists and critics continue to ask what the relationship might be between existing art forms and current political concerns. As spelled out in the volume's introduction, the aesthetics best attuned to this ongoing relationship cannot be reduced to a single artistic form or style. Rather, the volume as a whole points to a sensory aesthetics that allows for critical cognition of historical and material forces, as well as an ability to register both the allure and failure of twentieth-century communism. Today the sense of failure has been heightened by ever-proliferating reminders of the world revolution's defeat, as well as of the only limited gains made by the various liberatory movements that prevailed in the West after the Second World War. Causes like human rights, civil rights, and liberal multiculturalism came to fill the void left by socialist internationalism, but these are now being openly questioned – not least by persistent strife and inequality along the lines of class, race, and gender.

As a result, an international, politically engaged community continues to ask questions about the lessons of Marxist internationalism for our fragmented present. Several of the volume's contributions make clear how the Comintern sought to relate proletarian revolution to struggles around race and nation. Similarly, Eric Blanc has noted how an important innovation of Leninist Marxism was the rejection of an earlier radical tolerance for anti-Semitism and a new commitment to defending cultural and religious minorities in the name of Marxism.[10] Here, the Comintern's legacy has the potential to point not only to the defence of minorities against police violence and migrants against wanton detention, but also to connect such seemingly disconnected struggles in response to a failing world system – one defined, in both the West and much of Eastern Europe, by deindustrialization, a prolonged economic slump, and the seeming absence of a revolutionary proletariat.[11] Instead, in many of these places, both East and West, the displacements and crises of global capitalism have triggered uncritical nostalgia for lost greatness and stability, masterfully manipulated by an ascendant cohort of authoritarian-minded politicians.

In contemporary Russia, such uncritical, restorative nostalgia has often had a Soviet bent, reinforcing the need for caution when revisiting twentieth-century communism. Svetlana Boym prescribes what she calls "reflective nostalgia," combining mourning and melancholia in ways that allow for considerations of the present and future, not just the past. However, in 2017, amid an array of international conferences and museum exhibitions commemorating the Bolshevik Revolution's centenary, there was a tendency to relegate revolution to the past – to regard the event itself as an academic concern or historical curiosity, and the artworks emerging from it purely as museum pieces.[12] Against such tendencies, a growing body of activist scholarship repositioning Marxism as a critique of neoliberal globalization has sought to dispel the "perfume of 1917" via decentralized forms of insurgency and insurgent culture.[13]

If the 2017 centennial prompted mixed emotions as to how the Bolshevik Revolution ought to be commemorated, the 2019 centenary of the founding of the Comintern presents an opportunity to think beyond the Russian Revolution. The founding of the Comintern, while indeed part and parcel of Russia's revolutionary process, marked an international effort to reorganize national categories, to celebrate human labour, and to fight injustice. To be sure, these lofty aims often crashed against the rocks of Stalinist realpolitik, but the Comintern's failings, along with its successes, connected figures across multiple state and national lines. In its international, translocal aspirations but also in its shortcomings, the Comintern thus allows us to extract a shared legacy of workers', anti-colonial, and anti-racist activism from the ruin of the past. Our hope is that a reappraisal of art and literature associated with the Comintern will remind us of this lost legacy of leftist internationalism – one of historical encounters and aesthetic forms that reverberate wide and long, beyond the sectarian debates that marked the organization's demise. Ultimately, the broad coalition of artists and activists captured in this volume – many of them excluded from Cold War–era canons – all sought equality over barbarism, but failed to pre-empt the global fascism of their time. For our own time, Comintern aesthetics reminds us of a broad, sustained effort to think, feel, organize, and create on an international scale against historical catastrophe. Despite the difficulties of translating world revolution into local struggles, the will to cross these divides strikes us as the most crucial takeaway for the present.

This volume emerged out of conversations that we, as editors, shared in our individual work on leftist internationalism – Steven Lee on American and Soviet discourses of culture, revolution, and identity; and Amelia Glaser on the development of a Jewish literary internationalism that spanned continents. The project would not have been possible without the many conversations that have taken place with the contributors represented here and with colleagues and students who are actively engaged in understanding how leftist political structures changed art. In particular, we would like to thank those not included in the volume who served as brilliant discussants and speakers at the Berkeley conference: Emily Finer, Grace Lavery, Georgy Mamedov, Luis Martin-Cabrera, Eric Naiman, Sunyoung Park, and Dale Peterson. Steven Lee would also like to acknowledge the lively, multifaceted students in his Fall 2014 graduate seminar on "Comintern Modernisms," which helped to shape the project: Ernest Artiz, Jeehyun Choi, Thiti Jamkajornkeiat, Emily Laskin, Dominick Lawton, Poema Meyer, and Ariel Wind.

We are tremendously grateful to the University of California's Humanities Research Institute for granting us a short-term residency during which we assembled a second draft of this collection, as well as to the three graduate students who joined us in this process – Dominick Lawton and Daniel Valella of UC Berkeley and Teresa Kuruc of UC San Diego. Xiaojiao Wang, a graduate student at UC San Diego, joined us at a later stage for a second reading of the entire volume. We are grateful to a supportive and erudite editorial team at Toronto University Press, and want to thank, in particular, Mark Thompson, Robin Studniberg, and Carolyn Zapf. We would also like to extend our sincere gratitude to the many other sponsors of this long-running project. The April 2015 conference was hosted by Berkeley's Institute of International Studies and supported by the Institute of Slavic, East European, and Eurasian Studies (ISEEES), the Institute of East Asian Studies (IEAS), the Center for Korean Studies, the Townsend Center for the Humanities, the Department of English, the Institute for South Asia Studies, and the University of California Humanities Research Institute. ISEEES, IEAS, and the UC San Diego Jewish Studies program provided subventions for the volume's publication, with additional support from Berkeley English. Finally, we would like to thank our families, in particular Eran and Ina, for constantly reminding us to envision a better and more just world, always against the odds.

NOTES

1   Pascale Casanova, *The World Republic of Letters*, trans. M.B. DeBevoise (Cambridge, MA: Harvard University Press, 2004), 25.

2   For a collection of studies highlighting the translocal, as opposed to the transnational, see Tim Oakes and Louisa Schein, *Translocal China: Linkages, Identities and the Reimagining of Space* (London: Routledge, 2006); and Katherine Brickell and Ayona Datta, eds., *Translocal Geographies* (London: Routledge, 2016).

3   See Robin Kelley, *Hammer and Hoe: Alabama Communists during the Great Depression* (Chapel Hill: University of North Carolina Press, 1990). Beyond Ram's and Skakov's contributions to this volume, for recent discussions of Soviet modernity vis-à-vis Soviet peripheries, see Michael Kunichika, *"Our Native Antiquity": Archaeology and Aesthetics in the Culture of Russian Modernism* (Brighton, MA: Academic Studies Press, 2015); and Ivan Sablin, *Governing Post-Imperial Siberia and Mongolia, 1911–1924: Buddhism, Socialism, and Nationalism in State and Autonomy Building* (London: Routledge, 2016).

4   See Kris Manjapra, "Communist Internationalism and Transcolonial Recognition" in *Cosmopolitan Thought Zones: South Asia and the Global Circulation of Ideas*, ed. Kris Manjapra and Sugata Bose (New York: Palgrave Macmillan Transnational History, 2010), 159–77.

5   See Homi Bhabha, *The Location of Culture* (London: Routledge, 1994).

6   Anthony Pym has fruitfully theorized localization – a concept formerly reserved for software, products, and sometimes film – in its relationship to lexical translation. See Anthony Pym, *Exploring Translation Theories*, 2nd ed. (New York: Routledge, 2012).

7   Martin Puchner, *Poetry of the Revolution: Marx, Manifestos, and the Avant-Garde* (Princeton, NJ: Princeton University Press, 2005), 47–66.

8   Giorgio Agamben, "Language and History: Linguistic and Historical Categories in Benjamin's Thought," in *Potentialities: Collected Essays in Philosophy*, ed. and trans. Daniel Heller-Roazen (Stanford, CA: Stanford University Press, 1999), 48–61, quote at 54.

9   Pheng Cheah, *What Is a World?* (Durham, NC: Duke University Press, 2016), 8–9.

10 Eric Blanc, "Anti-Imperial Marxism: Borderland Socialists and the Evolution of Bolshevism on National Liberation," *International Socialist Review* 100 (Spring 2016), https://isreview.org/issue/100/anti-imperial-marxism.

11 For two views of the surplus populations that have emerged in the wake of mass industry and attempts to resituate race and nation vis-à-vis class, see "Brown v. Ferguson" and "Gather Us from among the Nations: The February 2014 Protests in Bosnia-Herzegovina," in *Endnotes* 4 (October 2015), https://endnotes.org.uk/issues/4.

12 One prominent exception was the Smart Museum of Art's *Revolution Every Day* exhibit, which juxtaposed Soviet and post-Soviet works – for instance, clips of

Dziga Vertov's *Three Songs about Lenin* (1934) with Cauleen Smith's *Three Songs About Liberation* (2017), featuring African American women speaking about slave emancipation and the civil rights movement. Its ingenious catalogue is organized as a day-by-day calendar, combining chronological history (covering 1917–41) with multiple other temporal vectors. See Robert Bird, Christina Kiaer, and Zachary Cahill, eds., *Revolution Every Day: A Calendar, 1917–2017* (Milan: Mousse Publishing, 2017).

13 Joshua Clover, *Riot. Strike. Riot: The New Era of Uprisings* (London: Verso, 2016) 145.

Contributors

Kate Baldwin is professor of English, communication, and gender studies at Tulane University. She is the author of *Beyond the Color Line and the Iron Curtain: Reading Encounters between Black and Red* (Duke University Press, 2002) and *The Racial Imaginary of the Cold War Kitchen: From Sokol'niki Park to Chicago's South Side* (Dartmouth College Press, 2016).

Katerina Clark is professor of comparative literature and Slavic languages and literatures at Yale University. Her present book project, tentatively titled *Eurasia without Borders?: Leftist Internationalists and Their Cultural Interactions, 1917–1943*, looks at attempts during those decades to found a "socialist global ecumene," which was to be closely allied with the anti-colonial cause. She is the author of *The Soviet Novel: History As Ritual* (University of Chicago Press, 1981); with Michael Holquist, *Mikhail Bakhtin* (Harvard University Press, 1984); *Petersburg, Crucible of Cultural Revolution* (Harvard University Press, 1995); with Evgeny Dobrenko, *Soviet Culture and Power: A History in Documents, 1917–1953* (documents with commentary) (Yale University Press, 2007); and *Moscow, the Fourth Rome: Stalinism, Cosmopolitanism and the Evolution of Soviet Culture, 1931–1941* (Harvard University Press, 2011).

Tony Day is the author of *Fluid Iron: State Formation in Southeast Asia* (University of Hawaii Press, 2002); the editor of *Identifying with Freedom: Indonesia After Suharto* (Berghahn Books, 2007); the editor, with Keith Foulcher, of *Clearing a Space* (Brill, 2002); and the editor, with Maya H.T. Liem, of *Cultures at War: The Cold War and Cultural Expression in Southeast Asia* (Cornell University Press, 2010).

Evgeny Dobrenko is professor of Russian and Slavonic studies at the University of Sheffield. He is the author of *The Political Economy of Socialist Realism* (Yale University Press, 2007) and co-editor with Natalia Jonsson-Skradol of *Socialist Realism in Central and Eastern European Literatures Under Stalin: Institutions, Dynamics, Discourses* (Anthem Press, 2018).

Enrique Fibla-Gutiérrez is a researcher, professor, and curator currently working on non-commercial cinema during the interwar period. He has published in the *Journal of Spanish Cultural Studies, 1895 Revue d'Histoire du Cinéma,* and *Screen,* among others, and is co-editor (with Masha Salazkina) of the forthcoming edited volume *Global Perspectives on Amateur Film History and Culture* (Indiana University Press, 2020).

Jonathan Flatley is professor of English at Wayne State University. The author of *Affective Mapping: Melancholia and the Politics of Modernism* (Harvard University Press, 2008) and *Like Andy Warhol* (University of Chicago Press, 2017), he is currently working on a book called *Black Leninism: How Revolutionary Counter-Moods Are Made.*

Amelia M. Glaser is associate professor of Russian and comparative literature at the University of California, San Diego. She is the author of *Jews and Ukrainians in Russia's Literary Borderlands* (Northwestern University Press, 2012), the editor of *Stories of Khmelnytsky: Competing Literary Legacies of the 1648 Ukrainian Cossack Uprising* (Stanford University Press, 2015), and the translator and, with David Weintraub, co-editor of *Proletpen: America's Rebel Yiddish Poets* (University of Wisconsin Press, 2005).

Marina Khrustaleva is an architectural historian, journalist, and curator from Moscow, Russia, currently living in Los Angeles. She was chair of an international NGO, Moscow Architecture Preservation Society (MAPS), and co-founder of the Center for Heritage Capitalization. Marina has curated multiple exhibition projects and public events on the Russian avant-garde, heritage preservation, land-art, public spaces, and city development.

Christina Kiaer teaches at Northwestern University, where she specializes in Soviet art. She is the author (with Robert Bird and Zach Cahill), most recently, of *Revolution Every Day: A Calendar* (Mousse Publishing, 2017) and is completing a book on socialist realism, *Collective Body* (University of Chicago Press).

Dominick Lawton is a PhD candidate in Slavic languages and literatures at the University of California, Berkeley. His work focuses on the poetics of material objects in early Soviet culture

Steven S. Lee is associate professor of English at the University of California, Berkeley, where he is also affiliated with the Center for Korean Studies, the Center for Race and Gender, and the Institute of Slavic, East European, and Eurasian Studies. He is the author of *The Ethnic Avant-Garde: Minority Cultures and World Revolution* (Columbia University Press, 2015).

Vladimir Paperny currently teaches at the University of California, Los Angeles and also continues to work in his design studio, doing graphic design, architectural photography, and video production. His *Architecture in the Age of Stalin: Culture Two* was published in Russian (Ann Arbor, 1985; Moscow, 1996, 2006), in English (Cambridge University Press, 2003, 2011), in Czech (Arbor Vitae, 2014), and in Italian (Artemide, 2017). His essay collections include *Mos Angleles, Mos Angeles-2*, and *Mos Angeles Selected* (NLO, 2004, 2009, 2018) and *Fuck Context?* (TATLIN, 2011). Most recently, he co-edited *The Architecture of Great Expositions* (Ashgate, 2015).

Harsha Ram is associate professor of Slavic languages and literatures and comparative literature at the University of California, Berkeley. He is the author of *The Imperial Sublime: A Russian Poetics of Empire* (University of Wisconsin Press, 2003) and is currently completing *The Scale of Culture: City, Nation, Empire and the Russian-Georgian Encounter*, a book on Russian-Georgian cultural relations, which seeks to theorize and instantiate the problem of geographical scale in literary analysis. His article in this volume is taken from a projected third volume on Russia's place in debates on world literature.

Masha Salazkina is associate professor of film studies at Concordia University. She is the author of *In Excess: Sergei Eisenstein's Mexico* (University of Chicago Press, 2009) and co-editor of the collection *Sound, Speech, Music in Soviet and Post-Soviet Cinema* (Indiana University Press, 2014). Her current book project traces a trajectory of materialist film theory through the discourses of early Soviet cinema, institutional film cultures of the 1930s–50s Italy, and critical debates surrounding the emergence of New Latin American Cinemas.

Snehal Shingavi is associate professor of English at the University of Texas, Austin and the author of *The Mahatma Misunderstood: The Politics and Forms of Literary Nationalism in India* (Anthem Books, 2013). He has translated Munshi Premchand's Hindi novel *Sevasadan* (Oxford, 2005); the Urdu short-story collection, *Angaaray* (Penguin, 2014); Bhisham Sahni's autobiography, *Today's Pasts* (Penguin, 2015); and, with Vasudha Dalmia, Agyeya's *Shekhar: A Life* (Penguin, 2018).

Nariman Skakov is assistant professor of Slavic languages and literatures at Stanford University. His teaching and research interests lie primarily in twentieth-century Russian/Soviet/post-Soviet literature and culture. He is currently working on a book dealing with late modernist experiments in the Soviet Union in the 1930s.

Xiaobing Tang is Sin Wai Kin Professor of Chinese Humanities at the Chinese University of Hong Kong. His most recent publication is *Visual Culture in Contemporary China: Paradigms and Shifts* (Cambridge University Press, 2015).

Katie Trumpener is Emily Sanford Professor of Comparative Literature and English at Yale and part of its graduate faculty in film and media studies. She has published repeatedly on East German film and literature, and is completing a book (*The Divided Screen: German Cinemas 1930–2000*, to be published by Princeton University Press) placing Germany's Cold War media war in a longer and broader historical context. *On The Viewing Platform: The Panorama between Canvas and Screen* (co-edited with art historian Tim Barringer) is forthcoming from Yale University Press.

Sarah Ann Wells is associate professor of comparative literature at the University of Wisconsin, Madison. She is the author of *Media Laboratories: Late Modernist Authorship in South America* (Northwestern University Press, 2017) and co-editor of *Simultaneous Worlds: Global Science Fiction Cinema* (University of Minnesota Press, 2015).

Bo Zheng, associate professor at the School of Creative Media of the City University of Hong Kong, is an artist and writer specializing in socially engaged art. His recent art projects include *Sing for Her*, a participatory installation created with Filipino domestic helpers in Hong Kong; *Plants Living in Shanghai*, a found botanical garden; and an open online course created together with ecologists and humanities scholars in Shanghai.

Index

emancipatory: emancipatory components of revolutionary impulse, 35–6, 67, 228, 230, 232, 249; goals of revolution as, 44, 48, 54; shift from, to confined, 232

Engels, Friedrich, 33–4, 282, 318, 475. See also *Manifesto of the Communist Party*; Marx, Karl

England, 86, 87; literacy exchange of, with India and Russia, 109–32. See *also* Great Britain

Entartete Kunst (*Degenerate Art*) exhibition (Munich), 453

Epstein, Melech, 282, 292

Èrdberg, Oskar, 92–5, 97, 103; "Around a Bowl of Rice" (*U vedra s risom*), 93, 103; *Die drei Grundsätze des Mister Kung, u.a. chinesische Novellen*, 92; *Kitaiskie novelly*, 92; "The Red Scarf," 94–5; *Tales of Modern China*, 92, 93

Ertürk, Nergis, 41–2

Esenin, Sergei, 439

España al Día (newsreel, Spain), 150

"españolada," 141, 142

Espina, Antonio, 144

Estraikh, Gennady, 288

Esty, Jed, 16, 17

Exclusivas, 143

factography, 152–3, 235, 293, 295, 352, 354, 380

Fadeev, Alexander, 426; *Rout*, 426

failure: as virtue, 12

fascism: aestheticized politics of, 18; as great threat to Jewish life, 284; International Conferences Against Fascism, 126–7; Popular Front against (*see* Popular Front). See *also* Spain

Faulkner, William, 200

Fauset, Jessie, 317

Feng Naichao, 259

Fenollosa, Ernest, 53; *The Chinese Written Character as a Medium for Poetry*, 53

Ferraz, Geraldo, 181. See *also* Galvão, Patrícia

Fibla-Gutiérrez, Enrique, 15, 133–69

Fichte, Johann Gottlieb, 282

film clubs, 133, 142, 145–9, 155, 156, 475, 478, 491. See *also* Cineclub Español; Cineclub Proa Filmófono

film education, 143, 149–51

Filmófono (production company), 138, 143, 151

Film Popular (PCE distribution and production company), 157

First Congress of the Toilers of the Far East, 202

Fischer, Ernst, 443

Fisher, Philip, 521; *The Vehement Passions*, 521

Fitzpatrick, Sheila, 23n21

Flammarion, Camille, 248; *L'atmosphère: Météorologie populaire*, 248

Flatley, Jonathan, 14, 18, 313–51, 381

Flavin, Dan, 468, 469; *1964* (sculpture), 468

Foley, Barbara, 416n11

Ford, James, 391

For Whom the Bell Tolls (Hemingway), 305

Foulcher, Keith, 206

Fourth International, 230

France: at centre of interwar avant-garde cinema, 143; *Candid* (newspaper), 463; Communist Party of France (PCF), 147, 156; *Le Monde* (newspaper), 433; Paris Exposition Internationale (1937), 457, 460, 462

Francis, G., 214; "Story of Nyai Dasima," 214

Freedom (US newspaper), 392–419. See *also* Childress, Alice; Robeson, Paul